*Practical Applications
of Psychology*

# Practical Applications of Psychology

FOURTH EDITION

Anthony F. Grasha
*UNIVERSITY OF CINCINNATI*

HarperCollins*CollegePublishers*

Acquisitions Editor: Catherine Woods
Cover Design: John Massey
Cartoonist: Dave Blanchette
Electronic Production Manager: Eric Jorgensen
Publishing Services: Interactive Composition Services
Electronic Page Makeup: Interactive Composition Corporation
Printer and Binder: R.R. Donnelley & Sons Company
Cover Printer: The Lehigh Press, Inc.

**Practical Applications of Psychology,** Fourth Edition

Copyright © 1995 by Anthony F. Grasha

All rights reserved. Printed in the United States of America. No part of this book may be used or reproduced in any manner whatsoever without written permission, except in the case of brief quotations embodied in critical articles and reviews. For information address HarperCollins College Publishers, 10 East 53rd Street, New York, NY 10022.

Library of Congress Cataloging-in-Publication Data
Grasha, Anthony F.
      Practical applications of psychology / Anthony F. Grasha. — 4th ed.
      p.   cm.
      Includes bibliographical references and index.
      ISBN 0-673-52340-3 (pbk.) : $30.00
      1. Psychology, Applied.      I. Title.
   BF636.G577      1995
   158--dc20                                                          94-29604
                                                                         CIP

95  96  97  98    9  8  7  6  5  4  3  2  1

*To Carol, Kevin, and Eric for adding dimensions to my life I other-wise would never have had. And to my parents, colleagues, and others I've met along the way who encouraged me to pursue the things in life that interested me.*

# Contents

---

**Chapter 2:**

## Becoming a More Knowledgeable Consumer of Information   43

---

**Chapter 3**

## Solving Problems and Making Decisions   81

## Chapter 4:   Learining and Retention Processes in Daily Living   121

## Chapter 5:   Modifying Our Behaviors   165

---

**Chapter 6:**
</br>
**Motivation in Everyday Life    203**

---

**Chapter 7:**                   **Interpersonal Communication   247**

---

**Chapter 8:**                   **Developing Interpersonal Relationships   293**

## Chapter 9:  Managing Our Relationships with Others   333

---

**Chapter 10:**        **Adapting to the Demands and Challenges of Daily Living   385**

# Preface

About twenty years ago I began work on the first edition of *Practical Applications of Psychology*. During this time period a number of things have changed in my life and within the field of psychology. Yet the underlying philosophy behind this text has remained the same. I continue to believe that psychological principles have a high potential for helping people deal more effectively with the demands and challenges of daily living. The success of the first three editions of this book suggested that a large number of people not only agreed with this philosophy but found the approach very helpful for learning about personal applications. This edition continues to explore personal applications of psychology, presenting concepts as diverse as critical thinking; everyday applications of research principles; problem solving and decision making; learning theory and behavior modification; attitude change, motivation, and personality theory; interpersonal communication and human relationships; managing conflict and stress; working effectively in groups; and personal growth and adjustment.

Each chapter has applications that will help people to understand themselves and others better, change behaviors if change is needed, and enhance their interactions with others. A major assumption underlying the text is that one cannot make the transition from theory to practice simply by reading about applications. Consequently, this book is explicitly designed to encourage applications to daily living. Built into each chapter is an experiential component. Involvement activities within each chapter illustrate particular concepts and personally involve you with the information. The aim is always to express *how you can use this information at work and in your career, in school, and in your personal life*.

Another goal of this book is helping people to understand many of the major aspects of human behavior that psychologists study. The content is selected from the psychological research literature, experiences of practitioners, and from my experiences in teaching everyday applications of psychological concepts. Though the book's content decidedly has a how-to flavor, I have carefully kept in perspective where the information comes from, with citations to appropriate literature.

## NEW TO THIS EDITION

I wrote the third edition seven years ago, and in the interval of time new developments and ideas for using psychology in everyday life have appeared in the literature. Thus, changes in features and format reflect new developments in the field as well as the comments of current users and reviewers of the third edition. Listed below are some of the additions to the content in this edition of *Practical Applications of Psychology*.

- Attempts have been made to present more of an integration of applications of the content to one's personal and family life, school, and job.
- The increasing interest in active learning strategies and reflective and critical thinking is developed to a much higher degree in this edition. Several changes have been made to the format of the chapters as well as to the end of chapter activities to involve readers more as they read. Chapter organizers at the beginning of each chapter present key questions readers can use to help structure the information. These questions become the basis for organizing the summary at the end of each chapter. In addition, several involvement activities have been integrated into the flow of the text .
- The emphasis on critical thinking also includes a new first chapter on important thinking processes. In addition, the first three chapters together form a section that emphasizes major concepts for critical thinking and its everyday applications in a variety of settings.
- More than half of the *Focus on People* and *Focus on Applied Research* boxes are new to this edition, and a number of new or revised applied activities can be found in the *Things to Do* and *Applied Activities* sections at the end of each chapter.

Besides the general considerations listed above, new content added to each chapter includes:

---

**Chapter 1:**     *Critical Thinking Processes in Everyday Life*

This chapter is new to this edition and focuses on several modes of thinking. Some are predictable, routine, and repetitive thinking habits that operate with little conscious awareness. Included here are automatic mental control processes and mindless thinking. The practical implications of each are presented, and they provide a backdrop for understanding the value of more deliberate and reflective thinking patterns. The nature of critical thinking is introduced, and the use of concepts related to critical thinking for understanding and explaining everyday behavior is presented.

---

**Chapter 2:**     *Becoming a More Knowledgeable Consumer of Information*

This chapter is now much more clearly focused on thinking critically about information that appears in the popular media, including advertising, news stories, and other information people are asked to digest every day. Overall, the chapter pulls together the content in a much more coherent manner focusing on how to correctly interpret information and avoid becoming influenced by facts and figures that are flawed. Specific examples of new material include: making distinctions among the different types of claims employed in the popular media to influence us; how to evaluate such claims; an expanded section on how blind luck and probability affect our daily lives; and a discussion of the illusion of correlation and additional ways to determine whether two or more events are related.

---

**Chapter 3:**     *Solving Problems and Making Decisions*

Formerly Chapter 9 in the third edition, this chapter illustrates how to use principles of critical thinking to solve problems and to make decisions. Expanded coverage occurs in the sections on personal barriers for effective problem solving and decision making; the use of heuristics and the role of bias in problem solving; and processes for making decisions. Here concepts related to making decisions under conditions of uncertainty are discussed, taking into account the role of personal losses and gains and the likelihood of something going wrong with a decision. Two heuristics for sorting through the pros and cons of various options are introduced, and additional coverage for developing contingency plans is presented. The chapter concludes with a new section on "getting unstuck," or what to do if a more rational process for decision making fails to work.

**Chapter 4:**                    *Learning and Retention Processes in Daily Living*

This chapter has been extensively revised to enhance the discussion of the applications of the information. Attempts were made to provide a better balance between learning information and skills and making clearer suggestions about the practical applications of this material. Expanded coverage includes: the role of time on task, active practice, the role of time management and organization in learning, how to effectively employ reinforcement, and the disadvantages of punishment and rewards. New coverage on how our memory system operates and how to learn and retain information better in school and other settings is included. In particular, an emphasis is given to the roles of overlearning, elaborating on information, and mental imagery and mnemonics on improving retention.

**Chapter 5:**                    *Modifying Our Behaviors*

Revisions in this chapter include expanded coverage on the operant model and its role in helping us understand how environmental stimuli influence our overt behaviors, thoughts, and feelings. New ideas for baselining and recording information in a behavior modification plan as well as additional suggestions for controlling antecedents and rewarding and shaping new behavior are discussed. The use of social support in helping people change as well as additional suggestions for applications of the material on observational learning, self-instruction, and mental practice are included.

**Chapter 6:**                    *Motivation in Everyday Life*

Changes include organizing the chapter around biological, cognitive, and environmental influences on motivation. The section on biological sources of motivation, including the discussion of thirst, hunger, sex, and general arousal and sensation seeking, is new to this edition of the book. Cognitive influences on motivation are discussed, with expanded coverage of the role of expectations, locus of control beliefs, and self-efficacy. Also new to this edition is a section on unconscious sources of motivation, including the presence of underlying motives in our fantasies and dreams.

The section on environmental influences contains new information about the role of incentives and intrinsic and extrinsic motives. A discussion of the implications of pursuing goals with positive and negative qualities, the resulting conflicts this produces, and how to resolve them appears for the first time in this edition. Achievement, power, and affiliation are discussed in terms of how underlying needs, cognitive expectations, and the value we place on incentives related to such motives jointly influence our actions.

**Chapter 7:**                    *Interpersonal Communication*

The literature supporting concepts and principles in this chapter has been updated, and a number of changes have been made in the content. New material is included on the functions that interpersonal communication serves in our lives and on the role of conscious and unconscious processes in our everyday conversations. The information on communication networks and patterns has been reorganized, and new material has been added to illustrate in a much more contemporary manner how accessibility, participation, and opportunities for a two-way dialogue enhance the nature and quality of our interactions. The manner in which distortions occur in the flow of information is covered in more detail, and examples that pertain to a variety of everyday situations are illustrated.

The section on noise in the communication channel has been expanded to include ways that it is purposely created to distort the meaning of a message. Expanded coverage includes the role of hidden agendas in our interactions, the interpersonal gap, and the role of interpersonal status and affect in everyday conversations. In particular the roles that status and affect play in perceptions of psychological size and distance and our communication styles are illustrated. A new section on attributes of the communication environment, including new work on the role of physical space, personal space, and the emotional climate of our conversations, appears at the end of this chapter.

---

**Chapter 8:**    *Developing Interpersonal Relationships*

This chapter has been substantially rewritten for this edition. The focus is now on the factors that influence the development, maintenance, and separation from interpersonal relationships. The content includes new and expanded coverage of the phases in relationship development; the role of liking, respect and trust; similarity in attitudes; the nature of social exchanges; stereotypes and prejudices; shyness; and the role of self-disclosure. New material on envy and jealousy appears, and the section on love has been enhanced to incorporate discussions of attachment styles, Sternberg's triangular theory of love, and styles of loving. Recent research on loneliness is highlighted, and a new section on separating from interpersonal relationships concludes this chapter.

---

**Chapter 9:**    *Managing Our Relationships with Others*

This chapter is new to this edition and deals with important interpersonal relationship skills needed to manage conflict, to handle attempts to influence us, and to enable each of us to become more assertive and gain control over our lives.

The coverage of conflict includes detailed descriptions of the functions conflict plays in relationships, factors that trigger it, and factors that serve to support and maintain disputes. Eight approaches to resolving differences among people are described, including helpful suggestions for how to employ each strategy in everyday life.

A discussion of interpersonal influence tactics and how to avoid being manipulated by them is designed to help with meeting two important interpersonal goals—namely, how to get others to do what we want and how to avoid being unnecessarily influenced by others. A number of suggestions for becoming more assertive in dealing with people are included. Discussed are ways to integrate assertive verbal statements with nonverbal messages, making requests, saying "no," giving and receiving feedback, and exercising one's interpersonal rights.

---

**Chapter 10:**    *Adapting to the Demands and Challenges of Daily Living*

This chapter was substantially revised and updated from the last edition. It is organized around the need to adapt to the challenges and demands of everyday life. Included is content on how to manage stress; ways to cope with the anxiety, unhappiness, and depression that may accompany unsuccessful attempts at coping; and the need to develop and maintain a positive and productive self-image. There is an updated discussion of the characteristics of physical and psychological stressors including a more current account of the underlying physiology of stress. There is an extensive discussion of how stressors are appraised and of the physiological, behavioral, emotional, and cognitive signs of stress.

The discussion of coping strategies is organized around the need to pursue three interrelated goals: preventing and reducing distress, seeking a comfortable level of arousal, and buffering and protecting ourselves against stressors. The section on developing physical hardiness through physical activity, diet, and good health habits is much more detailed, with many helpful suggestions included.

Anxiety and depression and ways to cope with them are related to problems in appraising and coping with stressors as well as other more traditional causes. A new section on optimistic and pessimistic explanatory styles and their role in depression is included. The chapter ends with a discussion of the role of our self-image in managing the demands of daily living and with suggestions for pursuing self-renewal goals.

This edition has new features, but some things remain the same: clear explanations; a personal writing style; and learning aids such as the key questions contained in the chapter organizers, a summary of the information in each chapter developed from the key questions, glossaries of important terms, personal application activities, and chapter outlines and crisp topic headings that help readers organize the information.

In an Instructor's Manual both teachers' and students' problems in teaching and learning about applications are discussed. Classroom procedures for involving students are covered, as are suggestions for coordinating classroom procedures with the content and activities in the text. Additional classroom activities are presented, along with test questions and a listing of audiovisual materials, and mini-lecutres with questions and activities based on these brief presentations.

## ACKNOWLEDGMENTS

The content and organization of this book carry many of my thoughts and feelings about the field of psychology and its personal applications. The book is not, however, a solo effort. It would not have been possible to complete without support from people behind the scenes. I particularly appreciate the encouragement and patience of my wife Carol and my two sons with the time I spent writing. My editor at Harper-Collins, Catherine Woods, and her predecessor, Meg Holden, both were very instrumental in getting the fourth edition underway. Catherine Woods did the lion's share of the editorial work, helping to move the book through the review and production process. She also was a wonderful person with whom to discuss ideas about the format and content of this edition. Lesly Atlas, the assistant editor on this project, also worked behind the scenes getting the manuscript and supporting materials into the hands of the right people.

I also want to especially recognize two of my former undergraduate students— Laura Lovejoy and Julie Sand. They worked with me on all aspects of this revision from the very beginning. They were very helpful in tracking down literature in the library, making copies of key articles, reading drafts of chapters from a student's point of view, and making suggestions to help the book become more "user friendly." They wanted to learn how a textbook was developed, and I think they acquired an enlightening and sometimes entertaining view of the process.

I want to thank a number of other people who worked behind the scenes on this textbook. Lois Lombardo coordinated the production process to ensure that all of the elements came together on schedule. Alice Solomon copyedited this edition and saw to it that the material was organized properly and that passages that needed to be were clarified. The designer, John Massey, developed a scheme for laying out the text and illustrations in an attractive manner, and took my primitive sketches and turned them into aesthetically pleasing professional illustrations. Finally, I appreciate the comments and suggestions of Nancy C. Armbruster, Mott Community College, Robert Baugher, Highline Community College, Kathy Herrington, West Virginia Northern Community College, Eve McClure, Highline Community College, Gene Olbert, Oklahoma Junior College, Randy Rice, Tidewater Community College, Patricia N. Taylor, Sumter Area Technical College, and Bruce Treichel, Loraine County Community College. They were the reviewers of the fourth edition who gave me the benefit of their experience as I worked on this book.

*Anthony F. Grasha*

# Critical Thinking Processes in Everyday Life

## Chapter Overview

Our ability to adapt is affected by a variety of cognitive processes. Some are predictable, routine, and repetitive thinking habits that operate with little conscious awareness. Other cognitive processes are more deliberate and reflective and help us to think critically about issues we face. Both modes of thinking are important components of our daily lives. Appreciating how we think and finding ways to think more effectively will be explored in this chapter.

## Chapter Organizers

*As you read, answer the questions that follow on a separate sheet of paper, and check your responses with those provided in the summary section.*

A variety of complex actions—including your ability to play a musical instrument, type a term paper, or drive a car—are performed by mental processes that operate automatically and without conscious guidance.

1. What types of mental errors occur when automatic mental control processes are not executed properly?
2. How can you protect yourself from the mistakes they sometimes produce?

In some of your conversations and interactions, you respond without attending to details in a rather routine and predictable manner. This mode of thinking is labeled **mindlessness.**

3. Do you know the three characteristics of mindless thinking?
4. What are the consequences of relying on this mode of thinking?
5. Can you think of ways to overcome mindlessness?

When you are faced with difficult and unpleasant events, absolute and extreme ways of interpreting these events may occur.

6. How do absolute and extreme ways of thinking affect your life, and what can be done to manage them?

Critical thinking represents a more conscious, reflective, and questioning approach to issues that we encounter every day.

7. What are three common patterns of thinking that are related to your level of intellectual development? How do they affect the way you think?
8. How can critical thinking be used to help you understand the terms, concepts, and principles that describe behavior?
9. Are you aware of how your personal assumptions affect both the questions you ask about human behavior and the answers you obtain?
10. Can you ask effective questions that will develop explanations for behavior?
11. When developing explanations about behavior based upon your observations, what should you do to ensure that they are accurate?

## The Lure of the Cult

For a period of 51 days in March and April of 1993, cult leader David Koresh held a small army of law enforcement officials at bay in Waco, Texas. Koresh viewed himself as a modern-day Jesus Christ. He attracted people by preaching that the end of the world was near and that he alone held the keys to salvation. He taught followers that everyone in the outside world was evil, while only cult members were good people. Apparently, for some of them, the message was effective! Over a period of several years, he attracted more than one hundred people to become members of a cult known as the "Branch Davidians." A well-armed compound was built outside Waco, Texas, to protect the cult members from outside influences. There, at Camp Apocalypse, he and his followers lived amid reports of drug abuse, child endangerment and abuse, kidnapping, and the stockpiling of weapons.

Cult members gave absolute authority over their lives to David Koresh. His followers lived in spartan quarters without central heat or indoor plumbing. Koresh's living quarters, on the other hand, were, relatively speaking, well furnished. David Koresh preached his version of scripture in almost daily Bible studies. Graphic sexual talk mixed with images of violence became a part of his biblical message. Followers were told that he would take on their sins. Thus, he was officially the only member of the cult permitted to have sexual relations with the women and to drink alcoholic beverages.

Children held a special interest for Koresh. He fathered at least seventeen children and he dictated how they lived and played together. Girls were permitted to sleep late, while the boys were required to rise as early as 5:30 A.M. for "gym," which included marching and other military-like drills. Staged fights were encouraged, with children who did not participate energetically enough harshly disciplined. Violent war movies and television programs were standard fare for the children.

His favorite form of punishment for children was paddling them for very minor offenses such as spilling a drink. The paddle was known as "the helper." Physical punishment was the discipline of choice, and it began at an early age. The children soon learned to develop both an awe and fear of Koresh. To reinforce his authority

Above account based on news reports from the Associated Press, *Time* magazine, and *Newsweek* Magazine during this period of time.

over the children, he taught them to refer to their parents as "dogs" and to see him as their only true parent. When they reached 11 years of age, the girls were given a "Star of David" to wear signifying they were ready to become one of his wives.

While trying to arrest David Koresh, four federal law enforcement agents were killed in a gun battle with cult members. What ensued was a 51-day siege of the compound by federal and local law enforcement agents. The drama was constantly in the news until its tragic end on April 19. That day, law enforcement officials attacked the compound with tear gas and armored vehicles. Acting on a vow never to surrender, Koresh's followers set fire to the compound.

The remains of 72 people were recovered from the compound, including those of 24 children who were placed in upstairs rooms where they could not escape. Koresh's body, along with the bodies of at least 7 members of the cult, had bullet wounds to the head, suggesting that what had transpired might have been a murder-suicide.

## CHARACTERISTICS OF EVERYDAY THINKING

"What on earth were people thinking about to follow this guy?" one of my students recently commented. The story of David Koresh raises a number of issues about the ways people think. For example:

- Why did his followers blindly accept his views of the world?
- Did people ever stop and ask questions about what he wanted them to do?
- How could they conclude from his behaviors that he had their best interests in mind?
- Did he "brainwash" them to think a particular way?
- Were his followers like robots mindlessly following whatever commands they were given?

It would be easy to point our fingers at the people in David Koresh's cult and to say, "they should have known better." However, blindly accepting and not thinking very critically about events in the world around us is a common human shortcoming. It arises because there is always a certain amount of uncertainty about what to think, say, or do. Some people, like those who followed David Koresh to their deaths, handle such uncertainty by not engaging in much detailed thought. They would rather have answers to their questions handed to them by some authority figure. A few procrastinate, or try to avoid dealing with their doubts and misgiving. Still others view the uncertainties of life as a challenge. They derive a considerable amount of satisfaction thinking about ways to understand and resolve the issues they face.

A variety of thought processes aids our attempts to understand the world around us. In his work, Richard Nelson Jones (1990) identifies more than thirty characteristics of thinking that play an important role in our lives. They include dreaming, analyzing, reflecting, judging, memorizing, concentrating, forgetting, reasoning, and a number of other aspects of our thought processes we normally take for granted. *Jones argues that if people want to live their lives more effectively, they must become aware of the advantages and disadvantages of their current modes of thought.* Otherwise, they are blind to patterns in their thinking that produce desirable or undesirable outcomes in their lives.

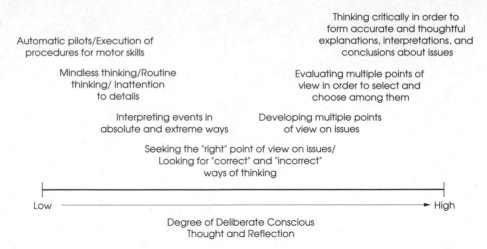

**Figure 1.1** *Thought processes that we use on a daily basis. The extent to which each depends upon using deliberate conscious thinking and reflection is illustrated by its placement along this continuum. Each of these thought processes and the role it plays in our everyday lives are discussed in this chapter.*

To aid this inquiry, several general modes of thinking are identified and examined in this chapter. Each can be thought of as lying along a continuum of conscious reflection and involvement as illustrated in Figure 1.1. At one end are modes of thinking that do not require a large amount of conscious effort. Examples include the automatic mental processes used to execute motor skill as well as other routine modes of thinking. They are employed every time you drive a car, swing a golf club, move your fingers on a computer keyboard, or respond to others in social situations in a predictable manner without attending to the details of what was said or requested.

At the other end of this continuum are more active, reflective, and deliberate thought processes. The latter are important to our ability to think critically and creatively about the complex issues we face. Examples include developing multiple perspectives on issues and thinking critically by questioning the validity of information, solving problems and making decisions, and generally probing beneath the surface of issues to discover what is really going on.

Combinations of both automatic and more deliberate mental processes are a significant part of our daily lives. Let us examine the characteristics of each of the thought processes in Figure 1.1 and the role they play in our everyday lives.

## THINKING ON AUTOMATIC PILOT

*Some psychologists estimate that a significant number of our daily activities occur without much reliance on conscious reflection or awareness* (Abelson, 1981; Schneider, Dumais, and Shiffrin, 1984; Norman, 1988). People have the capacity to develop routine and repetitive thinking habits that largely operate outside of conscious control. These are sometimes referred to as **automatic mental control processes** (Norman, 1980). Such thought processes are the mental equivalent of an automatic pilot. Like computer programs, they silently work in the background to control and direct a variety of our everyday actions.

*One set of actions is the sequence of motor skills we employ.* Consider for a moment how you arrived at school or at work today. If you drove your car, you did not consciously say to yourself, "open the car door, sit down, fasten the seat belt, put the keys in the ignition, make sure the transmission is in neutral, turn the key, release the parking brake, put both hands on the steering wheel, gently step on the gas pedal, and move forward." Instead, these skills were coordinated by mental programs of which you were largely unaware.

Such thinking processes allow us to handle a variety of tasks without conscious awareness. Thus, our mental capacity is saved for dealing with relatively more complex and important issues that demand conscious thought and deliberation. **Automatic pilots** make it possible to drive to school while mentally reviewing for a test or to mow the lawn while rehearsing a sales presentation. They also allowed a blue grass singer I recently watched to change a broken guitar string while continuing to sing. Without missing a beat, she reached into her back jeans pocket, pulled a guitar string from a packet, and, with little apparent effort, managed to fix her guitar.

## The Role of Automatic Pilots in Making Mistakes

Why would someone say to his or her spouse or best friend, "I hate you— no, I mean I love you." Or, why would a corporate manager dressing for a required company dinner start putting on her pajamas? Sigmund Freud saw hidden motives for all such slips. Our unconscious mind surfaces when we least expect it to and allows hidden wishes and motives to be satisfied. Thus, the husband hates his spouse but cannot consciously express it, and the corporate manager would rather go to sleep than to the required dinner.

Psychologist Donald Norman (1980, 1988), however, argues that failures in automatic mental processes provide a much simpler interpretation than do explanations

WHAT EVER POSSESSED YOU TO WRITE AN ANSWER TO A HISTORY QUESTION ON YOUR PSYCHOLOGY EXAM?

based upon a person's unconscious intentions. While automatic pilots normally serve us well, *errors in executing them may occur when people become tired, fatigued, rushed for time, or otherwise distracted.* Such mistakes fall into predictable patterns. Four very common errors that Donald Norman has identified in his work include the following.

1. *Selection errors. A mental control process related to what is needed is selected, but it is not the correct one.* Getting ready to give a dinner party, a friend placed an unbaked cake in the refrigerator and a bottle of white wine in the oven. The automatic control process for putting something into the oven was executed, but with the wrong object.

2. *Execution errors. An automatic pilot is executed but not completed.* On several occasions, I have walked into my office or my kitchen at home to retrieve a book or car keys and forgot why I was there.

3. *Interference errors. A stronger mental control process interferes with the execution of a relatively weaker one.* There is an intersection on the way to work where I can make a right turn to come to the university or a left turn to go downtown. Ninety-five percent of the time I turn right to go to work. However, when I want to go downtown, I sometimes have found myself turning right at that intersection. Usually this occurs when I am preoccupied and thinking of other things.

4. *Blending errors. Two or more automatic pilots are triggered and blended.* A student in one of my classes returned home after playing soccer and told himself "I'm going out tonight with my girlfriend, and I have to take a shower and wash my sweaty soccer clothes. Distracted by thoughts of the party, he turned on the shower and, without thinking, jumped in with his soccer clothes on.

## Three Ways to Manage Mental Errors

*1. Remain extravigilant, and monitor your actions under circumstances where you have experienced problems with automatic control processes in the past* Automatic pilots are activated to meet the demands of particular situations in our lives. Thus, the useful and nonuseful aspects of automatic thinking are likely to recur. Sometimes it helps to remind yourself of what occurred in the past before entering such situations and of the precautions needed to prevent a recurrence. I now remind myself to be careful when entering the intersection mentioned in the example above.

*2. Use the side effects of a miscue to guide and direct future actions* While preventing a miscue from occurring might not always be possible, once it occurs, certain side effects are produced. Drive your car at night without your lights on, and other cars typically start blinking their lights at you. Forget to put coffee in the coffeemaker in the morning, and the hot water that results is a less satisfying drink. Fail to pick up a date on time because of losing track of time, and your evening is often not as pleasant. Consider such side effects a "wake-up" call, and take immediate actions to correct the problem. Then develop mental notes on the steps you must take in the future to avoid such problems from recurring.

*3. Set up cues to break out of a habitual thinking pattern* When I write, for example, I tend to become so focussed on the task that I frequently lose track of time and other obligations. I have found that the alarm on my wristwatch is a wonderful reminder to exit the mental script that controls my ability to intensely focus and to ignore other concerns and demands (e.g., leaving home for work, attending a meeting, or fixing a meal).

## MINDLESS THINKING

*Besides executing complex sequences of motor skills, routine modes of thinking are involved in a variety of other actions, including our interactions with others.* For example, think about the last time you said to another person, "Good morning," "How are you today?" "I love you," or "Let's get together again real soon." Did you spend much time thinking about what you were saying? Did you really mean what you said? Did you think beforehand about other words you could have spoken?

If you answered "no" to each question, you were engaging in what psychologist Ellen Langer (1989a) labels mindlessness. *Mindlessness is the tendency to process information without attention to details in a rather routine and predictable manner.* As a result, our thoughts and subsequent behaviors occur without the benefit of much deliberation.

## Characteristics of Mindless Thinking

*Becoming Trapped by Categories* That is, categories or distinctions learned from past experience are rigidly used to guide present behavior. A physician friend remarked that when admitting an elderly patient to a hospital, she automatically prescribes "bed rest." This order instructs the staff to restrict the patient's mobility, and it is not always necessary. She simply prescribes "bed rest" whenever a patient fits the category of "elderly person." Similarly, some individuals automatically avoid contact with or dislike those classified as "Afro-American," "Mexican-American," "Jewish," "Italian." They may shun those who represent a cultural, religious, or ethnic group other than their own. A rigid adherence to categories also guides our likes and dislikes for foods (e.g., fast food, health food), music (e.g., classical, rap, top 40), political parties (e.g., Republican, Democrat, Socialist worker, Communist), occupations (e.g., police officer, minister, teacher, salesperson), and other aspects of daily living.

In effect, the characteristics of the category are assumed to apply across the board. Mindless thinking makes no exceptions, and it fails to address uniqueness and diversity. Thus, an elderly patient, one Mexican-American, or a single health food dish are automatically assumed to be like the other members of that category. Without conscious deliberation, someone or something is automatically made to fit an existing mold.

*Blindly Following Requests* In effect, behaviors are initiated without giving much conscious thought to questions such as, "Why am I doing this?" or "What other options for thinking and behaving do I have?" Such tendencies are particularly likely in, but not limited to, situations in which we engage in routine and repetitive tasks.

An interesting demonstration of this tendency was found in two research studies conducted by Ellen Langer (1989b). In one, she sent a memo to people working in a company, with the instructions, "Please return this memo to Room 247 immediately." Ninety percent of the people opened the memo and returned it without asking a single question. In another study, individuals standing in line to use a Xerox machine were confronted with a new arrival who wanted to use it. To gain access to the machine, all

this person had to say was, "Excuse me, I want to use this machine to make five copies because I need to make copies."

In effect, people responded to the familiar structure of what was said (i.e., "Please return this memo," or, "because I need to make copies"). Few people bothered to ask questions about details such as, "Why should I return this memo instead of putting it into a wastebasket?" "What is so special about your request to use this copier? Everyone using this machine needs to make copies."

Thinking mindlessly stopped when doubts or misgivings were raised about the request. For example, when the memo was a different color or shape than an ordinary office memo, fewer were returned. When the reason for using the copier was made to sound absurd (e.g., "I need to use the copier because an elephant is after me"), the request also was denied. In both cases, such information forced people to consciously attend to the content of the message and to ask, "What on earth is going on here?"

***Acting from a Single Perspective or Mindset*** Sometimes, people act as if only one set of rules applies to a situation. This limits their perceptions. For example, read the following passage, and, as you read, count the number of times the letter F occurs:

### FINAL FOLIOS SEEM TO RESULT FROM YEARS OF DUTIFUL STUDY OF TEXTS ALONG WITH YEARS OF FUNDAMENTAL SCIENTIFIC EXPERIENCE.

Based upon information in the first two words, a mindset develops that the letter F must appear at the beginning of a word. As a result, the number of times an F appears in other positions is missed. There are actually nine Fs in this passage.

In a rather amusing example of this characteristic of mindlessness, several hundred students were asked to rate various components of an introductory psychology course they had just completed (Reynolds, 1977). Students rated various lectures and films on a scale where A = excellent; B = good; C = average; D = fair; and E = poor. The eval-

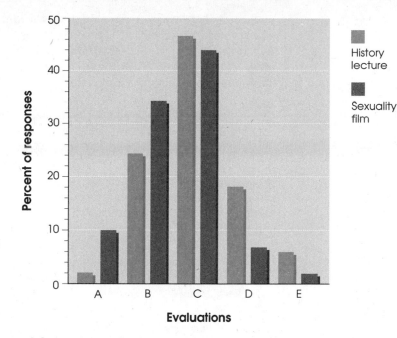

**Figure 1.2** *Distribution of evaluations of a lecture not given on the history of psychology and a film not shown on human sexuality (based on data in Reynolds, 1977).*

uations for the lecture on the history of psychology and the film on sexuality and communication are shown in Figure 1.2. As you can see, the evaluations were relatively good. *Unfortunately, the lecture was never given, and the film was never shown in the course!* The course ratings were apparently based on a mindset that "everything on this evaluation form is something I have experienced in this class." Or perhaps the students thought, "It's not a good idea to leave blank spaces on an evaluation form. I had better put something down."

***Failing to Consider Alternative Perspectives on Issues*** When people are faced with interpersonal conflicts, for example, Alfie Kohn reports that most of them view themselves as "right" and the other person as "wrong" and treat the problem in a "win-lose" fashion. Thus, individuals try to "win" to enable their "correct" point of view to prevail. In the process, a reluctance to seek a compromise tends to develop (Kohn, 1986). Similarly, when people are faced with multiple tasks at school or work, a common point of view is, "I have too many things to do and not enough time in which to do everything." Identifying how time is used ineffectively and exploring effective time management strategies may not occur to someone adopting the latter perspective.

## Consequences of Mindless Thinking

Ellen Langer reports that mindless thinking creates four unfortunate consequences.

***A Narrow Self-Image May Result*** A student once informed me that he failed to take more responsibility and initiative for learning material because "It's the teacher's job to teach me what I need to know." Another mentioned that she seldom tried more efficient ways for completing tasks because "I'm just an employee, and I do things the way I'm told by my boss." *In effect, such individuals saw themselves and others as members of rigidly defined categories.* As a result, definitions of their role as a "student" in the classroom or as a "subordinate" at work were restricted.

*Our Relationships with Others Can Be Adversely Affected* A former client had trouble controlling his anger. He managed a small company, and when employees seriously disagreed with him on issues or made mistakes, it was not uncommon for him to throw a "temper tantrum." He would yell and scream in an attempt to get people to do things his way or to correct deficiencies. His response was virtually automatic and quite predictable. Alternative ways to respond were examined, including the need to: redefine events in a less hostile manner, count to ten, view disagreements as sometimes helpful, and see mistakes as an opportunity to help employees learn. "I like what you are telling me," he often said. Unfortunately, he was not able to use such responses on a regular basis. *He was trapped by mindsets for responding in an angry fashion.* Unable to change his ways, he eventually decided that the frustration of dealing with people was not worth it. He left the business and retired early.

*Learned Helplessness May Develop* Repeated failures can produce a mindset that "I have no choice or control over what will happen to me." This sense of futility is called **learned helplessness**, and it may generalize to situations beyond those in which it was originally learned (Seligman, 1975). Several bad experiences in college math courses, for example, have led some students to conclude, "I'll never be good at math or at anything else in college." A couple of bad relationships can lead to thoughts like, "I'll never be able to form a lasting relationship with anyone." People naturally try to avoid the anxiety, depression, and other bad feelings associated with learned helplessness. In the process, they fail to seek other college courses in which to succeed or to form new relationships in which they could be happy.

*We Become Easily Influenced by Others* A common defense of people convicted of war crimes was "I was just following orders!" What they failed to do, however, was to question the orders they were given. Becoming susceptible to turning control over our lives to others is not uncommon. Some people, for example, join cults or other organizations in which they do not think for themselves and blindly follow the dictates of some leader. Read Focus on Applied Research 1.1 to gain additional insights into the tactics used to mold the thought processes of people who join cults.

## Three Ways to Defeat Mindlessness

*1. Recognize the signs of mindless behavior, and take actions to prevent a recurrence.* This is difficult while in the midst of a mindless act, but reviewing our actions afterwards and vowing "never again" can help. A neighbor responded to an advertisement for a well-known local hairstylist who "guarantees to make you a new person." From entering the salon to leaving, she was lured into its mystique. She later remarked to me, "I never questioned what they told me. I agreed to whatever they said I needed to have done with my hair." The result was predictable. She left with a cut and color highlights that gave her a "new look" she later regretted. Afterwards, she recognized her mindless actions and vowed to never repeat her mistake in the future.

In effect, mindlessness is defeated when people develop what Ellen Langer terms **mindfulness,** which, in an interesting play on words, is the exact opposite of mindlessness. Becoming aware of conditions where mindless thinking prevails begins to promote a sense of mindfulness. The next two strategies also help.

*2. Actively resist attempts by others to tell you how to think and behave* Otherwise we become puppets whose strings are pulled by others. Think for a moment, how often in the past two to three days you allowed other people to dictate what you should do. Most of us like to please, and it is natural to just do what is asked and not to spend much time asking "Why?" A more effective approach would be to practice using the following questions: *"What do I really want to do here?"* or, *What course of action is in my best interests?" "What do I stand to gain or lose by doing what others want?"* Such questions force us to pay conscious attention to the situation and to thoughtfully consider the best response.

*3. Search for ways to make decisions and to gain control over your life* Even making small decisions and gaining control over the little things in life lessens a sense of mindless futility and learned helplessness. Life begins to have meaning whenever we work to regain a sense of mastery and control. Sometimes, unexpected dividends occur, as illustrated in the results of the following study.

One group of residents of a nursing home were allowed to decide where to receive visitors, whether or not to see a movie, and were given control over the care of a houseplant. A second group that was similar in age and physical health was told the staff would help them to make such decisions. When compared 18 months later, the first group showed improvement in a number of areas. They were more active and alert; their health had improved; they were less anxious and depressed; they felt more in control of their lives; and, unexpectedly, the researchers found that fewer of them had died. The differences in death rates were impressive. Among the nursing home residents who were allowed to make even relatively small decisions, about 15 percent had died during the eighteen-month follow-up period. In the group where such decision making was discouraged, 30 percent of those in this group had died (Rodin and Langer, 1977).

## ABSOLUTE AND EXTREME WAYS OF THINKING

Everyone is susceptible at one time or another to repetitive thoughts and verbal statements that interpret events in absolute and extreme ways. "Extreme thoughts" suggest that disaster is right around the corner and include statements that contain words like *every, always, awful, terrible, horrible, totally,* and *essential.* Absolute words suggest we have no choice and include statements that contain works like *must, should, have to, need,* and *ought.* Such beliefs are learned throughout a lifetime of experiences and represent almost a knee-jerk reaction to unpleasant events. Albert Ellis (1987) labels such thoughts **irrational beliefs.**

One of the students in my class recently failed a test in her major. She was upset and said to herself, "This is the *most horrible* thing that could happen to me. I always mess up on important exams." A friend found that his girlfriend had walked out on

## Mindless Thinking in Cult Indoctrination Practices

The question of why otherwise normal people give up their worldly possessions and devote their lives to cult leaders is a fascinating one. A review of the research by David Myers (1993) and Edward and Ann Wimberly (1986) suggest that elements of "mindless thinking" play a major role in the process.

To begin, the process of indoctrination works best with people who are insecure and looking for simple answers to the complex issues of life. Contacts with cult members are rewarded by invitations to have dinner or to socialize with members. Potential new members are made to feel special and loved by existing members. Basic teachings of the cult are presented during conversations, with attention given to how the cult has found answers to the questions people want. In most cases, initiates are taught that the road to spiritual peace and salvation and the answers they want for their lives can be found through *blind allegiance to the directions and outlook provided by the cult leader.*

*Members become trapped by categories* for viewing the outside world. Typically, those on the outside are categorized as misguided and as enemies who wish to destroy the cult and what it stands for. Further indoc-

trination into the *rigid mindset of the cult* occurs through cult rituals, prayer sessions, and self-examination sessions where thinking that goes against accepted beliefs is discouraged. In order to lock in such beliefs, the cult isolates new members from outside influences. They begin to "practice what the cult preaches." *This makes it difficult to explore ideas that run counter to the cult's teachings.* New members soon find themselves justifying the cult's beliefs to others as they actively solicit new members to join or to raise money for the cult. Such activities reinforce their beliefs and make it less likely they will openly question the cult's teachings.

As with other forms of mindless thinking, changes in the situation can get people to ask, "What am I doing here?" or, "Why am I doing this?" As the leader's demands become more extreme, as flaws in a leader's character develop, or as the cult is shown to engage in illegal activities, some members snap out of their mindless allegiance. In turn, the leaders turn to the use of force and intimidation to control deviant members. Threats of harm to those who flee are made; beatings are administered for noncompliance; or drugs are used to neutralize disagreeable members.

him. He was upset and told himself, "This happens to me *every time* I get close to a woman. They *always take advantage* of me. I will *never be able* to have a close relationship with another woman again." A client was fired from his job and kept thinking," "A company *should treat* people better than that. They *ought to* help me find another job. I'll *never be able* to manage this by myself."

Such thinking is understandable immediately after an unpleasant event occurs. Unfortunately, when it persists, our ability to cope with events is diminished. If someone continues to believe, "I *will never* be able to have a close relationship with another woman again," two outcomes are likely. One is that negative emotions persist. The second outcome is that a "self-fulfilling prophecy" occurs. Actions in line with the belief are taken, and such thoughts are subsequently confirmed. My friend did not date for three months after the incident, and it was more than two years before he entered into another close relationship.

When irrational beliefs gain a foothold in our minds, they dominate how we think about situations. *They contribute to distorting our perceptions, keeping us frantic, and preventing us from taking constructive actions to resolve issues.* Thus, our levels of frustration and dissatisfaction with life increase.

## Three Ways to Manage Absolute and Extreme Ways of Thinking

With a little self-reflection, it is easy to identify the presence of irrational thinking. Once its presence is recognized, the thoughts that characterize it can be successfully challenged and their influence lessened. The following three things counter irrational beliefs.

*1. Examine the objective facts in a situation* What would an instant replay on television bring to light? *Example:* "A replay would show my girlfriend left me, but I was not treating her very well. I can honestly admit I helped to force her out of the relationship."

*2. Interpret events in a less extreme and a more balanced fashion* Seek and accept another valid way of interpreting the event that provides a more balanced perspective. *Example:* "The situation is not pleasant, but her leaving is not the end of the world. I have bounced back from such things in the past."

*3. Develop plans to overcome the problem and reduce negative emotions* *New ways of thinking need to be backed up with behaviors that support them. Example:* "I guess I made some mistakes in our relationship. Maybe it's not too late for me to apologize and to try and work on the relationship. I'll call her early next week and see if she is willing to talk about how we relate to each other."

Additional suggestions for managing irrational beliefs can be found in the section on stress management in Chapter 10. For now, it is important to recognize that they are a rather persistent part of how we think about events in our daily life.

How could the student who failed her test and the person who was fired from his job (mentioned earlier) employ the three more productive modes of thinking described above? What would they say to themselves, and how would they have to then behave differently to reinforce new ways of thinking?

# WAYS OF THINKING AND OUR LEVEL OF INTELLECTUAL DEVELOPMENT

Other thinking patterns that are prevalent in our everyday lives have been identified in research designed to assess stable patterns in how people think. In one set of studies, William Perry (1970, 1981) and Mary Belenky and her colleagues (1986) used in-depth interviews to identify patterns among individuals in their level of intellectual development. Participants in both studies were questioned about their views of learning and education, significant events in their lives, how they handled moral issues, as well as other concerns in their everyday lives. Attempts were made to identify the ways that people understood important issues in their lives. William Perry's interviews were conducted on a predominately male sample, while Mary Belenky and her colleagues interviewed 135 women.

While some differences were noted between the samples, there were many similarities across both studies. Both researchers found patterns in how people thought about things, and such modes of thinking differed in complexity. A summary of three such patterns of thinking common to both studies and their implications for everyday thinking are identified in Table 1.1. William Perry labels such modes of thinking "positions," while Mary Belenky and her colleagues refer to them as "ways of knowing."

**Table 1.1**                    Patterns in How People Think

| IDENTIFIED BY PERRY/BELENKY | DESCRIPTION OF THREE MODES OF THINKING AND THEIR IMPLICATION FOR CRITICAL THINKING |
| --- | --- |
| Dualism/Received Knowledge | Belief that information is either correct or incorrect, right or wrong, and that there are fixed ways of looking at the world. Reliance on authorities to determine how and what to think. *Implication: leads to difficulty thinking independently, generating alternative perspectives, and analyzing information.* |
| Multiplism/Subjective Knowledge | Ability to see that uncertainties, doubts, and unknowns exist and that these, in turn, naturally lead to multiple points of view. Have difficulty, however, developing reasons why some opinions would be better than others. Tendency to turn inward and not to rely as much on external authorities for answers. Men view having opinions as "every person's right," while women simply acknowledge that differences in opinion can be expected and are valuable. *Implication: leads to considering alternative points of view but without an ability to consistently formulate and employ criteria for deciding among them.* |
| Relativism/Procedural Knowledge | Recognition that points of view differ in quality and that good ones are supported by evidence and other criteria. Thus, discipline and legal, moral, religious, and other criteria are used to determine which opinions can be accepted or rejected or which need additional analysis. Men tend to rely more on objective, external criteria, while women tend to blend both external criteria and internal criteria such as their personal values and beliefs. *Implication: leads to independent thinking, analyzing information, and using appropriate criteria to draw conclusions.* |

Both researchers viewed these patterns as representing different levels of intellectual development. They were not thought of as fixed stages that someone entered and then leaves. *Rather, people were viewed as having preferences for certain modes of thinking that typically vary with their age and experiences, life circumstances, and, to a lesser extent, their gender.* In effect, as we become more mature, our capacity to employ more complex ways of understanding the world (e.g., relativism/procedural knowledge) increase. Yet retreating to less complex modes of thinking is not uncommon and often serves as a form of self-protection. Thus, someone might be able to use a broad relativist point of view when discussing the merits of a piece of poetry. When faced with time pressures at work to complete a task, this same person might ask his or her boss to "tell me exactly what I should think and do here."

## Dualism/Received Knowledge: Seeking the "Right" Point of View

Joanne Kurfiss (1988), for example, reports that the **dualism/received knowledge** modes of thinking emphasize "black-white," "correct-incorrect," or "right-wrong" ways of making judgments and forming opinions. She points out that such thoughts are encouraged by practices in certain educational settings. For example, such patterns are promoted by the use of true-false and multiple-choice exams and textbooks that present subject matter as consisting of a large number of correct or incorrect facts and concepts. Classroom procedures also contribute when few opportunities are provided for students to challenge a teacher's ideas or those in the text. Thus, students can easily develop the idea that "the teacher or some authority is always right." Similarly, parents encourage a dualism/received knowledge mode of thinking when children are taught that authorities are always correct, that there is always a "right" or "correct" thing to do, and that they are not to not ask too many questions.

## Multiplism /Subjective Knowledge: Developing Multiple Points of View

This mode of thinking develops when people begin to see that the world is not tied up in neat little packages and that authorities do not always have correct answers. Individuals begin to see that multiple viewpoints exist in the world and that authorities are not always right. Educational settings help to develop this position by exposing students to alternative points of view, and parents help when they encourage children to appreciate diversity in the world. While people can see multiple viewpoints in this mode of thinking, they typically lack the capacity to decide what points of view are, relatively speaking, better than others.

Research shows that a majority of college students and other adults rely on the dualism/received knowledge and multiplism/subjective knowledge approaches to analyzing and understanding issues (Belenky et al., 1986; King, Kitchener, and Wood, 1985). Such individuals want authorities to provide "correct, or right" answers and prefer to focus on expedient or simplistic explanations to complicated issues. They are concerned with "getting the facts" from what others say or from what they read. When asked to think for themselves about issues for which there is no clear answer, they may resist or become frustrated with not being able to form an acceptable response.

## Relativism/Procedural Knowledge: Evaluating Multiple Points of View

In spite of its usefulness for thinking broadly about more complicated issues, **relativism/procedural knowledge** as a mode of thinking is employed less often and is relatively uncommon even among college seniors and older adults (Kurfiss, 1988; Ryan, 1984). When this thinking style is employed, however, people typically see the need to probe beneath the surface of issues. For example, a question such as, "Is it proper for one human being to kill another?" is seen as having several answers. An individual employing a relativistic mode would not simply respond "yes" or "no." The answer would depend upon the context, and certain criteria would be used to form a response. Thus, someone might say, "If a person is on a battlefield, then killing would be justified, because your basic survival needs are threatened. However, if someone calls you a 'jerk,' killing that person must not be allowed on the basis of legal and moral principles."

The important point is that several possible answers are recognized, and the adequacy of each can be evaluated against relevant criteria. To develop this capacity, we need practice "thinking for ourselves." Experiences at school, work, and in other areas of life must provide opportunities for analyzing ideas and positions, debating points of view, writing position papers, having ideas challenged, and justifying one's position on issues. Opportunities for doing such things are not always taken advantage of or available. Thus, this is the least well developed mode of thinking.

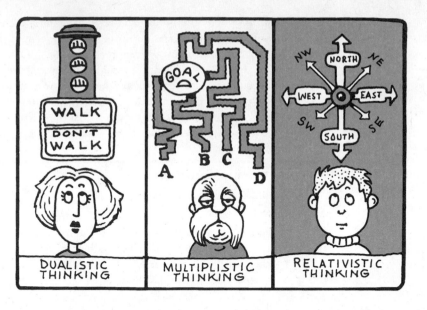

## CRITICAL THINKING

According to Diane Halpern (1989), the term **critical thinking** has a very special meaning. It is not, for example, the negative thinking we use when criticizing someone. Nor is it a thought that points to something as a "critical situation." Rather, people think critically when they ask questions like, "Given this information, what's the best decision I could make here?" or, "What are some alternative ways of looking at this issue?" Halpern notes that such thinking has the following three characteristics.

*1. Critical thinking has a purpose* It involves deliberate conscious thought and reflection that is directed towards accomplishing some goal. This can be solving problems, making decisions, applying information to our lives, or otherwise probing beneath the surface of issues and events to understand them better. This separates critical thinking from the routine and largely automatic thinking involved in brushing our teeth or driving the usual route to school or work and from the thinking involved in daydreams or night dreams.

*2. Critical thinking is reasoned* It emphasizes our ability to examine all of the information relevant to an issue or problem and then to form an accurate conclusion. Thus, a student who says, "I did poorly on the exam because I failed to use good study habits and my instructor did not emphasize some important points in class enough" is employing critical thinking. A thoughtful analysis of the information available went into developing that conclusion. A student who says, "It's the teacher's fault I did poorly on the exam" is simply being "critical" of the teacher but is not engaging in critical thinking.

*3. Critical thinking evaluates, in a constructive manner, more than one side of an issue as well as the positive and negative attributes of a situation* Someone thinks critically when he or she comments, "The salesperson showed me how this car is better than others on the market but did not mention ways in which it was worse," or when he or she asks, "What do I like and dislike about what my boss just said?"

*In order to think critically, we must go beyond the "dualistic/received knowledge" modes of thinking described in Table 1.1 and begin to use characteristics of a "relativistic/procedural" thinking pattern.* In effect, our thinking must remain flexible in order to enhance our understanding of the information we receive and the issues we face.

In spite of the benefits of critical thinking, research shows that people may not think critically because of a lack of knowledge about the methods and skills involved as well as little interest and motivation for doing so (Glaser, 1984, 1985). This is unfortunate because other studies demonstrate that skills to improve our thinking can be taught and that this knowledge helps us in almost all areas of our everyday lives (Halpern, 1989; Nickerson, 1986a, 1986b; Zechmeister and Johnson, 1992). This research also suggests that learning how to think critically cannot occur in a vacuum. Some focus is needed for learning about and applying principles of critical thinking. Thus, in the remainder of this chapter, specific suggestions for thinking critically will be introduced in the context of how we try to understand the reasons for our own actions and those of others.

## THINKING CRITICALLY WHILE ATTEMPTING TO UNDERSTAND BEHAVIOR

Understanding behavior involves analyzing, interpreting, or explaining certain events. This process might begin with questions such as: "Why did my Uncle Harry commit suicide?" "What made my friends Carlos and Sylvia get divorced?" "Why am I so afraid of taking exams?" On the other hand, a friend, newspaper article, or other source might provide us with a statement or principle about behavior. For example, "People with different personalities are attracted to each other." "People are basically selfish." "Beauty is only skin deep."

In effect, all of us face two tasks when trying to analyze and interpret our actions and those of others. One is to develop explanations or reasons for "why" certain actions occurred. The second is to judge the adequacy of those provided by others. Several principles of critical thinking can help us do both of these things more effectively. They are listed in Table 1.2.

## UNDERSTAND IMPORTANT TERMINOLOGY

### Make Sure Terms, Concepts and Principles Are Understood and Used Correctly

Perhaps you or someone else decided that Uncle Harry was severely depressed, Carlos and Sylvia had a power struggle in their marriage, and that your test taking was hindered by a fear of failure. How can you be sure such interpretations are justified? Do you understand what terms like "depression," "power struggle," and "fear of failure" mean? If not, your ability to use them or to evaluate whether others used them correctly will be affected. At times, people are tempted to be satisfied with a superficial understanding of the meaning of terms. This may be due to a lack of interest or to a belief that the time and energy to probe deeper is better spent elsewhere. It is also possible that potential embarrassment over appearing ignorant prevents someone from asking, "What does this mean?" or, "What do you mean when you say. . .?" When a candidate for local office states, "My office surveyed local citizens, and they are willing to

| **Table 1.2** | Thinking Critically When Developing and Evaluating Explanations About Behavior |

**Understand Important Terminology**
- Make Sure Terms, Concepts, and Principles Are Understood and Used Correctly
- Explore the Underlying Structure of Terms, Concepts, and Principles

**Recognize Underlying Assumptions**
- Identify the Assumptions that Underlie Explanations of Behavior
- Challenge Old Assumptions, and Develop New Ways of Thinking

**Use Questions to Facilitate Obtaining Relevant Information**
- Use Questions to Guide and Direct a Search for Information
- Ask Questions in the Form of Educated Guesses

**Pay Careful Attention to the Evidence an Explanation Is Based Upon**
- Distinguish Between Observations and Inferences
- Include Personal Qualities and Situational Factors in Explanations

**Explanations Must Fit Underlying Evidence**
- Sufficient Grounds for an Explanation Should Exist
- Explanations Must Not Be Too Far Removed from the Underlying Evidence

pay more taxes to get better city services," his views sound scientific. Before jumping on the bandwagon, however, explore how the candidate defined "surveyed." "Surveyed" could mean, "I talked to a few of my friends and neighbors," or "I hired an independent agency to do a scientific poll of citizens in the area." *Using dictionaries, learning key terms in textbooks, and, whenever possible, asking someone to explain what they meant are ways to avoid misinterpretations.* Taking such steps also makes it more difficult for others to purposely deceive us.

## Explore the Underlying Structure of Terms, Concepts, and Principles

If the meaning of some term, concept, or principle used to explain behavior continues to be elusive, follow the advice offered by David Perkins (1986, 1987). He suggests that we explore its underlying structure. People tend to treat terms and concepts as if they existed in a vacuum, that is, divorced of a context or frame of reference. Students, for example, may be asked to learn definitions of terms or to read about facts, concepts, and principles in psychology textbooks. Some do so without exploring the larger frame of reference in which the idea is embedded. Thus, a textbook presents a term such as "mindlessness," and a definition is conveniently provided. *Unfortunately, a limited understanding of what something means makes us more susceptible to influence by those with more knowledge.*

This intellectual laziness is very common. David Perkins argues that as a way out of this dilemma, any piece of knowledge or, for that matter, any object or event should be viewed as a **design**—that is, as a structure that is devised to accomplish a particular purpose. Most of us are more comfortable thinking of a car, jet plane, or tall building as representing a design. That is, the structure or form of such objects allows certain functions to occur (e.g., transportation, shelter). Ordinarily, terms, facts, concepts, principles, and math formulas are not thought of as representing designs. When they are, a comprehensive understanding of almost anything is possible. Listed below are four questions that David Perkins suggests we ask to understand what something means. Examples of how to use them appear in Table 1.3.

1.  What is its purpose?
    *(i.e., What is this term, concept, or principle designed to do or accomplish?)*
2.  How is it structured and organized?
    *(i.e., What are its components, and how do they relate to each other?)*
3.  What is an example or model case of it?
4.  What statements and reasons are used to explain and/or evaluate it?
    *(i.e., What statements and reasons explain what it is and/or help us decide whether or not it has achieved its purpose?)*

---

**Table 1.3**         Exploring the Underlying Structure of a Term, Concept, or Principle:
Four Questions to Ask

---

**Example 1: Exploring the term "mindlessness"**

*What is its purpose?*
Allows us to respond to questions, requests, and demands in a routine manner without devoting a great deal of conscious attention to our response.

*How is it structured and organized?*
Mindless thinking occurs when we become trapped by categories, we assume a single perspective when looking at things, and when we are engaged in relatively routine activities.

*What is an example, or model case?*
"I picked the wrong handouts for class from a pile of papers and passed them out to students before I caught the error."

*What statements and reasons are used to explain and/or evaluate it?*
Mindlessness is accompanied by low levels of self-awareness and awareness of what other people are doing. May produce problems for people by making them look silly. Also, may lead people who make mistakes to feel they have less control over their lives.

**Example 2: Exploring a proposed principle of behavior suggested by an advertisement for subliminal audiotapes designed to help people lose weight. Specifically, "People are influenced by messages that stimulate their unconscious minds."**

*What is its purpose?*
The audiotape and the accompanying message are designed to stimulate people to lose weight in a relatively easy and quick manner.

*How is it structured and organized?*
A message, "Do what is necessary to lose weight," is placed on a sound track at a sound level that makes it impossible to be consciously heard.

*What is an example, or model case?*
A local health food store plays the tapes to lure customers into the store.

*What statements and reasons are used to explain and/or evaluate it?*
Our unconscious mind hears the message, and it then stimulates actions designed to produce a weight loss. Testimonials from satisfied customers were used. The views of dissat-

isfied customers, however, were not given; nor were any scientific data reported. Why someone would listen to his or her unconscious mind is not explained very well. Many people fail to listen to a variety of loud and clear messages to lose weight from physicians, advertisements, and their conscious thought processes.

# RECOGNIZE UNDERLYING ASSUMPTIONS

Explanations typically reflect certain underlying **assumptions** about human nature. For example, consider the explanation of why a student named Carla quit college. One explanation is that "Carla decided to quit because of changes in her career plans." This explanation reflects a different assumption about human nature than one like, "the college forced Carla to quit." The first assumes that she made an independent decision to leave school. In the second, aspects of Carla's college environment are assumed to be at fault. Perhaps she was getting poor grades, her courses were not interesting, or she had friends who were quitting and she responded to peer pressure.

Underlying assumptions about human nature are always embedded in any explanation. *One advantage is that our assumptions help us develop a consistent set of beliefs about how the world operates.* We can then explain human behavior without appearing to be uncertain in our approach. *A disadvantage is that our assumptions may interfere with our ability to find other explanations.* They may function as blinders that allow us only to see in one direction. Thus, if I focussed on what the college did to force Carla to quit school, I might discount or ignore the role of personal problems or changes in her career plans.

The types of assumptions that underlie our explanations fall into several categories. Those identified by Lawrence Wrightsman (1992), based upon 30 years of research, are listed in Table 1.4. Such beliefs affect how we think and what we say or do.

| Table 1.4 | Assumptions About Human Nature |
|---|---|

Based on a 30-year research program, psychologist Lawrence Wrightsman has identified a number of assumptions about human nature that consistently appear in the beliefs each of us have about people. Of course, once they become a part of our belief system, they often appear in our everyday actions. Those that have appeared consistently across a variety of situations are presented below in the form of eight bipolar dimensions.

What assumptions about human nature would be present in the behaviors of a teacher who used three different exams in a large introductory psychology class and "watched those taking the exam like a hawk"? What belief about human nature listed below do you hold? How does each one appear in your actions?

- Trustworthy ——— Untrustworthy
- Rational ——— Irrational
- Willpower ——— Lack of Willpower
- Altruistic ——— Selfish
- Independent ——— Conforming
- Complex ——— Simple
- Similar ——— Different
- Stable ——— Unstable

If I believed that people were untrustworthy and irrational, I might think twice before deciding to walk among a group of strangers. On the other hand, if I thought that people were trustworthy and rational, I might be more willing to make friends with people I did not know. Wrightsman reports that a variety of behaviors—including our preferences for political parties, the friends we keep, and our selection of an occupation—are related to underlying assumptions about human nature.

*Our evaluations and judgments of people also are colored by underlying assumptions.* In one study, student ratings of their instructors were obtained on overall teaching ability, the clarity of classroom presentations, and the emotional climate between teacher and students. Students who held more positive views of human nature (e.g., trustworthy, rational, stable, altruistic ) gave more favorable evaluations than students who held negative views about human nature (e.g., untrustworthy, not rational, unstable, selfish). In addition, students who viewed others as dissimilar were able to identify differences in the teaching styles among instructors better than did those who assumed people were similar (Wrightsman, 1992).

## CHALLENGE OLD ASSUMPTIONS, AND DEVELOP NEW WAYS OF THINKING

In the field of psychology, new directions for explaining behavior occurred when people began to make new and different assumptions. When psychologists John Watson and B. F. Skinner suggested that mental events had little place in a science of behavior, the debates that followed led to new discoveries about the factors that influenced human behavior. In particular, psychologists began to focus on how stimuli in the environment triggered, shaped, and maintained our actions. As one example, the way in which rewards affected our actions was identified, and this led to many practical applications in education, therapy, and business settings. New assumptions led to alternative answers to questions such as, "What factors control the behaviors of people?"

*All of us can become more effective critical thinkers by broadening our perspective on the world around us.* This often adds additional interests to our explorations and new insights into what to think, say, or do. To accomplish this goal, it is helpful to play around with what we assume to be true about people and events in our lives. Two strategies for doing this include:

1. Using assumptions that are contrary to accepted beliefs, and
2. Reversing common assumptions to generate alternative perspectives and insights into behavior.

Each of these two approaches is illustrated in Focus on People 1.1. The goal of employing such strategies is to generate thoughts about alternative ways to conceptualize issues. The new ideas generated at first may appear strange, weird, or outrageous. Try not to reject them immediately. Instead, always identify potential "likes" as well as "dislikes" associated with new ways of thinking.

## USING QUESTIONS EFFECTIVELY

Many of our questions are stated in a rather general or casual manner. Consider for a moment the question, "Why do I become anxious when taking exams?" The explanation may lie in a lack of preparation; internal conflicts, such as a fear of failure; pressure

FOCUS ON PEOPLE 1.1
## Food for Thought

Sometimes new assumptions help us to "think a little crazy" in order to develop interesting and oftentimes new insights into human behavior. Making new assumptions also opens us up to asking questions in a different manner. *To do this:*

### 1. Use assumptions that are contrary to accepted belief.

*Assumption:* People agree to get married until "death do us part."

*Assumption that is contrary to accepted belief:* People agree to marry for five years with an option to renew the marriage contract for another five years.

*New Insights:* Eric Bienstock (1989) proposes that instead of a "lifetime contract," people might consider five-year renewable contracts. He suggests that this approach would give individuals an easy out if they made a mistake or were in an abusive relationship. Also, it would force those who wanted to continue in a marriage to be able to do so without worrying about a "lifelong commitment."

*New Questions:* Would a renewable contract force people to spend time, energy, and effort discussing their reasons for remaining together? Would partners treat each other better to avoid losing a spouse at contract renewal time? What problems would renewable contracts pose for raising children and making long-term plans?

### 2. Reverse common assumptions to generate questions that lead to alternative perspectives and insights into behavior.

*Assumption:* Students are assigned grades at the end of a course.

*Reversal:* Students are assigned grades at the beginning of a course.

*New Insights:* Roberta Borkat (1993), a professor of English, suggests giving everyone in a class an A after the second week. She argues that several benefits would occur. Students would be assured of a high grade point average, and no academic obstacles would stand in their way. Professors would be relieved of useless burdens and would have time to pursue their real interests. Even forests would be saved by the need to have less paper for books, compositions, and examinations.

*New Questions:* Her suggestion is, of course, stated "tongue in cheek." Let us play around with it and examine a variation of her idea. What might happen if everyone entering a class received an "A" and all they could do over the term was lose credit for poor work? Would the quality of the student work and teaching processes in such a class improve? What if all students were treated as if they were "A" students?

from peers or parents to do well; or the instructor may emphasize exams or the importance of getting a good grade. Thus, *finding an answer is facilitated when the search for information begins with a question that helps to guide and direct the process.* Something can be learned from the way psychologists do research into the reasons why people behave as they do.

## Ask Questions in the Form of an Educated Guess

It is helpful to state possible answers to questions before information is gathered. Observations, facts, and figures are then employed either to prove or to reject those tentative answers. This is called forming a **hypothesis**, or developing an educated guess about the answer to a question. How this process works with the formal study of behavior is shown in Focus on Applied Research 1.2.

As you can see in the research example, *a hypothesis, or educated guess, is not pulled out of a hat.* Past research, theories, and experience studying a phenomenon are used to form a hypothesis. *In a research setting, a good hypothesis is testable, and the procedures used to*

## Unmasking the Amazing Kreskin

George Kresge, better known by his stage name, "The Amazing Kreskin," was getting ready to appear before an audience of 700 citizens in Dunedin, New Zealand. Kreskin was unaware that he was about to become part of a psychological research study conducted by David Marks and Richard Kammann (1980).

At one point in his act, Kreskin faced the audience and said, "I'm going to send a number between one and fifty. I'll make both digits odd, but not the same odd digit. For example, fifteen would be okay, but eleven wouldn't do because the two odd digits are the same. Open the mental screen in your head and read what is on it."

Before reading further, open your "mental screen." Reread the instructions, and write two numbers you think Kreskin was "transmitting" in the space below.

First number:_____    Second number:_____

About four hundred people in the audience got the correct answers, and the audience went wild. Most of them thought Kreskin had ESP. Did you think of the numbers 37 or 35, as members of the audience did? Kreskin said he had thought of both numbers. Marks and Kammann, however, had another hypothesis. Kreskin was simply making use of a common response bias and not using ESP.

You are already familiar with this response bias if you think of the colors "red" or "green" when asked to quickly think of a color. Such response biases are called population stereotypes. They are simply rigid ways of responding that characterize a large group of people. Kreskin's instructions elicited certain response biases. By telling his audience both digits were odd, only ten digits between 1 and 50 could be correct. He used up 15 as an example, and 11 and 33 were eliminated because both digits are the same. Mentioning 11 and 15 also makes people select answers further away from them. Thus, the digits 31, 35, 37, and 39 become possible answers.

To test their hypothesis, Marks and Kammann had an assistant who was unaware of the purpose of the study read the instructions Kreskin gave to his audience to 200 students. After reading the instructions, they purposely thought of other things while pretending to transmit "mental messages."

The data confirmed their hypothesis. The number 37 was selected by 35 percent of the students, and the number 35 by 23 percent. Therefore, Kreskin could count on more than half of his audience selecting the numbers 37 and 35. When he told them he considered both numbers, a lot of people inappropriately began to feel psychic.

gather information allow it to be disconfirmed. Marks and Kammann (1980) tested the hypothesis that a response bias was responsible for The Amazing Kreskin's "powers" on a group of undergraduate students. Thus, their hypothesis was testable, and the procedure employed allowed it to be disconfirmed. The students' responses, for example, could have been evenly distributed among all of the possible two-digit odd numbers. If this had happened, their hypothesis would have been rejected.

A student in one of my classes wanted to understand why her new boss oversupervised employees. An educated guess was that he had high personal needs for control and influence. Thus, she observed his actions in a number of settings to see if evidence supported her point of view. She noticed, for example, that her boss was very opinionated only when discussing issues with subordinates. He appeared less so with people on or above his level in the organization. Also, at a company picnic, he closely watched his children and constantly disciplined them for minor bouts of misbehavior. When working with relatively inexperienced employees, he was much more controlling than he was with those with a lot of experience on the job.

On the basis of such observations, she concluded that her boss probably had strong needs to control and influence others. However, the evidence did not support her hypothesis as originally stated. Apparently, his needs to control were much more evident when dealing with people who had less rank or experience than he did.

*Hypotheses not only provide direction to the process of answering questions, they also keep professional and amateur psychologists honest.* That is, they prevent people from becoming "Monday morning quarterbacks" or becoming susceptible to the **hindsight bias.** Everyone has had the experience of believing that they "knew all along" the outcome of a political election, the Superbowl football game, or some natural disaster. After learning that two friends got divorced, this bias would be present if you said, "I knew this would happen all along. I just knew it." Perhaps you remember having a little doubt about the marriage, but once the outcome was known—suddenly you became absolutely sure the breakup was inevitable.

*The hindsight bias occurs whenever we project new knowledge into the past and then deny that the outcome information has influenced our judgment.* Scott Hawkins and Reid Hastie (1990) report that people have a difficult time recalling their initial thoughts and predictions. Thus, they simplify the situation and focus only on those factors that are consistent with the outcome. Evidence contrary to the outcome is ignored, or its significance is discounted. When two people get divorced, friends might focus on how they sometimes argued in public or occasionally went to a social gathering without their spouse. The fact they held hands in public and often hugged each other in front of friends is now not viewed as very important. The result of this distorted analysis is, "I just knew the divorce would happen." There are two actions we can take to overcome the hindsight bias.

1. *One is to consider how an alternative outcome might have occurred* (Fishhoff, 1975). That is, if, after the fact, "you knew two people would get divorced," think of reasons why they might have remained married. This will force you to consider all of the factors that were present and how you selected facts in order to "predict" the divorce.

THOSE MONDAY MORNING QUARTERBACKS BECOME A LITTLE SENSITIVE WHEN PEOPLE DISAGREE WITH THEM.

2. *Become skeptical.* Challenge the explanation given; look for alternative ways to explain something; or gather additional information to help us change our minds.

The latter advice, however, is sometimes easier said than done. *Changing our minds after providing an explanation is difficult.* The reason is that the most informative piece of information we can obtain is something that rules out a hypothesis or causes us to change our point of view. People are generally unwilling to challenge their cherished beliefs. Instead, they are likely to fall into a trap called the **confirmation bias.** This is a tendency to look for information that confirms current beliefs rather than looking for evidence that challenges it.

# PAY CAREFUL ATTENTION TO THE EVIDENCE AN EXPLANATION IS BASED UPON

## Distinguish Between Observations and Inferences

The raw data for developing explanations are the specific characteristics of the events and behaviors observed. In gathering such information, a common problem must be avoided. *This is the tendency to confuse what is directly observed with an inference or initial interpretation about the observation.*

To explore this distinction, take a dollar bill out of your purse or wallet, and lay it in front of you. Indicate whether the following statements about the dollar bill are observations or inferences by placing an "O" or an "I," respectively, in the spaces provided:

1. _____ There are some numbers on the dollar bill.
2. _____ This dollar bill will buy a hamburger.
3. _____ The dollar bill is very thin.
4. _____ Dollar bills have germs on them.
5. _____ This dollar bill is not counterfeit.
6. _____ A friend would be happy to receive this dollar.

You should have identified items 1 and 3 as observations and the remaining items as inferences. That is, your answer was derived by interpreting the information given and not from what you could directly observe. For example, at some fast food chains, your dollar could purchase a hamburger. At others, it is barely enough for a large cup of coffee. Determining that the dollar is counterfeit also involves forming an inference based upon an analysis of the quality of the paper, the ink, and other markings.

In much the same way, care must be taken when offering explanations for events and behaviors that occur daily. At a restaurant the other night, a waiter dropped a tray containing two desserts. I overheard someone at the table next to mine say, "He sure is clumsy." What was said is an inference and not an observation. The behaviors observed were that while walking across the dining room, the waiter raised the tray high over his head to avoid hitting a customer who was passing by. His hand tilted slightly to the right; the tray leaned sideways; and the two desserts slid to the side of the tray and dropped over the edge.

"Clumsy," then, is an inference and not something that was directly observed. It represents an opinion about an underlying characteristic of the waiter based upon a single observation. *In our daily lives, making firm judgments about someone's personality should only occur after multiple contacts and observations with an individual.* Therefore, concluding that the dropped tray was an "accident" caused by an unbalanced load is an interpretation that is much closer to the specific behaviors observed.

## Include Personal Qualities and Situational Factors in Explanations

*Behaviors are always a function of an individual's personal qualities as well as factors in the environment.* Included in our personal qualities or dispositions are such things as our hereditary characteristics, motives, emotional state, attitudes, and beliefs. Examples of environmental or situational influences include such things as the actions of other people, rewards, sanctions for behavior, hazards in the environment, and the formal and informal rules and expectations guiding behavior.

An **attribution** is simply an inference about the causes of an action. For example, if you are successful in school, you might attribute your performance to a strong need to succeed and to hard work. On the other hand, you might attribute a lack of success to uninteresting courses, bad teachers, or difficult tests. Both explanations focus on either personal qualities or situational influences, and thus they distort the fact that both factors played a role. Over time, certain biases or **attribution errors** affect our ability to objectively analyze and interpret our own actions or those of other people. Three types of errors identified in the literature are noted below (Kearl and Gordon, 1992).

*1. The Fundamental Attribution Error* Observers of behavior have a general tendency to focus on personal factors when describing the behaviors of others and to ignore or downplay environmental influences. Thus, a worker who has several accidents is viewed as "accident-prone" or "unlucky" rather than as someone who works in an unsafe environment.

*2. The Actor-Observer Bias* The tendency to look for personal explanations is greater when we focus on the actions of others rather than on our behaviors. As actors, however, we attribute our behavior to situational causes. Consequently, observers watching a coffee cup slip out of my hand may label me "clumsy" or "nervous." I am more likely to attribute the problem to a "slippery coffee cup." The latter tendency towards environmental explanations is stronger whenever we make a mistake or fail to perform well. Similarly, the tendency to look for personal characteristics as explanations of the behaviors of others is stronger if we dislike them or they engage in an action we dislike.

*3. Self-Serving Bias* Related to the actor-observer bias is a tendency to put ourselves in the best possible light. People are quick to take credit for their successes and to pass the buck for their failures. Generally speaking, we attribute our successes mostly to ability and effort and blame our failures on bad luck or other factors outside of out control.

As a general rule, the influence of situational factors is underestimated and that of personal factors is emphasized whenever people analyze and interpret the actions of others. The cause appears to be partly cultural. Western culture values autonomous individual action, internal motivation, and accepting personal responsibility. Consequently, a well-formed bias to look for personal dispositions develops, and it colors our interpretations of behavior. On the other hand, other cultures emphasize social relationships and obligations. Joan Miller (1984), for example, asked Americans and citizens of India to describe the causes of positive and negative behaviors they had observed.

The Americans emphasized personal attributions, and the people from India emphasized situational explanations.

*Furthermore, among people living in a Western culture, the emphasis on personal attributions appears to be arrived at mindlessly.* Instead of considering all of the evidence, Daniel Gilbert (1989, 1992) demonstrates people form attributions in a two-step process. First, people identify the behavior and make a quick personal attribution. This first step is simple and automatic, like a reflex. Second, critical thinking is employed to correct or adjust that inference so that it will account for situational influences. Such thinking requires attention, thought, and effort. If Gilbert's view is correct, fewer situational factors should be identified when observers cannot devote thought and effort to the event. Gilbert reports that this is indeed the case. When observers are distracted, fatigued, engaged in other tasks, or rushed for time, less attention is paid to situational influences on behavior.

Furthermore, people normally use the clues described in the scenario below before deciding that a behavior has been influenced by a situational factor. The more such clues are judged to be present, the greater the degree of situational involvement in the behavior. When distracted, however, people have a difficult time using them, and personal attributions prevail (Kelley and Mischela, 1980).

*Scenario:* Rodney files a grievance with the union after his supervisor accuses him of being lazy and reassigns him to another job. Did the supervisor's actions provoke Rodney to file the grievance, or was he just being irrational? A friend of Rodney's used the following clues to help her decide the supervisor's actions (i.e., a situational factor) were at fault.

- *Consensus:* Most people would engage in the same action if they were in that situation. "Rodney did what anyone else working here would have done if their supervisor accused them of being lazy. He filed a grievance with the union."
- *Distinctiveness:* What occurred is atypical or unusual for the person being observed. In effect, that individual has never engaged in the behavior before. "Normally, Rodney is pretty easygoing and takes criticism well."

• *Consistency:* The person reacts or would probably react in the same way every time the same stimulus or situation occurs. "What the supervisor said struck a nerve. He would probably do the same thing again."

## Managing Attribution Errors

Attribution errors distort interpretations of our actions and those of other people. They cannot be discounted or disregarded. *The best protection is to monitor explanations for the presence of both situational and personal qualities.* This is not to suggest that both factors are always present in equal amounts. Rather, the problem you are trying to control is to avoid ignoring one at the expense of the other.

To do this, try to find at least one example of each factor to explain why some event occurred. In an experimental setting, showing people a videotape of how some action looks from the perspective of both an actor and an observer helps. When this is done, more situational explanations for someone's actions become apparent (Storms, 1973). In our daily lives, however, this change in perspective can occur only if we empathize with the plight of another person. Putting ourselves in their shoes enhances our capacity to correctly explain their actions.

Of course, it also is possible to become a victim of attribution errors. Thus, each of us needs to protect ourselves from an unfair analysis of our actions. To guard against inaccurate judgments, help others think critically about your actions. Do the following:

*Call Attention to What Caused Your Behavior* Offer an alternative explanation, for example, "I'm sorry I dropped the vase; I pinched my fingers in the door this morning, and now I can't seem to hold things well."

*Point Out a Mistake, or Perhaps Joke About It* A frank acknowledgment will show you to be a competent person, and it will also let the other person know that the mistake is not typical of you. Thus, you might say, "What a terrible meeting I ran! I should never have let Sam and Jane take up so much time."

*Let Other People Know You Have Changed* Ask for another chance to show what you can do. In doing this, you might be honest, open, and sincere. You might say to your boss, for example, "Look, Phil, I know I didn't handle that customer well before; but I've done my homework, and I know I can be much more effective now."

# EXPLANATIONS AND CONCLUSIONS MUST FIT UNDERLYING EVIDENCE

Facts, data, observations, and other information about people and situations are the raw materials, or evidence, used to support various principles and conclusions about behavior. Ideally, there should be a good fit between the two. In most everyday situations, however, the fit between an explanation or conclusion and the evidence (i.e., information, facts, figures) supporting it is not perfect. Thus, the best we can do is establish (or at least hope) that the evidence is worthwhile.

A jury, for example, does not determine whether someone is "absolutely" guilty. Rather, the information, facts, and other evidence are weighed, and the defendant is found guilty "beyond a reasonable doubt." A physician assesses your symptoms and determines how likely it is that you have a particular disease. A weather forecaster examines patterns in the wind, humidity, air temperature, and pressure, and then he or she concludes there is a 70 percent chance of rain or snow. A public opinion poll reports that, "Survey results show 60 percent of the population is unhappy with the President's economic policies. The margin of error is + or − 3 percentage points." As you can see, explanations and conclusions cannot be absolutely guaranteed to be accurate. There is always the possibility of an error, as many jurors, physicians, weather forecasters, and pollsters have discovered.

The problem each of us faces in developing explanations and forming conclusions is nicely summarized by Robert Pinto and John Anthony Blair (1993) when they note:

> Even thoroughly trustworthy data can support conclusions in varying degrees. Sometimes data conclusively establish a conclusion; sometimes they render a conclusion probable but do not establish it conclusively; sometimes the data available make it reasonable to suspect the conclusion is true; and sometimes the data provide no real support for the conclusion at all (p. 4).

What we need are criteria for evaluating our explanations and conclusions. T. Edward Damer (1987) suggests that we ask whether the underlying evidence provides **sufficient grounds** for accepting a conclusion. *Sufficient grounds means that the evidence creates an overall pattern that suggests the interpretations or conclusion was reasonable and more likely to be correct than incorrect.*

## Three Criteria for Determining Whether Sufficient Grounds Exist

*1. The underlying evidence must be acceptable for sufficient grounds to exist* To be acceptable, support for an interpretation or conclusion about behavior must be:

- Readily available and a matter of public record
- Accurate, correct, and factual.

Let us examine each of the latter two aspects of whether information is acceptable.

*Being readily available and a matter of public record means that the underlying information, facts, and figures supporting something are accessible to anyone who wants them.* Unfortunately,

this is not always the case. A popular audiotape proclaims that people "using special memory-enhancing techniques can double their capacity to learn." The research backing its claims of enhanced learning is based upon inaccessible research by Bulgarian researchers. Similarly, UFO buffs for years have claimed that physical evidence of alien visits is lacking because the "aliens are careful to not leave any evidence behind" and a "government conspiracy to hide such evidence exists" (Randi, 1982). Of course, this means that only a "chosen few" have the information needed to support conclusions about powerful learning techniques and visits by aliens from outer space. Thus, such conclusions should be taken with a grain of salt.

*Evidence is acceptable when it also is accurate, correct, and factual.* Thus, it needs to be based upon information that has its roots in research findings or the views of experts or anyone else with legitimate knowledge in an area. *Incorrect facts, data, and other information invalidate any conclusion or explanation based upon them.* Unfortunately, a number of explanations regarding human behavior rest on little more than personal opinion. They "sound good" but lack a more scientific foundation. Such "facts" sometimes have become a part of the "folklore" of how people function. Consider the following examples identified by Carol Wade and Carol Tavris (1987).

1. *Opposites attract.* People seek relationships with those who have some quality they lack. Typically, this is more wishful thinking than reality. *Birds of a feather flock together* would be more in line with the research data. People tend to be attracted to those who are similar in looks, interests, religion, intelligence, age, and family background.

2. *Beauty is only skin deep.* The qualities beneath the surface of a person should play the major role in our attraction towards them. Individuals typically use this statement to try and convince others they are fair and democratic. Unfortunately what people say does not always relate to what they do. Research indicates that physical attractiveness is an important influence in our attraction to others literally from the moment an infant emerges from the womb. People considered physically attractive are perceived as more poised, likeable, sensitive, and desirable, and as leading more exciting, successful, interesting, and happy lives.

*2. The underlying evidence must be relevant to an explanation for sufficient grounds to exist* To be relevant, support for an explanation must be:

- Appropriate for the explanation it supports; also,
- The explanation or conclusion logically follows from it.

Let us examine the latter two aspects of when underlying support for a conclusion is relevant.

*"Appropriate" means the facts, data, and observations clearly apply to or are suitable for that explanation.* That is, it is not something drawn out of "left field" or "used just because it was handy." Assume that a friend of yours, Jakeba, recently quit her job. Two explanations are provided by two of her friends. One says, "Jakeba quit her job because the stars and planets were in an unfavorable alignment when she was born." Another says, "Jakeba quit because of conflicts with her boss and coworkers." The second would be considered a more appropriate explanation.

*The explanation or conclusion must logically follow from the underlying evidence.* Quitting one's job, for example, is one logical outcome of having unresolved conflicts with a boss and coworkers. Such conflicts make a job environment aversive and people are more likely to leave. It is certainly more logical than assuming an unfavorable horoscope reading was at fault.

*3. The explanation or conclusion is a better fit to the underlying evidence than anything else.* Selecting the first thing you thought of to explain or interpret something is generally not a good idea. A more appropriate explanation or conclusion might be overlooked. *The best safeguard here is to first consider other alternative explanations and to reject them before reaching a conclusion.* This may prevent us from "jumping to conclusions" or otherwise making hasty interpretations. It also keeps us from exaggerating the importance of any one explanation or conclusion.

## Explanations and Conclusions Must Not Be Too Far Removed from the Evidence Supporting Them

Sometimes thinking about alternative explanations or conclusions produces several that appear to meet the criteria for sufficient grounds (i.e., they appear reasonable and are more likely to be correct than incorrect). In such cases, it is important to select the one that is closest to the evidence. For example, a United States senator running for office recently claimed that "The 1 percent drop in unemployment is proof that our party's economic policies are working." An alternative explanation is that "the economy is improving, businesses are doing better, and thus they are hiring more people. Our party's economic policies are only one of several factors responsible for the drop in unemployment." Of course the latter explanation may not strike the emotional chord in voters that someone running for office wants to hit.

People may draw conclusions that go beyond the evidence for two reasons. One is a natural tendency to exaggerate. The other is that diverse facts, data, and other pieces of information are often present. They do not always agree, some may be inaccurate, and important details may be missing. In spite of all of this, some explanation must be provided. Pressure to say something takes over, and it is easy to miss the mark.

Table 1.5 contains three scenarios in which conclusions were drawn based upon underlying evidence. Before reading further, apply each of the three criteria to determine if there are sufficient grounds for accepting each conclusion (i.e., whether they are more likely to be correct than incorrect). *Sufficient grounds exist only if all three criteria are satisfied.*

All three conclusions fail the test for sufficient grounds for different reasons. The conclusion in *Scenario 1* is based on information that is unacceptable. The underlying evidence is *factually incorrect* and runs counter to the research findings that were *readily available* in the discussion of Tavris and Wade's work presented earlier. That evidence suggested that physical attractiveness *was* an important factor in whether or not we like someone. Thus, a more accurate conclusion is that *Nicole probably would not like Tom.*

The conclusion in *Scenario 2* is not based on relevant evidence. For this conclusion to be acceptable, the childhood beating should be an *appropriate explanation*, and Jason's actions as an adult should *logically follow* from that fact. Thus, we would have to figure out some way that a childhood beating on Friday the 13th would influence Jason's adult behavior on the same date. Having an unconscious need to get back at his father sounds mysterious. It is not, however, as appropriate or logical as other reasons, such as wanting money to pay off bills or to buy drugs.

The evidence in *Scenario 3* is probably factually accurate. However, Christie and Carl getting married is *not necessarily a logical outcome* of going to the movies and studying

**Table 1.5**    Is There Sufficient Grounds for Accepting Each Conclusion?

Sufficient grounds exist only if the conclusion meets each of the following three criteria: (1) The evidence is acceptable (i.e., readily accessible to anyone and accurate and factually correct); (2) The evidence is relevant (i.e., appropriate for the conclusion; the conclusion is a logical outcome of the evidence); (3) The conclusion is a better fit to the underlying evidence than any other alternative explanation. If not, what is a better explanation? *Check your answers with the discussion in the text.*

**Scenario 1: Facts, data, observations, and other evidence**
- Physical attractiveness plays a superficial role in whether we like someone.
- Tom is physically unattractive.

**Conclusion:**
Nicole would probably like Tom, because good looks are not all that important anyway.

**Scenario 2: Facts, data, observations, and other evidence**
- As a 10-year-old child, Jason was once beaten by his father on Friday, April 13.
- As a 35-year-old adult, Jason robbed Mrs. Adams of $100 on the evening of Friday, April 13.

**Conclusion:**
Jason robbed Mrs. Adams to fulfill unconscious needs to get back at his father for beating him.

**Scenario 3: Facts, data, observations, and other evidence.**
- Christie went to the movies with Carl last week.
- Carl and Christie studied together for their Calculus midterm exam.
- Carl introduced Christie to all of his best friends.

**Conclusion:**
Christie and Carl will get married one day because they are such good friends.

together. Also, the evidence fits other conclusions better than the one that they will get married. For example, saying that "Carl and Christie might continue to date," or, "Carl and Christie might remain good friends" would be more in line with the evidence.

# PUTTING IT ALL TOGETHER

The principles for critical thinking identified in Table 1.2 and discussed in this chapter can help you improve your own critical thinking. While they have been presented in isolation from one another, there are circumstances where combinations of such principles can be very useful. Their combined use may help to prevent the unfortunate consequences such as those illustrated in Focus on People 1.2. Try to apply what you have learned about critical thinking to this real-life situation. Use the following questions to help you think about the issues that are involved and to gain a deeper understanding about what has happened.

FOCUS ON PEOPLE 1.2

## Rush to Judgment

At a high school graduation ceremony, a school board member heard the principal instruct the audience that as a courtesy to everyone, "whoops, hoots, and hollers" were prohibited as the names of graduates were announced.

*In spite of the principal's plea, the proceedings were interrupted by screams and shouts by friends and family members of the graduates.* The member of the board began to tally the number of times the proceedings were interrupted by members in the audience who were Caucasian and by those in the audience who were Afro-American. The board member sent the tally of his observations, along with some comments, to an attorney who represented the school board on legal matters. The letter was leaked to the news media, and a controversy erupted.

The school board member presented the following information in the letter:

### CAUCASIAN GRADUATES

| Proceedings Interrupted | Proceedings Not Interrupted |
| --- | --- |
| 29% | 71% |

### AFRO-AMERICAN GRADUATES

| Proceedings Interrupted | Proceedings Not Interrupted |
| --- | --- |
| 74% | 26% |

The letter writer calculated that the rate of disruption (74%) among Afro-American audience members was two and one-half times greater than the rate (29%) among Caucasian members of the audience. "You will recognize," the board member wrote to the school board's attorney, "this is exactly the same disparity between racial groups as we see with student suspensions and expulsions."

The letter also stated, "This study contains no room for racist, insensitive judgment by teaching faculty, administrators, etc., as it was based only on the ability of family and friends to follow a simple request for the preservation of order. If there is a two and one-half to one racial disparity ratio by which black parents/relatives fail to adhere to common standards of civility, we should not be surprised that this behavior ultimately reflects itself in student performance and misconduct."

The school board member's conclusions were labeled racist, and members of the minority and white community called for a resignation.

Based on a story in the Associated Press, June 8, 1992.

- For the conclusions "parents encourage student misconduct" and "the board member is racist," list the evidence used.
- Do you understand what the term "racist" means? Use a dictionary, and/or apply David Perkins's questions for exploring the meaning of a term to gain a better understanding of this word. Is the term used correctly by the people involved?
- What assumptions about human nature identified in Table 1.4 are the school board member and people in the community making?
- What questions/hypotheses do you think the school board member probably used to direct his search for answers? Did such questions/hypotheses create any biases?
- Is the evidence you identified based on observations or inferences?
- Does it include both personal and situational factors?
- Are there "sufficient grounds" to accept it? That is, is it reasonable and more likely to be correct than incorrect given the evidence? To do this, determine whether the evidence is "acceptable" and "relevant" to each conclusion. What alternative explanations are there for the conclusions that were drawn?
- In the final analysis, do the conclusions stray too far from the underlying evidence?

## Summary of Chapter Organizers

Suggested responses to the chapter organizers at the beginning of this chapter are presented below.

1. *What types of mental errors occur when automatic mental control processes are not executed properly?* Automatic pilots guide our motor skills and allow us to save our conscious mental capacity for more important tasks. Errors occur when people become fatigued or otherwise distracted. Common errors include using a related but wrong process, blending two or more automatic pilots, interference among two or more control processes, and executing but not completing an automatic pilot.

2. *How can you protect yourself from the mistakes they sometimes produce?* To protect yourself it is important to remain extravigilant and to monitor your actions where problems have occurred in the past. In addition, the side effects of a miscue can be employed to guide and direct future actions. Lastly, use reminders to do things that help you break out of habitual patterns.

3. *Do you know the three characteristics of mindless thinking?* Mindlessness involves becoming trapped by categories or allowing past distinctions to rigidly guide present behaviors. Also, it is likely to occur anytime you blindly follow requests, act from a single mindset, and fail to consider alternative explanations for things.

4. *What are the consequences of relying on this mode of thinking?* Over time, a narrow self-image may develop when you limit how you see yourself. An inability to break mindless patterns adversely affects relationships. Learned helplessness may develop, and you can become too easily influenced by others.

5. *Can you think of ways to overcome mindlessness?* A good place to begin is to recognize the signs of mindless behavior. Then, resist attempts by others to prescribe how you should think. Question what you are doing, and actively search for ways to gain control over your life.

6. *How do absolute and extreme ways of thinking affect your life, and what can be done to manage them?* Such modes of thinking lead to distortions in your perceptions of reality; they contribute to your negative emotions; and they prevent you from taking a more constructive approach to resolving issues. To overcome them, such beliefs must be challenged, less extreme and absolute ways of thinking developed, and actions taken based on new ways of looking at situations.

7. *What are three common patterns of thinking that are related to your level of intellectual development?* How do they affect the way you think? The dualism/received knowledge style leads to difficulty thinking independently and analyzing information. Individuals in a multiplism/subjective knowledge mode have problems employing criteria to decide among their options. The relativism/procedural knowledge style leads to independent thinking and to employing appropriate criteria when making interpretations and forming conclusions.

8. *How can critical thinking be used to help you understand the terms, concepts, and principles that describe behavior?* Critical thinking involves taking a reflective and questioning approach to understanding behavior. Thus, important terms, concepts, and principles need to be defined and/or used correctly. This is not only true for how terms are employed, but how others do so as well. Whenever possible, exploring the underlying structure of terms, concepts, and principles is helpful for understanding them. Treating such things as a design or a structure adapted to a purpose forces you to test the depth of your knowledge about various terms, concepts, and principles.

9. *Are you aware of how your personal assumptions affect both the questions you ask about human behavior and the answers you obtain?* Your questions tend to reflect underlying views of human nature. Recognizing this can help you to identify biases and limitations in the explanations obtained about your own behaviors and the actions of others. Your personal assumptions also affect how your questions are answered and thus have implications for your continuing thoughts and behaviors. To broaden your base of knowledge about human behavior, it is sometimes useful to challenge your assumptions and develop new ways of explaining behavior.

10. *Can you ask effective questions to develop explanations for behavior?* Questions are helpful in organizing and directing our search for answers about behavior. Stating a question in the form of an educated guess or hypothesis is often useful. Then information supporting it can be obtained and alternative explanations eliminated. An educated guess also makes you less susceptible to the hindsight bias when explaining events.

11. *When developing explanations about behavior based upon your observations, what should you do to ensure that they are accurate?* When trying to understand and explain behavior, an initial step you should take is to not confuse observations with inferences. Furthermore, how personal qualities and situational factors contribute to any behavior must be identified. To do this well involves a sensitivity to such factors and taking care not to become trapped by attribution errors or biases. The fundamental attribution error, the actor-observer bias, and the self-serving bias act to distort your explanations and conclusions.

    Your explanations also should have sufficient grounds. This means they must be based on evidence that is acceptable (i.e., accurate and readily accessible), relevant (i.e., appropriate and logically related to a conclusion), and selected only after alternative explanations or conclusions are ruled out.

## Things to Do

1. Do groups such as fraternities, sororities, and political parties use tactics similar to those of cults described in Focus on Applied Research 1.1 to recruit new members? In what ways are their tactics different? Have you ever belonged to groups that encouraged "mindless allegiance" to a person or cause? What aspects of mindless thinking affected you?

2. Sit and observe the staff and customers at your favorite fast food restaurant for a half hour. List examples of things that are said and done that represent examples of automatic mental control processes and mindless thinking. Did any of these thinking processes produce problems for anyone?

3. Review Table 1.1 on common modes of thinking. Select a newspaper and/or news magazine. What statements in the news articles, editorial pages, and advertisements provide evidence for each style? Also examine statements in these sources that represent irrational beliefs. Who is using them, and what effects did such beliefs produce?

4. A recent newspaper headline said, "Two Junior High School Students Arrested in Plot to Kill Teacher." The students were angry because of bad grades and "wished the teacher were dead." Classmates began betting on whether they had the courage to do it and raised $250. The plan was for one student to stab the teacher while the other held the instructor down. A school official heard of the plot and

broke it up minutes before it was to occur. Pretend that you will design a study to discover why the students tried to kill their teacher. *Develop three hypotheses to explain their actions.* One should focus on personal qualities, the second on situational factors, and the third on how both types of factors jointly influence behavior. Which hypothesis do you think is the more likely explanation? Why?

5. What assumptions about human nature described in Table 1.4 would likely be made by the following people: a judge about to sentence a habitual criminal; a woman deciding whether to accept a marriage proposal; a salesperson trying to sell a customer a new refrigerator; a teacher who uses two to three forms of an exam in a large introductory class?

6. A woman wrote to the "Amazing Randi," a professional magician, to claim the $10,000 he offered to anyone who could document a psychic ability. She described how she would run to one end of a fish tank, stand there, and then "will" the fish to come to her. The fish would come to her end of the tank, and she claimed an ability to "communicate with goldfish." Refute her claim by using the concepts related to observation versus inference, self-serving bias, definition and clarity of terms, role of personal qualities versus situational influences on behavior, and the criteria of evidence being "acceptable," "relevant," and having "sufficient grounds."

## APPLIED ACTIVITIES

EXERCISE 1.1

**Developing Accurate Interpretations and Explanations**

**Scenario 1:**

Massimo Polidoro is a magician and investigator for the Italian Committee for the Investigation of the Paranormal. On a popular television talk show, he demonstrated what he claimed were "psychic powers" including bending and breaking a spoon with his thoughts, identifying a drawing in a sealed envelope, and making radish seeds germinate in his hand. He then invited viewers to bring broken watches and cutlery to their TV sets as he went into a "trance." The audience was told that "something" might happen in their homes, such as the watches ticking again or the cutlery becoming bent. Other strange phenomena might also occur. The television show's switchboard was jammed with telephone calls from all over Italy reporting "broken watches that were fixed, spoons that were mysteriously bent, a TV set that suddenly turned off, and a clock's pendulum that fell to the floor"(Polidoro, 1993).

- State a hypothesis that would guide and direct your search for answers to what occurred. What information would you need to support your hypothesis? How would you obtain this information?

- What type of attribution error are viewers likely to make about Massimo Polidoro? Give an example of what they would say.

- What personal and situational factors could help us understand the behaviors of people who called the television station?

- Is the conclusion that "psychic forces" were operating justified? Does the evidence fit the facts? Does the conclusion stray too far beyond the facts? Indicate whether it meets the criterion of "sufficient grounds" discussed in the text.

**Scenario 2:**

On a cold, snowy January evening, I arrived at the Northern Kentucky-Cincinnati airport around midnight and caught the only taxicab still waiting for passengers. The driver eager to talk, said, "Cold night outside, isn't it." I quickly replied, "Sure is," hoping that would be the end of it. Instead, he asked, "What do you think caused all of this bad weather?" Recognizing that my wish for a quiet ride home was unlikely to be granted, I replied, "I heard that a high pressure system over the Rocky Mountains was diverting cold air our way." "Don't think that's it," the driver quickly said. "You remember when they took those moon rocks off the moon a while back? Bad move. It just upset the balance of nature. That's why we've got problems with the weather."

- List the assumptions about the causes of the weather the taxi driver and I are making.

- How would those assumptions affect the types of questions we ask about the weather and the explanations we are likely to provide?

- Which one of us was right? Justify your answer.

**Scenario 3:**

A recent report in a newspaper noted that researchers had discovered that as the amount of ice cream sold during the summer in large urban areas increased, the number of burgularies and violent crimes increased. Assuming that those who commit crimes eat ice cream, would it be reasonable to conclude that eating ice cream causes people to commit crimes?

- Are there sufficient grounds to accept the latter conclusion? What criteria for determing sufficient grounds does the latter conclusion meet or fail to meet?

- What alternative explanations for the data are there? Which one(s) would provide a closer fit to the underlying evidence?

EXERCISE 1.2

**Exploring the Meaning of Terms, Concepts, and Principles**

Ensuring that we have a good understanding of terms, concepts, and principles is an important aspect of thinking more effectively. In the space provided, use the process suggested by David Perkins to enhance your understanding of the following terms and principles. Also, try this process on other issues that interest you.

**Exploring the term "Critical Thinking"**

- What is its purpose? (i.e., What is it designed to do or accomplish?)

- How is it structured or organized? (i.e., What are its components and how do they relate to each other?)

- What is an example or model case?

- What statements and reasons explain and/or evaluate it? (i.e., What statements and reasons explain what it is and/or help us decide whether or not it has achieved its purpose?)

EXERCISE 1.2
(*continued*)

**Exploring the principle "Assumptions about human nature underlie our thoughts and actions"**

• What is its purpose? (i.e., What is it designed to do or accomplish?)

• How is it structured or organized? (i.e., What are its components, and how do they relate to each other?)

• What is an example or model case?

• What statements and reasons explain and/or evaluate it? (i.e., What statements and reasons explain what it is and/or help us decide whether or not it has achieved its purpose?)

## Key Terms

*Actor-observer bias.*    Tendency for observers to emphasize personal factors as causes of actions of others but to emphasize situational factors when describing their own actions.

*Assumptions.*    The personal beliefs and theories that underlie what we take for granted about the world around us.

*Attribution.*    An initial conclusion about the cause of an action.

*Attribution error.*    Bias that favors either personal qualities of people or factors in the situation as causes of behavior. Ignores the fact that any behavior is influenced by both factors.

*Automatic mental control processes.*    Mental programs or scripts that automatically guide and coordinate a variety of motor skill sequences for accomplishing tasks such as driving a car or hitting a golf ball.

*Automatic pilot.*    Another term used to refer to automatic mental control processes involved in our ability to use complex sequences of motor skills without a lot of conscious effort.

*Confirmation bias.*    This is a tendency to look for information that will confirm what people currently believe rather than to look for evidence that challenges current beliefs.

*Critical thinking.*    Deliberate and reflective thinking designed to ask questions, to interpret information, and to draw accurate conclusions.

*Design.*    Refers to thinking of any piece of knowledge as a design—that is, as a structure adapted to some purpose. Thus, a key to understanding various terms, concepts, and principles is to explore their underlying structure and purpose.

*Dualism/Received Knowledge.*    Mode of thinking or cognitive style in which people want to develop correct or incorrect, or right or wrong, answers to issues. People with this style believe there are fixed ways of looking at the world, and they rely on authorities to tell them how and what to think.

*Fundamental attribution error.*    Tendency of observers when describing behaviors to emphasize personal factors and to deemphasize environmental influences.

*Hindsight bias.*    A tendency to incorrectly but confidently assume that the outcome of some event was obvious before it happened. Involves projecting knowledge gained from the event into the memory of that event and then denying that such information influenced one's judgment.

*Hypothesis.*    An educated guess about the answer to a question. In a research study, a hypothesis is a predicted outcome of the experiment.

*Inference.*    An interpretation or initial conclusion based upon an observation of behavior. A problem that sometimes occurs is for people to form an inference and assume they are describing a behavior.

*Irrational beliefs.*    Repetitive thoughts and verbal statements that interpret events in absolute and extreme ways.

*Learned helplessness.*    An acquired belief that people have little choice of or control over what happens to them and over their ability to influence others.

*Mindfulness.*    The tendency to process information by attending to details and using critical thinking processes to maintain and/or gain control over events in one's life.

*Mindlessness.*    The tendency to process information without attention to details in a rather detached, routine, and predictable manner. When one is engaged in mindless thinking, little conscious thought or deliberation is given to information received, requests made, or decisions about what actions to take.

*Multiplism/Subjective Knowledge.*   A mode of thinking or cognitive style in which multiple points of view about issues are acknowledged. Individuals turn inward and do not rely as much on external authorities for answers. People have difficulty with developing and using criteria to make decisions about which alternatives to accept or reject.

*Relativism/Procedural Knowledge.*   A mode of thinking or cognitive style in which people recognize that alternative points of view exist and that good opinions are supported with reasons. Individuals using this style are able to compare alternative points of view against academic discipline, legal, moral, religious, and other criteria in order to determine which ones to accept, reject, or to withhold opinions on.

*Self-serving bias.*   Tendency to put our actions in the best possible light by taking credit for our successes and attributing our failures to other factors.

*Sufficient grounds.*   Establishing whether an explanation or conclusion is reasonable and more likely to be correct than incorrect given the evidence used to support it.

# Becoming a More Knowledgeable Consumer of Information

### Chapter Overview

All of us are consumers of information. Every day we are bombarded with claims, facts, figures, and other data from the news media, advertisements, books, and our conversations with people. In this chapter, principles and concepts normally associated with how psychologists do research can be used to help you sort through such information and determine what is valid. Such ideas also will allow you to develop a more objective outlook on the world and make you less susceptible to needless influence from others.

### Chapter Organizers

*As you read, answer the questions that follow on a separate sheet of paper, and check your responses with those provided in the summary section.*

Every day, you are exposed to a variety of facts and figures in newspapers and magazines, on television, in casual conversations and through other sources?

1. What questions should you be asking to challenge the information you receive in the news media, advertising, and from other sources.

Advertisers, politicians, members of the news media and others make various claims or assertions to influence your choice of products, political candidates, and your point of view on issues.

2. Do you know four ways that various claims are stated?
3. What precautions should you take when evaluating a particular claim?
4. What types of evidence support a claim, and what can be wrong with it?

Sometimes, people try to influence you by quoting the results of research studies. Usually, different people, products, or services are compared, and data are provided to support the fact that one is in some way better than the others.

5. What do you have to watch out for when making comparisons?
6. How can you tell that the sample of people, products, or services used in the comparisons reported was adequate?
7. Are you able to determine the ways in which methods of observation and test procedures can distort the outcomes of the research reported to you?

You have heard statements such as: "There is a 50 percent chance of rain." "The average salary of college students is six dollars an hour." "Seventy percent of the doctors contacted recommended Pain-Away medication." "Alice is ranked number one in her class." "Violent crime is correlated with hot and humid weather."

8. What precautions should you take when interpreting terms such as "probability," "average," "percentage," "ranks," and "correlations"?

## A Little Magic in a Bottle. . .

The people gathered around the brightly colored horse-drawn wagon. The magic show and banjo music had just finished. A noisy crowd suddenly grew silent and focused its attention on the small stage in front of the wagon. Medicine Man Sam, as he was known to the people in the region, was about to speak.

"Step right up, folks. Don't be afraid to come a little closer," he said in a booming and enthusiastic voice. "What I have for you today won't hurt you at all. In fact, it's guaranteed to make you feel better, give you some energy, and let you live longer, or you get double what you paid for it back. And the best part of all is that it won't cost you a week's pay."

Medicine Man Sam paused to look at the faces of those in the crowd. A few appeared amused by the beginning of the sales pitch. A couple waved their hands in disgust and turned away. But as Sam had suspected, most were curious, and they stood in place waiting to hear whatever else he had to say.

"So far, so good, " he thought to himself. "I've got a few of these suckers ready to bite." The remaining words of his well-rehearsed sales pitch rolled off his tongue with ease. "For one little dollar the amazing benefits of Dr. Conn's Secret Snake Oil Tonic can be yours," he proclaimed. "This is no ordinary product," he noted while pausing and lifting his index finger high over his head to emphasize the point. "Nine out of ten people tell me that after one little sip they feel marvelous and have a new lease on life. And, I bet you didn't know that three out of four doctors recommend Dr. Conn's Secret Snake Oil Tonic when everything else fails."

Pausing briefly and gesturing with his arm to the chart on the side of the wagon, he confidently said, "The figures don't lie. You and I can both see that my tonic out-sells all the other leading brands two to one. Ladies and gentlemen, for all of these reasons and more, Dr. Conn's is the leading snake oil tonic on the market today."

Medicine Man Sam positioned himself for closing some sales with his favorite lines. "Now I ask you folks, can you afford not to have this highly effective product in your home? I'm not going to be here all day and my supplies are limited. Don't delay; step right up and get two bottles for the price of one while my limited supplies last."

His references to science and limited supplies worked. The crowd began to stir, and about a third of them began reaching into their pockets for money. A few children, dispatched by their parents, ran home to pick up loose change that was lying around the house. Medicine Man Sam encouraged everyone with money to come forward. Even as he handed out bottles to customers and collected their money, he kept working the crowd. In a loud but sincere tone of voice directed towards the skeptical members of the audience, he said, "Don't be bashful. Buy one bottle, and I'll give you a second bottle absolutely free."

Turning his head away from the crowd for a moment, he stared into the empty space ahead of him and said. "And you sir, madam— yes, you with the books in your hands. How many bottles of Dr. Conn's Secret Snake Oil Tonic do you want?"

## BECOMING A MORE EFFECTIVE EVERYDAY PSYCHOLOGIST

Would you accept Medicine Man Sam's offer and purchase a bottle of snake oil tonic? Perhaps you would refuse because you doubt the claims he made. Bear in mind, however, that such claims are used even today very successfully by people promoting a variety of products and services. You may already have succumbed to the lure of "money-back guarantees," "testimonials from satisfied users," "doctors and other authorities recommending the product," "limited supplies," "two-for-one offers," and "charts and graphs" that provide what appear to be objective data on an issue.

Today, multicolored horse-drawn wagons have been replaced by commercials on television and radio, the advertisements that appear in the newspapers and the magazines you read, as well as sales pitches by solicitors promoting a variety of products. To complicate matters, it is not always products and services that force us to critically evaluate what is said. Sometimes it is an idea or point of view someone wants us to accept. A presidential candidate needing our vote claims that the current president is solely responsible for the high rate of unemployment. A newspaper columnist states that the "war on drugs" is a failure and that the only way to eliminate the problem is to make drugs legal. Or, a self-proclaimed prophet argues that "the world will end the next time the orbits of the sun, moon, and the earth place them in a straight line with each other." While the methods used to deliver the message have become more sophisticated, you and I have something in common with people living in earlier times. *We have to decide whether or not the information and claims are valid.*

A good place to begin is to challenge the claims, facts, figures, results of research, and other information reported to us. To do this, having a set of guidelines would be useful. One source of such guidelines is principles associated with the research process in the field of psychology. Underlying this process are a number of questions that help psychologists to analyze and interpret data. Applying these same questions can help you become a more sophisticated consumer of information and less susceptible to purchasing a bottle of "snake oil."

## ANALYZING AND INTERPRETING INFORMATION YOU ARE GIVEN EVERY DAY: EIGHT QUESTIONS TO ASK

1. What is asserted or claimed to have occurred?
2. What evidence is offered to support the assertion or claim?
3. What is being compared, and is the comparison a fair one?
4. What problems exist with the sample of people and products studied?
5. Were representative test conditions used?
6. Were extraneous variables controlled?
7. How consistently did the event occur?
8. Was the statistical information presented and used appropriately?

Let us begin by applying the above questions to information that is designed to influence our attitudes and behaviors towards particular people, products, and events.

## 1. What Is Asserted or Claimed to Have Occurred?

An **assertion** is a statement that claims that something is true without offering objective proof that the statement is accurate. Sometimes such statements are based on incomplete information or a partial or faulty analysis of whatever evidence exists. Recently a friend told me that a mutual acquaintance named Harry was "cheating on his wife." He had seen Harry entering a movie theater on a weekday afternoon with a woman other than his wife. *Determining the accuracy of an assertion depends upon the outcome of gathering and analyzing additional evidence.* In this case, I later discovered that Harry was out with a coworker looking for a large auditorium in which to hold a sales presentation for his company. The movie theater was one of several possible locations they were visiting.

Before accepting various claims or assertions at face value, *treat what was said as one of several possible explanations, and examine what was claimed in more detail.* A good place to begin is to identify the type of claim that was made. Richard Mayer and Fiona Good-child (1990) note that assertions appear in one of four possible formats, each having particular advantages and disadvantages.

## Four Types Of Claims You Encounter Every Day

*1. Two or More Events Are Related* Sometimes your are told that two or more events are associated or related to one another. A recent newspaper article argued that people who exercise live longer than sedentary individuals. In this example, the events that were related were "exercising" and "living longer." *It is important not to jump to the conclusion that just because two things are associated, one of them, (e.g., "exercise") caused the other (e.g., "living longer") to occur.*

A similar thing happens with "guilt by association." Here, people may infer that you have certain characteristics just because of the company you keep. One of my students was accused by a neighbor of being rowdy and inconsiderate "just like your friends on the street." His best friend was playing his car stereo very loudly one afternoon and woke his neighbor's baby from a nap. My student was not there when the incident occurred but was placed in the same category as his friend.

*2. One Event Caused the Other to Occur* I recently received in the mail a brochure for a set of audiotapes labeled a "Mind Supercharger." The ad claimed it would synchronize my brain wave patterns into the "optimal psychological state for deep meditation and expanded awareness." Apparently the tapes have subsonic or subliminal messages on them. Thus, it says, "You won't actually hear anything, but you will sure feel it. It's weird, but it actually feels like angels are flying around inside your skull." Using this product, I'm told, will increase the sex drive, enhance psychic functioning, boost IQ, accelerate learning and memory, heighten mental awareness and perceptual acuity, transform fear and anxiety into soaring self-confidence, and, best of all, it will heal sickness and disease. The casual assertion here is that "listening to the audiotape" will "cause" all of the wonderful things listed above to occur.

Determining a "cause-and-effect" relationship demands that claims meet the four criteria listed below. Let's see whether the "Mind Supercharger" causes good things to happen when these criteria are employed.

1. *The two events covaried.* That is, a change in one was associated with or related to a change in the other. On the surface, at least, it looks like the use of the "Mind Supercharger" was associated with "satisfied users" claiming that it did wonders for their lives.

2. *The event that supposedly was the "cause" happened before the "effect" occurred.* As written, the advertisement makes it look as if the changes in people's lives only happened after the product was used. There is, however, no way for us to tell from the information given.

3. *The "effect" occurs when the factor identified as the "cause" is present and the "effect" ceases to occur when the "cause" is absent and/or removed.* Apparently, when people use the "Mind Supercharger" they report something beneficial happens in their lives. There is no way to tell whether the benefits would disappear if people stopped using the tapes. Of course, if people reported these same benefits while listening to soothing music, the value of the tapes would have to be questioned. In the latter case, the presence of the "special tapes" would not have caused anything special to occur.

4. *Other plausible alternative explanations have been ruled out.* For example, people who purchase the product typically expect it to help them. Also, they are probably motivated to change their lives. The question then becomes whether the content of the tapes, expectations that "these tapes will really help me," or the motivation of users to change produced the benefits. *The content of the tapes alone was not the only factor added to the lives of users.*

**3. Two or More People, Products, or Events Share the Same Characteristics** Thus, an off-brand product is advertised to be "exactly the same as the brand name," but it costs one-third less. Or, a political candidate tries to convince you that her views are similar to yours. Thus, when someone tries to convince you that two things are alike, think about apples and oranges. Like many things in life, they share some similarities (i.e., both are fruits and grow on trees). They also differ in significant ways, and those distinctions make all of the difference in the world. Never accept an assertion that two things are alike until you explore ways they might differ.

**4. Two or More People, Products, or Events Are Claimed to Be Different** The ingredients of two sinus and allergy medications *produced by the same manufacturer* were compared by a consumer group. The products used the same brand name but differed in color and the symptoms they were supposed to be most effective in reducing. The "green pills" were billed as a remedy for many ailments, including nasal and sinus congestion, running nose, sneezing, itchy and watery eyes, fever, and minor aches and pains. The "yellow pills" were marketed for sinus sufferers rather than for more generalized misery. The "yellow tablets" sold for over a dollar more than the "green tablets." In this case, the company claimed that the two pills possessed different properties and were sensitive to different types of ailments.

Unfortunately, *someone's claims that two things are different should not be taken as evidence that they necessarily vary in important ways.* As an investigator quickly discovered, the ingredients in both pills were identical! They only differed in color and price. "It's just a

**Table 2.1**            Exhibit A

Two scientific-looking individuals appear on your television. You immediately recognize
them as scientists because they are dressed in white coats and carry clipboards. They
walk toward two identical cars that are parked on an airport runway. The announcer's
booming voice says that the experiment is designed to determine which one of the two
identical cars will travel further than the other under the influence of a gasoline additive. The announcer's voice challenges you.

"Will car A, running on Super-Petrol with SX-100, outperform car B, running on Super-
Petrol with the SX-100 removed?" One test run is shown on the screen. No surprises
here. Car A travels farther than car B. "What you saw, folks, is what happened in 80 percent of the test runs we made. Can you afford to wait to use Super-Petrol with SX-
100? With gasoline prices as high as they are today, this scientifically proven product will
save you an average of six dollars on every tank of gasoline you use. Now how can you
go wrong?" the announcer confidently asks. "Run down to your nearest Super-Petrol
station, and buy the only product we sell, Super-Petrol with SX-100."

*Before you run to your nearest gasoline station, the eight questions listed in the text will help you
decide whether Super-Petrol with SX-100 is worth the trip.*

marketing strategy," an embarrassed spokesperson for the manufacturer told the
reporter (*Consumer Reports,* January 1991, p. 67).

*Let's apply what you have learned thus far to Exhibit A in Table 2.1. Which one of the four
types of claims or assertions listed above was used in the Super-Petrol commercial? The claim is
that a "cause-and-effect relationship" exists. The advertiser wants you to believe that Super-Petrol
with SX-100 caused Car A to travel further than Car B.*

How well do you think the evidence provided meets the three criteria for determining a cause-and-effect relationship listed above? It looks as if the use of the additive and
Car A traveling further than Car B were related. Also, it appears that Car A traveled further
only after the additive was employed. Remember, though, that before we can conclude
that a cause-and-effect relationship took place, alternative explanations have to be ruled
out. Perhaps you can think of some already. We will return to Exhibit A later on. *In the*

*meantime, the answers to the following questions will help you add to your list of alternative explanations.*

## 2. What Evidence Is Offered to Support the Assertion or Claim?

Identifying the type of claim made (e.g., one event caused another or one thing is different from another) is a good way to ensure that you understand the information given. The next step is to evaluate critically the evidence offered to support it. *To do this, begin with a wary eye on the source of the evidence. Some sources of evidence are more reliable than others and knowing this often provides valuable clues to the validity of a claim.* You encounter the following sources of evidence quite frequently on a daily basis, and each has certain disadvantages.

*Personal Experience and Opinion* Here, various personal experiences and informal observations are used as support for the accuracy of a statement. A writing teacher created a national controversy when she argued in the magazine *Academic Computing* that student papers produced on the Macintosh computer were inferior to those produced on an IBM PC (Levy, 1990). Mac papers allegedly were sloppy, contained many misspelled words and incorrect punctuation, and violated a number of the general rules of English. The Mac students' vocabulary also was reported to be simplistic and infested with slang.

Even the subject matter was alleged to be different. While her IBM PC–using students addressed themselves to weighty matters such as capital punishment and nuclear war, Macintosh-wielding students wrote about fast food, dating, and the cultural significance of Styrofoam peanuts used as packing materials. Apparently students tainted with "Macness" were turning out the essay equivalent of rock videos.

The problem is that such observations may be unique only to the time and place in which they initially occurred. Furthermore, personal biases distort such observations. A person committed to a particular computer brand, or any other product, has a psychological investment in the merits of that product. Thus, he or she may quite innocently discount the virtues of other products.

*Testimonials* The virtues of everything from athletic shoes to zippers, rug cleaning services, and political candidates are often supported with statements from various professional athletes, movie stars, physicians, lawyers, and other well-known public figures. Their endorsement adds credibility to a claim, because such people are often viewed as unbiased. *The flaw in reasoning here is that many people believe that public figures would not endorse something unless it worked or performed as claimed.* Unfortunately, in most cases, they have a "psychological or financial stake" in a product selling, a service being adopted, or a political candidate getting elected.

*Expert Opinion* Sometimes experts are quoted to enhance the validity of a claim. Statements such as "according to leading authorities" or "according to scientific research on the topic" are often used to support claims. However, some caution is needed. *In most cases, the expert's opinion is mostly window dressing.* It is designed to impress rather than to inform. *Also examine whether the expert is speaking about an area in which he or she has expertise.* Someone may be a Nobel Prize winner. If the prize, however, was won for work on genetic mutations, this individual's views on political candidates, health foods, and other products and services is likely worth no more than yours or mine.

*Research Findings*  You have undoubtedly noticed that politicians use the findings from surveys to justify their positions or as evidence for their popularity. In order to sell more of their products, food and soft drink manufacturers often proudly announce the results of consumer "taste tests" showing their products are preferred two to one over the "other leading brand." Attempts are made to influence how positively you should feel about where you live when the opinions of residents on the "quality of life" in various cities are placed in your local newspapers. And inevitably, comparisons among products are made with "the outcomes of various demonstrations" and "the use of facts and figures" to back up claims. After all, didn't Car A travel further than Car B when Super-Petrol with SX-100 was added to its gasoline tank?

It is important not to become intimidated by such data. To paraphrase a computer programmer's motto, "garbage in—garbage out." *That is, the facts and figures are only as good as the methods, processes, and procedures used to produce them.* The answers to the remaining six questions will arm you with information needed to interpret correctly the facts and figures from research findings designed to support various claims.

## 3. What Is Being Compared, and Is the Comparison a Fair One?

Advertisements, news articles, and other sources are filled with comparisons. Charts show one cigarette reduces tar and nicotine better than another. Data are presented to show that one political party's economic policies are better than another. Two pieces of identical dirty clothing are washed by two brands of detergent, and the clothes washed with Brand X are "whiter" and "brighter" than those washed with Brand Y. Or, a gasoline additive is added to the fuel tank of one car and it travels farther than another car. Before accepting the conclusion offered, you must determine whether the comparisons were adequate.

When advertisers, politicians, newspaper polls, and others in the popular media make comparisons based on "research data," you can expect the quality of that research to vary. To evaluate the information, you need to understand some of the terminology and principles associated with making comparisons. The following suggestions can help you.

*Evaluating Comparisons when Preexisting Differences Exist Among Groups*  The reading and math achievement scores of different high schools, for example, are published in the newspaper. Or, the "on-time" record of different airlines appears in an advertisement. The different high schools and airlines are called **grouping variables,** because they are naturally occurring groups that will be compared. Of course, the news stories and advertisements comparing such groups are often explosive. Schools that do not perform well (i.e., often in the inner city) are chastised; calls for educational reform are made; and teachers are blamed for not preparing their students. The airline with the best "on-time" record crows about it and suggests that the other airlines are not doing a good job.

The problem in comparing groups on the basis of preexisting characteristics is that they are seldom equal on all of the factors that matter. Teachers in all of the schools may have equivalent educations and training. Yet those teaching in the inner city have students from poor families who often live in high-crime areas and in environments where it is not easy to study. Teachers in the more affluent schools do not have students with such problems. Similarly, the airline with the best "on-time" record may only fly in warm climates and thus not have to contend with bad winter weather and congested airports.

*Evaluating Comparisons when Groups Are Purposely Made to Be Different From Each Other* For example, one group of cars is given a gasoline additive, while another does not receive it. Or, one group of students is provided with computers to help them learn foreign language vocabulary. Their vocabulary test scores are then compared to another group where a foreign language was taught in a traditional manner. Thus, an experimental setting is set up, and under such conditions it is important to understand the difference between two variables. Those factors that are manipulated are called **independent variables.** The measures taken of their effects are labeled **dependent variables.**

*Distinguish between experimental and control groups.* To assess whether any independent variable (e.g., presence of a gasoline additive, use of a computer to assist with foreign language learning) has an effect on the dependent variable (distance traveled, number of vocabulary items correct on a test), we need to compare it to something else. Comparison conditions are formally called **control groups** while the group in which the independent variable is manipulated is called the **experimental group**.

The performance of a control group can help us determine whether the independent variable actually made a difference in the dependent variable, or the measure taken. An adequate control group has one of two characteristics. It possesses all the attributes of the people, events, or products under study (e.g., cars, study programs, televisions, radios, cigarettes) except that it does not receive the independent variable. Or, the control group receives the independent variable in different amounts. In the latter case, it is known that the absence of the independent variable would produce no effect. As an example, in a study of how much practice it takes to learn to use a power tool or to speed-read, a zero-practice condition is not necessary. It is unlikely that the task could be mastered without practice.

*Take possible placebo effects into consideration.* An important exception to this generalization is the study of the influence of psychological treatments or drugs on behavior. If participants in an experimental group were told they were receiving a new drug to eliminate headaches, for example, they might think, "This drug will help me to get better." Thus, this expectation, and not the drug alone, might make their headaches lessen in intensity. Consequently, when drugs are tested, a control group that receives a **placebo,** or neutral substance (e.g., sugar pill), is needed. Then one can assess whether the expectation, the drug, or both affected participants.

*Placebo effects are rather powerful and must always be considered as a causal cofactor any time something is claimed to help you medically or psychologically.* Research, for example, suggests that up to one-third of the people given placebos for headaches, high blood pressure, anxiety, and other ailments report significant improvements in their conditions (Aronson et al., 1990). Similarly, people with a positive or optimistic mental outlook recover faster from illnesses. In one study, individuals with an optimistic mindset were compared to those who were more pessimistic. The optimists recovered from the common cold and influenza on average within four days compared to eight days for the pessimists (Peterson and Bossio, 1991). These authors also report that people with an optimistic outlook benefit more from psychotherapy and other psychological interventions designed to help them cope.

## Three Problems with Comparison Conditions

*1. A Control Group Is Absent* One example of this occurred in a special attempt to find a solution for juvenile delinquency. James Finckenauer (1982) notes a tendency for people to want a "quick cure" or panacea for the complex issues involved in delinquency. One such project he investigated was known as the Juvenile Awareness Program. Its premise was simple— "scare the devil out of the delinquents."

The program, popularly known as "Scared Straight," was initiated at Rahway State Prison in New Jersey and involved several hundred juveniles. Groups of juvenile offenders were sent to visit the prison for a day. There, a tour of the facility was followed by several hours of convicts shouting and screaming at the youngsters while describing in graphic detail the horrors of prison life.

Proponents of the program claimed that at least 90 percent of the youngsters participating did not commit crimes afterwards. Of course, such claims gained national attention, because the "quick fix" everyone wanted was in hand. An award-winning news special on the program was developed, and, predictably, law enforcement officials and politicians across the country began to embrace this "cheap cure" for juvenile delinquency.

James Finckenauer saw a number of problems with what was reported. To begin, he investigated the source of the claims of a 90 percent improvement and found them to be based on opinions, biased readings of court documents, and wishful thinking. A research study was then designed to determine what if any successes the program actually had. Information about the convictions and arrests of a group of people who attended the program was gathered from court records. These data were used to develop a comparison or control group of juveniles with similar offenses who did not participate in the Rahway sessions. After the first group completed the program, the court records detailing delinquent and criminal behavior of participants in both groupss were followed for a period of six months.

The findings were remarkable. Instead of the 90 percent cure claimed by proponents of the program, only 58.7 percent of the participants had no further delinquency or criminal entries on their records. Even more startling, 88.6 percent of those in the control group had no additional infractions of the law recorded in their court records. This led some people to wonder whether those delinquents visiting the prison were "Scared Crooked." Debate still continues on the value of such programs.

*2. The Comparison Conditions Lack a Critical Factor* Several years ago a new brand of window glass was advertised as far superior to its competitors in visual clarity. Unknown to the public at that time, comparative pictures of this brand with others on the market were deceptive. The window panes that supposedly held the new glass were empty. It is no wonder that the other brands were not as clear. The control group's window panes contained glass, a critical factor that was absent from window panes of the company promoting its products.

*3. One Group Is Accidently or Purposely Given Characteristics that Enhance a Favorable Outcome* This is a variation of the last principle. Instead of removing something from one of the groups, a factor is added that biases the comparison (Cooper and Richardson, 1986). Recently I read advertisements that compared pictures of the "old" and the "new " containers of a popular breakfast cereal, an instant soup, and a deodorant. The new packages were larger than the old packages. "The best part of all," the copy in the ads screamed, is that "the price is the same!" What's the catch?

The advertiser is relying on a **natural response** bias to control how you think and the conclusions you draw. A response bias is a predictable way that people respond to a stimulus. When looking at a larger and smaller package, people have a response bias that leads them to conclude that "bigger is better: it contains more, and if the price is the same, the bigger package must be a value."

Unfortunately, while larger in size, the new packages contained less product. Thus, when you originally paid $3.00 for ten ounces of deodorant in the "old" container (i.e., 30 cents an ounce), you now pay $3.00 for eight ounces in the "new," larger package (i.e., 37.5 cents an ounce). This gambit is a good way to hide a price increase from consumers; in the process, people think they have received more for their money.

## 4. What Problems Exist with the Sample of People and Products Studied?

One intent of most data collection is to be able to develop conclusions that apply to a large number of people. Thus, the people and the products tested should be representative of a larger population. They should not be biased toward a particular point of view or result. If I am interested in what people in this country feel about the Democratic Party candidate for president, I should question other people besides registered Democrats. Similarly, an all-purpose, all-weather tire that only stops trucks from skidding is hardly an all-purpose tire.

There are two general ways to get an appropriate sample. One is to choose randomly the people or products that will be tested. The other is to select them with regard to certain predetermined characteristics. A **random sample** is analogous to picking names out of a hat. Drawn from a larger sample of names or products, those that will be studied are picked *without any known biases* for selecting them. One method is to assign a number to the names in a telephone directory or to the products produced. To pick people or products randomly, a sample of numbers is drawn from a container that has all the possible numbers in it. In practice, when large samples are needed, this is usually done by a computer. A random sample guarantees that everyone has an equal chance of being selected.

A second method selects people or things because they have certain characteristics of interest. In testing a hair dye that gradually reduces grayness, only people with gray hair would be of interest. Consequently, a sample could be randomly selected from the general population of people with gray hair. Or the psychological characteristics of people who live in isolated areas of the country may be of interest. The effects of isolation might appear in family interactions or in the types of leisure activities chosen. A sample of individuals living in isolated rural or mountainous areas would be needed.

*Selecting a random sample ensures that everyone who participates has similar characteristics.* This is important for ensuring that the information obtained or observations made are representative of a larger population of people or products. Thus, the findings of a study cannot be attributed to some flaw or characteristics of the sample. In addition, data from a random sample help us to interpret fairly and accurately the information obtained.

In the state of Ohio, both Hamilton County and its largest city, Cincinnati, have for decades enjoyed a dubious national reputation as a highly conservative place to live. "Clean and safe and quiet and repressive," a writer for a national publication recently noted (Richmond, 1993). The bases for this writer's claims were interviews with several prominent citizens and newspaper stories of highly publicized attempts by various citizen groups and law enforcement officials to try to ban books, videos, art exhibits, and other forms of expression that they found offensive. An important question is whether or not the perception of the area as conservative is justified.

To find out, more is required than memorable news events and the opinions of a few of the county's citizens. Thus, the opinions of a random sample of residents of the county should be compared to those of a random sample of individuals representing other regions of the country. A local newspaper hired a respected public opinion organization to do this, and the data from those items where conservative views might be expected to dominate are shown in Table 2.2. Contrary to being different, the views of a random sample of county residents were for all practical purposes identical to those of people nationally. Thus, the writer mentioned above based his conclusions on a biased (i.e., nonrandom) sample.

*Let us return for a moment to Exhibit A in Table 2.1.* Do you think the cars described in the Super-Petrol experiment represented an adequate sample? Unfortunately, only two cars were used. Therefore, a representative sample was not tested. Although two cars of the same make and size were evaluated, in order to generalize, a variety of compacts, intermediates, and luxury cars ought to be examined. In this way we could determine if the additive works with different size engines and models.

## 5. Were Representative Test Conditions Used?

People are often tricked by surprisingly nonrepresentative test conditions. Cigarette advertisements, for example, sometimes contain data about how little tar and nicotine smokers consume with particular brands. Did you know that these estimates are determined by measuring how much tar and nicotine specially designed machines consume when smoking? The machines take one puff every 30 seconds and cannot inhale the smoke. Their "smoking" habits are unlike those of human beings. Thus tar and nicotine data reflect merely how much a machine—not a human being—will consume. When the blood samples of individuals are analyzed immediately after smoking, a different picture emerges. No significant differences in nicotine levels are found, regardless of what brand people smoke (Brown, 1983).

| **Table 2.2** | Random Samples Assist with Making Fair Comparisons | |
|---|---|---|
| **ITEMS** | **COUNTY RESIDENTS FAVORING** | **RESIDENTS OF U.S. FAVORING** |
| Tougher antiabortion laws | 40% | 41% |
| Mandatory death penalty | 70% | 72% |
| Cut military spending | 46% | 48% |
| Mandatory drug tests at work | 68% | 65% |
| School prayer amendment | 73% | 71% |
| Tax increase to reduce deficit | 29% | 28% |

Based on data from a survey commissioned by the *Cincinnati Post* and conducted by the University of Cincinnati's Institute for Policy Research. *Cincinnati Post,* October 25, 1990.

**Interaction effects** constitute one limitation on our ability to generalize. Such effects are quite common, because the variables that affect products and behavior seldom have the same influence under all conditions. For example, a gasoline additive might increase the distance compact and full-scale cars travel at sea level. In mountainous terrain, however, the additive might work only with compact cars. The combination of extra weight, hilly roads, and less oxygen makes a full-scale model burn gasoline less efficiently, even with the additive.

Interaction effects also appear in a variety of our actions, including recognizing the physical characteristics of individuals from ethnic and racial groups other than our own. In studies of facial recognition, Euro-American, Afro-American, and Hispanic participants were shown photographs of the faces of individuals within each group. Afterwards, they were asked to identify those individuals from a lineup of photographs that included those they had seen before. All students were better able to recognize the photographs of individuals from their own racial group than from another group (Platz and Hosch, 1988; Bothwell et al., 1989). This interaction is shown in Figure 2.1.

As with any research finding, once an interaction is identified, it is important to explain it. Psychologist June Chance (1985) notes that the differences in facial recognition are probably caused by a lack of experience interacting closely with members of different racial and ethnic groups. She finds that when people become more experienced living and working among individuals of other cultures and racial groups, they become attuned to differences in facial characteristics.

*Were representative test conditions used in the Super-Petrol study described in Exhibit A in Table 2.1?* The test conditions were not representative of normal driving conditions. Cars are rarely driven on airport runways as shown in the commercial. It would be nice to know how the gasoline performed under highway driving conditions, city driving,

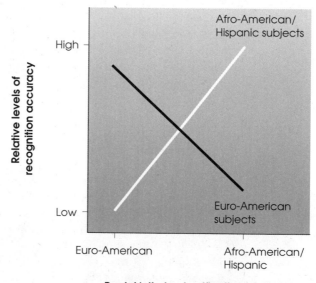

**Figure 2.1** *Illustration of an interaction effect from composite findings from research on the accuracy of facial identification as a function of the racial/ethnic composition of individuals in the photographs and the participants. Participants examined photographs and then later were asked to identify those that they remembered having seen before.*

in the desert, in rain, in snow, or in conditions of extreme cold. After all, cars are driven under a variety of conditions, and possible interaction effects of road and climate conditions should be examined. A good test of a gasoline additive should reflect how performance varies with changes in such conditions.

## 6. Were Extraneous Variables Controlled?

A good research design allows us to assess whether or not an outcome was due to the effects of the independent variable studied. To do this, extraneous, or unwanted, variables need to be controlled. **Extraneous variables** are cofactors that could interfere with the variable under study or that could give us the desired result even if the independent variable were not used. In the Mind Supercharger, mentioned earlier, people's motivation to change and the expectation the tapes would help them could have produced the positive benefits listed by "satisfied users." *Extraneous variables are considered controlled if they affect all of the people or products tested equally—or if care was taken to eliminate them before the research project began.*

Paying special attention to people is another common extraneous variable when studying human behavior. Knowing that they are being studied may make some individuals behave in line with what they expect the experimenter wants. This is called the **Hawthorne effect.** It was first identified in the now classic experiments carried out by psychologists Elton Mayo and Fritz Roethlisberger at the Hawthorne plant of the Chicago Western Electric Company over the period of 1924–1933 (Bramel and Friend, 1981).

Mayo and Roethlisberger studied the effects of changing working conditions on workers' productivity and satisfaction with their jobs. They varied such things as the amount of lighting in the plant, the number of hours worked, rest breaks, free lunches, and incentive plans for producing more electrical relays and other devices. Dana Bramel and Ronald Friend noted that most popular accounts of what happened suggested that no matter what the researchers did, productivity went up. Even when work conditions were made worse than they were originally, people worked harder and more efficiently.

The secret ingredient, however, was not the physical change in working conditions—even when it was good. Instead, *the attention shown to the employees by the experimenters and everyone else connected with the study was the critical factor.* The conditions of the experiment led to a more relaxed and casual style of interacting with the researchers and the workers' supervisors. Thus, being treated in a special way and knowing they were being observed were the most important factors in increasing workers' productivity. While it was an extraneous variable, the Hawthorne effect helped to sensitize management to the positive effects of developing good human relations with employees. It led to the "human relations" movement in industry, including the use of work teams and the involvement of employees in making more decisions about aspects of their work environment that affect them.

Sometimes, people have special characteristics that might influence their actions. They vary in their level of intelligence, motivation, resourcefulness, and other personal qualities. Thus, it would be important to ensure that the most able and least able individuals were distributed across the conditions studied. Otherwise, we could falsely conclude that a "new method of studying," or a "self-motivation program" was effective. The best way to control variations in personal qualities is to use **random assignment** of people to conditions. This is illustrated in the example shown in Focus on Applied Research 2.1.

---

### Do Students Sitting at the Front of the Class Receive Better Grades?

Most students have heard that those sitting in the front of the classroom receive higher grades than those sitting in the back of the class. Well, it's true! Or, perhaps it's best to say, the statement is true if one forgets about the need to randomly assign people to their seats.

Peter McDonald and Edgar O'Neal (1980) allowed 209 undergraduate students in an introductory psychology class to sit anywhere in class they wanted during the first half of the term. After the midterm exam, students were randomly assigned to seats. The effects of each arrangement were examined by comparing the number of items correct on the 50-item multiple-choice midterm and final exams.

The classroom was divided into six sections from the front to the back of the room. The comparisons shown below were for the 72 students in the front sections and the 87 in the rear sections. *The average exam scores for each condition are shown below.*

| | EXAM SCORES | |
|---|---|---|
| SEATING ARRANGEMENT | STUDENTS SELECT SEATS | SEATS RANDOMLY ASSIGNED |
| Front of Class | 34.0 | 32.2 |
| Back of Class | 31.7 | 32.8 |

Apparently, when students selected their seats, the relatively better students sat at the front of the class, with predictable results on the exam scores. When the instructor assigned the seats randomly, the differences in the average test score between the front and back of the room were largely eliminated.

---

*Were extraneous variables controlled in the Super-Petrol study?* Besides the gasoline additive, other factors could enable one car to travel farther than the other. Just as people in two conditions may have different characteristics, so may products. For example, one car will travel farther if it has a smaller engine, proper air pressure in its tires, a tuned engine, and closed windows. If the cars differed on such things, then extraneous variables were probably present and may have contributed to one car's traveling a shorter distance. It is difficult to tell based on the data presented whether or not such factors were controlled.

## 7. How Consistently Did the Event Occur?

When examining data, you should ask how often the event under study occurred. If it occurred consistently, then you are in a better position to say that the independent variable produced the effect. How can you tell if five out of ten customers selecting a particular brand of coffee or nine out of ten dentists choosing one brand of toothpaste represent a consistent and stable preference? A general understanding of the concept of probability can help you make your decision.

When one event is more or less likely to occur than another, you are dealing with **probability.** Before leaving home for work or school, you may listen to a weather report that says there is a 90 percent chance of rain. Of course, sometimes even with this forecast it will not rain. *A probability statement does not guarantee anything.* It is merely our best estimate or guess of the chances for some event to occur. When used properly, such estimates can help us avoid getting wet and even assist us in performing well on exams, as Focus on Applied Research 2.2 shows.

To decide to wear our raincoats, to select alternative B on an exam, or to take any action, we must first be able to answer an important question. What is the likelihood or probability of the event of interest occurring on the basis of chance or blind luck? If we knew this, we could then compare what was reported to us or what we observed against the probability that the event was a chance occurrence.

To assess how often something occurs on the basis of chance, you need to know how often that event might occur if there were no biases or other factors influencing the event (e.g., response biases, loaded dice, unfair comparisons). Then, divide this by the total number of events that are possible. Examples of how to do this are below:

1. On a multiple-choice test with 4 alternative answers, where only 1 answer can be correct, the likelihood that alternative B or any other answer is correct is .25. The probability is calculated by dividing 4 (the total number of events, i.e., possible answers) into 1 (the number of correct answers); 1/4 = .25.

2. When someone on a television commercial is given three cups of coffee and is asked to state which one is new Ultra-Taste coffee, the probability of selecting Ultra-Taste is .33. You divide 3 (the total number events, i.e., cups of coffee used) into 1 (the number of cups with Ultra-Taste in it); 1/3 = .33.

Once the probability of something occurring on the basis of chance is known, you can also determine the number of products, people, or events that might occur on the basis of chance. For example, if you are taking a multiple choice exam with 100 questions on it, you can expect to get 25 correct on the basis of chance; .25 × 100 = 25. Similarly, if 500 women were tested in the Ultra-Taste study, how many would select this brand of coffee on the basis of chance?

## Living With Blind Luck

One of the lessons of probability is that anything in this world could occur due to blind luck. This includes the chance that a nuclear war could occur, that your next plane ride will end in a crash, that an asteroid will crash into our planet causing a natural catastrophe, and that a single monkey could have written this book by chance (see Table 2.3). Fortunately for all of us, the probabilities of such events occurring are quite small. Still, the advice given by a very wise and astute fictional Asian detective—Charlie Chan—should be heeded. He once said, "*Unfortunately, coincidence allows itself the luxury of occurring.*" The incidents reported in Focus on People 2.1 suggest he had a point.

Most people find it difficult, however, to accept the fact that blind luck and coincidences are regular features of daily life. Time and energy are spent trying to identify patterns in random events or otherwise explaining them. One reason is that it is uncomfortable to live in a world in which some events are outside of our control. "There has to be a reason for this," we say to ourselves. To find explanations, some individuals turn to horoscopes, psychics, tip sheets on what lottery ticket numbers to play, or mystical writings. Or they decide it was "God's will."

A second difficulty in accepting blind luck as an explanation is that we lack information about what a chance event looks like. For example, which of the following two series of flips of a coin is more likely due to chance?

HTHTTHTHTHTHTHHTHTTHTHTHTHTHHTHTHTHTHT

HTTTTHHTTTTHTHTHHHHTHTHTHHHTTTTTHTHHT

## Using Probability to Get Higher Exam Scores

A number of researchers have studied strategies for taking exams and concluded that engaging in certain behaviors increases the likelihood of obtaining a higher score.

### Study 1:

Multiple-choice test items from instructor manuals developed by textbook publishers and examination items written by instructors were examined to determine what strategies would increase the likelihood of selecting a correct answer (Feder, 1977). The following strategies were found to increase the chances of selecting a correct answer if you do not know the answer.

- Select "true" over "false." Teachers tend to favor the positive side of things.
- Avoid answers with words like always, never, or seldom in them. Correct answers seldom use these words.
- If knowledge or applications of basic principles are tested, select the response that is oversimplified.
- Alternatives C or B are more often correct than A, D, or E.
- When dates, numbers, or rankings are needed for answers, avoid selecting the extremes.
- Select the longest alternative.

### Study 2:

Should you stick with an answer or change it on a multiple-choice test? There appears to be no big advantage to switching (Skinner, 1983). The answer-switching strategies of 68 students were monitored for a semester. The probability of making changes that were right or wrong follows: wrong to right = .52; right to wrong = .26; wrong to wrong = .22. Thus, you stand a chance of being correct 52 percent of the time and incorrect 48 percent of the time.

What is the best way to answer an essay exam? Answers to essay exams were analyzed to determine differences in the strategies employed by students (Gerena, 1981). Good students were more likely to employ certain strategies than were relatively poorer students. The strategies students with GPAs above 3.0 used most often are listed here:

- Express an opinion similar to that of the teacher.
- Quote books and/or articles.
- Rephrase arguments several times.
- Rephrase the questions conveniently.
- Do not admit you don't know the answer.
- Discuss extensively what you know and very little what you don't.

When presented with such a choice, Scott Plous (1993) notes that most individuals pick the top row. In reality, the second row more closely approximates what a random series would look like. People expect a random series of events to alternate between a "head and a tail" more often than a truly random series would. *Random events can occur in streaks, and this fact is not well known.* Many gamblers and sports fans unfortunately look beyond luck when they have a winning streak or when a favorite player encounters a hitting or shooting streak. In reality, studies show that after missing or hitting three shots in a row, professional and collegiate basketball players, for example, are just as likely to make as to miss the fourth shot. Similarly, stock prices are just as likely to rise as to fall after a streak of increases or decreases in price. Such data, unfortunately are ignored in the belief that "my luck will change." Thus, special insights, outstanding skill, and other logical explanations are developed. Everything, that is, except admitting that blind luck played a major role in the performance (Gilovich et.al., 1985).

**Table 2.3**                     Probability of One Monkey Writing This Book

There are approximately 1,400,000 letters and spaces in this book. My computer keyboard has 62 keys on it, including the space bar. The chance that a monkey would hit the correct key is 1/62. To write the book the monkey would have to select the correct key consecutively 1,400,000 times. The probability of doing this is 1/62, or .016 raised to a power of 1,400,000. To get some idea of how rare this event is, remember that: $.016^2 = .00002$; $.016^3 = .000004$; and .016 raised to the 1,400,000 power would be a figure that had a decimal point followed by enough zeros to fill every space on every page in this book.

*See, it is virtually impossible for a monkey to have written this book—I hope!*

Ignoring the role of chance in our lives can have unfortunate consequences. Sometimes, when caught in a run of bad luck, people say "my luck has got to change, things will fall my way soon." This belief is known as the **gambler's fallacy**. In a game of poker between two players of equal skill who are using a fair deck of cards, each player can be expected to win half of the games. In the short run, one player may have more than his fair share of winning hands. For the number of winning hands to even out might take a thousand or more games. In the meantime, the person who believes "my luck's got to change" could literally lose his shirt waiting for "Lady Luck" to smile on him. It sometimes takes a long time for one's luck to change. Just ask Anthony Young, a New York Mets baseball team pitcher. In July of 1993, he set a major league

---

**FOCUS ON PEOPLE 2.1**

### Strange But True

A colleague's house, located in the Cincinnati area, was burglarized. Among other items, the thieves took a set of antique silverware with a very unique pattern. The silverware was a wedding gift from his wife's grandmother when they married 25 years before. Several months later, his wife visited her mother in Fort Worth, Texas. They decided to visit a flea market in a small town outside of Fort Worth on a pleasant Saturday afternoon. Sitting for sale in one of the stalls was the stolen set of silverware. The police were notified, and the stolen property was recovered. The police traced the path of the stolen silverware from an auction house in Cincinnati to another in Dallas, Texas. The person purchasing it decided to try and sell it at the flea market.

In October of 1990, Intel Corporation, a major computer chip manufacturer, was suing another manufacturer of computer chips for infringing on Intel's 386 microprocessor. Intel had learned the company was planning to release a similar chip called the AM386. They learned of the infringement through an interesting coincidence. Both companies employed individuals named Mike Webb. Both Mike Webb's had checked into the same hotel in Sunnyvale, California, on the same day. Then, after both had checked out, the hotel received a package addressed to a Mike Webb employed by the AM386 company. The hotel misdirected the package to Mike Webb at Intel, who then initiated legal action against their competitor for copying their microprocessor design (Sullivan, 1990).

record for consecutive losses. In spite of it being highly improbable, over a two-year period he lost 24 straight games in which he was the starting pitcher. All of us, however, fall into the gambler's fallacy whenever we continue to purchase lottery tickets, stay with bad relationships and investments, and hang on to unpleasant jobs, all the time believing that "Lady Luck" will eventually smile on us. Rather than rely on Lady Luck, however, it is sometimes better to take constructive action to improve a situation.

How can you tell if a behavior you are observing or some other event of interest simply happened due to chance? After all, it would be nice to eliminate chance or blind luck as a possible alternative explanation. There are at least four things you can do using the following advice.

*1. Things that Occur with a High Degree of Frequency Are Often Not Due to Chance* A multiple-choice exam score of 95 out of 100 questions correct is probably due to studying hard rather than chance. A bar of soap that is selected 70 percent of the time from a shelf with ten competing brands is most likely a nonchance preference. Perhaps the brand had a good advertising campaign behind it, or it really was a superior product. *A word of caution is in order here.* Remember that in a small number of cases or a small sample, it is possible for something to occur quite frequently due to chance. On ten flips of a coin, it is possible to get eight or even ten heads when we might only expect five on the basis of chance. Similarly, 66 percent of the people tested preferring Decay Away toothpaste sounds good. But what if only three people were tested? Two out of three is 66 percent, as is 666 out of 1,000. *Chance also means the average number of times we can expect something to occur on the basis of blind luck.* Thus, a good-size sample of observations is needed to have confidence that an event that occurs with a high degree of frequency is not due to chance.

*2. Calculate How Often the Event Would Occur on the Basis Of Chance* Use what you learned earlier in this section to do this. As a rule of thumb, accept something that occurs at least 15 percent above what would be expected on the basis of blind luck as caused by some other factor. But remember what was said about the size of the sample above. Only when the number of people, products, or events is large should you do this. Better yet, use the procedure described below.

*3. Use Statistical Tests to Help You* If you want to know whether a single behavior or the difference between two behaviors is due to chance, statistical tests can help. Such tests help to determine when you can say, "I reject chance as causing the behavior or other events I observed." This means you have observed a **statistically significant** event, and what occurred represents a time when factors other than chance produced the effect.

*4. Take Some Advice from My Grandfather* He once asked me whether I would bet my life's savings that something was not due to blind luck. His point, of course, was that placing money on the line has a tendency to make us conservative. It is only after adopting such a cautious attitude that we should make decisions about data.

Reconsider Exhibit A in Table 2.1 for a moment. Did the performance of the car with Super-Petrol with SX-100 exceed what one might expect on the basis of chance? Remember that the television commercial showed only a single test but claimed that this represented what occurred 80 percent of the time. If true, the results were not a chance event if the testers ran a large number of tests. Bear in mind, however, that just because something exceeds chance, it is not necessarily true that experimental treatment produced it. It also is important to consider whether appropriate comparison or control conditions were used and whether extraneous variables influenced the outcome.

## 8. Was the Statistical Information Presented and Used Appropriately?

Any variable that affects a product or person is unlikely to do so in exactly the same way under all conditions. Variations can be expected. A gasoline additive may increase gasoline mileage, but it will do so somewhat differently among the various cars tested. Similarly, two students who spend the same amount of time preparing for an exam are likely to have somewhat different scores. One may get a score of 95, whereas another receives a score of 85.

Such variations in performance present a problem for describing how a number of various people or products actually performed. For example, what would you say when asked "How did students perform in a class you took on a recent exam?" It is unlikely that you would provide the exam scores of every person in class. Instead, your natural inclination would be to look for some way to summarize the performance of the group. You might say, "everyone did very well" or "everyone did poorly"; or perhaps other words would be used. One issue, however, in using a verbal description to summarize what happened is that not everyone would agree on what "very well" or "poorly" meant. Indeed, you might find as many different ways of describing the class's performance and interpretation of such descriptions as people taking it.

Fortunately, there are mathematical techniques for helping to describe, summarize, and analyze data. Such methods are called *statistics*, and they have the advantage of providing much more precision in summarizing and describing the performance of people and products. Common statistics with which you are familiar include the terms "*average,*" "*percentage*" (or proportion), "*rank order,*" and "*correlation.*" They often appear in magazines, newspapers, television, and other sources of information. Care must be taken in interpreting statistics, because they can be presented in a deceptive manner or purposely used to distort and manipulate your opinions. *You must recognize when they are used properly to avoid drawing false conclusions about events.*

*Average* This term is often abused, because when it is used, the type of "average" it refers to is typically not given. Consider the following news item from a local newspaper. I am sure you have seen similar things.

> The strike at the Monocorp freight warehouse continues into its fourth week. Management and the union are wide apart on wage discussions. A union spokesman claims that the average wage paid workers was $6.50 per hour, and they are demanding a $1.00-an-hour increase plus cost of living. A company representative said that the union was exaggerating the low wages. He said the average wage was $8.70 an hour and that the union's demands were obviously inflationary.

Two groups remain in conflict, workers miss paychecks to take care of their personal needs and families, and bitterness and frustration enter the lives of employees and company managers. Why? The reason is that each party is claiming that their calculation of the "average" wage is accurate. How can we tell who is correct? To do this, we need more information. Let us assume that we have the hourly wages for nine workers. They are: $5.00, $5.50, $6.50, $6.50, $7.50, $7.80, $8.00, $13.50, and $18.00. As is often the case when two sides argue over the "average," both are probably right. It depends upon which "average" you use; there are three of them.

1. *Mean.* The arithmetic **mean** is simply the sum of all the individual scores divided by the total number of scores. To obtain the mean wage, simply divide the total hourly wages of the employees by nine. You should get $8.70 per hour, which is the "average" that the company's management quoted.

2. *Median.* The **median** is the score that has 50 percent of the other scores above it and 50 percent of the other scores below it. In the wage distribution, the hourly wage that meets this criterion is $7.50 per hour. The union might have used this "average," because it was smaller than the mean. They did not, because there is a third "average" score that is even lower.

3. *Mode.* The most frequently occurring score in a distribution is the **mode.** A wage of $6.50 per hour is earned by two employees and therefore is the modal wage. This is the "average" the union used because it does the best job of suggesting that employees are underpaid.

The situation described above is not unusual in news reports of wage negotiations, the cost of doing business, the average number of clients served by an agency, and the reading or other abilities of students in a school system. Everyone can correctly quote the "average" and still select the one that gives them an advantage. *To avoid such deception, always ask what "average" is used.* Then you must decide whether it is the proper one to utilize. Understanding averages also may help you cope with the stress associated with unpleasant news, as Focus on People 2.2 illustrates.

*Steven Jay Gould's observations in Focus on People 2.2 regarding the median and life expectancy applies to any illness.* For example, the median number of years between the time when a person is diagnosed as HIV+ (i.e., as having been infected with the Human Immunodeficiency Virus) and the onset of a symptom of AIDS-related disorders (e.g., cancerous lesions like Kaposi's sarcoma or pneumocystic pneumonia) is 12 years (Root-Bernstein, 1993). Contrary to what most people think, being diagnosed

HIV+ is not an immediate death sentence. Half of the people with the diagnosis live longer than the 12-year median with those showing symptoms of opportunistic infections able to live at least 1 to 3 years with proper medical treatment. The hope is that one day a cure will be found. In the meantime, AIDS can be controlled through prevention. Health officials thus stress that people behave less promiscuously, that safer sexual practices be employed (such as the use of condoms), and that intravenous drug users not share or at least sterilize needles.

*How can you tell which average is the best one to use?* In general, the mean and the median are better than the mode. The mode is not very stable, because a change in only one score in a distribution may affect the mode. Also, it is not unusual to discover a tie for the score that occurs most frequently. In such cases, the distribution has more than one mode, and selecting "the mode" becomes a problem. For example, in a distribution of high school seniors' SAT scores, it would not be unusual to find ties among two or more scores in terms of how frequently they occurred. In such cases, the median or the mean would be a better choice of the "average score."

When there are extreme or rather odd scores, as in the distribution of wages shown above (e.g., one person made $18.00 per hour), the median is a better choice of the "average score." Thus, the median would be a better estimate of the "average." Usually, however, the mean will handle most situations that occur. When the scores progress in a rather orderly fashion from low to high, the mean is probably the best estimate of the "average." *You should be cautious anytime someone begins to use anything other than the mean to report data to convince you they are right.* They may be correct, but it is a good idea to beware of people bearing "fancy averages."

**Regression towards the mean** is the tendency for extremely high or low scores in a distribution to change over time. They change by becoming less extreme and moving relatively close to the mean. *Before illustrating why this is a problem in interpreting information, let us first examine what is happening.*

Think about the times you did extremely well on exams versus those instances when you did poorly. What factors made a difference in each case? When I ask people this question, they typically point to their level of motivation to do well, the amount of time and effort spent studying, and their level of test anxiety on the day of an exam. They also note how difficult it was to repeat exactly the same level of performance on two or more occasions. After a peak performance, for example, students typically report doing somewhat less well; after a poor performance, they report somewhat better test scores.

One reason this occurs is that the factors that produce a peak and poor performance are difficult to maintain at the same levels over time. They essentially vary randomly over time. Thus, when motivation levels fluctuate, and when effort and test anxiety change, the behaviors such factors influence also vary. Unless we understand this phenomenon, inaccurate interpretations of events can occur.

For example, athletes appear on the cover of *Sports Illustrated* magazine after having a peak performance. Typically, their performance drops, and sports fans begin to wonder if their favorite athlete was victimized by "the pressure of national recognition" or whether their idol "still has what it takes." Similarly, individuals who defy chance when first tested in an extrasensory perception (ESP) experiment almost always lose their "psychic powers" when retested. Believers inevitably argue that "the power ebbs and flows" and that conditions must be right for such "sensitive powers" to prevail. As most movie buffs will attest, sequels to popular movies seldom do as well at the box office as the original, and a poor script or acting is blamed. And on the football field, exceptional teams that play poorly in the first half inevitably do better in the second half. Sports

## Understanding the Median Gives a Cancer Patient Hope for the Future

Several years ago, Steven Jay Gould, a well-known biologist, learned that he was suffering from abdominal mesothelioma, a rare and serious cancer usually associated with exposure to asbestos. After surgery, he asked his doctor for references on the disease. His doctor told him there was nothing worth reading. In spite of this advice, Gould went to Harvard's medical library and began reading the literature about his disease. A few sentences into the first article made his heart sink. "Mesothelioma," the article said, "is incurable." The median life expectancy after surgery was eight months. He quickly realized why his doctor did not want him to read anything.

As a scientist, he also understood that a median life expectancy did not mean he would be dead in eight months. He knew that half of the people with this disease lived longer, and he began to read more to figure his chances of falling above the median. He discovered that the probability of living longer than eight months was dramatically increased if you were young, the disease had been recognized at an early stage, and if the newer treatments for it were employed. All of these factors applied to him.

Steven Jay Gould also found that the distribution of life expectancy above the median extended to several years, as illustrated in Figure 2.2. He was confident that with the new treatments he would receive, he could increase his chances for living several years beyond the median life expectancy of eight months. His prediction turned out to be correct. His knowledge of statistics and the meaning of the median gave him hope for the future and a positive mental attitude to help fight the disease. Without that knowledge, he might have become depressed and lost hope that he could have successfully fought the disease (Gould, 1985).

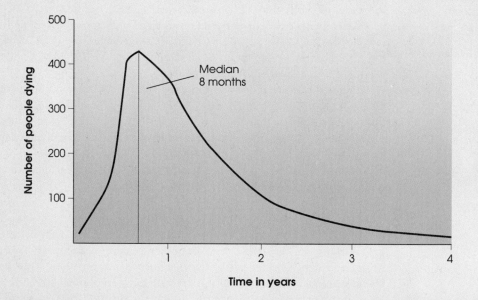

**Figure 2.2** *Distribution of deaths from the type of cancer Steven Jay Gould had. Note the sharp increase in deaths after diagnosis. The distribution of deaths above the median can stretch out for several years (based on data presented in Gould; 1985).*

commentators are quick to point out, however, that the coach's nasty half-time talk "must have put the fear of God into the team."

In effect, the changes noted above are largely due to the regression phenomenon. An exceptional football team more than likely would have done well in the second half, and the star athlete's performance would have dropped and recovered regardless of the appearance on the cover of a sports magazine. Interpretations for such increases and decreases, however, typically ignore this natural tendency for performance to rise or fall as an explanation. Instead, people search for plausible but largely inaccurate reasons to explain what occurred. In effect, the factors they identify (e.g., coach's halftime talk) are given more credit than they deserve for improving performance. Thus, anytime you note changes in extreme scores over time, exercise caution in interpreting the reasons for the variation.

*Percentage* I am sure you have seen statements like the following: "Eighty percent of the doctors sampled prescribe Pain Away headache tablets." "Sixty percent of the people present voted in favor of legalized abortion." The same principle applies here that was used as a caution flag when proportions were utilized to express the probability of an event. *You need to know the number of people, products, or events the percentage was based upon.* Eight of 10 physicians and 6 of 10 people at a meeting give you figures of 80 and 60 percent respectively, as would 800 and 600 out of 1,000 physicians. Which figures would you trust more?

A related problem is that sometimes the number of times something occurs is shown when calculating a percentage would be more appropriate. Seventy thousand people using a new product or service sounds like a high number. But if the total market is 20 million, it is just another of many products or services in that market. Less than 1 percent of the people use it. Whenever possible, try to determine a percentage when someone quotes you "the number of people" who do certain things.

*Ranks* It is not unusual to hear people discuss the top ten songs, the three best pitchers in baseball, the number one tennis player, or the best students in class. People are fascinated with knowing the best and worst, the first and last, the top and the bottom, or the least and most of almost anything. Like other statistics, rank ordering can be abused. There are two problems that can occur.

*First, remember that the "best" and "worst" are relative terms.* The top three brands of clothing in a fashionable store are often much better in quality than the top three brands in a discount store. They are generally not equivalent. Thus, an advertisement that says, "We sell only the top brands," should be taken with a grain of salt. *Second, the source of the ranks needs to be taken into account.* Manufacturers effectively set up test conditions that rank their products number 1. The same is true of politicians. They often hire polling organizations that show their candidate leading the pack among certain types of voters, on certain issues, or as not being as far behind the front runner as people believe. Staff members also stack rallies with a candidate's supporters to show how "popular" the candidate is.

*Correlation* When changes in one are associated with changes in the other, they are correlated. **Correlation** means that the two events covary or are associated. Our ability to detect covariations between events is important for navigating life. Thus, knowing that studying and exam performance are related, that drinking alcoholic beverages and driving a car is dangerous, and managing time leads to higher levels of productivity, helps us to adapt. Consequently, understanding correlations and how to tell when they are present or absent is an extremely important endeavor.

Correlations occur in different ways. An increase in one event may be associated with a corresponding increase in the other (e.g., the number of classes attended is associated with increases in exam score). This is called a *positive correlation*. Sometimes an increase in one event corresponds to a decrease in the second event (e.g., increases in failure experiences are associated with a decrease in self-confidence.). This is called a *negative correlation*. It is also possible that a change in one event is unrelated to a change in the other (e.g., how much a person weighs and their need for power). In the latter case, the two events are said to be not correlated. Figure 2.3 illustrates each type of correlation.

The correlation between two or more events can be represented mathematically. When this is done, a statistic called a *correlation coefficient* is obtained; it is symbolized by the letter $r$. This statistic can range from $r = -1.0$ (i.e., to indicate a negative correlation) to $r = 0$ (i.e., to indicate the events are unrelated) to $r = +1.0$ (i.e., to indicate a positive correlation). The larger the coefficient in either a positive or negative direction, the stronger the relationship between the two events that are correlated. Furthermore, while $r = 0$ means they are unrelated, in practice an $r$ of exactly 0 is very rare. To determine that events are related or unrelated, the *statistical significance* of each correlation coefficient is assessed, as shown in Table 2.4. Generally speaking, very small correlation

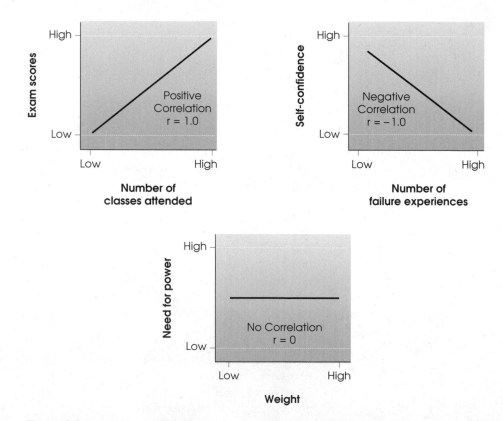

**Figure 2.3** *Examples of correlations between two events.*

| Table 2.4 | A Sample of Correlation Coefficients |
|---|---|

Listed below is a sample of the correlation coefficients taken from the research literature. Remember that the higher the correlation coefficient in either a positive or negative direction, the stronger the relationship. Can you explain why some of the factors below are correlated?

| EVENTS CORRELATED | CORRELATION COEFFICIENT ($r$) | STATISTICALLY SIGNIFICANT |
|---|---|---|
| Scholastic Aptitude Test scores and the height of students. | +.05 | No |
| Scholastic Aptitude Test scores and freshman grade point average. | +.38 | Yes |
| Adult vocabulary and math ability. | +.59 | Yes |
| IQ scores of identical twins reared together. | +.86 | Yes |
| IQ scores and college grades. | +.50 | Yes |
| Number of miles run in training and race times of runners. | −.73 | Yes |
| Grade point average and how close to instructor student sits. | +.35 | Yes |
| Number of main lecture points in lecture notes and examination scores. | +.68 | Yes |
| Length of alternatives on multiple-choice exams and whether or not that item is correct. | +.73 | Yes |
| Satisfaction with job and amount of reported stress on the job. | −.27 | Yes |
| Number of cigarettes smoked per day and amount of job stress. | −.01 | No |
| Amount of fat consumed in diet and amount of stress people report. | +.56 | Yes |

coefficients are not statistically significant, and thus the inference that they are unrelated is drawn. Care must be taken when interpreting such coefficients. Several things should be kept in mind.

*Correlation does not mean one event caused the other.* Of the 39 presidential elections for which a popular vote was recorded, the candidate with the longest last name has received more votes 27 times and fewer votes 7 times. The other 5 times, the candidates had names of equal lengths (Schaeffer, 1984). Such data suggest a high correlation between the length of a candidate's last name and the chances of winning. Does this mean that the length of a person's last name "causes" him or her to win the election? Should potential presidential candidates with short last names legally change their names to longer ones to ensure victory? Should Bill Clinton, who defeated George Bush in the 1992 presidential election, credit the length of his last name for the victory? Of course not. The length of a person's last name does not "cause" someone to win the election.

*Watch out for the* **illusion of correlation**. All of us have expectations that certain things must be related. This knowledge may be based on actual experience or someone may have told us what to expect. In effect, we bring an informal theory, or "intuition," about how two or more things should be related. One consequence of such beliefs is that we see associations that are not there or we overestimate any small degree of covariation that exists.

For example, some stockbrokers believe that stock prices rise with the length of the hemlines on women's skirts. Large gains in average stock prices have occurred when hemlines moved 10–15 inches off the floor (Allesandra, 1991). Others believe that a positive mental attitude gives individuals special advantages— it enables them to become successful in life. In both cases, people are more likely to focus on stories in newspapers, testimonials from friends, or the outcomes of research studies that support their point of view. What they ignore are instances where hemlines changed and stock prices remained the same. Or they forget about people with a pessimistic outlook who became successful. *In other words, they forget a principle mentioned earlier in this chapter, namely that the accurate testing of ideas demands that appropriate comparisons be made.*

Chris Wolff (1993) proposes one strategy for examining whether two events are associated. This is to set up a 2 × 2 **contingency table** as shown in Figure 2.4. Such a table allows us to determine how often an event occurs when the factor of interest is present and absent. After all, to show a relationship, information about both states of affairs is needed. Instead of focusing our attention on only those observations that suggest a relationship (i.e., the cell that gives us the illusion of correlation), the contingency table allows us to compare our observations to something else. In effect, it forces us to consider "the rest of the story"—in this case, how many times the presence and absence of an optimistic outlook was associated with success and the lack of success.

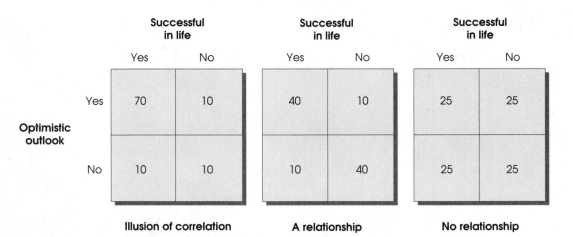

*Figure 2.4* *Three hypothetical examples of the use of a contingency table to examine whether or not mental attitude is related to success in life for 100 people. Note that the example on the left illustrates the illusion of correlation. The 70 people who had an optimistic outlook and were successful makes it tempting to conclude that the two factors were related. The data do not support this conclusion. If a positive mental attitude is important to success in life, then a relatively large number of people without an optimistic outlook should have no success in life. One would expect more than 10 people to appear in the lower right hand cell. The contingency table in the middle, however, illustrates what a clear association between a positive mental attitude and success would look like. The table on the right illustrates the absence of a relationship.*

Whether or not you have actual data to plug into a contingency table is not the important issue. Chris Wolff notes that the act of setting one up forces us to focus on the types of evidence we need to accurately and fairly conclude that two events were related. In particular, it counters a natural tendency to pay more attention to events that occur than to those that do not. As you can see in figure 2.4, how often something does not occur (e.g., lack of an optimistic attitude associated with a lack of success) is just as important in determining whether events are related as the number of times optimism and success are related.

Understanding the illusion of correlation helps us to avoid developing inaccurate conclusions. *The other side of seeing a correlation that does not exist is failing to identify one that does.* The illusion of correlation occurs because people expect two things to be related. **Invisible correlations,** however, result from the absence of an expectation that two variables will be related. As a result, identifying relationships among events that can help as well as produce harmful effects in our lives does not occur.

Until recently, associations between low dietary fiber and colon cancer were invisible, as was the connection between secondhand smoke and lung cancer, and other respiratory ailments. Similarly, many people still fail to see the connection between unprotected sex with multiple sex partners and the chances of contracting a sexually transmitted disease, including infection with the virus associated with AIDS. The belief that "it will not happen to me" is a common fallacy.

The reasons for not making such connections vary. Jennifer Crocker (1981) suggests that a lack of information, denying that certain events affect our lives, and the lack of ability to properly select and classify events that affect us are to blame. Identifying invisible correlations is just as important as properly interpreting those that are visible to us.

*When interpreting correlations, always ask what other factors might be responsible.* A newspaper article proclaimed that business managers who drank lots of coffee increased their chances of having heart attacks. "I'm going to stop drinking coffee and avoid a heart attack," a friend said after reading the article. I pointed out that business people who drank coffee often had hard-driving, stressful life-styles. Their stress-filled life-styles were probably the problem, and not coffee drinking per se. In addition to drinking less coffee, I suggested that my friend also might learn to manage stress better. Key questions to ask:

- "What's missing from the relationship I'm focusing on?"
- "What other factors could be related to those I'm looking at that might have produced the relationship?"

*Let us again turn our attention to Exhibit A in Table 2.1 for a moment.* Was the statistical information presented and used appropriately? The advertisers hope that viewers will think there is a correlation between the gasoline additive and the distance traveled. Problems with how the test was conducted and possible extraneous variables cast doubt on that conclusion. Also, a claim is made that similar results were obtained in 80 percent of the test runs. Is this percentage used appropriately? How do we know that it is not based on 4 out of 5 test runs? Would you be as impressed knowing it was 4 out of 5 rather than 80 out of 100? The number of test runs is missing. Finally, the commercial also stated that we would save an average of four dollars on every tank of gasoline. Did it use the average that showed the product in its best light?

*To further test your understanding of the eight questions to ask, complete Exercise 2.1 in the Applied Activities at the end of this chapter.*

## Summary of Chapter Organizers

Suggested responses to the chapter organizers presented at the beginning of this chapter are presented below.

1. *What questions should you be asking to challenge the information you receive in the news media, advertising, and from other sources?* Before embracing the accuracy and usefulness of such evidence and then using it to develop explanations, to form conclusions, and to otherwise make decisions, some caution is needed. Using questions to challenge information in these sources promotes a critical analysis of what they have to offer. The following eight questions are helpful in accomplishing the latter goal:
   1. What is asserted or claimed to have occurred?
   2. What evidence is offered to support the assertion or claim?
   3. What is being compared, and is the comparison a fair one?
   4. What problems exist with the sample of people and products studied?
   5. Were representative test conditions used?
   6. Were extraneous variables controlled?
   7. How consistently did the event occur?
   8. Was the statistical information presented and used appropriately?

2. *Do you know four ways that various claims designed to influence you are stated?* Before accepting at face value an assertion or claim, first identify the form in which it is offered. Claims or assertions are tyically stated as: Two or more events are related; One event caused the other to occur; Characteristics of one person, product, or event are said to be included in another; and One person, product, or event is different from another.

3. *What precautions should you take when evaluating a particular claim?* Each of the four forms that claims take must be interpreted with a grain of salt. If two events are related, don't assume that one caused the other to occur. When one event is claimed to cause another, assess whether the two events covaried, if the cause happened before the effect, whether the effect occurs when the factor identified as the cause is present and ceases when it is absent, and whether alternative explanations have been ruled out. When the property of one thing is included in another, don't automatically assume they are really alike; nor should you make the same mistake if an assertion says they are different.

4. *What types of evidence support a claim, and what can be wrong with them?* Personal experience and opinion are very common and suffer from the fact that such observations can be distorted and only may apply to the particular time and place where they occurred. Testimonials build on the prestige of those making a claim, but such individuals are not always objective. They may have a financial or psychological stake in what is offered. Expert opinion is sometimes used to impress more than to inform and best used when a person is not speaking outside of his or her area of expertise. Research findings often sound objective, but those reported in the mass media may be incomplete or suffer from inadequate methods, processes, and procedures used to produce them.

5. *What do you have to watch out for when making comparisons?* To claim that something produces an effect, it is important to be prepared to answer the question, "compared to what?" While important, comparisons are not always employed properly. When drugs are being compared, it is important that a placebo be used to control for the effects of expectations such as "I know this drug will help me." Also, it is

not uncommon to have a control or comparison group absent, or for comparison conditions to have a critical factor absent, or to be given characteristics that enhance a favorable outcome.

6. *How can you tell that the sample of people, products, or services used in the comparisons was adequate?* An important intent of gathering information is to draw conclusions that apply to a large number of people. Thus, ensuring that comparisons are based on information from samples that are random or selected without any known bias is important. If not, at least recognizing the limitations a more restricted sample places on interpretations is useful.

7. *Are you able to determine the ways in which methods of observation and test procedures can distort the outcomes of the research reported to you?* Two issues must be taken into account. If the test conditions adequately represent normal events, then the findings can be generalized to everyday life. Also, extraneous variables must be controlled to ensure that the factor under study is the likely cause of whatever outcome was observed.

8. *What precautions should you take when interpreting terms such as "probability," "average," "percentage," "ranks," and "correlations"?* Probability means that one event is more likely than another. It does not guarantee that something will occur. One must always consider the likelihood that some occurrence, no matter how compelling, was due to chance.

   Remember that there are three types of averages—the mean, median, and mode. They typically represent different numerical values, with the mode being the one that changes most dramatically when a new score is added to a distribution. When extreme scores are present, the median is a better estimate of the average. And because extreme scores over time naturally regress or move towards the mean of a distribution, care must be taken when explaining changes in extreme scores. Always ask the number of events associated with a percentage, and take claims of "we're ranked #1" or "ranked last" with a grain of salt. Ranks are often relative terms, and the source of any claims must be evaluated.

   Finally, a correlation implies that two events are associated. It does not mean that one event caused the other to occur. Attending to personal biases and experiences that make us think two or more things are associated helps us avoid the illusion of correlation.

## Things to Do

*The following activities are designed to help reinforce concepts covered in the chapter. Select those that interest you to test your ability to apply the information in the chapter.*

1. Look through your favorite magazine or watch television for an advertisement that makes claims based on research data. Analyze the data using the eight-question procedure outlined in this chapter. Having done this, how would you redesign the demonstration or research study so that it was improved?

2. Set up 2 × 2 contingency tables that would help you answer the following questions. Does cramming for an exam lead to higher test scores? Do people who attend church on Sunday have less misfortune in their lives? Is exercise associated with people living longer? Assume that you have data on 200 people to help you answer each question. What would the contingency table look like if a relationship were found to exist in each case? If there were no relationship? If the illusion of correlation was present?

3. Cable channels often have late night programs that sell a variety of products under the guise of a television show. They are technically called "infomercials," because they disguise (not very successfully) a sales pitch for exercise products, subliminal tapes, psychic readings, blenders, car cleaners, hair care products, memory-enhancing programs, and many other products. Watch an "informercial," and write a short two- to three-paragraph critique using concepts in this chapter for critically analyzing and evaluating information you are given.

4. Design a two- to three-minute presentation that you might use to "sell" your skills and abilities on a videotape that you would send to potential employers. Build into your presentation at least two to three deceptive uses of information based on the presentation in this chapter. Try to be as subtle as you can when doing this to help disguise the deceit. Share your presentation with a friend or classmate, and see if the type of dishonesty employed can be identified. Check your responses with your instructor.

5. Go through the newspapers and magazines around your home or apartment, and select statements and claims that you feel are the most deceptive. Critically analyze and evaluate each claim, and develop a "top ten" deceptive claims list. Are there any similarities among the statements that make them problematic?

## APPLIED ACTIVITIES

EXERCISE 2.1                    **Applying the Eight Questions for Analyzing and Interpreting Information**

### The Case of the Unhappy Housewives

Sheri Hite is a journalist who has studied the sexual preferences of men and women. Her research technique is to lay questionnaires around on tables, benches, chairs, and on the floor of bus terminals, city parks, sidewalks, restrooms, office buildings, and other public settings. The questionnaire items ask people to give information about the sex acts they enjoy, how often they have sexual relations, when they engage in sexual activity, where they do it, and with whom they typically engage in sex. They also are asked to provide details about what they like and dislike about their spouses, significant others, and casual sexual partners. About 10 to 15 percent of the questionnaires are then returned to her for analysis. In one of her studies she reports that 94 percent of American housewives are unhappy with their marriages and that 75 percent of them are having affairs (Hite, 1987).

1. What is asserted or claimed to have occurred?

2. What evidence is offered to support the assertion or claim?

3. What is being compared, and is the comparison a fair one?

4. What problems exist with the sample of people and products studied?

5. Were representative test conditions used?

6. Were extraneous variables controlled?

7. How consistently did the event occur?

8. Was the statistical information presented and used appropriately?

EXERCISE 2.2

**What Would You Do?**

*For each of the scenarios listed below that appeared in the popular media, critically analyze the information by answering the questions provided.*

**Scenario 1:**

In November of 1990, Iben Browning incurred the wrath of geologists and seismologists for projecting a 50-50 probability or likelihood of a major earthquake occurring along the New Madrid fault zone in Ohio and Kentucky in early December. He claimed the tidal action of the moon was exerting pressure on the earth's surface at the New Madrid fault zone. Browning had a Ph.D. degree in zoology and had worked for a nuclear weapons research site and a well-known cancer research center. Many people who lived along the fault worried about the earthquake destroying their homes. Some even packed up their belongings and left home during that period of time (based on an Associated Press story, AP, November 30, 1990).

- How credible is the source of the prediction?

- Is a 50-50 probability of something happening really a prediction?

- Is the prediction based on a possible "correlation," "the illusion of correlation," or "a potential invisible correlation" between the moon's tidal actions and pressure on the earth's surface?

**Scenario 2:**

Anthropologist James Schaefer examined the effects of barroom environment—music, lighting, decor—on the drinking behaviors of more than 5,500 patrons in bars that specialized in country and western themes. *He found that country music with a slow tempo of 60 beats per minute was more likely to lead to alcohol abuse than music with a faster tempo of 85 beats per minute.* The data gathered were the number of sips of a drink that people took while listening to certain songs. Classic country songs such as Kenny Rogers's "Lucille," Crystal Gayle's "Don't It Make My Brown Eyes Blue," and Willie Nelson's "Blue Eyes Cryin In The Rain" were particularly effective in encouraging drinking (Stone, 1989).

- Has a "cause-and-effect relationship" between the music and drinking been established? If not, what needs to be done?

- What "extraneous variables" could be operating here?

- Are the comparisons that are made to establish a relationship between drinking and the music adequate? If not, what kinds of comparisons would be better?

EXERCISE 2.3

**What's Wrong Here?**

*All of the statements below were taken from claims and assertions found in the popular media. Indicate in the space provided why you should be suspicious.*

- "No other smoking-cessation program works better than Quitters Anonymous."

- "Ache-Be-Gone contains twice as much pain relief medication as its competitors, and that's why it's the most effective product on the market today."

- Portions of an article in the newspaper read, *"The Last Body Count* was a very successful feature film and later video store release. Unfortunately, it was ranked last in its time slot when shown on network television. A news magazine show and three situation comedies competing with it were ranked higher in the ratings. Viewers are obviously losing their taste for violence on television."

- "According to industry records, last year, Trans-Caribbean Airlines had the best 'on-time' record of any other airline in the industry. Fly with us, and be sure of getting to your destination on time today!"

- "Students who use a word processor get higher grades."

- "This SAT refresher course is guaranteed to raise your combined SAT scores an average of 100 points higher than your PSAT or last SAT scores."

# Key Terms

*Assertion.* Making a statement or claim that something is true without offering objective proof that the statement is accurate. Determining the accuracy of the statement or claim depends on the outcome of gathering and analyzing additional evidence.

*Contingency table.* A table showing the different effects of two or more variables where the data reported are the frequency with which something occurs.

*Control group.* A comparison condition in a research study in which the experimental treatment is absent.

*Correlation.* A tendency for the measures of two events to vary together.

*Dependent variable.* The measure of performance used in a research study.

*Experimental group.* The condition in a study in which the experimental treatment is used.

*Extraneous variables.* Unwanted factors in a research study that could interfere with the experimental treatment or produce the same effect as the treatment.

*Gambler's fallacy.* Belief that a run of bad luck in games of chance or anything where chance plays a role will soon change in our favor.

*Grouping variables.* Using existing characteristics of people, products, or events to classify them into groups for purposes of making comparisons among them (e.g., gender, age, type of car, size of box product comes in).

*Hawthorne effect.* The tendency for people to behave a certain way because they are being observed and not because of the variables under study.

*Illusion of correlation.* A tendency to allow our expectations that certain things must be related to lead us to incorrectly assume that two events are correlated. One consequence of such beliefs is that we see associations that are not there or we overestimate any small degree of covariation that exists.

*Independent variable.* The factor that is under study and that is manipulated by a researcher.

*Interaction effect.* The tendency for combinations of independent variables to produce effects on behavior that are different from the influence of any one on them operating alone.

*Invisible correlations.* Not detecting an association between two events that play a role in our lives. This results from the absence of an expectation that two variables will be related.

*Mean.* The sum of all the individual scores in a distribution divided by the total number of scores.

*Median.* The score in a distribution that has 50 percent of the other scores above it and 50 percent of the other scores below it.

*Mode.* The most frequently occurring score in a distribution.

*Placebo.* A harmless neutral substance (e.g., a sugar pill, injection of water) used in research on the effects of drugs in order to assess how much the expectation of a cure affects the reactions of participants in a study.

*Probability.* The likelihood that an event will occur.

*Random assignment.* Putting people or products into the conditions under study without any known bias when making such assignments. This means, for example, that variations in people such as intelligence, motivation, anxiety, resourcefulness, and other qualities are distributed across the conditions under study.

*Random sample.* Selecting people or products to study without any known biases affecting the selection. This means that everyone has an equal chance of being selected.

*Regression towards the mean.* Tendency for extremely high or low scores in any distribution to move over time in the direction of the mean of the distribution to which they belong. For example, a competitive swimmer or track athlete has a distribution of performance times in his or her career. The exact same peak or very low times in these sports do not continue to occur. Typically, athletes find that after a peak performance or a very poor performance, their times tend to drop or improve somewhat, respectively.

*Response bias.* The predictable way in which people respond to certain stimuli.

*Statistically significant.* A term used to describe two events that are probably different because of factors other than chance. Typically, if we can assume that the observed difference would occur fewer than 5 times in 100 due to chance, then we say it is statistically significant.

## CHAPTER 3

# Solving Problems and Making Decisions

## Chapter Overview

Without the ability to solve problems and make decisions, managing current issues as well as our concerns for the future would be impossible. This chapter emphasizes how you can become more effective in dealing with the variety of problems you face. How to employ a process for solving problems and making choices will be examined in detail.

## Chapter Organizers

*As you read, answer the questions that follow on a separate sheet of paper, and check your responses with those provided in the summary section.*

Several ways of thinking and behaving interfere with your ability to solve problems and make decisions. They affect your levels of motivation and interest as well as the types of skills used to find solutions and courses of action.

1. What pitfalls should be avoided when tackling problems?

Sometimes people are not particularly excited about the prospects of finding solutions or courses of action to the issues they face.

2. Why is it important to accept the challenge a problem presents?

Perhaps the most important factor that guides and directs our attempts to solve a problem is how it is initially defined.

3. Are you aware of three criteria that can help you define a problem better?

Identifying the important facts and generating a range of alternatives also play a role in finding solutions to issues.

4. What steps can you take to ensure that you have perceived the important facts in a problem?

5. How can you develop a list of the best possible alternative solutions or courses of action regarding the issues you face?

Carefully evaluating the benefits and costs of potential courses of action is an important part of making a decision.

6. What process can you use to assess the strengths and weaknesses of various options?
7. What rules of thumb can help you sort through the pros and cons of your potential solutions or courses of action?
8. What should you do if you get stuck and still have a hard time deciding?

Having made a decision, there are several things to which you must still attend.

9. Why is it important to have a contingency plan for something going wrong?
10. Is your work finished when you have successfully identified a solution or course of action?

## Tragedy at Sea

During the height of tensions during the Iran-Iraq war, a number of United States Navy warships were in the Persian Gulf protecting the shipment of oil and other commodities. On July 3, 1988, the *USS Vincennes*, a high-tech warship, was on routine patrol when one of its helicopters was attacked by Iranian gunboats. The *Vincennes* moved into Iranian territorial waters to help and opened fire with superior weapons on the gunboats.

To some observers, this was like shooting at rabbits with a radar guided-missile. However, to Captain Will Rogers and the crew of the *USS Vincennes*, this was the combat for which they had trained for years. As the shooting at the gunboats continued, tension aboard the *Vincennes* remained high. They were still positioned inside Iranian waters, and uncertainty about possible attacks by Iranian missiles and F-14 fighter planes lurked in the back of their minds.

Besides the threat of Iranian attack, stress was higher than usual under such circumstances. Neither Captain Rogers nor the crew were combat veterans. This was their first hostile encounter outside of wargames and other naval simulations where the ship's captain had developed a reputation as a risky decision maker.

At 9:47 A.M. an Iran Air 655 airbus took off from Bandar Abbas, Iran, with 290 civilian passengers aboard on a commercial air route over the Persian Gulf. Almost immediately, the radar on the *Vincennes* picked up the airliner and fed information about the aircraft into a sophisticated computer system designed to identify airplanes as "friendly," "hostile," or "unidentified."

The computer initially labeled the aircraft as a commercial flight. Unfortunately, in the tension and semidarkness of the ship's command center, a crew member checking commercial flight schedules for the Persian Gulf missed the listing for the airbus. Direct radio contact with the plane was initiated; but the aircraft's radio channels were busy with air traffic control information and the plane did not receive the initial messages or later warning from the *Vincennes*.

By this time, Captain Rogers had taken complete control of the situation. He was directing the fight with the gunboats and was trying to monitor information provided by the computer and his staff about the unidentified airplane. There were simply too many things to think about.

Then something happened that psychologists call "scenario fulfillment"—you see what you expect. In the tension of the moment, anxious crew members tagged the unidentified aircraft as an F-14 fighter and reported that it was descending, picking up speed, and closing in on the *Vincennes*. A later review of the tapes from the warship would reveal that no such thing occurred. In reality the passenger plane was slowing down and climbing to 12,000 feet.

Captain Rogers was confronted with incomplete and inaccurate information. He had seconds to make a decision and accepted his crew's conclusion that the aircraft was hostile. He gave the command to fire, and two SM-2 surface-to-air missiles were launched. Within seconds, the airbus, with its crew and 290 passengers, was destroyed.

Based on accounts of the incident in *Newsweek* and *Time* magazines.

# PROBLEM SOLVING AND DECISION MAKING: TWO SIDES OF THE SAME COIN

Each of us needs to solve problems and make decisions under a variety of circumstances. Some of them, like the situation faced by the captain of the *Vincennes*, are tension arousing. Incomplete information exists; there is little room for error; and quick decisions are needed. Other circumstances, while not life threatening, are just as important and demand our best efforts to manage them. Included here are such things as where to invest money, what career path to choose, whether or not to marry, how to resolve a personal problem, choosing what car to purchase, and deciding how to decorate a room or repair a small appliance.

Problem solving and decision making are sometimes treated in the literature as if they were separate topics. In reality, they are very much interrelated. To solve **problems** we have to make a number of important **decisions.** We must decide, among other things: how to adequately define our problem; what information is most important; which alternative **solutions** are possible and which one would be the "best" choice; and how to implement a particular solution or course of action. Having to deal with problems forces us to make decisions.

Similarly, whenever we say to ourselves, "I have got to make a decision. What should I do?" we are responding to a problem in our lives. That is, we are reacting to something for which we do not have a readily available response. The need to make a decision reflects the fact that we have a problem. *Consequently, suggestions for improving one process ultimately help us to do the other more effectively.*

# A PROBLEM-SOLVING AND DECISION-MAKING PROCESS

## 1. Identify and Avoid Common Pitfalls

Most of us can enhance our problem-solving and decision-making abilities. A good place to begin is to assess the extent to which certain problem-solving and decision-making attitudes and behaviors are present in your daily life. This should help identify

areas where you are already strong and weak. Before reading further, please complete the activity in Exercise 3.1 in the Applied Activities section at the end of this chapter.

What was your score on each item of the rating scale? How satisfied are you with your current ability to solve problems and to make decisions? One reason people with low scores feel less satisfied is that each statement represents a common pitfall to problem solving and decision making. This is obvious when the attitudes and behaviors within each statement are used often in our lives. Let us examine several reasons why the items in the scale represent relatively ineffective attitudes and behaviors.

*Ignoring Problems* Paul Watzlawick (1974) has observed that many of us have a tendency to deny that problems exist. Some persons seem to have learned early that "hear no evil, see no evil, and speak no evil" were less risky ways to behave. Thus, they hope that things will not get worse, that the problem will go away, or that it will solve itself. Such people engage in "magical thinking."

The problem with this strategy is that our problems often get worse instead of better. To choose not to take action when it is needed leaves us vulnerable to whatever occurs as the problem gets worse. Two married friends used to tell me, "Jan and I argue more than other couples, but that's just the way we are. It's nothing to get excited about, since we like each other." Two months later, they had filed for divorce.

Daniel Wheeler and Irving Janis (1980) find that people may adopt two styles to avoid problems or make decisions. They are called **complacency** and **defensive avoidance.** Complacency occurs when people fail to see the signs of some danger or simply ignore them. They continue to do things as they always have. Many people ignore hurricane or tornado warnings, the connection between lung cancer and heavy smoking, and physical symptoms that suggest serious illnesses. Defensive avoidance occurs when people see that a problem exists but believe they have little hope of finding a solution. *There are three forms of defensive avoidance that people use.*

1. *Rationalizing the problem.* People make up reasons why the problem does not exist or convince themselves that, "It can't happen to me." Most heavy drinkers and smokers are aware of the dangers of their habits. Many continue to tell themselves, "Nothing has happened so far."

2. *Procrastinating.* Individuals simply put off taking any action. They tell themselves, "Nothing needs to be done about it now; I can take care of it later." Thus, problems and the need to make decisions are avoided. Some students ignore their poor performance early in a term thinking they can overcome it later.

3. *Passing the buck.* People might pass the buck by saying, "I'm not the one who needs to do something about that problem," or "I'm not the one responsible for making the decision. It's Janet's job to solve that problem and to make that kind of decision." Buck-passing is a common problem in large organizations. There, the responsibility for solving a problem or making a decision often can be pushed up, down, or sideways in the organization.

*Becoming Overly Optimistic* As a general rule, it is helpful to be optimistic about your ability to find solutions to problems. Martin Seligman (1991) reports that optimists are more willing to challenge the problems they face, to persist until a solution is found, and, when necessary, to seek assistance from others. There is, however, a negative side to such optimism. Too much of it may lead us to spin our wheels on issues for which there are no good solutions. Seymour Sarason (1978) argues that effective problem solvers and decision makers must know "when to cut their losses." They know when to stop expending time and energy on things that are unlikely to be resolved.

*Using Past Solutions for Present Problems* When our electricity or telephone service fail in our homes, most of us take actions that worked well in the past. Similarly, when faced with a conflict with another person, the chances are good you behave as you did in the past. You might argue, fight, cry, turn your back and leave, or try to reach a mutual solution. While this strategy works in some circumstances, Paul Watzlawick and his colleagues (1974) note that "old problem-solving habits do not necessarily fit new situations." Sometimes they make the problem worse or create new problems. There are two ways that we typically use past solutions for new problems.

1. *Applying more of the same.* This occurs when we simply use more of a certain solution to solve a problem. This strategy is seen when we raise the thermostat in our homes as the temperature drops. Yet this only raises our heating bills and consumes more of a scarce natural resource. To counter pornography or drug smuggling, stiffer laws are passed, more law enforcement officers are hired, additional jails are built, and court time to handle the additional arrests increases. Drug smuggling, however, continues to flourish in spite of such efforts.

2. *Taking actions that are just the opposite of those found in the problem.* When we find a friend, for example, who is feeling sad or depressed, our natural tendency is to try to cheer him or her up. Often the attempt fails. Why? Because people typically resent attempts to control their emotions. It only increases their feelings of failure and the sense that something is wrong with them. In this case, doing just the opposite of how the person is feeling does not address the real issues with which the person is struggling.

*Seeking Perfect Solutions* Some of us are simply not satisfied unless we get things just right. Paul Watzlawick and his colleagues suggest that this strategy gets us nowhere. Not only do perfect solutions seldom exist, but they may lead us to embrace solutions that sound good but are ineffective. A neighbor of mine tried to find a way to achieve perfect health. She became "hooked" on exercise and a "vegetarian diet." Unfortunately, she exercised too much, injured her back, and had to quit for six months. She also grew tired of vegetarian meals and went back to her old diet with which she quickly gained an additional five pounds. As usually occurs with people who embrace "perfect" solutions, she was convinced she had done the right thing and was willing to do it all over again as soon as her injury healed.

*Trying to Solve Problems and Make Decisions Quickly* There is a tendency in our culture to get things done quickly. Irving Janis and Leon Mann (1977) observe that rushing to solve problems or make decisions is seldom effective. The quality of the solution typically suffers. Such warnings often are not heeded with tragic results sometimes occurring, as illustrated in Focus on People 3.1.

Under pressure for quick solutions and decisions, people can become trapped by a process labeled **decision freezing.** Psychologist Arie Kruglanski notes that this aspect of decision making is characterized by premature commitment to a course of action. The pressure for a quick decision leads people to bypass an important step in the problem-solving and decision-making process. This is the part in which all available options are considered before making a final judgment. When this step is skipped, people become indifferent. They begin to rely on "wishful thinking" (i.e., everything will be alright), and information that opposes the decision is discounted or ignored. In effect, indecision and ambiguity become stressful, and any action is seen as preferable to none at all. Kruglanski argues that decision freezing occurred among decision makers associated with the space shuttle *Challenger* mishap.

*Selecting the First Alternative Considered* A very common mistake in problem solving and decision making is to select the first solution that occurs to us. Initial ideas,

## Deadly Consequences of Making a Quick Decision

*In 1986 the space shuttle* Challenger *exploded on launch, killing all crew members.* On the surface, the cause was defective parts that connected the solid-fuel rocket boosters to each other. Beneath the surface was a perceived need to launch as soon as possible. In the process to ensure a speedy liftoff of the *Challenger*, many observers noted that normal decision-making procedures of the National Aeronautics and Space Administration (NASA) were circumvented.

*Pressure for a quick decision came from many sources.* NASA officials wanted to secure congressional funding through displays of cost-effectiveness and productivity. Thus, they wanted to launch 15 space shuttles in 1986 and to increase that amount to 24 a year by 1988. There was intense public interest in the "Teacher in Space" program, and a corresponding wish to use it to demonstrate NASA technology. Freezing weather already had delayed the launch more than twenty hours, and NASA did not want to disappoint the general public or compromise the interest in the Teacher in Space program. The latter interest, of course, could translate into increased public sentiment for continued funding for NASA. All of this created a powerful psychological "pressure cooker" in which NASA officials fixated their sights on launching the shuttle and became largely impervious to contrary facts.

*One of those contrary facts were some misgivings about the safety of the launch on the part of engineers working for Morton Thiokol,* the company that manufactured the solid-fuel rocket boosters. Top management at Thiokol, while initially sympathetic to the arguments of their engineers, soon began to sing a different tune. Their vice president for engineering later testified that he initially opposed the launch but changed his position after being told to take off his engineering hat and to put on one representing management.

*Why did officials at Thiokol also begin to favor a decision to launch?* Dependent upon NASA for $400 million a year in business, they could identify with the plight of NASA officials to not delay the launch further. A false sense of security set in. Everyone recognized that there had never been a mishap with a shuttle launch and that estimates for a failed launch were expected in only 1 out of every 100,000 launches—an estimate, by the way, that was revised soon after the *Challenger* incident.

Above account based on information appearing in *Time* and *Newsweek* magazines during the period of the accident.

unfortunately, may not be the best. We must develop a habit of generating alternatives and not evaluate any one until we have such a list. My son's school sponsored a father-son day. One activity was to spend the morning making plaster casts of animal tracks. As we gathered at the school to board a bus, it began to rain. Almost in unison, people said, "That does it. There goes the morning. No way we can make animal tracks in the rain. Let's cancel." Fortunately, one of the fathers knew the value of generating alternatives. He suggested the group go to the gym and make plaster casts of each father's foot, along with that of his son. While the "animal tracks" we made were not those originally planned, it was a fun morning.

*As a general rule, it is a good idea to strive for a minimum of at least three alterative solutions.* Joseph Keating (1984) reports that this helps overcome the tendency to rely on shortcuts, past habits, and other simplistic solutions. Such solutions often function like aspirin or a cold tablet in providing temporary relief from a cold. They do not lead to long lasting resolutions of a problem. In many cases, Keating notes, the initial ideas for a solution are likely to be overly simplistic. It is better to stretch ourselves to determine whether we can develop something better than our initial ideas.

*Misuse of the Representativeness and Availability Heuristics* Amos Tversky and Daniel Kahneman (1982) note that people often resort to certain **heuristics,** or rules of thumb, when trying to make decisions and solve problems. The advantage of heuristics is that they reduce the time and effort required to make reasonably good judgments and decisions. The disadvantage is that they lead to biases in our responses.

The **representativeness heuristic** is a tendency to make judgments by asking whether an event conforms to our preconceived idea of it. For example, many people believe in visits by aliens from outer space. Thus, reports of strange objects and lights in the sky are seen as evidence of flying saucers and visits by aliens from outer space. Natural explanations (e.g., weather balloons, ball lightning, optical illusions), although more likely to be correct, are given less weight.

The **availability heuristic** is a tendency to make decisions based upon what is most vivid, easily recalled, or otherwise available in our memory. Thus, events that appear in the news media or that capture your imagination are perceived as more likely to occur than a relatively ordinary event. For example, when asked to estimate their chances of getting injured in the Middle East from a terrorist attack or a car accident, people believe the terrorist attack is more likely (Tversky and Kahneman, 1982). In reality, an injury from a car accident is more likely. Of course, most automobile accidents are seldom front page news stories. Terrorist attacks, however, become major news events.

*Letting Other People Make Decisions for You* People have entered careers, taken courses, gotten married, bought products, and done other things they eventually disliked because they let someone else make the decision. Gordon Miller (1978) states that this seldom works. Most of us forget that even if someone else makes a decision, we are the ones who must live with it. Miller argues that we need more control over our lives. Making our own decisions is one effective way of establishing control.

*Lack of Confidence* Barry Anderson (1980) and Irving Janis and Leon Mann (1977) report how important it is to have confidence in such skills. Good problem solvers and decision makers have confidence in their abilities. Studies show that people with relatively high levels of confidence examine a variety of alternative solutions and use "lessons learned" from their past attempts to solve problems. Those with relatively low levels of confidence in their ability were very dependent upon others and would not take the risk to think on their own (Phillips et al., 1984). Consider how the following ideas might help you increase your confidence.

1. *Sit back periodically, and imagine yourself successfully solving a problem or making an important decision.* Morris Stein (1974) has demonstrated that using images in this way increases people's confidence in their problem-solving abilities.

2. *Obtain the knowledge and information you lack and, if necessary, get other people to help you.* Other people, books related to the content areas of your problem, and the ideas in this chapter might help. Having the knowledge to tackle certain problems is just as important as knowing how to employ a problem-solving and decision-making process effectively.

3. *Whenever possible, break your problem into manageable units.* The steps to use in solving problems and making decisions that follow in this chapter suggest one way to do this. They break the process of problem solving and decision making into stages. Or

you might find that some issues naturally have several parts. Why not work on one part at a time? Think about how you planned your program of study at school. You most likely did an overview and worked out the details a semester or academic quarter at a time. An important payoff is that as you complete each part, your confidence in your skills will probably increase.

*Believing You Lack Intelligence and Creativity* An old saying attributed to Thomas Edison is that genius is 1 percent inspiration and 99 percent perspiration. Herbert Simon, a Nobel Laureate, spent about a hundred hours a week for years doing the work for which he won the Nobel Prize (Hayes, 1989). Other research supports the idea that not only are persistence and hard work components of success in such areas, but the overwhelming majority of people have the basic intellectual and creative skills needed to find reasonable solutions to the problems they face.

Studies also show that the correlation between an individual's IQ and overall scores on problem solving averages about + .66 (Sternberg and Detterman, 1986). As you might remember from the discussion of correlation in Chapter 2, this suggests the two factors are related but that other factors also were involved.

*For example, Keith Simonton suggests that chance may play a role.* He notes that all of us employ intellectual processes that contain ideas, images, symbols, abstract concepts, rhymes, snippets of memory, and other elements that interact when solving a problem. In effect, the mental elements are like a child with a pailful of Legos. Simonton argues that some people simply have more mental elements to work with, while others possess the equivalent of a Lego starter set. Both can be creative, but those with a more diverse set of "Lego pieces" or mental elements have an advantage. In effect, with more of these elements present, they have a higher probability of combining ideas and images into a novel and creative product (Simonton, 1988).

A somewhat different point of view is offered by Teresa Amabile (1983). Rather than focusing on characteristics of the person, she focuses on the product. She states that "a product or response is creative to the extent that appropriate observers independently agree it is creative"(p. 31). *What is creative, then, depends to some extent upon whatever biases observers have about appropriate solutions.* If the outcomes of your thinking processes match those biases, then you are likely to be considered a creative problem solver. This is why forms of music (rock and roll), art (Picasso's abstract cubism style), dance (Martha Graham's modern dance movement), scientific theories (Darwin's evolutionary perspective), and a variety of inventions (automobiles, television) were initially discounted. Their creators were considered "inept," "dreamers," "out of the mainstream," and even "a bit weird." It took time for people to recognize the creativity in such things.

Along similar lines, other nonintellectual factors are involved. *The chances of developing a creative product increase when people have sufficient freedom from other responsibilities.* Men in a traditional family setting probably have an advantage. Household tasks and child-rearing responsibilities are more likely to take time away from a woman than a man. This may be one reason why studies show that successful men marry as often as men in the general population. Successful women are more than seven times as likely to remain single (Hayes, 1989). *Furthermore, people need an environment where their efforts will be encouraged and supported.* Creative solutions to a variety of problems are more likely to occur when external controls are minimal. This includes such things as time pressures, negative evaluations, and interference by others (Amabile, 1983).

## 2. Accept the Challenge a Problem Presents

Accepting the challenge of a problem is a necessary first step in trying to solve it. To do this, a problem must not be perceived as an obstacle, crisis, or burden. When a problem is viewed as a challenge rather than a threat, two very positive things occur. One is that people become open to alternative ideas for solving it. This was demonstrated in a study of business managers (Tjosvold, 1984). They were presented with a series of problems to be solved with subordinates. Those who saw the problem as a challenge listened and used the ideas of their subordinates. Managers who perceived the problems as a crisis were less open and less willing to listen to ideas from subordinates. Second, people persist toward solutions when problems are perceived as challenges. Students, for example, who viewed difficult test items in this way persisted in solving them, while those who did not tended to stop working on them (Klein and Weitzenfield, 1978).

## 3. Carefully Define the Problem

How a problem is initially stated guides and directs our attempts to solve it. In effect, the solution obtained is strongly influenced by the way a problem is initially defined and stated. For example, consider the following scenarios.

> Helen teaches geography and wants her students to appreciate the length of various rivers and river systems around the world. In class one day, she asks her students the following questions: "Is the Mississippi River longer or shorter than 500 miles?" If you were in class, what would you say?

> How long would you estimate the river's length to be?_____

> *Comment:* Most people in groups where I have used this scenario decide the Mississippi River is longer than 500 miles, and the average estimate of its length is about 980 miles. However, when asked if the river is longer or shorter than 5,000 miles, most decide it is shorter, and the average estimate of its length is around 1,970 miles. Decisions about the river's length vary considerably depending upon the frame of reference (i.e., 500 vs. 5,000 miles) employed in how the problem was initially defined and stated.

> Your dog was rolling around in the grass and leaves on your lawn. He is dusty and dirty and needs a bath. Unfortunately, you do not have any dog shampoo around the house. What would you do to wash your dog?

> *Comment:* When stated this way, people typically respond by suggesting that their own shampoo or a simple bar of soap will do the job. However, a somewhat broader set of responses occurs when the problem is stated as "Unfortunately, you do not have any dog shampoo around the house. How would you separate the dirt from your dog?" In addition to using their own shampoo or soap, vacuum cleaners, dry towels to wipe the dust and dirt off, and spraying the dog off with a garden hose are added to the list of solutions.

As you can see in the examples above, how a problem is stated may lead us towards certain solutions or not allow us to consider all of the available options. As James Adams (1986), a leading figure in the problem–solving literature, notes:

Inadequately defining the problem is a tendency that is downright foolish on an important and extensive problem-solving task. A relatively small time spent in carefully isolating and defining the problem can be extremely valuable both in illuminating possible simple solutions and in ensuring that a great deal of effort is not spent only to find that the difficulties still exist—perhaps in even greater magnitude (p. 23).

Let us examine several issues involved in adequately defining a problem.

*Isolate and Locate the Source of the Problem* This means finding the part of the environment that is most likely responsible for the issue. A source can be one of three things. *First, the source of a problem might be other people in your life.* An organization I once consulted with was having trouble keeping its staff washrooms clean. They were used by staff and visitors. Management issued washroom keys to its staff and had visitors use a public washroom in the building. Unfortunately, the washrooms remained as messy as ever. The problem was incorrectly linked with visitors and not members of the organization. Once this was called to the staff's attention and washroom rules were discussed with people, the appearance of the washrooms improved.

*Second, the source of a problem might be some object in your environment.* A neighbor's car radio went out whenever he approached a local radio station. He complained to the station manager that its equipment was causing his radio to malfunction. As far as the radio station manager knew, my neighbor was the only person with this problem. Thus, it seemed unlikely that the radio station's equipment was in some way responsible. He had one of his technicians check my neighbor's radio. The technician found a loose wire that apparently turned the radio off when it was jarred by potholes in the street near the station. Those same potholes jarred the radio back into operation. Properly locating the problem led to a solution.

*The third source of a problem might be a relationship.* Whenever we have an interpersonal problem, a natural tendency is to blame the other person. "It couldn't be my fault," we might think to ourselves. Interpersonal problems are much easier to resolve when the relationship is viewed as the source.

A former neighbor and his wife, for example, used to argue over who would take the garbage out to their garbage cans, located in their backyard. One would think this would be a simple problem to solve. At the very least, the chore could be rotated. Unfortunately, whatever strategy they chose, one of them would inevitably break the deal. Each blamed the other for being absentminded, stubborn, and purposely irritating. They eventually entered counseling for other problems in their marriage and discovered that the techniques they employed to manipulate and control each other interfered with their relationship. Their therapist pointed out that the garbage became a symbol for "who is the garbage person in this relationship" and, by implication, the low-status person in the marriage. The source of the issue was not the garbage per se, but unresolved control and authority issues in their relationship.

*Avoid Vague Problem Definitions or Those that Contain a Solution* Once the source is located, a more formal definition of the problem can be developed. A good definition should not restrict efforts towards finding an answer. *Our efforts are easily hindered when a problem is defined in overly general terms or if the definition includes a specific solution.* Stating a problem as "my roommate bugs me" or "how can I effectively threaten my children to get them to behave?" are both inadequate problem statements. In the first statement, it is not clear what aspect of the relationship is a problem. Is the roommate noisy, messy, or not paying his or her fair share of the expenses? Spending some time locating the source might lead to a better problem definition such as, "What is causing me to have that funny feeling in my stomach?" In the second example, a solution is embedded in the problem statement (i.e., how to effectively threaten my children). The underlying issue that needs to be resolved is how to discipline children better. Thus, a more constructive problem statement might be, "What are some possible ways to effectively discipline my children?"

Given the information above, what faults do you find with the following problem definitions?

- "What is the meaning of life?"
- "What type of raffle should our club hold to raise money?"
- "What is the best thermostat to buy to help me keep all of the rooms in my apartment warmer during the winter?"
- "What can I do to get Jan to stop irritating me?"
- "Why don't I feel like myself today?"

Did you notice that the first and last problem statements were too general to guide and direct the process of finding a solution? Can you see how the others have a solution embedded in the problem statement? *How would you restate each problem statement in order to improve it?*

***Reframe or Restructure a Problem Definition*** There are times when the definition does not seem quite right; our attempts to solve the problem lead us to dead ends; we feel like we are spinning our wheels; and the possible solutions just don't make much sense. According to Edward DeBono (1992a, 1992b), the latter conditions are often clues that the problem definition needs to be reframed or restructured. What is needed is a new perspective on the issue. *DeBono notes that developing a new way of conceptualizing a problem refocuses our energy and enhances our interest and motivation to find a solution.* Two examples of the effects of reframing a problem are illustrated in Focus on People 3.2.

DeBono terms the process of reframing or restructuring a problem definition to promote a more creative solution as **lateral thinking.** The suggestions made in Focus on People 3.2 to change the labels on the buttons and to install mirrors near the elevators are examples of lateral thinking. The opposite, or **vertical thinking**, is seen in people who restrict their problem definitions. They use what is to them the most logical way to approach an issue. To replace the window curtain motors or to build more expensive elevators are examples of vertical thinking. Both thinking processes yield solutions, but lateral thinking is more likely to generate a more creative and effective solution.

*Another important aspect of reframing a problem is to ensure that it is stated in a positive or optimistic manner.* When two different groups were told that a particular problem was solved by at most 1 in 10,000 people or by 1 in 10, many more solutions were obtained from the latter group (Adams, 1986). Similarly, if given a choice, what problem would you prefer to work on? "How can I keep myself from losing $10,000?" "What can I do to make $10,000?" A majority of those I ask report they would rather work on how to make $10,000. Viewing problems as challenges, opportunities, and in a more positive light is much more motivational. It also puts us in a better frame of mind to deal with

*The Case of the Backward Curtain* A colleague of mine was in the hospital suffering from a bad back. He was confined to his bed and was dependent upon others to do many things for him. One of the few tasks he could do for himself was to open and close the curtains in his room by pressing buttons on a console beside his bed. But when he pressed the button labeled "Open," the curtains closed; pressing "Close" opened the curtains. A hospital maintenance man was called to fix the mechanism. He defined the problem as a defective motor that controlled the curtain and began to disconnect the motor when my colleague suggested, "Couldn't we look at this problem differently? The curtains will open and close properly if the labels on the buttons are switched." The maintenance man agreed, and the problem was solved quickly and inexpensively. In effect, my colleague had reframed the problem as "how to get the direction of the curtains to coincide with the labels on the buttons."

*The Case of the Slow Elevators* A former client worked for an engineering consulting firm that had consulted with a manager of a large office building.

The manager was receiving an increasing number of complaints about the elevator service, particularly during rush hours. When several of the larger tenants threatened to move out unless the service improved, the manager decided to look into the problem. Engineers from the consulting firm were called to make recommendations about increasing the speed of the elevator service. They made three alternative but expensive recommendations: adding new elevators, replacing existing elevators with faster ones, and adding a central computerized control system to route the elevators to congested floors. Unfortunately, the earnings of the building would not support any of the possible solutions. An assistant to the building manager solved the problem. Instead of defining the problem as "how to speed up the elevator service," he reframed and defined the problem as "how to make people who wait for elevators less impatient." He suggested that full-length mirrors be installed on the walls of the elevator lobbies. This gave people something to do while waiting (e.g., looking at self or other people, fixing hair and makeup), and their impatience decreased.

issues. How would you recast the following problem statements to make them more positive?

- "What can I do to get through this lousy chemistry course I'm taking?"
- "How can I keep my spouse from wanting to leave me?"
- "What will I do if I can't find a job after I graduate?"
- "What can I do about this stupid haircut I have?"

## 4. Identify the Important Facts

Any problem has many different characteristics. Some of the attributes are very important for developing a solution or trying to choose what action to take. Others will not be very helpful. Alec Mackenzie (1972) refers to this as the 20-80 rule. As a rule of thumb, 20 percent of the facts account for 80 percent of what is going on. These are what he labels the "vital few" among the "trivial many." *Good problem solvers and decision makers are able to focus on the important facts.*

Using the 20-80 rule, what critical elements would be needed to solve each of the following problems?

As I was going to St. Ives,
I met a man with seven wives.

Each wife had seven sacks;
Each sack had seven cats;
Each cat had seven kits.
Kits, cats, sacks, and wives.
How many were going to St. Ives?

If you have both black and brown socks in your drawer mixed in the ratio of four black and five brown, how many socks will you have to take out to make sure of having one pair of the same color?

Assume that you are going to purchase a new car. As you know, you will have quite a range of sizes, shapes, and performance levels. Using the 20 80 rule, how would you simplify things so you could efficiently solve the problem?

Mary is 21 years old, and her father died 2 years ago. She is concerned about her mother's social life. Her mother is 48 years of age, goes shopping, plays bridge, works out at a local sports club, and attends an occasional movie with her girlfriends. Her mom seldom dates and otherwise appears to be reasonably happy. Mary, however, thinks her mom's social life is rather dull and would like to see her do more, including having some male companionship. What factors should Mary consider in order to solve this problem?

Perhaps you discovered the following facts using the 20-80 rule. In the St. Ives problem, only the fact that "I" was going to St. Ives is important. In the sock problem, the four to five ratio is irrelevant. Out of any three socks pulled from the drawer, any two are bound to be the same color. In selecting a car, you could consider everything relatively unimportant except the car's gasoline mileage, how many people it comfortably seats, and its cost. These three facts will quickly eliminate a lot of models. In thinking about Mary, the important fact is why Mary is so concerned about her mother's social life. Just because it does not meet Mary's standards is no reason to assume her mother has a problem.

The ability to sort relevant from irrelevant information is obviously important for solving problems and making decisions. Certain ways of perceiving the world affect our ability to do this. In particular, our ability to isolate stimuli and ideas from the background in which they appear plays an important role. Before reading further, complete the activity that is contained in Figure 3.1.

Based on how accurate people are on a task such as this, they can be categorized as **field independent** or **field dependent** (Witkin and Goodenough, 1981). Individuals who easily find hidden figures similar to those contained in Figure 3.1 are labeled field-independent. Those who cannot find the correct figures or have difficulty locating them are labeled field-dependent. In the latter case, the background in which the figure is buried interferes with their ability to identify it.

Field-independence and field-dependence are more than just personality characteristics that describe our ability to pick certain stimuli out of a background. They also represent opposite ends of a continuum that describes how we prefer to perceive our environments and process information. Such **cognitive styles** have been related to our ability to solve problems and to make decisions. Individuals with a field independent style tend to prefer working on problems that deal with numerical data, complicated facts, and abstract and theoretical issues (Romming, 1984). Their field-dependent coun-

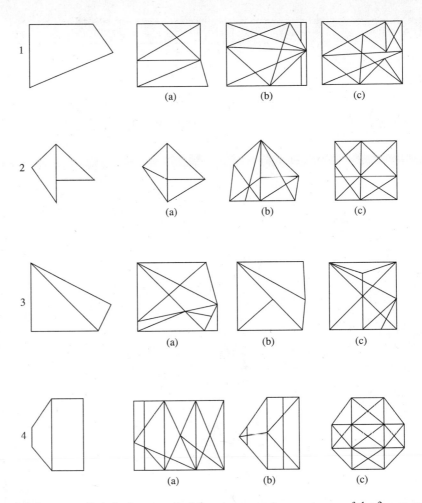

**Figure 3.1** *Try to find the figure on the left as it appears in one or more of the figures on the right.*
*Answers: 1(b),(c); 2(a),(b); 3(a); 4(a), (b), (c)*

terparts, however, are much more comfortable working on problems and issues that are more interpersonal in nature (Mezof, 1982). A summary of the relative strengths and weaknesses of each cognitive style for solving problems appears in Table 3.1.

*Identify Who Owns the Problem Besides identifying the critical elements in a problem, a second important fact to identify is who owns the responsibility for resolving the issue.* In a relationship problem, both parties are typically responsible and must jointly try to solve it. Yet in other areas of our lives, problem ownership and the responsibility for resolving it might reside with someone else. Consequently, it is important to avoid taking responsibility for solving someone else's problem.

The case of Mary mentioned earlier is one example of this principle. She was apparently more concerned about her mother's social life than was her mother. Even if her mother were dissatisfied, Mary could not solve that problem. Her mother would have to recognize the problem and become committed to resolving it. Similarly, many of us are legitimately concerned about friends smoking cigarettes or abusing drugs, not

**Table 3.1**    Field-Independence, Field-Dependence, and Problem Solving

| FIELD-INDEPENDENT INDIVIDUALS | FIELD-DEPENDENT INDIVIDUALS |
|---|---|
| • Good at analyzing and structuring the components of problems in order to solve them. | • Not as good at analyzing and structuring the components of problems in order to solve them. |
| • Work well on problems that involve lots of attention to detailed numerical calculations and the need to manage a diverse set of complicated and technical facts. | • Do not find problems that involve detailed numerical calculations and the need to manage a diverse set of complicated and technical facts very interesting. |
| • Enjoy working on abstract and theoretical problems. | • Find problems that have more of a concrete focus and less of a theoretical focus more interesting. |
| • Not very comfortable working on interpersonal problems. | • More comfortable working on interpersonal problems. |
| • Sample cues in problem in order to select those needed to solve a problem. | • Have more difficulty finding the right cues needed to solve problems. This is particularly true of problems of a theoretical and technical nature. |
| • Prefer to work alone when solving problems and making decisions. Less likely to request help from others. | • Prefer to work with others when solving problems and making decisions. |

taking steps to find a job, gaining too much weight, cheating on their spouse, or otherwise behaving inappropriately. We want them to change and sometimes intrude in their lives to "help them." Such efforts typically do not work, because the people who own the problem are unwilling to accept responsibility for their actions. You might offer to consult with them. But they have to take responsibility for resolving the issue. Who owns the problem in the following examples? What would you do if you found yourself in each situation?

1. Natalie rushes into her instructor's office in tears. She says, "Because of you, I can't join a sorority this term. The C from your course gave me just a little less than the 2.0 average I needed to join. What are you going to do to help me?"

2. Damon and his roommate continually argue about what television shows to watch. One day Damon asks his roommate, "What are you going to do about the television problem?"

3. Melissa finds herself bringing more and more work home from the office. When asked why she works so hard at home, she replies, "I can't get everything done at the office. People under me are not doing their jobs well, so I have no choice but to correct their mistakes."

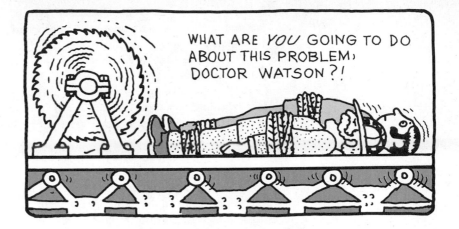

***Develop and Employ Appropriate Representations of Elements in a Problem***   As you have just seen, identifying the important facts and critical elements in a problem is not always easy. Quite a number of facts, figures, ideas, and relationships among components of the problem must be kept in mind. When the need to do this is added to our liabilities in selecting information, processing it, and remembering it, the task of solving a problem becomes even more complicated. Thus, we need to find ways to select elements, summarize and combine them, and otherwise organize them in order to work on them.

Normally, people accomplish the latter goal by relying upon internal representations of the elements in a problem. *In effect, the parts of a problem are converted to auditory and visual images, and we "listen to" or "see" the parts in our heads.* As an example, John Hayes (1989) reports how such internal representations help to solve math problems. In one study, participants were given math problems such as $28 \times 7 = ?$ or $356 + 892 = ?$ They could not use a pencil and paper to solve them. Instead, they had to rely on auditory images by vocalizing the problem or upon visual images by imagining the problem in their heads.

Hayes noted that bilingual people tended to vocalize math problems in the language in which they originally learned certain math processes. One person did elementary mathematics in Catalan, his first language, and more advanced math in Spanish, the language used in later schooling. Another learned arithmetic in Hong Kong on an abacus and continually moved her fingers whenever she vocalized math problems.

A blind participant imagined numerals as Braille patterns or as bars of color with each digit having its own unique color. Other people were able to visualize images of the numerals in a math problem, including marks indicating borrowing or cancellation. Two of Hayes's participants complained that the 2 by 4 card that contained the math problem presented to them had no room to "write their answers." They solved this dilemma by imagining the answer in the space above the problem or by imagining a piece of paper taped to the bottom of the card.

In many cases, internal representations do more than simply allow us to vocalize or visualize specific elements of a problem. With more complex issues, internal representations provide a model that also guides and directs our approach towards solving the problem. Susan Sontag (1989), for example, describes how images and metaphors for diseases such as AIDS affect how a medical problem is conceptualized. She notes that the major metaphor physicians employ when faced with the problem of understanding and treating diseases such as AIDS is the battlefield metaphor. AIDS is caused by an "invading organism, the human immunodeficiency virus (HIV)" that "destroys" the body's "defenses" and then ultimately "kills" its "victims" by leaving them to the mercy of other "invading organisms." Of course when faced with an "attack," we either need to "strengthen our defenses" or find "weapons" that will eliminate or neutralize the "invaders."

A battlefield as a representation of the problem of how to cure people of a disease has limitations. It ignores or discounts other ways for managing illnesses. In the search for "weapons," ideas for prevention and the use of alternatives to traditional medicine may be overlooked. A similar thing occurs when the problem of "how should I teach a class" is addressed. An instructor who represents the teaching-learning process as "filling containers" will teach differently from someone who imagines that the teaching-learning process is like "coaching a baseball team" or "being a midwife" (Pollio, 1987; Grasha, 1990). In much the same way, a supervisor who describes working with people as "pushing a brick across the street with your nose" is likely to possess a somewhat limited approach to solving work-related problems.

Because of limitations in our ability to keep all of the critical elements and facts of a problem in our heads, John Hayes (1989) and James Adams (1986a) emphasize the importance of also developing external representations of issues. Making a list of the important facts; developing a table or chart; or drawing a figure, diagram, map, or sketch can help us to visualize and verbalize components of a problem. The external representation should capture the important facts and the relationships among them to help us make competent decisions for solving a problem.

The next section illustrates ways to develop options for solutions to the problems we face. Many of the examples used contain additional ideas for how problems and their components can be represented.

## 5. Generate a Range of Alternative Ideas for Solutions or Courses of Action

It is important that we generate a range of alternatives before deciding upon a solution or making a decision. You remember from the discussion earlier that failing to do this is a common pitfall in solving problems and making decisions. People often have to force themselves to do this for two reasons. Tendencies to select the first option considered typically arise out of our impatience to complete the task. In the process we may select a simplistic solution or one that is based on past habits for thinking and reasoning. In the latter case, rather rigid and persistent assumptions creep into our efforts to resolve a problem.

The term **set** is used to describe the latter reactions. A good example of this tendency is a set that assumes familiar objects cannot be used in nontraditional ways. This is called **functional fixedness.** What happens is that we fixate on the common or usual use for an item. Recently, I needed a screwdriver to tighten the handle on a kitchen cabinet. I became frustrated when I could not find a screwdriver that was thin enough. My wife came to the rescue. She gave me one of the knives from the cabinet and asked me if the tip might work. It did, and the problem was solved. Thinking of a knife as something to cut things with or to spread butter on bread interfered with my viewing it as a screwdriver. Have you ever had a similar experience with some other object?

***Form an Idea Tree*** Many problems have a number of possible answers among which the actual solution is sure to be found. A three-letter anagram puzzle (e.g., BTI) has six possible combinations of the letters. To find which of the six is a solution, we can represent the problem in the form of an idea tree similar to the one in Figure 3.2. An idea tree simply groups possible solutions in an orderly fashion. In this case, answers having B, T, and I as the first letter were listed together. An idea tree also can help with everyday problems, as illustrated in Figure 3.3.

***Use Metaphors*** Using a metaphor or analogy to represent the problem or some part of it is often helpful in developing alternative solutions. We need to consciously ask ourselves what object, person, place, or thing is similar to our problem or already solves it in ways that we might be able to adapt. Such approaches have been employed in a variety of problem-solving situations. Gordon Prince (1970) developed a number of suggestions for systematically using metaphors in problem solving. Examples based on his suggestions are illustrated in Table 3.2.

***Brainstorm Ideas*** This method for generating ideas was developed by Alex Osborn (1963) to help groups solve problems. His goal was to create an atmosphere in which a large quantity of ideas would be produced. Osborn argued that out of a large number of ideas, a new combination of previously unrelated things might occur. The five rules for brainstorming by yourself or in a group setting are simple. They are:

1. List as many ideas as you can within a specified time period (e.g., fifteen to thirty minutes).
2. Do not be overly concerned about how practical the ideas are, simply list them.
3. Defer any evaluations or criticisms of your ideas until after the listing period is over. Otherwise, you are likely to prematurely eliminate useful ideas.
4. After the listing period, try to combine and improve the ideas generated so that they will be more useful to you.

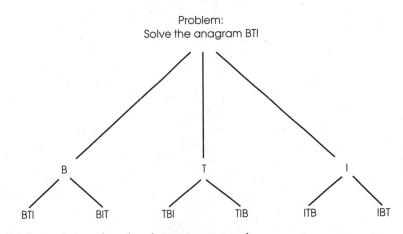

**Figure 3.2** *An idea tree for a three-letter anagram puzzle.*

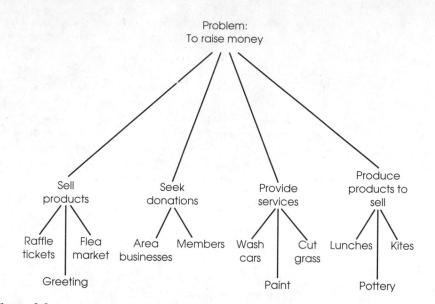

**Figure 3.3** *An idea tree for a money-raising problem. Keep in mind that this tree can be extended even further. For example, are there any ways that money can be raised in new categories or under those already listed? In addition, the types of raffles, greeting cards, or lunches can also be expanded. Some idea trees may never be complete as long as we are resourceful and imaginative in our thinking.*

5.  After completing number 4, eliminate the ideas that you feel are not useful, cannot be improved, or simply are not desirable.

*List Attributes* In a classic work on problem solving, Robert Crawford (1954) noted that new ideas occurred by the improvement of characteristics or attributes of existing things or by the transference of such attributes from one situation to another. By breaking some problems into their components, it is possible for us to generate ideas that will lead to a solution. Automobile designers solve their problems in this way. They break the characteristics of an automobile into categories like body size, color, shape, horsepower, seating capacity, and decoration. They then make improvements in each of these characteristics from one year to the next. Creating a television series often involves the transfer of characteristics from one situation to another. Rival television producers transfer the characteristics of a hit show and use them to form a "new" series. Although this solves their production problems, it tends to leave a number of police, medical, Western, and comedy shows looking quite similar.

The improvement or transference of attributes to generate interesting ideas is quite easy to do. Begin by listing the attributes of the situation. Alternatives to the listed attributes are then formulated. Finally, pick various combinations of the alternative attributes and try to imagine an interesting solution to the problem. Table 3.3 illustrates this process for the problem of designing a new type of credit card.

Remember that as long as we can identify the basic characteristics of any problem, we can use this technique. For example, designing a new format for teaching a class

| Table 3.2 | Three Ways to Create Metaphors |
| --- | --- |

*Fantasy Analogy*  Imagine an ideal but farfetched solution to the problem and see where it leads you. You might ask, for example, "Could the problem solve itself?" After all, who ever heard of a problem solving itself? But what if it could? How would it do it? Someone probably answered these questions in developing a self-sealing tire, a no-frost refrigerator, a self-cleaning oven, and permanent-press slacks.

A student in one of my classes was concerned about having a good social life during the school year. She imagined that she was the only woman on campus and that all the guys wanted to take her out. This gave her the idea to have a party where there were more males than females attending. She said it worked. She got a lot of attention and quite a few dates as a result.

*Direct Analogy*  During World War II, sonar was developed when engineers recognized that a ship on the surface of the ocean was "blind as a bat." Bats, of course, employ sound waves to find objects, and the same principle was used in sonar. Pringles potato chips were developed when product developers at Proctor and Gamble recognized that some cookie manufacturers stack cookies in a round container. Why not, they reasoned, make potato chips a uniform size and shape and do the same thing?

A friend moved into an apartment with two people she barely knew. She used direct analogies by asking the following question. How is establishing a new relationship like getting a new puppy to adjust to a new home? How is establishing a new relationship like meeting your boyfriend's parents for the first time? A colleague wanted to create the illusion of more space in his apartment. He thought of a magician trying to form such an illusion. This led him to use mirrors on some walls, to build in "hidden compartments" for shelf space, and to purchase smaller pieces of furniture that would make everything else look spacious by comparison.

*Personal Analogy*  Imagine yourself or get others to imagine they are an element of the problem. Thinking of yourself as a piece of dirt attached to a shirt might lead you to discover new ways to separate dirt from clothing. A colleague of mine was involved in teaching police officers to become more sympathetic to rape victims. Talking about the trauma the women faced and their needs did not generate much discussion or ideas about how the officers could become more helpful. Things changed, however, when he led the officers through the details of an imaginary rape in which they were the victims. After this experience, the police officers were more responsive and had ideas about how they could become more helpful.

might be done by generating alternatives to these attributes: format of class; teacher-student interactions, testing procedures, type of students; location of the class; and time of day that it meets. Or we might want to discover some new ways to study by finding alternatives to the following attributes: time of day to study, location of study area, study materials, studying alone or with others, principles of learning to use, and type of information to study. How would you design a new soap opera for television?

*Use a Checklist*  A checklist is a series of questions that directs your attention to components of the problem. Your responses to such questions generate a series of ideas that might assist you. Table 3.4 gives an example of a checklist that I have used in my

**Table 3.3**  An Example of Attribute Listing

*Fill in the blank spaces with ideas that you have for other alternatives to those shown.*

*Problem:* Design a new format for a credit card.

**ATTRIBUTES OF CURRENT CARDS**

| Rectangle | Plastic | Raised Letters and Numbers | Multicolored |
|---|---|---|---|

**ALTERNATIVES**

| | | | |
|---|---|---|---|
| Square | Metal | Concave letters and numbers | Black |
| Circle | Glass | No letters and numbers | White |
| Triangle | Wood | Magnetic impressions | Green |
| _____ | _____ | _____ | _____ |
| _____ | _____ | _____ | _____ |

**What Solution(s) Are Suggested?**

Randomly combine elements associated with different attributes to see what ideas occur to you—for example, a credit card that looks like a coin. Identification information and available amount of credit could be coded as well. Card is dropped into a coin slot apparatus that is connected to a central computer. Credit check could be run and the purchase price automatically subtracted from the amount of available credit.

---

work. Based on the type of problems you face, you might want to modify it and add questions that would help stimulate your thinking.

*Working Backward* Sometimes we basically know what we want as an outcome to the problem. Allen Newell and Herbert Simon (1972) note that a rule of thumb, or a *heuristic,* called "working backward," is helpful here. This method helps us to break the steps we must take to reach our solution into manageable units. An example of this approach appears in Figure 3.4. As you can see, it assists us to generate alternatives when the solution is known.

## 6. Evaluate the Alternative Solutions

I recently received a phone call from a branch manager of a local corporation. He and his staff had attended a workshop on creative problem solving. Among other things, they had learned how to generate alternative ideas for solutions and courses of action. "My problem," he said excitedly, "is how to pick the best option from the list. Isn't there any advice you could give me?"

Unfortunately, there is no easy answer to his question—a question most of us have had to face when making decisions. Gordon Miller (1978) states that this is often a source of frustration and tension and that it is easy to become trapped by two facts associated with making a choice. *One is that we will probably never be aware of all the alternatives.* It is possible that we missed some ideas regardless of the technique used to generate them. Also, our world changes. A new option may suddenly appear in the future, and those we currently have may disappear or become useless. *The second fact is that we*

| **Table 3.4** | A Checklist for Stimulating Ideas |
| --- | --- |

Answer the following questions in relation to the problem you have. Remember that not all of the questions may be applicable. Skip those that are nonapplicable to your issue.

1. List the attributes and characteristics of your problem. How can some of the following things be changed?
   - Physical dimensions (larger, shorter, taller, smaller, wider, borders)
   - Social dimensions (number of people, communication patterns, leadership, norms, roles, goals)
   - The way things are ordered (right-left, up-down, first-last)
   - The time element (faster-slower, longer-shorter)
   - The cost (more-less, high-low)
   - The texture (rough-smooth, hard-soft, wet-dry, heavy-light)
   - The function (do more, do less)
2. What parts of the problem can be:
   - rearranged
   - reversed
   - combined
   - minimized
   - magnified
   - substituted for by something else
   - altered
   - completely eliminated
3. How can you do the following:
   - change the physical environment
   - produce new learning
   - go against tradition
   - change the values people have
   - make use of emerging trends
   - change attitudes and opinions
4. Based on the ideas you thought of, what are two or three possible solutions to the problem? Which one do you like best? Which one do you like least? What are the reasons you have for your selection?

*will usually not be able to experience all of our alternatives before choosing.* There simply may be too many of them; or, the cost in terms of time, energy, and money to consider all of them is often too great. Consider the plight of someone playing chess. Some experts estimate that the total number of possible moves in a game is $10^{120}$ (Newell and Simon, 1972). In spite of this, anyone wanting to play must decide which is the best move to make at any given moment, and everyone tries to do the best he or she can.

In much the same way, each of us must take whatever alternatives were generated and make decisions regarding the best solution at a given moment in time. Thus, it is hard to provide a definitive response to the question "what is the best option to select." A general guideline, however, is to first evaluate the options that are available to you.

*Use Criteria to Evaluate Alternatives* The best way is to assess each alternative against whatever criteria apply to a situation. Some issues have preestablished criteria for determining the best solution or action to take. The problems you encounter in mathematics, statistics, and laboratory work in school have certain guidelines already established. The criteria may be based on some theory, the types of results most other people obtain, or the preferences of your instructor. Once you know such things, you can select the response that best meets those criteria.

Most of the time, however, things are not as clear as they could be. How do you know the best way to redesign a credit card? What are the most important safety features needed in an automobile? What is the most effective method for disciplining a child? Daniel Wheeler and Irving Janis (1980) suggest several general criteria that can be applied to almost any problem.

1. *Tangible and monetary benefits and costs.* Included are such things as money, materials, supplies, equipment, number of people required, distance to travel, and other things that can be seen, heard, or touched.

2. *Intangible and personal psychological benefits and costs.* Included are the time and energy required, deadlines, emotional consequences for self/others (e.g., happiness, excitement, anxiety, frustration), changes in attitudes and beliefs of self/others, effects on relationships, thoughts and feelings about yourself, and other things that have no material value or substance.

3. *Likely acceptance of ideas by others.* Good decisions not only must be of high quality (i.e., they have important tangible and intangible benefits), but often they must be acceptable to someone other than ourselves.

With each of the three criteria listed above, any alternative solution or course of action will have a number of pros and cons associated with it. A problem, however, is likely to develop. As Benjamin Franklin noted, "People cannot keep all the pros and cons in mind at one time." Franklin advised writing down the criteria and then balancing off the pros against the cons for each alternative. He suggested something similar to a financial balance sheet. To accomplish this goal *each alternative must be evaluated along the same lines.* Thus, if financial cost or the materials needed are factors with one option, the financial cost and materials associated with the others also need to be examined. Similarly, if one option has emotional consequences or affects relationships in certain ways, then the role the same factors might play in the other options needs to be assessed. Otherwise, we have no common ground to balance off the pros and cons.

One example of how Franklin's goal can be accomplished is illustrated in Table 3.5. To set up such a table, do the following:

1. Select one of your options and brainstorm a variety of pros and cons for each of the criteria. No need to be bashful here. List as many as you want.
2. Use this initial organization to develop a list of the pros and cons for each of the other options.
3. If a new consideration develops when listing the pros and cons of any alternative that applies to the others, use it as a basis to evaluate all of the alternatives.

## 7. Select a Solution or Course of Action

Evaluating your alternatives against criteria as illustrated in Table 3.6 should help identify the relative strengths and weaknesses of various options. It does not tell you, however, what is the best solution. The problem is that several options typically exist, and each has a variety of pros and cons. Do you select the alternative with the most benefits? The fewest costs? Is the option that allows you to avoid having a major loss the best route to take? Or is it the one where the benefits exceed the costs by a certain ratio?

*The Role of Perceived Gains and Losses* To make a choice, it is first necessary to understand how our perceptions of what we stand to gain or lose affect our capacity to choose a course of action. To do this, it is necessary to focus on the list of benefits and costs associated with each option, as illustrated in Table 3.5. Ellen Siegelman (1983) and

**Table 3.5**       Deciding Where to Go for a Summer Vacation

*Problem:* Which new location to visit for a summer family vacation

*Special Considerations:* All of the benefits and costs are pretty much equal in terms of their importance. Thus, select the option where the number of +'s exceed the −'s.

**ALTERNATIVES**

| RELEVANT CRITERIA | KIAWAH ISLAND<br>SOUTH CAROLINA | DISNEY WORLD/EPCOT CENTER<br>ORLANDO, FLORIDA |
|---|---|---|
| Tangible and Monetary<br>Benefits/Costs | − Will cost about $1,800 when transportation, meals, and lodging are accounted for.<br>+ Money for a short vacation later on will be available.<br>+ Place to stay easy to obtain. | − Will cost about $3,000 when transportation, meals, and lodging are accounted for.<br>− Money for a short vacation later on will not be available.<br>− Housing is sometimes difficult to get. |
| Intangible and Personal,<br>Psychological<br>Benefits/Costs | + Will be able to spend quality time with my wife and children.<br>+ Should be able to relax on beach.<br>− Children may get bored with just the beach.<br>+ Not as far from home, so less frustration traveling with children.<br>+ Friends have not visited, so children can share a unique experience.<br>+ A new experience for the children. Not a new experience for my wife and me. | + Will be able to spend quality time with my wife and children.<br>− May not relax as much, as the pace will be hectic.<br>+ Children not bored<br>− Some frustration involved in traveling 900 miles with a 9- and 10-year-old.<br>+ Friends at school have visited, so children would have something in common with them.<br>+ A new experience for everyone. Will add some excitement to our life. |
| Likely Acceptance<br>of Idea by Others | − Children may not like it.<br>+ Wife would prefer the island and beach better.<br><br>Total: 8 +'s and 3 −'s | + Children will probably like this place.<br>− Wife may not like carnival atmosphere.<br><br>Total: 5 +'s and 6 −'s |

Lola Lopes (1983) note that the benefits associated with any option represent our gains if that course of action works out as planned. Similarly, the list of costs represents our losses if our choice does not work out. Thus, if the island vacation described in Table 3.5 is a success, the family is happy, and no money was wasted. Otherwise, family members are unhappy and several thousand dollars were wasted.

The term **personal stake** is used to label the potential gains or losses associated with a decision. Personal stakes can be tangible or intangible. They include our gains or losses stated in terms of money, personal property, power, prestige, recognition, status,

**Table 3.6**

Deciding What Job Offer To Accept

*Problem:* What job offer should I accept after I graduate?

*Special Considerations:* Use the 1–5 rating scale described in the text to rate how important each benefit/pro and cost/con would be for choosing that option. Select the option with the largest difference between the +'s and −'s.

|  | ALTERNATIVES | |
| --- | --- | --- |
| **RELEVANT CRITERIA** | **MANAGER OF FAST FOOD RESTAURANT** | **SELLING REAL ESTATE** |
| Tangible and Monetary Benefits/Costs | +5. Pays $24,000 salary. <br> +3. Decent future earnings. <br> + 4. Medical benefits are provided. <br> − 3. Long hours. <br> − 5. Extensive supervision required. <br> + 3. Two weeks paid vacation. | − 2. Paid on % of sales. <br> + 5. Potential for very good future earnings. <br> − 3. Must contribute to benefits. <br> − 3. Long hours. <br> + 5. No employees to supervise. <br> − 3. No paid vacation |
| Intangible and Personal, Psychological Benefits/Costs | − 2. Advancement opportunities poor. <br> + 5. Could learn enough to one day run my own business. <br> − 4. Not much room for creativity. | + 4 Advancement opportunities good. <br> + 5. Could learn enough to one day open my own office. <br> + 3. Possible to be creative. |
| Likely Acceptance of Idea by Others | + 1. Friends would not mind. <br> − 1. Parents might not like it. | + 1. No problems with friends <br> + 1. Mother sold real estate and would be happy. |
| Sum of Ratings <br> (+ Sum) − (− Sum) = | (21–15) = 6 | (24 − 8) = 13 |

respect, and self-confidence. Such things normally play an important role in the choices we make and must be taken into account. And they may bias our decision making if we are not careful.

Research reveals that people behaved differently when faced with accepting a sure gain versus taking a loss. *When faced with a sure gain, people tend to take it rather than take a chance on losing something.* Most people, for example, decide to purchase an item as soon as it goes on sale rather than wait for further markdowns. They don't want to take a chance on someone else purchasing the item. Many stock market investors sell as soon a short-term gain is made rather than holding a stock for the long haul. They want to avoid the possibility of the stock market taking a turn for the worse. Rather than waiting to preregister for the next term, some students sign up for popular courses immediately after the registration period begins. They are afraid of getting closed out of a class.

*When faced with accepting a sure loss, people tend to make risky decisions* (Kahneman, Sloric, and Tversky, 1982). Rather than cut their losses, many individuals continue to "throw good money after bad" in poker, blackjack, and other games of chance. They hold out for the slim chance that they can eventually recover their losses. Or, even though we are unlikely to improve, some of us continue to invest our time and energy in unproductive and dissatisfying jobs, projects, and relationships. Studies demonstrate that once we invest time, energy, and money in something, our commitment increases, and it is difficult to "pull back." (Dawes, 1988). People prefer to hang on at any cost to avoid admitting defeat or to accept a loss.

Both biases can create problems for us. Sometimes, accepting a sure gain is a sensible and prudent course of action. At other times, avoiding a little risk could prevent us from attempting something more exciting or adventuresome. We then miss an opportunity to add something to the quality of our lives. Going to the beach for a vacation every year is beneficial. But going on a cruise ship, hiking in the wilderness, or taking a trip to the Grand Canyon might be more stimulating as well as a productive learning experience. Taking some risk is one way to stretch ourselves to grow and develop.

*Of the two biases, accepting a risky alternative when faced with a loss is more likely to produce problems.* One reason is that if something goes wrong, we are stuck with the loss and the misery it produces in our lives. Second, when faced with a loss, people have a tendency to "try to recover it." In effect, they try to protect themselves but typically end up losing more, as Focus on People 3.3 illustrates.

*Making Choices in the Face of Potential Gains and Losses* Personal stakes are always present, no matter what decision we try to make. What varies is the amount to be gained or lost and which one strikes us as more important. In spite of having to assess

---

### FOCUS ON PEOPLE 3.3
### How Not to Cut Your Losses

In an advertisement campaign, the maker of Cutty Sark Scotch once offered $3 million to anyone who could capture the Lock Ness Monster. The benefits of the campaign were apparently high, but some executives began to get cold feet. "What if someone caught the monster," they reasoned. "We would be out several million dollars." To protect themselves, they purchased an insurance policy with Lloyd's of London. In return for a $7,000 premium, they agreed among other things to allow Lloyd's to keep the monster if it were caught. Had they thought about it more and concentrated more on what could be gained, the company would have realized that the owner of the Lock Ness Monster could make untold millions of dollars (Lopes, 1983).

Scott Warner, a stockbroker for a major company, lost $6 million of his company's money in 12 hours by trying to cover his losses in a downward spiral of the stock market. Instead of selling his holdings and accepting a relatively smaller loss, he selected a riskier course of action. He decided to invest more money to purchase additional stocks that were suddenly cheaper. "When the market turns around," he reasoned, "I'll make a killing and easily cover my earlier losses." Unfortunately, the market did not turn around, and he was fired for incompetence.

and agonize over our potential gains and losses, a decision must be made. Thus, what is needed is a decision-making process that can do two things. One, it should help us sort through the benefits and costs associated with each of our options. Second, it should help us to minimize the problems that sometimes occur from selecting a sure gain or an overly risky alternative. *One strategy is to select the alternative that has the most number of benefits/pros and the fewest costs/cons.* Research shows that taking the time to assess your options in this way leads to higher quality decisions than does a more casual or global approach (Dawes, 1979). This strategy is particularly useful when you feel that the importance of any consideration for selecting an option is relatively equal. Thus, in making a decision about a vacation, as described in Table 3.6, the availability of housing is considered about as important as your family's happiness when deciding where to take a vacation.

Sometimes, however, some considerations are much more important than others. Think about selecting a particular job for a moment. It is unlikely that having to drive 2 miles to work would be perceived as just as important in selecting a job as the salary you were paid. The chances are that the money would be a more important consideration. Consequently, a strategy for making a decision should weigh that factor more. One way to do this is to develop a list of pros and cons for each alternative, just as was done earlier. Next, rate how important the pros and cons associated with each alternative are for selecting that option. Use a 1 2 3 4 5 rating scale where:

- 1 = "Compared to all the other considerations for making a decision about this option, this factor is of minor importance."
- 5 = "Compared to all of the other considerations for making a decision about this option, this factor is very important."

*Under such conditions, your second decision-making rule is to choose the alternative that yields the highest numerical difference between the pros and cons.* An example of this latter process is shown in Table 3.6. An additional advantage of this process is that it forces us to evaluate the importance of various considerations. In this way, we can obtain a clearer picture of why certain options are more or less attractive to us.

Can you trust the numerical values obtained by a process that is still, to some extent, subjective? One answer to this question is provided by Eugene Zechmeister and James Johnson (1992) in their comments about numerical procedures similar to the one described in Table 3.6.

> We recognize that these numbers are imperfect, but they are still much better than unsystematic and biased judgments. What tells you more about a student's academic performance—the fact that he has a 2.2 GPA or his self-report that he does "great" in school. We can and do trust numbers, and in view of all the careful and systematic work we put into generating them, we can be perfectly trusting of the numbers we arrive at by managing decisional information in such a systematic manner (p. 238).

Robyn Dawes (1988) reports that neither of the two rules of thumb presented here will yield a perfect solution. Nor do they necessarily specify an optimal course of action. *Rather, such rules of thumb help us select with more confidence the alternative that is most likely to satisfy most of our important needs and goals.*

***If Necessary, Look for Ways to Get Unstuck***   In most cases, the rational process described above will lead to a solution. But there also are times when you continue to feel stuck.

You still cannot make up your mind. What should you do? Consider the following advice.

*Put the problem aside for awhile.* As strange as it might seem, do nothing. Relax, read a book, take a vacation, or sleep on it for a while. This is called **incubation.** If it is successful, the idea for a solution should flash effortlessly into your mind. You might have a "Eureka!" or "Aha!" experience. Incubation may work because putting the problem temporarily aside provides a rest and allows us to recover from fatigue. It may also give us a chance to consider parts of it during some of our other activities. You have probably had the experience of some part of a problem "popping" into your head while you were walking, reading, or eating a meal. Or our cognitive activity might continue to work on the issue while we are engaged in other activity. Regardless of how it works, Barry Anderson (1980) reports that incubation is effective only after a period of conscious work on the problem.

*Dream about the problem.* Pat Garfield (1974) argues that we can make our dreams work for us. Dream content, she suggests, reflects issues and events in our daily experiences. Thus, dreaming about our problems or about decisions we must make sometimes yields interesting solutions. Pat Garfield describes a number of problems that were eventually solved in this way. She describes how the German chemist Friedrich A. Kekule had tried for years to find the molecular structure of benzene. He reported dreaming as he dozed in front of a crackling fire one cold night in 1865:

> Again the atoms were juggling before my eyes . . . my mind's eye, sharpened by repeated sights of a similar kind, could now distinguish larger structures of different forms and in long chains, many of them close together; everything was moving in a snake-like and twisting manner. Suddenly, what was this? One of the snakes got hold of its own tail and the whole structure was mockingly twisting in front of my eyes. As if struck by lightning, I woke . . . (p. 60).

This dream led Kekule to the realization that the benzene molecule was a closed carbon ring. When he reported his discovery at a scientific convention in 1890, Garfield reports he said, "Let us learn to dream, gentlemen, and then we may perhaps find the truth." To use our dreams to problem solve, Pat Garfield notes that we must listen to them. It is too easy to dismiss a dream. One technique is to get into the habit of recording our dreams. She suggests writing a description of the dream *immediately* upon awakening. This provides a written record, and from it we might find a solution to a problem—provided, of course, our dream was related to the problem. Garfield, however, suggests that we do not have to leave this to chance. She indicates that with practice, it is possible to steer our dreams in certain directions. Telling ourselves that we want to dream about a certain thing seems to work for some people. Perhaps you would want to try to do this and see if it works for you.

*Examine your decision-making style.* Ellen Siegelman (1983) reports that sometimes difficulties in reaching a decision reflect problems in the style or preferences people have for making decisions. Thinking about the ways that our style affects deciding what to do may suggest ways to overcome the problem. A description of three styles she has identified appears in Table 3.7. Which one best describes you, and how might it facilitate and hinder your approach to selecting solutions and courses of action in your life?

*Follow your heart.* Spencer Johnson (1993) suggests that when all else fails, do what "feels right for you." From his point of view, this means using our intuition to examine how we feel about any particular solution or course of action. Such feelings often incorporate a tremendous amount of information about a situation. Johnson notes that if a particular course of action does not feel right, then it probably isn't. He also cautions against making decisions based on fear. Using fear or anxiety as a guide seldom brings about a good result. In the final analysis, the important questions are:

- Does my decision show I am honest with myself?
- Does my decision show that I trust my intuition and it feels right?
- Does my decision suggest that I deserve better?

Spencer Johnson argues that a "yes" or "no" answer to each question can be very helpful in deciding whether or not to pursue a particular course of action.

**Managing the Uncertainty that a Decision Will Not Work Out as Planned** No matter how a course of action is selected, there is always one additional decision remaining. *This is deciding what you will do if your choice fails to work out as planned.* After all, if all decisions worked out as planned, there would never be any costs or potential losses associated with a choice. Unfortunately, this is not the case. Unexpected events have a tendency to intervene between the time a decision is made and the outcome we hoped to achieve. Such events include chance happenings, freak accidents, severe weather,

| Table 3.7 | Three Common Decision-Making Styles |
|-----------|-------------------------------------|

The following are characteristics of three decision-making styles identified by Ellen Siegelman. Which style appears to best characterize you? How does it facilitate and interfere with your ability to make decisions?

**Cautious style**
- Prefers to make secure rather than novel choices.
- Produces as many options as possible and continually reviews them.
- Relies on reason and mistrusts feelings when making decisions.
- Believes there is just one right decision in a situation.
- Thinks about desired outcomes and tends to focus on personal losses.
- Anxious about making choices.
- Having made a decision, may worry about it or want to change it.

**Balanced style**
- Values making secure and novel choices equally. Sees value in both.
- Produces a number of options but stops after a reasonable search.
- Uses reason and feelings when deciding what to do.
- Believes there is no one right answer. Works to find one that is good enough.
- Thinks about desired outcomes and considers both personal losses and gains.
- Feels both anxiety and excitement when making choices.
- Having made a decision, rallies behind it and tries to learn from it.

**Risky style**
- Prefers to make novel rather than secure choices.
- Makes a quick overall survey of options and hopes something will click.
- Relies almost exclusively on feelings rather than reason when deciding.
- Tends to choose the first option that "feels right."
- Assumes desired outcomes will occur and that personal gains will prevail.
- Feels mostly excitement about making choices.
- Having made a decision, takes action without much additional thought.

injuries, sudden changes in economic conditions, other people trying to sabotage our efforts, and many other unexpected happenings in life. In effect, they become the fly in the ointment of any decision-making processes.

Recently, a neighbor's daughter wanted to look good and to impress the person accompanying her to an outdoor concert. She tried on a number of outfits from her wardrobe until she found something she liked. Unfortunately, an unexpected rainstorm at the concert left her drenched and looking, in her words, "like some character from a horror movie." The outfit chosen did not allow her to look good at the concert. The unforeseen rainstorm took care of that. However, she apparently impressed her date, because he asked her out again.

The likelihood that such intervening events will adversely affect our choice is labeled **risk** when it can be objectively assessed and **uncertainty** when it cannot be precisely calculated. The likelihood of bad weather is a good example. If a weather report says the chance of rain is 90 percent, the probability of rain is precisely stated. Thus, we know the *risk* associated with deciding to leave an umbrella or raincoat at home. On the other hand, if we step outside, look at the sky, and try to guess what the weather will be, the chance of rain cannot be precisely estimated. All we can say is, "Well, it looks like it might rain" or, "It doesn't look like rain." Such subjective estimates reflect our uncertainty about the weather.

*Even though uncertainty cannot be precisely calculated, it lurks in the background of our thoughts about potential choices.* It is communicated through our anxiety levels, hesitations to act, hunches about what will work or not work, feeling overwhelmed with choices, and our general discomfort level. People also express doubt about an outcome when they say things like: "I'm not completely sure this will work; there are too many things that could go wrong here" or "It's a crapshoot whether or not our plan will pan out; I'm feeling uneasy about moving in this direction."

*Try to identify things that could go wrong.* Investors in the stock market, for example, know that unforeseen changes in the economy might occur and lower their earnings. Car owners and bus and airplane travelers are aware that equipment failures could lead to added expense, delays, injuries, or death. During rush hour, commuters know that delays due to traffic jams, accidents, and road construction may occur. Most couples thinking of marriage know that relationships can be affected by unforseen personality conflicts, pesky relatives, and disputes over money, work, and sex.

*Build in safeguards to protect yourself if something goes wrong.* Everyone, of course, hopes that unforeseen events will not occur. But effective decision makers build in safeguards to protect themselves "just in case something goes wrong." Experienced stock market investors, for example, put their money into a variety of stocks and bonds to "spread out the risk." Commuters create a "cushion of time" and leave for work 30 minutes earlier "just in case traffic gets bad." Many car owners purchase an extended warranty as a "safeguard" to protect their out-of-pocket expenses when the manufacturer's warranty expires. Some couples sign prenuptial agreements as a "backup plan" in the event something goes wrong with the marriage.

Another way to protect yourself is to take advantage of some advice offered by Irving Janis and Leon Mann (1977). They strongly encourage people to develop a contingency plan for something going wrong as the last step in making a decision. To do this, *try to imagine that your solution fails.* One way is to reassess the pros and cons associated with the alternative that was chosen. Imagine a scenario where the disadvantages were much more important than initially thought. Or have a friend play "devil's advocate" and give your reasons why your course of action will not work. Janis and Mann find that people who explore a "worst-case scenario" inoculate themselves against something going wrong. They subsequently feel more secure about their choice and are better able to handle any criticism it might produce. And if things fail to work, they are prepared with a contingency plan.

## 8. Implement and Monitor Your Solution or Course of Action

After everything is said and done, it is still necessary to continue to monitor and evaluate your solution or course of action. Sometimes corrections need to be made. There is also no reason to get locked into a choice forever. Circumstances change, and a good solution or decision today may not work as well in the future. Sometimes it is helpful to have a "self-destruct" deadline in mind. Pick a date several weeks or months into the future, and tell yourself you will not continue to employ your course of action unless you have good evidence it works. This might help you monitor what you are doing to have the evidence you need for the "self-destruct" deadline.

## *Summary of Chapter Organizers*

Suggested responses to the chapter organizers at the beginning of this chapter are shown below.

1. *What pitfalls should be avoided when tackling problems? Some people ignore problems* or otherwise rationalize, procrastinate, or try to "pass the buck." *An overly optimistic attitude* may lead to more time spent on issues than they are worth. *Employing past solutions for present problems* may trap us in old problem-solving habits that do not fit current situations. *Seeking perfect solutions* ignores the fact they do not exist and it uses up much of our time and energy. *Trying to solve problems and make decisions quickly* typically affects the quality of the decisions.

   When selecting the first alternative considered, other solutions are left out. Having at least three options is a good idea. *People also err when they make judgments based on preconceived ideas or on what information is most readily available in memory. Letting other people make decisions for you* forces you to live with someone else's way of thinking. *A lack of confidence* in our skills and believing that we *do not have the intellectual capacity or creativity to resolve issues* keeps us from trying hard enough.

2. *Why is it important to accept the challenge a problem presents?* People who perceive the issues they face as obstacles or burdens are not as effective in obtaining solutions. Their low interest and motivation interferes.

3. *Are you aware of three criteria that can help you define a problem better?* A good problem statement isolates and locates the source of the problem. Also, it is not overly general, nor does it contain a solution embedded within it. Finally, it is reframed or restructured when the definition does not seem quite right or attempts to solve it lead to dead ends.

4. *What steps can you take to ensure that you have perceived the important facts in a problem?* Good problem solvers and decision makers are able to separate the "vital few facts" from the "trivial many." Identifying important facts includes determining the critical elements in a problem and who owns responsibility for resolving the issue. Having an appropriate visual or verbal representation of the problem also allows us to keep before us the critical elements.

5. *How can you develop a list of the best possible alternative solutions or courses of actions to the issues you face?* A number of techniques can help including forming an idea tree, using metaphors, brainstorming, attribute listing, using a checklist, and working backwards.

6. *What process can you use to assess the strengths and weaknesses of various options?* The best way is to list the criteria that apply and then balance off the pros against the cons for each of the options considered.

7. *What rules of thumb can help you to sort through the pros and cons of your potential solutions or courses of action?* Two that research shows are beneficial are to select the solution that has the most number of benefits/pros and the fewest number of costs/cons associated with it. The second is to assign ratings to the considerations for selecting an option. This takes into account the fact that some benefits/pros and costs/cons are more important than others when formulating a decision. It also allows us to appropriately consider the role that potential gains and losses play in making decisions and not to be overly influenced by one or the other. Research shows that both strategies are better than trying to decide in a more casual or global manner.

8. *What should you do if you get stuck and have a difficult time deciding?* Under such conditions put the problem aside for a while, and let it incubate; dream or fantasize

about the issue to allow your imagination to take hold, examine your decision-making style for problems it may present; and, if all else fails, follow your heart.

9. *Why is it important to have a contingency plan for something going wrong?* There is always a certain amount of uncertainty or risk that a selected course of action will not work out. Thinking in advance of what could go wrong and developing a plan just in case is often helpful. If the unexpected occurs, you are prepared.

10. *Is your work finished when you have successfully identified a solution or course of action?* In some sense, it has just begun. Once a decision is made, it is necessary to continue to monitor and evaluate how well it is working out. Circumstances change, and a good solution today may not work as well in the future.

## Things to Do

1. Use concepts from this chapter to analyze what went wrong in the *USS Vincennes* incident described at the beginning of this chapter. Focus upon the following issues: the pitfalls in problem solving and decision making that were present; how gains and losses associated with a course of action influenced the decision; the likely role of the captain's decision-making style on the outcome.

2. What criteria for a good problem definition do the following problem statements violate? How would you rewrite each one? "How much of a pay raise should I give George to get him to work harder?" "How can police security be increased to better protect shoppers in the parking lot of this mall?" "How can I get my sister to spend more time with her husband and children?" "Sylvia asked me to figure out how she can make more money. What should I tell her?"

3. For the following problems, use the method that is suggested for generating alternative ideas for solving it.
   - (Form an Idea Tree) You have just inherited $500,000. What is the best way to invest this money?
   - (Use Attribute Listing) How can you design a better mousetrap?
   - (Brainstorming) How could someone complete a college degree in half the time?
   - (Working Backwards) Select a current task you recently completed. How much time did you spend on it? How could you have finished it in half the time?
   - (Idea Checklist) What could you do to redecorate your bedroom?

4. Pick any two of the problems listed in number 2 above. List the options you want to consider further, and develop a list of pros and cons for each option. Based on information in the text, how would you sort through the pros and cons?

5. What are some of the personal barriers that prevent you from becoming a more effective problem solver and decision maker? List each barrier, and think of at least one thing you could do to overcome it. Share your ideas with a friend, and see if your friend could suggest other ideas for you to follow.

6. Select a problem in your life for which you are currently stuck trying to figure out what to do. Use information in this chapter to assess your decision-making style, and identify factors in your style that might be getting in the way of making a decision. Also, try the advice for "following your heart" given in the chapter. What does this process suggest you should do to resolve your problem?

## APPLIED ACTIVITIES

EXERCISE 3.1

### Identifying Common Problem-Solving and Decision-Making Concerns

Rate each of the following statements using the rating scale described below. Try to respond as honestly and objectively as you can.

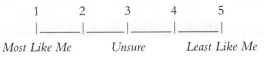

$$1 \qquad 2 \qquad 3 \qquad 4 \qquad 5$$
| \_\_\_\_\_ | \_\_\_\_\_ | \_\_\_\_\_ | \_\_\_\_\_ |

*Most Like Me*     *Unsure*     *Least Like Me*

_____ I typically ignore a problem and hope that it will go away.

_____ I am overly optimistic that any problem can be resolved.

_____ I rely on solutions or courses of action that worked well in the past.

_____ I am seldom satisfied unless I have a perfect solution or course of action.

_____ I use preconceived ideas about what will work and what to do.

_____ I find myself selecting solutions that are most vivid in my mind.

_____ I believe in solving problems and making decisions quickly.

_____ I usually select the first solution or course of action that occurs to me.

_____ I have a tendency to let other people make decisions for me.

_____ I do not have confidence in my ability to solve problems or make decisions.

_____ I do not have the intelligence or creativity to solve problems.

Sum your ratings. As a general rule, scores between 11 and 33 suggest that people will have some dissatisfaction with their ability to solve problems and to make decisions. Scores above 33, in my experience, are associated with people who are more satisfied in their capacity to resolve issues in their lives.

For the items on which you gave yourself scores of 1 or 2, what are some actions you could take to lessen the impact of that factor in your life? List your ideas on a separate sheet of paper.

EXERCISE 3.2    **Solving a Personal Problem**

The following activity is designed to remind you of important chapter concepts as you try to resolve an issue in your life. The issue selected can be anything. Try to pick something that is currently a concern, is important to resolve, and for which you would like to try the ideas in the chapter. Several prompts are given throughout this activity to help you focus on relevant material from the chapter.

**1. Identify and Avoid Common Pitfalls**
- "I am aware of the eleven pitfalls in trying to solve problems and make decisions and the ones that typically affect me." If not, complete Exercise 3.1 before proceeding.
- "I will pay particular attention to the following two to three pitfalls as I try to work on the problem I have selected for this activity." List each in the space provided below, and indicate what actions you will take to avoid them.

**2. Carefully Define Your Problem**
- List your initial problem statement in the space provided.

- How well does your initial problem statement meet each of the following criteria?

    The source of the problem is isolated and located. Yes____ No____

    The statement is not overly general. Yes____ No____

    The problem statement does not contain a solution. Yes____ No____

- If your problem statement fails to meet one of the criteria, it needs to be restructured or reframed. Do this in the space provided below.

- Recheck this new problem statement against the three criteria listed above.

**3. Accept the Challenge a Problem Presents**

    I see this problem as a challenge. Yes____ No____

    I am committed to finding a solution. Yes____ No____

If you answered "no" to either item, you may want to select another problem before proceeding with this process. If so, reanswer question 2.

## 4. Identify the Important Facts

•List the critical elements and facts associated with this issue.

•Who owns this problem? That is, is it something you alone are responsible for resolving, or should other people be involved? If so, list them below.

•What is an external representation of the problem and its elements that can help you to verbalize and visualize what you need take into account? Take your critical elements and facts listed above, and on a separate sheet of paper, develop a representation of your problem. Your representation can be a table or chart, a drawing or figure, a diagram, a map, a sketch, a metaphor, or anything else that will help you to verbalize and visualize important elements.

## 5. Develop Alternative Solutions or Courses of Action

•Pick one of the processes for generating alternative solutions, and use it on a separate sheet of paper. List the name of the method used and the alternatives you developed in the space below.

Method employed:

Possible solutions or courses of action:

Have you generated at least three alternative solutions? Yes_____ No_____

If not, think about your problem and identify a minimum of three. List any new alternatives in the space provided.

In using one of the methods for generating alternative solutions, did you prematurely evaluate any options and thus eliminate one from consideration? Yes_____ No_____. If "yes," and there are several, pick one to two of them, and list them above so that you can continue to consider them further.

## 6. Evaluate the Alternative Solutions

•On a separate sheet of paper, set up a table similar to Table 3.6 in the text. Follow the instructions given in the text for setting up such a table. Then list the pros/cons, benefits/costs, and gains/losses associated with each alternative course of action.

**7. Select a Solution or Course of Action**
- If your benefits and costs for each option are pretty much equal in terms of how important a role they will play in the decision you will make, select the option that has most benefits and the fewest costs.
- Otherwise, assign weights to each of your pros and cons, as illustrated in Table 3.6. Select the option that has the largest difference in the numerical weightings between the pros and cons.
- List your decision below, and indicate what method you used.

- If necessary, take steps to become unstuck. If you still feel stuck obtaining a solution, briefly indicate how the following ideas from the text might help you.
  1. Put the problem aside for awhile and incubate it.
  2. Dream about the problem.
  3. Examine your decision-making style as it applies to this problem from Table 3.7 in the text. Describe the pros and cons of your decision-making style for selecting a course of action.
  4. Follow your heart.
- What is your contingency plan in case the decision you made above does not work out? Briefly indicate what you plan to do in the space provided.

**8. Implement and Monitor Your Solution or Course of Action**
- How will you monitor your solution or course of action to continue to assess whether it is effective?
- Identify a self-destruct date upon which you would be willing to give up your solution or course of action unless you have evidence it is working well.

# Key Terms

*Availability heuristic.* A tendency to make decisions based upon what is most vivid, easily recalled, or otherwise available in our memory. People judge dying from an accident more likely than a stroke because they can remember more examples of accidents and accidental deaths.

*Cognitive style.* A preferred pattern for gathering information, processing it, and forming various judgments and opinions that are then employed in our attempts to solve problems and make decisions.

*Complacency.* A personal style for problem solving and making decisions in which people fail to see the signs of some danger or simply ignore it.

*Decision.* The choice we make from among alternative ideas for solutions or courses of action.

*Decision freezing.* Characterized by premature commitment to a course of action. The pressure for a quick decision leads people to bypass a detailed examination of the available options to the selected course of action.

*Defensive avoidance.* A personal style for problem solving and making decisions in which we fail to take actions because of the belief there is little chance of finding a solution.

*Field-dependence.* A perceptual and cognitive style in which people have difficulty separating a stimulus from the background in which it occurs. Individuals with this attribute also find it somewhat difficult to solve problems that are technical and theoretical in nature. Much more comfortable working on interpersonal issues and concerns.

*Field-independence.* A perceptual and cognitive style in which people find it relatively easy to separate a stimulus from the background in which it occurs. Individuals with this attribute are less comfortable working on interpersonal issues and concerns than they are on problems that are technical and theoretical in nature.

*Functional fixedness.* A tendency to assume that a familiar object (e.g., a knife) cannot be used for something else (e.g., a screwdriver).

*Heuristic.* A rule of thumb, or general approach, to finding a solution. Dividing fractions by the least common denominator is an example of a heuristic.

*Incubation.* A method for finding a solution in which we put the problem aside for a while and try not to think about it. The solution sometimes emerges as "Eureka" or as an "Aha" experience.

*Lateral thinking.* A method of thinking about a problem in which we try to reframe or restructure it in some novel or unusual way to obtain a solution.

*Personal stake.* The tangible and intangible gains or losses associated with a decision.

*Problem.* Anything for which we do not have a ready response.

*Representativeness heuristic.* Tendency to make judgments by relying upon how well an event represents our preconceived idea of something. If people believe they are poor tennis players, if they played poorly one day, they are likely to decide they also will perform poorly the next time they play.

*Risk.* The chances that some intervening event might interfere with a decision achieving a desired result. This likelihood can be objectively measured (e.g., the probability that flipping a coin will produce the head you predicted).

*Set.* A tendency to approach problems with a somewhat rigid and persistent way of thinking.

*Solution.* A combination of new or existing ideas that will work in a given situation.

*Uncertainty.* The chances that some intervening event might interfere with a decision achieving a desired result. This likelihood cannot be objectively measured, and thus subjective estimates are employed (e.g., how certain you feel that your choice of a career will make you happy).

*Vertical thinking.* Working a problem or trying to make a decision in a very logical, orderly fashion. Doing long division or solving an algebraic equation is an example of vertical thinking.

# Learning and Retention Processes in Daily Living

## Chapter Overview

Acquiring new behaviors and remembering what was learned is a universal concern. To do these well, the factors that produce changes in our skills and knowledge must be well understood. In this chapter, the aspects of our everyday experiences that affect our capacity to learn and remember will be explored. Suggestions for promoting effective learning and retention will be provided.

## Chapter Organizers

*As you read, answer the questions that follow on a separate sheet of paper, and check your responses with those provided in the summary section.*

Learning is not a spectator sport. There is no substitute for spending time on the tasks that will help you develop your knowledge and skills.

1. What are some things you could do to enhance the quality of the time you spend trying to learn?

Practicing and receiving feedback are important elements in helping you to learn a variety of things.

2. Do you know two things you can do to ensure that you will receive the maximum benefits from the time spent practicing?
3. When trying to acquire new information and skills, what characteristics should the feedback you receive have?

Behaviors that are rewarded are more likely to increase in frequency.

4. What are several things you can do to use rewards effectively as well as to avoid their potential negative side effects?
5. Is it better to provide a reward every time a desirable response occurs or just some of the time?

6. What happens when behaviors are no longer rewarded?

Unpleasant or aversive stimuli are sometimes used to help you acquire desirable behaviors.

7. What are three ways that unpleasant stimuli influence your actions?
8. How can punishment be used effectively?

How you structure and organize a task affects your performance.

9. How does organizing and planning your time help you to learn?

Learning depends upon your ability to remember previous ideas and behaviors.

10. How does your memory system work?
11. What causes you to forget information?
12. How can you improve your ability to remember?

## The Man Who Never Forgot Anything

Alexander Luria (1982) was the most distinguished Soviet psychologist of his generation. In his book *The Mind of a Mnemonist,* he described a case study of a man he referred to as S, a person who never forgot anything. His feats of memory were mind-boggling, and they included:

- Repeating lists of 70 words or numbers after a single presentation. He could do it just as easily in reverse order as he could from beginning to end. All that he required was that there be a three- to four-second pause between each element in the series.
- The ability to reproduce the series of words or numbers that had been presented to him a week, a month, a year, or even many years earlier. During such sessions, he would sit with his eyes closed, pause, then comment: "Yes, Yes . . . This was a series you gave me once when we were in your apartment . . . You were sitting at the table, and I was sitting in a rocking chair . . . You were wearing a gray suit, and you looked at me like this." Having established the context, he would reel off the series precisely as he had been given it.
- An uncanny ability to remember the details of every conversation he had ever had and the details of every book he had ever read. Even if the conversations or the books were read in his childhood, he could reproduce them.

His ability to form images to things he experienced gave him his phenomenal memory. He had the ability to convert sounds into visual images of different colors. When he was taught the words of a Hebrew prayer as a child, for example, the words settled into his mind as puffs of steam or splashes of color. When listening to a tone with a pitch of 3,000 cycles per second, he saw a whisk broom that was a fiery color and sparks flying off of it.

When repeating a series of words, he ordered the visual images the words produced by attaching each one to objects along a roadway or street he visualized in his mind. He would take a mental walk along the street, and as he encountered each color, it in turn, triggered the word he had memorized. On one occasion he got stuck remembering a particular word during his mental walk. "It's by the street lamp," he said, "but I can't see it. Oh I know, the street lamp was on at the time." In his mind he turned on the lamp, and the word flashed into his mind.

# CHARACTERISTICS OF LEARNING

Most of us do not possess the capacity to learn and remember as well as the individual Alexander Luria studied. What we can do, however, is rather remarkable. A complete list of what is learned in a lifetime would fill every page in this book. Yet the variety is impressive and includes skills and knowledge needed to prepare foods, drive a car, master course content, stay healthy, communicate and interact with others, and many other things. Each of us has the capacity to acquire the knowledge and skills needed to adapt to a lifetime of change in our lives. Without the capacity to learn, we would have little more than instinctive reactions to the demands of our environment. Personal control over our lives would be impossible.

**Learning** *is a relatively permanent change in our skills and knowledge as a function of our experiences.* Let us briefly examine components of this definition of learning. *Relatively permanent* implies that as long as we continue to use what is acquired, it is generally available to us. *Changes in our knowledge and skills* means that something new has been added to our repertoire of thoughts and actions. Everything that we learn occurs *as a function of our experiences* with events we encounter daily. Certain things, however, must happen in our experiences in order to learn effectively. The remainder of this chapter explores the factors involved and how you can employ them to enhance your ability to learn.

# FACTORS THAT AFFECT ACQUIRING INFORMATION

## Time on Task

There is no substitute for spending time on whatever you want to learn. Research clearly shows that the "total amount of time spent on a task" consistently runs a close second to general ability in predicting how much will be learned (Corno and Mandinach, 1983). In academic settings, one aspect of time on task is showing up for class. In one study, 84 percent of the students receiving at least a B grade reported that they were almost always in class. Of those who had a C- or lower grade, 53 percent were absent on a regular basis from their classes (Lindgren, 1969). Of course, simply showing up for class is not the issue.

The quality of the time spent acquiring information rather than the number of hours or minutes spent is the important issue. Successful students use their class time effectively. They concentrate on what is going on, participate in discussions and take much more complete notes than their less successful counterparts (Hawley et al., 1984). Research suggests that when taking notes, students capture important points by summarizing or paraphrasing ideas in their own words and later organizing the information into an outline or a chart that captures key points (Carrier and Titus, 1979; Kiewra et al., 1988).

Successful learners also ask questions when they don't understand something. Unfortunately, in spite of the importance of asking questions, some people fail to do so. They either readily accept whatever information is provided, or they are too embarrassed or uncomfortable to ask.

Why do some students choose not to ask questions? Jan Collins-Eaglin (1992) reports that *the most important barrier are beliefs that their questions are silly or dumb or that having questions means they are somehow inadequate or stupid.* Such students typically mis-

read the silence in class. They interpret the lack of questions by classmates as a sure sign that their classmates understand the content. She notes that minority students are also uncomfortable asking questions if the teacher is a member of a different ethnic or racial group. In such cases, students believe their lack of knowledge will be exposed and this will reflect badly on their ethnic group.

*Time on task is also important for learning skills needed to do a job well.* Robert Morrison and Thomas Brantner (1992) examined the factors that facilitated or hindered employees learning a new position. They found the most important factor was time spent on the job struggling with the demands of that position. This was true regardless of whatever ability and skill levels participants initially possessed and the type of job they were asked to learn.

## The Role of Practice

With practice, correct and appropriate responses tend to occur more frequently over time, as illustrated in Figure 4.1. Also note that there are individual differences in terms of how much people benefit from the same amount of practice. Thus, in designing learning experiences for ourselves or others, do not assume that everyone learns at the same rate.

*Active Practice Must Be Emphasized* Passively paying attention to information or "going through the motions" when learning a skill is unlikely to be effective. Based on a review of the research literature, Charles Bonwell and Jim Eison (1991) report that teaching and learning strategies that encourage active practice enhance the acquisition and retention of information. From the learner's point of view, this means that the time spent on a task should have the following characteristics.

- Appropriate levels of interest and motivation to learn are present.
- Attention is focused on the task.
- A goal for what must be learned is established and pursued.

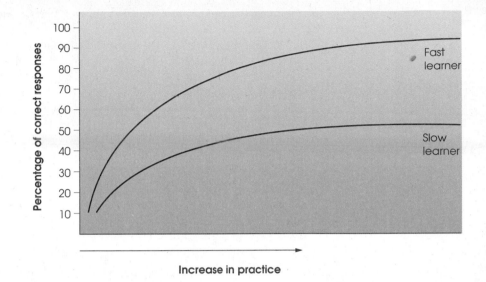

**Figure 4.1** *Acquisition curves for a fast and slow learner.*

- Questions are asked when something is not understood.
- Feedback is sought in order to learn from one's mistakes.
- Attempts are made to integrate and to establish connections among various ideas or the components of a skill.
- Rote repetition is discouraged.
- Critical thinking processes such as analyzing, synthesizing, and evaluating information are emphasized.
- Whenever appropriate, ideas about and experiences with the information are written down and/or discussed with others.

Study techniques such as the SQ3R method also encourage active practice. This procedure, developed by Francis Robinson (1970), is something anyone can use while reading a textbook to actively practice information. SQ3R stands for Survey, Question, Read, Recite, and Review. Here is how it works. First, survey what you must read. Glance over the chapter, and notice what is covered and how it is organized. Then take the first section and ask yourself a *question* or several questions before beginning to read. Textbooks are organized into sections to help this task. Write your questions down, because you will need a record of them. *Read* the section, and then *recite* an answer to the questions. If you cannot answer your questions, *review* the section to find the answer. This procedure should be used for each part of the textbook you are reading. It can also be used as a method to review lecture notes or notes you took on an outside reading.

*Distribute Your Practice over Time* How practice on a task is spaced also is important. Should practice of a task be concentrated in short periods of time, or should the same amount of practice be extended over a longer time period? Students, for example, often wonder whether it is better to cram the night before an exam or to study and review over a period of days or weeks preceding an exam. **Massed practice** is equivalent to cramming the night before, and **distributed practice** is equivalent to studying the same amount over a longer period.

A generalization from the research literature is that people learn relatively easy tasks just as well with massed as with distributed practice. On difficult tasks, however, distributed practice enhances learning (Underwood, 1970; Demster, 1988). This effect is particularly noticeable with verbal material. Robert Bjork (1979) reports that distributed practice typically leads to twice the amount of information recalled. For such improvements in retention to occur, the interval between practice periods must be relatively long, such as 24 hours or more (Zechmeister and Nyberg, 1982). In an unusual illustration of retention after spaced practice, adults were tested on basic algebra 50 years after they took college math courses. A surprising amount of information was retained. Those who performed best had taken math courses spread out over four years of college. The distributed practice effect also is most noticeable when information must be recalled rather than recognized. *Thus, distributed practice would be expected to help you more with essay, fill-in-the-blank, and short-answer exams than with multiple-choice tests.*

The general disadvantages of massed practice should not surprise you. *Research clearly shows that cramming is an ineffective way to learn.* It taxes your ability to process and remember information, lowers your energy levels, produces fatigue, and strokes the fires of test anxiety (Zechmeister and Nyberg, 1982).

The sleep-before-you-learn-approach may not always be helpful. *A short period of sleep just before new learning may increase forgetting.* In one experiment, students slept for either thirty minutes or one, two, or four hours. Soon after awakening, they memorized lists of words and were tested four hours later for recall of the material. Their ability to remember was impaired. Essentially, that "groggy" feeling after awakening is a form of sedation that interferes with cognitive functioning. Research suggests it is better to remain active and to wait about an hour after awakening before starting to study. This is

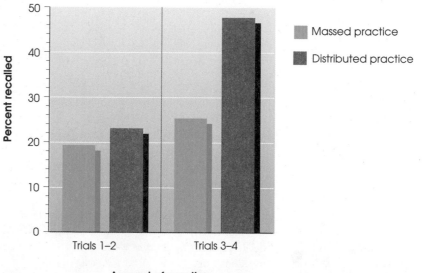

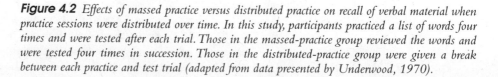

**Figure 4.2** *Effects of massed practice versus distributed practice on recall of verbal material when practice sessions were distributed over time. In this study, participants practiced a list of words four times and were tested after each trial. Those in the massed-practice group reviewed the words and were tested four times in succession. Those in the distributed-practice group were given a break between each practice and test trial (adapted from data presented by Underwood, 1970).*

particularly true if you have had less than five hours of sleep before studying (Hoddes, 1977; Karacan, 1981).

## The Role of Feedback

The purpose of feedback in learning is to reduce the extent to which people make errors. Both external and internal sources of feedback or **knowledge of results (KR)** are used. External sources include feedback from teachers, supervisors, or the speedometer on an automobile, and the sights and sounds of a personal computer. Some word processing programs, for example, will "beep" if you misspell a word while typing, and the visual display immediately shows mistakes in writing, data entry, and drawing. Internal sources of feedback include such things as perceptions of progress on a task and various cues from body movements and thinking processes. When driving a car, internal feedback from your leg muscles indicates how much pressure to apply to the gas pedal and to the brakes.

*Feedback Is Most Effective when It Is Immediate* This is particularly true for tasks in which similar responses must be made in quick succession (Bilodeau and Bilodeau, 1961). Everyday examples of this type of task are learning to drive a car, using a computer keyboard, swimming, or shooting a rifle. For an exam, immediate feedback is beneficial only if further exams rely on knowledge and skills tapped by earlier exams (McKeachie, 1993). In many content areas, however, this is not the case. Subsequent exams may cover different historical periods, outside readings, or completely new content areas.

*Feedback Must Be Detailed, Specific, and Constructive* That is, detailed information regarding what is wrong as well as specific suggestions for how to improve in the future should be given. As an example, writing skills generally are improved when people are provided with detailed constructive feedback during the early stages of a task. Barbara Walvord (1990), for example, examined the writing practices of college teachers across a variety of disciplines. She found that a letter grade on a paper or instructor comments on the finished product did little to improve future performance. Instead, writing improved when students received ongoing, constructive feedback on initial outlines and drafts of a paper. Similarly, Deborah Miller and Mary Kelley (1991) reviewed a number of studies on factors that enhanced the academic achievement of children. They concluded that achievement was enhanced when parents or guardians provided specific, constructive, and regular feedback on homework assignments.

Similar effects of constructive feedback can be seen in other areas of our lives. Some electrical utilities, for example, use digital meters to provide consumers with daily feedback on energy use. They also give customers specific suggestions for actions to take to reduce the amount of energy consumed. Customers given such information reduce energy consumption by 10–20 percent (Stern, 1992). In an effort to improve safety practices, a city's vehicle maintenance employees were provided with a daily graph depicting safety violations (e.g., improper use of tools, failure to use goggles or to clean up spilled oil). They also were given training in proper safety procedures. Over a 40-week period, this feedback led to a 47 percent increase in the use of proper safety procedures (Komaki et al., 1980).

Feedback is a valuable component of acquiring a variety of behaviors at work, in school, and in other areas of our lives. There are times, however, when those most responsible for providing feedback fail to do so. Or, they do not give it in ways that are helpful.

*Therefore, you must take some initiative to obtain the feedback you require.* Otherwise, your performance is likely to be less capable and accompanied by tension and frustration.

## The Role of Positive Reinforcement

Rewards are pleasant stimuli occurring after a response occurs; they increase the likelihood of that response recurring. They are labeled **positive reinforcers** and include such things as money, food, praise, spending time with someone you enjoy, pampering yourself, and engaging in favorite activities such as watching television, gardening, or just goofing off. The effects they produce can be rather dramatic and affect a broad range of everyday behaviors.

*Rewards Increase the Frequency of Desirable Behaviors* Rewards improve performance on the job, in sports, and, in school. They lead to better health care practices and exercise habits, enhance communication and relationship skills, and literally affect almost everything we say and do. The trick is to discover what people find rewarding and to use it to increase desirable behaviors. For example, the retail selling behaviors of 41 sales clerks (i.e., quickly waiting on customers, friendliness) and absences from their workstations were improved by using positive reinforcers (Luthans et al., 1981). Interviews were held that identified that paid time off from work, equivalent cash payments, and tickets to enter a company-sponsored drawing for a paid vacation would be rewarding. Table 4.1 shows how the behaviors of the sales clerks were modified through the use of rewards.

*Positive Reinforcers Can Help to Reduce the Frequency of Bad Habits* In the latter case, the frequency of behaviors that oppose undesirable actions are increased through the use of rewards. In one study, rewards such as self-praise and engaging in favorite

---

**Table 4.1**   Frequency of Selling Behaviors and Absences From Workstation

The average frequency of appropriate selling behaviors and average number of times each sales clerk was absent from his or her work station was recorded for 20 days to establish a baseline. The positive reinforcer intervention was run for the next 20 days (intervention phase), and then the positive reinforcers were removed for 20 days (postintervention phase).

**SELLING BEHAVIOR**

| PHASE OF EXPERIMENT | EXPERIMENTAL GROUP | CONTROL GROUP |
|---|---|---|
| Baseline | 370 | 373 |
| Intervention | 433 | 362 |
| Post-intervention | 424 | 354 |

**ABSENCE FROM WORK STATION**

| PHASE OF EXPERIMENT | EXPERIMENTAL GROUP | CONTROL GROUP |
|---|---|---|
| Baseline | 286 | 282 |
| Intervention | 225 | 293 |
| Post-intervention | 226 | 297 |

activities were used to help individuals lose weight. People were reinforced for avoiding situations where they were tempted to eat high-calorie foods, for eating more nutritious snacks, and for exercising more often. Significant reductions in weight loss were obtained and maintained over time through the use of positive reinforcement (Agras, 1987). In another study, excessive trash was reduced and additional landfill space was gained by giving homeowners lottery tickets for recycling glass and newspapers (Diamond and Loewy, 1991). Failing to use seat belts was overcome when fast food restaurants rewarded customers who used them with food coupons. Within days, the usage of seat belts doubled (Geller, 1985).

*Positive Reinforcers Work Best Immediately After a Response*  Reinforcing people before they use an appropriate behavior typically does little good. Many children have been allowed to go to the movies because they promised to do household chores or homework later. Such promises are sometimes conveniently forgotten. In addition, the association between a behavior and reward is best made immediately after the response occurs.

Although not an ideal situation, most of us can tolerate delays in obtaining rewards for several reasons. One is our ability to symbolically relate the delayed reward to the appropriate behavior. Taking a test and waiting two weeks for a good grade still rewards good study habits. Students simply remind themselves of the study behaviors that produced the reinforcement. Similarly, receiving a sales bonus several weeks after making a big sale rewards good salesmanship. A salesperson easily ties the reward to the behaviors behind the sale.

*Another reason people can tolerate delays in reinforcement is that behavior is seldom learned or maintained by a single reward.* In everyday life, several reinforcers become associated with a behavior. Thus, a good grade and sales bonus also may be associated with self-praise or positive remarks from a teacher or sales manager. Stimuli that acquire reward properties through their association with established positive reinforcers are called **secondary reinforcers.** Even though the grade or sales bonus is delayed, these secondary reinforcers immediately reward the behavior and allow a person to wait for later reinforcers.

## Reinforcement Schedules

When teaching a new response, it is usually effective to reinforce an appropriate response each time it occurs. The latter technique is called a **continuous reinforcement** schedule. While continuous rewards are important for initially developing a behavior, it is possible to continue responding with fewer rewards. **Partial reinforcement** is a process whereby behaviors are rewarded only after a certain number of responses occur or after a given interval of time. Partial reinforcement schedules encountered in everyday life are presented in Table 4.2.

*Partial Reward Schedules Help to Maintain Behaviors Over Time*  They help our actions eventually to come under self-control or to allow other rewards in our environment to influence them. All of the reward schedules have gaps produced by time or by the number of responses that were not reinforced. *Such gaps provide opportunities for other internal and external rewards to become associated with our actions and to gain control over them.*

A student in one of my classes taught his 7-year-old daughter to keep her room clean and tidy. He began by giving her 50 cents a day to clean up her room, which she quickly learned to do. After four weeks of paying her every day, he began to pay her 50

| **Table 4.2** | Common Reinforcement Schedules |
| --- | --- |

*Continuous:* A reinforcer is given each time a response occurs. It is the fastest way to establish a new response.

*Fixed ratio:* A reinforcer is given after a certain number of responses occur. Examples include getting a salary based on producing a fixed number of units of a product on an assembly line or a sales bonus based on the number of units sold. If the number of responses needed to obtain a reinforcer is high, a pause in an individual's responding will occur after the reward is given. To eliminate such pauses, the number of responses required for a reinforcer should be kept low. Think about what happens to your studying behavior immediately after an exam. The decrease most students experience is an example of the pause.

*Variable ratio:* A reinforcer is given after a variable number of responses. That is, an individual may receive a reinforcer for every tenth, fifteenth, or twentieth response. In laboratory situations, attempts are made to give the reinforcer for an average number of responses (e.g., an average of every tenth response). In our daily lives we encounter variable ratio schedules when we play golf, poker, or slot machines. Every response is not reinforced, nor is the reinforcement given after a predetermined number of responses. A high-handicap golfer usually has few "rewarding" shots. Their occurrence is somewhat erratic since it is hard to predict when a good shot will be made.

*Fixed interval:* A reinforcer is given after a fixed interval of time, provided the response has occurred at least one time during that interval. This can be hourly, weekly, or even monthly. Your pay at work and the grades you receive in school occur on a fixed-interval schedule. You might be paid once a week or once a month. Your grades are given after midterm exams and after final exams. People tend to increase their responding just before the reinforcer is given and to decrease it afterward (e.g., cramming before an exam and relaxing afterward). We learn that the next reward cannot occur for a certain amount of time, so there is no need to rush things.

*Variable interval:* A reinforcer is given after variable intervals of time. It might occur sometimes once a week, while at other times it might occur once every third or fourth week. We could, if we wanted, figure out the average amount of time until we get a reward. This is done in the laboratory to give rewards on such a schedule. Variable-interval schedules are not typical in our everyday affairs. Examples are "pop" quizzes in a class. They are typically not given after every hour of class. Similarly, a salesperson or consultant might have to wait for a paycheck. Thus, he or she gets paid sometimes every other week, but at other times it's every third, fourth, or perhaps fifth week. It depends on when people decide to pay for the product or service.

cents every other day. In the meantime, he began to increase the number of compliments he and his wife gave her for a clean room. Because of the additional attention she received, his daughter also began to enjoy having a tidy room. She soon learned to clean her room to earn compliments and because of the self-pride and pleasant atmosphere a clean room created. Money was no longer needed.

***Partial Reward Schedules Allow Behaviors Leading to Distant Rewards to Be Maintained***
Sonia Goltz (1992) reports that many organizations escalate investments of time, money, and other resources in activities that do not result in immediate rewards. This includes such things as strategic and long-range planning, market research, research and

development for new products, test marketing new products, and spending resources on managerial and sales training programs. In fact, in many cases, there are continuing costs and losses associated with such activities. *She finds that managers are more willing to make decisions to spend resources where the immediate payoffs are small if they were partially rewarded for doing this in the past.* In effect, they learned to expect that long-term payoffs would occur in spite of short-term costs and losses.

## The Extinction of Learned Responses

When responses are no longer followed by the rewards that control them, **extinction** occurs. That is, the behaviors eventually weaken and cease to occur. Most of us would stop working if our bosses failed to pay us. Similarly, our career plans would quickly change if we discovered that jobs were no longer available. *Extinction, however, is not the same as forgetting a response.* The response is held back because there is no longer an incentive to perform, but it will return when the reward is again used. Thus, if your employer gave you the back pay owed and continued paying you, your good work habits would soon return to normal.

*Because people often reinforce undesirable behaviors in others, extinction can help to break such bad habits.* Sometimes young children misbehave in order to get the attention of a parent or guardian. Temper tantrums, pounding a toy on the floor, or talking in a loud tone of voice are typical behaviors. Thus, they learn that such actions will get an adult to pay attention to them. Ignoring the behavior removes the reward and puts such behaviors on extinction. Of course, any behavior placed on extinction sometimes will reappear because of **spontaneous recovery.** Occasionally, children will revive the behaviors that were ignored. Continuing to disregard them should cause them to once again go away.

*Resistance to Extinction*  Sometimes behaviors resist extinction. Positive reinforcers that normally control them are removed, and the behavior continues. There are two reasons for this. *One reason behaviors resist extinction is that they were initially learned or maintained under partial reinforcement schedules.* Thus, the expectation that the reinforcement will occur next time is well developed. For example, when teaching a young child to use a spoon or fork to feed itself, plenty of attention, smiles, and praise are initially provided. As the child learns how to feed itself, a partial reward schedule takes over, and the external rewards become less frequent. Yet the expectation that "a reward might sometimes occur" maintains the proper use of forks and spoons even after a caretaker decides that positive reinforcers are no longer needed.

*A second explanation for resistance to extinction is the fact that our actions also come under the control of internal rewards (e.g., self-praise) or other external reinforcers in the environment.* A good friend was out of shape, gaining weight, and decided to cure these problems by getting more exercise. He joined a health club and began to jog, lift weights, and swim on a regular basis. His goal was to work out four times a week for an hour. Each day that he kept his schedule, he rewarded himself by watching a favorite television program. After six weeks, he stopped reinforcing his exercise with watching television. His interest in exercising, however, did not decline. One reason was that he would congratulate himself after working out by saying "nice job," "keep it up," or "you're doing real well." He made friends at the club and began to exercise with other people. Everyone was very helpful, and friendly, and they complimented each other. The latter rewards replaced watching television.

## Negative Side Effects of Rewards

While the role of rewards in acquiring behaviors might appear to be rather straightforward, they sometimes can have a number of negative side effects (Balsam and Bondy, 1983):

*Positive Reinforcers May Affect People and Events Beyond the Initial Behavior of Interest* It is difficult sometimes to do just one thing, and reinforcing certain actions may produce unintended repercussions. When the state of Michigan enacted a law to control highway litter, a 5–10-cent deposit was required on the sale of all soft drink and beer cans and bottles. State officials reasoned that the trash was now valuable, and people would be less likely to throw away something of value. If some did, those who collected trash would be rewarded for returning the cans and bottles. During the first year of the program, highway litter was cut by 70 percent. Unfortunately, several unintended effects occurred. Because the litter law encouraged the recycling of metal cans and glass bottles, it caused the loss of 213 jobs out of 900 in the beverage bottling industry in Michigan. Supermarkets also were forced to hire new employees to handle returnables. This cost one chain $2.6 million and forced it to raise food prices (UPI wire story, September 18, 1979).

*People May Concentrate on Earning a Reward and Make Performing Desirable Behavior a Secondary Goal* Managers become frustrated with workers whose only ambition appears to be to "get a paycheck at the end of the week." Teachers occasionally become disappointed because some students "grub for grades" or look for loopholes in the grading system instead of focusing on learning course content.

*The Effects of Positive Reinforcers May Not Generalize to Other Situations* Clients in psychotherapy at times maintain appropriate behaviors because of the support and caring attitude of a therapist. Once therapy is terminated, old patterns of behavior may reappear.

*External Reinforcers May Undermine Intrinsic Rewards* When people are rewarded for doing something they normally enjoy, they may begin to lose interest in continuing the task. Thus, when workers are given incentive plans for continuing to perform highly challenging and interesting jobs, they often report losing interest in those tasks (Dessler, 1982).

*The Wrong Behaviors Are Inadvertently Reinforced* In somehouseholds, getting young children to sleep becomes a battle of wills. A child throws a temper tantrum and continues to cry after being put to bed. In many cases, a parent or guardian gives in and picks the child up. In effect, the temper tantrum is rewarded. In some cases, rewarding misbehavior can become a major social problem, as illustrated in Focus on People 4.1.

*Rewards May Lose Their Attractiveness in the Long Run* Praise for a job well done has more value to someone starting out on a job than to a ten-year veteran. To an "A" student, the first "A" received in school means more than the last. In one study, increases in the size of the bonus a worker received (expressed as a percentage of current salary) was not always viewed as highly attractive. A point of diminishing returns was reached where people placed less value on the bonus (Worley et. al., 1992). Essentially, what happens is that experience with certain rewards may cause people to

## The Rewards of Misbehavior

A clique of middle-class boys, many of them top high school athletes in Lakewood, California, formed a group known as the "Spur Posse." One of their favorite activities was to keep a competitive count of how many girls they had bedded and fondled. Some claimed individual tallies into the sixties with girls as young as 10 years of age.

The incidents made national headlines when seven of the girls filed rape, sexual molestation, and other charges. Adding to the controversy was the callous attitude of the boys towards their behaviors and the belief they had done nothing wrong. They portrayed some of their victims as "sluts" and talked as if they were somehow entitled to sex with them.

Some of their parents apparently shared their sentiments. The father of one 18-year-old said, "Nothing my boy did was anything any red-blooded American boy wouldn't do at his age." Another dad said, "We used to talk about scoring in high school. What's the difference." A mother, throwing up her hands, said, "What can you do? It's a testosterone thing."

A number of rewards probably contributed to their actions. Some of the boys may have had their attitudes and behaviors inadvertently rewarded by parents who found little wrong with their actions. Since they hung out together, they also gained social recognition from each other for their actions. And, as often happens in such cases, the participants became celebrities. National talk shows, including Phil Donahue, Oprah Winfrey, and many others had them on as guests. Not only did they receive national attention for their misdeeds, but the talk show producers rewarded their participation with fancy hotels, free meals, new clothes, and stretch limousines for transportation.

Based on accounts in *Newsweek* and *Time* magazines.

discount their importance or to lose interest in them. Thus, the overuse of any given reward should be avoided.

## The Role of Negative Reinforcement

Some aversive stimuli increase the likelihood of responses that either remove them from a situation or that prevent such stimuli from recurring. They are labeled **negative reinforcers.** Aversive stimuli are events that are unpleasant to us, such as pain, loud noises, bright lights, and electric shocks. When unpleasant stimuli occur, people try to remove them by escaping (e.g., running from a burning building or closing a window to shut out street noise) or by taking actions to avoid experiencing them (e.g., stopping at a red light to avoid having an accident or changing a baby's diaper so a child will play quietly and not cry). The former response is called an **escape response**, while the latter is labeled an **avoidance response.** What type of response is involved in the actions described in Focus on People 4.2?

While escape and avoidance responses are common and helpful components of our daily behaviors, sometimes problems develop. Some people abuse drugs to escape from their problems or smoke cigarettes to lessen internal tension and frustration. Many of our fears and phobias are avoidance responses. A nephew of mine had a bad experience speaking in front of a class and began to fear other situations that involved public speaking. Courses that required student presentations were avoided, as were jobs where speaking to groups of people was necessary. Such behaviors often are difficult to unlearn. People never give themselves a chance to see that the dreaded consequence is greatly exaggerated or probably will not occur.

FOCUS ON PEOPLE 4.2

## Garbage Collectors Teach a Smelly Lesson

Tokyo, Japan, has some of the world's most detailed trash separation rules. Burnable wood, papers, and other debris must be separated from nonburnable cans, bottles, and batteries. Strict controls are needed, because the city produces 5 million tons of trash a year, and its largest landfill will fill up by March of 1996. Consequently, it is understandable that garbage collectors for the Bureau of Public Cleansing do not tolerate people who violate the rules.

The latter lesson was taught to people in Daimachi, a neighborhood in the Tokyo suburb of Hachioji. People were not following the rules, and the garbage collectors placed a sign up reminding them of the regulations. A significant number of people continued to ignore the rules anyway. The last straw occurred when someone responded by putting a bag of garbage on top of the sign.

After that, the garbage crews let the residents of Daimachi know who was in charge. Bags piled up first in the door yards of apartment buildings. Soon they began to take over parking spaces. After a few weeks they began to overflow onto sidewalks. Halfway into the fourth month, they merged in to a stinking, unbroken, block-long ridge about four feet high. A small, steady stream of murky, smelly fluid flowed half a block down a gutter to a storm drain.

The residents finally caved in. They pledged to obey the regulations, and the mounds of garbage were finally removed. Of course, they only did so after being given a lesson on the powers of negative reinforcement.

Based on a story in the *Baltimore Sun*, December 22, 1992.

## The Role of Punishment

Behavior that is punished tends to occur less frequently, and this can occur in a number of ways. *One is to allow inappropriate behavior to lead to natural and logical unpleasant consequences.* Sometimes learning from experience can be effective. A neighbor had a difficult time getting her son ready on time for school. He was slow in the morning and seemed to drag his feet. His mother rushed around in the morning trying to get him ready. One day, she decided not to do anything. He missed the school bus, and she refused to drive him to school. The following day, he was ready on time for the bus.

*In addition, some times an unpleasant stimulus is deliberately given after a response.* A parent slaps a child for misbehaving, or a manager docks the pay of workers who show up late. *Finally, something pleasant is taken away after an inappropriate behavior.* A child eating a bowl of ice cream begins to throw it on the floor, and the ice cream is removed. Or, a football player makes several bad plays and is removed from the game. A teenager returns home late from a party, and her parents forbid her to go out with friends for two weeks. In each case, a person is deprived of something he or she normally enjoys as a way to decrease some undesirable behavior. Such punishment is called a **response cost,** as in, "that'll cost you."

While punishment is a relatively popular method for controlling behavior, it has taken its "licks" as a means of controlling behavior. When aversive stimuli are used to punish, a number of problems are likely to occur (Walters and Grusec, 1977; Balsam and Bondy, 1983). Frustration and anger often develop and people may focus more on "getting even" than on learning anything new from the experience. Or, as sometimes happens, they avoid situations or become fearful in places where they were punished. This make further learning difficult.

Perhaps the biggest problem is that some people do not know the distinction between punishment and abuse. Punishment is designed to help people learn. *Abuse, on the other hand, is the use of aversive stimuli to purposely and unjustly mistreat another person. Abuse involves using severe levels of aversive stimuli than are necessary to correct a behavior.* This typically happens when people try to dominate and control another person, or, when they take their anger out on others because they cannot handle their personal frustrations in more acceptable ways. Several examples of the latter problem are described in Focus on People 4.3.

In spite of such problems, research evidence suggests that when used with care, common sense, and in a nonabusive manner, punishment can be an effective means of controlling behaviors (Avery and Ivancevich, 1980; Parke, 1977). To do this, the following principles for administering punishment should be kept in mind:

*Punishment Is More Effective When Applied Immediately* Examples of violations of this principle are rather common. I recently observed a supervisor reprimand an employee for something that occurred two days earlier. A neighbor waited until late afternoon to punish a child for misbehavior that occurred that morning. Delays in administering punishment do not suppress undesirable responses very well. They also leave someone confused, because actions leading to the punishment are less likely to be as well remembered.

*The Magnitude of the Punishment Should "Fit the Crime"* In supermarkets and department stores, for example, frustrated parents spank young children for touching boxes and cans of food or running ahead of the shopping cart. A verbal reprimand or

---

### FOCUS ON PEOPLE 4.3
## Abuse Disguised as Punishment

The use of corporal punishment to discipline children has been an issue of debate among teachers, school administrators, and parents for a number of years. The majority of school systems in the United States permit it, but the practice has, in some cases, gotten out of hand. Students have been punished in ways that are humiliating and that border on impinging on their constitutional rights not to be subjected to cruel and unusual punishment (Hyman, 1984). In such cases, what happens to them would better be labeled abuse. Irwin Hyman reported the following examples to illustrate what some adults consider to be "fair punishment" but what by any reasonable standards would constitute abuse.

- A Georgia high school student was forced to take part in a punishment drill called running the "gauntlet" for quitting the football team and then returning. His teammates lined up and punched and kicked him as he ran between two lines of teammates. He sustained a large gash over his eye requiring stitches, and X rays revealed a possible hairline fracture.

- A Florida youth was paddled for misbehavior in the classroom by a teacher. He was hospitalized for four days after being paddled and upon release was confined to a wheelchair for several weeks.

- A Missouri high school principal caught three boys with cigarettes in their pockets. He gave them a choice of either paddling or eating the cigarettes. Two of the boys chose to eat a total of 18 cigarettes. Both immediately developed medical problems. One sustained a kidney infection, while the other irritated an ulcer and vomited large amounts of blood.

Irwin Hyman also notes that students have been abused by being stuck with pins, standing on their toes for long periods of time, having parts of their hair cut, lying on a wet shower floor for long periods of time, and being tied to a chair with a rope. He argues that criminals have more protection from abuse and unusual forms of punishment than do children in our schools. What do you think?

taking the child out of the area until he or she agrees to behave would be much more appropriate, given the severity of the offense.

*Punishment Must Be Consistently Applied* People need to know what to expect if they misbehave. Thus, the expectations of parents, coaches, supervisors, and teachers for appropriate behavior should be shared and the consequences of misbehavior clearly stated. Otherwise, attempts at "beating the system," "cheating," or "seeing what I can get away with" will increase.

*Punishment Should Be Limited to Specific Responses* A client of mine used to beat his son because "he was stupid." A caller to a radio talk show I was on said that he periodically beat his children once a week whether or not they needed it. "It will make them better people," he said. Such actions are inappropriate and would better be labeled abuse. Punishment is best used to correct specific acts of misbehavior in order to help people learn a proper way to do something very specific. It should never be used indiscriminately to correct something as global as "stupidity" or to make someone a "better person."

*Punishment Should Be Humanely and Sensitively Applied* The worst abuses occur when people use it to "get even," to "teach someone a lesson he will never forget," or when they are caught in a fit of personal anger and rage. *A humane use of punishment means that the physical and psychological well-being of the other person will be preserved.* Alternatives to aversive stimuli should be emphasized. For example, using a response cost procedure and taking away children's privileges, having them do extra household work to pay for breaking a household object, or having them stand in a corner or stay in their rooms are humane alternatives to beating.

## The Role of Organization and Planning

Learning takes a certain amount of discipline, and the tasks we want to learn and master must become a priority in our lives. To do this, it is important both to set aside time to learn and to develop a plan for engaging in tasks designed to help us acquire information and skills. Without a certain amount of organization and planning, such things as practice, feedback, and reinforcement will do us little good.

*Effective Time Management Aids Learning* Bruce Britton and Abraham Tesser (1991) administered a time management questionnaire to 90 college students at the beginning of their freshman year. Four years later their cumulative grade point average (GPA) was obtained, and the attitudes and behaviors that were the best predictors of GPA were identified. Table 4.3 shows which ones were associated with higher grades.

Short-term planning and attitudes towards the use of time were the best predictors of college grades. Together they were a better predictor of GPA than was a measure of general academic ability (i.e., students' SAT scores). Teresa Hoff Macan and her colleagues (1990) also report that students' time management skills were related to better grades. In addition, those who managed their time well had less stress. They also were more satisfied with school and their lives in general.

Do different types of planning and scheduling make a difference on grades? According to Daniel Kirschenbaum (1982) and his colleagues, the answer to that question is yes. In this study, the use of flexible monthly planning in combination with rewards to encourage participants to persist in achieving their goals was compared to

| **Table 4.3** | Time Management Practices of Successful Students |
| --- | --- |

The following behaviors and attitudes were among the best predictors of the cumulative grade point average of students after four years of college.

**Short-Range Planning**

Make a list of things to do each day.

Plan a day before starting it.

Schedule activities that must be done.

Have a clear idea of what must be accomplished next week.

Set and honor priorities.

**Attitudes Toward Time**

Do not do things others ask me to do that interfere with school work.

On school days, spend more time with schoolwork than other activities.

Believe there is room for improvement in how time is managed.

Make constructive use of time.

Seldom work on assignments the night before they are due.

Do not continue with unprofitable routines or activities.

Adapted from information presented by Britton and Tesser (1991).

other methods. The results of this rather remarkable study are illustrated in Focus on Applied Research 4.1.

Flexible monthly planning in conjunction with weekly and monthly rewards led to better performance in school than did the other methods. One reason is that people do not have to feel bad about themselves if they miss a day or two. There is still time to make up the work. The rewards also provided an incentive to stick with the plan. Finally, Daniel Kirschenbaum reports that students using monthly plans felt much more in control of their time. In effect, the schedule did not control them. They controlled their schedule.

# REMEMBERING WHAT WAS LEARNED

Our ability to learn also depends upon our ability to remember previous ideas and behaviors. After all, to acquire information, we must take it into our memory system. This involves encoding it in some form such as a verbal label or mental image, storing it for later use, and then later retrieving the material. Thus, learning and retention are interdependent processes. In trying to understand retention, variations on two major theories appear in the literature. They are the **memory system approach** and the **levels-of-processing** point of view.

## The Memory System

*Sensory Register, Short-Term, and Long-Term Memory*   One retention model suggests that three interrelated memory components are involved—a sensory, short-term, and long-term memory system (Atkinson and Shiffrin, 1968). Initially, information from the environment enters a **sensory register.** This is a brief sensory trace of the

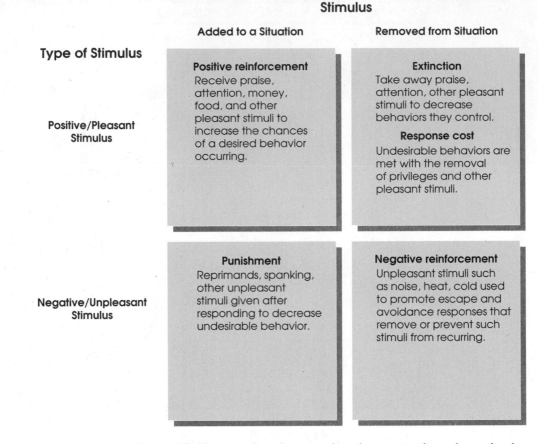

**Stimulus**

| Type of Stimulus | Added to a Situation | Removed from Situation |
|---|---|---|
| **Positive/Pleasant Stimulus** | **Positive reinforcement** Receive praise, attention, money, food, and other pleasant stimuli to increase the chances of a desired behavior occurring. | **Extinction** Take away praise, attention, other pleasant stimuli to decrease behaviors they control. **Response cost** Undesirable behaviors are met with the removal of privileges and other pleasant stimuli. |
| **Negative/Unpleasant Stimulus** | **Punishment** Reprimands, spanking, other unpleasant stimuli given after responding to decrease undesirable behavior. | **Negative reinforcement** Unpleasant stimuli such as noise, heat, cold used to promote escape and avoidance responses that remove or prevent such stimuli from recurring. |

**Figure 4.3** *The ways that pleasant and unpleasant stimuli can be employed to change and modify behavior.*

information and occurs in each of our senses. For example, with visual information, the rods and cones in our eyes begin to send a pattern of nerve impulses along the optic nerve to visual centers of the brain. This pattern forms a "visual image," or copy, of the stimulus, which usually lasts no longer than 1.5 seconds. With auditory stimuli, the auditory nerve and hearing centers in the brain are stimulated. An "echo" remains and generally disappears completely within 3 to 4 seconds (Sperling, 1969; Cowan, 1988).

Visual and auditory images are unprocessed or unanalyzed sensory information. However, if we focus our attention on aspects of this sensory input (e.g., a point a teacher makes in class, a sentence in a book), our brains begin to analyze it for importance and meaning. This cognitive processing condenses sensory information, identifies important features and patterns, keeps the major details, and allows us to later retrieve it. This further analysis of the sensory information takes place in two stages. One involves the **short-term memory** system and the other the **long-term memory** system.

Short-term memory takes visual and auditory information from the sensory register and transforms it into an acoustic code. This acoustic code stores information for a relatively short amount of time (e.g., less than a minute) and has limits on how much can be stored. The short-term memory for information that is presented once lasts for about thirty seconds and has a limited capacity of seven plus or minus two units of information. That is, after a single presentation, about five to nine items of information are retained for a relatively short period of time.

FOCUS ON APPLIED RESEARCH 4.1

## Improving Grades with Monthly Planning

During their second semester in college, 63 freshmen volunteered to participate in an 11-week study improvement program (Kirschenbaum et. al., 1982). Participants were assigned to one of three groups. One group was taught how to develop specific daily hour-by-hour schedules. This included what they would study and where and when they would do it.

The second group was shown how to develop a moderately specific monthly schedule, as illustrated in Figure 4.4 (see next page). Note that this schedule asks participants to identify what needs to be done in their courses over a four-week period. Instead of planning a specific time to do something, people simply indicate, for example, that they have Monday, Wednesday, or Sunday to read their chemistry assignment and to

complete the problems in Chapter 2. They were free to do the assignments any time they could during these three days. If they did nothing on one day, they had to catch up on their work on the remaining two days. Also note in Figure 4.4 that there was a weekly reward as well as a monthly reward for completing all study assignments successfully.

The third group was not taught how to develop a schedule. An additional control group of students not enrolled in the program but having similar academic abilities was used.

*The effects on student's grade point averages before and after the eleven-week study skills course and six months and one year afterwards are shown in Figure 4.5.*

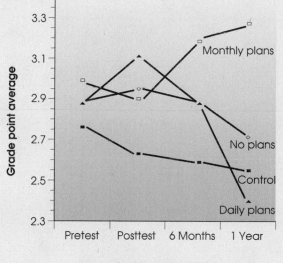

**Figure 4.5** *Changes in GPA as a function of the type of study plan participants developed.*

(D. S. Kirschenbaum et al. Specificity of planning and the maintenance of self-control: One year follow-up at a study management program. *Behavior Therapy,* 1982, *13,* 232–240. ©1982 by the Association for Advancement of Behavior Therapy. Reprinted by permission.)

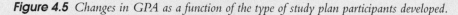

Without rehearsal designed to maintain the information, the memory loss occurs rather rapidly, as shown in Figure 4.6. With **maintenance rehearsal** and some preliminary organization of the information, it can be retained in short-term memory for relatively longer periods of time. Think about what most people do after reading a telephone number from the directory and then walking a short distance to a phone. They maintain the number in short-term memory by repeating it several times and organizing it to facilitate retention. Thus, the numbers 5128716784 are repeated and organized

## Continued

### Example of a Monthly Plan

Flow Chart: Plans for This Month

Name _____    For Month _____

Today's Date _____

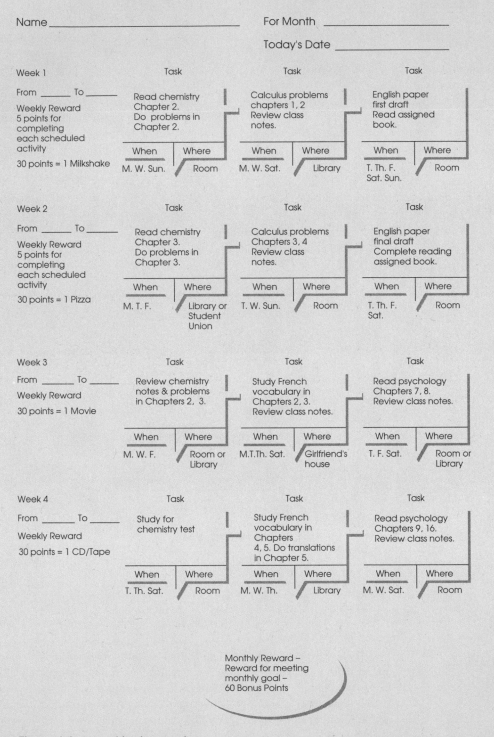

| Week 1 | Task | Task | Task |
| --- | --- | --- | --- |
| From _____ To _____ | Read chemistry Chapter 2. Do problems in Chapter 2. | Calculus problems chapters 1, 2 Review class notes. | English paper first draft Read assigned book. |
| Weekly Reward 5 points for completing each scheduled activity | When: M. W. Sun. / Where: Room | When: M. W. Sat. / Where: Library | When: T. Th. F. Sat. Sun. / Where: Room |
| 30 points = 1 Milkshake | | | |

| Week 2 | Task | Task | Task |
| --- | --- | --- | --- |
| From _____ To _____ | Read chemistry Chapter 3. Do problems in Chapter 3. | Calculus problems Chapters 3, 4 Review class notes. | English paper final draft Complete reading assigned book. |
| Weekly Reward 5 points for completing each scheduled activity | When: M. T. F. / Where: Library or Student Union | When: T. W. Sun. / Where: Room | When: T. Th. F. Sat. / Where: Room |
| 30 points = 1 Pizza | | | |

| Week 3 | Task | Task | Task |
| --- | --- | --- | --- |
| From _____ To _____ | Review chemistry notes & problems in Chapters 2, 3. | Study French vocabulary in Chapters 2, 3. Review class notes. | Read psychology Chapters 7, 8. Review class notes. |
| Weekly Reward | When: M. W. F. / Where: Room or Library | When: M.T.Th. Sat. / Where: Girlfriend's house | When: T. F. Sat. / Where: Room or Library |
| 30 points = 1 Movie | | | |

| Week 4 | Task | Task | Task |
| --- | --- | --- | --- |
| From _____ To _____ | Study for chemistry test | Study French vocabulary in Chapters 4, 5. Do translations in Chapter 5. | Read psychology Chapters 9, 16. Review class notes. |
| Weekly Reward | When: T. Th. Sat. / Where: Room | When: M. W. Th. / Where: Library | When: M. W. Sat. / Where: Room |
| 30 points = 1 CD/Tape | | | |

Monthly Reward –
Reward for meeting
monthly goal –
60 Bonus Points

**Figure 4.4** *A monthly planning sheet.*

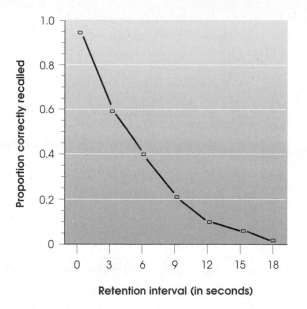

**Figure 4.6** *Retention of three consonants over 18 seconds. Subjects hear three consonants and then have to count backward by threes from a given number (e.g., 458). After an interval, they are asked to recall the consonants. Under these conditions, forgetting is quite rapid (adapted from Peterson and Peterson, 1959).*

into "chunks" by breaking them up into their parts (e.g., 512-871-6784). The number is then associated with the name and other characteristics of the person to whom it belongs.

This process is rather fragile and easily disrupted, as illustrated by a study of people trying to remember new telephone numbers (Schilling and Weaver, 1983). The telephone company wanted the operators to say "Have a nice day" after giving the number. Participants who listened to "Have a nice day" made twice as many errors recalling unfamiliar telephone numbers as did people not given the salutation. Apparently the operator's message interfered with their ability to use rehearsal to remember the numbers.

Short-term memory is basically our working memory. It is the memory for the things that are the focus of attention at the moment. Some of what we deal with at any given moment in time is also likely to be useful in the future. Thus, it needs to be transferred into long-term memory. To do this, information undergoes **elaborative rehearsal.** This occurs when information is actively analyzed and related to material that is already stored. When studying, you use elaborative rehearsal when you encounter a new term or concept (e.g., short-term memory) and ask, "What are the unique features of short-term memory?" "How is it similar and different from the sensory register or long-term memory?" This elaboration transfers selected material to long-term memory and into a more permanent memory code (Melton, 1963). It is later retrieved into short-term memory in order for us to put it to use.

Elaboration transfers the information into a memory code that has several characteristics (Tulving, 1972). One is information about the time something was learned and the context in which it was learned. This is called **episodic memory** or the memory for episodes in your life. Memories of your high school graduation or first job are examples of information stored in this manner. Second, the basic meaning of words and concepts are stored without reference to their time and place in your experiences. This is called **semantic memory** and resembles an encyclopedia more than an autobiography. The meaning associated with information in long-term memory also includes mental images associated with material that was learned. Third, items we learn also are coded with a verbal or semantic code and with a mental imagery code. The ability to imagine what something looks like aids retention.

Of course, we learn and remember more than verbal information. A variety of motor skills such as driving a car, swimming, playing a musical instrument, and other skills are acquired. They also are retained for long periods of time. **Procedural memory** is a term used to refer to this third type of information that is stored in long-term memory. When a motor skill is needed (e.g., you want to ride a bike), each part of the procedure is recalled without your awareness and automatically triggers the next component in the sequence (Squire, 1987). Procedural memory does not rely on verbal labels. This can be seen by trying to describe how you ride a bike, balance yourself on one foot, or do a complicated dive off a diving board.

## The Levels-of-Processing Approach to Understanding Memory

From this point of view, memory is seen as an active process in which information is analyzed at various levels and later reconstructed (Craik, 1979; Lockhart and Craik, 1990). For example, when given something to learn, e.g., the word "table," you could analyze it in terms of its physical features (i.e., how many letters it has), how it sounds (i.e., does it sound like Mable?), or what the word means (i.e., define a table and give two examples). The first is a rather shallow analysis that involves a simple letter count. To decide whether it sounds like something involves a little more mental effort, while analyzing aspects of its meaning takes the most mental effort. The additional mental effort should pay off in how well something is remembered, and this appears to be the case.

The levels-of-processing view argues that the rapid forgetting of material presented once is due to the shallow acoustic analysis given to it. The persistence of information in long-term memory is related to the deeper level of processing it receives. That is, information is transformed into a memory code based on meaning. Thinking about what something means is a more complex and difficult cognitive task than analyzing the information into an acoustic code.

*Processing information to a deeper level implies spending time to attach relevant semantic and imagery codes.* This can occur automatically, or we might need to consciously force ourselves to do it. For example, when meeting someone new for the first time, you might categorize their facial features as "friendly" or "intelligent." This analyzes the face to a deeper level and increases your chances of later remembering it. Similarly, giving his or her name additional meaning would also improve retention. Ask yourself several questions after being introduced, such as "What does this name sound like?" "What does he or she do for a living?" "What images does the name remind me of?"

# EXPLANATIONS FOR FORGETTING

## Decay of the Memory Trace

The decay of the memory trace for information appears to be a factor in the loss of information in sensory memory. Also, when the rehearsal of information is prevented, decay of the memory trace probably accounts for forgetting in short-term memory.

When information is rehearsed in short-term memory or when it is subsequently transferred to long-term memory, factors other than the decay of the trace are responsible for our inability to remember.

## Failure to Retrieve Information

Our long-term memory system is thought to have an unlimited capacity. Once information enters, it stays there forever. The failure to remember something is not due to information dropping out of the system. Rather, memory losses reflect problems with people's ability to retrieve some of the knowledge they possess. Think of storage in long-term memory as similar to the storage of books on shelves in a library. Thus, long-term memory can be improved by giving information good "call numbers" (e.g., strong verbal and imagery codes) when it is initially teamed or by searching the "shelves" properly to find it.

*Our emotional state at the time of learning and the time of recall affects retention.* When the mood a person is in during learning matches the mood he is in when asked to recall, retention is improved. When instructed to feel sad, people remember more unpleasant past experiences than when instructed to feel happy (Ellis and Ashbrook, 1989). Similarly, individuals remember more happy childhood experiences when instructed to experience a happy mood (Bower, 1981; Snyder and White, 1982). Such research suggests that part of the memory code for the things we learn contains information about our emotional state at the time of learning. This relationship is illustrated in Figure 4.7.

Emotional cues may help to facilitate retrieval up to a point. Extremely strong emotions when trying to recall something, for example, interfere with rather than facilitate our ability to remember. During a classroom exam, for example, students who are highly test-anxious do not perform very well (Loftus, 1980).

Overall, with the exception of reading information from the sensory register, the retrieval of information in short- and long-term memory is a dynamic process. It is

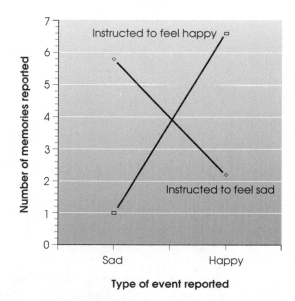

**Figure 4.7** *Number of memories reported when participants were instructed to feel happy or sad and then to report experiences of the past week (based on Snyder and White, 1982).*

more than simply finding its call number and pulling it off of the appropriate library shelf. *Recall forces us to reconstruct, reproduce, or recreate the original information from a variety of memory codes.*

## Interference Among Memory Traces

Memory traces for old and new information may interfere with each other. This often happens when the old and new information is similar. Thus, confusion occurs over what response is correct. When an old memory interferes with something learned recently, **proactive interference** has occurred. The birthdays of old boyfriends and girlfriends might make it difficult to remember new friends' birthdays; or concepts in sociology learned last term interfere with learning how psychologists explain similar events. **Retroactive interference** occurs when a new memory interferes with an older memory. Remembering the accomplishments of fourteenth- and fifteenth-century monarchs on a history test is more difficult after you studied sixteenth- and seventeenth-century monarchs a few days before the exam.

# IMPROVING YOUR MEMORY

## Overlearn Information

**Overlearning** refers to a special kind of practice that enhances our ability to remember the knowledge and skills we acquire. To overlearn something, it must be practiced beyond the time that it takes to acquire it. Overlearning is one reason why most of us can remember the words to popular songs, nursery rhymes, poetry, and foreign language vocabulary years after initially learning such things. Singing a favorite tune to yourself, for example, when it first appears on the record charts adds more than a little enjoyment to your life. Practicing it long after you have learned the words and melody increases your ability to remember it.

In a review of the research literature, James Driskell, Ruth Willis, and Carolyn Cooper (1992) report that the effects of overlearning apply to a variety of job-related skills as well as those used in hobbies and sports. Training beyond the point of initial proficiency allows people to gain additional practice as well as feedback on how well they execute a response. And when the retention of cognitive information versus skills are compared, overlearning is a powerful factor in the retention of both but is even more so for motor skills (Driskell et. al., 1992). With verbal information as well as with skills, overlearning works by strengthening the memory trace for what was practiced. Such research suggests that people retain information at least twice as long after overlearning it.

There are a number of ways to obtain the benefits of overlearning. *To begin, develop a habit of periodically reviewing information you obtained in class sessions and readings.* When preparing for an exam, go over your notes one to three more times after you feel that "I really know it." Look for opportunities while riding the bus, taking a walk, or waiting for an appointment to rehearse mentally information you have just learned.

*Rereading a textbook or a set of readings also produces the benefits of overlearning.* In some cases, people who reread did better on tests of retention for facts, concepts, and principles than those who took notes, outlined, or summarized the written information (Anderson, 1980; Barnett and Seefeldt, 1989). The benefits on retention of rereading for students with relatively low and high levels of academic ability are illustrated in Figure 4.8. Finally, when acquiring new skills, continue to practice beyond the point where an initial proficiency is obtained. This is particularly true of skills that you might only use periodically.

## Categorize Information

*Grouping information helps, because it enables us to overcome limitations in our short-term memory system.* The magic number 7 plus or minus 2 describes the number of items people can handle in short-term memory after a single presentation (Miller, 1956). When telephone numbers, credit card numbers, addresses, and other information exceed 9 items of information, they become much more difficult to remember. One way to overcome this problem is to "chunk," or regroup, larger amounts of information into smaller groupings. Thus, the number string 1776198420011942 is remembered better if it is not thought of as a series of single digits. Instead, think of it as the years 1776-1984-2001-1942. Or a group of 28 letters   N-F   L-F-B I-I-B-   M-U   S -A-N-A   S-A-M-T-V-V   C   R-I-R   S-C-B-S   can be remembered much better if they are chunked as:

   NFL    FBI    IBM    USA    NASA    MTV    VCR    IRS    CBS

Similarly, the words "time," "stick," "stitch," "in," "softly," "carry," "a," "speak," "a," "saves," and, "nine," "big" are a lot more meaningful when put into the sentences: "A stitch in time saves nine" and "Speak softly and carry a big stick."

Figure 4.9 illustrates how chunking leads to an exceptional memory. Essentially, looking for patterns allowed both subjects to exceed the limits of the magic number 7 plus or minus 2. This skill, however, takes time to develop and can be observed in other areas. Football coaches and people who had played but not coached were asked to look at diagrams of plays for 5 seconds. They then were asked to reconstruct the X's and O's, arrows, and other elements of the play. When logical and legitimate football plays were shown, the coaches were far superior in reproducing that play. They recalled an average

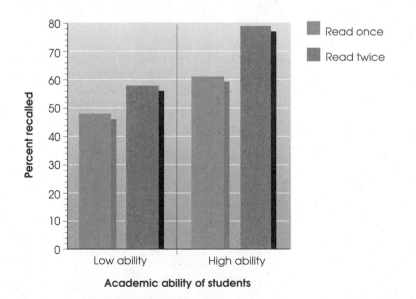

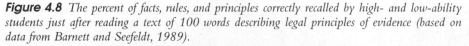

**Figure 4.8** *The percent of facts, rules, and principles correctly recalled by high- and low-ability students just after reading a text of 100 words describing legal principles of evidence (based on data from Barnett and Seefeldt, 1989).*

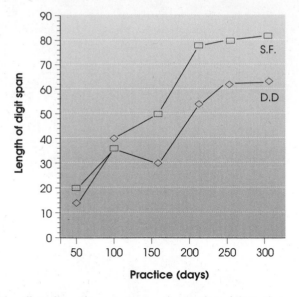

**Figure 4.9** *The effect of practice on increasing the number of digits that can be recalled after a single presentation. Normally, people can remember a string of random numbers 5 to 7 items long after a single presentation. Both S. F. and D. D. were college students who developed personal systems for chunking digits that were presented to them. They were able to remember random strings of numbers 60 to 80 digits in length after a single presentation. S. F. was a long-distance runner and categorized sequences of numbers into a set of running times. For example, he would remember 3,492 as 3 minutes and 49.2 seconds ("a near world record"). In addition, he used digits to represent years, and thus 1944 would be remembered as "near the end of World War II." He taught D. D. how to use his system.*

("Exceptional, Memory," by K. A. Eticsson and W. G. Chase. *American Scientist* 70:607–614, 1982, Fig. 1, page 608. Reprinted by permission of *American Scientist,* journal of Sigma Xi, The Scientific Research Society.)

of 22 elements, while the non-coaches remembered about 6 elements. The coaches were able to use their superior knowledge of patterns in the plays to later reproduce them. When the plays shown were illogical (i.e., violated the rules for a good play), both groups remembered about 5-9 elements (Garland and Barry, 1991).

Our cognitive system often groups related information into appropriate categories naturally. This facilitates being able to retrieve information and helps us relate one thing to another. *You can help this natural tendency by looking for ways to categorize information.* Sentences such as, "Several keys were needed to form a word" and, "The notes were sour because the seam split" become meaningful when assigned to categories like "typing a letter" and "playing a bagpipe." *Assigning information to categories enhances retention, because it gives information additional meaning.*

One way to benefit from "chunking" is to organize your notes from presentations, outside readings, and major points from the text into a combined outline. Organizing information to be learned pays off. Donald Dickinson and Debra O'Connell (1990) reported that students with high test scores spent an average of 43 minutes a week organizing information from readings and class notes. Those with low test scores spent an average of 10 minutes per week organizing material.

When developing an organization, topic headings within outside readings or a textbook might suggest categories to use. For example, you could use this technique to combine information from this book and class sessions. Helpful categories might include things like Characteristics of Reinforcement, Problems with Punishment, and Techniques for Improving Memory. Related information then can be grouped into categories using a traditional outline format similar to one found in a detailed table of contents in most textbooks.

On the other hand, information can be combined by creating a **cognitive map** (McCagg and Dansereau, 1991; Gold, 1984). A cognitive map is a special way to categorize information to give it personal meaning. Pictures, charts, drawings, or diagrams are used to form an accurate but personally meaningful representation of something you want to learn. One example of a cognitive map to represent characteristics of our memory system is shown in Figure 4.10. Note that related concepts are grouped together and the relationships between various categories are shown. Research shows that students who use a cognitive map to organize information have significantly higher exam scores than those who study the same information employing normal study techniques (McCagg and Dansereau, 1991).

## Elaborate on Information

Elaborate or embellish information that you are learning. This will force you to analyze it in more detail and to process it to a deeper and more meaningful level. There are a number of things that can help here.

*Get Beyond the Facts, and Integrate Information* When studying for multiple-choice exams, many students tend to focus on specific facts. Yet, when preparing for essay exams, they tend to focus on basic facts as well as trying to integrate those facts into a larger context. The latter strategy processes information to a deeper level. It also improves scores on multiple-choice exams. Paul Foos and Cherie Clark (1984) demonstrated this by telling two groups of students to expect an essay or a multiple-choice exam. Both groups were given the multiple-choice exam, and those who prepared for the essay exam made the highest exam scores.

*React to What You Are Learning in Writing* Paul Hettich (1976) advises people to record their reflections, ideas, and any new insights about information in a journal. This would include relating material to your past and present experiences. Cynthia Hynd (1990) and her colleagues also recommend annotating or writing comments, reflections, and ideas in the margins of a book you are reading. In effect, you have an ongoing dialogue with the author. She reports that students who either keep journals or write comments in the margins perform better on exams than those who do not. Furthermore, people who placed comments in the margins of a book did better on multiple-choice exams. Both techniques were equally effective with essay exams.

Some people underline or use an outliner pen to highlight important information. Can this substitute for keeping a journal or writing comments in the margins of a book? Research suggests that it is not as effective, but it is better than doing nothing while you read. In a discussion of the research on this issue, Linda Johnson (1988) reports that highlighting or underlining important material enhances retention under certain conditions. This is when people think about the meaning and implications of ideas they are reading before deciding what to highlight or underline. Thus, they are

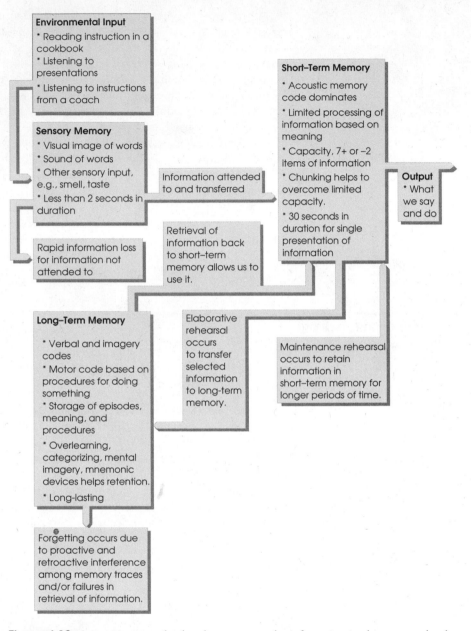

**Figure 4.10** *A cognitive map developed to represent the information in the text on the three components of our memory system. A cognitive map can be a picture, chart, drawing, diagram, or any other device that provides an accurate but personally meaningful organization to information.*

going beyond merely rehearsing the information to mentally elaborate on it. When people focus on individual sentences rather than the relationships in the whole paragraph, only information in the underlined sentences are retained rather than an overall sense of important issues and concepts.

*Ask Yourself Questions About the Material and Try To Answer Them* The SQ3R technique described earlier was one way to do this. Simply writing a question and trying to answer it anytime one occurs to you is another. Robert Bjork (1979) finds that *the best questions get us to look at the broader implications of terms, concepts, and principles we want to master.* Particularly effective for enhancing retention are questions that make us figure out how a concept applies in different contexts or settings. An example of such a question in a history course would be: "What implications did the Watergate break-in have for governmental self-regulation, potential candidates for the presidency, and how other nations viewed the United States?" In a psychology class, it might be: "How does a conditioned response help us explain the reactions of Pavlov's dogs in his laboratory, a fear of heights, and test anxiety?"

## Use Mental Imagery

Before your children acquire a language, they undoubtedly categorize people and objects in their environment using **mental images.** Familiar things are recognized because they match some internal representation of them. As we grow older, less emphasis is placed on images. The use of words to categorize people, objects, and other events becomes more important because of the stress on verbal learning in our society and school systems.

In spite of such training, people still manage to use images. At one extreme are individuals with *eidetic,* or photographic, memories. Such people are able to remember all the details of a photograph or visual scene and even entire pages of a textbook. In addition, the storage of information in memory involves assigning meaning to information often in the form of a verbal and imagery memory code (Bower, 1970). This typically occurs automatically without much conscious thought on our parts.

However, since information assigned an imagery code is learned faster and remembered longer, consciously forcing ourselves to form images of information to be learned can improve our memory. For example, in learning a new name, associate a mental image to the name. The infamous John Doe gets transformed into an image of that person with a deerlike face. Concepts like the flow of electricity, the structure of molecules, and historical events can be transformed into real or imaginary images. Thus, the flow of electricity is visualized as similar to water flowing through pipes, and imagining vivid battle scenes can assist with remembering important details of warfare during the American Civil War.

## Use Mnemonic Devices

**Mnemonic devices** are memory aids, and a variety of them are available to help enhance our retention. Such memory aids work because they enhance our ability to associate or link things we want to learn together. Mnemonic devices essentially create a distinct memory code (i.e., stressing verbal and imaginal information), and they help to organize, chunk, and structure material. As a result, less memorable information becomes almost "unforgettable." In effect, such devices facilitate our ability to encode information and to later retrieve it. Several examples are illustrated below.

*Acoustics* Acoustics are short phrases in which the first letter of each word functions to help you to recall something. The order of notes E, G, B, D, F on the lines of a musical scale are remembered with the phrase "*Every Good Boy Does Fine.*"

*Rhymes* A rhyme, on the other hand, connects items in a short rhyming phrase or poem to help you remember. One that many of us have used for placement of "i" and "e" when spelling is "I before E except after C." The number of days in the month becomes, "Thirty days hath September, April, June, and November. All the rest have 31, except February, which stands alone." One of my students employed the following rhyme to remember characteristics of our memory system.

> Like magic, the sensory register disappears quick.
>
> It takes repetition, however, to make short-term memory stick.
>
> Elaborate and add a little meaning into this mix,
>
> And, your long-term memory will soon be fixed.

*Music* Various types of music also have memory-enhancing qualities. For example, Richard Yalch (1991) reports that 60 percent of prime time television commercials use musical jingles to help make the message memorable. He finds that brand names of products are recalled significantly better when used in a jingle than when the message is simply spoken.

In another study, information about minerals was remembered much better when it was presented in the form of a song (Chazin and Neuschatz, 1991). Another showed that dramatic improvements in remembering the original 13 colonies in the United States were obtained when their names were attached to the tune "Yankee Doodle" (Gfeller, 1986). Repeating names, dates, definitions of terms, and foreign language vocabulary in cadence with the beat of a piece of music (i.e., typically classical music) has long been a suggestion found in popular study programs (cf. Lofland, 1992). Recent experimental evidence is beginning to suggest that such advice may have some merit.

*Acronyms* These are memorable words that are formed out of the first letter of each item in a string of words that would otherwise be difficult items to associate. RICE, for example, stands for advice on taking care of an ankle sprain (i.e., *R*est, *I*ce, *C*ompress, *E*levate), while HOMES helps us to remember the names of the great lakes (i.e., *H*uron, *O*ntario, *M*ichigan, *E*rie, *S*uperior). Another student in my course used the acronym TRAP to remember key elements of learning presented earlier: *T*ime on task, *R*einforcement, *A*ctive practice, and *P*unishment. One person even developed a nonsense word PREFAT in order to add *E*xtinction and *F*eedback to the above list of key elements in learning.

*Narratives* These are short storys that contain the items to be remembered. Instead of trying to memorize by rote repetition, the story puts what would otherwise be disconnected words into a meaningful context. To see how this works, first repeat the 12 items in the following list once; pause for 5 seconds, and try to write them in order. Next, form a short story that connects each of the words together. Consider the example below.

1. Automobile   2. Railroad   3. Book   4. Monkey   5. Wallet   6. Carpet

7. Watch   8. Hand   9. Key   10. Window   11. Neck   12. Door

> I patiently waited in my *automobile* by a *railroad* crossing reading a *book* while a slow freight train passed. To my surprise, a *monkey* climbed into my car and grabbed my *wallet* and threw it on the *carpet*. He then reached for my

*watch;* but I smacked his *hand,* and he retaliated by snatching my car *keys* and throwing them out the *window.* I grabbed his *neck,* opened the *door,* and threw him on the passing train.

Narrative is a very powerful device for enhancing retention. In one study, participants learned 12 lists of disconnected words with each list containing 12 items. People in the "narrative group" were required to recall the words by making up a story about them. Those in the control group were not given any special instructions. Overall, everyone eventually had to learn 144 items. *Control group participants recalled an average of 14 percent of the items, while the "narrative" group recalled an average of 94 percent of the items* (Bower and Clark, 1969).

*Substitutions* Robert Sandstrom (1990) reports that converting relatively abstract material into something that is concrete makes it more easily remembered. The name Makowski, for example, would be hard to remember. But if you substitute a picture formed from the sounds in the name, it becomes easier to remember. Thus, imagine the name as your Ma on a Cow that is Skiing down a hill. Another popular substitution replaces numbers with letters in the alphabet (Budworth, 1991). In this case, digits are substituted for consonants in the alphabet, and vowels are then used to fill in the gaps so that a memorable word or phrase can be formed. In translating the word or phrase back to numbers, the consonants are then substituted for the numbers. Table 4.4 illustrates how to do this.

*Keywords* Richard Atkinson (1975) developed a clever system to use mental imagery to facilitate learning foreign language vocabulary. The idea is to take a foreign language word, (e.g., the Spanish *caballo,* which is pronounced cob-eye-o) and to isolate a sound in its pronunciation that has an English equivalent. In this case the English sound "eye" can be heard in its pronunciation. This sound is called a *keyword.* The idea is to form an image of the English sound and the translation of the foreign word. *Caballo* means "horse" in Spanish. Thus, an image might be formed of a horse kicking an eye or perhaps a horse with a giant eye coming out of its head. Several examples of this method with other foreign languages appear in Table 4.5 and Figure 4.11.

Keywords do not have to be single words. They could include several words, phrases, or even partial words. The method also is not confined to foreign languages and has been employed in a variety of settings where learning vocabulary is an issue (cf. Rosenheck et al., 1989; Roberts, 1985; Troutt-Ervin, 1990). Consider the following examples.

1. *Geology.* The mineral pyrite is used in the manufacture of explosives. To learn the characteristics of this mineral, assign the keyword "pie" to pyrite. Assign the keyword "sticks" to represent its hardness level of 6, and use the image of a box of dynamite to represent the mineral's major use. Now combine them. Imagine a pie resting on a box of dynamite that is on top of a burning pile of sticks. And above all, "watch out!"

2. *Botany.* Angiosperms are flowering plants. Think of the key word "angel," and imagine an angel holding a bouquet of flowers in her hands.

3. *English vocabulary.* A demagogue is a "rabble rouser." Imagine a "Demon Hog" causing trouble by chasing people around a house. Or, "taciturn," which means "disin-

| **Table 4.4** | A Substitution System for Converting Numbers to Words or Phrases |

The steps to follow include:

- Memorize a list of consonants that are associated with the digits 0–10. The list below is one that I have used to teach this system.
- Substitute one of the consonants for each digit in a string of numbers.
- Add vowels when necessary between the consonants to form a memorable word or phrase or a memorable nonsense word or phrase.

0 = Z, S: The letter Z appears in the word zero, and the number 0 is all curves, as is the letter S.

1 = T, D: Both have a single downstroke.

2 = N, H: They have two straight lines in them.

3 = m, Y: They have three lines in them.

4 = R, W: R is the last letter in the word four, and the letter W has four lines in it.

5 = V, L: The latin V means 5, and L is 50.

6 = b, J: The letter b resembles a 6, as does a mirror image of the letter J.

7 = C, K: The extension of the letter K partially resembles the backslash on the number 7, and the sound of the letter C resembles the beginning sound of the word seven.

8 = f, g: A longhand letter f and g look like a figure eight.

9 = p: A mirror image of the letter p looks like the number 9.

10 = X : In latin, X means 10.

**Examples:**

*Birthdate: 6-7-70*                6 7 7 0
Substitute consonants for numbers: J C K S or BCKS
Add vowels where needed to form a word or phrase: JaCKS, BaCKS, or perhaps two imaginative words such as Bee CaKes

*Bank card access code: 64153*        6 4 1 5 3
Substitute consonants for numbers: BRDLY
Add vowels where needed to form a word or phrase: BRaDLeY

*Telephone number: 871-6484*        8 7 1 6 4 8 4
Substitute consonants for numbers: FKD BRGR
Add vowels where needed to form a word or phrase: FaKeD BuRGeR

---

clined to conversation," could be represented by the phrase "Take his turn." Imagine a person who refuses to take a turn when talking to other people.

The keyword method decreases the amount of time needed to learn vocabulary and enhances the retention of terminology. It works better when people make up their own keywords, and overall, it is superior to traditional methods of learning vocabulary. This is illustrated in Focus on Applied Research 4.2.

*Method of Loci* The famous Roman orator Cicero invented an early system called the *method of loci*. He used the images associated with walking to different parts of his

**Table 4.5**     Examples of the Keyword Method with Foreign Languages

|  | KEYWORD | TRANSLATION | IMAGE |
|---|---|---|---|
| *German* | | | |
| Der Tisch | (tissue) | table | Pieces of tissue paper coming out of a slit in the middle of a table. |
| *Russian* | | | |
| Linkor | (Lincoln) | battleship | A battleship with a statue of Abraham Lincoln on the deck. |
| *French* | | | |
| La Porte | (port) | door | A door on a ship with a large porthole on it. |
| *Spanish* | | | |
| Casa | (castle) | house | A castle built on top of the roof of a ranch-style house. |

**Figure 4.11** *Examples of keyword images.*

FOCUS ON APPLIED RESEARCH 4.2

## The Effects of the Keyword Method on Learning and Retention

The following studies illustrate the effects of the keyword method on the learning and retention of vocabulary.

*English vocabulary: (Roberts, 1985)*

*Instructions:* Definitions of 20 unfamiliar words had to be learned in 10 minutes.

*Data:* Percent of the definitions correctly recalled immediately as well as on a retention test given one week later are shown.

| | TIME OF RECALL | |
|---|---|---|
| | **IMMEDIATE** | **ONE WEEK** |
| Keyword Group | 69.0% | 40.6% |
| Traditional Learners | 62.3% | 21.0% |

*Botany terminology for plant groups (Rosenheck et al., 1989)*

*Instructions:* Participants asked to learn terms associated with a classification system for 16 plant groups in 24 minutes.

*Data:* Percent of the definitions correctly recalled immediately as well as on retention tests given two days and two months later are shown.

| | TIME OF RECALL | | |
|---|---|---|---|
| | **IMMEDIATE** | **TWO DAYS** | **TWO MONTHS** |
| Keyword Group | 84.4% | 83.1% | 38.1% |
| Traditional Learners | 66.9% | 55.2% | 22.9% |

garden to learn the order of ideas in his speeches. Cicero made up images of important words in his speech and associated them to objects in his courtyard that he passed while walking through it. The order of the objects he passed helped him to organize the order of the points in his speech. Thus, his first point, about soldiers needing new clothes, was formed into a mental image of soldiers in new uniforms wading in a fountain at the entrance to his courtyard. Dramatic improvements in recall can occur. In one study, participants memorized a list of 32 words. One group used rote memorization, while the other used the method of loci. The rote memorization group recalled 25 percent of the list, while the second group was able to recall 78 percent (Crovitz, 1971).

*Peg Systems* Here you memorize a standard set of "peg words," or mental hooks to which you attach things that you want to learn (Lorayne, 1990). This is not unlike having hooks in a closet on which you hang coats, hats, or other articles of clothing. Such systems are particularly good for learning and recalling items in a particular order. Exercise 4.1 in the Applied Activities section is designed to teach you a peg system that you should find useful in a number of areas of your life.

Overall, mnemonic devices enhance our ability to acquire and remember information in a variety of contexts. Perhaps their biggest advantage is that they force us to use our imaginations to help us learn. In effect, they add a little interest to our labors and help us to make learning fun.

## Summary of Chapter Organizers

Suggested responses to the chapter organizers presented at the beginning of this chapter are presented below.

1. *What are some things you could do to enhance the quality of the time you spend trying to learn?* Successful learners use their time on all aspects of a learning task effectively. In academic settings, they show up for class, concentrate on what is going on, participate in discussions, and take much more complete notes than their less successful counterparts. Successful learners also ask questions when they don't understand something.

2. *Do you know two things you can do to ensure that you will receive the maximum benefits from the time spent practicing?* One important principle is to use active practice. This includes such things as focusing attention on a task, establishing goals for what must be learned, and integrating and establishing connections among various ideas or components of a skill. Active practice also involves using critical thinking and discussing ideas and experiences with others. When reading information, techniques such as SQ3R help us to do some of the latter things. In addition, practice should be distributed, or spaced, over time. Massed practice, or cramming, has been shown to be less effective in acquiring information because it promotes fatigue and interferes with our ability to process information.

3. *When you are trying to acquire new information and skills, what characteristics should the feedback you receive have?* Feedback, or knowledge of results, is most effective when it is given immediately, when it is detailed and specific, and when it is constructive.

4. *What are several things you can do to use rewards effectively as well as to avoid their potential negative side effects?* Rewards, or positive reinforcers, increase the frequency of desirable behaviors and also help to reduce the frequency of bad habits. In the latter case, the frequency of behaviors that oppose undesirable actions are increased through the use of rewards. Positive reinforcers also work well when they are provided after a response and without a long delay. Sometimes problems occur in using rewards. They include the fact that a positive reinforcer may affect actions in addition to the one that was rewarded. Also, people may concentrate on earning a reward and make performing the desirable behavior a secondary goal. Sometimes behaviors learned do not generalize to other situations, and external rewards may undermine intrinsic interests in a task. It is not unusual to find inappropriate behaviors inadvertently rewarded or to see that rewards lose some of their attractiveness in the long run.

5. *Is it better to provide a reward every time a desirable response occurs or just some of the time?* When initially learning a response, rewarding a desirable behavior each time it occurs is recommended. As a response develops, switching to a partial reinforcement schedule is helpful. Partial rewards may occur after a fixed or variable number of responses or intervals of time.

6. *What happens when behaviors are no longer rewarded?* When a positive reinforcer that controls a behavior is removed, extinction occurs. The behavior eventually ceases. Behaviors learned under conditions of partial reinforcement resist extinction much better than those learned under continuous reinforcement.

7. *What are three ways that unpleasant stimuli influence your actions?* Aversive stimuli can punish a response and thus decrease its frequency of occurrence. Or, it can be used to teach someone an escape or avoidance response that will terminate or prevent the stimulus from happening.

8. *How can punishment be used effectively?* Punishment is used effectively when the magnitude is appropriate for correcting the misbehavior, and when it is consistently applied, limited to specific responses, and used humanely. In the latter case, care is taken to preserve the physical and psychological well being of the person receiving it.

9. *How does organizing and planning your time help you to learn?* Such things help people to focus their time and energy on a task and orient them towards important things they should review and study.

10. *How does your memory system work?* One model suggests that three interrelated memory systems are involved. They are the sensory register in which sensory traces of information initially appear; a limited-capacity short-term or working memory system; and an unlimited-capacity long-term memory. Attention to features of a stimulus places information in short-term memory. Rehearsal helps to maintain it there, while elaborative rehearsal transfers material into long-term memory. A second point of view is that information undergoes analysis at three levels: an acoustic analysis, a structural analysis based on physical features, and one based on meaning. The deeper the processing, the better information is learned and remembered.

11. *What causes you to forget information?* Forgetting does not occur simply with the passage of time. Instead, over time memory traces may interfere with each other. Proactive interference occurs when an old memory of something learned affects retaining new information, while retroactive interference happens when a new memory interferes with an older memory. Failures in retrieving information also may contribute to a memory loss, as do certain drugs and strong emotions.

12. *How can you improve your ability to remember?* Memory can be improved by over-learning material, chunking or categorizing it, elaborating on information, employing mental imagery, and by using mnemonics or memory aids.

## Things to Do

1. Think about what happened to you yesterday. Develop a list of how your behavior was affected by positive reinforcers, negative reinforcers, and punishment. Where did you encounter them? Who used them? Did you feel manipulated?

2. Watch two of your favorite soap operas or situational comedies. Develop a list of the ways the actions of the characters were influenced by positive reinforcers, negative reinforcers, and punishment. Do you think that interactions you engage in are based on the extent to which they are rewarded or punished by other people?

3. Select two news stories from a newspaper or magazine. What role did positive and negative reinforcers and punishment play in the actions that people took. Would people have behaved differently if the reinforcement and punishment was different? Give some examples to state your point your view.

4. If a friend told you she was having problems getting good grades in school, what principles of learning from the chapter would you tell her to use to improve her grades? What if your friend told you she wanted to get promoted at work? What principles from the chapter might be useful in helping her to get ahead in the business world?

5. Try using the following mnemonic strategies to do the following activities.

   • Acoustics to memorize a grocery or shopping list.
   • Rhymes to learn the names of people that you have a hard time remembering.

•The method of loci to learn the major points in a presentation you must give or that you would like to give.

•A narrative to memorize your schedule for the next couple of days.

•The letter–number substitution method to memorize telephone numbers or credit card or other account numbers you need to have at your fingertips.

•The keyword method to learn vocabulary in your courses or in a foreign language you are currently taking.

•The peg system to learn a list of concepts or principles in a class you are taking.

6. What are two or three deficiencies that you have as a learner? List them, and indicate how concepts and principles from this chapter can help you.

7. Do you think the romantic attachment between two people is based on principles of positive reinforcement? Give examples of how this could be the case. Do you believe that love is nothing more than two people exchanging rewards, or is something else involved? What else do you think plays a role?

## APPLIED ACTIVITIES

EXERCISE 4.1

**Learning a Mnemonic Peg System**

Perhaps you are a bit skeptical about the use of mnemonics and mental imagery to improve your ability to learn and remember. The following demonstration should give you some personal data for deciding whether such techniques are likely to be useful to you. *Please read the four instructions* before proceeding.

1. For this demonstration use the list of words at the bottom of this page.
2. Take out a sheet of paper with a 1" × 1/2" rectangle cut in it. When I tell you to do so, you will expose each word in the list in order. Each word is a natural association for a number from 1 to 20. Colleagues of mine, Julius Persensky and R. J. Senter, developed the list for some research they were doing in mnemonics. The rationale for each item in the list is rather obvious, except perhaps for the following: 2 = pair of dice; 8 = eight ball in a set of pool balls; 13 = baker, since 13 is a baker's dozen; 14 = heart, since February fourteenth is Valentine's Day; 15 = pool balls, since there are 15 pool balls in a set; 16 = girl, since sweet 16 is often used in that context; 19 = a calendar, since every year in this century begins with 19; 20 = cigarettes, since there are 20 cigarettes in a pack.
3. Expose each word, and try to form a mental image of the item. You might imagine one-dollar bills as wallpaper in your room or a giant tricycle sitting outside your home. As soon as you form your image, go on to the next item. Try to be creative in forming images.
4. As soon as you are finished, write the lists of words in the order in which they occurred. Give yourself one point for each item that is in the correct order.

5. Use the images to help you learn lists of information for a class or for other things you want to learn in a particular order (e.g., shopping lists, historical dates and events, birthdates of friends and relatives). Consult Figure 4.12 for an example of how to do this.

*A list of 20 words:*

| | |
|---|---|
| Dollar bill | Football team |
| Dice | Dozen eggs |
| Tricycle | Baker |
| Four-leaf clover | Heart |
| Hand | Pool balls |
| Six-pack | Girl |
| Seven-up | Magazine |
| Eight ball | Golf course |
| Baseball team | Calendar |
| Bowling pins | Cigarettes |

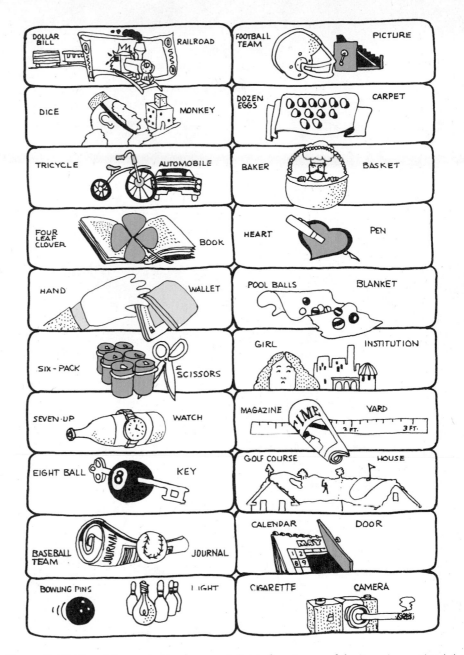

**Figure 4.12** *Use of the twenty item mnemonic list to form images of the items in exercise 4.1. Why not try to use them with a new list?*

EXERCISE 4.2

## Using Learning Principles to Help You Prepare for an Exam

A number of ways to use learning principles were suggested in this chapter. This activity combines them with some additional information into a format to help you improve your study habits.

**Background Information.**

Analyses of study habits clarify that transmitting principles for improving such habits is not enough. Other things need to happen as well.

- *Problems that need to be corrected must be identified.* To do this you need to analyze your current study habits and identify potential problem areas.
- *The motivation to change undesirable habits must be present.* No suggestions for change, including those in this activity, will work unless you are committed to using them.
- *A structure that will facilitate change should be used.* The procedure in this exercise is one example of such a structured format.

### Step 1:

Use a separate sheet of paper to develop a flexible monthly study plan like the one shown in Figure 4.4. *To gain experience with the process, work on only one or two courses initially.*

1. List the activities you need to do for the next four weeks in each of the courses for which you want to use the flexible monthly schedule (e.g., outside readings, text-book chapters to read, special projects or assignments to be completed, review of notes).
2. List each activity in the order in which it must be completed. Use personal or instructor-imposed deadlines to decide the order to complete activities.
3. Remember that an important part of this process is flexibility. Schedule time for each activity on more than one day, as shown in Figure 4.4.
4. Identify places where you plan to complete each of the activities.
5. *View the plan that you established above as tentative and subject to modifications after you have had a chance to use it.* Later on in this process, you will be given an opportunity to modify your initial schedule.

### Step 2:

Answer the following questions in the space provided.

1. Are the study areas you identified in Step 1 conducive to thoughtful studying? That is, can you really get some work accomplished? Yes_____ No_____. If no, choose a more appropriate place to study and prepare classroom assignments.
2. The flexible monthly planning process has provisions for a weekly as well as a monthly reward. List five to seven things you find rewarding in the space provided (e.g., snacks, watching television, buying new clothes). Which of the latter rewards can be used as weekly rewards, and which one(s) could be used as the monthly reward for your study plan?

### Step 3:

Begin to implement your plan. Since the specific time periods you will study will be determined on a day-to-day basis, establish reasonable time periods. As a general rule, give yourself a five- to ten-minute break for about every 90 minutes you study. If you should miss doing something on one of the days in your schedule, you still have time later on in your schedule to do the work. Try not to allow unfinished business from one week to fall into the next week. Thus, set reasonable goals for what you can accomplish, and stick to them. Use the weekly and monthly rewards as incentives for you to keep yourself on a reasonable schedule.

**Step 4:**

Select the learning principles discussed in the chapter that you feel you need to use more often in preparing for an exam. Place a check next to those principles listed below that you want to use more often. Think about what you need to do in order to make those principles work for you. Make sure that you completely understand each of the principles that you want to concentrate on. Integrate each of the principles selected into your study plan. In the space provided, indicate how, when, and where you will integrate the principles selected.

- Establish goals for what you want to learn. Make sure that you are clear about what it is you need to know (e.g., definitions of terms, applications of information).

- Spend quality time on all aspects of your studying. This includes the time you spend in class. Make sure that you take complete notes and that you ask questions when you do not understand something.

- Emphasize active practice. Review your notes and textbook periodically, and use the SQ3R system to help you focus and concentrate on the material.

- Space your studying, and avoid cramming the night before an exam.

- Do not study too soon after awakening, especially if you are getting up in the middle of the night to study. Allow yourself at least 45 minutes to get yourself completely awake and alert.

- If you are not sure why something was not done satisfactorily, ask for feedback. Remember that good feedback is specific and constructive.

- Overlearn information. Periodically review what you are learning in class and reread books and readings at least once.

- Chunk information to be learned into relevant categories. This can be done as an outline or by using the cognitive mapping technique described in the text.

- Elaborate on the information to be learned. Do this by reacting to what you are reading and studying in writing. Use annotative notes in the margins of your textbook or study notes. In addition, ask yourself questions as you read.

- Use mental imagery and mnemonic devices to help you organize, chunk, and structure information.

**Step 5:**

In addition to the above ideas, keep the following general principles in mind.

1. Stress understanding rather than rote repetition. Prepare for an exam as if you were going to make a presentation on the information. Try to make information as personally meaningful as you can.
2. Avoid studying when you are tired or fatigued. It is easier to study when you are fresh and relaxed.
3. Study in a quiet, pleasant atmosphere, and keep your study area free of distractions. Remember, it is difficult, if not impossible, to do two things at once. In reality, you switch one or the other on and off. Thus, three hours of studying while listening to the radio or watching television is less than three hours of studying.
4. Observe, talk to, and perhaps study with someone who has good study habits. Try to integrate that person's actions into your behavior.

**Step 6:**

*Assess how the ideas in this activity worked for you.* After two weeks, what corrections need to be made? After one month, what are two to three specific things you can do to make it work better for you the next time?

## Key Terms

*Avoidance response.*    A response taken to prevent an aversive stimulus from occurring.

*Cognitive map.*    A method for categorizing or grouping information using words or pictures. The intent is not only to place related information together, but to show how information across categories is related.

*Continuous reinforcement.*    A reinforcement schedule in which a reinforcer is administered every time a behavior occurs.

*Distributed practice.*    Spacing the total amount of practice on a task over a period of time.

*Elaborative rehearsal.*    Rehearsing information by doing more than simply repeating it to oneself. Underlying patterns and meaning in it are identified and used to help remember it.

*Episodic memory.*    The storage of information in memory regarding the period of time something was learned and the context in which it was learned.

*Escape response.*    A response taken to get away from or to terminate a negative stimulus.

*Extinction.*    The cessation of a response after a reinforcer that controls the behavior is no longer administered.

*Knowledge of results (KR).*    Feedback given when performing a task to help reduce the number of errors or the degree to which incorrect responses occur.

*Learning.*    The relatively permanent changes that occur in our thoughts and behaviors as a function of our experiences.

*Levels-of-processing approach.*    The theory that looks at our memory system in terms of how deeply information is processed.

*Long-term memory.*    The part of our memory system in which information is stored for extensive periods of time.

*Maintenance rehearsal.*    Repeating something like a new telephone number or street address to oneself in order to keep it readily available in short-term memory.

*Massed practice.*    Extensively practicing a task within a short period of time.

*Memory system approach.*    A way of understanding our memory system by breaking it up into a sensory register and a short- and long-term memory store.

*Mental imagery.*    The pictorial representation of information in our memory system.

*Mnemonic device.*    A memory aid or strategy for helping us to remember.

*Negative reinforcer.*    Aversive stimuli (e.g., shock, pain, loud noise) that increase the strength of responses that are successful either in removing the unpleasant stimuli from a situation or in preventing them from occurring.

*Overlearning.*    Reviewing or repeating information beyond the point at which it is mastered.

*Partial reinforcement schedule.*    A schedule of reinforcement in which a reinforcer is given less than every time a response occurs. The reinforcer might be administered after a fixed or variable interval of time or after a fixed or variable number of responses.

*Positive reinforcer.*    Stimuli that increases the strength of a response when added to a situation immediately following the response.

*Proactive interference.*    Memory loss due to an old memory interfering with something learned recently.

*Procedural memory.*    Memory for rules, associations, and other information needed to produce various motor skills and actions. Information in procedural memory operates without conscious awareness.

*Punishment.*    Aversive stimulus that eliminates or decreases the strength of a response when administered after a response occurs.

*Response cost.* A form of punishment where a privilege or some other normally pleasant stimulus is withheld if an undesirable response occurs.

*Retroactive interference.* A cause of forgetting in which a new memory interferes with the ability to remember something learned in the past.

*Secondary reinforcers.* Stimuli that acquire the ability to reinforce behaviors through their association with established reinforcers.

*Semantic memory.* Storage of items based on the meaning associated with the information.

*Sensory register.* Part of our memory system that receives information from the environment and retains it as a visual or auditory image.

*Short-term memory.* Storage of information for relatively brief periods of time—usually less than a minute.

*Spontaneous recovery.* The reappearance of a response after extinction. When a response occurs through spontaneous recovery, it is not as strong as it was before and will go away if it is not rewarded.

CHAPTER  5

# Modifying Our Behaviors

### Chapter Overview

Most of us are interested in modifying some aspect of our own or someone else's behavior. To do this well, we must design processes for learning based upon sound principles of behavior modification. This chapter explores the role of environmental stimuli, social factors, and certain cognitive processes such as self-instruction and mental practice in helping people to change.

### Chapter Organizers

*As you read, answer the questions that follow on a separate sheet of paper, and check your responses with those provided in the summary section.*

Strategies for change based upon the application of principles of learning are available to help you modify your behaviors, thoughts, and feelings.

1. What are two assumptions that underlie different approaches to changing behaviors, thoughts, and feelings?

Our overt actions, thoughts, and feelings are influenced by stimuli in the environment.

2. What are the ABC's of behavior, and how do they explain the connection between environmental stimuli and our actions, thoughts, and feelings?
3. Can you list seven parts of a process for modifying behavior that stresses our gaining control over environmental stimuli to help us change?
4. Why is it important to identify specific goals or target behaviors you want to change, and what is the best way to do this?
5. Do you know how to monitor and record information that will help you to better understand a behavior you want to change?
6. What are some ways to effectively manage the stimuli that control your actions?

Observing and modeling the actions of others can be an effective way not only to learn new things but to modify the way that we behave, think, and feel.

7. What are some things you have learned by modeling other people?
8. Do you know the critical elements involved in following a model that can help you learn effectively?

Our thoughts play an important role in changing our behaviors and may facilitate or hinder our efforts.

9. What are some things you can say to yourself to help modify your actions?
10. Why is mental practice often an effective part of modifying behavior? What can you do to make it an effective part of your life?

## A Case Of Writer's Block: Behavior Modification to the Rescue

A short time into his career as a college teacher, Victor Stevens became concerned about the lack of time he was spending on his professional writing. To change this habit, he sought advice from the late B. F. Skinner, one of the most noted psychologists of this century (Stevens, 1978).

Skinner suggested he first establish a specific place where he could restrict his activity to writing and be free of other distractions. Victor Stevens chose a room in his basement that he carpeted and into which he put a desk, typewriter, and chair. Next, Skinner told him to record the amount of time spent writing in this setting and to graph it. To automate this task, he hooked a timer to the light on his desk so that it was turned on and off with the light. The timer then recorded the amount of time he spent writing at his desk. Finally, B. F. Skinner told him to post a daily record of the amount of time spent writing where he could monitor his progress. Following this advice, Victor Stevens placed his graph on the wall in front of his desk.

Skinner's advice worked to some extent. While Stevens was writing more, he was spending less than an hour a day on his writing. Writing alone was not rewarding enough. He discussed the problem with some of his students, and this led to an informal seminar on techniques for controlling behavior. Students also developed projects including losing weight, getting more exercise, studying more, and cutting back on smoking. Each week the seminar met, Stevens and his students shared their graphs reflecting the progress they had made.

For the teacher and his students, dramatic changes occurred in their ability to modify their habits. Both found that the time together sharing their progress was a good source of support and a very rewarding experience. Talking with others, getting our ideas recognized, and receiving positive feedback and compliments are important social rewards. In Stevens's case, such rewards led to dramatic increases in the amount of time spent on his writing. His output increased from an average of 30 minutes a day before the seminar to 2 hours a day afterwards. In a 310-day span, he recorded over 400 hours of work that resulted in completion of a book chapter, an edited book, a major journal article, and two grant proposals.

## MODIFYING BEHAVIOR

Do you have habits you would like to change in yourself or in others? Most people do. A teacher, for example, might want to reduce disruptive behaviors among students; a business manager needs her salespeople to learn how to increase product sales; a coach wants to improve the performance of athletes; and a parent might want to have family members interact more efficiently. There is nothing devious or sinister about this. The individuals mentioned above face problems in their interactions with those around them, and behavioral changes are needed.

At one time or another, most of us also wanted to change or modify some of our habits. Popular examples include trying to get more exercise, lose weight, reduce cigarette smoking and the consumption of alcoholic beverages, enhance communication skills, or improve study habits. In such cases, the problem was not how to manage other people better, but how to manage ourselves more effectively.

Strategies for change based upon the application of principles of learning are available to help us modify our behaviors, thoughts, and feelings. The techniques draw upon learning principles that emphasize the control and use of environmental stimuli, observing and imitating others, and changing aspects of how we think in various situations.

Methods for producing change also tend to emphasize different things. Some methods focus on the control of environmental stimuli to change overt behaviors—those actions we can see ourselves or others performing. *The underlying assumption is that once more desirable overt behaviors occur, less desirable thoughts and feelings associated with them will decrease.* Young children sometimes throw a temper tantrum to get what they want. The jumping around and screaming is reinforced whenever someone pays attention to it. Thus, a parent might be taught to manage a youngster's temper tantrum by ignoring it. Removing the reward should place such behaviors on extinction, and the internal anger and rage also should dissipate.

Other strategies for change focus more on the thoughts and emotions that guide and direct our responses to situations in our lives. *The underlying assumption is that behaviors will improve when undesirable thoughts and feelings are managed.* Some students, for example, become very anxious when confronted with an exam. Their anxiety increases, and they think, "I can't cope with this exam. It's too hard, and I'm going to fail." To manage this problem, test-anxious students can be taught how to substitute positive thoughts for their normally negative self-appraisals. Thus, they are shown how to overcome self-defeating thinking with self-talk like, "You studied hard for this exam, you know the material, and you can do well. Just concentrate and take it one question at a time." In addition, test-anxious students are shown how to substitute the calming influence of relaxation for the unpleasantness of anxiety. With their thoughts and emotions under control, test performance normally improves.

In practice, both types of strategies are employed alone or in combination. Research shows that when used properly, self-talk and relaxation are effective in modifying a variety of behaviors, thoughts, and feelings—including those noted above (Martin and Pear, 1988; Watson and Tharp, 1993). *These authors also report that people typically do not fail at changing behavior because the techniques don't work; rather, they fail because they don't use the techniques.* Or, they use them in a halfhearted manner. It is not uncommon to hear someone say, "I tried that strategy once, and it did not work." To derive benefits from the ideas and techniques for modifying behavior presented in this chapter, one must actively practice them just like any other skill.

# ENVIRONMENTAL STIMULI AND BEHAVIOR MODIFICATION

## The Use of Operant Conditioning Principles

Using **operant conditioning** principles to modify behavior has its roots in the work of B. F. Skinner. It emphasizes how stimuli that follow responses influence them. Such stimuli are labeled **consequent stimuli,** and examples include the use of positive reinforcers or rewards as well as aversive stimuli used to punish certain actions. The responses such stimuli control and maintain are called **operants,** because they operate or produce effects in the environment. Operants are responses that are voluntarily emitted. Familiar examples include selecting a television program, walking to a restaurant, and turning on an air conditioner to cool a room.

Operants make up a large part of our daily responses. The process through which they are acquired is called **operant conditioning,** and three basic elements must be presented for such learning to occur. The elements are called the ABCs of behavior and they are described below and in Figure 5.1.

*Antecedent Stimuli*  Such stimuli precede a behavior and can affect our actions in one of two ways. In *operant conditioning,* antecedent stimuli function *as cues or signals that certain responses will be reinforced or punished*. They are called **discriminative stimuli** (S$^d$), because they help us to *discriminate, or distinguish*, between things in our environment that will lead to rewards or punishment from those that do not. Thus we can make appropriate choices about what actions to take. They include such things as the coin slot on a candy machine or a teacher's announcement of an upcoming exam. When faced with such stimuli, we might decide to purchase a snack or to start studying in order to prepare for an exam. Such choices increase the chances of obtaining a reward (e.g., the snack, getting a good grade on an exam). Other choices, such as waiting until the last minute to study, could lead to a low grade on the exam.

There is a second type of antecedent stimuli that affects our actions. They "automatically trigger" certain responses, thoughts, and feelings. Such "triggers," for example, cause various reflexes to occur (e.g., removing our hand from a hot object, closing our eyes in the wind), or they initiate overlearned habits or responses (e.g., automatic response sequences discussed in Chapter 1, such as bringing our car to a stop at a red light, or, quickly reaching for a piece of chocolate as soon as it's offered). They also initiate a variety of thoughts and emotions, such as feeling anxious when an exam is passed out in class and thinking "I'm not going to do well on this test."

*Behavior*  These are specific actions that occur in the presence of antecedent stimuli. Thus, you put money into the candy machine, apply pressure to your brake to stop your car, and hug or shake the hand of your friend you have not seen for awhile. In addition to overt actions being influenced by antecedents, it is also important to note that they may "cue" or "trigger" various thoughts and feelings. When faced with preparing for an exam, some students treat it as a challenge; they become energized and think "I know I can do well on this test." They typically decide to study hard. Others automatically become anxious and spend a lot of time worrying or thinking "No

## The ABCs of Behavior

| Antecedents $\longrightarrow$ | Behavior $\longrightarrow$ | Consequences |
|---|---|---|
| "Discriminative stimuli" or cues for deciding what response to initiate | | C+ Pleasant stimuli (e.g., positive reinforcers or rewards) |
| | | C− Aversive stimuli (e.g., punishment) |
| Coin slot $\longrightarrow$ | Decide to put money in machine to buy a snack $\longrightarrow$ | C+ Get a favorite snack |
| Exam date announced by teacher $\longrightarrow$ | Choose to wait until the last minute to study $\longrightarrow$ | C− Get a low grade on the exam |

| Antecedents $\longrightarrow$ | Behavior $\longrightarrow$ | Consequences |
|---|---|---|
| Stimuli that automatically "trigger" certain responses, thoughts, and feelings | | |
| Crib in bedroom/ lights turned off $\longrightarrow$ | Baby gets angry and throws a temper tantrum $\longrightarrow$ | C+ Baby gets attention |
| Exam passed out in class $\longrightarrow$ | Anxiety and self-defeating thoughts occur $\longrightarrow$ | C− Get a low grade on the exam |

**Figure 5.1** *Common examples of ABCs of behavior.*

matter how hard I study, I'm going to fail this exam." Their subsequent efforts at studying are then hampered.

*Consequences* Overt behaviors and our internal thoughts and feelings are typically followed by pleasant or unpleasant stimuli. When the consequent stimulus is pleasant, that is, a positive reinforcer or reward, the behavior is likely to increase in frequency. Thus, you will continue to put money into candy machines to receive a sweet treat, to stop at an intersection to avoid an accident or traffic ticket, and to hug or shake the hand of a friend in order to obtain a warm greeting in return. Most young children would rather stay awake and play with their parents or guardian. A temper tantrum occurs, and someone returns to calm the child. Such attention is generally reinforcing, and the youngster learns to throw a temper tantrum to get attention.

When the consequent stimulus is unpleasant (e.g., punishment is administered), the behavior is likely to decrease in frequency. Thus, if failing to brake leads to an accident or traffic citation, you are less likely to run a stop sign in the future. Or, for test-anxious students, exams arouse anxiety and self-defeating thoughts; performance suffers; and a low grade typically results. This, of course, leads to more anxiety about flunking out of school and additional negative thoughts about oneself. Taking exams and anything associated with them, including studying, soon become aversive, and people begin to avoid them.

# USING PRINCIPLES OF OPERANT CONDITIONING TO MODIFY BEHAVIOR

Methods for using operant conditioning principles to change behaviors have become very popular. Behavioral modification techniques have been taught to teachers, sales managers, military officers, therapists, parents, coaches, and ministers just to name a few of the types of people trained in their use. In addition to providing processes to help manage other people and to create more pleasant and effective environments, *behavior modification also can help us change personal behaviors.* When used to modify or change our actions and thoughts, behavioral techniques are sometimes called **self-management procedures.**

The process described in this section to modify behavior is simply an elaboration of the basic elements of operant conditioning discussed earlier. It has the following seven parts:

1. *Identify the problem, and select a specific target behavior.*
2. *Monitor how much of the target behavior currently exists.*
3. *Control antecedent stimuli.*
4. *Break response chains.*
5. *Manage consequent stimuli.*
6. *Obtain social support.*
7. *Monitor and record progress towards changing behavior.*

Let us now examine each of the components in more detail.

## 1. Identify the Problem and Select a Specific Target Behavior

To modify our own or someone else's behavior, specific behavioral goals or outcomes that a change process will achieve must be stated. Such behavioral goals or outcomes are called **target behaviors.** To begin to think about target behaviors, it is sometimes helpful to first state them in general terms. Friends and neighbors have said to me that they wished they could reduce their cigarette smoking, lose some weight, or play golf better. Colleagues have often said they want their students to learn the content, have good attitudes, or act creatively in the classroom. Such statements represent good ways to initiate thinking about behavioral changes we might want in ourselves or others.

The latter statements, however, are too general to design specific learning experiences that will achieve the proposed changes. Instead, it is important to be more detailed and specific about how many cigarettes to cut back on, how much weight to lose, and what content must be learned and to what degree. More appropriate targets would include statements like; "I want to reduce my smoking by a total of ten cigarettes a week," "I need to lose 15 pounds," or "I want my students to be able to list ten famous events in history between 1800 and 1870."

Research demonstrates that having clear and specific goals for modifying behavior has several advantages. They focus our time and energy in specific directions and enhance our motivation and commitment to learn (Cervone et al., 1991; Kirschenbaum, 1985). More important, these authors note that having some objective in mind helps us identify what knowledge and skills are needed to make changes in our actions. We are then in a better position to acquire what is needed.

*Select Targets That Are Important to You* The risk of failure lurks in the background anytime attempts to change behavior are made. There are two things people typically do that produce failures. One is not pick the most important target behavior. A close friend was concerned about losing weight and improving her study habits. She was 40 pounds overweight but had close to a dean's list grade point average. She had said on a number of occasions that losing weight was very important to her. Yet she decided to work on her study habits. Why? "Because they are easier for me to do something about." Within two weeks she had completely lost interest in improving her already good study habits. *To maintain interest in a behavior modification plan, select target behaviors that are really important to you.*

*Do Not Try to Do Too Much at Once* A mistake is to assume you can quit smoking within a week, lose 40 pounds in a month, improve your grade point average overnight, or run a marathon two months after starting a jogging program. Trying to do too much at once only sets you up for a failure experience and a lot of frustration. Learning to change takes time, sometimes a great deal of time. There are two things you can do that will lessen the chances of biting off more than you can chew.

1. *Work with a single behavior.* Exercise 5.1 identifies two or three specific targets for each statement. We are usually confronted with alternative ways of obtaining our goals. Any one of the alternatives in Exercise 5.1 is probably desirable. It is difficult, however, to develop and use behavioral change plans for everything at the same time. It is much better to pick one alternative. An easy way to do this is mentally to rank order your alternatives in terms of importance. That is, you establish priorities among your options and select the one that is most important to you.

2. *Think of the specific behavior as composed of several interconnected units.* Many of our actions can be thought of as links on a chain. Rather than try to change a target behavior all at once, work on each link in the chain. For example, I might want to jog a mile each day, or I might want my son to pick up all his toys each day. It is unlikely, however, that I will be able to get either to happen all at once. I might look at the task of jogging as composed of quarter-mile subunits. Similarly, picking up toys could have subunits of 3, 6, 9, and 12 toys. Or losing weight by cutting out "junk food" snacks might be done in increments of 3, 6, 9, 12, and 15 snacks per week. Reducing smoking might be done by gradually cutting back 4, 8, 12, 16, 20, and 24 cigarettes a week over a period of time.

Analyzing a response into its component parts is important for the process of reinforcing behaviors. We will later examine how to reinforce behaviors using such information. For now, it is important that you be able to analyze a response into reasonable subunits.

*State Target Behaviors in a Positive Manner* What would you rather do: lose 25 pounds of body fat or reduce the number of calories you consume each week? Stop biting your nails or keep your hands at your side or on a desk? Cease being a nicotine addict or reduce the number of cigarettes you smoke? Raise a miserable grade point average or spend two more hours a day studying? In each case, both parts of the statement will

accomplish the same goal. How you package your target behaviors is important to maintaining interest in the plan. Stating the target in terms of "body fat," "nail biting," or "nicotine addiction" may keep you from focusing on taking constructive actions. To change behavior, develop a positive attitude and state your targets accordingly.

*Increase the Strength of Replacement Behaviors* Replacement behaviors are target behaviors that are alternatives to engaging in the bad habit. In some cases they are incompatible with the bad habit. For habits such as eating high-calorie snacks, smoking, drinking alcoholic beverages, or using abusive language, it is not enough simply to try to reduce their occurrence. It is also a good idea to increase behaviors that will replace the bad habit. A plan for consuming fewer high calorie snacks, for example, might also contain a plan for increasing the amount of exercise and the number of nutritious snacks that will be eaten. Furthermore, people who want to reduce their smoking might find activities that are difficult to do while smoking. When the urge to smoke occurs, instead of lighting up, people might garden, wash their car, rake leaves, ride a bike, take a shower, meditate, or play a sport such as tennis or racquetball.

Before reading further, complete Exercise 5.1 in the Applied Activities section at the end of this chapter. It is designed to help you learn to state target behaviors in a more detailed manner. Bear in mind that when beginning a personal change plan, initial target statements may be somewhat general. Thus, your initial statement might express a need to study more hours, exercise more frequently, or eat fewer snacks. After thinking about the problem and/or gathering baseline data as described in the next section, you will have more information to be much more specific in what you need to do.

## 2. Monitor How Much of the Target Behavior Currently Exists

Target behaviors specify what alterations in our responses are necessary. To measure any change, information about the current state of our behavior is needed. This is best done by gathering **baseline data.** Baseline data can answer such questions as: "How many cigarettes do I currently smoke?" "How many calories do I consume in a day?" "How far do I jog each day?" and "How much content do I require my students to learn about a particular topic?"

Obtaining baseline data does three things. It provides a performance level from which to monitor changes in our behavior. While you may want to cut your cigarette smoking in half, it is important to know precisely the number of cigarettes currently smoked. Thus a target of a 50 percent reduction is made from a clear frame of reference. In addition, baseline data may suggest modifications in your target. Given the current state of your habit, you might decide that you want to accomplish more or less of a change. Finally, as the process for recording baseline data discussed below shows, you gain information about other aspects of the behavior that may need your attention.

*Recording Baseline Data*  Keeping a diary is a useful way to gather baseline data. The diary should include information about the ABCs of the responses you wish to modify. You should note the stimuli that cue or trigger the behavior you wish to change. Thus you might record that you smoked a cigarette while standing around with friends who smoked or you failed to study because your friends asked you to go to a dance with them. The responses recorded should include overt behaviors as well as thoughts and feelings associated with that situation. It also is useful to record the consequent stimuli that follow the response. In this way, you can gain insights into the reinforcers that have gained control over your actions.

*Furthermore, record information about specific aspects of the behavior you wish to change.* Thus, you can determine the amount of time your target behavior takes, its frequency, or the amount of something consumed when engaged in the behavior. Thus, you could record the number of cigarettes smoked each day, the amount of time spent studying, or the amount of calories consumed at a meal. Of course, for certain problem behaviors, you might want to record more than one of these responses. For example, the number of snacks eaten as well as the number of calories consumed might be of interest. Or, the number of times you sat down to study as well as the amount of time you spent at each sitting might be of interest.

*Try not to focus only negative information.* A record that consists only of behaviors you are performing poorly or unpleasant thoughts and feelings is discouraging. Try to record positive instances of behaviors, thoughts, and feelings as well as negative ones. Research suggests that this assists with maintaining your motivation and commitment to change. It also helps us to focus on the progress being made as well as any problems (Johnson-O'Connor and Kirschenbaum, 1986). Thus, you might want to note the times you successfully exercise, study, or eat nutritious foods as well as the times you fail to do so.

*Record information about your target behavior as soon after it occurs as possible.* Waiting until you have a private moment or the end of the day will lead to inaccurate information getting recorded. Also, recording devices should be readily accessible and tied to the particular habit you want to change. A small notebook that you can carry or that fits in a shirt pocket or purse is often useful. If studying is a problem, use paper in the back of a course notebook. Between-meal snacks could be monitored by a record sheet kept on your refrigerator or kitchen cabinet door. Similarly, a chart kept near your exercise gear could be used to record information about your physical activity.

Finally, baseline information should be recorded until a clear pattern or picture of the behavior begins to emerge. *You should stop when you have a good sense of how often the target behavior occurs and what antecedent and consequent stimuli are associated with it.* For most things, three to five days is generally an adequate amount of time, provided the behavior of interest occurs relatively frequently during that time period. An example of a format for recording baseline information appears in Table 5.1.

**Table 5.1**      Recording and Using Baseline Data

*Part 1:* Record diary entries on important incidents associated with the target behavior.

*General Target Behavior:* Increase the number of sales reports I write.

| TIME OF DAY | ANTECEDENT STIMULI | BEHAVIORS, THOUGHTS, EMOTIONS | CONSEQUENCES |
|---|---|---|---|
| M. 8:10 A.M. | Boss called on telephone to talk about his new office decorations. | Put aside report I was working on for 40 minutes and talked to him. | I was pleased with the advice I gave him. However, I spent 40 minutes with him instead of writing. |
| M. 8:55 A.M. | Coffee cart | Put report down and had coffee and doughnut. Felt guilty for eating junk food. | Enjoyed chance to relax. But break took 20 minutes away from work. |
| M. 9:10 A.M. | Pile of reports | Finished one and began another. | Felt good to see the pile of work begin to shrink. |
| M. 9:40 A.M. | Wife called | Put report aside and talked with her for 20 minutes. Thought "I'll never finish." | Had fun discussing weekend plans. But, felt guilty because time was taken from work. |
| M. 9:45 A.M. | Vendor called | Stopped work on reports to talk to him. | Was helpful but took too much time. |
| M. 11:05 A.M. | Department head called | Talked about a customer. Thought, "too many other things to do." | Spent 30 minutes on what should have been a 10-minute item. |
| M. 11:40 A.M. | Reports on desk | Worked well on two reports | Congratulated myself. |

Sometimes when our actions are monitored, changes in behaviors occur. Almost everyone has had the experience of a teacher, coach, or parent observing them and "more desirable behaviors suddenly appearing." Monitoring ourselves and becoming self-aware may lead to reductions in smoking, of eating too much, or it may promote more exercise. Self-monitoring and recording baseline information often change behaviors we care about in a more desirable direction (Bornstein et al., 1985; Mace and Kratochwill, 1985). We react to being observed, and this effect is called **reactivity.** Michael Mahoney and Carl Thoresen (1974), however, note that the changes produced by self-monitoring and recording do not last very long. In order to influence behavior in the long run, we must follow the remaining five steps in the behavior modification process. They are:

3. Control antecedent stimuli.
4. Break response chains.

| Table 5.1 | Continued |
|-----------|-----------|

*Part 2:* Record the frequency, amount of time, or quantity of something the behavior consumes.

*General Target Behavior:* Increase the number of sales reports I write.

*Recording Start Date:* May 10

Number of reports completed, day 1–5

|        | 1 | 2 | 3 | 4 | 5 | AVERAGE |
|--------|---|---|---|---|---|---------|
| Week 1 | 6 | 8 | 7 | 5 | 6 | 6.4 |
| Week 2 | 5 | 7 | 6 | 7 | 5 | 6.0 |

*Part 3:* Use information from the diary to identify antecedent stimuli and consequent stimuli that either facilitate or hinder the target behavior from occurring. In some cases, this analysis also might identify other behaviors that must be brought under control if the initial target behavior is to be achieved. In this case, it appears that the telephone calls disrupt report writing and cause some worry about completing tasks, but talking on the phone is rewarding.

*Part 4:* Using information obtained from the diary and recording the frequency, amount of time, or quantity of something the behavior consumes, revise the general target behavior, and make it much more specific. Follow the guidelines in the text for ensuring that such targets are reasonable.

*Specific Target Behavior 1:* Want to increase the average number of sales reports I write to eight per day by June 12.

*Specific Target Behavior 2:* Need to screen telephone calls so that low priority calls are returned at my convenience and do not interrupt my report writing.

*Part 5:* Use information from the diary to identify ways to gain personal control over the antecedent and consequent stimuli that hinder or facilitate the target behavior. Here, the disruption caused by telephone calls could be prevented by having a secretary, answering device, or voice mail system take telephone calls. Outside of high-priority calls, they could be returned when it is more convenient to do so. Since the telephone calls are rewarding, this individual could use talking on the telephone as a reward for completing all or part of the writing goals for that day. Of course, other antecedents (e.g., a small sign on the desk as a reminder to "stay on task") or other rewards (e.g., a favorite snack at the end of the day, chance to watch an enjoyable television program) also could be used.

5. Manage consequent stimuli.
6. Obtain the support of other people.
7. Monitor and record your progress.

## 3. Control Antecedent Stimuli

What typically happens when you encounter the following stimuli: "Don't Walk," "Wet Paint," "Fast Food Restaurant," "Snack Machine," "Cigarettes," "Get Out of the Way, Quick!" or "Danger"? You probably take some action in their presence that allows you to obtain a reward or to avoid an unpleasant stimulus. Thus, such stimuli may serve as cues or information for helping you to decide what actions to take. They may also automatically trigger certain productive or undesirable habits, thoughts, and feelings. Thus, antecedent stimuli need to be managed, and there are three things that can be done to accomplish this goal.

*1. Remove Stimuli that Act as Cues for or that Trigger Problem Behaviors from a Situation* If snacking occurs whenever the television set is on, consider placing the snack in a closet out of sight. My youngest son only sucked his thumb when a particular blanket was in his hand. Removing the blanket "cured" the thumb-sucking habit. A friend smoked whenever he had a cup of coffee in his hand. Giving up coffee reduced the number of cigarettes he smoked.

*2. Avoid Situations in which the Antecedent Stimuli Normally Appear* A friend found himself engaging in too many casual conversations at work and not getting as much done as he wanted. He began to stay away from areas of the office where such conversations normally took place, and his productivity increased.

*3. Add New Antecedent Stimuli in order to Increase the Chances of a Desirable Behavior Occurring* In some families, for example, conversation at meals is almost nonexistent, limited to a few comments, or used to berate children for misdeeds. In effect, such stimuli become associated with unpleasant consequences instead of lively dinnertime conversations. Richard Green (1984) and his colleagues found an interesting way to change this by modifying the antecedent stimuli. They designed placemats that provided conversational topics (e.g., what was the most exciting thing you saw happen today) and games (e.g., try to name as many animals as you can that begin with the letters of the alphabet) that the whole family could participate in. Compared to traditional placemats or no placemats, their Table-Talk placemats generated more social and educational conversations. Several examples of antecedent stimuli that trigger undesirable habits and suggestions for managing them are presented in Table 5.2.

## 4. Break Response Chains

Many of our behaviors can be viewed as a chain of interconnected responses. Many bad habits maintain themselves because one action leads to another. A friend leaves his office and along with several coworkers walks across the street to the nearest bar. They sit at the same table and order a couple of drinks before going home. This is done every day, and because my friend loves imported beers, he is gaining weight. *One way to break this chain would be to take some action incompatible with going to the bar.* Such an action works best if it comes early in the chain. Thus he might go to the track or gym after he leaves his office.

*A second technique for breaking a chain is to complicate the process of enacting a behavior.* For example, reaching for a cigarette and stuffing it in your mouth is much more difficult if the pack is wrapped in three layers of aluminum foil and is locked in a desk drawer. If drinking too much coffee is a problem, put your cup down every time you take a sip and ask yourself, "Do I really want another sip?" Such methods make the behavior less automatic and mindless and provide time for you to think about what you are doing.

Review the target behaviors you identified in Exercise 5.1 at the end of this chapter. Were any of them responses that might be modified by controlling antecedent stimuli or breaking response chains? How would you do this?

## 5. Manage Consequent Stimuli

You know from the discussion earlier that consequent stimuli exert an important influence on our actions and those of other people. Such stimuli can be used to our advantage to help us modify behavior—that is, if we understand how to employ them effectively. The following seven sections contain several principles for using such stimuli to modify behavior.

*1. Stress the Use of Positive Reinforcement* The research literature on behavior modification suggests that whenever possible, positive reinforcers should be employed to change behavior. As you learned in Chapter 4, care must be taken when aversive stimuli are used to avoid unpleasant emotions and counterproductive responses that interfere with learning. *And when used as self-punishment in a self-management plan, the evidence is quite clear in showing that aversive stimulation simply does not work.* In some cases, it may only make things worse by increasing your frustration levels and making some problem behaviors more resistant to change. Also, people who rely on self-punishment in personal change plans are less likely to carry out their plans (Worthington, 1979; Shiffman, 1984).

It is also important to select a reinforcer that is appropriate for the behavior you want to modify. An ice cream cone is fine as a reward for studying hard for a test. However, it is probably not a good reward to use for sticking to a diet. Similarly, no single reinforcer is likely to work in all situations. Praising staff for getting reports finished on time is effective but unlikely to sustain long-term performance. People still expect to receive a paycheck for the overall job they do.

*2. Select Positive Reinforcers That Are Likely to Influence the Behavior You Want to Change* Six types of positive reinforcers that we might consider employing occur through:

1. Our social interactions with other people.
2. The things we do to reduce our physiological needs.
3. The stimuli in our environments that we find attractive and pleasant.
4. Our ability to reinforce ourselves verbally.
5. Our ability to use mental images to reinforce desirable actions.
6. Using responses we enjoy doing to help us modify problem behaviors.

Examples of each type are presented in Table 5.3.

*3. Reinforce a Behavior Immediately After It Occurs* Rewarding yourself or someone else before you make an appropriate response typically does little good. Furthermore, the association between a behavior and reward is best made immediately after the response occurs. Sometimes, however, certain tasks make a delay between the response and the reinforcer desirable. A teacher may find it difficult to give each child an M and M candy every time he or she responds correctly. There may be too many who deserve a reward at the same time, or it might be close to lunch or dinner. In a similar way, I

**Table 5.2**                    Examples of Antecedent Stimuli Associated with Common Habits

| HABIT | ANTECEDENTS | METHODS FOR CONTROLLING |
|---|---|---|
| Eating too many high-calorie foods | Candy bars<br>Ice cream<br>Potato chips<br>Magazine ads for luscious desserts<br>Food storage cabinets<br>Snack machines<br>Snack food aisles in stores<br>Hunger pangs anxious thoughts | Remove all high-calorie snack foods from house. Wrap all foods that require no preparation in lots of plastic, wax paper, or aluminum foil. Place more desirable foods in cabinets where you normally keep high-calorie snacks. Avoid snack machines and store aisles where such foods are sold. Never go grocery shopping when hungry. Try to resolve personal problems instead of using food to soothe them. |
| Smoking too much | Pack of cigarettes<br>Smell of smoke<br>Work pressure<br>Drinking coffee<br>Having a drink<br>Talking on phone<br>Finishing a meal<br>Waiting for bus<br>Driving in car<br>Reading magazine<br>Cocktail party<br>Friends who smoke | Don't carry cigarettes with you. Learn to manage time and stress to reduce pressure in ways other than smoking. Restrict smoking to certain time periods and places. Do busy work with hands, doodle, or play with paper clips. Put something in mouth beside cigarettes (e.g., gum, carrot, celery.) Switch to tea after dinner. Leave table after a meal, and take a walk. Leave parties early when people smoke. Develop friendships with nonsmokers. |
| Lack of exercise | Sedentary friends<br>Socializing after school or work<br>Sedentary leisure activities like watching television, reading newspapers, and watching participation sports. | Find friends who are more active and pursue sports and other types of physical activity you enjoy with them. Keep pictures of people exercising and reminders to do so around the house. Read magazines and articles on physical activity. Join a health spa, and use it several times a week. Curtail time watching television and other sedentary activities to allow time for physical activity. |

might want to reward myself with a soft drink after I jog a certain distance. It is possible that I might not be thirsty enough, or a soft drink may not be conveniently available.

One way to deal with the latter problem is through the use of **token rewards** or by simply keeping records of how many reinforcers have been earned. The teacher might give the students plastic chips, and I might simply keep a record of rewards I owe myself in a notebook. In this way, a symbolic reward is given immediately, and the actual reinforcers can be obtained at a later time. Using tokens also help us to change undesirable behaviors that normally receive very powerful and immediate reinforcers, such as smoking cigarettes, drinking too much coffee, or eating junk foods. The tokens provide a symbolic but immediate reward and a continuing reminder that a tangible reward will come later. Such a reminder assists with overcoming the tendency for delays in rewards to make them less effective (cf., reinforcement discussion in Chapter 4). Receiving token rewards helps us to bridge the gap between executing a desirable behavior and when it receives a tangible reward.

*4. Do Not Demand Too Much Effort for Too Little Reward* Positive reinforcers are effective because people derive benefits from them. Research shows that the benefits are assessed against the effort it took to obtain a reinforcer. William F. Whyte (1972) calls this the **cost/benefit ratio.** If the benefits the reward provides are not worth the effort (i.e., do not provide satisfaction), people are not likely to work for the reward. Giving an 11-year-old child a nickel every week for cleaning his room each day is probably expecting too much. Similarly, some students will not take a class if they believe the amount of work required exceeds the number of credit hours they would earn. And many people have refused a job offer and later said, "You can't believe what they wanted me to do for so little money!" Any reward has to be worth our time and energy to pursue it. Failing to heed this principle often leads to failure in the use of positive reinforcers.

An important area in which the cost/benefit ratio must be examined is efforts of less-developed countries to control their population growth. One issue is to determine an effective reinforcer to get people to use contraceptives and other family planning methods. Such rewards must fit the culture and be perceived as having clear benefits that exceed the costs of obtaining them. Several that have been tried successfully are illustrated in Focus on Applied Research 5.1. Such efforts also are supported by government policies that promote family planning and by ongoing educational efforts that demonstrate their value.

*5. Reinforce Each Successive Approximation to Your Target Behavior* In Chapter 4, we saw that learning takes place gradually over time. A change in behavior is seldom completely correct the first time we or someone else tries it. A reinforcer may be adequate for the target behavior, but we need not wait until the complete response occurs before reinforcing it. Components of the total response should be rewarded. Thus, each of our little successes is reinforced. This process is called **shaping** a behavior. There are three ways to do this.

1. *Reward each subunit of a target behavior until it is mastered.* Jogging one complete mile, for example, might be viewed as composed of quarter-mile units. Reinforcers could be earned after completing each quarter-mile unit. Points might be earned and "cashed in" later for a treat. Or a pat on the back for running one quarter of a mile or some other appropriate distance could be given. When one unit was mastered, a reward would be obtained after completion of the next subunit. Thus, earning a point, a pat on the back, or a soft drink would occur only after jogging one-half of a mile. Obtaining additional reinforcement would then depend upon mastering the next component.

2. *Administer a portion of the total reinforcer for completing a part of the target behavior.* A number of daily behaviors are shaped in this way. Students earn credits in each course that count towards the total number needed for graduation. Salaried employees earn a part of their yearly salary for each week worked. A student in one of

**Table 5.3**  Examples of Six Types of Positive Reinforcement

| | |
|---|---|
| *A. Social* | |
| Approval of another person's behavior | "That was a nice job you did." |
| | "I appreciate the time and energy you took to do this." |
| Paying attention to another person | "That looks interesting; can you show me how it works?" |
| | "I'd like to have the other people see what you are doing." |
| Giving affection | "I like you." |
| | "Let's spend more time together." |
| *B. Physiological needs* | Food: potato chips, peanuts, pretzels, cookies, favorite meal. |
| | Liquids: water, soft drinks, beer, wine, milk shakes, ice cream sodas. |
| | Sex: sexual relations with another person. |
| *C. Pleasant or attractive environmental stimuli* | Going to a movie, attending a concert, sunbathing, taking a drive in the country, buying new clothes. |
| *D. Verbal self-reinforcement* | "I did very well on that problem." |
| | "I think that I'm performing extremely well." |
| | "I'm really doing a good job." |
| *E. Mental images* | "I can imagine myself taking my time on my tennis backhand. I almost see the ball going over the net low and past my opponent. People are applauding my stroke, and I win the set." |
| | "I imagine studying in my room for three hours. In class the next day, I visualize the teacher asking people to answer questions about the assignment I studied. I answer, and my teacher smiles at me and says, 'Good comment'." |
| *F. Responses we enjoy* | "I like to jog a lot. I'll only allow myself to run if I have completed the reading for class the next day." |
| | "I enjoy watching TV. But I've been late for class too much. I will only allow myself to watch TV if I show up on time for all my classes that day." |

FOCUS ON APPLIED RESEARCH 5.1
## Behavior Modification and Family Planning

It is estimated that approximately 77 percent of the world population lives in less developed countries characterized by higher than average mortality and illness rates and widespread unemployment and poverty. At least 500,000 women die each year from pregnancy-related causes, with 99 percent of these deaths occurring in developing countries. Many more women in such countries suffer from serious health problems as a result of unwanted pregnancies. Worldwide, over 1 billion people live in absolute poverty or are too poor to buy enough food to maintain their health or to perform a job. Overpopulation is widely believed to present significant barriers to solving many of these concerns. In spite of such problems, the 1990s have seen faster increases in human population than any other decade in history.

In a review of the literature, John Elder and Jacqueline Estey (1992) report how behavior modification techniques have assisted developing countries to help their population manage the size of their families. Rewarding people for using contraception and undergoing sterilization has played a major role in such efforts. Some examples include:

*Monetary Rewards:* Money is by far the most frequent type of reinforcer offered for family planning. In the Tamil Nadu program in India, a small payment of 30 rupees (about $7.00) was paid to men and women volunteering to be sterilized. The payments were designed to compensate people for the time and energy they expended undergoing the procedure. It also was

assumed that people would see the value of the procedure for their long-term health and ability to raise existing children better. This program was very successful and averaged 3.42 sterilizations per thousand people. In other states in India not offering such incentives, the number of sterilizations was 1.00 per thousand people. Other programs have paid women a small sum each month not to have more than three children and to space their second and third children more than three years apart. The money is redeemed when they reach the end of their childbearing years.

*Material and Social Rewards:* Material reinforcers include food, powdered milk, priorities for housing, clothing, or even umbrellas. In the states of Kerala and Gujarat in India, the latter reinforcers led to 63,000 vasectomies in a 30-day period. In Thailand, women in rural areas were urged to space their next pregnancy with a pig. An acceptor of family planning would be given a 2-month-old piglet upon promising to continue to use fertility control methods during the pig's fattening period. Once the pig reached a 90-kg. weight, women would become eligible for another pig if they did not become pregnant (i.e., the initial pig was not taken away). In a 3-year period, no woman agreeing to the arrangement had given birth. In some cases, "gold medals" and special clothing with insignia have been used as awards for those who successfully participated in family planning. Social rewards used were recognition and praise for using contraceptives or for delaying births for a period of time.

---

my classes used a clever variation on this principle to help her write term papers. She would list the tasks needed to complete the paper (e.g., read certain articles, develop an outline, write a first draft, etc.). She then put $25 into a jar and made each part of the task worth a certain amount of money (e.g., each article read, $0.50, outline $3.00, first draft $8.00, etc.). As the task was completed, she withdrew the money and spent it on whatever she wanted to buy.

3. *Reinforce and learn the final response in a sequence of related actions before we reinforce and learn the earlier responses.* In toilet training young children, the first thing to reinforce and learn would be to sit for a few minutes on the potty. Normally this is the last response in the sequence of using a toilet. The children would then be taught to pull their pants down and to sit on the toilet. Eventually each aspect of the sequence of notifying a parent, walking to the bathroom, undressing, and sitting on

the potty is reinforced. Remember that all this training is achieved by reinforcing and learning responses later in the sequence first. How would you use this method to teach a young child to dress? How could you use this method to teach a worker to assemble an automobile engine or typewriter? Can you think of other responses for which the procedure might be appropriate?

**6. Shift from Continuous Reinforcement Once a Target Behavior Is Acquired** Obtaining a reinforcer each time a target behavior is completed is not always practical or possible in our daily lives. Initially, responses are reinforced on a continuous basis because they are learned faster. Behavior modification plans, however, should eventually rely less on continuous reinforcers. The goal is to wean ourselves from the control of external reinforcers. Our actions need to come under self-control. Thus, exercise continues because it makes us feel good, or good study habits are used because we then have more time to socialize.

Also, attempts should be made to bring behavior under the control of reinforcers that occur naturally in our environments. To do this, it is important to set a "reinforcement trap." The behavior becomes trapped by naturally occurring stimuli. Thus, external rewards are initially used to shape an exercise program. In the process, we lose weight, feel and look better, and find that others admire us more. We socialize more often and get comments on how nice we look. Paying attention to these natural reinforcers breaks our dependence on rewards that are self-administered.

While this shift may occur without any effort on our part, sometimes we need to assist the transfer to naturally occurring consequent stimuli. There are two things we might try. *One is to actively monitor the natural rewards that accompany changes in our actions.* By forcing ourselves to pay attention to their occurrence, we facilitate the chances of our actions coming under their control.

**7. A Second Strategy Is to Shift to a Less-than-Continuous Reinforcement Schedule** As you learned in Chapter 4, once some competency with a behavior is acquired, it is not always necessary to receive a reward every time. In fact, it is possible to continue responding with fewer reinforcers. The different reinforcement schedules (e.g.,

SHAPING BEHAVIOR

continuous, fixed- and variable-interval, and fixed- and variable-ratio) you learned about can be helpful when modifying a behavior. It is easy to use them. Once you see progress in modifying a behavior, shift from a continuous schedule to either an interval or ratio schedule. Make the shift gradually. For example, if I wanted to use a fixed-ratio schedule, I might first use it so that 75 or 80 percent of my responses were reinforced. Once an adjustment was made to this schedule, I could increase the number of responses needed for a reinforcer. The important point is not to shift too rapidly to a schedule that produces only a few reinforcers.

## 6. Obtain the Support of Others

It is oftentimes difficult to change our actions by ourselves. We might benefit from a shoulder to cry on or a person who can offer advice and encouragement. Or we might need another person to know about our plan because it keeps us honest and committed to our plan. It is sometimes easy to fool yourself about your progress, but another person may not be as easily deceived.

In clinical settings, a therapist helps people in these supportive ways. In your daily lives and for less severe problems, a friend, spouse, roommate, parent, or classmate may help. That person may simply listen and make comments on your plan. Or that individual might join you in helping to modify a behavior. A graduate student I worked with wanted to ensure that she finished her dissertation on time. She worked up a schedule and had weekly goals. She enlisted her husband to help. She put $200 into a jar and instructed her husband that for every week she failed to achieve her goal, he was to send $25 to her least favorite charity. Her husband only had to do this once. This procedure is called a response-cost because a failure to reach a goal costs you a positive reinforcer. It takes one other person to be used effectively. How might it be used to improve study habits, reduce smoking, or to consume less calories?

An alternative is to contract with another person to help you with your plan. The contract specifies your target behavior, how you will try to control the behavior, and what the other person needs to do to help. *When obtaining help from another person, do not*

| **Table 5.4** | A Sample Contract |
| --- | --- |

*General Target Behavior:* I want to stop eating junk food snacks.

*Specific Target Behavior:* I will stop eating candy bar snacks. In their place I will substitute healthy, nutritious snacks.

*Date:* March 20

*Contract between:* Susan Mann
Betty Conn (roommate of Susan Mann)

*Agreement:* Susan Mann—I agree to stop eating candy bars between my regular meals. I recorded my consumption of candy bars for the past seven days, and I eat 18 candy bars a week. I will begin my plan the first week by cutting back 2 candy bars a week. I will continue to cut 2 candy bars a week over the next nine weeks. At the end of the nine weeks, I will have eliminated them from my diet. In their place, I will substitute pieces of fruit, vegetables, nuts, and other wholesome snacks.

*Agreement:* Betty Conn—I agree to help Susan cut out candy bars from her diet. I will meet with her each night for ten minutes to discuss her progress. We will review her records of candy bars consumed and check that against her goal of eliminating two bars a week. I will comment on anything I notice that suggests she is losing interest or not following her plan properly. I will also check to see what nutritious snacks she is beginning to eat and make favorable comments on this.

*Consequences:* Susan Mann—For each week I meet my goal, I will put $4 aside into a fund to buy a new pair of slacks. If I fail to meet my goal during a week, I will do Betty's laundry and ironing for that week, and I will contribute nothing to the fund for the new slacks.

*Consequences:* Betty Conn—I will praise Susan for keeping her schedule and offer encouragement. If she achieves her goal of eliminating candy bars from her diet by the end of the ninth week, I will do her laundry and ironing that week.

*Review:* We agree to discuss this plan every two weeks and see if it is working well and to make any needed modifications.

*Signed:*

---

*use others to punish you when you fail to stick to your contract.* This often leads to bad feelings and arguments. Inform the support person that the only time he or she can assist is when you are exhibiting desirable behaviors. The contract is signed. Putting names on it ensures that both parties agree, and it increases your commitment to the process.

At first glance, such details may seem unnecessary. However, contracts that lack such details seldom produce desired results. In one study, students developed a contract with another person to improve study habits. One group formed very specific contracts, while the other group's contracts were less detailed (Seidner and Kirschenbaum, 1980). Those with specific contracts were much more enthusiastic about their plans to change behaviors, increased the amount of time spent studying, learned new study skills, and followed the details of the contract. An example of a contract that has the elements needed to increase the chances of success appears in Table 5.4.

Research shows that support and help from others is a key ingredient in whether a personal change plan will work (Hall, 1980). Having other people involved is particularly effective when trying to modify difficult habits such as losing weight, cigarette and

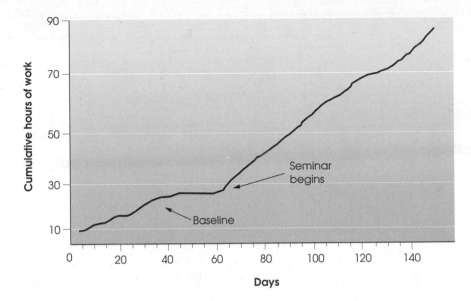

**Figure 5.2** *A cumulative record of writing behavior. The amount of time the psychologist described in the beginning of this chapter spent writing each day is added together for the baseline period and after the informal seminar began. Note the increase in writing that occurred after the seminar and the social support and rewards it provided. A cumulative graph allows one to check the total amount of a desirable behavior quickly and to note changes in the rate by which it occurs. (Adapted by permission from V. J. Stevens, Increasing professional productivity while teaching full time: A case study in self-control.* Teaching of Psychology, 5, *1978, 203–204.)*

alcohol consumption, delinquent behaviors, getting more exercise, and maintaining good health habits. In many cases, it is not necessarily the number of positive reinforcers they help to deliver that makes the difference. Rather, it is the overall support that they provide for your efforts to change (Cohen and Lichtenstein, 1990). When social support and reinforcement are introduced, the effects on behavior can be rather dramatic, as illustrated in Figure 5.2.

## 7. Monitor and Record Your Progress When Modifying Behaviors

Baseline data are not the only records needed. It is also important to record progress toward achieving a target behavior as well. Behavioral changes take time, and monitoring our progress will allow us to assess if a plan is working. What, if any, adjustments should be made can then be determined. To keep such records, you need only extend in time the procedures you used for the baseline data. A suggested way to do this appears in Table 5.5.

Some responses are difficult to monitor alone, and a little common sense is needed. A friend of mine wanted to improve his golf swing and needed information on the length of his backswing, the position of his wrists, and his hip movements. Trying to monitor his movements and swing the club only made things worse. He solved the problem by asking one of his playing partners to watch each component for him. He was then able to keep accurate records.

**Table 5.5**                          A Record-Keeping Format

*Specific Target Behavior:* Want to increase the average number of sales reports I write to eight per day by June 19. (Note: This example extends the analysis begun in Table 5.1)

*Baseline Recording Began:* May 10

*Behavior Mod. Plan Began:* May 24

*Control of Discriminitive Stimuli:* Will use my voice mail to screen telephone calls so I don't pick up the phone every time it rings. Also will put a small sign on my desk to remind me to finish a complete report before doing anything else.

*Reinforcement Plan:* Unless it is an emergency, I will allow myself to talk on the telephone only after I have completed a minimum of three reports. Each day that I meet my target, I will allow myself to select one of the following: a favorite dessert, a movie from the video store, an hour to read a favorite book, or time to watch two of my favorite television shows.

**Days of the Week**

|      | 1 | 2 | 3 | 4 | 5 | Total |
|------|---|---|---|---|---|-------|
| 5/10 | 6 | 8 | 7 | 5 | 4 | 30 |
| 5/17 | 7 | 6 | 5 | 8 | 5 | 31 |
| 5/24 | 8 | 7 | 6 | 8 | 6 | 35 |
| 5/31 | 7 | 8 | 7 | 8 | 7 | 37 |
| 6/7  | 8 | 8 | 7 | 7 | 8 | 38 |
| 6/14 | 8 | 8 | 8 | 8 | 8 | 40 |

*Specific Target Behavior:* I want to reduce my smoking by two cigarettes a day until I cut my smoking habit in half.

*Baseline Recording Began:* March 7

*Behavior Mod. Plan Began:* March 14

*Control of Discriminitive Stimuli:* Will walk away from people while they are smoking. Will chew gum or take a brisk walk when urge to smoke occurs.

**Days of the Week**

|      | 1  | 2  | 3  | 4  | 5  | 6  | 7  | Total |
|------|----|----|----|----|----|----|----|-------|
| 3/7  | 32 | 36 | 28 | 30 | 32 | 31 | 30 | 219 |
| 3/14 | 34 | 32 | 30 | 30 | 28 | 26 | 26 | 206 |
| 3/21 | 26 | 24 | 24 | 22 | 20 | 18 | 16 | 150 |
| 3/29 | 16 | 14 | 14 | 15 | 14 | 13 | 14 | 100 |

*Reinforcement Plan:* Will give myself ten points each day that I meet my goal. Every time I accumulate thirty points, I will treat myself to a movie.

# SOCIAL-BASED APPROACHES TO MODIFYING BEHAVIOR

## Imitation Learning

What was something you think you learned by watching other people? Who was the person you observed, and how were your responses similar? Listed below are three reactions to these questions from students in my classes. Can you identify with any of them?

1. Sometimes I act just like my mom when I get angry. It is really weird. My mom usually throws things around when she gets mad and then bursts into tears. I find I have a similar emotional response when I get really mad.

2. I practice four or five times a week, but what really seems to help is to watch someone who is better than me. I don't mean a real professional. Just someone who plays a bit better than I do. The professionals are just too good. Watching them doesn't help me as much.

3. I've got a good one for you. Last night I was leaving a restaurant, and they had small bowls at the cash register with the names of waitresses on them. They were marked "tips" and each had a few dollars in it. I usually don't tip at the fast food places, but seeing the money in the dish and watching other people put a couple of quarters in them as they left influenced me. I dropped 50 cents into the dish marked with my waitress's name. It wasn't much, but then again I seldom leave a tip.

Perhaps you have had similar reactions. Observing other people and imitating their behaviors are important influences on our learning. Modeling the actions of others helps us to learn various skills, emotional responses, socially appropriate behaviors, and even aspects of our sex roles.

*Developing Skills*    Observing other people is often a first step in acquiring a new skill or enhancing an existing one. We might, for example, learn how to swing a golf club, play tennis, cook a meal, make a dress or sport coat, drive an automobile, or do the latest dance steps. We then try the skill ourselves and obtain feedback and perhaps a pat on the back. The feedback and rewards for imitating a model are essential elements of learning from our observations of other people (Bandura, 1986).

In one study, supervisors were taught management skills using principles of imitation learning. Forty supervisors were assigned to a group that received training on how to model behaviors or to a control group. The training was designed to improve their ability to motivate employees, to handle complaints, and to overcome resistance to change. Films of supervisors successfully handling such problems were shown to the modeling group. Participants then practiced the skills they observed. Compared to the control group, supervisors exposed to the models received higher performance ratings on the job, acquired their skills quickly, and were judged to have better interpersonal skills by their superiors (Latham and Saari, 1979).

*Developing Socially Appropriate Behaviors*    Most of us return favors; periodically contribute to charities; display good manners at meals and social occasions; and are willing to help a friend, neighbor, or a stranger who needs assistance with a task. Such behaviors are learned, and research suggests that imitating models helps us acquire such responses. *Models provide a definition of socially appropriate behavior, and observing a model is sometimes more effective than simply telling someone to "do the right thing."*

One example of the latter tendency occurred in a study in which 11,051 students attending 66 high schools were asked to donate blood (Sarason et al., 1991). One group of students was shown an informational slide show about blood and its uses and asked to donate. The second group viewed a slide show that also showed a number of students giving blood and the popularity of high school blood drives. The group shown a model had 16.9 percent more donations to the blood bank than the group simply given information and asked to donate blood.

*Learning and Expressing Our Emotions*    As children we learned to express various emotions by observing the actions of people we admired and respected. Children who have highly anxious parents, for example, behave more anxiously than do other children. Also, our fears of snakes, spiders, and other things are strongly influenced by observing models (Ollendick and King, 1991).

Anger, anxiety, frustration, and other unpleasant emotions are not the only ones we might acquire by imitating others. We also learn in part how to express joy, excitement, happiness, serenity, relaxation, and other pleasant emotions in similar ways. Many of us developed ideas of how to show affection toward the opposite sex, to hug and kiss, or to make love by trying to imitate a respected model.

While models for emotional responses are sometimes people we know directly, this is not always the case. We learn a number of pleasant and unpleasant emotional reactions by watching films and television. We might identify with an actor and actress and get angry or show affection like they did. Television and movie violence acts as a stimulus for existing aggressive tendencies and leads to a breakdown in the inhibitions that existed against violence. Violent models also activate violence-related thoughts and suggest specific ways for carrying out such tendencies (Belson, 1978; Zillmann, 1989; Bushman and Geen, 1990).

To be fair, you must recognize that pleasant emotions and other socially acceptable behaviors are also stimulated by models on television and in the movies. David Loye (1978) showed that some television shows make people feel less aggressive; these people also report feeling more satisfied with themselves and other people after watching them. Susan Hearold (1986) reported that after watching programs that demonstrated prosocial behaviors, viewers' scores on tests of prosocial behavior increased. This was particularly true of their willingness to help other people in need.

*Developing a Gender Role*   Many of our masculine and feminine behaviors are learned through male and female role models. Such models helped us learn appropriate behaviors for our gender. We may have imitated our parents, relatives we admired, famous actors and actresses, and close friends who displayed traditional masculine and feminine behaviors.

In the United States, James Doyle notes how boys are encouraged to imitate war heroes, famous male athletes, and successful businessmen. Many women, on the other hand, are exposed to role models who teach them to cook, sew, care for babies, and engage in other behaviors that are considered feminine (Doyle, 1983). Apparently, the models different cultures provide for men and women to imitate are rather similar. A typical finding is that around the globe, girls spend more time helping with housework and child care, while boys spend more time in unsupervised play (Edwards, 1991).

Even if people are exposed to them for brief periods of time, masculine and feminine models exert very powerful effects. In one study, college women were shown a number of television commercials. Some were shown commercials in which the women played passive roles while men played authority figures. Other women were shown commercials with the same content but with women as the authorities. The participants then had to engage in a variety of tasks, including a four-minute public speech. Judges assessed how independent, conforming, and self-confident the women were on the tasks. Those who watched women in independent, self-confident roles displayed more independence, less conforming behavior, and more self-confidence (Jennings, Geis, and Brown, 1980).

## Using Imitation Learning Principles

*Select a Role Model*   Obviously, imitation learning is an important learning process in our lives. The principles associated with modeling others can be used to develop a

| **Table 5.6** | Characteristics of Effective Models |
| --- | --- |

The research literature suggests the following characteristics are associated with effective models.

**Personality Characteristics**
- Warm and friendly personalities.
- Worthy of respect because of their competence, prestige, and intelligence.
- Similar to us with respect to sex, age, socioeconomic status, and physical characteristics.

**Competence with Skill**
- Are able to perform the skill we want to master.
- Perform the skill at a level that is normally one or two steps above our level or are able to perform at this level if asked.
- Are not perfect and occasionally make a few mistakes when performing the skill.
- Get rewarded for performing the skill or at least can demonstrate that positive rewards can be normally expected after completing the behavior.

**Ability to Teach Skill**
- Can break the skill up into its component parts to demonstrate it.
- Can organize the behavior according to how difficult it is.
- Can teach the skill by beginning with least difficult aspects and moving to most difficult components.
- Can talk about, label, and summarize what they are doing as they perform the skill.
- Can help you master particular parts of the skill by verbally or manually guiding your actions if needed.

variety of interpersonal, academic, and job-related skills. To do this, we must pay attention to the factors that research demonstrates makes imitation learning effective and apply them to our lives.

A good place to begin is by finding a model who can help you learn the skills you wish to acquire. The work of Albert Bandura(1986) identifies several characteristics of effective models, which are presented in Table 5.6. A model does not necessarily have to be a person with whom we normally interact. Television and radio personalities, sports figures, cartoon characters, actors in instructional audiotapes and videotapes, and people pictured preparing recipes, fixing cars, and making clothes also may help us acquire certain behaviors. Some people are even able to learn to write by studying a model's writing, as Focus on People 5.1 illustrates. Of course, if it is necessary to ask questions or to have the model coach you, his or her physical presence is certainly needed.

*Attention, Retention, and Motivational and Physical Movement Processes* Selecting a model who has certain characteristics is a first step in using the components of imitation learning. In addition, there are several other things to consider. Research by Albert Bandura demonstrates that people benefit most from models when they take steps to pay attention, to retain what the model does, to maintain their motivation, and to ensure that they are effectively employing the skills learned. *Attending means that one must notice the details of the model's behaviors.* What does the model do to swing a golf

FOCUS ON PEOPLE 5.1

## On Becoming A Best-selling Author

During the nineteenth century, a popular device for becoming a good author was for people to copy Shakespeare. Individuals using this technique hoped that by copying his writings, aspects of his style would rub off on them. Since no one has matched Shakespeare's skill and style, it is doubtful the technique worked as well as people thought it would.

While copying someone's writing does not work, it is possible to profit from consciously trying to model and imitate some of the things established writers do. This was demonstrated by best-selling author Robin Cook. Before writing his first novel, *Coma*, Robin Cook was an opthamologist and clinical instructor at Harvard Medical School. He had never written a novel before, and his only writing experience had been scientific articles. He was convinced, however, that he could write a good mystery.

To write his novel, he read and studied more than 100 best-selling mystery and adventure novels to discover the devices their authors used to capture and hold the reader's attention. He did this by taking notes on those features of the books that built excitement and held the reader's interest. The plot devices that were used frequently and that appeared to work best were incorporated into his story. The result was a best-selling novel titled *Coma* that told the story of how a woman medical student unraveled mysterious deaths at a hospital. It was read by millions and became a popular movie. It also became the first in a long line of best-selling novels by this author (based on a story in *People*, October 22, 1978).

club, make a dress, or dance with grace on the dance floor? Once we attend to such things, it is important to compare how the model's actions differ from ours. This discrepancy helps us to develop a plan for what we want to do. Furthermore, the model's behavior must be retained. A period of time might pass before we have the opportunity to try what the model did. This could be a few seconds or minutes or, in some cases, several hours or days. Labeling what the model does, taking notes, or summarizing what occurs helps us to remember. Motivation can be maintained by observing the rewards the model receives. Of course, we must remind ourselves that successful imitation of the behavior can be rewarding for us as well. While trying the behavior, giving ourselves a few pats on the back and even earning the admiration of others is motivational. Finally, we should also have the physical abilities to copy the model's actions. With physical skills such as playing a particular sport, certain muscles might need to be developed through practice and exercise before we can imitate successfully. Suggestions for employing these components are listed in Table 5.7.

Observational learning typically occurs in the background of our lives. We are not always aware of following a model. When the components of the model are made explicit, however, people are in a position to make changes in their lives (Bandura, 1986). A planning process for utilizing imitation learning principles is presented in Exercise 5.2 in the Applied Activities section at the end of this chapter.

## *COGNITIVE-BASED APPROACHES TO MODIFYING BEHAVIOR*

Cognitive approaches to modifying behavior try to achieve changes in behavior by altering thought patterns, beliefs, attitudes, and opinions. Such methods attempt this by getting people to change how they talk to themselves and/or try altering their self-

| Table 5.7 | Using Important Processes in Imitation Learning |
| --- | --- |

**Attention Processes**
- Pay attention to factors that distinguish the model from you.
- Keep yourself alert to notice details of the model's behavior.
- Use all of your senses to help recognize important behaviors the model demonstrates.

**Retention Processes**
- Summarize what the model does.
- Take notes on how the model behaves, and review them periodically.
- Create labels to describe what the model is doing (e.g., closed stance, firm left arm/wrist).

**Motivational Processes**
- Encourage and reward yourself for progress made in imitating.
- Watch others receive rewards for successful imitation.
- Focus on the encouragement that others give you for trying to change.

**Physical Movement Processes**
- Develop physical abilities through practice and exercise in order to copy model's actions.
- Observe yourself perform the physical activities. Determine if they meet the standards to successfully reproduce the model's behavior.
- Get feedback from others on how well your behavior matches that of the model.

images and those of the world around them. Many of the methods were developed by therapists who sought to help people resolve problems in their lives. The methods have since found a variety of applications in therapy, sports, education, and other areas of our lives.

## Self-instruction

Most people take instructions from teachers, coaches, parents, and others who are trying to show us how to do something. Such instruction not only gives us the steps to do something, but also includes words of encouragement. Donald Meichenbaum has developed ideas for modifying behavior based on the philosophy that people can teach or coach themselves (Meichenbaum, 1977, 1986). His methods have been used to help people to overcome negative self-images; to cope with emotions such as anxiety and depression; and to perform better on a variety of interpersonal, communication, and sports skills.

When dealing with negative emotions, for example, Meichenbaum tries to teach people to relax and to say comforting things to themselves. The emphasis is not on eliminating negative feelings but on giving people an alternative to letting their emotions rule them. Studies (cf. Mahoney and Lyddon, 1988; Rehm, 1988) have shown that the following ideas are useful:

- Repeat helpful reminders to yourself to relax (e.g., "Be calm, relax those tense muscles, and take it easy, there is no reason to overreact. This is only a test and not the end of the world").

- Reinterpret or reframe problems differently (e.g., "My anxiety over taking this test is not dreadful, and if used right it can help me to prepare better").
- Replace self-defeating thoughts with incompatible ones, including those that contain positive self-instructions (e.g., "I can handle this test," versus, "I'm not going to do well").
- Remind yourself of helpful actions to take ("I need to fall back on the basics of studying to do well").
- Remember to self-reward desirable behaviors (e.g., "I spent three good hours studying, and I deserve a pat on the back").

Research shows that self-instruction can help people cope with unpleasant emotions. In clinical settings it sometimes reduces anxiety levels enough that people are able to take less of certain drugs such as Valium to control anxiety. In one study, for example, self-instructional strategies cut in half the amount of Valium needed to control anxiety (DeVogue, Minor, and Karoly, 1981). Furthermore, people who try to change difficult behaviors such as eating patterns or who try to give up drugs or get more physical activity sometimes relapse into old habits. When this happens, it is not unusual for them to feel guilty, blame themselves, and give up. Included are saying things to themselves like, "I've failed at this again. I can't seem to change. I've got no long lasting willpower." Helpful self-instructions include things like, "Old habits are difficult to break. I had a relapse here, but that's to be expected. It happens a lot, and I just need to learn from this mistake and try not to repeat it again in the future." The latter instructions are much more helpful in getting oneself back on track (Marlatt and Gordon, 1985).

An example of how self-instruction was used by a company president to reduce anxiety over giving a speech and to enhance his confidence in public speaking skills is presented in Focus on People 5.2. As you read, think of how the same techniques might be used to make you more confident about speaking in public.

## Mental Practice

In Chapter 4, the role of mental imagery in improving memory and acquiring new behaviors was discussed. Mental imagery can also be used to change certain habits or to enhance our ability to perform. In particular, mental imagery is effective when used to engage in **mental practice,** or rehearsal of a skill. Athletes, for example, who imagine themselves performing a skill before competition tend to do better than those who do not (Mahoney and Auner, 1977). High jumper Dick Fosbury, for example, often frustrated both the crowd and the officials by insisting on "mental practice" before he jumped. Fosbury, who revolutionized the style of high jumping, used to spend several minutes at the runway. He reported that he was "jumping in his head" and that he sometimes missed. When his mental rehearsal resulted in failure, he picked himself up out of the pit and made another fantasized attempt. Fosbury refused to make an actual approach to the bar until he had successfully cleared it in his head (Mahoney and Auner, 1977).

Studies show (cf. Suinn, 1983, 1989) that mental rehearsal is most likely to benefit you when:

- You possess the physical ability needed to execute the skill.
- It is used in conjunction with regular practice.

**FOCUS ON PEOPLE 5.2**

## Using Self-Instruction to Overcome Anxiety over Public Speaking

A company president I consulted with was shown how to use self-instruction to reduce a mild case of anxiety over public speaking. He was worried about giving a speech to company stockholders because the company was not doing as well as last year. He was taught to use several aspects of self-instruction.

*Remind himself to relax.* He was taught to control his breathing and loosen tension in his face, neck, and upper body muscles. When tense, he told himself how to reduce some of the tension (cf. Chapter 10 for examples of such techniques).

*Reinterpret the fear.* That is, say things to himself that made the fear of public speaking less aversive. Thus, he said such things to himself as, "The fact that I'm nervous before giving a speech does not mean I am going to screw up the talk. My anxiety is just a natural way my body prepares me to become alert to do a good job."

*Focus on helpful actions by thinking of successful speaking practices.* Because he had enjoyed success in the past, a checklist of key things he did when giving a talk was developed. Furthermore, he was asked to mentally rehearse his checklist of successful behaviors before practicing his talk and before giving it to the stockholders. Finally, he reminded himself of occasions when items on his checklist were used successfully and how well his talk was received.

*Reinforce himself for doing a good job.* He was instructed to make reinforcing self-statements immediately after he had practiced his speech successfully and after he had given it to the stockholders. "I did everything I said I was going to do well. I knew I could do a good job. That was a very fine speech I made, and my boss looked impressed."

Everything worked out well for him. The stockholders were disappointed in the company's performance but liked his ideas for turning the situation around. One of his ideas for new products received a large round of applause. Self-instruction made the situation much more tolerable for him.

- You are motivated to learn and able to concentrate and focus on the components of the skill.
- The mental images formed are concrete and vivid.
- The mental images follow the sequence of how the skill is normally executed.
- You are able to imagine yourself in control of the situation and confidently executing the skill.
- You are relaxed and not anxious when mentally performing the skill. Typically, people are taught a method for relaxation and then practice while lying down or sitting quietly in a comfortable chair (cf. examples of relaxation methods in Chapter 10).
- Whenever possible, you try to have one last mental rehearsal just before engaging in the skill.

Mental practice, when used as the only intervention, is most beneficial for those who are adequately prepared physically. In sports, for example, the higher the ability level, the more benefit people derive from such practice (Zecker, 1982).

When combined with self-instruction procedures, mental practice can be even more effective, as Focus on Applied Research 5.2 illustrates. As you read, try to imagine yourself using similar techniques to play your favorite sport better, to prepare for an exam, or to improve your performance on certain work skills.

## Brainpower Golf

Daniel Kirschenbaum and Ronald Bale are psychologists, and avid golfers, who were convinced that cognitive-behavioral methods could be used to improve a person's ability to play the game (Kirschenbaum and Bale, 1980). To test their thinking, they analyzed what the pros said about the mental side of golf by reading 68 instructional golf books and two years of issues from *Golf Digest* and *Golf Magazine*. Based on this reading and their knowledge of behavioral psychology, they developed a training program based on self-instructional and mental imagery principles. Golfers were trained in how to use such techniques. The specific techniques used were:

*Deep-muscle relaxation.* Golfers were taught how to progressively tense and relax 12 muscle groups. Golfers used their knowledge to remind themselves to relax specific muscles a few minutes prior to their tee time or when needed during a rematch.

*Use of a planning checklist.* A review of each shot by using a checklist was made before taking it. The checklist was carried in a notebook and included such things as: lie of the ball, turf condition, potential hazards, wind, club selection, break of green, and distance to green and hole.

*Mental practice.* Before each shot, golfers were instructed to imagine the shot they wanted to take while holding the club. They were taught to picture such things as the feel of the shot, the swing they would take, the flight of the ball, and the ball landing in the target area.

*Positive self-monitoring.* After finishing a given hole, the golfers reviewed everything they had done well with each club they used. To prevent becoming their own worst enemy, they were told to "file away the poor shots in their memories" and "recall them after the game."

*Positive instructional self-statements.* Golfers were taught to develop a list of statements that would motivate them and prevent them from becoming anxious. The statements included such things as "Play your own game at your own pace," "You've made great shots with this club before," or "Your competence as a golfer does not depend upon your performance in any particular game."

Compared to their performance before training, golfers on college teams reported the program was very helpful, and data showed it reduced the number of strokes they took over 18 holes by an average of 1.5 strokes per round. At their level of competition, one to two strokes often determines who wins or loses.

There are a variety of other approaches for modifying our behaviors, thoughts, and feelings. Those presented in this chapter have emphasized changing overt behaviors by managing environmental stimuli, modeling others, and using mental processes such as self-instruction and mental practice. You will find discussions of other methods in Chapters 6, 8, and 10 of this book. There you will find suggestions for how to gain control over important attitudes, values, and beliefs that help to guide and direct your actions. Also, techniques for managing your emotions in interpersonal relationships and for reducing stress will be discussed.

## Summary of Chapter Organizers

Suggested responses to the chapter organizers presented at the beginning of this chapter are presented below.

1. *What are two assumptions that underlie different approaches to changing behaviors, thoughts, and feelings?* Change strategies tend to emphasize changes in overt behaviors and/or underlying thoughts and feelings. Those directed towards overt behaviors assume that as more desirable behaviors occur, less desirable thoughts and feelings associated with them also will decrease. Methods that focus on modifying underlying thoughts and emotions assume that changes in thoughts and feelings also will affect the behaviors they guide and direct. Sometimes both types of strategies are combined in a behavior modification plan.

2. *What are the ABCs of behavior and how do they explain the connection between environmental stimuli and our actions, thoughts, and feelings?* The ABCs of behavior refer to stimuli that precede our actions (i.e., antecedent stimuli) and consequent stimuli (rewards and punishment). In a learning process called *operant conditioning*, behaviors, thoughts, and feelings are influenced by such antecedent and consequent stimuli. Antecedents provide information to help us decide whether certain actions will lead to a reward or punishment (e.g., a sign on a park bench that says "Wet Paint"). Failing to heed the sign will get your clothes dirty and effectively punish your actions. Some antecedents also automatically trigger desirable and undesirable behaviors.

3. *Can you list seven parts of a process for modifying behavior that stresses our gaining control over environmental stimuli to help us change?* When using operant conditioning principles to modify behavior, it is important for you to do the following: identify the problem, and select a specific target behavior; monitor how much of the target behavior currently exists; control antecedent stimuli; break response chains; manage consequent stimuli; obtain social support; and monitor and record progress towards changing behavior.

4. *Why is it important to identify specific goals or target behaviors you want to change, and what is the best way to do this?* Having clear target behaviors or goals in mind provides direction to your attempts to change. It is often helpful to begin the process with a general statement of what you would like to do (e.g., I need to study more). After you become more familiar with the problem by thinking about it and/or reacting to information gathered from a diary and recording baseline data, a more specific statement of what you want to do can be determined (e.g., I need to increase the amount of time I spend studying by 6 hours a week). Besides being specific, targets should be important to you; they should not force you to do too much at once; and they should be stated in a positive manner.

5. *Do you know how to monitor and record information that will help you to understand a behavior you want to change better?* Monitoring information is best done by keeping a diary of the ABCs of behavior associated with your target as well as recording either the frequency, duration, or amount of something the behavior of interest consumes. It is also important not to focus only on negative information but to monitor things you do well. Information should be recorded as soon after it occurs as possible as well as until a clear pattern of when, where, and how often the behavior of interest occurs.

6. *What are some ways to effectively manage the stimuli that control your actions?* Both antecedent stimuli and consequent stimuli can be managed. Troublesome antecedent stimuli can be removed or avoided, or you may want to add new

antecedents that promote desirable behaviors to a situation. When managing consequent stimuli, stress the use of positive reinforcement, and whenever possible, try to avoid the use of punishment. Behaviors should be rewarded immediately after they occur, and you should not demand too much effort for too little a reward. Successive approximations to your target behavior should be reinforced as well as eventually trying to shift from continuous reinforcement once a target is acquired.

7. *What are some things you have learned by modeling other people?* Observing models and trying to imitate their actions is an important part of your ability to learn. Modeling helps you to acquire a variety of skills, to develop socially appropriate behaviors, to express emotions, and to know how to act in your gender role.

8. *Do you know the critical elements involved in following a model that can help you learn effectively?* Good models are people you admire and respect, who are just above you in their ability level, who make mistakes, and who are similar to you in gender and personality. Learning from a model also involves employing several interrelated processes. You need to focus attention on the model, take steps to retain to what the model does, maintain your motivation to observe, and ensure that you have or can acquire the physical skills to follow a model.

9. *What are some things you can say to yourself to help modify your actions?* Self-instruction is a useful tool for modifying our behaviors, thoughts, and feelings. It works best when you repeat helpful reminders to yourself, reframe problems in a more productive manner, replace self-defeating thoughts with more helpful statements, remind yourself of helpful actions to take, and try to self-reward desirable behaviors.

10. *Why is mental practice often an effective part of modifying behavior? What can you do to make it an effective part of your life?* Mental practice helps you to focus on certain behaviors and to mentally rehearse how you will behave in particular situations. It works best when you possess the physical ability to execute the skill; it is used in conjunction with regular practice; you are motivated to learn; the mental images are concrete and vivid; they follow the sequence of how the skill is normally executed; you can imagine yourself confidently executing the skill; you are relaxed when thinking about how to employ the behavior; and you have one last mental rehearsal just before engaging in the skill.

## Things to Do

1. Let your imagination run wild. Pretend that you are in absolute control of your work environment. Your boss and coworkers will do whatever you tell them to do. Design a work environment that is based on principles associated with operant and respondent teaming. Pay particular attention to such things as pay and salary schedules, work schedules, discipline problems, organization of your work unit, everyone pulling his or her fair share of the work, and promotions.

2. In Focus on Applied Research 5.1, the use of behavior modification techniques to limit family size in developing countries was illustrated. Are you in favor of such strategies, or do you believe they go against a right of every human being to have as many children as he or she wants? Should such strategies be adapted to countries other than those considered "less developed"?

3. Using the ABCs of behavior and the example of the process shown in Figure 5.1, diagram how each component can be used to have shoppers return shopping carts when they take groceries to their cars, influence people to use parking meters at

the end of a block rather than in the middle, increase the number of people who ride a mass transit system, encourage married couples to have no more than two children, reduce the number of people who are on welfare, get people to put litter into garbage cans in a city park.

4. A number of our behaviors are acquired through observational or imitation learning. Think about your life for a moment, and develop a list of skills, ways of expressing emotions, socially appropriate behaviors, and aspects of your gender role that you acquired in part through imitation learning. Who did you use as a model, and when in your life did you acquire such things?

5. How would you employ self-instruction and mental practice to help you successfully acquire the skills in activity 4 above?

6. Ted is having trouble meeting deadlines at work. He takes on more work than he can handle and tries to do everything perfectly. As a result, he falls short of his goals. He completes tasks later and does not do the quality job he thinks is necessary. His boss has told him that he has to "get his act together" or he will be terminated. You are asked to work with Ted to help him improve his performance on the job. What ideas from the discussion of stimulus-based approaches to behavior modification, social approaches, and cognitive approaches would you suggest that Ted use? Give a reason for why you choose each principle, and suggest how Ted might put it to good use in his life.

7. Imagine that whenever a friend enters his living room, the television set is turned on, and he then walks to the kitchen to get a snack. Afterwards, your friend sits down in a comfortable chair and lights up a cigarette and eats a snack. This behavior continues into the evening, and eventually he discovers there is little time left in the day to study. What advice would you give your friend for breaking this response chain? What would you suggest he do to learn a more desirable response?

## APPLIED ACTIVITIES

EXERCISE 5.1
**Developing a Behavior Modification Plan**

Having just read about the components of developing a behavior modification plan, use each of the steps outlined below to develop a plan for a changing one of your behaviors. If you are uncertain of what is involved in each step, refer to the appropriate section in the chapter. Use the space provided to develop your plan.

1. Identify a Target Behavior
   A. Identify a behavior that is important to you and that you would like to change. State a general target behavior, and then convert it into a statement that is much more specific.
      i. General target behavior statement:



      ii. Initial thoughts about a specific version of the target behavior:



   B. What reasons do you have for wanting to change, modify, or acquire the behavior listed above? List the pros and cons of the changes you would like to make.
      i. Pros:                                    ii. Cons:



2. Monitor Baseline Behavior
   A. Develop a format for recording baseline data. Use the diary and chart formats described in the text. Outline generally what you will do in the space provided. You will need a small notebook in which to record your baseline data.







   B. Reevaluate your target behavior.
      i. What antecedents influenced the behavior?



      ii. The consequent stimuli that control the behavior:

C. Did your diary and baseline suggest anything about your initial target statement? Does it have to be revised in any way? Restate your target behavior if neccessary.

D. If you are modifying a bad habit, state a replacement behavior target you will try to increase as you attempt to decrease the habit. Ensure that your replacement target is specific and that the behavior has been broken into smaller manageable units.

3. Control Antecedent Stimuli

Based on information obtained from your diary, what antecedent stimuli are associated with the behavior you want to change? What can you do to ensure that they will not influence your actions? Indicate how one or more of the following ideas might be used in your plan.

i. What can you do to remove antecedent stimuli associated with problems in your life?

ii. How can you avoid situations in which antecedents either cue or trigger responses you want to change?

iii. What stimuli could you add to a situation to help initiate desirable behaviors?

4. Break Response Chains

Is the behavior you are trying to modify tied in with a sequence of actions? Would breaking one part of the sequence help you to change it? What is the sequence, and how might you break it up?

5. Manage Consequent Stimuli

A. What specific rewards will you use to modify your behavior? Use Table 5.3 for ideas and select positive reinforcers that are likely to influence the behavior.

B. How can you break your target behavior into interconnected subunits? List the subunits in the space provided.

C. How, when, and where will you reward the behavior and/or each subunit connected with it?

D. Is the cost/benefit ratio adequate? Are you demanding too much effort for too little of a reward? Yes _____ No _____ If yes, what adjustments will you make?

E. Once your target is acquired, indicate how you plan to manage the shift to an intermittent schedule.

6. Obtain the Support of Other People
   A. Can you enlist the aid of other people to help you change? A minimum requirement might be to have someone to share your plan with and with whom to periodically discuss your progress. Would forming a contract with someone help you to modify your behavior? If a contract is desirable, outline the types of things you would like to see in the contract in the space provided. Write the complete contract on another sheet of paper using the model provided in the text. Be sure that you and the other person sign it.

   B. Who will you get to provide the social support you feel is needed?

7. Monitor and Record Your Progress
   Outline ideas for a table, chart, or graph to monitor your progress. You can continue to use the format you established when you baselined your general target behavior. Use another sheet of paper to record your progress and follow the suggestions in the text.

EXERCISE 5.2    **A Planning Process for Using Principles of Imitation Learning**

**List two or three skills you would like to learn or to modify.** Pick those that you feel you could acquire by observing and imitating another.

**Example:** Learn to interview for a job; write a term paper.

**Select one of the skills listed above that you feel you would have the best chance of acquiring.**

**Example:** Learn to interview for a job.

**Select one or more models using the criteria for a good model in Table 4.5.**

**Example:** My friend Fred who just got a job after several interviews. Also, I would like to watch a videotape on interviewing skills at the career center on campus.

**What will you have to do to make the best use of the model(s) you selected?** What are some things you must do to maintain attention, enhance retention, keep yourself motivated, and help yourself develop appropriate physical skills? Is there anything you need to tell your model to do? Consult Tables 5.6 and 5.7 for ideas.

**Example:** I'll ask Fred to describe what happened at the job interviews and to show me how he answered some of the questions. I'll pay close attention to what he says and summarize what I think he is doing well and see if he agrees with me. I'll ask him to throw a few questions at me and have him critique how well I performed. While watching the videotape on interviewing skills, I'll take good notes and try to develop a checklist from the videotape of good interview practices. As I start to learn some things, I'll pat myself on the back a few times. I'll also remind myself that if I learn some things, I will get a job.

   Implement your plan. Evaluate how your attempts to imitate are working out, and make any needed corrections to ensure success.

## Key Terms

*Antecedent stimuli.*   Stimuli that occur before we respond and that exert an influence on that response. Some antecedent stimuli act as cues or provide information that certain actions will lead to a reward or punishment (e.g., a "Wet Paint" sign on a bench). Others automatically trigger reflexes and other automatic habits and sequences of behaviors (e.g., removing one's hand from a hot object, slowing a car down as you approach a busy intersection).

*Baseline data.*   The level of performance before behavior is manipulated by rewards and punishment.

*Behaviorism.*   A theoretical approach to human behavior that attempts to break our actions into stimulus and response components. Behaviors are then explained in terms of how various stimuli affect responses.

*Consequent stimuli.*   Those stimuli that occur after a response occurs. Some consequent stimuli reward behaviors and thus acquire the capacity to control our actions.

*Cost/benefit ratio.*   The ratio of the benefits a positive reinforcer produces relative to the costs involved in performing an action that leads to a reward. People generally continue responding when the benefits of the rewards they receive exceed the costs of responding.

*Discriminative stimulus.*   A stimulus that occurs before a response and that acts as a cue or signal that a particular action will be rewarded or punished.

*Imitation learning.*   A process of acquiring behaviors based on observing a model and then imitating what the model does. This process is also called *modeling* or *observational learning.*

*Mental practice.*   The use of mental imagery to rehearse or practice a sequence of actions.

*Operant conditioning.*   A learning procedure that emphasizes the role of positive and negative reinforcers in controlling our behavior.

*Operants.*   Behaviors that a person voluntarily emits and that are usually considered to be under conscious control.

*Reactivity.*   The tendency for behaviors to change in a more desirable direction when they are self-monitored and recorded.

*Response cost.*   A technique for taking away positive reinforcers every time an inappropriate response *is* made.

*Self-management procedure.*   The use of behavior modification principles to modify or change our actions and thoughts.

*Self-instruction.*   A process for learning that has people coach themselves into thinking and doing things in a certain manner.

*Shaping.*   A process of learning in which each successful attempt at making a part of a complete response is rewarded.

*Target behavior.*   The specific behavioral outcomes or goals that people work toward.

*Token reward.*   A symbolic reward that is given after a desirable response (e.g., giving a poker chip to reward a child's behavior in school. The chips can be traded in at a later time for other rewards).

## CHAPTER 6

# Motivation in Everyday Life

### Chapter Overview

Motivation refers to the factors that initiate, guide, and maintain your behaviors towards obtaining certain goals. They include a variety of biological and learned needs, expectations and values, and incentives in your environment. This chapter examines such factors and provides insights as well as practical suggestions for how to manage the motives that operate in your life.

### Chapter Organizers

*As you read, answer the questions that follow on a separate sheet of paper, and check your responses with those provided in the summary section.*

Our behaviors do not exist in isolation from our biological makeup.

1. In what ways does your genetic makeup motivate your actions?
2. How do needs and drives affect your actions?

Thirst, hunger, and sex are three motives that have a strong biological component as well as being affected by other influences in our lives.

3. Are you aware of how physiological, cognitive, and environmental influences affect thirst, hunger, and sex?

Arousal refers to your general level of alertness and activity.

4. Do you know how low and high levels of arousal affect your performance?

Sometimes the things that motivate you are outside of conscious awareness.

5. How do unconscious motives affect your actions?

At times, various personal beliefs initiate, guide, and maintain your actions.

6. How do various expectations, beliefs about being in control of your life, and personal values influence your behaviors?
7. What steps can you take to manage such beliefs?

Factors in your environment also act to motivate your behaviors.

8. In what ways do environmental factors motivate you?

Achievement, power, and affiliation needs account for a number of our actions.

9. How do needs for achievement, power, and affiliation appear in your life?

All of the needs that affect you are not created equal. At a given moment in time, some appear to have a higher priority for being expressed than do others.

10. How does Abraham Maslow account for the way your needs are expressed?

---

### Name That Motive!

Why would people do the following things?

*If you don't like me—I'll find someone else for you.* A West German woman, Anita von Schilling, paid a marriage broker the equivalent of $2,000 to find her ex-husband a new wife. She was so determined to get the best possible woman for him that she insisted on interviewing all applicants. Candidate number one was too dull, number two was too spoiled, and number three was too talkative. Both Mrs. Schilling and her ex-husband agreed on number four—an unmarried woman with a handicapped child. At last report the two women had become best friends (*Daily Record,* Glasgow, October 28, 1982).

*It's a bird, it's a plane, no it's . . .* Larry Walters was a truck driver who became bored traveling the highways. To add some excitement to his life, he built and flew his own "aircraft" to 16,000 feet. The takeoff was without incident, but the landing was a little rough when he became entangled in a power line. His "aircraft" was a lawn chair supported by 42 helium balloons, which he popped one by one with an air gun when he decided to land. The Federal Aviation Administration was not amused. They fined him $1,500 for flying an "unauthorized aircraft" (*Time,* August 29, 1983).

*Neither wind, nor snow, nor rain, nor a dead body deters a dedicated golfer from his game.* Officials at a local golf course in Winter Haven, Florida, covered Dennis Carter's body with a sheet right where he died on the sixteenth green. Because of a mix-up by the local police, the body stayed there two hours. His three golfing partners decided to call it a day, but other friends and neighbors in his 40-member golf league played through. "It was a real shock to all of us, but there was really nothing we could do," said one of his best friends (Associated Press, September 14, 1988).

*Oh well, the exam was not all that important anyway.* At the University of Colorado at Boulder, 580 French language students were taking a final exam in a gym when the Lady Buffalos basketball team showed up. Rather than force the athletes to reschedule their practice, the instructors excused the test takers and gave them all As. Apparently, practice makes perfect—by late January the Lady Buffs remained undefeated. (*College Reports,* December 1992).

---

## THE NATURE OF HUMAN MOTIVATION

As you can see from the examples above and your own everyday experiences, people do a lot of ordinary and extraordinary things. The question of "why" someone behaves in a particular way has intrigued everyone from great detectives trying to solve crimes, poets describing human nature, managers looking for ways to improve worker productivity, and ordinary people trying to develop a little willpower and motivation. The search for answers often lead to questions such as: *"What's the motive here?" "Why would anyone do that?" "How can I motivate myself?"*

**Motivation** refers to the factors that initiate, guide, and direct our behaviors towards certain goals and that maintain our actions while particular goals are being pursued. *Such processes may be biological in nature* (e.g, seeking food or water to lessen the discomfort produced by physiological mechanisms associated with hunger and thirst). Or, *the motivational mechanisms may involve modes of thinking and ways of relating to aspects of our environment.* For example, a student receives a good grade on a midterm math exam and concludes, "I knew I could do well." She becomes optimistic about doing well in the future, imagines herself getting an A on her report card, and consequently spends extra time and energy preparing for the final exam. Similarly, all of us want to obtain certain goals that exist in our environment. Thus, we may work overtime in order to earn enough money to purchase a new car. To maintain the rewards of social recognition and acceptance from friends, some of us might decide to purchase clothes and listen to music that meets with the approval of friends.

# BIOLOGICAL INFLUENCES ON MOTIVATION

## Genetic Factors

*Instincts* An **instinct** is a behavior pattern that is unlearned, expressed in a uniform and consistent manner, and occurs in every member of a species. Such things as nest building in birds, the mating rituals of animals in the wild, a spider spinning a web, or the work of a colony of bees in producing honey are to a large extent genetically programmed. With human beings, however, it is difficult to find complete and uniform sequences of behavior that are easily classified as instinctive.

*Human behavior is much more flexible and diverse, and it is guided and shaped by genetic as well as by environmental and cognitive influences.* For example, it is not uncommon to hear references to a "maternal instinct." No one would deny that biological factors play a role in mating and reproduction. They are not, however, the whole story. Studies of mate selection among men and women in 37 cultures have identified several types of influences (Buss, 1991; Cosmides and Tooby, 1987). One set appears to represent biological motives that are common across cultures. For men, important factors in selecting a mate were physical characteristics that made women desirable as sexual partners and as people who could bear children. For women, the most important factors were signs that a male was healthy and strong and could protect them and provide for a family. A second set of influences varies across cultures and is not genetically programmed. Included here were the different emphases cultures gave to marriage as a way to gain recognition and status within a community, to express romantic love, to bring factions in communities together, and to increase the wealth of a family. Finally, within a given culture, personal thoughts and feelings about marriage and having a family play a role. Some couples, while very much in love and enjoying whatever recognition and status marriage provides—consciously choose not to have children. Others make similar choices because unpleasant childhood experiences have "turned them off to wanting children."

## Needs and Drives

Internal biological states within people that help to initiate, guide and direct, and maintain behavior are called **needs.** Biological or physiological needs such as hunger, thirst, and rest are behind common behaviors such as eating Big Macs, drinking water, and sleeping eight hours a night. They operate by creating a state of internal tension or arousal that initiates actions that will try to satisfy the underlying need. This state of physiological arousal is labeled a **drive.** *Think of the drive as the increase in the energy and tension you experience when a need such as hunger, thirst, or sex is not satisfied and/or when your ability to satisfy that need is threatened.* Therefore, a person who is deprived of food for 24 hours will experience a relatively high level of drive, as will someone who is hungry but does not have enough money to purchase food.

One way we respond to drives is to reduce the internal tension in order to achieve a state of *homeostasis*—the maintenance of a balanced or constant internal state of tension. A familiar analogy is how a thermostat regulates the temperature in a room. A sensor monitoring the room temperature detects a change; a response system such as a furnace or air conditioning system is turned on; and it continues to function until a desired temperature level is achieved.

*Thirst* Satisfying our thirst illustrates how this homeostatic process operates within us. Our bodies become thirsty either through the direct loss of fluids (e.g., sweating, bleeding, diarrhea) or by consuming too much salt (Logue, 1991; Schmidt-Nielsen, 1994). In both cases, the body's normal balance of water and minerals such as sodium is disturbed. When fluids are lost, for example, nerve cells or receptors in an area of the brain known as the hypothalamus emit an antidiuretic hormone that reduces the amount of water our kidneys secrete. A loss of water also causes receptors in the heart and kidney to detect subsequent changes in blood pressure. Our kidneys release the hormone renin, which in turn acts on nerve cells in the hypothalamus to create the sensation of thirst and to initiate drinking. Thus, the volume of body fluids is restored to normal level.

Eating too many pretzels, potato chips, or salted nuts, on the other hand, creates a water-sodium imbalance in the fluids inside and outside of our cells. Salt contains sodium-chloride, and thus potato chips, pretzels, and salted nuts create an imbalance in the amount of sodium in the fluids outside of our cells. This increase in sodium causes fluids within our cells to be released in order to restore the water-sodium balance. Our cells dehydrate, and the fluids must be replaced. Fortunately, receptors in the hypothalamus are sensitive to such elevations in the levels of sodium; we become thirsty and drink a variety of beverages.

*Managing our need for liquids:* Water, soft drinks, sport replacement fluids, and other beverages help us to restore a loss of fluids and any sodium-water imbalance. Unfortunately, some popular ways of satisfying a thirst, such as drinking beer, wine, coffee, and carbonated beverages, are not very effective "thirst quenchers." Such beverages tend to dehydrate us and leave us wanting more to drink. While this is good news for the manufacturers of such products, it does not help us regulate our sodium-water balance for very long.

*How people satisfy their thirst illustrates that care must be taken when explaining an underlying need in strictly biological terms.* An internal biological mechanism is certainly present. However, people try to satisfy their thirst with a variety of beverages—many of which are heavily advertised in newspapers, magazines, and on radio and television. Advertising is a situational factor designed to influence the particular way our thirst is satisfied. Such ads highlight the flavor of the drink (e.g., fruit juice, chocolate milk, flavored soft drinks) and/or the pleasurable effect produced by the alcohol or caffeine in beer, coffee, or tea.

Advertisements also imply that reducing our thirst with plain ordinary water is "boring" and that other rewards are easily obtained from other liquids. After all, why worry about our sodium-water balance when we can drink certain cola drinks and be "hip;" consume beer and add a little "excitement and fun" to our lives; develop a "healthy life-style" through fruit-flavored carbonated water; and satisfy our needs for "romance and passion" by drinking various wines and liquors. Such appeals, if mindlessly followed, may lead to unpleasant consequences including consuming more sugar and caffeine than is necessary and falling victim to the downside of alcoholic beverages including "hangovers," impaired judgments, reckless and careless behaviors, and an increased risk of automobile and other "accidents."

Stop and ask yourself the questions, *"Why am I drinking this and what do I hope to accomplish?" "What alternatives are there to the liquids I am currently consuming?" "Is this something that is in my best interests to do?"* Responding to such questions makes drinking anything less of a mindless act and helps us recognize that choices, including healthier ones, are available.

*Hunger* Our bodies try to seek a balance between food intake and energy requirements. As with thirst, internal regulatory mechanisms try to maintain a level of homeostasis. This regulatory system includes neural pathways in several areas of our brain including the hypothalamus and sensors that monitor nutrients in our bloodstream. Areas of the hypothalamus, for example, tend to stimulate as well as inhibit food intake, while sensors in our brain and livers provide feedback to our nervous system about the levels of glucose or blood sugar, fat, and various amino acids or proteins in our blood stream (Pinel, 1993).

A popular way to picture homeostasis in eating is in terms of an internal standard, or **set point,** around which body weight is regulated (Schwartz, 1984). This set point is best thought of as a range of weight (i.e., 140–146 lbs) rather than a specific weight (i.e., 143 lbs.). The reason is that our weight normally changes with diet, exercise, aging, pregnancy, and other factors. Essentially our body tries to maintain this weight range and to correct deviations when we fall too far below or above the range. Our body generally does a good job of maintaining our weight, even under unusual circumstances, as illustrated in Focus on People 6.1.

*Coping with our need to eat:* How much and what we eat is under more than biological control. Judith Rodin (1985, 1989) finds that some people are highly responsive to the sights and sounds of food. Pictures of food in magazines or the noise associated with its preparation stimulates a rise in insulin levels. As a result, blood sugar falls, and sensations of hunger increase. Family and cultural influences also play a role. People learn that sharing meals and eating certain kinds of foods brings them closer to each other and their origins. Social pressures to eat make people feel guilty about refusing to do so. Culture also shapes what foods will be seen as acceptable ways to satisfy our hunger. Worldwide, people salivate or are repulsed by hamburger, fried grasshoppers, octopus cooked in its own ink, the eye of a camel, dog and cat meat, and a variety of snails, snakes, and bugs.

Some individuals also find themselves attracted to certain foods like chocolate because it "makes me feel good" or to vegetables because they are "good for you." Food

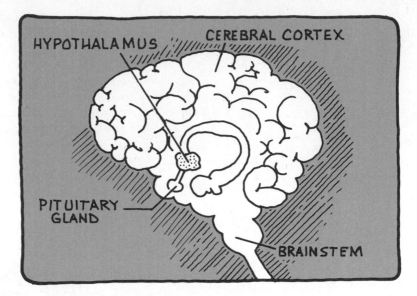

not only satisfies our hunger, but for some it becomes a medicine that treats a host of real and imagined physical and psychological ailments.

Because of personal insecurity, cultural pressures, advertising, and the physical shape of popular models, actors, and actresses, some of us may view ourselves as too fat or too thin. Of the two, being too fat typically is viewed as the worst sin. People then try to lose weight in order to achieve a "socially desirable image." And, they get plenty of help. A multibillion-dollar industry caters to our needs to diet and lose weight.

*Unfortunately, most attempts at dieting end in failure in the long run.* Rather than lose weight, the majority of dieters gain about 10–15 percent more weight than they lost within a year of quitting a diet. The average amount of weight lost through dieting averages out to about a *7–8-pound* gain. Thus, the quip "I lose the same 8–10 pounds every time I go on a diet," has a basis in reality. Most people would be much better off not dieting at all rather than subjecting themselves to the "dieting yo-yo." Frequent swings in weight gains and losses through dieting not only create stress but affect our general health and well-being.

One reason is that genetic factors play an important role in the size and shape of our bodies. Thus, everyone who tries to reshape the dimensions of their body is to some extent fighting "mother nature." Furthermore, going on a strict diet slows down the body's **basal metabolism**, or the amount of energy it expends in a resting state maintaining basic biological functions such as digestion, breathing, and neural activity. For example, depending upon body size and gender, people need about 1,200–1,900 calories a day to maintain basic bodily functions.

*Dieters may unwittingly suppress their metabolic rate.* Susan Wooley (1979) and her colleagues report that depriving ourselves of food and eating foods low in carbohydrates, as many popular diets suggest, tend to lower our metabolism. One outcome is that fewer calories are needed to maintain basic functioning, and people are able to conserve energy. In effect, we become more efficient in using calories. This is probably a remnant

### Help—A Little Weight Needed!

Most people are aware of how difficult it is to lose weight. But what would you do if you had to gain some weight?

This was the problem 7'6" professional basketball player Shawn Bradley faced. Sports columnist Rick Reilly (1993) reports that the Philadelphia 76ers took a chance on Bradley and selected him with the No. 2 pick in the draft. Bradley was a former center for the Brigham Young team and had only played one year of college ball before doing two years of missionary work in Australia.

The problem was that he weighted 245 pounds and was skinny for his height. Undoubtedly, he faced getting beat up in the battles that occur under the boards in the National Basketball Association. Soon after Bradley reported to the team, a decision was made to get him bigger and stronger. Shawn Bradley began a strength and conditioning program designed to build his muscles. He also began to eat a 7,000-calorie-per-day diet. The diet included six meals a day with plenty of 1,000-calorie milkshakes, pancakes, double chocolate cakes, triple decker sandwiches, eggs, cereal, milk, juice, cheeseburgers, french fries, steaks, and large quantities of almost anything else he wanted to eat.

How much weight did he gain? Over a four-month period, he added an inch and a half to his chest, took an inch off his waist, his body fat dropped from 13 percent to 10 percent of his body weight, and his muscle strength had increased. *Unfortunately, his 7,000-calorie-a-day diet did not add a single pound to his body.* He still weighed 245 pounds.

He may eventually gain the extra 30 pounds the team wants. His plight, however, illustrates how difficult it is for a physically active person to gain weight.

of our evolutionary history, when primitive people had to endure long periods of time when food was scarce. They needed ways to conserve energy and to avoid losing too much weight. Many diets force our body to react as if a famine occurred, and our energy needs are reduced (Franken, 1988).

This low metabolism is like a furnace that is stoked down and needs less fuel. As people grow weary of their diet and begin to eat normally again, their metabolism does not change as quickly as their eating habits (Logue, 1991). They now feed a sluggish furnace with rich fuel, and this excess energy is converted into fat. Early in our evolutionary history, this was a very adaptive response. When food was plentiful, a low metabolism would help people to gain weight and to build stores of fat to draw on for a future famine. Today, this additional weight frustrates dieters, and they blame a lack of willpower rather than their altered metabolism.

Peter Miller (1983) reports that a much better strategy for losing weight is to do things that do not adversely affect your metabolism. *This includes limiting weight loss to 1–1 1/2 pounds a week, getting regular exercise, eating well-balanced meals, and not skipping meals.* Your body tolerates and adjusts much better to *small and gradual reductions in weight loss,* and they are tolerated much better over time. Many dieters, however, are impatient. They want quick results and thus rush to crash diets that suppress their metabolism. *Exercise provides a metabolic boost* during and after exercising so that more rather than fewer calories are burned. Also, exercise leads to a loss in weight due to reductions in body fat much more than does dieting. *Nutritious meals are important for our general health, and not skipping meals keeps our metabolic rate up.* Thus, the habit of many dieters to skip breakfast or lunch only keeps their internal furnace sluggish and inefficient in burning calories. Other ideas for managing your weight are presented in Table 6.1. Also, specific suggestions for eating better to develop the physical hardiness needed to cope with the stressors of everyday life can be found in Chapter 10.

*Sex* Our sexual response satisfies both biological and psychological needs. Besides its reproductive function, sex is a source of pleasure and helps to create an intimate bond between two individuals. Also, when our sexual needs are satisfied, our self-image and sense of well-being are enhanced. *Our motivation for sexual activity is affected not only by physiological factors, but, like hunger and thirst, by cognitive and environmental factors as well.*

Sex hormones, estrogen in females and testosterone in males, are important components of the physiology of sex. They have two effects. One is that such hormones direct the development of male and female sex characteristics during puberty, including muscle development and facial and body hair in males and breast development, menstruation, and the widening of hips in females. Thus, the mature bodies of men and women reflect the action of these hormones.

Sex hormones also are associated with our sex drive. These hormones influence sexual arousal through their effects on the hypothalamus, which monitors blood hormone levels and activates the neural circuits involved in arousal. *The sex drive in humans, however, is not as strongly determined by hormones as it is in lower animals.* Natural daily and monthly fluctuations do not greatly affect sexual desire in men or women (Byrne, 1982; Harvey, 1987). In women, for example, sexual desire can continue and sometimes increase after menopause, when estrogen levels are very low.

This does not mean that such hormones are unrelated to our sex drive. Rather, the levels of these hormones increase when we are sexually aroused by other sources of stimulation that play a role in our overall levels of sexual arousal. For example, such things as erotic pictures and tapes, sensuous advertisements, romantic movies and novels, and explicit written descriptions of sexual activity create sexual arousal. Elevations in hormone levels, breathing, blood pressure, penis erection, vaginal secretions, and orgasms can occur in response to stimulation from such sources (Kelley and Byrne, 1991). Being in the presence of attractive people also plays an important role in sexual stimulation. For example, James Dabbs (1987) and his colleagues had male college students talk separately to other males and females. Their testosterone levels rose in both social situations, but they were especially high after talking with the female students.

*Our imaginations affect sexual desire, suggesting that our brains may be our most significant sex organ.* Individuals with spinal cord injuries have no genital sensations but can still fantasize about sex and feel sexually aroused (Willmuth, 1987). Nearly all men and about 40 percent of women tested have dreams that sometimes contain sexual imagery that lead to an orgasm. While wide awake, daydreams, memories of prior sexual activities, and fantasies about "what it would be like to have sex with . . . " are often arousing (Wells, 1986). When asked to read stories describing sexual encounters, the level of arousal is higher when people can imagine themselves as the central character (Dekker and Everaerd, 1989). During sexual intercourse, many people also fantasize about having sex with imaginary lovers, a former lover, groups of people, having oral-genital sex, and other sexual images.

Our imaginations aside, cultural practices, and religious and moral codes affect the expression of sexual desire. In the Marquesas Islands in French Polynesia, for example, children as young as 3 years of age are encouraged to masturbate. Most engage in casual homosexual contacts during their youth, and as adolescents, they have sexual activity with an adult of the opposite sex, who instructs them in technique (Suggs, 1962). In

| **Table 6.1** | Suggestions for Losing Weight Sensibly |
|---|---|

*Keep track of your weight and what you eat.*  Start a graph of your weight, and leave room for making about two to three entries a week for three months. Hang the chart in a closet or bathroom. Use your daily calendar or a small notepad to record what you eat, the amounts you eat, and the calories you consume. Information about calories in a variety of foods is available in most bookstores. You may also want to include the time of day and situation (alone, with friends, in car, in kitchen, watching TV, and so on). This will help you to feel in control of the process of losing weight and will give you information to reduce your intake. For example, you might only eat high-calorie snacks when watching television or studying, and thus corrective actions can be taken.

*Determine how many calories you need to maintain your current weight.*  As a general rule, for every 3,500 calories you do not use up, you gain one pound. To figure out how many calories you need each day to maintain your weight, multiply your weight by 12 if you are inactive, by 15 if you engage in moderate physical activity, and by 18 if you engage in strenuous activity—for example running six to ten miles a day, playing three to five sets of tennis daily, or swimming one mile or more.

*Reduce your daily consumption of food by 200–300 calories below the number needed to maintain your weight.*  Keep it at this level until you stop losing weight. Then reduce your calories by another 200–300 calories until you stop losing weight again or have achieved your goal. Weight is best lost slowly (i.e., 1–1 1/2 pounds a week). The faster it comes off, the higher your risk of gaining it all back again.

*Eat a nutritious diet, but do not eat less than a range of 1,200–1,600 calories a day.*  It is difficult to supply your body with adequate nutrients when calories are severely restricted. Also, you will feel hungry and will crave food, making the diet very unpleasant. Other consequences include a loss of muscle tone, excess fatigue, other health problems, and a depressed metabolism. Include fresh fruits, vegetables, whole gain breads and cereals, and meats that are not high in fat in your diet. Refrain from eating large amounts of high-calorie processed foods and high-fat fast food restaurant items. Reduce but don't completely eliminate something you enjoy (e.g., pasta, hamburger). You will only increase your craving for them.

*Increase your physical activity.*  Take the stairs instead of elevators, park farther away from your destination, walk instead of driving to nearby places, and exercise more frequently. Exercise increases your metabolic rate, burns calories, and, when combined with a diet, helps with losing weight (e.g., 200 calories exercise + 300 calorie reduction in diet = 500 calories per day, or 3,500 calories per week.)

*Form or join a group dedicated to helping people lose weight.*  Group support and pressure contribute to successful weight reduction. Professionally supervised groups may be especially helpful because of the additional expertise they provide.

contrast, our society is not as open regarding sexual expression. Various church groups teach their members that sex is only for reproduction; in some states laws prohibit certain forms of sexual expression, such as oral or anal sex; and strong prejudices exist towards homosexual activity.

*Meeting sexual needs and having rewarding sexual experiences:* In spite of the existence of a variety of constraints on sexual behavior, people manage to satisfy their sexual needs in a variety of ways, as illustrated in Table 6.2. While not everyone engages in all

| Table 6.2 | Meeting Sexual Needs |
|---|---|

**People meet their sexual needs in a variety of ways.**

*Sexual Preference*

| | |
|---|---|
| Heterosexual | 91% |
| Homosexual/Bisexual | 6% |
| Not sexually experienced | 3% |

*Frequency of Intercourse*

| | |
|---|---|
| Men | 66 times/year |
| Women | 51 times/year |
| Separated | 66 times/year |
| Widowed | 8 times/year |
| Under age 40 | 78 times/year |
| Age 41–50 | 67 times/year |
| Age 51–60 | 46 times/year |
| Age 61–70 | 23 times/year |
| Over age 70 | 8 times/year |

*Extramarital Affairs*

| | |
|---|---|
| Men | 34% |
| Women | 20% |

*People at Risk for AIDS*

| | |
|---|---|
| Five or More Sexual Partners, Casual Partners, Male Homosexual or Bisexual Partners | 5.5% |

*Aroused by Erotic Literature*

| | |
|---|---|
| Men | 89% |
| Women | 92% |

of the behaviors illustrated in this table, all of us have considered what sexual experiences are appropriate for us. There are several things you might want to consider when thinking about how to have rewarding sexual experiences. They are presented in Table 6.3. *Based on your experiences, what would you add to this list?*

## Arousal

**Arousal** refers to the body's general level of alertness and activity as reflected in muscle tension, heart and respiration rates, and patterns of electrical activity in the brain. It varies from deep sleep through normal wakefulness to extreme excitement. Factors that contribute to our arousal include needs and drives, the intensity of the stimuli in our environments, encountering novel events, and using certain drugs such as the caffeine in coffee. Our level of arousal may facilitate or inhibit our ability to perform a variety

| Table 6.2 | Continued |
|---|---|

**Number of Hetereosexual Partners**
Men
(since age 18)  12 partners/year
Women
(since age 18)  3 partners/year

**Masturbation**
Men  94%
Women  63%

**Oral–Genital Sex**
Men  72%
Females  69%

**Anal Sex**
Men/Women  32%

**Group Sex**
Men  33%
Women  18%

**Perception of Having
Engaged in "Kinky" Sex**
Men  19%
Women  28%

**Sexual Pleasure from
Inflicting/Receiving Pain**
Men  3.5%
Women  3.2%

Based on information contained in the reported frequency of sexual activity in data from a survey by The National Opinion Research Center at the University of Chicago (1990) and Hunt (1974).

of daily behaviors. This relationship between arousal and performance is called the **Yerkes–Dodson law** and is illustrated in Figure 6.1.

When the level of arousal is too high, performance deteriorates. John Adams (1980) reports that this occurs for several reasons. *Under high levels of arousal, the most recently learned behaviors are often dropped in favor of old habits.* A neighbor spent time with a therapist learning alternative ways to discipline his children. Instead of screaming or beating them, he discovered that ignoring some of their actions, withholding privileges, and talking about solutions to problems were helpful. One hot and humid summer day, however, he was rushing to finish mowing his lawn before it rained; his telephone was ringing; and his two youngsters were fighting on the deck. He separated them, cursed each of them, and without thinking, slapped them on their buttocks.

In addition to finding that old behaviors replace those most recently learned, *John Adams also finds that high arousal interferes with a person's ability to solve problems and make*

| **Table 6.3** | Developing Rewarding Sexual Experiences |
|---|---|

*Get accurate information.* Popular books can be helpful, but they often err on the side of sensationalizing some aspect of sexuality. A course on human sexuality or a textbook in the area will contain much more accurate information.

*Don't look for magic buttons and techniques that will bring you sexual bliss.* Advertisements, books, videotapes, and a variety of other sources promise techniques and even products that are "guaranteed to enhance your love life." Our sex life, however, is most satisfying when two people use it to communicate their mutual desire, love, and appreciation for each other. There are no magic love potions or devices that will make you a marvelous lover if the latter ingredients are not present. Most couples could enhance their sex lives better by working on conflicts and communication problems that are interfering with their relationship. Such things create distance in all aspects of a relationship.

*Become aware of the cultural pressures that play a role in your attitudes and beliefs about human sexuality.* In our culture, men are expected to perform at almost every and any opportunity. Women are expected to respond whenever their lovers initiate sexual activity. Such expectations reduce the range of sexual responses possible and take away from the spontaneous expression of sexual desires. They not only make focusing on the sensual experiences more difficult but can create tension and other problems.

*Understand that family and religious influences often shape your views about your sexuality.* Sometimes parents or guardians do not discuss sex or do so in hushed tones; or, myths about sexuality are reinforced (e.g., masturbation is harmful to your health). In some families, sexual abuse of children is a problem, and such activities can leave lasting scars. Similarly, some people learn that various forms of sexual expression are sinful. Problems develop when such beliefs are internalized as "the absolute truth" and "final word" on the subject. Feelings of guilt and sexual inadequacy typically follow.

*Behave in a sexually responsible manner.* Treat your body with respect, and demand that others do likewise. Respect yourself by not allowing others to use your body as a toy. Respect yourself and your partner by using contraception. Unwanted pregnancies and sexually transmitted diseases, including AIDS, can be prevented. The use of condoms is a necessity and right now one of the most potent defenses against infection by the HIV virus that is implicated in causing AIDS.

*Take a proactive stance to deal with any sexual problem you find difficult to resolve.* Seek professional help for the problems in your sex life. Therapy for sexual issues is typically very successful. If you are victimized by someone (e.g., date rape, sexual harassment), report the offender. This helps you to begin gaining control over your feelings and helps to protect others from becoming victimized.

*decisions.* The reason is that good problem-solving and decision-making strategies are put aside. In the haste to reduce tension, alternative solutions are not carefully considered; quick decisions are made based upon the first idea presented; and the opinions of other individuals are not sought.

While high levels of arousal can become disruptive, *remember that people vary in terms of what they consider to be a high or low arousal level.* A person who normally enjoys periods of quiet reading may find a ride on a motorcycle very exciting. Someone who normally rides a motorcycle might experience that same ride as relatively unexciting. That person, however, might also find reading a book unpleasant. Similarly, rather than finding high levels of arousal disruptive and seeking ways to reduce them, some people

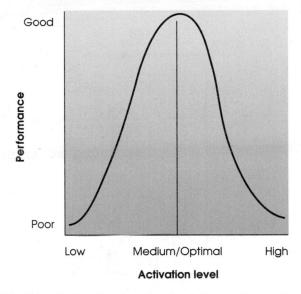

**Figure 6.1** *The Yerkes-Dodson law. A medium level of arousal is considered optimal for performance.*

actively seek ways to maintain arousal and add excitement to their lives. This latter tendency is called **sensation seeking.** Tendencies towards sensation seeking are highest among 17–24-year-olds, and then such tendencies gradually begin to decline.

Marvin Zuckerman and Frank Farley (1986) suggest that people are probably born with tendencies towards sensation seeking. Those with low arousability are not very responsive to mental or physical stimuli. Thus, they need rather high levels of stimulation to "rev" them up to optimal levels. Others may be very responsive physiologically to stimulation. They therefore choose low levels of stimulation to calm their hyped-up nervous system. Individuals with neither very high nor very low levels of arousability seek some middle ground.

*There appears to be a constructive and destructive side to sensation seeking.* In his research, Frank Farley finds that some thrill seekers pursue constructive mental stimulation by becoming artists, scientists, or entertainers. They may enjoy playing competitive sports or derive pleasure from driving sports cars or working long hours on novel and creative projects. Other individuals, unfortunately, seek high levels of arousal in a destructive manner. Mentally, they become criminal masterminds, schemers, and con artists. Physically, they may enjoy violent, delinquent, and criminal behavior. Similar results between sensation seeking and socially unacceptable behaviors have been noted in samples of nondelinquents. Michael Newcomb and Linda McGhee (1991) examined the life-styles of 595 nondelinquent adolescents over a three-year period. Deviant behaviors such as using illicit drugs occurred much more frequently among adolescents who were high sensation seekers

## Managing Uncomfortable Levels of Arousal

*Seek Appropriate Levels of Sensations for a Given Activity* Typically, this is our *optimal level of arousal,* and it varies depending upon our personal preferences for sensations and the task we want to perform. People report feeling best and performing much better

when arousal falls within their optimal range (Ford et al., 1985). This optimal level of arousal when listening to soft music or reading a book, however, is going to be lower than the level needed to compete in a tennis match or game of basketball. To obtain this optimal level, we might need to raise or lower our level of stimulation. After returning from a hard-fought tennis match, someone would have to relax and "calm down" before being able to concentrate on reading a book. Similarly, to compete in a game of tennis, we might need to "psych ourselves up," engage in warmup activities, and otherwise increase a relatively lower level of arousal.

*Develop a Small-Win Mentality* This means breaking problems into smaller parts, pursuing each part, and developing some successes in tackling each aspect of the problem. Thus, a large, unmanageable problem suddenly becomes a series of smaller, manageable ones, and a person's arousal level declines. Karl Weick (1984) refers to the latter strategy as a "small wins philosophy." Having a series of "small wins" along the way to resolving a much larger issue can be very motivating. This strategy is used by Alcoholics Anonymous (AA), an organization that seeks to have alcoholics stop drinking alcoholic beverages for the remainder of their lives. To an alcoholic, this goal seems impossible. To make it manageable, AA stresses the need for people to stop drinking for one day, or even one hour at a time. Thus, the impossibility of lifetime abstinence is scaled down to the more workable task of not taking a drink for an hour, or the next 24 hours. Each hour and day an alcoholic refrains from drinking becomes a small success, or win.

# COGNITIVE INFLUENCES ON MOTIVATION

## Unconscious Motives

One of the world's richest men, J. P. Morgan, was reported to have said, "Someone always has two reasons for doing anything—a good reason and the real reason." In looking for the real reasons behind a person's behavior, it is important to understand that conscious and unconscious needs and drives affect behavior. People are sometimes very much aware of the motives behind their actions. Purchasing a pizza or a new suit or studying hard for an exam are actions that are motivated, respectively, by hunger, wanting to look attractive, and trying to achieve success. On the other hand, we might be unaware of the reasons for other behaviors. Sigmund Freud, for example, noted that the motives for some behaviors lie within our unconscious mind. People are not consciously aware of these motives, but they exert control over their actions (Freud, 1937).

In Freud's view, unconscious motives reflect past conflicts that we have forgotten and various sexual or aggressive impulses of which we are unaware. For example, Freud saw creativity in art, music, and literature as expressing unconscious sexual impulses. Given the tremendous preoccupation of popular music, for example, with romance, making love, and intimate relationships—perhaps he had a point. Similarly, a 40-year-old student described how he continually failed in the business world. He believed he lacked the motivation and skills to succeed in a business. Through psychotherapy, he learned how a fear of achieving more in life than his father was causing his unhappiness. By holding himself back, he avoided the guilt of surpassing his father's achievements.

*Getting in Touch with Unconscious Motives* To do this, you first must be willing to examine your actions honestly and objectively. To accomplish this goal, my colleague Daniel Kirschenbaum and I discovered that people had to spend sufficient time answering the question, "What made me behave the way I did?" We developed several suggestions for ways individuals could become more consciously aware of the factors that guided and maintained their actions. They included not discounting or disregarding completely what others say about us; examining our fantasies and dreams for underlying motives; and discussing our concerns and behaviors with people who can provide a more objective point of view (Grasha and Kirschenbaum, 1986). Let's examine each point in more detail.

1. *Try not to discount or disregard completely the reactions other people have to what you say and do.* There is a natural tendency to deny and reject what others say about us. *Instead, first ask yourself what is valid about their point of view.* A person I know at the sports club where I work out, Robert, would ask people to play tennis and then find some excuse for quitting when he fell behind. He blamed the hot sun, the tension of the strings in his racquet, a sore elbow, and anything else that was convenient. After pulling his bag of excuses on one of his close friends, he was asked why he was so afraid of losing. His reaction was predictable. He denied his fear of losing

and insisted that he had a sore elbow. A few days later he called his friend and admitted his fear of losing a match.

2. *Try to identify the motivations in your fantasies and dreams.* The dreams you have at night and your daydreams contain an abundance of information about your motives. For example, imagining someone asking you out not only suggests an interest in that person but may be an indication of your desire to overcome loneliness. Research on dreams suggests three things about our ability to interpret them. One is that some dreams might not be interpretable. They are merely collections of memory fragments gathered during the day and replayed at night. For dreams that are more than unrelated memory fragments, professional help is sometimes helpful in unraveling them. A third is that there are many aspects of our dreams that we can interpret ourselves (Cartwright, 1977; Sheras et al.,1983). Consider how the ideas in Table 6.4 might help you.

3. *Discuss your concerns and behaviors with friends, parents, or even a professional counselor.* Sometimes other people are able to provide a more objective viewpoint on our motivations. A student in one of my classes was constantly angry about how teachers treated him. He interpreted poor marks on term papers or exams as well as anything said in class as a personal attack on him. One day in a fit of rage over a low exam grade he shouted at his professor, "You treat me just like my old man. You never give me credit for the good things I do!" In a talk with him after this incident, he said his father was highly critical of him but that he could never confront his father. Unfortunately, anyone in authority who judged him received part of the anger he had reserved for his father. Based on that insight, he sought professional counseling to learn to deal with his feelings more effectively.

## Expectations

**Expectations** are beliefs that anticipate or estimate how we and others will or should behave. Barbara Bank (1992) notes that expectations are present in several areas of our lives, including statements about what we hope to become in the future (i.e., type of career path, get married and raise a family); the informal rules others establish for how we should behave in social situations (i.e., sit quietly, raise cane, help others); and our estimates of whether our actions will lead to success or failure. Such beliefs compel us to respond in certain ways and thus are important for initiating, guiding, and maintaining our behaviors.

*The Role of Personal Expectations in Our Successes and Failures* Russell Jones (1977) reports that personal estimates about our actions leading to successful outcomes are good predictors of achievement in school, on the job, and for our success in relationships. Norman Feather (1987) also finds that the best predictors of whether unemployed workers looked for other jobs were expectations that such searches would be successful. In both cases, people with average or less than average ability were able to do well because they expected to succeed.

An overall anticipation that our behaviors will or will not lead to something productive is only part of the story. According to Albert Bandura (1982, 1986), our beliefs in **self-efficacy** also must be examined. Self-efficacy is our judgment about our perceived capabilities to organize and execute courses of action required to attain particu-

**Table 6.4**                     Ideas for Interpreting Dreams

*Motivate yourself to remember dreams.*   Everyone dreams about four to six times a night; there is plenty of potential material to use. Unfortunately, people remember only about 10 percent of their dreams. To recall more of your dreams, take the point of view that dreams are interesting and worthwhile experiences. Before going to sleep, say, "I am going to remember the dreams I will have tonight."

*Keep a dream diary.*   Keep a notepad or a tape recorder near your bed. When you awaken, lie still and try to recall what you were dreaming. Just let your thoughts wander, and search for fragments of various dreams. Since we are usually in a stage of sleep associated with dreaming just before awakening, the chances of capturing at least the last dream of the night are pretty good. Record the details of what you remember.

*Look for themes in your dream diary.*   Concentrate on studying a recurring dream or a number of dreams that you have had. Avoid the temptation to make too much out of a single dream. Try to relate dream events to concerns and issues you are facing in your waking life. Use the following questions to help interpret symbols, events, and themes in your dreams.

- *Does the symbol or theme represent something literal in my life?* Sometimes a dream replays an event we recently experienced. Thus, parents, friends, and events may appear as they did in reality. Dreaming about an argument you had with a friend could represent a concern that you need to mend some fences.

- *How do themes in the dream relate to problems in my waking life?* A student reported a recurring dream in which he sat on his front lawn and watched a storm approach. He did not move until he was drenched by the rain. He recognized that he procrastinated a lot and saw the dream as a reminder of this problem.

- *How are specific dream symbols like me?* Dreaming of a tornado could represent a destructive side of you; losing tickets could signify a fear of losing important things in life; and pulling onions from the ground could symbolize tears and sadness. *Take the point of view that they mean nothing unless you can relate them to themes in your waking life.* Check your interpretations against waking thoughts, feelings, and conflicts. Looking for universal symbols and meanings is seldom helpful.

- *Form a dream study group.* Find other people who are interested in talking about dreams. Share your dreams and your interpretations with each other. Discussing dreams can be fun, and it takes some of the mystery out of them.

lar goals. Such capabilities include our ability to control our thoughts, emotions, and motor skills when executing a particular task. Self-efficacy has two components. One is the perception that we possess the skills and abilities to achieve certain goals. The second is our estimate that if those skills and abilities are used, a positive outcome will follow. *Perceptions of self-efficacy underlie global pronouncements regarding our abilities such as "I think I can" or "I have what it takes."*

Albert Bandura reports that perceptions of self-efficacy predict grades in school, the development of social skills, smoking cessation, career choices, coping with feared events, and the performance of sales people. Without some degree of self-efficacy, people are unlikely to try new things or to change unsatisfactory aspects of their lives. They become immobilized and lack the confidence to take the necessary risks associated with change. Furthermore, when an individual is learning something new, self-efficacy

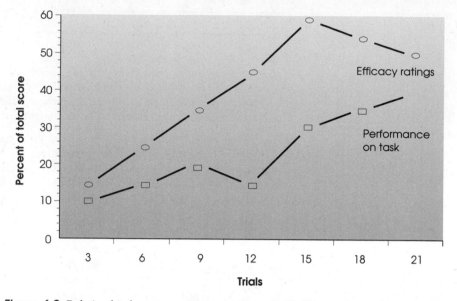

**Figure 6.2** *Relationship between participants' ratings of self-efficacy or how competent and confident they were that they could do the task and that their efforts would lead to a productive outcome. From Bandura, A. (1982). Self-efficacy mechanism in human agency.* American Psychologist, 37, *122–147. © 1982 by the American Psychological Association.*

typically increases at a faster rate than does correct performance on a task, as illustrated in Figure 6.2. Dale Schunk (1992) reports that this relationship between learning and self-efficacy is a two-way street. Among students learning new material in classes, for example, he finds that a higher sense of self-efficacy enhances performance. However, as people learn and comprehend more, they obtain positive feedback about their performance. This feedback, in turn, enhances feelings of efficacy and their motivation to continue with a task. Four factors produce an effective level of self-efficacy.

1. *The number of success experiences on a task—particularly if they occur early in learning.* This is why breaking tasks up into manageable units often facilitates the acquisition of skills and information. Success on a part of a larger task tends to motivate people to continue trying.

2. *Observing models we admire and respect obtaining productive outcomes from their efforts.* This boosts our confidence and feelings of competence. Effectively, we say to ourselves, "If they can do it, then there is no reason why I can't."

3. *Listening to others when they try to boost our morale.* Uplifting messages can boost our energy levels and give us an impetus to try harder.

4. *Correctly interpreting information from our physiological states.* Emotional cues often provide important signs that we can do something. It is important not to misread such information. A little anxiety before an exam, for example, is normal and not a sign that failure lurks around the corner. Similarly, becoming excited over a large state lottery jackpot is also normal. It is not, however, a sign that you should spend large sums of money on tickets or that "lady luck will smile upon you."

## Locus-of-Control Beliefs

Positive and negative outcomes resulting from efforts to achieve some goal also develop our perceptions of personal control. In particular, such outcomes lead people to develop ideas about what produces rewards in their life. Individuals whose efforts typically lead to positive outcomes develop an **internal locus of control.** They form an expectancy that future behavior will be rewarded and the belief that they are the "captains of their fate" (Rotter, 1975). Thus, they are likely to see promotions at work or good grades in school as due to their hard work and persistence.

On the other hand, people whose efforts frequently produce a less than adequate performance develop an expectancy that they cannot control important outcomes in their lives. Such individuals develop an **external locus of control.** Externals believe that luck, fate, or powerful others control most aspects of their lives. They perceive that whether they get rewarded is largely outside of their control. Thus, promotions at work or good grades are likely to be seen as due to getting the right breaks or other factors beyond their immediate control.

*Internals Have an Advantage when Facing the Demands of Daily Living* Such individuals are typically assertive, extroverted, and self-directed, and they feel powerful. They have tendencies towards prosocial behaviors and are very interested in developing relationships (Miller et al., 1986; Benassi et al., 1988). They also differ in their motivation to communicate with others, as illustrated in Focus on Applied Research 6.1. Some of the other advantages of an internal locus of control, based upon findings in the research literature, are presented in Table 6.5.

Julian Rotter (1975) and Jerry Phares (1973) note that our beliefs in locus of control are not fixed. That is, they are learned through our past experiences and can be modified. Events that occur in our environments may temporarily or permanently alter

## Locus Of Control, Television Watching, and Interpersonal Communication

Alan Rubin (1993) was interested in whether locus-of-control beliefs affected people's motivations to communicate in two areas. One was through direct interpersonal contact and the other was through the use of television. Television was examined because it helps to connect and disconnect people from each other. And for some individuals, viewing programs may aid their ability to initiate conversations or serve as a substitute for talking to people.

Four hundred people completed questionnaires assessing their locus-of-control beliefs, their motives for interpersonal communication, as well as their motives for watching television, their willingness to engage in interpersonal communication, and their satisfaction with it. Patterns among the responses to the questionnaires were then identified.

Rubin found that individuals with an internal locus of control tended to prefer engaging in interpersonal modes of communicating, while externals were less interested talking with others. *Externals were more anxious when communicating and found such interactions to be less rewarding and satisfying. Externals also were heavy viewers of television.* This occurred partly because of the anx-

iety externals felt in interpersonal situations, but also because of a general distrust of the world around them.

For externals, television served several important functions. It allowed them a means of escape from an environment they distrusted; they could either avoid or better manage the time spent communicating with others; and they obtained needed information without having direct contact with other people. News and television talk shows, for example, often served as an acceptable alternative to direct interaction for those with an external locus of control.

*Rubin notes that those with an external locus of control were not totally reclusive. They were simply motivated to communicate in a more ritualistic manner.* Although more anxious and less satisfied communicating, they often preferred having other people around them while watching television. Thus, conversations could be initiated by or directed towards things that were occurring in a particular show. There was less pressure on externals to develop a topic of conversation, and such discussions could be kept rather brief in order to not disrupt viewing a program.

the degree to which people assume an internal or external position. Disappointments in the outcome of some event (e.g., an election, an argument), negative feedback on an exam or some task at work, and upheavals in our lives (e.g., natural disaster, relationship breaking up) may alter our beliefs. When such things occur, people tend to become somewhat less internal than they were beforehand. Also, when treated with kindness and respect for their initiatives, people tend to become more internal in their locus-of-control orientations.

## Promoting an Internal Locus of Control

*Assume More Responsibility for Tasks at Work and School* Volunteer to do things that other people normally take on. Initially, select tasks that are relatively easy to do and that have the best chance of being accomplished successfully. If you find yourself working with other people on a project, volunteer, if possible, to manage the project. Again, initially select something that is relatively easy and that has a good chance of succeeding.

*Try New Activities Rather than the Usual Safe and Secure Ways of Doing Things* Try a new sport, a new food, a new way to travel home from school or work, or anything else that will get you to break old habits. People who have strong external beliefs in locus of

| Table 6.5 | Characteristics of People with Internal or External Locus-of-Control Beliefs |
|-----------|---------------------------------------------------------------------------------|

| INTERNALS | EXTERNALS |
|-----------|-----------|
| Persist in the face of failures. | Give up more easily. |
| Work at tasks for long periods of time. | Do not spend as much time on tasks. |
| Cope better with stress in their lives | Do not adapt as well to stress |
| Tend to be less susceptible to anxiety. | Tend to be more susceptible to anxiety. |
| Welcome and meet new challenges in their lives well. | Do not like new challenges and handle them poorly. |
| Seek as much information as they can about events that are likely to affect their lives. | Tend to just let things happen and are not as curious about things that might affect them. |
| Take remedial actions to try and overcome their shortcomings. | Not as likely to take remedial actions to correct their shortcomings. |
| Get good grades in school and high scores on achievement tests. | Typically obtain lower grades and do not score as high on achievement tests. |
| Not very susceptible to depression. | More susceptible to feeling depressed. |
| Try to take control of as many parts of their lives as they can. | Sit back and wait for things to happen to them. |
| Tend to be more successful and to earn more money than externals. | Tend not to earn as much money as internals. |
| Are more interested in politics and more likely to vote in elections. | Not as interested in politics and tend not to vote in elections. |
| More likely to complete college and to obtain graduate degrees. | Less likely to complete college and to obtain graduate degrees. |

control often engage in behaviors that reinforce those beliefs. Trying and enjoying something new will help you to see that you can control aspects of your life.

*Consider Changing Aspects of Your Current Environment* Ask yourself some of the following questions: How do my current friends, acquaintances, and other people in my life contribute to my locus-of-control beliefs? What types of people do I need to associate with to help myself change? What is it about my current job or school that contributes to my believing I am not as much in control of things?

## Values

**Values** are the stable beliefs that underlie and are observed in our behaviors across a number of different situations in our lives. Based on surveys of what people believe, Milton Rokeach (1979, 1984) reports that most people value, to some degree, the following things:

| | | | |
|---|---|---|---|
| Family security | Accomplishment | Pleasure | Social recognition |
| Wisdom | Inner harmony | Happiness | A world of beauty |
| Equality | Salvation | Self-respect | National security |
| Mature love | Freedom | True friendship | |
| A world at peace | Comfortable life | An exciting life | |

Norman Feather (1992) demonstrates that our values function like needs and, thus, affect several components of our actions. *Values affect a person's willingness to initiate actions designed to accomplish certain goals.* Someone who values "a world of beauty," for example, is more likely to contribute to and participate in organizations that support protecting wilderness areas and reducing pollution. *Values also affect the degree of effort people put into an activity and how well they persist in pursuing certain goals.* In a study of unemployed people, Norman Feather reports that those who valued a strong work ethic tended to work hard throughout their lives. When faced with the loss of a job, they also persisted for longer periods of time in their search for a new position. *Finally, values affect the choices we make in life.* Someone might choose between becoming a police officer versus a grocery store owner, or between staying home to read on Saturday night versus attending a party. Important values that underlie such choices are authority versus autonomy and privacy versus socializing.

## Examining Your Values: Three Questions to Ask

*What Do I Currently Value, and Am I Satisfied with What I Value?* A 30-year-old student in one of my courses devoted most of her time to her job. One day, she asked the question, "What do I want to do for the next 35 years of my life?" It became clear to her that she currently valued her job more than her personal life. This, she decided, was unacceptable. She wanted to place more of an emphasis on personal growth. She developed new hobbies, began a physical activity program, modified her diet, and discussed marriage with her boyfriend.

*What Discrepancies Exist Between What I Value and My Behaviors?* People sometimes believe one thing and consciously or unconsciously behave in ways that are counter to such beliefs. When they become aware of this, **cognitive dissonance** is generated. Cognitive dissonance is a state of internal tension that some people characterize as feeling "tense," "anxious," "guilty" or generally as a dislike for their current actions. *Such tension may motivate people to do something about it, including bringing their behaviors in line with their values.* It is not unusual to find people who value being on time. Whenever they are late for work or a social engagement, frustration sets in, and they can be heard to say, "I'm sorry, being late like this is just not like me." Typically, they take steps to ensure that it does not happen again.

*What Discrepancies Exist Among the Things I Value?* Inconsistent beliefs alone also create cognitive dissonance and corresponding pressures to realign them. In a classic research study, Milton Rokeach (1979) created cognitive dissonance by first having people rank-order the personal importance of the 18 values presented earlier in this section. Participants who ranked "freedom" higher than "equality" were informed that this meant they were interested in their own freedom more than that of other people. This, the researchers said, was a sure sign of prejudice and racist beliefs. Most of us would not want to be thought of in such unflattering terms and would probably take steps to reduce the cognitive dissonance this information caused. This is exactly what Milton Rokeach discovered. On a second administration of the value-ranking task, the differences in how freedom and equality were ranked were considerably less. Also, follow-up mail solicitations revealed that people with initially large discrepancies were more willing to join and contribute to organizations such as the NAACP and other organizations concerned with civil rights.

# ENVIRONMENTAL INFLUENCES ON MOTIVATION

## Incentives

**Incentives** are external stimuli or goals within the environment that motivate our actions (Bolles, 1975). Common examples include driving 30 miles to a restaurant that serves excellent food, studying hard in order to get an "A" on a test, training to run a race in order to increase the chances of winning a trophy, and working overtime to earn extra money to purchase a new car. In the latter examples, "good food," "excellent grades on exams," "a trophy," and "extra money" were incentives or goals that people pursued by driving long distances, studying hard, training, and working overtime.

In effect, incentives are the goals we pursue in our quest to either reduce certain drives (e.g., driving 30 miles to a restaurant to reduce our hunger) or to obtain something we consider important and personally valuable (e.g., studying hard in order to obtain a good grade in a course). Regardless of what attracts us to them, when incentives are removed, performance generally declines.

This latter point was illustrated in a study of whether students would perform well on a final exam if it did not count toward their final grade (Morgan, 1978). Students taking an educational psychology course were placed in one of two groups. One group was told the final exam would count toward their final grade. The other group of students was informed that the exam only would count if they earned a superior grade. In the second group, the final exam might help a grade, but it would not hurt the grade they had already earned from two previous exams. The results are shown in Table 6.6. While many students do not enjoy exams, the data suggest that they are effective incentives to help motivate people to study.

**Table 6.6**                          Do Final Exams Provide an Incentive for Students to Study?

**Percentage of Students with Final Exam Scores that Were Higher Than, the Same as, or Lower Than Scores on Their Two Previous Exams**

|  | FINAL EXAM SCORE | | |
|---|---|---|---|
|  | **HIGHER** | **SAME** | **LOWER** |
| Final exam counted toward course grade | 42% | 50% | 8% |
| Final exam could not lower course grade | 0% | 29% | 71% |

*Some incentives are more attractive than others.* Those that people prefer to work harder to obtain are described as having a higher **incentive value** than other things. Similarly, goals perceived as highly rewarding have a higher incentive value than those viewed as aversive. As you might expect, people are drawn to things that are rewarding and tend to avoid pursuing aversive goals. Thus, if given a choice, most people would rather relax on weekends than go to work. Engaging in leisure time activities is generally considered more rewarding.

## Problems Pursuing Incentives: Goal Conflicts

Incentives provide problems for us when choices among goals with different incentive values must be made. Two or more goals may have similar positive features (e.g., each goal leads to fame and fortune), negative features (e.g., pursuing each goal leads to a loss of income and self-esteem), or combinations of both positive and negative qualities. Under the latter conditions, a **goal conflict** occurs. This is a dilemma or confusion caused by trying to choose among goals that vary in their incentive values (i.e., the attractive and unattractive qualities they possess). Typical reactions include becoming indecisive or tense, withdrawing from situations, avoiding a decision, and seeking reasons to justify one course of action over another (Epstein, 1978).

## Identifying and Resolving Common Goal Conflicts

*Approach-Approach Goal Conflict* This happens when we must choose among goals with incentive values that are equally attractive or desirable. Think of such everyday events as choosing which shirt would go best with a new suit, what movie to take someone to on a first date, or which of several new job offers to accept. Approach-approach conflicts usually are easier to resolve. All that is needed is to find one or more reasons that one alternative is better than another. Thus, the shirts may cost the same, but one has a more flattering color; your choice of a movie is narrowed down to two comedies, and you select the one that received the better review; or, the jobs have similar salaries and benefits, but you choose the one that is closer to home.

Resolving an approach-approach goal conflict is a balancing act. *We place the positive aspects (pluses) of each alternative on an imaginary scale, then note which side of the scale is heavier.*

*Avoidance-Avoidance Goal Conflict* Sometimes we face choosing among goals whose incentive values leave us "caught between a rock and a hard place." Such choices are exemplified by wanting to graduate on time but finding you have to choose one of two unpopular required courses to take this term. Also imagine that you have two invitations to a party this Saturday evening. Both involve driving 40–45 miles, and both will have some people you dislike attending. Attending either party is uncomfortable and anxiety arousing.

Such conflicts can be resolved by engaging in a negative balancing act. *The negative qualities (minuses) associated with each alternative are placed on an imaginary scale, and this time the heavier side loses.* In selecting from two undesirable required courses, for example, we might choose one that requires fewer unpleasant reading assignments or exams. Which party to attend could be resolved by going to the one hosted by a close friend. In effect, we choose the lesser of two evils.

*An alternative way to resolve an avoidance-avoidance conflict is to identify another option that has more positive qualities.* On occasion, this leads to creative solutions. Some students petition their department or college to drop a required course. They usually present evidence that they have had similar work or that taking the course presents problems for completing graduation requirements on time. Rather than spend time with a "loser" or staying home alone, some people might find a completely different social activity to pursue.

*Approach-Avoidance Goal Conflict* Sometimes a single goal has both attractive and unattractive qualities. We are hungry, and a dish of ice cream looks very tasty at the moment. Unfortunately, the good taste comes at the expense of the calories in the sugar and fat, and keeping our weight under control is important. Two or more goals also may have both attractive or unattractive features. This is called a **double approach–avoidance conflict.** One of my students, Raymond, wanted to have a date for the university's homecoming dance. He faced a dilemma in trying to decide who to ask. While he enjoyed the company of his friend Carmen, she did not get along with several of his other friends. Tanya socialized well with his friends, but he did not enjoy her company as much. Deciding on a date was a problem.

Such conflicts often leave us in a particularly difficult bind. Generally speaking, there are three ways to resolve the conflicts produced by goals that have both positive and negative qualities. *Additional reasons for making one alternative more attractive than the other are identified.* Here each option is placed on an imaginary scale, and positive aspects (pluses) are added. Raymond, for example, recognized that Carmen lived on campus, and thus he would not have to borrow someone's car to pick her up. *A new alternative that has the positive characteristics of both of the other alternatives under consideration is sought.* Raymond tried to find another person whose company he enjoyed and who got along with his friends but was unable to do so. Or, recognize that there is no perfect solution in such cases. *Just go ahead and pick one of the alternatives.* Making any decision sometimes relieves the stress associated with goal conflicts, and doing this is generally better than doing nothing at all (Janis and Mann, 1977).

## Extrinsic Versus Intrinsic Motivation

There are two types of benefits associated with the incentives people pursue. They include tangible rewards and those that occur through the subjective thoughts and feelings of the person seeking a goal. **Extrinsic motivation** is the causal factor that

underlies the pursuit of the tangible rewards associated with particular goals. **Intrinsic motivation** is the causal factor that underlies the pursuit of the subjective aspects of particular goals, that is, the interest and personal enjoyment the goal generates. In most environments, both factors are important. However, intrinsic factors tend to occur much more frequently than do extrinsic factors.

In a study of worker motivation, for example, a random sample of 1,035 workers was asked to rate the importance of 18 aspects of their jobs. The rank order of the factors affecting motivation in the workplace is shown on the left-hand side of Table 6.7.

| Table 6.7 | The Relative Importance of Intrinsic and Extrinsic Factors in the Workplace and in the College Classroom |

| **RANK OF EACH WORKPLACE FACTOR** | **RANK OF EACH CLASSROOM FACTOR** |
|---|---|
| 1. Opportunity to do interesting work | 1. Enthusiasm of the teacher |
| 2. Having responsibility over a task | 2. Studying course material that is perceived as personally relevant and important |
| 3. Being valued for work that I do | 3. Having a well-prepared and organized teacher |
| 4. Having influence in organization | |
| 5. Amount of money I make | 4. Assignments and course material are challenging but "doable" |
| 6. Ability to achieve | |
| 7. Having pleasant coworkers | 5. Students are actively engaged in classroom learning through hands-on activities and discussions |
| 8. Job security | |
| 9. Ability to use skills and knowledge | |
| 10. Chance for promotion | 6. Variety and novelty are present in the assignments and classroom learning techniques |
| 11. Having a fair boss | |
| 12. Meaningful work | |
| 13. Fringe benefits | 7. Students feel they have good rapport with their instructors and that teachers are approachable |
| 14. Comfortable and clean working conditions | |
| 15. Convenient hours of work | |
| 16. Contribution to society | 8. Course material is made real, concrete, and understandable through the use of appropriate examples |
| 17. Job status | |
| 18. Working for a good company | |
| Based on data by Elizur (1984) | Based on data by Sass (1989) |

The right-hand side displays the top 8 factors affecting motivation in the college class-room from a sample of 700 students (Sass, 1989). The students were asked to list specific aspects of classes that influenced their level of motivation. *Note that among the top 8 factors in both environments, intrinsic factors appear more frequently than extrinsic factors. How would you rank each factor shown in Table 6.6 in a job that you currently hold? In one or more of the courses that you are now taking?*

*Sometimes External Rewards May Undermine Intrinsic Motivation* People subsequently lose interest in the task, and their performance may deteriorate. *For external rewards to have such an effect, an interesting task is performed to which external rewards are not normally expected* (Deci and Ryan, 1980, 1985). Such tasks usually are not routine. They challenge our skills, creativity, and problem-solving ability and they arouse our curiosity and emotions. When people suspect that they are being "bribed" to do something they enjoy or that they are doing it "for the money," a problem develops. Most of us want to feel in control and thus resist others' efforts to manipulate us.

In playing the stock market, or blackjack, or in collecting sales commissions and bonuses, on the other hand, external rewards would interfere less with a person's interest in the task. Normally, external rewards play an important role in such activities. Someone expects to receive them, and it is unlikely such activities would continue in their absence.

*Enhancing Intrinsic Motivation in the Workplace* Michael Matteson and John Ivancevich (1987) report that employee satisfaction and productivity are improved when occupations are perceived as intrinsically motivating. In job redesign efforts, they argue that factors that emphasize intrinsic motives should be stressed. To be successful, however, such efforts must ensure that both employee satisfaction and performance are enhanced. Attention to the following five principles can help to accomplish the latter goal:

1. *Variety should be present in the tasks that employees perform.*
2. *People need a certain amount of autonomy to do their jobs.* Managers should avoid the tendency to over-supervise every little detail of a job. Employees often respond well to opportunities to handle tasks and problems in their own ways.
3. *People work better when they can identify how their efforts contributed to a final product or outcome of a task.* Essentially, employees need to feel ownership for a product or outcome and to recognize that "I made a difference."

4. *Regular feedback on how well an employee is performing needs to be provided.* Not only does this allow corrections to be made, but the positive aspects of feedback often make people feel good about their efforts.

5. *Opportunities to work on tasks and/or to discuss job-related issues with other employees need to be a part of the work environment.* This allows for ideas to be shared and for people to recognize each other's contributions and to have some of their social needs met.

## COMBINED EFFECTS OF NEEDS, EXPECTATIONS, AND THE INCENTIVE VALUE OF GOALS

The influences of needs, expectations, and the incentive value of various goals have been discussed in isolation from each other. *For some of our motivations, however, all three factors simultaneously influence our actions.* This combined influence can be seen in the needs for achievement, affiliation, and power.

### Achievement

How would you respond to the following questions?

1. Do you want to become highly successful in life? Yes_____ No_____
2. Do you want to accomplish something really unique in your lifetime? Yes_____ No_____
3. Do you enjoy doing things better than other people? Yes_____ No_____
4. Do you think that effort and ability are the most important things in becoming successful? Yes_____ No_____
5. Do you always try to improve on what you are doing? Yes_____ No_____

People who answer "yes" to each question typically have a high need to *achieve. The need to achieve is defined as a desire to compete successfully with standards of excellence* (McClelland, 1985a; Atkinson and Raynor, 1978). While there are differences among people, most of us have at least a small amount of interest in getting ahead. Being able to satisfy the need for achievement over time produces a number of desirable consequences. People learn to persist on tasks, to take initiative, to assume personal responsibility for doing things, and to set realistic goals for themselves. High needs for achievement also are associated with obtaining status, wealth, and personal and professional fulfillment (Chusmir, 1989; Ruf and Chusmir, 1992).

Both David McClelland and John Atkinson argue that three factors influence the level of achievement motivation. They are:

1. *A learned need or drive (i.e., internal energy or tension).* This develops from childhood and other experiences where excellence and competition are stressed and where successes are rewarded with praise and affection. In addition, we model people we admire and respect, who also have strong needs for achievement.

2. *An expectation (i.e., cognitive factor) about whether or not our attempts to satisfy this need are likely to be successful.* This develops from having success experiences on a task in the past. It is also related to believing we have the skills to do well and that our efforts will be productive.

3. *The incentive value of goals (i.e., an environmental factor).* These are the positive and negative qualities associated with the goals that someone wants to pursue.

Thus, for people to achieve and get ahead in life, they must have an appropriate amount of the internal need or drive to achieve, expect success on tasks that will help them meet this need, and value obtaining goals that represent an accomplishment.

*Individuals with a High Need to Achieve Are Realistic About What They Can Accomplish* John Atkinson finds that people high in the tendency to achieve success are very realistic about what they can accomplish. They do not willingly accept tasks or goals that are beyond their capabilities. They do not, for example, seek the most prestigious occupation. Instead, Atkinson reports, they are more likely to prefer a career that offers reasonable amounts of success and rewards. People low in the need for achievement are more likely to settle for an easier but low-paying job or to make an attempt at a "prestige" job that is beyond their capabilities.

Furthermore, people high in achievement motivation strive for satisfaction from accomplishing a challenging task or goal. A challenge for them is not something that is too easy or too difficult. Rather, Atkinson reports that the challenge is best defined as a goal or task that is of intermediate difficulty. This is seen in the types of careers they select, the courses they take in school, and how they play sports. They strive for careers that offer reasonable chances for success; they take courses that challenge them but ones they know they can pass; they set goals in sports that are not too easy or too difficult. When given a choice of running a 3-, 6-, or 9-mile race, a person high in achievement and a good runner probably would select the six-mile race. On the other hand, a person low in achievement might select very easy or very difficult goals and tasks.

*The Fear of Failure Is Associated with the Need to Achieve* To understand how the fear of failure affects achievement, consider the following aspects of your life. You take an exam, and your responses are graded. You might try to cut costs at work, and your boss assesses how successful you were. You might write a book, paint a picture, build a house, or try other things that could lead to failure. The **fear of failure** is the anxiety that occurs when a challenge is faced and you are concerned about your ability to handle it. It affects how people behave in school and work situations and the goals they try to achieve.

In one study, John Atkinson (1978) measured the need for achievement and fear of failure among a group of college students. Achievement motivation was assessed from the content of the stories they wrote to pictures on a projective test called the Thematic Apperception Test. The fear of failure was determined from responses to a measure of test anxiety. Performance on a variety of tasks was related to whether or not students had high or low levels of each motive. The results of this study appear in Table 6.8. Note the differences in performance depending upon participants' levels of achievement and the fear of failure.

People vary in terms of how much the fear of failure affects their lives. For some, it is not much of a problem. They succeed because they enjoy the challenge of a task and do not worry much about failing. For others, it detracts somewhat from the positive feelings associated with their successes. And for still others, it drives whatever tasks they try to complete successfully. When faced with a challenge, their immediate response is to figure out how to avoid failing. They run scared and sometimes are successful at what they try. Their successes, however, are not motivated by strong needs to achieve or to obtain satisfaction by meeting challenges. Rather, they result from trying to keep themselves from "falling flat on their faces," "looking silly," "getting a harsh evaluation from someone," or "losing their honor." Such individuals view getting ahead as anxiety arousing, a struggle, and they are typically less satisfied with their accomplishments.

**Table 6.8**

The Effects of the Need for Achievement and Fear of Failure on Performance

**Task: Persistence on Exam, Exam Performance, and Interest in School**

| NEED FOR ACHIEVEMENT | FEAR OF FAILURE | HIGH PERSISTENCE | HIGH EXAM SCORES | HIGH INTEREST IN SCHOOL |
| --- | --- | --- | --- | --- |
| High | Low | 73% | 67% | 78% |
| Low | High | 25% | 25% | 36% |

**Task: Ability to Set Realistic Job Goals**

| NEED FOR ACHIEVEMENT | FEAR OF FAILURE | REALISTIC JOB GOALS | UNREALISTIC JOB GOALS |
| --- | --- | --- | --- |
| High | Low | 75% | 25% |
| Low | High | 39% | 61% |

*People Who Fear Failure Use Several Strategies to Avoid Failing* Several research studies have identified strategies that people employ to avoid failing (cf. Barry, 1975; Flett et al., 1992). The tactics employed are described in Table 6.9 and a more detailed examination of one of them—cheating—appears in Focus on Applied Research 6.2.

*Some Individuals Also Display a Fear of Success* For some the need to achieve is low because they actually fear becoming successful. Initial research by Martina Horner (1978) suggested that this fear was a problem more for women than men. Later research has found that the problem affects both men and women. People who fear success tend to worry about social rejection or disapproval from their less successful peers. They also may fear losing control over their independence and autonomy if they become too successful. And as Sharon Fried-Buchalter (1992) notes, some even come to see themselves as imposters. Instead of internalizing their successes, they discount them and instead believe they have somehow fooled the world about their capabilities. She notes that people who see themselves as imposters not only fear success but also failure. They worry about harsh and negative evaluations from other people, including someone uncovering their imagined "deception."

*People with High and Low Needs for Achievement React Differently to Their Successes and Failures* Bernard Weiner (1972) and Daniel Bar-Tal (1978) report that people high in achievement motivation tend to believe that ability and effort are responsible for their successes. Those with a low need for achievement believe whatever successes they have are due to factors outside their control. They attribute their successes to easy tasks or to luck.

When they fail, those with a high need to achieve dig in and work harder. They say to themselves, "I know I have the ability, and if I try harder, I will eventually succeed." People low in achievement tend to stop trying when they fail. They do not believe their skills and abilities make much of a difference in their successes. Consequently, they may wait for easier tasks or for their luck to change.

*Our Need for Achievement Can Be Modified* An important implication of David McClelland's work is that we can learn how to increase our willingness to achieve. In a

| **Table 6.9** | Strategies Employed by People Who Possess a Fear of Failing |
|---|---|

*Easy tasks or goals are attempted.*  Success is ensured by doing easy tasks. Students who use this strategy may attend easy schools, take routine courses, or major in less difficult areas. Employees may avoid challenging jobs and promotion opportunities.

*Difficult tasks or goals are attempted.*  This effectively ensures that they will fail. Since the task is difficult, people do not criticize them as much. After all, there is less shame in failing at a difficult task. One of my students switched his major from psychology to physics. He disliked his new major intensely but continued it. When asked why, he responded, "It's better to flunk out of physics than psychology."

*Tasks are attempted with a lack of investment.*  By not working too hard on a job assignment or studying for an exam, the potential for failure is handled with an attitude of, "I'm really not all that interested in this."

*Procrastination increases.*  People have a difficult time getting things done on time or wait until the last minute to complete tasks. This stems in part from the anticipation of meeting with disapproval from individuals who have more perfectionistic standards.

*Superstriving occurs.*  Individuals make a supreme effort and work beyond their capabilities. They run scared, become successful, and they often end up exhausted and "burned out."

*Lying and cheating sometimes are used to get ahead.*  Dishonesty typically yields only temporary relief from the anxiety over failing. Yet cheating is popular in many areas, including the college classroom.

---

### FOCUS ON APPLIED RESEARCH 6.2
### Dishonesty in the Classroom

In separate studies, Donald McCabe (1991) and Stephen Davis and Cathy Grover (1992) and their colleagues reviewed the research literature on academic dishonesty and gathered data from more than 12,000 students across a variety of institutions and disciplines. On the surveys, students were asked to respond to a variety of questions about their experiences with cheating in the college classroom. Several of the prominent findings from these studies included:

- *Sixty-one percent of undergraduate college students cheat* at some point in their college careers. This includes buying term papers, falsifying bibliographies, copying answers on exams, and plagiarizing papers and lab reports.
- *Eighty-five percent of business students admitted to cheating* at least once during their college careers, and 74 percent of engineering majors, 67 percent of science majors, and 63 percent of humanities majors also cheated in some way at least once.

- *In spite of the prevalence of cheating, 90 percent of those sampled answered "yes"* when asked, "Is it wrong to cheat."
- *Women tended to cheat less than men,* and students in small private institutions were more honest than those in large public and private universities.
- *Cheaters tend to have a fear of failure,* to be less intelligent than other students, to need social approval, to be more impulsive, and to have a poor work ethic.
- *Less than 2 percent* of those who cheat are caught.

### Sample of Reasons Given:
- "There's no other choice. If I don't cheat, I'll get Cs and Ds because I will fall to the bottom of the grading curve—behind those who cheat."
- "I really don't think it would be possible to have any free time here if I did not cheat."
- "Generally when someone cheats, it's like adultery. What they don't know, ain't going to hurt 'em."

classic demonstration of using psychological principles in an applied setting, businessmen in Hyderabad, India, were trained to develop the characteristics of people with a high need for achievement. Owners of small and medium-sized businesses learned how to do the following six things:

1. *To engage in self-study* where they become sensitive to the presence of achievement motivation in their own thoughts and actions. Based on such information they were able to assess what skills they had that would help them get ahead and what new skills they might need to learn.
2. *To think creatively and imaginatively* about steps they could take in their businesses to become more successful. This included setting goals for the future activities in their businesses.
3. *To establish moderate goals* they had a realistic chance to obtain.
4. *To take initiative and responsibility* for getting things done in their lives. They were taught not to wait around for other people to make things happen to them.
5. *To attribute their successes more to their skills, ability, and effort,* and less to easy tasks and luck.
6. *To think positively* and imagine themselves becoming successful as a result of the actions they took.

After the motivation training, the businessmen were much more active than those who were not shown how to enhance their needs for achievement. They participated more in community affairs, started new businesses, invested more money in expanding their businesses, and employed over twice as many new people over a two-year period than did the untrained businessmen (McClelland, 1978, 1985b).

## Power

Please answer the following questions.

> Do you like to watch and/or play competitive team sports? Yes_____ No_____
> Do you try to persuade others to accept your ideas about issues? Yes_____ No_____
> Do you prefer to be in charge of things? Yes_____ No_____
> Are you concerned about your reputation? Yes_____ No_____
> When angry, do you verbally or physically attack others? Yes_____ No_____
> Do you try to wear the most stylish clothes you can? Yes_____ No_____

David Winter (1976, 1988) reports that people who have needs for power typically possess the characteristics described above. The *power motive* is a concern for having impact on others, arousing strong emotions in others, or maintaining one's reputation and prestige. Like achievement, three factors affect our attempts to gain or use power. They are: an internal need or drive to feel powerful, personal expectations or estimates of whether our efforts to obtain influence will be successful, and the incentive value of the goals we pursue.

For example, two people may have the same level of need or drive to run for a seat on city council. One person, however, believes she can be successful in a campaign and values the goal of being a city council member. The other candidate either may not estimate his chances of success as high or does not value obtaining a "relatively low-level political office." In the latter case, he is likely to drop out of the race or spend less effort and time trying to get elected.

*Power Is a Rather Complex Force in Our Lives* Research shows no consistent tendencies for one sex to score higher than the other on tests of power motivation (Winter, 1988). In addition, both men and women had similar interests in obtaining "socially appropriate" indicators of power such as prestige and the ability to exert leadership. Some gender differences, however, occur when the abuse of power is examined. Tendencies to express power in socially unacceptable ways are stronger in men than in women. High needs for power are associated with drinking alcoholic beverages, driving recklessly, gambling, verbal and physical aggression, sexual and physical abuse of partners, and tendencies to be overcontrolling in close relationships. While women also may engage in such actions, they are not as strongly related to their need for power.

*Also, early and current family history appears to play a role in socially unacceptable displays of power.* David Winter notes that such behaviors occur less frequently among men and women who had younger siblings around when they were growing up. Having children as adults also moderates socially unacceptable displays of power. Experiences in nurturing or caring for others may dispose people to find more socially acceptable ways to express their power motives.

When power is misused in other areas of our lives, problems may occur. *It can interfere with our relationships.* When your goal in life, for example, becomes simply to have an impact, whatever the cost, the need for power interferes. You may find that other people cease to trust you or that they are afraid you are out to use them. People with a high need for power have a difficult time establishing close interpersonal relationships. They are less satisfied with such relationships, and they tend to break up with their partners more often.

When people satisfy this need in more socially acceptable ways, good things happen. They may find themselves seeking leadership positions in social clubs and other organizations. Because they are comfortable wanting to have an impact, they are able to get others to accept and implement their ideas.

## Affiliation

To what extent are the following behaviors a part of your everyday life?

Do you like to make friends and be with other people? Yes_____ No_____

Do you have a lot of interest in joining clubs, giving parties, or visiting other people? Yes_____ No_____

Before deciding, do you typically seek advice from others? Yes_____ No_____

Do you want more other people to approve of you? Yes_____ No_____

A "yes" response to each item would suggest a high need for *affiliation*. The need for human contact is a deeply rooted need in all but a few individuals. And like achievement and power, it is susceptible to the joint influence of an underlying need or drive, our expectations that we can successfully form relationships, and the value we place on a given relationship.

For example, two students in my class recently expressed an interest in wanting to meet new people (i.e., both had an underlying need to affiliate). An opportunity to join a student bowling league was presented to both of them. Only one person accepted the invitation. The other declined and told me he did not make friends easily and that bowling was not something he enjoyed. In effect, his expectations for successfully forming relationships were low, and the goal of joining a bowling league was not valued very highly.

*It Is Better to Seek Moderate Levels of Affiliation* People with moderate levels of affiliation tend to be more satisfied with their social interactions. When individuals become overly concerned with affiliation, they run the risk of conforming blindly to the desires of others. Or they become dependent on others to tell them what to do and how to do it. Elizabeth Mazur (1989) also reports that among women, high needs for affiliation are associated with negative moods. She suggests that some women may have higher expectations than do men that encounters with others will be enjoyable. People in their lives, unfortunately, do not live up to such expectations, leading them to feel sad and disappointed. On the other hand, those relatively unconcerned with affiliation have difficulties with intimate relationships and are suspicious of others. They withdraw from social contact and consequently miss opportunities for personal growth.

*Anxiety Increases the Need for Affiliation* There is an old saying that "misery loves company." Having others around us when we are anxious may help us feel better. *Having people who take a more active role in helping us to cope is much more effective.* In one study, patients who were going to have heart bypass surgery preferred someone who had just had surgery as a roommate. The dominant reason given was the superior information that someone who had already been through the experience could provide (Kulik and Mahler, 1990).

## THE INTEGRATION OF HUMAN MOTIVES: THE VIEWS OF ABRAHAM MASLOW

According to Abraham Maslow (1970), *the variety of needs that play a role in our everyday lives should not be thought of as unrelated to each other.* An important aspect of Maslow's thinking is that at any given moment in time, various needs compete for expression. At this moment, your need to sleep, eat, or relax may be pitted against your need to achieve at work or school or to spend time with friends.

### Maslow's Hierarchy of Needs

Not all needs, however, are created equal. Maslow proposed that our needs can be arranged into a hierarchy where basic survival needs (e.g., hunger, thirst, sex, seeking shelter) have a higher priority for expression than do other needs. They must be *reasonably well satisfied* before people attempt to fulfill higher-order personal growth needs such as forming friendships, seeking status, or trying to achieve their potential in life. When we are hungry or thirsty, for example, our thoughts are directed toward obtaining food or something to drink. Other things are relatively unimportant until our hunger or thirst is satisfied.

This hierarchy of needs is described in Exercise 6.1 in the Applied Activities section. Completing this activity will help you to identify the variety of needs that compete for expression in your life. It will also help you consider ways to do something about your needs that are currently unmet.

## *Summary of Chapter Organizers*

Suggested responses to the chapter organizers presented at the beginning of this chapter are presented below.

1. *In what ways does your genetic makeup motivate your actions?* Instincts play a much more important role in the motivation of lower animals than they do in human beings. However, many so-called human instincts, such as the "maternal instinct," are affected much more by cognitive and environmental factors.

2. *How do needs and drives affect your actions?* Needs are internal biological and learned states. They operate by creating a state of internal tension or drive that leads to actions that will try to satisfy the underlying need. This internal tension is reduced in order to achieve a state of homeostasis, or balance, in this tension.

3. *Are you aware of how physiological, cognitive, and environmental influences affect thirst, hunger, and sex?* Thirst is related to a loss of water through dehydration as well as a sodium-water imbalance in cellular fluids. Our thirst is satisfied by a variety of beverages, including some that are not healthy for us. *Hunger* is regulated by your body's attempts to seek a balance between food intake and your energy requirements. A homeostasis is achieved through regulatory mechanisms in the hypothalamus and sensors that monitor nutrients in your bloodstream. Eating is affected by family and cultural influences as well as any personal insecurity about your body image. Oftentimes people try to control their weight and body image by going on a diet. Unfortunately, most diets fail, because dieters unwittingly suppress their metabolic rate by cutting calories too much, failing to obtain adequate physical activity, and not eating well-balanced meals. *Sexual activity* is not driven in human beings as much by sex hormones such as estrogen and testosterone. In humans sexual arousal is affected more by cognitive and environmental factors than hormone levels. Erotic pictures, tapes, sensual advertisements, romantic movies, and your fantasies are much more important.

4. *Do you know how low and high levels of arousal affect your performance?* Arousal refers to your body's general level of alertness and activity. The Yerkes-Dodson Law shows that both high and low levels of arousal can affect your performance. Low arousal leads to boredom, while high arousal may produce less effective behaviors including those involved in problem solving and decision making. One way to handle high levels of arousal is to reduce the complexity of the problems you face by adopting a "small-win" attitude. Rather than reducing stimulation, sometimes you may seek stimulation to keep yourself aroused. High-sensation seekers tend to like excitement in their lives, while low-sensation seekers prefer less excitement.

5. *How do unconscious motives affect your actions?* Unconscious motives operate outside of our level of conscious awareness. Such motives can be identified by honestly and objectively examining your behaviors for clues to such motives. To do this, do not completely discount the reactions others have about you; try to identify the motivations in your fantasies and dreams; and discuss your concerns and behaviors with friends, parents, or even a professional counselor.

6. *How do various expectations, beliefs about being in control of your life, and personal values affect your actions?* Expectations about success and failure, for example, predict achievement as well as success in relationships. Self-efficacy beliefs are perceptions about your competence and confidence to execute actions and to obtain particular goals. Locus-of-control beliefs affect whether you feel in control of your life. Internals believe they are the "captains of their fate," while those with an external

locus of control attribute success to luck, fate, or easy tasks. Personal values affect your tendency to engage in behaviors that are compatible with them.

7. *What steps can you take to manage such beliefs?* Self-efficacy beliefs can be managed by doing things that lead to success experiences, modeling people who do well, taking words of encouragement to heart, and interpreting physiological cues appropriately. Internal locus-of-control beliefs are enhanced by taking responsibility for tasks, trying new things, and changing your environment to become more successful. Issues with values are corrected by resolving discrepancies among them and making behaviors compatible with your values.

8. *In what ways do environmental factors motivate you?* Incentives are external stimuli or goals that motivate our actions. Most goals have positive and negative qualities, and this produces conflicts in choosing among them. Approach-approach conflict occurs when two or more goals have equally attractive qualities; approach-avoidance appears when the qualities are equally unattractive; and approach-avoidance conflicts result when goals have both positive and negative qualities.

9. *How do needs for achievement, power, and affiliation appear in your life?* The need to achieve is the desire to compete successfully with standards of excellence. When this need is high, you might select moderately difficult tasks, persist at tasks, and seek feedback. Sometimes a fear of failing or a fear of success interferes with your ability to do well. The *need for power* reflects your wanting to have an impact on others, to arouse strong emotions, and to maintain a reputation. Men and women do not differ on their needs for power, but men have stronger tendencies to direct their needs for power in socially unacceptable ways. The *need for affiliation* reflects your need for social contact. You are better off seeking moderate levels of affiliation as well as the support and advice of others when you are feeling anxious.

10. *How does Abraham Maslow account for the way your needs are expressed?* Maslow believed that your needs have different priorities for being expressed. Before the personal growth needs (i.e., seeking status, trying to achieve one's potential in life) at the top of the hierarchy can be pursued, basic survival needs such as hunger, thirst, and seeking shelter must first be reasonably satisfied.

## Things to Do

1. Review the scenarios at the beginning of this chapter. What motives discussed in the text do you think initiated, guided and maintained their behaviors? Where are intrinsic or extrinsic factors more important? What role did locus of control and self-efficacy play in the actions taken?

2. Pick up your favorite magazine, and look at the advertisements. Try to identify the biological, cognitive, and environmental factors that are used to motivate you to purchase a product or to take some action.

3. Based on what you know about achievement, affiliation, and power needs, which of these needs are likely to be seen in a police officer, a teacher, a minister, a business manager, a homemaker, and a salesperson?

4. Using the information for scoring statements for the presence of the needs for achievement, affiliation, and power described in Exercise 6.2, determine the presence of each motive in favorite song, two to three pages from a novel that you are reading, a letter a friend sent you, a mail order solicitation for money.

5. Review the information on the need for achievement in the text. List the characteristics of people who have high needs for achievement. What qualities do you

currently possess? What are some actions you would have to take to adopt the qualities that you do not currently possess?

6. Describe a situation in which your level of arousal (i.e., tension and stress) is uncomfortable because you have too much to do and not enough time to complete the task. Review the section on the "small-win philosophy," and think of ways you can break the problem into smaller components that must be completed in order for everything to be completed; order the tasks that need to be finished, beginning with those that would be easiest for you to complete and ending with those that are relatively more difficult; as much as possible, begin working on your easiest tasks, and move on to the next only after you have completed the one before it.

7. Most people are bored or have areas of their lives that are not very exciting. List two to three new activities that would allow you to obtain sensation seeking levels that you would prefer. What factors would keep you from trying each activity? List the pros and cons, and select one that has the most positive or the fewest negative outcomes. Try this new activity for several days, and assess its pros and cons.

8. Carry a small notebook with you for eight to ten hours. About twice an hour, record the daydreams you are having. Use the information in Table 6.4 to help you interpret your daydreams. Or, record your dreams immediately after awakening for a period of three to four days and also use the information in Table 6.4 to help you interpret them. Did your fantasies help you to: Identify a problem in your life that is unresolved? Suggest a solution to a problem? Help you identify and deal with your feelings towards another person? Suggest future goals for your life?

## APPLIED ACTIVITIES

EXERCISE 6.1.

**Abraham Maslow's Need Hierarchy in Your Life**

Psychologist Abraham Maslow (1970) suggested that our motives can be organized into a hierarchy, with basic survival and safety needs at the bottom and social, self-esteem, and self-actualization (i.e., our attempts to achieve our potential in life) on the upper levels of this hierarchy. This activity is designed to help you explore some of the implications of Maslow's thinking in your life.

**Part 1.**

Think about the activities you engaged in during the past two to three weeks. Next, review the list of needs presented below, and place a check next to those you remember trying to satisfy. Then, concentrate on one or more examples of how you tried to satisfy that need, and rate how satisfied you were satisfying that need.

```
        1              2             3            4             5
        |_____|_____|_____|_____|
      Very        Moderately      Neutral     Moderately      Very
   Dissatisfied   Dissatisfied                 Satisfied    Satisfied
```

| MASLOW'S NEED HIERARCHY | TRIED TO SATISFY | SATISFACTION RATING |
|---|---|---|
| *Physiological* | | |
| Hunger | _____ | _____ |
| Thirst | _____ | _____ |
| Sex | _____ | _____ |
| Sleep | _____ | _____ |
| Rest | _____ | _____ |
| Exercise | _____ | _____ |
| *Safety* | | |
| Shelter | _____ | _____ |
| Protection | _____ | _____ |
| Physical | _____ | _____ |
| Psychological | _____ | _____ |
| Economic | _____ | _____ |
| *Social* | | |
| Displaying love and affection | _____ | _____ |
| Seeking friendships | _____ | _____ |
| Affiliating with others | _____ | _____ |
| *Self-esteem* | | |
| Developing confidence | _____ | _____ |
| Seeking independence | _____ | _____ |
| Achieving something | _____ | _____ |
| Obtaining influence | _____ | _____ |
| Obtaining knowledge | _____ | _____ |

Gaining recognition             _____             _____

Obtaining status             _____             _____

Seeking respect             _____             _____

*Self-actualization*

Trying to achieve your potential             _____             _____

Engaging in self-development             _____             _____

Behaving creatively             _____             _____

Displaying an acceptance of self             _____             _____

Displaying an acceptance of others             _____             _____

## Part 2.

Pick one or two needs that received the lowest satisfaction ratings, and develop an action plan to increase your ability to satisfy them in the future. Similarly, pick one or two needs you did not check that you would like to spend time working on in the future. What are several specific actions you must take?

Action Plan: Low-Rated Needs

Action Plan: Needs Not Rated but of Interest for Future

## Part 3.

Maslow suggested that people are more satisfied with their attempts to meet needs lower in the hierarchy than those that were higher. Do your ratings suggest this was true for you? Yes_____ No_____. Give a brief reason for your response.

Abraham Maslow also noted that people tend not to pursue higher-order needs (i.e., social, self-esteem, self-actualization) unless they were able to satisfy their physiological and safety needs. Is this true of how such motives operate in your life? Yes_____ No_____. Give an example to support your response.

Can you think of an exception to this principle in your actions and those of other people (e.g., people starving themselves to make a political/religious statement)?

EXERCISE 6.2    **What Do You Value?**

Rank-order the list of values below in terms of how important they are as guiding principles in your life. Assign a rank of 1 to the value that is most important and a rank of 18 to the one that is least important. Place your response in the spaces provided.

_____ 1. Family security          _____ 10. Salvation

_____ 2. A world at peace         _____ 11. Inner harmony

_____ 3. Freedom                  _____ 12. Equality

_____ 4. Self-respect             _____ 13. National security

_____ 5. Happiness                _____ 14. Mature love

_____ 6. Wisdom                   _____ 15. A world of beauty

_____ 7. A sense of accomplishment _____ 16. Pleasure

_____ 8. A comfortable life       _____ 17. An exciting life

_____ 9. True friendship          _____ 18. Social recognition

The number to the left of each value in the list above corresponds to how a national survey of people rank-ordered each value.

• In what ways are your ranks similar to and different from the national sample? How would you explain this?

• How happy are you with the way you ranked your values? Give an example of how your three top-ranked values appear in your life.

• Are there any discrepancies between any of the values you ranked in your top ten and your behaviors? If yes, list one to two examples. If no, how are you able to keep your behaviors in line with your values?

• Are you uncomfortable in any way with how you rank-ordered your values? Which values would you like to see as a more important part of your life?

EXERCISE 6.3

**Assessing the Presence of Achievement, Affiliation, and Power Motives in Your Behavior Using a Projective Test**

Study the picture on the next page for a few seconds. Then write a story about the picture on a separate sheet of paper. Be sure to include in your story the following: What is happening? Who are the people, and what has brought them together? What has led up to this situation? What are the people thinking and saying? What do you think will eventually happen? Work rapidly, and try not to spend more than five to eight minutes writing your story.

Listed below are brief descriptions of the types of things that could appear in your story that would key the presence of each motive. Take each sentence in your story and see if it matches one of the descriptions in the list. Mark each sentence for the presence of each motive. Determine the number of sentences that can be classified according to achievement, affiliation, or power needs. *It is quite possible that none of your sentences or only a few can be classified according to the descriptions in the list. Remember that each need does not occur in everything we do or say.* A sample story I wrote is scored for you on the next page to illustrate how to do it.

**Keys to the Presence of Each Motive in a Story for Exercise 6.3**

Score each sentence that you can by putting the number (e.g., Ia, IIc, IIIa) that best describes what is occurring in parentheses at the end of the sentence. Add up the number of sentences that relate to each motive.

I. *Achievement:*
  a. A concern for doing well is shown by an individual(s).
  b. High standards are set by someone.
  c. An individual is concerned about getting ahead.
  d. Someone is interested in accomplishing a long-term goal.
  e. The story or someone in it is involved in obtaining a unique accomplishment.
  f. A person wants to be better than someone else.
  g. A person wants to take personal responsibility for his or her success or failures.
  h. Someone in the story wants feedback on how he or she did.

II. *Affiliation:*
  a. An individual is interested in establishing a collaborative relationship with other people.
  b. A person expresses a need to make friends with someone else.
  c. Someone is interested in seeing that the needs of other people are met.
  d. An individual indicates that he or she wants to be liked by another person.
  e. Someone is interested in joining a club, having a party, or visiting others.

III. *Power:*
  a. Someone wants to influence or control another person or group.
  b. A strong desire for competition with other people is expressed.
  c. An individual wants to control the flow of information.
  d. A person shows a high need for status.
  e. Someone is interested in the impact of what he or she does on other people.
  f. People engage in activities that led to stress and conflict, for example, arguing, shouting, demanding, punishing others, or making strong commands.

### Example of story

The men and women are members of a sales department in a business organization. They are meeting to talk about their sales for the year. In past years, their group has had the lowest sales in the history of the company. This year, they have done better than any other department. *(I-a)* Their boss is telling everyone around the table that he expects them to maintain at least the same high performance level next year. *(I-b)* He says he is proud to be associated with this group and looks forward to working with them next year. *(II-a)* The woman with her back to the group is about to leave the room. She is angry with the other members of the group for not listening to her. *(III-f)* She thinks they were lucky to have done so well this year and wants them to spend more time realistically talking about the reasons for their success. *(III-c)* The person who is sitting on the edge of the table and talking to the others is telling them how helpful the feedback they gave him earlier in the year on his sales techniques was to him. He wants to know if there is anything else they can tell him now about his selling procedures that will help him next year. *(I-h)* He wants to do even better next year. *(I-c)* In all, the group members are happy, and they will want to have a party later on to celebrate. *(Il-e )*

### The scoring of the sample story.

| MOTIVE | NUMBER OF OCCURRENCES |
|---|---|
| Achievement | 4 |
| Affiliation | 2 |
| Power | 2 |

## Key Terms

*Achievement need.*   A learned need that is characterized by behaviors directed toward becoming successful and meeting an internal standard of excellence.

*Affiliation need.*   A learned need that is characterized by behaviors directed toward forming friendships and working closely with other people.

*Arousal.*   The body's general level of alertness and activity as reflected in muscle tension, heart and respiration rates, and patterns of electrical activity in the brain.

*Approach-approach goal conflict.*   Tension, frustration, and indecision encountered when choosing among incentives or goals that have equally attractive or desirable qualities.

*Approach-avoidance goal conflict.*   Tension, frustration, and indecision encountered when a single incentive or goal has both attractive and unattractive qualities.

*Avoidance-avoidance goal conflict.*   Tension, frustration, and indecision faced when choosing among incentives or goals that have equally unattractive or undesirable qualities.

*Basal metabolism.*   The amount of energy our body expends in a resting state maintaining basic biological functioning such as digestion, breathing, and neural activity.

*Cognitive dissonance.*   A state of internal tension aroused when people feel responsible for holding inconsistent beliefs or when their actions go against what they believe.

*Double approach-avoidance conflict.*   Tension, frustration, and indecision faced when choosing among two or more incentives or goals that possess both attractive or unattractive features.

*Drive.*   The energy level mobilized when a need is not satisfied.

*Expectations.*   The estimates that people make about what will or is likely to happen in the future.

*External locus of control.*   The belief that luck, fate, or other people control most aspects of our lives and the reinforcements we obtain.

*Extrinsic motivation.*   Forces in the environment that pull our behaviors in particular directions.

*Fear of failure.*   The anxiety that occurs when a challenge is faced and we are concerned about our ability to handle it and the possibility of receiving negative feedback from others.

*Incentives.*   The specific goals people pursue in trying to satisfy their needs. Essentially, incentives are the forces within the environment that impel our actions.

*Incentive value.*   The degree to which a goal, object, or stimulus has pleasant or unpleasant qualities.

*Instinct.*   A behavior pattern that is unlearned, expressed in a uniform and consistent manner, and that occurs in every member of a species.

*Internal locus of control.*   The belief that people can guide and direct their lives and are responsible for obtaining whatever reinforcements they receive.

*Intrinsic motivation.*   Internal factors that motivate or push our actions in certain directions.

*Goal conflict.*   A dilemma or confusion caused by trying to choose among goals that vary in their incentive values or the positive and negative qualities they possess.

*Locus of control.*   The beliefs people have about what controls events in their lives and how reinforcements are obtained.

*Motivation.*   Refers to processes that initiate, guide, and direct our behaviors towards certain goals, and that maintain our actions while particular goals are being pursued.

*Motive.*   An internal or external force that impels people towards certain goals in life.

*Needs.*   Internal biological or learned states within people that help to initiate, guide, and direct behaviors towards achieving certain goals.

*Optimal arousal level.*   The level of stimulation that leads to productive and satisfying levels of performance.

*Power need.*   A learned need that is characterized by behaviors that reflect a high degree of interest in controlling and influencing other people and in competing with others.

*Projective test.*   A device for measuring some of our personal characteristics. It requires us to react to stimuli that are basically neutral or ambiguous. Consequently, our perceptions reflect some of our personal attitudes, values, and needs.

*Self-efficacy.*   Our judgment about our perceived capabilities to organize and execute courses of action required to attain particular goals.

*Sensation seeking.*   Tendency for people to actively seek ways to maintain and add sources of excitement to their lives.

*Set point.*   An internal standard around which body weight is regulated.

*Values.*   The important and stable ideas, beliefs, and assumptions that underlie and are observe, in our actions across a number of different situations. They help to initiate, guide, and maintain our actions in a variety of situations.

*Yerkes-Dodson law.*   States that performance is optimal at intermediate arousal or levels of drive.

# Interpersonal Communication

## Chapter Overview

To enhance your ability to interact with others, several critical components of your ability to communicate must be understood. They include the functions interpersonal communication serve, the factors that facilitate and hinder your conversations, the role of body language, your communication style, and the role of the physical environment and the emotional climate on your everyday interactions. This chapter will help you to appreciate how the latter factors operate in your life and to understand the steps you can take to manage them more effectively.

## Chapter Organizers

*As you read, answer the questions that follow on a separate sheet of paper, and check your responses with those provided in the summary section.*

Interpersonal communication has several general characteristics.

1. Do you know five functions that interpersonal communication serves?
2. What role do conscious and unconscious processes play in your everyday conversations?

Different communication channels operate in your everyday life.

3. How do various communication channels affect your interactions?
4. What is body language, and how does it affect your ability to communicate?
5. Are you aware of how environmental, semantic, and emotional noise interfere with your conversations?

The messages that you send and receive from others have multiple meanings, and their meaning can be easily distorted.

6. How do the latent and manifest content of a message differ?
7. What are hidden agendas, and how do they influence your conversations?
8. Are you aware of how your beliefs filter the messages you receive?

A variety of formal and informal rules determine certain patterns in how, when, and where you can communicate with others.

9. What are the critical characteristics of your communication patterns?

Interactions reflect differences in status and the type of emotions displayed.

10. What role do status and affect play in perceptions of your impact relative to other people and the emotional distance in your interactions?
11. How do status and affect influence the communication style you use?

Communication occurs within a physical and psychological environment.

12. What role do physical space, personal space, and the emotional climate play in facilitating and hindering your interactions?

## Breaking the Code of Silence

For centuries, the Trappist monks' way of life was rugged and lonely. They lived in near-total silence, forbidden to talk to the other monks with whom they lived and worked. The lack of communication made it difficult for them to meet their needs for acceptance by others. It also made it difficult for them to check whether their thoughts and perceptions of the world were shared by others.

As you might imagine, not being able to talk to others led to misunderstandings among the monks. One monk, Brother Timothy, described a trial by noise. Each night as he lay in his bed he could hear the board in the bed of his neighbor squeak at every toss and turn. Brother Timothy did not feel that he could use sign language or other formal channels to remedy the irritation. Nor could he fix the board, since there was a rule prohibiting a monk from touching the property of another. One day while riding in a wagon with the monk who had the squeaking board, one of the boards in the wagon began to squeak. Brother Timothy got the other monk's attention and pointed to the squeaky board and then made a childlike gesture with his hands resting on his face to signify "sleep." This message was not understood, and the other monk looked at Brother Timothy as if he were crazy.

Frustrated, Brother Timothy asked the head of the monastery for permission to talk. He then told him about the squeaky board and how he could not get it fixed. The head of the monastery then had the board fixed. Unfortunately, the monk with the squeaking bed had to eat his meals on the floor of the dining hall for a week as penance. In spite of not being allowed to talk, he was somehow expected to know a problem existed.

In 1969, the Trappist monks were allowed to permanently break their code of silence. All monks could now make brief oral communications without asking for permission. A year later, dramatic results occurred in their lives. The monks reported they were more aware of themselves; their relationships with other monks had improved; they felt closer to other people; and they had a greater appreciation for silence when it occurred.

Based on a description of life in a monastery in a study by Jaska and Stech, 1978.

# *INTERPERSONAL COMMUNICATION HAS SEVERAL FUNCTIONS*

As the story of Brother Timothy illustrates, the relative absence of interpersonal **communication** makes life much more difficult. Without it our ability to give and receive information, to manage interpersonal conflicts, and to work with others on solving problems and making decisions would be seriously impaired. Furthermore, our ability to communicate plays an important role in meeting certain needs. Research demonstrates that our everyday conversations help us satisfy six primary interpersonal motives: pleasure, affection, inclusion, escape from other activities, relaxation, and control and influence over others (Rubin et al., 1988, 1992). The variety of ways such needs are fulfilled is illustrated in Focus on Applied Research 7.1.

*Perhaps the most basic function our everyday conversations serve is to ensure that a relationship will continue into the future.* Steve Duck proposes that whether our conversations are profound, insightful, or simply mundane, they help to lure or persuade someone we like into a deeper level of involvement with us (Duck, 1990; Duck et al., 1991). *In effect, any intimate, social, or business relationship has an element of unfinished business that needs to be perpetuated through regular conversations.* Thus, what appear to be ordinary statements such as, "When can I get back to you with this proposal?" "Let's discuss what we want to do next weekend," and "When's the best time to reach you later on this week?" have a much deeper purpose. Such statements are not simply about proposals, weekend activities, and time. Rather, they encourage people to develop a mental image of a continuing relationship with another person.

## Unconscious and Conscious Control of Interpersonal Communication

The production of sounds as well as who, how, and what to talk about occur without much conscious reflection and control. Dale Hample (1987) notes that so much happens so quickly in a conversation that conscious control is difficult to maintain. Instead, he argues that people enact prior scripts that were developed when similar situations were encountered in the past.

Such scripts are examples of the automatic mental control processes described earlier in Chapter 1. They allow us to converse with little conscious effort, although we may do so in a somewhat rigid and inflexible manner. Political candidates, business managers, and salespeople, for example, typically find themselves needing to get the same point of view across to numerous individuals and groups. They speak in well-rehearsed sentences, and the words flow essentially unchanged from one occasion to the next. Similarly, when people introduce themselves to each other, the same ground is covered effortlessly every time. Also, unconscious mental scripts are operating whenever you find yourself discussing one topic with someone while thinking about something else.

While some aspects of communication appear "mindless," others have a more "mindful" component. Janet Bavelas and Linda Coates (1992) point out that people also plan what to say in advance. Conscious control allows us to correct ourselves when speaking, to change topics, to avoid saying the wrong thing at the wrong time, and to provide a fresh perspective on issues. Along similar lines, Michael Motley (1992) argues that conscious control is evident whenever we enter unfamiliar or troublesome situations, an uncomfortable delay occurs in a conversation, or when we want to express our displeasure with someone but wish to avoid further conflict. Finding the "right words to say" is important in such circumstances.

# MULTIPLE COMMUNICATION CHANNELS ARE EMPLOYED

## Speaking and Writing

The communication channel is the route by which messages are conveyed. Our patterns of communicating tend to encourage or discourage the use of certain channels. Housel and Davis (1977) report that the face-to-face channel produces more accurate messages and higher levels of satisfaction among people. An important reason for this is that verbal and nonverbal messages are both present. This makes it easier to interpret what is said and more difficult to hide things.

While writing is not totally dissatisfying, the telephone is the next preference people have for communicating. As the phone company suggests in its advertisements, "The telephone is the next best thing to being there." Howard Muson reports that the telephone has certain advantages when compared to face-to-face communication (Muson, 1982). Someone can solve complex problems and process information just as efficiently over the telephone as in person. Thus, a lot of money and travel time can be saved. When negotiating, the party with the stronger case has a better chance of imposing it on the weaker party over the phone.

People also are less easily deceived and manipulated on the telephone than in person. Those out to "con" you have a more difficult time doing this on the phone than in person. Finally, people disagree more on the phone than in person. They feel more comfortable disagreeing when they do not have to see the other person.

## Body Language

Body language refers to the various arm and hand gestures, facial expressions, tones of voice, postures, and body movements we use to convey certain messages. According to Irving Goffman (1959), they are the things we "give off" when talking to other people. Goffman notes that our body language is generally difficult to manipulate at will. Unlike our verbal utterances, we have less conscious control over the specific body gestures or expressions we might make while talking. Unless we are acting on a stage or purposely trying to create a certain effect, body language occurs automatically without much thought on our part.

Michael Argyle (1972) notes that body language *helps us to communicate certain emotions, attitudes, and preferences.* A hug by someone close to us lets us know we are appreciated. A friendly wave and smile as someone we know passes us lets us know we are recognized. A quivering lip tells us that someone is upset. Each of us has become quite sensitive to the meaning of various body gestures and expressions. This sensitivity is rather remarkable. When shown films of people expressing various emotions, individuals were able to identify the emotion correctly 66 percent of the time even when each frame was exposed for one twenty-fourth of a second (Rosenthal, 1974). *Body language also supports our verbal communications.* Vocal signals of timing, pitch, voice stress, and various gestures add meaning to our verbal utterances. We may speak with our vocal

FOCUS   ON   APPLIED   RESEARCH   7.1

## Meeting Interpersonal Needs in Our Conversations

Elizabeth Graham (1993) and her colleagues administered tests assessing communication needs, communication style, and self-disclosure to 905 people. Examining the patterns among the measures, they discovered that satisfying various communication needs depended upon who people talk to, how they do it, and the topics discussed, including the amount of self-disclosure that occurred. The major findings included:

*Who People Talk To:* Certain individuals are more likely to help us satisfy particular needs, as shown in the table below. Conversations with spouses/lovers, close friends, and family members overall were more effective in helping people to satisfy needs for pleasure, affection, inclusion, and relaxation than were the other relationships. Participants reported that no single relationship was more effective than any other in helping participants to satisfy their needs for control and to escape from other tasks.

*How People Talk to Each Other: A friendly communication style* was perceived as helpful in meeting needs

for pleasure, affection, inclusion, and relaxation. *Becoming dominant or assertive* in conversations were effective strategies for satisfying needs for inclusion, escape, and control. *Behaving in a lively or animated fashion* also was useful in satisfying needs for inclusion, but in addition it helped people to meet their need for relaxation. Finally, *assuming a dramatic posture* when talking to others helped to meet needs for escape and control.

*What People Talk About: Discussing less intimate and personal topics* was associated with participants satisfying their needs for pleasure and affection. On the other hand, *discussing highly intimate and personal topics* was important for meeting needs for inclusion, control, and as a means to escape or avoid other tasks.

*Source*: Graham, E. E., Barbato, C. A., and Perse, E. M. The interpersonal communication motives model. *Communication Quarterly, 41,* 172–186. © by Eastern Communication Association, University of New Haven, West Haven, CT 06516

### INTERPERSONAL COMMUNICATION MOTIVES*

| PERSON CONTACTED | PLEASURE | AFFECTION | INCLUSION | RELAXATION | ESCAPE | CONTROL |
|---|---|---|---|---|---|---|
| Stranger | 2.6 | 3.0 | 2.2 | 2.3 | 1.8 | 1.9 |
| Coworker | 2.9 | 3.4 | 2.5 | 3.0 | 2.1 | 1.8 |
| Close Friend | 3.4 | 3.9 | 3.5 | 3.3 | 2.0 | 1.8 |
| Family Member | 3.1 | 3.8 | 3.1 | 2.9 | 2.1 | 1.9 |
| Spouse/Lover | 3.4 | 4.0 | 3.5 | 3.3 | 2.1 | 2.1 |

* Mean scores on the Communication Motive Inventory. The higher the scores reported, the stronger the presence of that particular motive.

organs, but we converse with our whole body. Body language helps us to decide when it is time to stop talking, to interrupt someone, or to shift topics. A summary of research (Mehrabian, 1981; Guilford, 1991; Burgoon, 1991) on other aspects of body language and the role they play in our conversations is presented in Table 7.1.

## Interpreting Body Language Accurately

What do you do when you do not understand a word? The chances are you ask someone or look it up in a dictionary. Unfortunately, with the exception of nonverbal signals used by referees in various sports and users of specialized sign languages, there are no

**Table 7.1**          Components of Body Language and Their Functions

**Body Contact**  The way we touch other people, where we touch them, and who touches whom usually expresses affection, intimacy, comfort, and, in some cases, dominance and power. *Examples:* Good friends may hold hands or put their arms around each other to show affection. Lovers kiss and touch each other's erogenous zones. People with more power and status tend to touch those with less more often. Physicians and nurses often comfort a patient by touching. Males touch females more in nonsexual interactions, and the touches of other more dominant individuals like kings, queens, and faith healers are often valued. A handshake suggests less dominance, while handholding conveys informality and intimacy.

**Body Orientation**  Where we sit or stand in relationship to others generally signals certain attitudes like our willingness to cooperate, to become competitive, to dominate, to be friendly, and our relative status. *Examples:* Standing or sitting on a higher level from other people is generally reserved for people who are more dominant or of higher status. Sitting on the same level next to another person signals a willingness to cooperate or otherwise behave in a friendly manner.

**Body Posture**  The way that we walk, sit, and stand often indicates our emotional state, status, how much we like other people, whether we are friendly or hostile, and our relative dominance. *Examples:* When people are dejected they often assume a meditative pose, head down and hands clasped behind their back. Walking with rapid arm swinging usually suggests we are on top of things. Standing upright, relaxed, and maintaining good eye contact often suggests that you like and are interested in another person. When the status of two people is equal, both may sit in a relaxed position or stand together. When there are status differences, the person with less status often has to stand or, if sitting, is in a much less relaxed posture.

**Gestures**  Various movements of our hands, feet, and other parts of our body often signal our emotions, help us to complete the meaning of verbal utterances, and may replace speech. *Examples:* Clenching our fists may be a sign of aggression, and continually touching our face could signal anxiety. Wiping our forehead indicates we are tired, and bringing our hand to our face, putting our chin on the palm, and extending the index finger along the cheek suggests that we are evaluating something. Folding our arms across our body may indicate we are defensive or do not want to be bothered. Opening our arms to someone suggests friendliness. Pointing at the end of a sentence helps us to give emphasis to what was just said. Waving our hand to someone as they approach says hello, and waving as they leave communicates good-bye.

dictionaries for the nonverbal cues we see every day. There is no place we can turn that will tell us *definitely* what a particular body cue means. For people interested in "reading others like a book," the problem with nonverbal messages is that a given posture or gesture has no universal meaning.

The best we can say is that various body postures, gestures, and facial expressions typically represent certain meanings. We must be careful when interpreting nonverbal cues. The following principles should help you to do this with a higher degree of accuracy:

*Focus on More than One Nonverbal Cue*  Several nonverbal cues often occur together. Each gesture is like a word in a language. In order to understand the message, we must structure the words into sentences that express complete thoughts. The various gestures

| **Table 7.1** | Continued |
|---|---|

**Head Nods** This is a special kind of gesture and helps us to show interest in others, to reinforce them, and to synchronize speech. *Examples:* Nodding our head while someone talks shows interest in what was said and may also communicate, "That's a good point, I agree." Ceasing to nod our head may suggest we want to speak. The more we nod our heads, the longer the other person is likely to talk.

**Facial Expressions** Changes in our eyes, brows, mouth, and other facial features are often associated with our emotional state. *Examples:* Displeasure or confusion might be displayed by a frown; envy or disbelief by a raised eyebrow; and antagonism by the tightening of jaw muscles and squinting of the eyes. Happiness is often communicated by a broad smile, while a simple smile with lips closed could suggest we are mildly pleased at something.

**Eye Movements** The location and length of our gaze suggests our interest and emotions and helps us to synchronize our discussions with other people. *Examples:* Looking at people a lot when they talk conveys interest. A long gaze at someone we like conveys interest and affection, while a similar gaze at someone we dislike may convey displeasure or hostility. Our pupils typically dilate when we are interested in something or emotionally aroused. We often seek eye contact when talking to someone to help us get feedback on how the other person is responding. Ending a long utterance with a gaze signals that it is the other person's turn to speak.

**Vocal Expressions** The loudness, pitch, speed, voice quality, and smoothness of our speech is related to our emotions; they help us to synchronize our discussions and are useful indices of dominance and power. *Examples:* Anxious people tend to talk faster than normal and at a higher pitch. A depressed person talks slowly and usually at a lower pitch. When angry and aggressive, we usually talk louder. Pauses in our speech provide punctuation, and stress and pitch also show whether a question is being asked and provide emphasis. People who are dominant are much more confident and precise when they speak. Individuals with less power tend to have more hesitancy and self-doubt in their expressions. Individuals with more power and status typically interrupt those with less power more often.

**Appearance** How we dress and groom ourselves serves the purpose of self-presentation. It typically signals something about our self-image and our needs to have an impact on others. *Examples:* Dressing sloppily and keeping ourselves dirty may suggest we do not care much for ourselves. Dressing informally often suggests we are relaxed, while wearing a suit to work helps to convey the image that we are "ready for serious business." Dressing better than others signals our needs for status and wanting to have an impact on people.

should be congruent with each other. You might hear people laugh or smile. Does this mean they are happy? What if their lips also quivered, their hands were shaky, sweat formed on their brow, and they kept shifting their position? You then might conclude that they were displaying a nervous laugh or smile.

*Focus Both on What People Say and What They Do* Someone who says, "I really like you," while looking at his or her shoes is not very believable. Similarly, when the words do not match the body language, people become uncomfortable and may misinterpret

what was said. Harry Triandis (1994) provides a tragic example of this latter point. Many Arabs, he notes, believe that a truly sincere person will not equivocate with a moderate statement but rather will express ideas forcefully and with some exaggeration. When former Secretary of State James Baker met in Geneva in January of 1991 to negotiate a compromise with representatives of Iraq's president Saddam Hussein, he very clearly and calmly said, "The United States will attack if Iraq does not move out of Kuwait." Saddam Hussein's half-brother was present and called Hussein to inform him that, "The Americans will not attack. They are weak, they are calm, they are not angry, they are only talking." Triandis notes that Baker should have delivered his message in an angrier tone, including pounding his fist on the table for emphasis. Had he done so, perhaps the death and destruction of Operation Desert Storm could have been avoided.

*Focus on Nonverbal Cues if People Say One Thing and Do Another* When in harmony, verbal and nonverbal messages improve our ability to understand a communication. When this occurs, people are behaving in a congruent manner. Yet people do sometimes say something and then contradict it with their nonverbal behaviors. When this occurs, they are described as behaving incongruently. I recently observed a local political candidate say in a speech, "I'm really interested in having a dialogue with young people." As he talked, however, he shook his fist and finger at the audience. Typically, we have less control over our nonverbal messages. Thus, they are a better indicator of how someone thinks and feels.

*Focus on the Context when Interpreting Nonverbal Messages* Sometimes the meaning of a nonverbal cue is modified by the particular environment or circumstances in which it occurs. Wild applause and screaming means one thing if a rock concert has just ended. It means another if the concert is an hour late in beginning. Desmond Morris (1977) observes that the circle formed by making a ring with the thumb and forefinger of one hand has different meanings across cultures. It means OK to an American or Englishman regardless of whether the person making it smiles. In France, it means OK only if the person is smiling; otherwise it means zero. To the Japanese, the same sign stands for money.

# NOISE IN THE CHANNEL INTERFERES WITH UNDERSTANDING MESSAGES

A message in a communication channel can be viewed as a signal that exists in a background of noise. Sources of noise include environmental, cognitive, and emotional factors that ultimately interfere with the clarity of a message. To be received or understood, a message must be stronger than the background of noise. Otherwise, an inaccurate interpretation of the message may result, causing misunderstanding, as illustrated in Focus on People 7.1.

## Managing Noise in Our Messages

Try to make your messages clearer (i.e., increase signal strength), or reduce the amount of noise. Redialing a telephone number to get a "clear" line or turning off environmental distractions helps to reduce environmental noise. Asking people to define a term or to explain what they mean helps to reduce a common source of semantic noise. Emotional noise can be reduced by working on fixing problems in a relationship as well as waiting until you and another party cool down before discussing issues.

---

### FOCUS ON PEOPLE 7.1
### The Perils of Semantic Noise

*The Case of the Pesky Goose* Four maintenance employees of the Columbus, Ohio Zoo became fed up with a pesky Australian goose and fed the bird to a cage full of cheetahs. Zoo officials called the incident the result of a "terrible misunderstanding" between a maintenance supervisor and four employees. The employees asked what could be done about the bird's frequent pecking attacks on them. "Go ahead and feed it to the cheetahs" the supervisor said while smiling. The supervisor's answer was meant to be an off-hand remark, one similar to "Go jump in the lake." Unfortunately, the message was embedded in semantic noise, because the maintenance employees did not understand the intended meaning. They interpreted the supervisor's words literally. They failed to understand that saying such things while smiling meant the supervisor was joking around with them. The employees were suspended from work for two weeks and had to reimburse the zoo for the cost of the goose (based on a *Cincinnati Enquirer* story, March 10, 1982).

*The Case of the "Trash Talking" Basketball Players* National Basketball Association referees are trying to cut down on the amount of violence in the game. Fist fights and brawls periodically break out, as do increases in flagrant fouls. During the 1992–1993 season, such fouls increased an average of 43.5 percent (Reilly, 1993). League officials were concerned and decided that part of the problem were the "verbal taunts" players leveled at each other (e.g., "Say, be sure to catch CNN tonight. You just made Play of the Day.") Thus, a crackdown on taunts was in order. The problem for the referees is that players also engage in "trash talk" (e.g., "Hey man, I just flushed your butt.") Thus, the refs had to decide whether the statement was a "taunt" or just good natured "trash talk." *The differences between the two are sometimes rather subtle, and thus a form of semantic noise occurs.*

*Examples: Trash Talk:* "Damn, who cuts your hair, Ray Charles?" *Taunt:* "Damn, who cuts your hair, Pete Rose?" *Trash Talk:* "Man, you got no J." *Taunt:* "George Miken called. He wants his jump shot back."

*While various sources of noise naturally enter a variety of verbal and written communications, sometimes they are purposely introduced to make it more difficult for people to communicate.* Home team crowds at football games scream and shout so loudly at critical moments in a game that the visiting team quarterback has a difficult time communicating signals to his team. Thus, this environmental noise becomes part of the home team advantage. Or, in order to manipulate your opinions or to disguise "what really happened," semantic noise is placed in a message. William Lutz (1989) labels the latter tendency **double-speak.** This is the use of language that makes the bad seem good, the negative positive, and the unpleasant attractive. Several examples of doublespeak are described in Table 7.2. *When successfully employed, doublespeak prevents people from asking "too many questions" and thinking critically.*

# OUR MESSAGES HAVE MULTIPLE MEANINGS

## Manifest and Latent Content

The meanings of our messages go beyond the words spoken. Consider the statement from a student who says with tears in her eyes, "Michael did not ask me to the homecoming dance, but that's OK with me." Or, a husband who tells his wife while pounding his fists on the table, "Of course I'm not angry." The words used as well as how we use them convey information to other people. Interpretations that focus on the surface meaning of the words may miss important information. What are ignored are the underlying attitudes, values, and feelings in the message.

A distinction between the **manifest content** and the **latent content** of our messages can assist us in understanding this process. The manifest content refers to the idea or fact that is conveyed. "Michael did not ask me to the homecoming dance, but that's OK with me." Or, " Of course I'm not angry." The latent content, however, refers to the things that our words, sentences, and physical gestures symbolize about our attitudes, values, feelings, and motives. A latent analysis represents a more in-depth analysis. Thus, we would recognize the rejection and disappointment in the student's response above and the anger that is behind the husband's words.

Berkeley Rice (1981) reports that an analysis of the latent and manifest content of messages plays an important role in the evaluation of threats from terrorists, kidnappers, and assassins. People specializing in such analyses look for evidence of underlying intentions and needs in the messages reviewed. A threatening message, "You will be killed," sent to the president of the United States would be viewed as passive and impersonal. However, the message, "I will kill you" would be taken more seriously, because it reflects a personal commitment to do something. Similarly, common human needs for attention, belonging, respect, power, and control underlie threats such as, "I demand to talk to the press or I will kill the hostages"; "Release the prisoners from our organization you are holding and send them to us"; or "Do not underestimate our ability to attack at any time."

## Hidden Agendas: People May Try to Hide What They Really Mean

Many of our conversations contain information that is openly shared. Both parties are honestly trying to discuss something and are not withholding information. In such cases, the manifest content is clearly understood, and people are not "playing games"

**Table 7.2**                    Doublespeak in Everyday Life

The following are categories of "doublespeak" identified by William Lutz. Remember that not all examples of euphemisms, jargon, bureaucratese, and inflated language represent "doublespeak"—only those that intentionally introduce semantic noise to distort the truth or to deceive you. *I've included some of my favorite examples to illustrate each category. Can you think of other examples?*

**Euphemisms:** These are inoffensive or positive words or phrases used to avoid having to employ a harsh, unpleasant, or distasteful word or phrase. Examples: The United States Army refers to the destruction of nonmilitary targets and the killing of innocent civilians as "collateral damage." In medicine a "negative patient care outcome" means the patient died. A premium ice cream maker does not add extra fat to our diet but fills our need for "fun, excitement, and surprise." A large manufacturer of consumer goods cuts costs that do not translate into consumer benefits by laying off 13,000 workers. The reason given was that the company had too many "nonvalue added inefficiencies."

**Jargon:** This is the specialized language of a trade or profession. *Examples:* An airline wishing to avoid telling its stockholders of the crash of a plane listed in its annual report a loss stemming from "the involuntary conversion of a 727." A bad neighborhood in Chicago is referred to as a "challenging urban environment."

**Bureaucratese:** This is the piling on of words and trying to overwhelm people with words. An economic advisor to the U.S. president comments on the Social Security retirement system by saying, "It is a tricky problem to find the particular calibration in timing that would be appropriate to stem the acceleration in risk premiums created by falling incomes without prematurely aborting the decline in the inflation-generated risk premiums."

**Inflated Language:** Language designed to make the ordinary seem extraordinary or to make everyday things seem impressive. *Examples:* Used cars are "preowned," sales people in many stores are now "sales counselors," an electrical utility sends its customers monthly "energy documents" instead of bills, and a manufacturer makes "stress reduction machines" rather than office copiers.

with each other. Their attitudes, motives, and feelings are rather apparent. At other times, people intentionally try to withhold information, how they feel, and their motives from each other. A physician may not tell a patient everything she knows about a medical problem. She wants the patient to remain optimistic about the chances of recovery. When discussing a common reading, some students do not tell the teacher they failed to read the article carefully. Or, one partner in a relationship fails to inform the other how he really feels about an issue in order to avoid further conflict.

From the speaker's point of view, the information withheld becomes a hidden agenda if it is used to influence or manipulate the thoughts and behaviors of another person (e.g., a physician withholding information in order to keep a patient optimistic about the chances of a full recovery). From the listener's point of view, such information becomes a psychological blind spot, and it remains hidden from view (e.g., the teacher does not recognize that some students failed to carefully read the article). The relationship among the open, hidden, and blind elements are described in Figure 7.1.

*Effects of Hidden Agendas on Relationships* Marlin Potash (1990) notes that hidden agendas remain beneath the surface as part of the latent content of a message. While

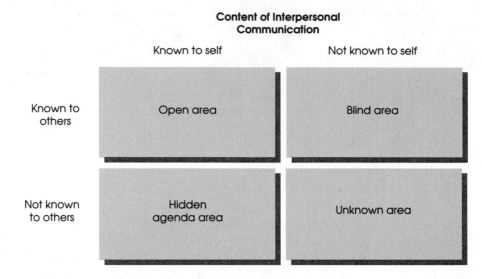

**Content of Interpersonal Communication**

**Figure 7.1** *The JOHARI Window. This model of interpersonal communication was developed by Joseph Luft and Harry Ingram. It illustrates how the content of a message can be openly shared or hidden from view. The hidden agenda and blind areas present problems in communicating because essential information is withheld or one party is unaware of things that might help clarify issues. The unknown area represents forces such as unconscious needs for control and authority that may interfere with our interactions. Effective communication is characterized by a large open area and relatively smaller hidden, blind, and unknown areas.*

such things represent information that is withheld, she finds that they influence our ongoing interactions. The reason is that the manifest or surface meaning of what is said must be altered to disguise the existence of the hidden agenda. The physician says, "Oh, don't worry about this problem getting worse, everything will be alright," or a student tells the teacher, "I can't answer that question because I did not pay much attention to that point."

Furthermore, attempts to disguise the hidden agenda may not feel right to the receiver of the message. *The way words are phrased, tone of voice, lack of eye contact, and other gestures combine to make the receiver suspicious.*

A patient becomes suspicious of his physician's response and talks to friends about his medical problem. Collectively, they provide bits of information that suggest his physician "has not told me everything." Such suspicions may lead to a lowering of trust in the doctor-patient relationship. Finally, the presence of a hidden agenda inevitably leads people to feel frustrated or anxious or to question their ability to adequately cope with the situation. One partner in a marital conflict might become frustrated and feel unable to cope with the situation until "he tells me more."

Figure 7.2 illustrates several signs that hidden agendas may be operating in your conversations with others. Typically, more than one is present in a situation.

*Managing Hidden Agendas* An important task is to reduce our psychological blind spots by uncovering any hidden agendas that may be present. Our goal is to increase the amount of information that falls into the open area of our interactions. Fortunately, four things can help you to accomplish the latter goal.

1. *Diagnose accurately that a hidden agenda is present.* Watching for the cues to the presence of hidden agendas listed in Figure 7.2 will help.

2. *Once you are sure that something is there, take some initiative to bring the agenda to the surface.* You might say such things as, "I'm concerned because we are not getting anywhere. Let's talk about how we feel about the issue." Another tact is to say, "I'm concerned about how things are progressing. I have a feeling that a related problem is. . . . What do you think?" When agendas are laid out on the table and discussed, they are typically easier to handle.

3. *Do not behave in such a way as to make people feel guilty or defensive about hidden agendas.* These agendas are legitimate aspects of your relationships with others. Saying such things as, "I can certainly expect that each of us might see things differently, and there is no reason to feel guilty about wanting different things" is often helpful.

4. *Develop a habit of discussing with others the manner in which you work and interact together.* The focus on such discussions is not on the product but on how you arrived at the product. In one-on-one situations, simply sit down periodically and talk about how issues were handled. In groups, schedule evaluation time at the end of a meeting, or hold special evaluation sessions to discuss factors that facilitated or hindered the group's ability to work together.

# MESSAGES ARE FILTERED THROUGH OUR ATTITUDES, VALUES, AND BELIEFS

## The Interpersonal Gap

It would be nice if everything we said was understood exactly as intended. Unfortunately, this is not the case. Messages are filtered by listeners' attitudes, values, and beliefs; consequently, changes in their meaning may occur. Someone who distrusts others and is skeptical of what people say, for example, will interpret the words "I like you a lot" differently from someone who is more trusting. A skeptic might think, "He doesn't really mean that, he's only saying it to get on my good side." A more trusting person will accept the message and treat it as a genuine expression of affection. The difference in interpretation between what the "speaker said" and what the "receiver heard" is called the interpersonal gap. Other examples include:

Lisa: "I'm really feeling angry. That's the last time I want to see you do that."

Manuel's interpretation: She is always blaming me for things. I wish she would stop.

Jasmine's interpretation: It was my fault. She is right. I'll try to do things differently in the future.

Courtney's interpretation: She's got to be kidding. What I did could not be that important.

*Preventing the Interpersonal Gap* The interpersonal gap is largely a function of differences in backgrounds and experiences. When people's past experiences do not overlap, differences in attitudes, values, and beliefs are likely to be present. Thus, people

## The Signs of Hidden Agendas

* **People become evasive** when questioned. They don't give a straight answer, and it becomes difficult to carry on a conversation with them.

* **Anxiety and suspicions develop** that "things are not what they seem."

* **Tension, anger, and frustration occur** for no apparent reason.

* **Long-winded discussion** on a topic that goes nowhere.

* **The same responses are given** no matter how a question is phrased.

* **People beat around the bush** with phrases like "get my drift," or "I'm sure you know what I mean."

* **Critical information is omitted** from a conversation.

* **What you are told is different** from what you know to be true.

* **Difficulty staying on a topic** or drifting from one topic to another.

* **Conflicts occurring** for no apparent reason.

* **Problems that were presumably "solved"** recur at a future date.

* **Inconsistencies are present** in what a person says and how it is said. A friend makes barbed comments while smiling and appearing happy.

*Figure 7.2*

run the risk of misunderstanding each other. Neither person's perceptions are necessarily wrong—they simply see things differently.

*To bridge this gap, take steps to understand what someone is really saying.* Asking questions, summarizing and paraphrasing what someone said, and otherwise checking our perceptions helps to accomplish the latter goal. Manuel might ask, in a sincere manner, "Who do you see at fault for what happened?" Courtney might ask, "I didn't think what I did was all that important. Would you help me understand why you feel that way?" Both would try to paraphrase or summarize what Lisa said to ensure that they heard what she intended.

## COMMUNICATION NETWORKS OR PATTERNS DEVELOP IN OUR INTERACTIONS

Participants in interpersonal communication are not always equal. In effect, certain **communication networks** or patterns evolve that control the nature and quality of the contacts people have with each other. Such patterns are based on formal and informal rules that determine who controls the flow of information, the availability of people to each other, the amount of participation that is possible, and the degree to which one- and two-way dialogues occur. Let us examine each component in more detail.

## Communication Networks Affect the Flow of Information

Some individuals have a more central or important position in a communication pattern and thus are able to regulate how, when, where, and for how long contacts will occur. A physician, for example, typically controls the conversation when a patient presents a medical problem. A medical history is taken, and the patient answers questions. After a physical exam and any needed laboratory tests, she tells the patient the likely diagnosis and prescribes a treatment. During these interactions, the doctor is pretty much in charge of what will be discussed and for how long a conversation will take place. On the other hand, in a developing intimate relationship, any partner can initiate a topic for discussion and share opinions, and there are few constraints on how much time the conversation might take. As many young lovers have noticed, "I can't believe we spent that much time talking to each other!"

In a classic set of research studies, Harold Leavitt (1951) noted that people who control the flow of information tend to be most satisfied with the interactions that are made. *Leavitt found that people in leadership positions or those otherwise in a position to control who talks to whom tended to be the most satisfied with the quality of the interactions.* This can be a problem, since those in charge also may assume that everyone feels the same way. In some settings, this may mean that communication problems are overlooked until they get worse and a crisis subsequently emerges.

For example, a good friend once told me, "My husband was the most surprised person in the world when I sued for divorce. He had no idea things were that bad between us." She then described a very dominant person who tried to control what was discussed, including getting the last word in on an issue. It is no wonder he was surprised by his wife's actions. *He was more concerned with being in charge than with listening to her concerns.*

## Communication Patterns Determine the Accessibility of People

In effect, constraints or barriers may exist that determine how people become available to each other. To talk to your physician, for example, you typically need to set up an appointment or to have a receptionist screen your call. Most of our friends and colleagues, unless they are busy, place few restrictions on our access to them. The president of your school, the head of a large corporation, or the mayor of your city, on the other hand, are less accessible. Communicating is not easy and often must be undertaken through a chain of command via memos or through subordinates. Typically, an appointment is needed; meetings are usually held for short periods of time; and a staff member does the follow-up work. Inaccessibility can be frustrating and may contribute to the perception that others don't care about you.

## Networks Affect the Amount of Participation Among Members

A communication pattern regulates the flow of information and the accessibility of people to each other. Thus, the amount of participation among members is affected. This has implications for how satisfied individuals are with their interactions and their

ability to work together in order to solve problems and make decisions. *When communication patterns allowed people to easily share ideas, their satisfaction with their interactions increased, and the quality of a group's decisions tended to improve* (Mullen et al., 1991). Similarly, other studies show that *the ability to participate in solving work-related problems was the most important predictor of the number of innovative ideas generated* (Monge et al., 1992).

## Communication Patterns Can Facilitate or Hinder Two-Way Dialogues

A lecture hall, for example, provides lots of opportunity to listen but very few opportunities to respond. Research shows that such settings promote a **one-way communication** pattern in which the teacher talks and students, for the most part, listen. For example, 70 percent of the time in a typical college classroom is spent with the teacher talking. Of the remaining time in a class period, students spend about 15 percent of it either responding to questions or asking questions and 15 percent remaining silent (Bonwell and Eison, 1991). When snuggling close to someone you care about, you and your partner have opportunities to talk and to listen. Thus, a **two-way communication** pattern is established.

Communication networks vary in terms of how much one- and two-way communication they permit. These are relative distinctions, but in general, a one-way pattern occurs whenever one person dominates a conversation. A two-way pattern occurs whenever two or more people are able to respond. A one-way pattern is not necessarily bad, and a two-way is not always good. Research shows that each has strengths and weaknesses (cf. Tesch, Lansky, and Lundgren, 1972), and the findings of such studies are presented in Table 7.3.

## Networks May Distort the Meaning of a Message

Constraints on the flow of information and a relative lack of two-way dialogues may modify the meaning of a message as it is passed among people. Three types of distortion can occur (Hawkins and Preston, 1981).

*1. Sharpening, or the Selective Perception and Retention of Facts, Occurs* Oftentimes, this means that the information mentioned first or last or those aspects of a message that are emotionally laden or very graphic are retained. Workers may hear that a foreman

| **Table 7.3** | Characteristics of One- and Two-Way Communication |
| --- | --- |

**One-Way Communication**
1. The listener has little or no opportunity to respond immediately.
2. The speaker must make assumptions about the listener's skill level, prior training, and understanding of the material being communicated.
3. It is difficult for a common language to develop as issues are presented.
4. A lack of involvement and interest can occur in the listener.
5. It encourages dependence on the speaker and discourages initiative and independence on the listener's part.
6. Since it encourages dependency, it can also lead to hidden hostility and frustration.
7. It can lead to frustration and anger on the part of individuals receiving one-way communications that are not clear.
8. It takes less time to transmit messages.
9. Compared to two-way, it is often less accurate, since people experience difficulty in obtaining clarification of messages.

**Two-Way Communication**
1. Two-way patterns allow for a better flow of information between and among individuals.
2. Because of the opportunity for immediate feedback, many of the assumptions that one makes about skill level of the listener, prior training, and understanding of the information get tested immediately.
3. It allows for a shared language to develop through discussion.
4. It leads to more involvement and interest on the part of each person in the communication.
5. It can encourage less dependence on the speaker and more initiative and independence on the part of the listener(s).
6. It takes more time for a message to be transmitted.
7. It is more accurate than one-way communication and can assist people in developing a better-quality product.

"chewed out" a coworker. What is not heard is that their coworker deserved it and that the feedback was intended to be constructive.

*2. Leveling, or Making the Message Shorter, Takes Place* This makes the message easier to grasp. However, the shorter version that remains typically fits the listeners' biases. Consequently, a person who fears for his job will hear about possible layoffs but assume they will only affect part-time employees.

*3. Assimilation Occurs* The facts or details that remain after a message is sharpened or leveled are made into a coherent story. How such processes operate is shown in Focus on People 7.2.

Several factors play a role in creating such distortions. *One is that people do not always listen to what is said.* Indeed, Steven Covey (1989) notes that one of our shortcomings as communicators is a tendency to think about what to say next rather than listening to what someone is telling us. As a result, we obtain only part of the message. Summarizing and paraphrasing what was said as well as checking important facts before repeating them to others help to overcome this tendency. *Furthermore, our ability to remember all of the information in a message is limited.* As you learned in Chapter 4, without actively rehearsing information, we quickly forget it. Asking questions, repeating key points, and taking notes also enhance our understanding of what people tell us. Finally, when we are overloaded with tasks, distracted, rushed for time, or otherwise under stress, a certain amount of "tunnel vision" develops. People can't deal with everything, so they selectively tune into parts of a message to help simplify things.

*Overcoming Distortions* The responsibility for correctly interpreting a message, however, does not rest solely with the receiver. The person sending it also is

---

### FOCUS ON PEOPLE 7.2
## The Man Who Tried to Outlaw the Words "Input" and "Feedback"

An English professor who also served as the academic vice president of a large Midwestern university became impatient with memos and letters sent to him using the words "input" and "feedback." He sent a memo to all administrative staff suggesting that people "act like the civilized people that they were" and not use such words.

His first memo had little effect. Thus, a second one was sent charging anyone who used the words outside of their accurate and technical meanings a 25-cent fine. Fines would be contributed to the Library Book Endowment Fund. As a further penalty, a person who wrote these words in a multiple-copy communication would pay an additional 25 cents for every 25 copies duplicated. Alternatives to the offending words were suggested (e.g., response, reply, or answer for "feedback," and ideas, feelings, or contribution for "input").

Since very few faculty members on campus received his memos, they had to rely on second-hand information about what the academic vice president had said. Listed below are a few of the things that were heard on campus.

- The academic vice president thinks people who use words he dislikes are uncivilized and should be fined 25 cents (sharpening).
- The academic vice president wants control over everything people write (leveling).
- The academic vice president is on a power trip and wants to control everything. He's looking for ways to embarrass people he considers uncivilized by fining them 25 cents for using words he dislikes (assimilation).

accountable. *A helpful attitude is to assume that as the sender of a message, you are responsible for seeing that it was received.* All too often, people assume that just because they said something or wrote a memo on an issue, they have done their job. One consequence is that they may later say, "I just don't understand how people missed that deadline, I sent it to everyone in a memo." "I told him more than once how to do it, yet he still screwed things up." When sending a message, ask those receiving it to acknowledge they received and understood it. In addition, reduce the chances that a message might be misunderstood by following the suggestions in Table 7.4.

Examples of common communication networks are shown in Figure 7.3. Can you see how such patterns affect the flow of information, the accessibility of people, and the degree of participation among members? Which one of the networks do you think is likely to have the most amount of distortion in the messages received?

# INTERPERSONAL STATUS AND AFFECT INFLUENCE OUR ABILITY TO COMMUNICATE

An effective dialogue is sometimes difficult because status and affect differences among people interfere. **Status** refers to differences in the amount of influence and power or how dominant one person is relative to another. *Status is often based on factors such as the*

| Table 7.4 | Overcoming Distortions In Communication |
|---|---|

The following suggestions are based upon research into factors that help to overcome distortions in interpersonal communication (Hawkins and Preston, 1981).

- *Reduce the number of people through whom a message must travel.* Ask yourself who must hear the message, and skip those who do not. A word of caution applies here. This should only be done if you are sure that the people skipped will not resent not getting the message or become suspicious if they hear you overlooked them.

- *Limit the amount of information in a message.* Try to keep your messages as simple as possible. When they become too complex, people tend to focus on parts of what is said and thus distort.

- *Place important information at the beginning of a message.* Misunderstandings increase when important information is placed in the middle of a message. Give the important points first, and build upon them as you continue to communicate. This helps to ensure that people hear the details of what you are trying to say.

- *Incorporate redundancy into your messages.* The repetition of the essential parts of a message reinforces the message. This might be done while you are communicating verbally or in writing or when you summarize what you said.

- *Put important messages in writing.* When a person is reading what you have written, there is essentially one link between you and the receiver. Develop the habit of following up important conversations with a letter outlining major points and areas of agreement and/or disagreement.

- *Obtain feedback on what you said or wrote.* Do not assume that people understand what was said. Ask them questions and/or ask them to summarize or paraphrase or otherwise acknowledge what they heard. Preface such requests with a statement that you want to ensure that you are not misperceived.

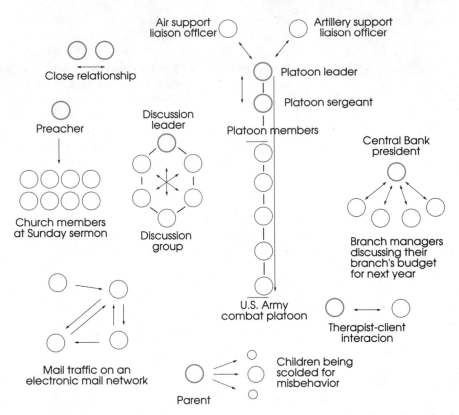

**Figure 7.3** *Examples of Communication Networks. The arrows represent the tendency for the communications among members of the group to be one-or two-way. The absence of arrows suggests that there is relatively little communication among members of the network at a given moment in time. Note how some members of a network play a more central role in initiating and receiving messages. Others do not communicate; or, whom they can directly communicate with is restricted. For example, in a discussion group, all members have easy access to each other. In the army platoon, the air support officer talks directly to the platoon leader, who relays information to other members of the group. During a sermon, church members typically listen and do not talk to each other.*

*amount of expertise and knowledge, assertiveness, independence, and leadership one person displays relative to another.* **Affect** refers to the emotional tone that exists between two or more people. *It includes such things as how friendly, warm, cooperative, and accepting they are of each other.* As you know from experience, when another person has considerably more status than you and/or when you dislike him or her, your ability to communicate is diminished. Subordinates, for example, may not feel free to share thoughts and feelings with a boss they cannot trust or respect. Students may be afraid to ask a teacher questions because they feel intimidated by the expertise and knowledge of the teacher.

## Psychological Size and Psychological Distance

One way to approach the problems that status and affect sometimes produce in our relationships is to examine the concepts of **psychological size** and **psychological distance** (Fuhrmann and Grasha, 1983; Grasha, Ichiyama, and Kelley, 1986). Psychological size is a convenient label for the perceived impact one person has relative to another. People who are perceived as psychologically big have a high potential for influencing and controlling other individuals. Similarly, the degree of positive and negative affect in a relationship is called *psychological distance.* The greater the perceived distance among individuals, the more negative affect or unpleasant emotions there are likely to be in those relationships.

One way to assess the degree of psychological size and distance in an interaction is to have people use circle drawings to represent important thoughts and feelings about those relationships (Grasha and Ichyiama, 1990). A summary of several research studies employing the drawing task appears in Focus on Applied Research 7.2 on page 270.

*Consequences of Psychological Size and Distance* Differences in titles, expertise, facility with language, and other factors are common among people. We cannot make them go away. They naturally contribute to establishing certain perceptions of size and distance between people. *Such variations in psychological size and distance may facilitate or hinder our attempts to interact.* Whether such perceptions help or interfere depends upon a person's comfort level with differences in status and affect. Some people adapt well to subordinate positions in life and do not overly resent those who are above them. Others do not adapt well and resent people above them. It appears that personally appropriate levels of size and distance are needed to establish a satisfying relationship. Close, intimate relationships work well, for example, when both parties perceive themselves as having relatively equal levels of psychological size and view themselves as rather close to each other (Gifford, 1982; Pollock et al., 1990).

*Perceptions that the levels of psychological size and/or distance are inappropriate may produce tension in a relationship.* The latter point came home to haunt me, as illustrated in Focus on People 7.3 on page 271. In other circumstances (e.g., on the job, in a classroom, meeting a powerful political figure for the first time), people may feel intimidated by someone they perceive as psychologically bigger than they are. Feeling intimidated may not be completely without a reason. A boss or teacher may use his or her position to put employees or students in their place. The employees and students dislike a boss or teacher who does this. Others may expect the person who is "psychologically bigger" to solve their problems, to see that all goes well, to take care of them, or to tell them how to do things. This dependence can lead to apathy and a lack of initiative.

Along similar lines, the distance in the circle drawings reflects how much two or more people like or dislike each other. The greater the psychological distance in a relationship, the more negative are the feelings people have towards each other.

Married couples in conflict, for example, report more psychological distance than do married couples who are not distressed (Christensen and Shenk, 1991). Like other people in relationships where negative feelings prevail, distressed couples reported less constructive communication, were somewhat uncomfortable in the presence of their partner, and tended to avoid or withdraw from conversations. On the other hand, perception of positive feelings makes other individuals appear closer to us, and the interactions are much more satisfying.

*Diminishing Unpleasant Levels of Psychological Size and Distance* The first step is to recognize that they are a problem in your relationships and to identify whether status or psychological-size concerns prevail and/or if the concerns deal with affect or psychological distance. Specific suggestions for managing psychological size and distance issues are presented in Tables 7.5 and 7.6 on pages 271–272 and in Exercise 7.1 in the Applied Activities section. Such suggestions, however, are more likely to help you if you begin by asking yourself, "What can I do to facilitate a change in this relationship?" Take some responsibility for the problem, and avoid the temptation to wait for someone else to change first. *Everyone is part of the problem by what they said or did, or by what they failed to say or do.*

## Communication Styles

People display their status and the extent to which they like and dislike others in various ways. As a result, certain preferred ways of interacting, or **communication styles**, emerge in our interactions with others. Our communication styles reflect "how" we prefer to interact with others (Bavelas and Coates, 1992). One way to describe communication styles is in terms of how interpersonal status and affect are represented in them (Carson, 1979; Snyder and Ickes, 1985; Andrews, 1989). Figure 7.4 (page 273) illustrates four styles formed by different combinations of status and affect, and a description of each is given in Table 7.7 (page 274). *Which one do you tend to use most often in your daily interactions?*

As you can see from the descriptions in Table 7.7, communication styles reflect how people try to control and influence each other. In addition, the styles describe how people normally respond to other individuals. Observations of interaction patterns reveal that people most often respond in certain predictable ways to each style. A hostile-dominant style will often dictate a hostile-submissive reaction. Similarly, a friendly-dominant style will often lead to a friendly-submissive response (Andrews, 1989).

Such differences occur because of a tendency to respond in a complementary manner to the amount of status displayed by others and in a corresponding way to the affect people display. *In terms of status, a complementary response means that when one person behaves in a dominant fashion, the receiver of the message will respond in the other direction.* Consequently, a relatively more submissive response occurs. Similarly, when one person behaves in a submissive manner, the receiver of the message will respond in a relatively more dominant way. In other words, submissive individuals are unlikely to elicit the same amount of submissiveness in people with whom they interact.

There are certain advantages for responding in this way. *The rewards people obtain in the interactions will be greater, and the personal costs of interacting will be minimized.* Thus, when subordinates respond in a relatively friendly-submissive manner to a friendly-dominant boss (e.g., by cheerfully doing what the boss wants without questioning him), each person obtains certain rewards. The boss feels that employees respect and like her, and the employees may receive good personnel evaluations for following her directives. Similarly, a parent who is hostile-dominant (e.g., gets angry and hollers at children) is rewarded when the children behave in a relatively hostile-submissive fashion (e.g., they stop misbehaving but resent the parent for bothering them). The parent enjoys the control such actions yielded, and by behaving submissively and keeping their resentment to themselves, the children do not make mom or dad angrier.

*In terms of affect, a corresponding or reciprocal response means that people return the same type of affect they receive from others.* Consequently, a friendly person will normally receive in return a friendly overture from another. Similarly, a hostile person tends to yield a hostile response in others. Once again, there is an adaptive function to how people return affect. Taking a friendly approach on average makes others more receptive to what you have to say. They listen better, and forming a relationship is easier. Becoming angry, on the other hand, alerts others that you are unhappy with what and/or how something was said and are ready to defend yourself. Based on this information, they may choose to modify their approach or to continue in an unfriendly manner.

Of course, our interactions are not always as neat and tidy as just described. For example, Dominic Infante (1992) and his colleagues report that verbally aggressive people (i.e., those who tease, swear, ridicule, and threaten others) do not completely turn others into sheep. Instead, people respond in a less dominant manner, but the tone of the response is nevertheless hostile-dominant in nature. Other research shows that when people "fire volleys" at each other, the interactions eventually cease, or people try to discover a less antagonistic way of relating to each other (Devogue, 1980).

## Two Implications of Our Communication Style

*We Help to Create Our Social Reality*  Because of the way people normally respond to each other, they effectively tell others how to treat them. If your peers easily become annoyed or avoid talking with you, perhaps you come across in an overly opinionated manner or with an angry edge to your words. A somewhat hostile-dominant response will lead to less friendly gestures in others. Similarly, if you feel dominated by others in conversations, perhaps you agree too readily with what they have to say. Or if people are always asking you to do favors for them, maybe you give in too often to their requests. In both cases, a friendly-submissive response yields more dominant behaviors in other people.

To change the way others react, you must modify your style and not wait for them to change. For example, if you are unhappy behaving in a hostile-submissive fashion, you may want to develop an ability to describe your feelings, to manage anger in constructive ways, and to learn how to assert yourself more. Similarly, changing unpleasant aspects of a friendly-submissive posture involves spending time meeting your needs and learning how to become more assertive in dealing with people.

*People with Rigid Styles Have a Difficult Time Changing*  For example, a very rigid hostile-dominant person is unlikely to respond in a friendly manner to a friendly-dominant style. More likely, a rigid hostile-dominant individual will perceive the friendliness as hostility and wonder what the other person "really wants." Similarly, a rigid hostile-submissive individual also would perceive the friendliness as hostility, because such people rarely receive friendly overtures from others.

When dealing with rigid people, special techniques must be used. The best way to deal with a hostile-dominant person is from a position of strength. In a one-to-one interaction, adopt a posture that is neither friendly or unfriendly. Think to yourself, "no big deal here, so you are a little angry, I don't have to respond in the same way." Think of the anger as bait, and don't bite on it. *Pretend you are a computer, and just talk about the facts before you in a very logical way*

In a group situation, get others to join you in establishing a solid front. A client and several people in his office were having problems with a very aggressive employee from another department who tried to browbeat people. To avoid confrontations, they usually gave in to this person and later regretted their decisions. At my suggestion, they became much more assertive and refused unreasonable requests from this employee. In effect, they presented a united front that prevented the hostile-dominant employee from running over them.

Sometimes people are overly submissive either in a hostile or a friendly manner. In such cases, to make them take some initiative, it is a good idea to become more submissive than they are. One of my students was concerned about her new boyfriend. He was shy and always relied on her to decide where to go on dates. She felt like she was taking too much responsibility for their social life and wanted him to make some decisions. The next time he responded with, "I just want to do whatever you think is best," she said, "I don't know where we should go either. I've run out of ideas and need some

FOCUS ON APPLIED RESEARCH 7.2

## Psychological Size and Distance in Relationships

Participants in three studies were asked to represent the relationship they had with another person using circle drawings. After completing the drawings, a twenty-two-item rating scale that indicated what aspects of interpersonal status and affect were present in the drawings was completed. The drawing data (1/4 normal scale) are shown below along with a brief explanation of the reasons participants gave.

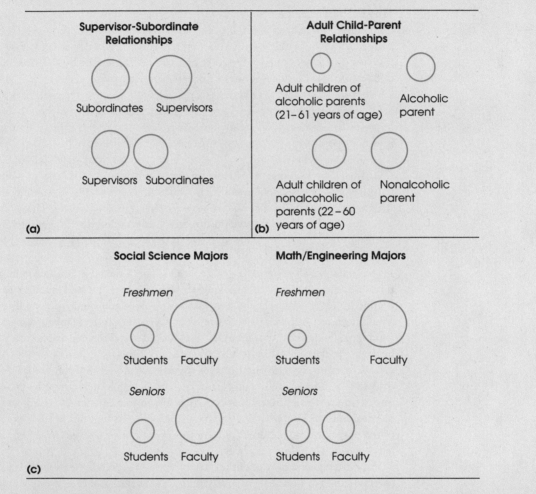

**Supervisor-Subordinate Relationships**

Subordinates    Supervisors

Supervisors    Subordinates

(a)

**Adult Child-Parent Relationships**

Adult children of alcoholic parents (21–61 years of age)    Alcoholic parent

Adult children of nonalcoholic parents (22–60 years of age)    Nonalcoholic parent

(b)

**Social Science Majors**

Freshmen

Students    Faculty

Seniors

Students    Faculty

**Math/Engineering Majors**

Freshmen

Students    Faculty

Seniors

Students    Faculty

(c)

**(a)** *Subordinates drew their psychological size larger than their bosses drew them. Subordinates also saw themselves as having much more knowledge and expertise than their bosses gave them credit for possessing. Supervisors perceived less psychological distance and a more positive emotional climate in the relationship than subordinates did (Salzmann and Grasha, 1991).*

**(b)** *Adult children of alcoholic parents (ACAs) perceived their psychological size as smaller than did an adult child of a nonalcoholic parent. They reported feeling less dominant and competent in their relationships with parents. Compared to adult children of nonalcoholic parents, ACAs also described the psychological distance as large and the emotional climate as very negative (Grasha and Homan, 1994).*

**(c)** *Social science freshmen's and seniors' perceptions of their relationship with faculty were similar. The distance was viewed as friendly, and both groups held similar perceptions of their knowledge and expertise. Math/engineering majors saw their relationship with faculty as much less friendly as freshmen and their psychological size was smaller. As seniors, math/engineering majors' perceptions of their knowledge and expertise were higher; they were not in as much awe of their faculty; and the psychological distance was friendlier (Grasha, Ichiyama, and Kelly, 1986).*

## A Matter of Size

My wife was recently intrigued with the concepts of psychological size and distance and suggested that we draw our relationship. She produced a drawing depicting both of us as having circles that were of equal size, and they were drawn close together. My drawing, had the circles positioned close together, but I drew hers about one-quarter of an inch smaller than mine. You would not have thought someone would have noticed, or made a big deal out of it. Of course, my experiences using the task suggested otherwise. The circle drawings come to symbolize the relationship and generate a considerable amount of interest.

She quickly asked, "Why did you draw me smaller than I drew you?"

For a few seconds, I was at a loss for words. I knew that telling her it was just a mistake would not work, so I came clean. "To be honest, Carol," I said, "I did it because I think you give in to me more often than I give in to you."

My spouse just paused for a moment and looked at me. Then she looked at the drawing again and said, "Well the least you can do is explain what you meant."

We spent the next four hours discussing "who gives in to whom and why." In retrospect, the conversation was rather productive and helped both of us see an aspect of our relationship we had previously not talked about.

So if you think this task is trivial and that circles don't mean a whole lot, accept a little challenge. The next time you find yourself with a friend or spouse and have nothing else to do, consider drawing a couple of circles and talking about them.

---

**Table 7.5**    Managing Psychological Size Issues in Relationships

*The following ideas have been found to help people manage status issues in a relationship.*

- *Increase personal expertise in an area.* Become knowledgeable about a topic, or develop needed skills in order to feel more competent and less intimidated by others.

- *Watch the overuse of status and titles.* Constantly demanding that people address us by a title or reminding others of our status may unnecessarily increase our perceived status relative to others.

- *Control the use of formal mannerisms.* Some people come across in a very formal manner or appear rigid and uptight. They talk, walk, stand, and generally behave in a way that makes others feel one down.

- *Watch the use of high-status body language.* Making others sit while you stand to carry on a conversation, or vice versa, conveys a higher degree of status. Similarly, talking with arms folded and a frown on your face and using a very firm voice conveys higher status to another person.

- *Make your language, how you dress, and other aspects of self-presentation compatible with the person with whom you interact.* People who are better dressed and who use complicated or technical language often convey a higher degree of status to those who cannot do such things. Doing less of such things will lower one's perceived status, while doing more will increase it.

- *Empower other people to do things for you.* Giving people a chance to become more responsible, to take initiative, and to demonstrate leadership helps to increase their status and in the process decreases the relative differences in psychological size between you and them.

- *Invite others to share their knowledge and expertise.* This conveys your willingness to accept their skills, makes them feel better about their competencies, and contributes to a decrease in the relative differences in psychological size between you and them.

**Table 7.6**                    Managing Psychological-Distance Issues in Relationships

*The following ideas are designed to encourage more positive emotions in relationships.*

- *Put your "critical parent" aside.* Don't make a major issue out of every little thing that is not going your way.
- *Try to fix the problem and not the blame.* No one likes to be blamed for something going wrong. It only adds to an already tense situation. Instead, look for ways to learn from a mistake and to take corrective actions that fix the problem.
- *Direct feedback towards another person's behaviors* and not his or her personality. Calling people "stupid" or other names seldom helps. Provide specific feedback on behaviors that must change.
- *Pursue joint goals.* When people share a common task, it is not unusual to find that they begin to like and appreciate each other more.
- *Look for pleasant activities to do with another person.* Doing things that two people find enjoyable is often contagious. Not only do such things help to take one's mind off a problem, but people find they can enjoy each other's company.
- *Talk about the problems between you.* This clears the air; it shows the other person that you care, and it sets the stage for solving a problem.
- *Reduce competition, and increase the amount of cooperation in the relationship.* Competitiveness often breeds anger, suspicion, and mistrust. Looking for ways to cooperate in finding mutual solutions to issues can overcome such emotions and/or prevent them from occurring.
- *Look for ways to compliment and reward the other person.* Recognizing and appreciating someone else's point of view, appearance, and/or accomplishments demonstrates that you care about that person.
- *Avoid using criticism, sarcasm, ridicule, punishing remarks, and terminal statements (i.e., cutting people off or not accepting their point of view) in conversations.* Such things tend to make others angry and create distance between yourself and other people.
- *Let the other people know what you appreciate about them.* Unless you say something, they may never know what you like and assume the worst.

help." When it became clear they would go nowhere unless he responded, he made a few suggestions. Apparently he did not want to suggest activities because he was afraid she would not like him if she did not have a good time.

# THE COMMUNICATION ENVIRONMENT AND OUR INTERPERSONAL INTERACTIONS

Such things as temperature, humidity, noise, crowding, a lack of privacy, and the physical arrangement of objects and people play a role in how and when we can communicate. People may become easily irritated with others when the temperature and humidity are high or find it difficult to talk to someone in a noisy, crowded bar or between chairs that are spread too far apart. The environment in which our interactions occur, however, is not simply physical. Psychological factors such as our perceptions of personal space and the emotional climate of a setting also play a role. Recently, my son's girlfriend told me, "I had to get out of my house. I was feeling closed in by everyone, and the atmosphere was really tense." Together, the physical and psychological elements in a situation are labeled the **communication environment.**

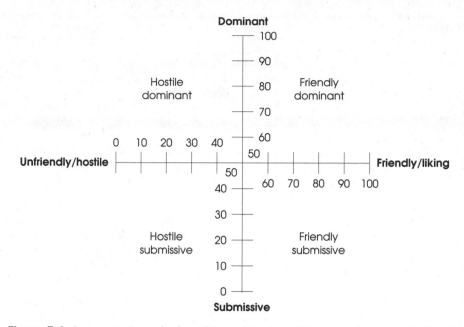

**Figure 7.4** *Communication styles formed by combinations of interpersonal status and affect.*

## The Role of Physical Space

According to Fritz Steele (1973), people are not as aware as they should be of the important role the physical environment plays in interpersonal communication. Most of us, he argues, could improve our relationships by becoming more environmentally competent. **Environmental competence** refers to our ability to understand how the arrangement of people and objects (e.g., furniture, rooms, pictures) influences our ability to communicate. People who are environmentally competent are also able to change physical settings to improve communications. They typically ask, "What am I trying to accomplish in the way of an interaction here?" "Is the physical setting conducive to the type of interactions I want?" "What needs to be changed to make the setting better for my goals?" Each of us could ask such questions before convening a meeting, making a presentation, discussing a personal problem, or holding a party. We might then find the setting working for us instead of against our plans.

*Physical Space Affects Several Aspects of Our Interactions* To become more competent in using the environment, we must recognize that physical settings affect our interactions by encouraging or discouraging social contact and by their symbolic meaning. The latter refers to the capacity of physical settings to convey messages regarding our status and relative influence.

   *Social contact.* The arrangements of objects in the physical environment has a tendency either to push people together or to push them apart. One aspect of a classic series of studies by Robert Sommer (1969) was the important effect the arrangements of chairs had on our ability to communicate. He reported that the placement of chairs across a corner of a table was the most effective grouping for encouraging seated conversations between two people. Chairs placed across the table from each other were second, and side-by-side placements were the worst possible arrangement. One reason is that visual contact has a tendency to make people more responsive to each other.

**Table 7.7**         Four Common Communication Styles

**Hostile-Dominant** Aggressive, arrogant, competitive, rigid; meets interpersonal goals at others' expense. Typically communicates a sense of pride and independence in combination with a contempt or disdain for others. Tends to test people and is generally very critical. Provokes a fearful respect or a resentful submission from those with whom he or she maintains ongoing relationships. Misperceives friendly gestures and sees them as ploys to "get something from me." Manages conflict by competing and trying to "win." Most comfortable in relationships with people who behave in a hostile-submissive fashion.

**Hostile-Submissive** Passive aggressive and generally resists the influence of others by not doing what they want, doing it slowly and/or poorly, or by showing that he or she really resents being asked. Tends to feel picked on by other people. Conveys a lack of faith in self in conjunction with a wariness, resentment, and mistrust of others. Has a difficult time forming close relationships with other people. The terms "self-criticism," "weakness," "cynicism," "depression," and "feelings of alienation" describe a person with this style. Perceives the world as comprised of people who are more dominant and hostile. Manages conflict by "avoiding with anger" or in a passive-aggressive manner. Is most comfortable in relationships with partners who are relatively more hostile-dominant.

**Friendly-Dominant** Appropriately assertive and achieves goals without stepping on toes of other people. Is interested in the welfare of other people and is generally flexible in dealing with people. Likes to offer guidance, sympathy, support, and leadership to others. Behaviors tend to convey self-confidence, strength, and basically warm feelings toward others. Has the ability to adopt any of the other styles if situations arise in which it appears beneficial to do so. Manages conflict by looking for a compromise and prefers collaborative efforts to resolve issues. Most secure when involved in close, friendly, protective relationships with dependent others who have friendly-submissive styles.

**Friendly-Submissive** Tends to be dependent on others, does what is asked, and makes few demands. Seeks comfort in helping others and is often self-sacrificing. Wants to be accepted by people and goes out of his or her way to cooperate and to socialize. Takes a relatively passive role in interactions but does so in a warm and friendly manner. Such a person sometimes appears to be helpless, uncertain, and somewhat anxious and in need of the advice and guidance of other individuals. Manages conflict either by avoiding issues or accommodating or giving in to another person. Most secure when involved with people who have a friendly-dominant style.

They then interact more often. Overall, the most desirable physical arrangement for obtaining maximum communication among all individuals is as nearly round a table or seating arrangement as possible.

The arrangement of the physical setting is obviously important for social contact. Fred Steele (1973), however, reports that many people treat a physical setting as fixed and unchangeable. In reality, he argues, many objects in our environment are **pseudo-fixed features of the physical space.** Chairs, tables, lamps, and other features can be moved or changed. The problem is that we have a bias to leave things as they are or are afraid to "disturb what someone else has set up."

*Symbolic aspects of arrangements.* Good examples are the locations of spaces and how they are set up. David and Toni Campbell (1988) report that lounge areas in a building

## Elements of Style

In addition to interpersonal status and affect, other research suggests that our style of communicating also is influenced by the following factors.

*Social Rhythms.* When people in conversations are comfortable with each other, a smooth rhythmic flow of interaction keeps them involved with each other. The conversation has a "beat" to it, with certain words or phrases emphasized, pauses held for particular periods of time, and words delivered at a particular pace. Most people speak and move in coordinated pulses of about a second's duration. When one person's style does not match the rhythm of the other, the conversation falls apart. A New Yorker, for example, generally expects a shorter pause than a Californian. Thus, as the Californian is waiting for what seems like a decent pause, the New Yorker perceives an awkward silence and jumps in to fill the void. The Californian then thinks the New Yorker was rude and aggressive (Douglas, 1987).

*Sex Roles.* Men interrupt faster and much more often than women do, and men touch women more than they do other men. Males tend to shift conversations to their preferred topics, whereas women are more apt to respond supportively. Women, on the other hand, tend to give more active encouragement to their boyfriends or husbands talking about themselves, while men listen less well and are less likely to help bring the thoughts and feelings of a partner out. When personal problems were discussed, men tended to change the subject and to start discussing a problem of their own.

Females ask nearly three times as many questions as males, make statements in a questioning tone, add questions at the end of a sentence (i.e., "Don't you think?"), lead off conversations more with a question, and are much more hesitant in their speech. In general, women tend to be more polite, tentative, and less aggressive than men in their style of communicating (Kohn, 1988).

*Nonverbal Behaviors.* Our body language contributes to our styles as communicators by determining how much we come across as *expressive (i.e., bland or dramatic), animated (i.e., active, quick, and forceful), expansive (i.e., how constricted or elaborate our posture appears), and coordinated (i.e., how jerky or smooth our body movements seem)* (Gallaher, 1992). Women tend to be more expressive, while men are more expansive and animated.

*Culture.* Americans tend to value informality and egalitarianism. In English, for example, the pronoun "you" can be employed to refer to one's lover, child, teacher, boss, or hair stylist. Oriental languages typically have different words for "you" depending upon who is being addressed or different tones to convey different degrees of familiarity, formality, and respect. Americans discuss politics and religion less often than Europeans, but Europeans and Latin Americans are more likely to view arguing as an enjoyable pastime. Unlike Asians, Americans are less patient with extensive "get acquainted rituals" i.e., "Hi— how are you?" and they refer to the future more in conversations (Althen, 1992).

were perceived as "more inviting" and led to more communication among people if they were conveniently located. Similar lounges inconveniently located were perceived as "less inviting," and the quality of the interactions among those using the space was lower. Paula Morrow and James McElroy (1981) asked 100 college students to examine slides of faculty offices. The offices were set up purposely to reflect different aspects of office design. After viewing each slide, the students rated the office in terms of comfort, welcomeness, and what personality characteristics an occupant might possess. They found the following.

1. *An open desk placement* (i.e., where people could sit alongside a faculty member) received higher ratings for comfort and welcomeness than a closed arrangement (i.e., where the faculty member was behind the desk). It also led to people's perceiving the occupant of the office as more interested in helping students, friendlier, and somewhat more extroverted.

*An example of a room arrangement that restricts interpersonal communication.*

2. *Messy offices* were perceived as less inviting, but the occupants were perceived as busier than those in tidy offices. The occupants of tidy offices, on the other hand, were perceived as more organized, friendly, and interested in students.

3. *The presence or absence of status symbols* had little impact on visitor feelings of comfort or welcomeness. It did result in higher ratings on the faculty member's interest in research and in getting ahead in life as well as service to the school.

4. *Male students* rated all office arrangements more positively than did female students.

## The Role of Personal Space

*Four Personal Space Zones* Edward Hall (1959) was an early pioneer in the study of personal spatial territories or zones within which certain types of behaviors and communications occur. Violations of the norms for each zone lead to certain nonverbal messages being triggered. The four personal zones identified by Hall are as follows.

1. *Intimate distance.* This personal zone covers a range of distance from body contact to 18 inches. Relationships between a parent and child, lovers, and close friends occur within this zone. Only those we like and have affection for are allowed to enter this zone. Also, how physically attractive people are to us, our apprehensions about close contact, and the degree to which we would rather avoid touching someone play a role (Anderson and Sull, 1985). When people try to enter without our permission, they violate our expectations for appropriate behaviors. We typically tell them to stay away from us or push them away (Burgoon and Walther, 1992). *Why do you think we allow a doctor to easily violate our intimate-distance zone?*

2. *Personal distance.* The spatial range covered by this zone extends from 18 inches to 4 feet. Activities like eating in a restaurant with two or three other people, sitting on chairs or the floor in small groups at parties, or playing cards occur within this zone. Violations of the zone make people feel uneasy. People usually divide the

amount of table space into equal parts and become irritated if someone places a plate or glass in their space. David Buller (1987) reports that our uneasiness can be exploited. Participants in his study were more willing to sign a petition if the person requesting it moved closer than 4 feet. They signed to get the person from intruding in their personal space. *Have you ever become uneasy by someone violating your personal space?*

3. *Social distance.* Four to 12 feet is the social-distance zone. Business meetings, formal dinners, and small classroom seminars occur within the boundaries of the social-distance zone. Discussions concerning everyday topics like the weather, politics, or a best-seller are considered acceptable. For a husband and wife during a party to launch into a heated argument in front of ten other people would violate the accepted norms for behavior in the social zone. *What would violate the social-distance norms in a classroom?*

4. *Public distance.* This zone includes the area beyond 12 feet. Addressing a crowd, watching a sports event, and sitting in a large lecture section are behaviors we engage in within this zone. As is true for the other zones, behaviors unacceptable for this zone can trigger nonverbal messages. At a World Series game a young male took his clothes off and ran around the outfield. Some watched with amusement on their faces, others looked away, and a few waved their fists at the culprit. The respective messages were, "That's funny," "I'm afraid or ashamed to look," and "How dare you interrupt the game." *How would you have reacted?*

## The Role of the Emotional Climate

The *emotional climate* refers to the overall emotional tone of our conversations. There are times when everyone is in a good mood, people are happy, and the conversations are pleasant. Participants describe such conversations as "fun," "productive," "enjoyable," and in other positive ways. People typically value and prefer such contacts with others.

On the other hand, the emotional climate in a setting is described as "tense," "unpleasant," "nasty," and in other negative ways. Often this occurs because people become threatened by something that was said. They become defensive and begin to think, feel, and act as if they were under attack. Or they become guarded in what they

say and how they say it. When this happens, a defensive *emotional climate* develops. People become less interested in trying to understand each other. Instead, tensions increase, arguments occur, people try to impress each other with what they know, or communication is cut off. Furthermore, Jack Gibb (1978) also reports that individuals begin to distort what is said. The amount of emotional noise in the conversation increases, and this interferes with accurately processing what was said.

*Four Factors that Underlie Tendencies to Become Defensive* Glen Stamp and Anital Vangelisti (1992) report that the following elements underlie our tendencies to become defensive:

1.  *A self-perceived flaw that we refuse to admit to others. Example:* "I'm not very good at initiating conversations with other people."
2.  *A sensitivity to that flaw: Example.* "I tend to be overly touchy about this and prefer not to talk about it with anyone."
3.  *A perception that one is under attack. Example:* "I feel like my desire to keep to myself is being challenged here."
4.  *The attack focuses on this flaw. Example:* "I thought she was pretty aggressive in accusing me of not really caring about other people just because I keep to myself and don't ask them a lot of questions."

These authors also noted that women reported greater feelings of defensiveness than did males. Both sexes, however, were just as likely to reciprocate in kind when someone tried to make them defensive. This, of course, only added to the tension in the interaction.

*A Checklist for Creating Defensive Communication Climates* Table 7.8 contains a checklist of items that are guaranteed to create a **defensive communication** climate.

| Table 7.8 | How to Create a Defensive Communication Climate |
| --- | --- |

Most of us do not purposely try to create a defensive communication climate. There are, however, actions we might unwittingly take or employ because of prior habits that do this very well. Check those items listed below that you find yourself using in your life on a regular basis. *What actions could you take to avoid using them as much in the future?*

- *Order* others to do something without giving them an explanation for why.
- *Threaten* people to get something accomplished. Saying such things as "If you don't do this, I'm going to . . . " or "I'm warning you, this is your last chance."
- *Tell others* you know exactly how they should or ought to behave.
- *Criticize* people without giving clear reasons or descriptive feedback.
- *Lecture* someone when they do something wrong about the terrible things they did.
- *Call people names* as an expression of anger (e.g., "idiot," "jerk," "creep").
- *Accuse* someone of doing things "to get even," "to spite me," or "to make me feel bad").
- *Analyze* the underlying motives of others and then making sure you tell them.
- *Interrogate someone in the guise of asking questions.* "Now, I'm not going to ask you again, where did you put the . . . "; "I can't believe that, what really happened?"
- *Withdraw from* the conversation, and refuse to discuss the issue anymore.
- *Use sarcasm or humor* to make fun of what another person said or did.
- *Blame others* for what happens by telling them, "It's your fault the project failed. I had nothing to do with it."

Unfortunately, each of them is used a lot in our conversations. As you read, check those that you use in your interactions with other people. Think about the effect those you checked had on recent discussions.

*Attitudes and Behaviors That Reduce Defensive Communication Climates*  One approach is to engage in the behaviors described in Table 7.8 less often. Another approach is to make certain attitudes and behaviors part of our communication styles. Jack Gibb (1978) has outlined four actions that will help us to do this.

1. *Become less judgmental and more descriptive when giving feedback.* Focus on behaviors when providing feedback, and ensure that when questions are asked, there is a genuine interest in obtaining information.
2. *Develop a problem-solving orientation with people.* Our goal in interactions should not be to persuade others to accept our view of things. We must collaborate with people in defining problems and seeking solutions.
3. *Try to empathize more with other people and their concerns.* Don't dismiss or discount what someone says just because you disagree with it. Try to appreciate what they have to say although you may not always agree.
4. *As much as possible, treat other people as equals.* Instead of viewing yourself as better, try to trust others, to participate in projects with them, and to attach little importance to differences in talent, ability, and status.

## Communication Skills That Reduce Defensive Communication Climates

*Active Listening Skills*  Listening involves more than hearing the words a speaker says. *The goal should be to search for the meaning and understanding behind the words.* Theodore Reik (1972) refers to this process as "listening with the third ear." Other authors such as Steven Covey (1989) note that we must first understand what someone is saying before we can have any hope of their understanding us. When people feel we comprehend their situation, they often become less defensive and more willing to share ideas. *Active listening involves the following skills.*

*Paraphrasing.*  This is a way of ensuring that you understand the ideas and feelings as they were intended. When we paraphrase, we put into our own words the ideas and feelings we have heard.

*Scenario 1:*

Daughter:  Susan has been going to the movies with Alice a lot and staying over for activities after school. Her mother hardly gets to see her anymore.

Mother:  Are you saying that you and Susan don't do a lot of the same things anymore? *(Paraphrase of content)*

Daughter:  That's true; she just does not want to do the things I want to do. I remember how much fun we used to have together.

Mother:  It looks like she's acting very independent and wants to do things on her own. *(Paraphrase of content)*

Daughter:  I'm feeling angry about her attitude. I wish she would begin to act like her old self.

Mother:  You sound frustrated and want her to revert back to how she used to be-have. *(Paraphrase of feeling and content)*

*Summarizing a message.* Here we condense what was said in the same words the speaker used. Stopping the conversation periodically to summarize ensures a better understanding of the points covered.

### Scenario 2:

Elaine:  I've just heard the company is going to merge with United Industries. I'm told that it will make us the second-largest company in the field. Apparently, the deal has been in the works for six months. So far there is no talk about how the top positions will be affected. I don't think that you or I need to worry about our jobs. This new operation will need all the help it can get.

Jerome:  Let's see if I understand. Our company has been negotiating a merger with United Industries for the past six months. It was approved, and things will probably not change much at the top. We don't need to worry about our jobs. Is that accurate?

Elaine:  Yes, that's correct. All of this sounds exciting to me.

*Validating what was said.* This is particularly helpful when conflicts develop in a conversation. While summarizing helps to ensure that people attend to what is said, John Gottman (1976) encourages people also to validate in order to step into the shoes of the other person.

### Scenario 3:

Marie:  I'm a little concerned that you were not on time for dinner at my parents' house the other night. My parents and I were worried that you were in some kind of trouble. I know your car would not start, but you could have tele-phoned.

Marcus:  I understand that my tardiness made all of you anxious and that you thought something awful happened to me. I felt so bad about it that I was embarrassed to talk during dinner. *(Note that Marcus summarizes what Marie said and validates by indicating he can see Marie and her parents' point of view.)*

Marie: I think I understand how anxious you were, and that helps me to understand why you were so quiet at dinner. *(Summarizes and validates what Marcus said.)*

By summarizing and validating, you are not saying "I agree with you" or "You are right and I am wrong." You are just admitting that another point of view makes sense. Sometimes that is all another person wants to hear. If you have trouble validating, you might say something like, "Can you help me see things from your perspective?"

*Reflecting others' feelings.* Here the receiver periodically verbalizes the sender's feelings. It is not an easy process. This is because we usually react to another person's feelings with an emotional response. A person gets mad at us, and we get angry in return. To promote understanding, sometimes it is helpful to reflect the speaker's feelings. For example, "Jamal, you sound worried about something. What is the problem?"

*Describing Your Feelings* Instead of acting out your feelings, learn to describe how you feel. A participant in a workshop reported how a friend became angry after she borrowed a mixer and forgot to return it. Her friend, Sharon, unfortunately, was having a party that weekend and needed the mixer. Sharon eventually confronted the workshop participant and said, "What a stupid thing to do. You ruined my party, because I really needed that mixer. You should have your head examined if you forget things so easily!"

Sharon expressed her feelings by yelling and screaming. A better way to handle this situation would have been for Sharon to describe how she felt. She might have said, "I feel angry because I was not able to use my mixer for the party. It cost me extra money to buy snacks. Next time, let's set a date when something you borrow from me needs to be returned."

When describing your feelings, try to include the following:

- *"I" message.* Use *I* instead of you. To say "I feel" rather than "you made me feel" is less accusatory. It also establishes the fact that you own your feelings. The other person is less likely to think he or she is responsible for your emotions. As a result, when negative emotions are described, they are likely to be less defensive.
- *Feeling label.* Describe your emotional response by labeling it. "I feel angry."
- *Describe the situation.* Specifically describe what happened that led you to feel a certain way. "I'm angry because I was not able to use my mixer to make snacks for a party."
- *Describe consequences.* Indicate what costs or benefits the situation produced. "I was not able to make snacks and thus had to spend extra money for the party."
- *Behavioral prescription.* Suggest what the other person and you might do in the future to help you feel differently. "Next time, let's set a specific deadline for returning something."

Describing your feelings helps others to see how you feel, provides people with insight into the effects of their actions on you, and suggests ways to resolve a problem. It does all of this and lessens the chances of someone becoming defensive.

*Although it is a very useful skill, active listening is not always appropriate.* It is best used when the conversation is conveying important information and/or when positive or negative emotions are present. In the latter case, it is important to acknowledge those emotions and to determine the reason for their presence. Active listening is not necessary when the conversation is casual, covers relatively unimportant information, or when two or more individuals are simply having fun talking. Finally, when used, active listening techniques should not be employed so frequently that they become distracting.

## Summary of Chapter Organizers

Suggested responses to the chapter organizers presented at the beginning of this chapter are presented below.

1. *Do you know five functions that interpersonal communication serves?* Communication helps you to give and receive information, to manage interpersonal conflicts, and to work with others on solving problems and making decisions. It also helps you meet interpersonal needs of pleasure, affection, inclusion, escape, relaxation, and control over others. The most basic function is to ensure that a relationship will continue into the future.

2. *What role do conscious and unconscious processes play in your everyday conversations?* Aspects of your conversations under unconscious control include the production of speech and the content of what is said. People sometimes appear to enact prior scripts developed when similar situations were encountered in the past. In other situations, such as the need to change topics, to correct what was said, or to avoid a conflict, there is a conscious or "mindful" component to what is said.

3. *How do various communication channels affect your interactions?* Human communication uses light waves in sending and receiving written and nonverbal messages; sound waves in speaking and listening; touch, and the molecules in the gases that affect our receptors for smell. Combinations of the verbal and nonverbal channels produce more accurate messages and higher levels of satisfaction among people. The telephone ranks second, with an added advantage of making it more difficult for others to manipulate or to "con" you.

4. *What is body language, and how does it affect your ability to communicate?* Body language refers to various arm and hand gestures, facial expressions, tone of voice, posture, and body movements used to convey certain messages. It helps you to communicate certain emotions, attitudes, and preferences. It also supports your verbal communications by controlling the pauses, timing, and pacing of your conversations. When interpreting body language, try to focus on more than one nonverbal cue; focus both on what people say and what they do; focus on nonverbal cues more if people say one thing and do another; and pay attention to the context.

5. *Are you aware of how environmental, semantic, and emotional noise interfere with your conversations?* Noise can come from your environment, from not understanding the meaning of words or phrases (i.e., semantic noise), and from being overly emotional. In such cases, it is difficult to hear what was said, and distortions in interpreting a message are likely.

6. *How do the latent and manifest content of a message differ?* The manifest content of a message is the literal meaning of the idea or fact conveyed. The latent content refers to things that words and physical gestures symbolize about someone's attitudes, values, feelings, and motives. Understanding a message involves paying attention to both factors.

7. *What are hidden agendas, and how do they influence your conversations?* Sometimes people may withhold information from you in order to influence or manipulate your thoughts and behaviors. This information becomes a hidden agenda. When hidden agendas are present, you may feel frustrated about the interaction; the same problems appear to recur; other people appear evasive; and the conversation appears to be going nowhere. To counter them it is necessary to first diagnose their presence and to take initiatives to bring them to the surface without making someone else feel guilty or defensive.

8. *Are you aware of how your beliefs filter the messages you receive?* The messages you send and receive are filtered by your own and other people's attitudes, values, and beliefs. Thus, two individuals interpret the same message differently, producing an interpersonal gap.

9. *What are the critical characteristics of your communication patterns?* Certain formal and informal rules govern how you communicate and create certain patterns or networks. Such patterns affect the flow of information, how accessible you are to others, the degree of participation that is possible, and the extent to which a two-way dialogue can occur. Sometimes a pattern becomes a barrier to communicating, and messages are distorted.

10. *What role do status and affect play in perceptions of your impact relative to other people and the emotional distance in your interactions?* How much more status (i.e., dominance, knowledge, expertise) you perceive yourself having relative to other people affects your perceptions of psychological size. Unfortunately, large differences in psychological size can be uncomfortable and affect the nature and quality of your interactions. Similarly, the extent to which positive and negative emotions are present affects your psychological distance from others. A large psychological distance will prevent effective interactions.

11. *How do status and affect influence the communication style you use?* Combinations of status (i.e, dominance-submissiveness) and affect (i.e., unfriendly-friendly emotions) are present in all of your interactions. People generally return a less dominant or submissive response than you give and the same type of emotions you display. Combinations of status and affect produce hostile-dominant, hostile-submissive, friendly-dominant, and friendly-submissive communication styles.

12. *What role do physical space, personal space, and the emotional climate play in facilitating and hindering your interactions?* The physical environment influences social contacts and conveys certain symbolic messages (e.g., your status, how open you are to talking with others). Personal space refers to spacial zones within which certain types of behaviors and communications occur. They include intimate-distance, personal-distance, social-distance, and public-distance zones. The emotional climate refers to the overall emotional tone that is present in your interactions. In particular, negative emotions can create a negative emotional climate and lead to tension-filled and unproductive discussions.

## Things to Do

1. Review Figure 7.3 in the text. Study each of the communication networks that are represented for a few minutes. In the space provided, answer the following questions. *Use knowledge about the flow of information, accessibility of people to each other, the degree of participation, and two-way dialogues among people to answer the following questions.*

   • In which one of the patterns are people likely to be most satisfied with their interactions? The least satisfied?
   • Which one(s) are likely to lead to good problem solving/decision making?
   • Which pattern(s) are likely to lead to distortions in the meaning of messages?

   Next, draw a communication network that you participate in using Figure 7.3 as a model. Describe how the information flow, accessibility, and participation affect your satisfaction, the ability of people to solve problems make decisions, and how the meaning of messages tends to be distorted.

2. Review Table 7.2 and the four categories of Doublespeak. Read carefully the articles, editorials, and advertisements in a couple of newspapers or news magazines to find other examples of doublespeak. Which one of the categories does each example fit? Are some used more than others? Can you tell if some people (i.e., government officials, educators, advertisers) tend to use such language more than others?

3. Watch a soap opera or other drama on television. Observe how people talk and react to each other. Identify instances where the following communication styles occur: hostile-dominant, hostile-submissive, friendly-dominant, and friendly-submissive. How do they affect the interactions that occur?

4. Hold a nonverbal party. The first hour, all the guests may communicate only nonverbally. No one is allowed to speak.

5. Based on what you have read in this chapter, what are five things that you could change in your own behavior that would improve your interpersonal communications?

6. Monitor a conversation that is occurring near you for ten minutes. Using the categories of body language described in Table 7.1, what are some of the specific things you see occurring? What functions do you think the various aspects of body language serve in the conversation?

7. How do psychological size and distance facilitate and hinder the interactions between students and teacher, a minister and members of the church, a police officer and motorist stopped for a traffic violation, a salesperson and customer, two people in love, and a couple about to get divorced?

## APPLIED ACTIVITIES

EXERCISE 7.1

### Managing Psychological Size and Distance in Relationships

This activity is designed to help you explore the psychological size and distance components of a relationship in which you are involved. It will also help you to see the relationship between aspects of psychological size and distance and the communication styles described in the text. *Please follow the directions below.*

**Focusing on a Relationship**

1. *Select a relationship in which you currently have some tension and would like to do something about it.* The issues in the relationship do not have to be extremely difficult and could be something that is only mildly bothersome to you. Briefly describe the situation, and indicate the nature of the problem.

2. *On a separate sheet of paper, use circle drawings to represent your thoughts and feelings about the relationship.* Use the size of the circle that you draw for yourself and the other person as well as the distance between the circles to represent your thoughts and feelings. Remember, there are no correct ways to draw any relationship. *Before drawing the relationship, take a minute or two to think about the types of interactions you normally have with this person.*

3. *Complete the following 22-item rating scale.* The rating scale is designed to help you identify the reasons why you drew the relationship as you did.

**Analyzing the Drawings**

4. *Examine your drawings to determine the general nature of the problem in the relationship.* Remember that differences in size reflect variations in status between two people (i.e., expertise, knowledge, dominance). The distance in the drawings reflects the degree to which the emotional climate is positive and pleasant or negative, tense, or unpleasant. The closer the two circles are to each other, the more positive the emotional climate. Do your drawings suggest that the problem is related to uncomfortable status differences, a negative emotional climate, or both? List your reasons in the space provided below.

### Grasha–Ichyiama Psychological Size and Distance Scale: Status–Affect Rating Scale

The 22 items listed below describe some of the reasons why people draw relationships a certain way. Thus, these items also represent your perceptions about a relationship. The items are arranged in sentences that have two adjectives that describe the end points on a rating scale. For the relationship you just drew, complete the sentences by assigning a rating that best describes how you think and feel about your interactions with that person.

1. When interacting with the other person, I feel like I have_____.
   Less expertise 1 2 3 4 5 6 7 8 9 More expertise

2. Towards the other person, I am_____.
   Very critical 1 2 3 4 5 6 7 8 9 Very accepting

3. When interacting with the other person, I am_____.
   Very passive 1 2 3 4 5 6 7 8 9 Very assertive

4. Towards the other person, I am_____.
   Very impatient 1 2 3 4 5 6 7 8 9 Very patient

5. When interacting with the other person, I am_____.
   Very submissive 1 2 3 4 5 6 7 8 9 Very dominating

6. With the other person, I am_____.
   Very competitive 1 2 3 4 5 6 7 8 9 Very cooperative

7. When interacting with the other person, I am_____.
   Very compliant 1 2 3 4 5 6 7 8 9 Very demanding

8. Towards the other person, I feel_____.
   Very distant 1 2 3 4 5 6 7 8 9 Very close

9. When interacting with the other person, I am_____.
   Very bashful 1 2 3 4 5 6 7 8 9 Very outgoing

10. Towards the other person, I feel_____.
    Very unaffectionate 1 2 3 4 5 6 7 8 9 Very affectionate

11. When interacting with the other person, I am
    Very unaggressive 1 2 3 4 5 6 7 8 9 Very aggressive

12. Towards the other person, I am_____.
    Very inconsiderate 1 2 3 4 5 6 7 8 9 Very considerate

13. When interacting with the other person, I am_____.
    Very timid 1 2 3 4 5 6 7 8 9 Very assertive

14. With the other person, I am_____.
    Very irritable 1 2 3 4 5 6 7 8 9 Very easygoing

15. When interacting with the other person, I feel_____.
    Very incompetent 1 2 3 4 5 6 7 8 9 Very competent

16. Toward the other person, I feel_____.
    Very cold 1 2 3 4 5 6 7 8 9 Very warm

17. When interacting with the other person, I have_____.
    Less influence 1 2 3 4 5 6 7 8 9 More influence.

18. Towards the other person, I feel_____.
   Very unfriendly 1 2 3 4 5 6 7 8 9 Very friendly
19. When interacting with the other person, I have_____.
   Less status 1 2 3 4 5 6 7 8 9 More status
20. With the other person, I feel_____.
   Very tense 1 2 3 4 5 6 7 8 9 Very relaxed
21. When interacting with the other person, I feel_____.
   Less knowledgeable 1 2 3 4 5 6 7 8 9 More knowledgeable
22. Towards the other person, I have_____.
   Mostly negative feelings 1 2 3 4 5 6 7 8 9 Mostly positive feelings

5. *Examine the rating scale to identify specific reasons for your drawings.* There are two things you will need to know to do this. First, the odd-numbered items on the rating scale are descriptors of interpersonal status. The even-numbered items are descriptors of interpersonal affect.

   a. *Obtain a status scale score* by summing the ratings you assigned to all of the odd-numbered items (i.e., 1, 3, 5, 7, etc.). Your status score is_____.

   *Obtain an affect scale score* by summing the ratings you assigned to all of the even-numbered items (i.e., 2, 4, 6, 8, etc.). Your status score is_____.

   b. *Plot your scores on the chart shown in Figure 7.4. The intersection of the two scores will identify the communication style you are employing in this interaction.* What are the advantages and disadvantages of this style for resolving the problem? To help you answer this question, examine the descriptions of each communication style in Table 7.7.

   i. Your communication style:_____

   ii. Advantages of your communication style in this situation:

   iii. Disadvantages of your communication style in this situation:

c. *Place a check mark next to the rating scale items that you assigned the highest and lowest ratings.* Review those items, and place a second check mark if you believe they are contributing to problems in the relationship. Remember, not every item receiving a high or low rating is likely to be a problem. In the space below, list no more than two to three of these items, and give a reason for why they contribute to one or more problems you experience in the relationship (e.g., being too impatient makes it difficult for me to listen, and I act impulsively; lacking expertise makes me feel insecure, and thus I don't think this person respects me very much).

**Solutions**

6. *How can you change the items you identified as problems on the rating scale?* One way is to think about how to integrate the descriptor opposite to the one that is a problem into your life (e.g., become more patient by counting to ten before responding; walking away from a situation to collect my thoughts; obtain needed expertise on my job by getting special training).

7. *Use the suggestions in Tables 7.5 and 7.6 for managing psychological size and distance.* Select one to two items from these tables, and indicate how you could use them to help improve the situation.

EXERCISE 7.2:

**Improving the Use of Physical Space to Enhance Communication**

A number of principles for changing the way you think of and use physical space to improve your everyday communications were discussed. Follow the planning process outlined below to begin to put those principles to use in your life.

1.  Think of a situation in your life in which you are typically not satisfied with the quality of the interactions that occur. Try to pick a situation in which you suspect that the physical environment plays at least a partial role in the problem. Imagine yourself having a conversation in that setting, and then briefly describe why you are dissatisfied with the interaction.

2.  Draw the physical features of the environment mentioned above in the space provided below. Indicate where the furniture is, where you and other people stand and sit, the color of the walls, how well lit the setting is, and other furnishings that are present. Try to draw as complete a description of the setting as you can.

3.  Review the section on the effects of physical space on communication in the text. Which concepts and principles apply to the setting that you described above? List them in the space provided, and provide a reason why they are factors. Are there other aspects of the physical setting not in the text that you think are important to consider? List them as well. Are there also factors other than the physical setting that play a role?
    •Factors identified in the text.

    •Other aspects of the physical setting that you believe played a role that were not discussed in the text.

4.  Based on your analysis, what actions should you take to enhance the quality of the interactions that occur in the setting described above? Remember that changing aspects of the physical setting may not completely solve the problem you are having. However, they often contribute to problems and thus must be taken into account. Develop your action plan in the space provided below.

EXERCISE 7.3:      **Reflection of Feelings**

One problem I find in working with people is that they are at a loss for words to describe feelings or they use the same words constantly. How many feeling words can you think of besides "angry," "happy," " sad," "afraid," or "frustrated"? How many others do you use? What is likely to be the long-term effect of using the same words all the time?

To begin to practice describing feelings, try to use as many different words as you can. Table 7.9 is a list of emotional words. Use them to complete the reflection-of-feeling statements used in the following conversation:

Me: Wow! I just can't wait until the Fourth of July comes around. That is going to be some picnic.

You: You sound as if you are feeling _____.

Me: I'm not sure what I have to do to please you. You're always making tough demands on me.

You: You are _____. Is there anything that I can do to change the situation?

Me: This is a pretty tough assignment. I just don't know if I can handle it.

You: It seems to me that you are _____. What are some of the options you have to do the assignment?

Me: That was a really neat movie. I wouldn't mind seeing it again.

You: What was it about the movie that made you feel _____?

| Table 7.9 | Common Emotional Description Terms | | | |
|---|---|---|---|---|
| | afraid | frustrated | loved | shaky |
| | angry | grateful | mistreated | shy |
| | annoyed | happy | nervous | silly |
| | anxious | hated | offended | superior |
| | ashamed | hopeful | optimistic | sympathetic |
| | awed | humilated | peaceful | tense |
| | bored | hurt | pleased | thrilled |
| | bothered | impatient | precarious | trusting |
| | calm | inferior | protective | uncertain |
| | concerned | insecure | proud | wonderful |
| | confident | irritated | rejected | worried |
| | content | jealous | repulsed | |
| | eager | joyful | sad | |
| | excited | lonely | satisfied | |

## Key Terms

*Affect.* The positive or negative emotional tone that exists in conversations among two or more people.

*Assimilation.* A form of distortion in communicating wherein the facts or details in a message are shortened or certain facts are selectively perceived.

*Body language.* Sending messages by using facial expressions, body gestures, changes in posture, and tone of voice.

*Communication.* An interpersonal process in which verbal and nonverbal messages are shared and understood by two or more people.

*Communication environment.* Characteristics of physical space and the psychological components (e.g., personal space, emotional climate) of an interaction that influence our ability to interact.

*Communication network.* The restrictions that exist in the flow of information among people. Communication networks or patterns may enhance or reduce the transmission of messages among people.

*Communication style.* A preferred or typical way that people communicate with each other.

*Defensive communication.* Perceiving what another person says or does as a personal attack.

*Describing feelings.* Communication skill in which a verbal description of how one feels is made instead of outwardly expressing that emotion.

*Doublespeak.* The deliberate use of words and phrases to create semantic noise in order to conceal and distort the meaning of a message. Often used by others to manipulate our opinions or to prevent us from thinking critically about issues.

*Environmental competence.* The ability to understand how the arrangement of people, furniture, and other room objects affects communication.

*Interpersonal gap.* Differences in the interpretation of messages due to people filtering the message through their attitudes, values, and other beliefs.

*Latent content.* What our words and sentences symbolize about our underlying attitudes, values, feelings, and motives.

*Leveling.* A form of distortion in communicating in which a message becomes shorter as it moves from one person to another.

*Manifest content.* The idea or fact that is conveyed in a message.

*Noise.* The environmental, cognitive, and emotional factors that interfere with messages being received and/or interpreted properly.

*One-way communication.* A pattern of communication in which most of the messages are directed toward the listener without the listener having an opportunity to respond.

*Paraphrasing.* Putting into our own words the thoughts and feelings of the other person. This communication skill helps someone know that we understand what he or she is saying.

*Personal space.* The personal territories or zones we interact in and within which we allow only certain types of behaviors to occur.

*Pseudofixed features of physical space.* Those aspects of our physical environment that can be changed or moved but that we treat as if fixed.

*Psychological distance.* The perceived positive or negative affect that exists between two or more people.

*Psychological size.* The perceived impact or influence that one person has on another. It relates to the relative differences in status or affect that exist between two or more people.

*Reflection of feelings.* Communication skill whereby we describe the speaker's feelings. It helps to show that we understand how the speaker feels.

*Sharpening.* The selective perception and retention of certain facts to the exclusion of others.

*Status.* The amount of influence and power one person has relative to another.

*Summarizing.* Communication skill whereby we condense what the speaker says in his or her own words.

*Two-way communication.* A pattern of communication in which two or more parties have the opportunity to both send and receive messages.

*Validating.* Indicating to another person that you can understand his or her point of view.

## CHAPTER 8

# Developing Interpersonal Relationships

### Chapter Overview

Forming friendships and other close relationships is an important part of everyday life. This chapter discusses how relationships form, barriers to developing them, the emotions that normally accompany our interactions, and how to cope with such issues. Factors that contribute to relationships breaking up and how to cope with separations also are presented.

### Chapter Organizers

*As you read, answer the questions that follow on a separate sheet of paper, and check your responses with those provided in the summary section.*

All of us need other people around us, and our satisfaction in life is related to how well our relationships are going.

1. What are several benefits that interpersonal relationships provide for you?
2. Do you know the different characteristics of relationships as they develop?

A number of factors are needed in order for friendships and other close relationships to form.

3. What role do liking, respect, and trust play in forming relationships?
4. How do similarity in attitudes, familiarity with people, living close to them, physical attractiveness, and the exchange of social rewards affect whether you will like another person?

Several barriers may interfere with your developing friendships.

5. Are you aware of how some personal characteristics, including shyness, can make it difficult to interact with others?
6. How do stereotypes and prejudices interfere with your interactions?
7. Why is self-disclosure important to forming close relationships?

Love, envy and jealousy, and loneliness are important emotions in your interactions.

8. Do you know the characteristics of love, the ingredients that comprise different types of love, and the different styles of loving people engage in?
9. How do envy and jealousy affect your relationships?
10. How do important qualities of loneliness appear in your life?

A significant number of relationships, formed with good intentions, tend to break up over time.

11. What causes relationships to break up, and what are some actions you might take to ease the pain of a separation?

Would you be willing to donate one of your organs to help the person you loved? Would you give up your life for a friend? Fortunately, very few people have ever had to answer these questions. But a mutual commitment, affection, and generosity underlie the important friendships and other close ties we form with people. The remainder of this chapter explores how such associations develop, the problems they force us to confront, and how to cope with them.

---

### The Boy Who Gave His Heart to the Girl He Loved

Fourteen-year-old Donna Ashland sat in a hospital bed eating ice cream, unaware that her boyfriend had died and that his heart was beating in her chest. Donna, on the verge of death from a progressive degeneration of the heart, received her boyfriend's heart in a heart transplant operation a few hours after he died of a brain hemorrhage.

Felipe Garza, age 15, had met Donna several months before, and they were going steady for two months prior to his death. He was in love with her and enjoyed the time they spent together. When he learned that Donna was seriously ill, he became depressed and began to tell people, "I'm going to die so I can give my heart to Donna."

While he appeared to be in excellent health, his sister told doctors that he occasionally complained of headaches and blackouts. When the pain in his head increased and he had difficulty breathing and walking, he was taken to a hospital, where he died. His parents remembered his wish to save his girlfriend, so they consented to the heart transplant operation.

Was it a quirk of fate? An act of God? Or, did Felipe Garza's death represent the ultimate sacrifice for the girl he loved?

———
Based on a UPI News Service story, January 7, 1986.

---

## INTERPERSONAL RELATIONSHIPS ARE IMPORTANT TO ALL OF US

In spite of the difficulties we will encouter, all of us are drawn to developing and maintaining friendships and intimate relationships with others. Few people can live the life of a hermit or recluse for very long. Even contemporary hermits living deep in the woods periodically surface to visit with friends and associates. Forest rangers often have friends nearby, if not spouses and lovers on the premises. Henry David Thoreau, the nineteenth-century philosopher and "recluse" of Walden Pond, lived so close to other people that he abandoned his cabin whenever he smelled something good cooking for dinner.

We need other people in our lives because our survival as well as our ability to meet a variety of needs depends upon establishing and maintaining relationships. When interviewed about their friendships and intimate relationships, people list several benefits, including meeting needs for affiliation and friendship, giving and receiving comfort and affection, obtaining emotional support, receiving advice and assistance with problems, influencing others, and developing a positive self-image (Reisman, 1979; Brehm, 1992).

## Relationships Take Time to Develop

Sharon Brehm (1992) reports that relationships do not progress in a lockstep fashion through various stages, but that certain themes appear to be more prevalent early versus late in a relationship. For example, when the specific relationships of couples are compared, a variety of different patterns of development typically emerge over time. Thus, she argues, it may be more appropriate to view "stages" as "phases" that take place at different times for different couples. Several of these themes are summarized in Table 8.1.

## Factors That Promote the Development of Relationships

*Liking, Respect, and Trust* Zick Rubin defines **liking** as a positive attitude toward another person that has two characteristics. *To like someone, we must first respect them and believe that they are trustworthy* (Rubin, 1973). Rubin also notes that once a decision to like someone is made, a bond begins to develop. People then report admiring the qualities of the liked person, consider them to be rather mature individuals, and often desire to have their qualities. Of course, such thinking is sometimes based more on wishful thinking than the actual qualities of a person. The euphoria of having just met someone who appears likable may cloud our judgment. Thus, it is important to maintain an open mind and a certain amount of objectivity about people until their actions confirm your initial impressions. Our respect and trust is something people need to earn and should not be given away lightly.

John Rempel (1986) and John Holmes (1989) suggest that answers to three questions can help us make decisions about whether to trust someone. Each is based on an important element of trust.

1. *How predictable is that individual?* A predictable person is someone whose behavior is consistent—consistently good or bad. An unpredictable person keeps us guessing about what might happen next. Such volatile people may make life interesting, but they don't inspire much in the way of confidence.

2. *Can I depend upon him or her?* A dependable person can be relied upon when it counts. One way to tell is to see how a partner behaves in situations where it is possible to care or not to care.

3. *Do I have faith in that person?* Are you able to go beyond the available evidence and feel secure that your friend or partner will continue to be responsible and caring? We have faith in another person when our doubts are put aside and we feel safe in a relationship.

*In effect, trust is a form of interpersonal glue.* It helps us to form and to maintain our bonds with others and provides a sense of security in relationships. Trust takes time to form and is often very fragile. It is easily broken by a single misdeed or broken promise. Before taking actions that might affect a relationship, it is important to ask, *"Will my friend or partner continue to trust me if I do this?"*

**Similar Attitudes**   The amount of interpersonal attraction and liking is also related to the number of attitudes people have in common. What really counts, however, is the amount of perceived rather than measured similarity. After all, we do not administer attitude scales to people we meet. Instead, we infer from their words and actions what they believe. Unfortunately, our yardstick is not very accurate. Individuals who were strongly attracted to one another tend to overestimate the degree to which they shared similar beliefs (Berscheid, 1985; Berscheid et al., 1989).

One reason similar beliefs are important is that a partner is more likely to agree with us and thus reward our thoughts. Also, if we like someone's views, we may anticipate a good time with them in the future. Finally, it may be that perceived similarity allows us to say things to ourselves like: "He's so much like me. I bet he'll like me a lot, too." The idea here is that people are attracted to men and women who have the mirror image of their qualities. Zick Rubin (1973), however, suggests that such similarities are probably more important early in the development of a relationship.

Later on, differences in beliefs also become important in maintaining interactions. You have probably heard the saying "opposites attract." Research suggests that successful couples often complement each other's qualities (Brehm, 1992). Provided that beliefs, values, interests, and personal characteristics are not too extreme, such differences contribute to making another person interesting, and they add to the novelty and excitement of the relationship.

**Familiarity**   Just being with people increases the chances of liking them and becoming friends. In a classic research study, Theodore Newcomb (1961) paired dormitory roommates based on their beliefs, attitudes, and values. Some pairs were matched, while others were dissimilar. He discovered that regardless of the amount of similarity in beliefs, roommates liked each other more than they did other people. In another study, people were asked to stand in a room and observe each other for different amounts of time. When asked whom they liked more, they picked those they were exposed to most. *This occurred even though they were not allowed to talk to each other or had never seen each other before* (Saegert, Swop, and Zajonc, 1973).

**Physical Proximity**   People who live, work, and interact in close proximity are more likely to become friends. In the workplace, those who work next to each other are more likely to become close friends than people who are only a few feet away (Berscheid, 1985). The same principle holds for developing more intimate relationships. In spite of superhighways, modern transportation systems, and increased mobility among people, we hold a special place in our hearts for people from our hometown. So much so that the person we marry is more likely to have grown up in our hometown than anywhere else (Ineichen, 1979).

**Physical Attractiveness**   An important belief in our culture is that what is beautiful must be good. Thus, people want to develop relationships with individuals who are perceived as attractive. Alan Feingold (1992) reports that attractive individuals are perceived as more sociable, dominant, sexually warm, mentally healthy, and intelligent. One consequence of such perceptions is that attractive individuals also are rated as more desirable for dates, marriage, and sex. While both sexes admire people who are physically attractive, men place a higher premium on it. Most men stress physically attractive dating partners more than women do. When asked to rank-order 13 characteristics most sought in a mate, men ranked physical attractiveness third, while women ranked it sixth (Buss, 1985). Women are more likely to date less attractive men.

Feingold also notes that personal perceptions of attractiveness affect our self-image and actions much more than do more objective measures of physical attractiveness (e.g., cultural standards and ideals regarding height, weight, body build, and other physical characteristics). This latter point is important. Many people deviate from cultural standards and ideals for what is ordinarily considered beautiful or handsome. Nevertheless, most of them like themselves and don't worry about the fact that they will never appear as models in a fashion magazine. This healthy self-image is contagious and is one reason they are able to form lasting friendships and intimate long-term relationships. *Thus, how you judge yourself is probably more important to your peace of mind than meeting the expectations of others.*

Consequently, there is no need to feel bad if you are less than extremely beautiful or handsome. *Remember that very few people would receive high ratings on physical attractiveness, and yet they still manage to have a good time.* And when people seek someone to date and marry, they typically find partners who are similar to themselves in physical appearance. One reason is that it is very difficult to find our ideal person in real life, and some compromises must be made. Another is that many of us believe we are less likely to be rejected if we approach people who are similar to us in physical attractiveness.

*Obtaining Rewards* Sharon Brehm (1992) reports that people tend to seek the company of those who reward them and dislike those who do not. In any social interaction, various rewards such as information, affection, status, money, skills, and attention are exchanged. Such rewards promote a willingness to continue the relationship. Brehm notes that happy couples act in more positive, rewarding ways towards each other than unhappy couples. Also, the level of rewards in relationships among friends and intimate couples is a good predictor of whether or not they will break up. Those who stay typically perceive a greater increase in rewards than those who leave.

Obtaining rewards, however, is only one part of the picture. George Homans (1974) and Peter Blau (1964) also pointed out that our interactions cost us something. Interactions take time, energy, commitment, money, and sometimes lead to unpleasant outcomes or emotions. Whether we continue to interact and begin to like someone is related to the amount of satisfaction obtained from such interactions. Satisfaction only occurs when our rewards exceed our costs. Otherwise, people tend to discontinue the relationship and seek another where the potential for a payoff is greater. Bear in mind that no absolute standards exist for how much the rewards of a relationship should exceed the costs. Rather, our past experiences with people establish a minimum "payoff" against which we compare our current interactions. Any friendship or intimate relationship that falls below this minimum is discontinued.

## BARRIERS TO FORMING RELATIONSHIPS

Some individuals have a difficult time forming friendships and other relationships with people they otherwise like and admire. While this may not be currently a major problem in your life, almost everyone has at one time or another experienced this concern. Some of the causes include personal characteristics that rub others the wrong way,

**Table 8.1**                                 Themes in the Early and Late Phases of Successful Relationships

| TIME FRAME | THEMES |
| --- | --- |
| **Early** | |
| *Initiating* | • People become aware of each other in social settings and begin to establish rapport with each other.<br>• Relatively easy topics, weather, hobbies, movies, and other superficial issues are discussed. |
| *Idealizing* | • Initial evaluations occur based on perceptions of physical appearance, common interests, and personality.<br>• Similarity in attitudes and values assessed, but they are often biased by what people want to see. |
| *Intensifying* | • Individuals begin to feel more comfortable with each other.<br>• Premium placed on spending more time with each other.<br>• Begin to do favors for each other, and generally help each other meet their needs to feel part of a relationship. |
| *Integrating* | • Perceptions change from "you" and "me" to "we."<br>• Start to empathize with each other's concerns and lend a sympathetic ear to the problems that each has. |
| *Bonding* | • Sexual intimacy occurs.<br>• Self-disclosure increases, and people begin to share their most intimate hopes, dreams, and fears with each other.<br>• Help each other to find solutions to issues in their lives.<br>• Able to understand and appreciate areas where their attitudes and values are similar and different.<br>• Begin to share future goals that involve each other.<br>• Commitment and identity as a couple deepens.<br>• Appreciate each other more and are better able to accept each other's limitations. |
| *Differentiating* | • Individual interests are explored, and they may spend less time doing things together.<br>• Do not rely as much on relationship for satisfaction in life. |
| *Reaffirming* | • In spite of emerging differences in attitudes and interests partners continue to trust each other and perceive their relationship as an important part of their lives.<br>• Discuss issues and work together to successfully perform long-term relationship roles such as husband-wife, mother-father, grandparents. |
| **Late** | |

Descriptions based on Schwartz and Schwartz, 1980; Murstein, 1987; Knapp and Vangelisti, 1992.

being shy, allowing stereotypes and prejudices to interfere with our interactions, and a lack of self-disclosure.

## Personal Characteristics That Interfere

John Reisman (1979) reported that people who had a difficult time forming close relationships shared a number of characteristics. They were somewhat depressed; lacked a good sense of humor; and had very few outside interests and hobbies. As a result, they had very little to share with others. When conversations did develop, these people were often critical and tended to think their opinions were better than others'. Overall, they took relatively little interest in what others were doing and failed to give people credit for their achievements. Finally, some were simply afraid of forming friendships and

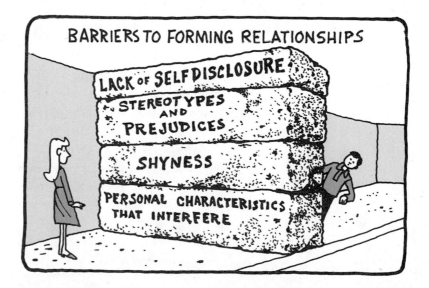

close relationships. They were either unable to trust others or worried about their capacity to give and receive affection.

## Coping with Personal Characteristics That Interfere

Perhaps some of the personal characteristics listed above apply to you. While it is difficult to change one's personality, it is possible to select specific goals that you can work on to enhance your ability to interact with others. To begin, consider whether integrating the following ideas into your life-style might help you.

- *Assess how aspects of your personality may bother others.* Take a chance and ask someone whose opinion you value how they perceive you in everyday interactions and how others might see you. Select something you learned from such discussions to make at least a small change in your behaviors.
- *Develop one or more new interests, and discuss them with others.*
- *Look for ways to compliment people more on what they say and do rather than criticizing them.*
- *Remember that the rewards we give to others help to enhance interactions.* Thus try to praise and agree more with the opinions of others, and take more of an interest in what they do and say.

## Shyness

How many of the items in Table 8.2 tend to describe you? According to Phillip Zimbardo (1975, 1977), the characteristics listed in this table describe a typical shy individual. I suspect that most of you reading this did not think that every item applied to you.

---

**Table 8.2**  Are You a Shy Person?

*Check the statements below that typically describe your thoughts and actions.*

_____ I am usually silent in the company of strangers or with members of the opposite sex.

_____ I frequently avoid eye contact with other people when talking to them.

_____ I tend to speak in a soft, quiet voice.

_____ Rather than talk to other people, I read a book, take a walk, or do something else by myself.

_____ I am rather self-conscious and concerned about what other people think of me.

_____ I tend to downgrade myself and what I can do.

_____ I am generally uncomfortable in social situations and don't like them.

_____ When I am around other people, I sometimes have "butterflies" in my stomach.

_____ When I am around other people, it is not unusual for me to blush.

_____ In social situations, I often feel my heart rate increase, and I can hear myself breathing faster.

_____ Even though I appear calm to other people in social situations, inside I feel anxious and apprehensive.

Perhaps only a few did. This is not unusual, because in Zimbardo's research, 80 percent of his national sample rated themselves as shy at some time in their lives. Forty percent considered themselves presently shy, and the majority of shy people reported they did not want to be labeled as shy. This means that more than 100 million Americans believe they possess shy qualities. And of these, 25 percent would perceive themselves to be extremely shy.

*Shyness Is Best Viewed as a Continuum* At one end of this continuum Phillip Zimbardo finds people who choose shy qualities because they are more comfortable with things, ideas, or their work. They prefer to be left alone, but they are not afraid to interact with others when necessary. The middle ground of shyness consists of those who lack self-confidence, have inadequate social skills, and are easily embarrassed. They are reluctant to ask someone to do them a favor or to demand better service at a restaurant, appliance store, or automobile service center. At the far end of the continuum are people who suffer traumatic episodes of anxiety over relating to other people. They are highly self-conscious and extremely awkward in interactions. While they may appear calm on the surface, they are almost in a state of panic. Shyness is a prison from which they see no escape or time off for good behavior.

*Shyness Grows out of a Negative Self-Concept* Arthur Wassmer (1978) and Jonathan Berent (1993) report that when people have a poor self-image, they usually behave in a shy manner. Why is this so? One reason is that people who do not think they are very competent are simply worried about exposing their thoughts, ideas, and behaviors to others. Individuals withdraw into a world where they remain self-conscious and highly critical of themselves. Their lack of social contact does not give them a chance to be appreciated by others and to have their ideas rewarded.

*Is it bad to be shy?* The answer depends upon whom you ask. Phillip Zimbardo considers shyness a social disease that is reaching epidemic proportions. He notes that our society seems to encourage an increase in isolation, loneliness, and separation. The incidence of shyness appears to rise along with such trends. Arthur Wassmer considers it a problem because it keeps people from making contact with each other. Shyness makes it difficult to meet new people or to make new friends. It also prevents people from speaking up for their rights. Shyness encourages us to be self-conscious, to criticize ourselves, to have few positive thoughts about ourselves, and to stay away from others. Robert Montgomery and his colleagues (1991) also report that shy people consider themselves to be less attractive and that they lack the social skills needed to develop or to benefit from social support networks. In effect, they remove themselves from the valuable social benefits that only other people can deliver.

*Occasional Periods of Shyness May Have Some Benefits* In small amounts, shyness may promote periods of private reflection, or help us think through problems and develop creative solutions. In work settings shy individuals are often found to have good aptitudes for a job and are just as intelligent and hard working as their more verbal counterparts (McCroskey and Richmond, 1979). One implication of such findings is that organizations run the risk of losing talented people if they systematically exclude shy people. Organizations should consider placing shy individuals in positions where their shyness is not a liability. Thus, high-profile jobs that emphasize interpersonal skills would not be a good choice. Offering special training programs in social and communication skills also would help. In the final analysis, whether shyness affects the quality of our lives determines whether it is bad. If it makes us unhappy or unable to relate to people when we have to interact, then it is a problem.

*Shyness Is Acquired in a Number of Ways* No single factor determines shyness. Phillip Zimbardo, for example, suggests that some individuals may have overreacted to some events in their past lives. They may have "looked silly"; people may have "laughed at them"; or they may have felt "on the spot, with everyone judging them." They then became anxious over getting embarrassed in social situations. For others, the risk of being rejected is so painful they would do anything to avoid it. *Thus, minimizing interactions makes the chances of personal embarrassment and rejection less likely.* Furthermore, cultural values may promote shyness. In Japan and other Asian countries, shy qualities are considered desirable. It is also possible that parents or other respected people in our lives modeled shy behaviors. Thus, imitation learning may be partly responsible.

Whatever the original source of the shyness, a self-fulfilling prophecy is usually set in motion that traps people in their shyness. One way to depict how this happens is illustrated in Figure 8.1 and in the description presented below.

1. *A social situation occurs, and anxiety develops.* Withdrawing from social contact temporarily reduces this anxiety. Reflecting upon why they behaved in this way, people label themselves as shy.

2. *In turn, this label initiates a script* that provides information from life experiences regarding how to behave (e.g., "I'm basically shy, so I should just sit here and not get involved with other people").

3. *Following the script informs others about how to treat them.* The body language of shy people puts out clear nonverbal signals that they do not wish to be bothered. Others pick up such signals and may think, "He looks like he wants to be alone, so I won't bother him." Or, "I'll just say hello and then find someone more interesting to talk to."

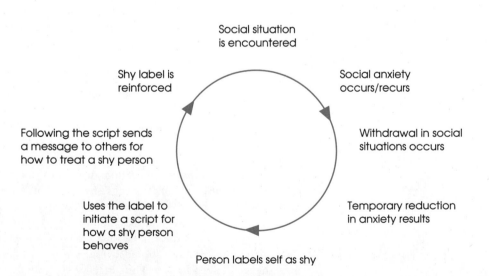

**Figure 8.1** *The Shyness Cycle. Depicted is one way a self-fulfilling prophecy for behaving in a shy manner develops and is maintained in social situations.*

4. *Someone who is shy then interprets the withdrawal or lack of interest on the part of others as confirming his or her self-image.* Thus, the label is verified. Someone might then think, "See, I knew that person wouldn't like me."

5. *The thoughts and actions described above are not effective in permanently reducing social anxiety.* It returns when the same or another situation is encountered, and thus the process repeats itself.

## Coping with Shyness

Students sometimes tell me, "I wish I weren't so shy, but I don't know what to do about it." Fortunately, clues for how to change are contained in the literature mentioned in the previous section. Of course, you should first decide that you really want to do something. One or more of the following ideas could help.

*Follow a Role Model* You may know someone you like and respect who has overcome shyness successfully. Or you may know someone who interacts well in social situations in ways you would like to copy. Talk to that person, observe his or her behavior, and think of ways you can do the same things he or she does. The principles for following a model discussed in Chapter 5 should give you several additional ideas for how to imitate successfully.

*Use Your Imagination* Let your imagination help you rehearse what you plan to do. Try to picture the specific things you will do in a social situation. Be sure to imagine that you are doing everything just as you want and that you are successful. Think about the reactions of other people. How will they react when they no longer see you as self-critical, shy, depressed, or not having fun?

*Try a New Behavior in Which You Think You Will Be Successful* As we all know, nothing succeeds like success. It is a great morale and self-confidence booster. When trying a new behavior for the first time, do it in a situation in which you think you are likely to be successful. Then think about taking on things that are more difficult.

*Focus on Some of Your Positive Qualities People* who are shy typically have a negative self-concept. It is not unusual to be shy and overly critical of yourself. Jonathan Berent recommends that you make lists in writing of your good and poor qualities. Then practice concentrating on the good things. Each day you should take a few minutes aside and think about your good points. This will tend to disrupt thoughts that you are not worth much.

A related technique is to stop negative thoughts from intruding (Watson and Tharp, 1993). Here is one way these authors suggest using this strategy. Whenever a self-critical thought or evaluation enters your mind, say to yourself out loud, "Stop." Then relax your muscles for a moment, and say, "Calm." Your goal is to get a short break in the undesirable thought. If you fail to get the break, repeat the process as many times as needed until the thought does not intrude. Remember to use this technique as soon as the critical thought occurs and every time it recurs.

*Soften* Acting shy may give people the impression you are not interested in them. Arthur Wassmer provides several nonverbal cues we can practice in our relationships to convey interest. He uses the word SOFTEN to summarize them: S (Smile), 0 (Open posture), F (Forward lean), T (Touch), E (Eye contact), N (Nod).

Instead of frowning at people or giving them a blank expression, we should smile more often. To get out of the habit of crossing our arms or legs or crunching ourselves into a corner of a chair or wall, we should open our posture a bit. Rather than turning our backs, walking away, or maintaining our distance, we should lean forward toward people. Giving people a friendly handshake and even a hug or kiss if appropriate would help us touch more. Looking at the walls, ceiling, or floor when we talk does not convey interest. Maintaining eye contact does. An occasional nod when people talk to us says that we are listening and interested. These nonverbal techniques help us to improve our basic social skills. You do not, of course, have to be shy to integrate them into your life-style.

## Stereotypes and Prejudices

One of our characteristics is that, "given a thimbleful of facts, we often rush to make generalizations as large as a tub." When we do this with people, we are guilty of stereotyping. The preconceived rigid beliefs about other individuals are called **stereotypes**. They are mental shortcuts that help us categorize people, places, and events in our lives. Thus, someone might label Jews as "stingy," whites as "untrustworthy," police officers as "mean," blacks as "lazy," Japanese as "cunning," Hispanics as "cruel and aggressive" and the Irish as having red hair, drinking lots of whiskey, liking to fight, wearing green, and losing their tempers quickly.

*Problems develop, however, when we ignore the individual differences that exist among members of any group.* Research suggests that this tendency is widespread and makes people imagine that any single member of a group must fit the group's stereotype. This bias leads to a belief that the stereotype was confirmed and thus allows it to continue (Schlusher and Anderson, 1987).

On the other hand, Robin Fox (1992) notes that the ability to stereotype has survived in our evolutionary history because such thought processes are sometimes adaptive. After all, consider how difficult life would be if you had to relearn the function of a chair, pen, car, or anything else everytime you encountered one that was a different shape or color. Similarly, knowing what a person does and how he or she can help you is facilitated if you can categorize people by their titles (i.e., teacher, doctor, lawyer) or by the uniforms they wear. When a stranger approaches on a dark street with a knife in hand, the label "dangerous adversary" automatically appears in our mind, and evasive actions are quickly taken.

When we combine a stereotype with strong feelings about a person, object, or event, we have a **prejudiced attitude**; that is, an attitude that has rigid beliefs and strong feelings about another person. Prejudices can be learned, but according to psychologist Harold Fishbein (1992), they also may reflect underlying protective mechanisms that are part of our evolutionary history. According to this view, our ancestors needed to ensure the cohesion of their families, tribes, or nations in order to survive. Thus, anyone outside of the group was seen as a threat to established rules of interaction, male dominance, food supplies, and to the group's women and children. Strangers were thus met with suspicion, fear, and hostility. Fishbein argues that the tendency to reject people outside of our primary social groups persists into the modern world. Unfortunately, in a modern multicultural society, such tendencies interfere with our ability to establish meaningful relationships that cross ethnic and racial lines.

Although the word "prejudice" is most often used today to describe "negative pre-judgments of others," positive prejudices also exist. We might think of someone as an "exceptionally fine modern artist," "a great statesman," or a "lovable humanitarian." At the other extreme, we might call someone about whom we hold negative prejudices a "nigger," "wop," "spick," or a "crazy nut."

*Negative Stereotypes and Prejudices Lead to Unfair Perceptions of Others* Melinda Jones (1991) reports that research generally shows that blacks and Hispanics are consistently described in less favorable terms than are whites. In a work environment, when someone is labeled a "union leader," managers immediately feel they will not understand management's point of view. Managers also expect that union leaders will behave uncooperatively and will show rigidity in their thinking (Zalkind & Costello, 1976). Focus on Applied Research 8.1 illustrates how stereotypes and prejudices can override otherwise good evaluations of people.

*Negative Stereotypes and Prejudices Lead to the Unfair Treatment of Others* Rigid beliefs often lead people to dislike certain individuals and to consider them as unimportant. As a result, there is **discrimination** against them. Discrimination is the differential treatment of individuals because they belong to a particular social group. At one time in our history, legal and social pressures were used to not allow women to vote; blacks had to ride in the back of the bus; gays and lesbians were thrown out of military service; and insensitivity made people with physical handicaps endure difficult access to many public buildings. Although such practices are currently illegal, and conditions have improved, we have a long way to go before complete equality is achieved for everyone.

Patricia Devine (1989) views discrimination as a natural outcome of the fact that negative stereotypes and prejudices are overlearned and automatically activated in the presence of a stereotyped group member. *Because such beliefs are thought to be valid, they are then used to justify actions taken by members of a majority group against minorities.* For example, slavery was justified before the Civil War because it fit stereotypes of blacks

---

FOCUS ON APPLIED RESEARCH 8.1

### I Really Think You Are Great, But...

Undergraduate business students (n = 249) were asked to describe typical Japanese and American managers on a number of dimensions (Powell, 1992). Participants evaluated each manager's perceived leadership style and the extent to which he or she conformed to masculine (i.e., independent, assertive) or feminine (i.e., understanding, warm) sex role stereotypes. In addition, they indicated which manager would have the most satisfied subordinates, who would have the most productive subordinates, who would be the better manager, and whom they would prefer to work for.

Japanese managers were rated as more effective in getting a job done, having the most productive subordinates, and as better managers overall. The Japanese manager also was viewed as less independent and assertive but more understanding and warm.

*In spite of giving them more positive evaluations, only 17 percent of the students said they preferred to work for a Japanese manager.* In effect, the Japanese managers' superior skills were recognized, but they were not fully accepted as potential bosses by the students. Gary Powell suggested that underlying prejudices about working for someone from another culture and negative attitudes towards Japanese business practices carried more weight.

The results of his study suggest that *people have a difficult time putting their stereotypes and prejudices aside, even when they can recognize the superior qualifications that a member of a minority group possesses.*

as "docile, happy-go-lucky, and somewhat unintelligent people." With such characteristics, they were believed to be suited for little else than serving as slaves (Devine and Sherman, 1992). These authors note that once the slaves were freed after the Civil War, the stereotype changed. Blacks were now perceived as savages who, without the constraints imposed by slavery, would revert to their primitive and animalistic nature. It is no wonder that many members of minority groups feel they cannot win. *The stereotypes change to keep them in a one-down position.* Such beliefs have made it more difficult for minorities to gain equal job opportunities and the high status positions that white people have enjoyed in our society.

Believing that people are not very important and disliking them may lead to unspeakably horrible events. The systematic attempt to exterminate Jews in Nazi Germany, the mass murders of Vietnamese civilians during the Vietnam War, the terrorist bombings in the Middle East, and the "ethnic cleansing" in the civil war in the former Yugoslavia, are examples of people acting on stereotypes and prejudices. Apparently, it is easier to kill someone who has been degraded by such labels as a "dirty bastard," "scum of the earth," "Kraut," "Gook," or any other name that dehumanizes an individual or group.

*Of course, negative stereotypes and prejudices do not always lead to killing and maiming others; but they usually take a toll on the human spirit.* Gilda Lopez and Nancy Chism (1993) demonstrated one way this occurs in their study of gay and lesbian students. They note that students reported being on guard and wary of the prejudices of other students and teachers. Thus, they were afraid to disclose their identity in situations in which they felt the instructor might retaliate. In particular they feared receiving lower grades, being made an "object" in class, or being patronized by receiving special treatment. Brief profiles of two of the students they interviewed are shown in Focus on People 8.1.

Research shows that there is a self-serving bias that is built into negative stereotypes and prejudices. Such beliefs make it easier for people to discriminate. An interesting set of mental gymnastics takes place. Because someone is labeled in derogatory ways, people think they deserve whatever treatment they receive from others (Zimbardo, Ebbesen, and Maslach, 1977). Furthermore, not only are those discriminated against considered deserving of bad treatment, but "they brought it on themselves through their thoughts and actions." *By "blaming the victim," those who persecute others can wash their hands of responsibility.*

## Learning to Cope with Your Stereotypes and Prejudices

*Look for the Unique Qualities in Others* Take time to consciously reflect on the personal qualities and characteristics that people have. Research shows that this can revise or reduce the tendency to quickly place someone into a category (Rajecki et al., 1992). *Personal contacts also can teach you about how much you have in common with others.* Rajecki reports that whites often discover that their black coworkers share their attitudes toward management. Heterosexuals soon discover that not all gay men are "swishy and sexually promiscuous" and that gays and lesbians are often prominent members of their communities.

*Try to Cooperate and Work Together with People You Sometimes Stereotype* At work or in classroom situations, sometimes you have to form teams to work on projects. In some cases, people have choices about who to work with on tasks. Take some initiative to work on tasks with someone who is a member of a group whom you stereotype or

## The Cost of Being Different: Effects of Lesbian and Gay Prejudices

### Jody:

Jody is a junior in the honors program, majoring in women's studies. She is energetic, outgoing, affectionate, and an animated speaker. She has very short hair and wears no make up. She says that people attribute her appearance to her feminism and do not recognize her lesbian identity until told.

In class, she feels very comfortable talking about lesbian issues as well as the issues facing other oppressed groups. She is aware that there is some negative reaction to her. Sometimes she sees other students rolling their eyes and hissing while she talks; other times, she feels that instructors are trying to placate her and move on to safer topics very hastily. She must also bear hearing teachers say things that are false such as, "There were no gay or lesbian people in colonial times. We can't dwell on irrelevant issues."

Her activism sometimes brings her close to burnout. She gets tired of answering questions such as, "In lesbian couples, who is the man and who is the woman?" The burden of educating others at times seems unreasonable to her. Jody also chooses her courses carefully, based on advice she hears within her community on which instructors are receptive.

### Gregg:

Gregg is a sophomore with a major in mechanical engineering. He comes across as a serious, intelligent, and likeable college student. Although his friends and family now know of his identity, he is still reluctant to come out publicly, fearing violence or verbal attacks that he does not feel strong enough to handle. Gregg views his mental agony as "hellish," and he has difficulty concentrating on his coursework. He once told a friend, "I'm one step short of a nervous breakdown." The worst part was that he felt so alone.

He hadn't anticipated the overt and subtle ways fellow students and teachers show their disapproval of gay men. When he hears students snickering about "faggots" and "fruitcakes," he cringes. When teachers tolerate homophobic remarks by ignoring them, he feels furious but not empowered to take the initiative. He is hoping that one day he will feel strong enough to confront such negative stereotypes and hatreds. For now, he is silent. He is reluctant to write about gay topics, fearing there will be grade retaliation or that his papers will be considered too "personal" rather than scholarly. Gregg also recognizes he is majoring in a field where there is discrimination against gay men, so he has to be very cautious about his identity—something he will have to do for the rest of his life.

Cases are based on descriptions of problems encountered by students in Gilda Lopez and Nancy Chism's article *Classroom Concerns of Gay and Lesbian Students, College Teaching, Summer 1993*. Selections are used with permission of Heldref Publications.

with whom you typically have little contact. If a positive emotional climate for working together can be established (cf. the suggestions in Chapter 7 for doing this), research suggests that negative attitudes can change.

In one study, researchers measured the attitudes of black, white, and Chicano children toward each other. To improve negative attitudes, the children were divided into small groups. Within each group, each child was assigned a part of the lesson, which only he or she learned for that day. Each group then had to learn the entire lesson by learning a different piece of it from other group members. Grades improved for children in the cooperative groups, and the black, white, and Chicano children came to like one another better (Aronson and Osherow, 1980).

## Lack of Self-Disclosure

Those who share their ideas, interests, experiences, and feelings with others generally have more friends and develop long-lasting relationships more easily than those who do not (Jourard, 1971). Relationships depend upon developing trust and respect for others, the belief that we are honest and open with others, and the discussion of shared interests. As self-disclosure increases, people report more emotional involvement in friendships and a greater satisfaction in dating relationships and marriage (Hendrick, 1989). The association between self-disclosure and feeling close to another person is reciprocal. Self-disclosure fosters intimacy and trust, and, in turn, intimacy and trust encourage more self-disclosure (Miller, 1990).

Some people appear to be better at self-disclosing than others. Kathryn Dindia and Mike Allen (1992), in an analysis of 205 research studies, found that women from Western societies typically reveal more about themselves to new acquaintances than do men. This was particularly true when women were talking to other women. Women-women interactions were highest in self-disclosure, male-male lowest, and opposite-sex self-disclosure was in between. Disclosing intimate details of one's life to a new acquaintance also was perceived as more appropriate for women than for men. When males engaged in such actions, however, they were more likely than their female counterparts to be viewed as maladjusted. Women also disclosed more to people with whom they had a long-standing relationship, such as a spouse, parent, or close friend.

Sidney Jourard argued that men suffer major mental and physical health problems because the male sex role discourages self-disclosure of their problems and concerns. This is particularly true of men who have a rather traditional view of how men should behave. Traditional men are supposed to keep a "stiff upper lip" and not reveal their feelings to others. One result of playing a traditional male sex role is that many men miss opportunities to obtain advice and help with their problems. Men who have more traditionally feminine qualities (i.e., empathy, understanding, warmth, ability to express emotions) in their personal makeup are much better at self-disclosing across a variety of situations (Shaffer et al., 1991).

There are some disadvantages to self-disclosure as well, particularly if there is too much of it. Camille Wortman and her colleagues (1976) note that talking too much about ourselves early in a relationship may not facilitate the development of friendship. People might attribute your high self-disclosure as an indication you are too immature, insecure, phoney, or that you tell everyone such things. Other people like to believe they are special to you. Waiting awhile before sharing your most intimate thoughts and feelings leads people you meet to believe you are interested in them and want the relationship to continue and deepen. Too much self-disclosure as a continuing habit in our relationships is not good either. When someone knows everything there is to know about us, there is little room for the surprises that increase interest and reduce boredom in our relationships.

*The advantages of self-disclosure seem to lie somewhere between not talking about yourself and doing it too much.* But talking about ourselves in at least moderate amounts is not easy. There is some risk involved. Fears for some people are that the other person may not reciprocate, that what is said might be unacceptable to a partner, or that they may conclude that the other individual is not willing to share friendship and love. Such anxieties are seldom justified. The advantages of self-disclosure, in my experience, far outweigh the disadvantages. What do your experiences suggest about this last statement?

## Increasing Self-Disclosure

How much you reveal about yourself is a personal choice. You need to consider your needs for privacy and discretion, the disadvantages of too much self-disclosure, and the advantages of disclosure in forming relationships. In my experiences, few people disclose so much that they are likely to experience problems. Most of us could probably benefit from increasing the amount of self-disclosure in our relationships. Suggestions for how to do this appear in Exercise 8.2 at the end of this chapter.

## THE EMOTIONAL SIDE OF RELATIONSHIPS

The list of emotions that appear in our interactions is impressive. They include feelings of liking others, love, jealousy, anger, frustration, tension, guilt, anxiety, sadness, grief, and loneliness. Such emotions add excitement and interest to our interactions. But they also make life difficult.

### Love

When asked what they want most out of a intimate relationship, 53 percent of the men and women responding to a national survey wanted love (Rubinstein, 1983). When approaching the question from a psychological point of view, Zick Rubin (1973) views love as a set of attitudes about others. Rubin also sees love as involving an attachment and caring between two or more people. He reports that people love others when they:

- *will do almost anything for them.*
- *seek them out when they feel lonely.*
- *feel possessive toward them.*
- *become concerned for their welfare.*
- *believe it would be hard to get along without them.*

Rubin finds that we can like or have a positive attitude about other people without loving them. But we do not love others unless we like them. Compared to those who merely like a partner, those in love with someone perceive a partner differently. Lovers report that they understand their partners better, they feel as if they were meant for each other, are willing to place their partner's happiness above their own, and believe more strongly in sexual communion (i.e., see sex as a merging with the beloved) (Hendrick and Hendrick, 1988). People in love have an intense desire to share discoveries, feelings, and opinions with their partners; they are more relaxed, less worried, and more creative and spontaneous with each other.

Adults in love also engage in actions that have a childlike quality to them. They may coo, sing, talk baby talk, and use affectionate babylike names for each other (Shaver and Hazen, 1988). In other studies Phillip Shaver (1988) and his colleagues report that adult intimate relationships tend to have other things in common with earlier developmental stages. They find that secure, avoidant, and anxious-ambivalent attachment styles found in childhood tend to appear in adult intimate relationships. Each is described in Focus on Applied Research 8.2.

*The Ingredients of Love: Intimacy, Commitment, Passion* From Robert Sternberg's (1988) viewpoint, there are several varieties of love that develop from combinations of three ingredients: "intimacy," "commitment," and "passion." **Intimacy** refers to warmth, closeness, and sharing in a relationship. **Commitment** is an intent to maintain a relationship in spite of the difficulties and costs that may arise. **Passion** represents the intense sexual and erotic desire for another person. How they combine in various

## FOCUS ON APPLIED RESEARCH 8.2

### Attachment Styles in Adult Relationships

More than 600 participants were asked about recollections of their relationships with their parents and were also questioned about their current experiences and feelings in romantic relationships. A description of each of the three attachment styles that emerged from this study is briefly described below. *Which one tends to describe you?*

### Secure:

I find it relatively easy to get close to others and am comfortable depending upon them and having them depend upon me. I don't often worry about being abandoned or about someone getting too close to me. I can commit to a relationship.

### Avoidant:

I am somewhat uncomfortable being close to others. It is difficult for me to trust them completely, and it is not easy for me to allow myself to depend upon them. I get nervous when anyone gets too close, and often my partners want me to be more intimate than I am comfortable being. I find it difficult to make a strong commitment to another person.

### Anxious/Ambivalent:

I find that others are reluctant to get as close as I would like. I often worry that my partner doesn't really love me or won't want to stay with me. I want to merge completely with another person, and this desire sometimes scares people away. I tend to be clinging, demanding, and very emotional.

The secure style was found to be associated with people having more positive outcomes in adult relationships and was present in the majority of the participants (56 percent). The remainder of the participants were in the other two categories. Those who reported avoidant attachments with their parents (i.e., feelings of rejection) found it difficult to trust and self-disclose with a partner and were generally uncomfortable with closeness as adults. Anxious-ambivalent types had both positive and negative feelings towards their parents, feeling both accepted but also rejected during childhood. They reported experiencing strong sexual attraction and love at first sight followed by concerns about whether the relationship would last. It is also difficult for them to develop a sense of autonomy.

forms of love is shown in Figure 8.2, and the reported level of each component of love over time is depicted in Figure 8.3.

*Types of Love* We can identify four types of love:

1. *Empty, liking, and infatuation. Empty love* represents a relationship in which people feel committed, but not very warm or close, and passion is largely absent. Unfortunately, some marriages drift into this state where people stay together for the "sake of the children" or because "no one else would have me." *Liking another person* is a fundamental building block of interpersonal relationships. For it to develop, a sense of intimacy or closeness that includes mutual respect and trust must be present. *Infatuation represents an intense desire for another person* and may precede a more lasting and deeper relationship. It is an erotic attachment in which people report feeling "turned on" by someone else. Mutual respect and trust as well a sense of commitment to a relationship are largely absent when infatuation is present.

2. *Passionate/Romantic love.* Ellen Berscheid and Elaine Walster-Hatfield (1978, 1988) define romantic love as an intense absorption with another person. Partners tend to long for and to seek fulfillment in each other. They are generally in ecstasy at finally having won each other's love. *One problem is that passionate love typically leads to unrealistic expectations.* There is no way our partner can live up to what we expect. Complete fulfillment in another person is more of a fantasy than a reality of everyday life. Each of us has many needs, and it is unlikely that any one person will satisfy them all. Yet passion-

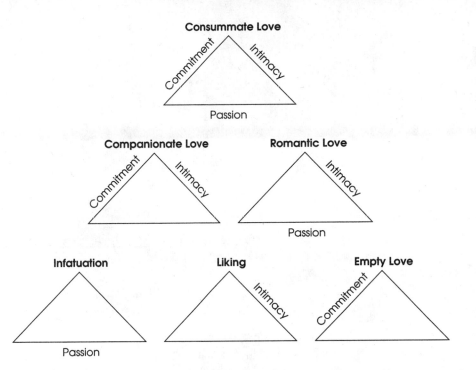

**Figure 8.2** *The Triangles of Love. Robert Sternberg identifies different types of love in terms of how intimacy, commitment, and passion combine. Several common forms are represented above. Any component shown indicates that it is an important feature or occurs at a relatively high level. The absence of a component suggests that it is a relatively unimportant feature or is present in relatively small amounts.*

ate love tends to blind people to this fact. The result is that tension and frustration enter the relationship.

*Another issue is that romantic love may lead us to ignore how dissimilar another person is.* When romantic or passionate love develops, partners tend to ignore differences in the attitudes and values they and a partner possess. Each partner may misperceive or misremember them as similar to their own or simply become more accepting of the differences (McClanahan, 1990).

*When caught up in passionate or romantic love, partners also may ignore developing problems in a relationship.* Conflicts, sources of tension, and irritating habits are overlooked and ignored. "I don't want to hurt his or her feelings" is a comment often heard by people in love. The mistake is to assume that love will overcome all obstacles. Unfortunately, this emotion is not an all-purpose Band-Aid. It cannot cover up problems in a relationship for long. If unattended, they will eventually build up until the bubble breaks, as the case of Harry and Sally, presented at the beginning of Chapter 9 illustrates.

Robert Sternberg reports that the flames of romantic or passionate love eventually cool over time. It is very difficult to maintain the intensity found in the early stages of a relationship. Some couples, however, worry when they discover that the intense passion they felt for each other is no longer there. They may question whether something is wrong with themselves or their partner. In reality, it is natural for a steady relationship to settle down. The demands of daily living, raising children, and work pressures force

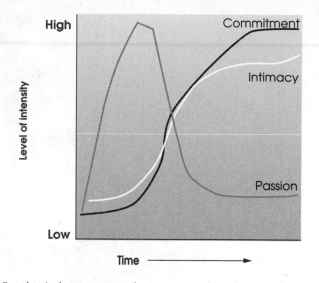

**Figure 8.3** *Sternberg's theory suggests that passion peaks early in a relationship and begins to drop in intensity while intimacy and commitment build gradually.*

people to concentrate on things other than their partners. This does not mean that passionate moments are gone forever. Rather, they are typically not of the same intensity or duration as they were when the relationship began (Schultz, 1984).

*3. Companionate love.* This is the less intense but steady concern, warm attachment, and caring we feel for another person. It is the glue that maintains long-term relationships and forms as intimacy and commitment increase over time. Research suggests that measures of the level of commitment and intimacy are one of the best predictors of whether a relationship continues (Hendrick et al., 1988). When relationships settle into companionate love, people are much more realistic about what they can expect from each other. They do not expect their partners to be perfect and understand that they may both like and dislike them. People are realistic and recognize that love will not solve their problems.

*4. Consummate love.* In Sternberg's typology, this represents an "ideal" for any short- or long-term relationship. All three ingredients are present, which leads people to have a close interpersonal engagement. Maintaining consummate love for extended periods of time is not easy, because simultaneously keeping passion, commitment, and intimacy at appropriate levels is difficult. Relatively few couples perceive their relationship in such terms, but a majority feel that at one time or another they have enjoyed moments of consummate love.

*Styles of Loving* Some people appear to have certain loving styles, or preferred ways of engaging in close relationships (Lee, 1976; Hendrick and Hendrick, 1986). Each of these styles is briefly described in Table 8.3. The Styles of Love scale developed by Clyde and Susan Hendrick is used to examine the extent to which the six styles appear in our intimate relationships. *They report that all of us are essentially a blend of each style, but some dimensions are stronger within our personality makeup than others.* In research using the Styles of Love Scale, men have higher scores than women on both passionate and game-playing love. Females, in turn, score higher on friendship, logical, and possessive love. The presence of passionate and unselfish love leads to satisfaction with a

**Table 8.3**    Styles of Loving

| LOVE STYLES | SAMPLE ITEM MEASURING EACH STYLE |
|---|---|
| *Practical (Pragma)* | I consider what a person is going to become before I commit myself to a relationship. |
| *Game Playing (Ludus)* | I have sometimes had to keep two of my lovers from finding out about each other. |
| *Passionate (Eros)* | My lover and I became emotionally involved rather quickly. |
| *Friendship (Storge)* | Love is really a deep friendship, not a mysterious mystical emotion. |
| *Unselfish (Agape)* | I cannot be happy unless I place my lover's happiness before my own. |
| *Possessive (Mania)* | I cannot relax if I suspect that my lover is with someone else. |

*Based on information in Hendrick and Hendrick, 1986, 1988*

relationship, whereas game-playing love produces low levels of satisfaction. Hans Bierhoff-Werner (1992) also finds people with a strong sense of practical love remain in relationships longer and have fewer intimate partnerships. The number of children couples have is closely related to the presence of the unselfish style of loving in their personal makeup. *Exercise 8.3 at the end of this chapter is designed to help you examine how such styles appear in your life.*

*Coping with Love* To prevent the problems that passionate love and its eventual decline present, you and your partner must discuss your differences. As problems arise, talk about them, or find a friend or counselor who can help you discuss them. Openly share your expectations for the relationship. Discuss how you expect each other to behave and what you hope the relationship will do for each of you. Similarly, nurturing your love for a partner over the long haul also needs to be accomplished. Companionate love demands that certain attitudes and behaviors be present in a relationship for it to work. Suggestions for managing companionate love in long-term relationships are described in Focus on Applied Research 8.3.

## Envy and Jealousy

- A client recently told me, "I wish I did half the business that Paul's company did. I don't know how he does so well, but I'd like a little of his magic to rub off on me."
- A woman interviewed on a recent "tabloid" television show said, "I told him that if he ever stepped out on me again I would kill him. He thought he was slick about it this time, and was he ever surprised when I told him what I knew. I'm only sorry I didn't finish the job on him. I don't care what happens to me, I got him good this time."

The statements above represent envy and jealousy, respectively. Both emotions are present in a variety of our daily interactions and appear to be triggered by similar events across different cultures (Hupka and Zaleski, 1990). Unfortunately, these two emotions are sometimes confused with each other. The characteristics of each can be better understood by examining situations that produce envy and jealousy.

FOCUS ON APPLIED RESEARCH 8.3

## Managing Companionate Love

Interviews with more than 200 dating, engaged, and married couples identified several attitudes and behaviors that help maintain a relationship over long periods of time (Walster and Walster, 1978). *What would you add to this list?*

### Personal Contributions
- Being sociable, friendly, and relaxed in social settings
- Being thoughtful about sentimental things like birthdays and anniversaries
- Being an intelligent, informed person and sharing ideas

### Day-to-Day Contributions
- Contributing to household responsibilities such as grocery shopping, making dinner, house cleaning, and car maintenance
- Contributing incomes to a joint account

### Sociability
- Being easy to live with, possessing a sense of humor, and not being too moody
- Being a good companion and suggesting interesting activities to do together
- Discussing your day and showing an interest in what your partner did that day

- Trying to fit in with your partner's friends and relatives

### Decision Making
- Taking your fair share of responsibility for making and carrying out decisions that affect both of you

### Appearance
- Being a physically attractive person
- Giving attention to clothing, cleanliness, exercise, and good eating habits

### Emotional Contributions
- Responding to your partner's personal concerns and emotional needs
- Not taking your partner for granted
- Being openly affectionate by touching, hugging, and kissing
- Working to make the sexual aspect of the relationship mutually satisfying
- Living up to your agreements about extramarital relations
- Committing yourself to your partner and to the future of your relationship
- Respecting your partner's need to be a free and independent person

*Envy* This is a desire to acquire something that another person possesses. People are envious when they wish they could have a house or car that a friend owns, a promotion that a coworker received, the kind of close relationship enjoyed by other couples, or anything else that they currently lack in their lives. Peter Salovey and Judith Rodin (1989) note that when experiencing envy, individuals are generally unhappy and feel inferior because of not having something they want. Typically, this occurs in situations in which people we like or associate with have things or take actions that threaten our definition of ourselves. Someone who defines him or herself as successful might become envious if a coworker was given a larger raise, a close friend purchased a more expensive car, or a friend received a higher grade point average.

On a more positive note, Salovey and Rodin report that most advanced societies use envy to encourage the talents, abilities, and productivity of their members. Thus, a little envy can become a motivational device. Someone may want the same pay raise a coworker received and vow "to work much more effectively with people around here to impress my boss." A coach might tell the seventh person on the depth chart of a basketball team, "if you really want to play in the starting five, you're going to have to work harder in practice." Or, a mother might tell her teenaged daughter, "If you want some of the nicer things in life, you are going to have to get advanced training after high school."

*Jealousy*  On the other hand, jealousy is a fear of losing something to which we have become attached. We are jealous when we fear losing a dating partner or spouse to another person or when we feel excluded from the company of someone we like or love. Peter Salovey and Judith Rodin (1989, 1985) report that when caught in the grip of jealousy, people experience multiple emotions, including sadness, fear and anxiety, and, most of all, anger. Besides the anger, their survey of 25,000 readers of *Psychology Today* magazine revealed that people act out their jealous feelings by:

- *Looking through their spouse's, or lover's belongings for unfamiliar names and phone numbers.*
- *Calling a spouse or lover unexpectedly just to see if he or she is there.*
- *Listening in on a telephone conversation of a spouse or lover or secretly following him or her.*
- *Extensively questioning a spouse or lover about previous or present romantic relationships.*

Jealousy is more likely to occur in relationships where people adhere to rigid definitions of their sex roles (Clanton and Smith, 1977). These authors also report that it serves a variety of functions. *Jealousy is used to gain power and control over another person.* "The next time you talk to him at a party, I'm going to get angry and not speak to you," I overheard a friend tell his date at a recent social gathering. *Expressing jealousy facilitates catharsis*, or the release of tension, within us. We are less likely to verbally or physically attack someone if we can talk about our feelings. Finally, *jealousy may legitimize retaliation.* Sometimes, this emotion leads to a demand for justice. We might think, "If my partner has an affair, then it's OK for me." Or, it might be employed as an excuse to withdraw from or break up a relationship.

The hardest feelings in a relationship to endure are those that arise from a fear of losing someone with whom we are sexually intimate. Sexual jealousy is more difficult

to cope with, because we often measure our self-worth and the health of our relationship in terms of sexual fidelity (Berscheid and Fein, 1977). While a problem in most intimate relationships, sexual jealousy is higher among people who are not married (Salovey and Rodin, 1985). One reason is that unmarried couples tend to see their relationships as less committed than those of married couples.

When asked to rate their levels of jealousy, men and women had equal scores (Adams, 1980). This contradicts the popular stereotype that women are more prone to jealousy. Women, however, reported that they were more likely to try to make their partners jealous. When a third person threatens an intimate relationship, men tend to concentrate more on saving face. They get angry, sulk, and try to make their partners feel sorry for them. They are also more willing to terminate the relationship, whereas women try to rehabilitate the bond with a partner and otherwise save the relationship (Nadler and Dotan, 1992).

## Coping with Envy and Jealousy

*Reframe Your Thinking*  Instead of saying, "Joyce's new car is just another indication of how much better she is than me," reframe the situation as, "Just because she is able to afford a new car is no reason for me to see myself as a failure. If I keep working hard and saving my money, I'll be able to afford a new car one day as well." Similarly, remind yourself that "just because my girlfriend talks to other guys at a party does not mean she dislikes me. She's just being sociable and taking an interest in what other people are doing."

*Gain Control over Your Imagination*  Envy and jealousy have the same effect as an engaging movie or novel. Our imagination takes over, and elaborate fantasies and bad feelings result. One of my students remarked, "Now that a colleague was awarded the promotion I wanted, he's going to eventually end up as my boss and make life miserable for me." Another told me, "I keep daydreaming that my wife is seeing someone else when she's out of town on her business trips." Instead of letting your fantasy life run wild, test the reality of your fantasies. What hard evidence is there that such suspicions are correct? And if you are comfortable doing so, talk about your feelings and try to determine whether or not there is anything to be concerned about.

*Take Steps to Build Your Self-Confidence*  Envy and jealousy flourish when our self-confidence in our skills and abilities is low. Consider doing things that help you feel better about yourself. Pick one or more activities and learn to do them well. Make yourself as knowledgeable as you can about the world around you. Share what you are learning with your partner and other people. Such actions help to build self-confidence and contribute to the image of yourself as an exciting and worthwhile person. You may find the ideas for improving your self-image discussed in Chapter 10 helpful, as well.

## Loneliness

Feeling lonely is something that most of us have experienced at one time or another in our lives. So much so that a number of facts and myths exist about this emotion, as illustrated in Table 8.4. Before reading further, determine the accuracy of your knowledge about loneliness.

**Loneliness** is a warning sign that our ability to connect with and remain attached to other people is in trouble. Robert Weiss (1974), for example, notes that each of us

| **Table 8.4** | Facts and Myths About Loneliness |
| --- | --- |

*To test your knowledge about loneliness, indicate whether you think each item is mostly true (T) or mostly false (F). Each item is discussed in the text.*

\_\_\_\_\_ Loneliness is a warning that our ability to connect with and remain attached to other people is in trouble.

\_\_\_\_\_ Loneliness is sometimes a sign of a personal problem.

\_\_\_\_\_ Feelings of sadness and depression are a part of feeling lonely.

\_\_\_\_\_ Lonely people may feel alienated and different from other people.

\_\_\_\_\_ Most people incorrectly assume other people have more friends than they do.

\_\_\_\_\_ Every year, at least 50 million people in the United States find themselves feeling lonely.

\_\_\_\_\_ People in their late sixties, seventies, and eighties are less lonely than younger adults.

\_\_\_\_\_ Loneliness is particularly intense during adolescence.

\_\_\_\_\_ People who live alone are more likely to say they are lonely than are those who live with other people.

\_\_\_\_\_ People who have high-level jobs or who work in prestigious occupations are less lonely than other employees.

\_\_\_\_\_ Loneliness varies with the time of day and time of the week.

\_\_\_\_\_ People report being more lonely during the holiday seasons.

Sum the number of statements you marked "mostly true" and those you marked "mostly false." Based on the research literature, each of the statements above is mostly true. *The reasons for each statement can be found in the discussion in this section of the text.*

---

has two important social needs. They are a need to feel attached to someone in an intimate relationship and a need for community. The latter is provided by friends who share our interests, people we work with on common tasks, and other important individuals in our lives. When such needs are not met, most of us begin to feel lonely. Thus, he views the onset of loneliness as an early warning that we are experiencing difficulties in our friendships and intimate relationships.

*Feeling lonely is both a contributor to feeling sad and depressed as well as a personal problem in and of itself.* When lonely, people report feeling one or more of the following things: unloved and uncared for, unable to disclose their private thoughts to others, alienated and different from other people (Beck and Young, 1978). They also report having low self-esteem and feeling generally inadequate. Lonely people tend to attribute their lack of social relationships to their own inadequacies and typically blame themselves for whatever problems they experience (Snodgrass, 1987; Jackson and Cochran, 1991).

*Most of us feel lonely when there is a mismatch between our actual social contacts and what we might desire.* What we desire, however, is based on a somewhat distorted view of the world. Most of us try to determine how many friends we should have by estimating how many friends others have. Scott Feld (1991) reports that such estimates are usually biased and incomplete. Those he studied reported having about 2.5 close friends in

their lives. They assumed, however, that other people had more friends than they did (i.e., an average of 3.4 close friends). *So persistent is this tendency to overestimate the number of friends others have that he concludes as many as 67–75 percent of us are likely to end up feeling socially deprived after making such comparisons.* This distortion may help to account for why 50 million people in the United States report that they are currently lonely.

People in their late sixties, seventies, and eighties tend to see themselves as less lonely than adolescents and younger adults (Perlman, 1991). One reason is that older adults may have made a better response to loneliness and, thus, cope better. Adolescents and young adults, on the other hand, are struggling with the questions "Who am I?" and "What should I do with my life?" They typically have stronger relationships with peers. Establishing an identity, however, takes a lot of private soul-searching and time away from other people. And, because peers are so important, even a brief absence may trigger lonely feelings.

Having other people around is no guarantee that someone will not feel lonely. While people who are unmarried and unattached are more likely to feel lonely, some report feeling lonely even when others are in their lives. They still perceive a lack of ability to get close to others and to share their thoughts and feelings (Rubinstein and Shaver, 1982).

Also, contrary to popular belief, it is not very "lonely at the top" of an organization. *Those with high-level jobs or who work in prestigious occupations report being less lonely than other employees.* This happens in spite of the fact that they work longer hours, are more committed to their organizations, and spend less time with their families (Bell et al., 1990). These authors speculate that the myth of "lonely at the top" developed because high-status people are expected to demonstrate superior abilities and greater sacrifices. The real victims in such circumstances may be the leader's spouse and other family members who depend upon him or her for companionship.

Loneliness varies with time of the day, week, and the time of year. Carin Rubenstein and Phillip Shaver (1982) found that evenings, weekends, and the winter season were the loneliest times for people. The exceptions were those who lived in warm, sunny climates during the winter. Holidays, in particular the Christmas, Chanukah, and

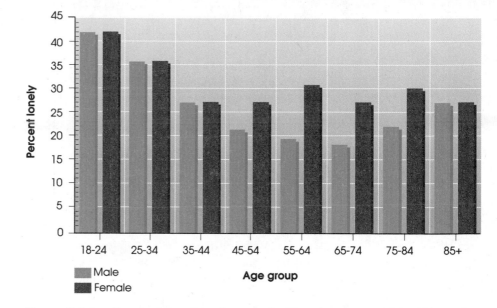

**Figure 8.4** *Loneliness and Age. Data shown are based on the responses of 25,000 people to questions about how lonely they currently felt (based on information reported by Perlman, 1991).*

New Year's holidays, were considered very lonely by those who had few friends or weak family ties.

## Coping with Loneliness

What can you do to combat periods of loneliness? While it is difficult to give an answer that will help in all situations, consider how taking preventive action, reducing discrepancies, and reestablishing contact with people might help.

*Taking Preventive Action* Using Robert Weiss's point of view mentioned earlier, the onset of loneliness is a warning that something is wrong with our relationships. You might consider using this early warning to take preventive action. When you begin to feel lonely, assess what is occurring in your relationships. Where are the trouble spots? Identify problems, and think of things you might do to overcome problems before they get out of hand. Enlist the aid of your close friends to help you figure out what to do. If possible, raise the things that are issues with the people involved. In relationships, sometimes "a stitch in time saves nine."

*Reestablish Contact, and Become Active* The Rubenstein and Shaver (1982) study mentioned earlier showed that people who did nothing, overate, watched television, or abused drugs only worsened their loneliness. Similarly, spending money, going shopping, or taking a drive in a car was also ineffective. People who called a friend, joined a club, or took time to visit someone were much more effective in coping. Another related strategy is to find new friends and people with whom to interact.

Sometimes this is a lot easier and even more fun than trying to work on reestablishing old relationships.

*Forget Yourself and Help Others* Doing things for others sometimes is helpful. This takes your mind off your problems and allows you to experience the joy of helping another person. Such things as volunteer work at a hospital or nursing home, coaching a kids' soccer or baseball team, tutoring other students, or becoming a foster parent, big brother, or big sister are all excellent ways to get involved.

*Identify the Cause of Loneliness* To do this it is important to make a distinction between events that precipitate or trigger loneliness and those that maintain them. Events that precipitate loneliness include such things as traveling, divorce, promotions to new jobs, or losing someone close to you. Precipitating events occur in our environments and generally we have very little control over them. Loneliness is maintained by such things as low self-esteem, fear of rejection or intimacy, a tendency to blame oneself for the problem, or becoming overly dependent on others. Factors that maintain loneliness are basically our thoughts and behavior patterns. We often have more control over them than we think. *A problem occurs when people continue to blame the precipitating events but fail to pay attention to the thoughts and behavior patterns that maintain loneliness* (Peplau and Perlman, 1982).

The distinction between precipitating events and factors that maintain loneliness is important. The latter account for much of the experience of loneliness. They must be dealt with if such feelings are going to be brought under control. In one study, Anne Peplau and Daniel Perlman (1982) studied the explanations people gave for being lonely. They found that individuals who believed the condition was permanent and due to a defect in their personality were least likely to overcome the problem. They would think, "I'm lonely because no one could ever love me. I'll never be worth loving." People who did not let such thoughts overwhelm them handled loneliness better. They viewed the cause as temporary and changeable. They would think things such as, "I'm lonely now, but I won't be for long. I'll stop feeling sorry for myself and get out of the house and meet some people."

# SEPARATING FROM RELATIONSHIPS

"Splitting up," "going our own separate ways," and "getting divorced," describe a rather frequent occurrence in close relationships. Dating relationships, engagements, marriages, and various living arrangements with people have a tendency to end. Some of the separations grow out of people trying relationships so they can gain the experience needed to make a long-term commitment. Sometimes such relationships simply go nowhere and end. At other times, a variety of problems get in the way of a couple's satisfaction.

Divorce among married couples is the most well-documented and studied of the various ways relationships end. Currently, about 50 percent of all marriages end in divorce, and the rate is higher among people who remarry (Brody et al., 1988). For comparisons, only about 1 percent of marriages ended in divorce during the latter part of the nineteenth century. About one-half of all divorces occur within the first seven years of marriage, with the first two to three years being an especially vulnerable time period. The actual rate of divorce may only represent the tip of the iceberg. It is unknown how many marriages end in nonlegal separations or how many married people stay together in an empty, essentially dissolved relationship "for the sake of the children" or because they lack the motivation to find a more satisfying relationship (Grasha and Kirschenbaum, 1986).

## Reasons for Breaking Up

*Boredom and Changing Interests*  In one study, researchers followed over 200 couples for a two-year period (Hill, Rubin, and Peplau, 1976). During this time period, more than one-half of them broke up. *Seventy-eight percent of the men and women listed boredom as the major reason for separation.* Apparently, their romantic, passionate love had cooled, and there was little else between them. Couples reported other reasons, including differences in hobbies, interests, religion, intelligence, and education.

*Sexual Attitudes and Differences in Expectations*  Almost 46 percent of the men and women in the latter study felt that their sexual attitudes contributed to the separation. Arguments about the frequency and type of sexual activities became major barriers to living happily together. Finally, their ideas about the relationship differed. Conflicts developed over whether they could date other people, whether a marriage would take place, and who made important decisions.

*Role Conflicts*  Among married couples and those couples living together in long-term relationships, conflicts over each partner's role become important reasons for why people separated (Blumstein and Schwartz, 1983). For example, an important conflict is whether each partner should play traditional gender roles (e.g., the man earns a living and the wife stays home and takes care of the house). Conflicts occur when women want more freedom to pursue career and other interests and their male partners want to hold them back. Additional tension occurs when married women work and they are still expected to do more than their fair share of household and child-rearing chores. In effect, they find themselves with two full-time jobs.

*Poor Communication Patterns*  Observations of and interviews with couples in happy and unhappy marriages indicate that how people communicate is important. Couples who divorced were openly very critical of each other; they avoided and withdrew from discussing important issues between them and became defensive when talking to each other (i.e., irritable, angry, feeling attacked). This was in contrast to happily married couples, who talked more to each other, kept channels of communication open, showed more sensitivity to each other's feelings and needs, and were more skilled at finding mutually agreeable solutions to their problems (Gottman et al., 1989, 1992).

*Problematic Attachment Styles*  Earlier in this chapter, secure, avoidant, and anxious/ambivalent ways that people relate to one another were described. Judith Feeney and Patricia Noller (1992) report that the ability of people to handle distress in relationships is related to such styles. People with a secure style acknowledge negative feelings and turn to others for support. Avoidant individuals tend to keep problems to themselves, while those with an anxious/ambivalent style are very dependent on a partner. Thus, people with the latter style are afraid to confront issues because they fear losing their partner. When a breakup occurs, Feeney and Noller found that those with an avoidant style were most "relieved that it was over," while partners with an anxious/ambivalent style were the least prepared for a breakup. They were very surprised that the relationship terminated and most upset with having to separate.

While some people suffer more than others, breaking up is seldom easy, and the resulting stress takes its toll. Separated and divorced people are more susceptible to physical illness and psychological problems (Masterson, 1984; Mirowsky and Ross, 1989). These authors suggest that separations often leave people without the emotional support they need and life appears more uncertain and unstable. Furthermore, anger towards a former partner and worrying about "what I did wrong" also enter one's life. During the first year after a divorce, for example, many persons feel psychologically inadequate. They believe they have been failures as spouses and parents. Of course, the costs of breaking up are not only psychological, as Focus on People 8.2 illustrates.

## Coping with Separation

Separations challenge us to form new relationships or to strengthen existing ones. Initially, this is difficult to do if you have been married or otherwise involved with someone for an extended period of time. You may not feel like spending time with people, or you may not have many single friends. In spite of such problems, it is possible to bounce back. Consider how some of the following ideas might help you:

*Find a Support Group* The chance to talk to those with similar problems is helpful. The lessons others have learned working through a separation may be just what you need. In most cities, groups are organized to deal with specific problems. Parents Without Partners, Singles Social Club, Divorced and Single Parents Group, and various social groups for people who are single again exist. Many colleges and universities also offer courses in marriage and divorce, interpersonal communications, personal growth and adjustment, and coping skills for daily living. Such courses often provide a chance

FOCUS ON PEOPLE 8.2
### The Cost of "Splitting Up"

It's usually the words "I don't love you anymore, but let's just be friends" that enrages jilted lovers. Those words, signifying the end of a relationship, once produced tears, temper tantrums, angry phone calls, and perhaps a threat or two. But now the stakes apparently are getting higher, since a federal jury in Chicago awarded a woman $178,000 because her fiance ended their seven-week engagement.

The court's decision and the suit itself have more than a few legal experts and romantics scratching their heads. As one person familiar with the trial said, "Dating and love and an engagement should be fun, a time when you can find out about another person. But now it looks like if you don't kiss me tonight, that's going to cost you $3,000."

The jury disagreed that it was simply a matter of the heart. Jurors found that the plaintiff's fiance violated the Illinois Breach of Promise Act when he sent a postcard abruptly breaking off marriage plans. Although he told her she could keep the engagement ring, worth $19,000, and a $10,000 bank account, it was not enough. The jury awarded her $93,000 in damages for pain and suffering, $60,000 for the loss of income she suffered from being emotionally distraught, and $25,000 for psychiatric counseling expenses.

As another observer of the trial noted, "If you promise somebody something, you could wind up giving them money. You've got to watch yourself."

Based on an account in the *Chicago Tribune,* November 24, 1993.

to share experiences, to work on the issues people face, and, not incidentally, to meet new people.

*Follow a Role Model* You may know someone you like and respect who has adjusted to the breakup of a relationship. Talk to that person, and borrow whatever ideas you find useful. You might even find the suggestions for following a model presented in Chapter 4 useful in this situation.

*Stop Putting Yourself Down* It is easy to think the worst about yourself, to pity yourself, or to blame yourself for what happened. Being overly critical of yourself will get you nowhere.

One way to handle such thoughts is to think of alternatives that counter them or, at least, thoughts that give a balanced perspective on the situation or that put you in a more positive light. For example, the thought, "Monty left me because I get too angry with him" can be countered with "I may have gotten angry, but so did he. He kept too many things to himself and then would blow up. It's hard to build a relationship with someone who refuses to talk about problems." The goal of such thinking is to ensure that a balanced perspective is maintained on your self-critical thoughts.

## *Summary of Chapter Organizers*

Suggested responses to the chapter organizers presented at the beginning of this chapter are presented below.

1. *What are several benefits that interpersonal relationships provide for you?* Not only is your survival dependent upon forming close relationships, but such bonds also have other benefits. These include helping you in meeting needs for affiliation, receiving comfort and affection, obtaining emotional support, receiving advice and assistance with problems, influencing others, and developing a positive self-image.

2. *Do you know the different characteristics of relationships as they develop?* Relationships appear to move through various phases as they develop. Early in a relationship people become aware of each other, establish rapport, and begin to do favors for each other. Perceptions change from "you" and "me" to "we." Later on, sharing future goals that involve each partner, developing a commitment and identity as a couple, and successfully performing long-term relationship roles such as husband-wife and mother-father become important.

3. *What role do liking, respect, and trust play in forming relationships?* Liking someone represents a positive attitude towards another individual. To like people, you must first respect, and believe they are trustworthy. You are more likely to trust someone if you see that person as predictable, and as someone you can depend upon. You need to be able to have faith that someone will be responsible and caring.

4. *How do similarity in attitudes, familiarity with people, living close to them, physical attractiveness, and the exchange of social rewards affect whether you will like another person?* The perception of someone having similar attitudes to yours is important in the initial stages of a relationship. Later on, differences in beliefs and being able to tolerate such differences become important. In addition, just being familiar with another person as well as living relatively close to that person increases your chances of liking him or her. Physical attractiveness is something that both sexes claim is important for liking someone. Typically, people are likely to find someone to date and marry who is similar to themselves in physical appearance. Finally, the exchange of social rewards with others enhances satisfaction. You are likely to stay in relationships only when the rewards exceed the costs beyond some minimum payoff that you find attractive.

5. *Are you aware of how some personal characteristics, including shyness, can make it difficult to interact with others?* Personal characteristics such as becoming depressed, lacking a sense of humor, and having few outside interests and hobbies play a role in people experiencing difficulties in forming relationships. Shyness is another quality that might produce problems for some people. People who are shy tend to be highly self-conscious and awkward in social situations. While it sometimes is a problem, it is also a quiet quality that many people may appreciate.

6. *How do stereotypes and prejudices interfere with your interactions?* Stereotypes are rigid beliefs that you might have towards other people. They are mental shortcuts that help you to categorize others into particular groups. Problems are likely to develop, however, if you ignore the individual differences that exist among members of a group. A prejudice is an attitude that has rigid beliefs and strong feelings towards another person. Both negative stereotypes and prejudices may lead someone to categorize people unfairly and initiate actions in which you might engage in discrimination. Both stereotypes and prejudices may lead someone to justify unfair actions and to keep others in a one-down position.

7. *Why is self-disclosure important to forming close relationships?* Those who share their ideas, interests, and feelings generally have more friends and develop long-lasting relationships. Self-disclosure fosters intimacy and trust, and, in turn, the intimacy and trust encourages more self-disclosure. Males adhering to traditional sex roles tend to have more problems self-disclosing than do women. While important, the advantages of self-disclosure appear to lie somewhere between not talking about yourself and doing it too much.

8. *Do you know the characteristics of love, the ingredients that comprise different types of love, and the different styles of loving people engage in?* Adults in love often become attached to others in a secure, avoidant, or anxious-ambivalent style. Several varieties of love develop from the degree to which ingredients of intimacy, commitment, and passion are present. People appear to adopt a number of styles of loving that are described as practical, game-playing, passionate, friendship, unselfish, and possessive.

9. *How do envy and jealousy affect your relationships?* Envy is a desire to acquire something that another person possesses. Envy leads to feelings of unhappiness, anxiety, and inferiority. Sometimes envy can be motivational and get people to take the actions needed to obtain what they desire. Jealousy, on the other hand, is a fear of losing something to which we have become attached. When jealous, people experience multiple emotions, including sadness, fear and anxiety, and, most of all, anger. Jealousy is often used to gain power and control over others, to release emotional tension, and to legitimize retaliation.

10. *How do important qualities of loneliness appear in your life?* Loneliness is a sign that our ability to connect and remain attached to others is in trouble. When lonely, people often report feeling depressed, alienated, and different from others. Most individuals feel lonely when there is a mismatch between their actual social contacts and what is desired.

11. *What causes relationships to break up, and what are actions you might take to ease the pain of a separation?* Most people list boredom as the major cause of a separation. Differences in attitudes and interests as well as conflicts over the roles each partner should play also contribute to dissatisfaction. How people communicate also is important. Relationships in which each partner avoids discussing issues and withdraws from conversations and in which angry encounters are prevalent tend to break up much more frequently. Seeking support groups, following the advice of someone who has been through a separation, and not putting oneself down help when someone deals with the stress of separation.

## Things to Do

1. Review the themes that appear in relationships that are described in Table 8.1. Think about two friendships or close relationships you have with other people. Which themes are you currently dealing with? Which one or more have you dealt with in the past? What are some things you have had to deal with that are not reflected in this table?

2. Watch your favorite soap opera or dramatic series on television. Which one or more of the styles of loving described in the text appear to be present in the lives of the characters? Do conflicts portrayed between characters reflect incompatible differences in their styles of loving?

3. List each of the barriers to forming close relationships discussed in the text and give a brief explanation of how each one has affected your life during the past two to four years. Which one of the barriers produced the most problems for you? What did you do to overcome it?

4. Stereotypes and prejudiced attitudes are among factors that distort our judgments about other people. To begin to understand such beliefs and how they affect you, do the following. For each of the following groups, answer the questions listed below: (a) men, (b) women, (c) Mexican-Americans, (d) black people, and (e) white people. How are members of each group portrayed in the movies, on television shows, and in newspaper and magazine advertisements? For each group, list three to four adjectives, short phrases, or other descriptors that appear to represent stereotypes or prejudices. In what ways are such characteristics accurate? Inaccurate? How are the actions of other people towards members of each group influenced by such labels? What would have to happen for the stereotypes and prejudices to change? What factors in daily life prevent such beliefs from changing?

5. How are the emotions of close relationships (love, envy, jealousy, loneliness) dealt with in popular music? List three to four songs that deal with such themes. How does the songwriter see the role of each emotion in people's lives? Are these emotions exaggerated in such songs, or do you think the role they play in people's lives are shown in a realistic fashion? If you wrote a popular tune about one of these emotions, what would the first four to five lines of your song say?

6. Pretend that the government has just declared that shyness is a "social disease" and declared a "war on shyness." What techniques could be used to eliminate shyness on a mass scale? What might happen to shy individuals that you know? How much better or worse off, would the world be if shyness could be eliminated?

7. Sometimes people "collude in their own craziness." That is, they do things that make things worse for themselves. Based on your experiences, what are three to four things that people say, do, or fail to say or do that contribute to problems in their interpersonal relationships?

## APPLIED ACTIVITIES

EXERCISE 8.1

### A Process for Practicing the SOFTEN Technique

As with any new technique you would like to try, it is important to be familiar with it before trying it out. The ideas listed below for practicing the SOFTEN technique can help you to integrate it better into your life-style.

### Part A: Becoming Familiar with the Process

1. Take a break for five or ten minutes. Make yourself comfortable. You might want to sit in a comfortable chair or to lie down. Close your eyes, breathe softly, and try to relax. Imagine yourself meeting a person you consider to be a good friend. Think about discussing something that the two of you will find exciting. Imagine yourself talking. What are you saying? How is your friend responding?
2. As you talk, think about yourself using the nonverbal cues in the word SOFTEN. To do this, pick one of the cues that interests you most. Imagine yourself using it as you talk with your friend. After using it several times, pick another one of the nonverbal cues in the SOFTEN formula. Gradually introduce each cue; one at a time seems to work best. Resist the temptation to use all of them at once. Your goal during this part of the process is to become familiar with each one and to visualize how you might use it.

### Part B: Practicing by Yourself

1. Having practiced in your imagination, try this part of the activity the next time you have a full-length mirror handy. Stand in front of the mirror. Relax and again imagine that you are talking to your friend. Practice each of the nonverbal cues in SOFTEN as you carry on a conversation with yourself in the mirror.
2. Try to be natural and not to overuse any one cue. Again, gradually introduce each cue, and try not to use all of them at once.

### Part C: Practicing with Others

1. When you feel at ease with each cue from practicing in your imagination or in front of a mirror, begin to use them in your everyday conversations. Do not use all of them at once. Do not do too much at once. Use only one cue, and do so until you feel you can use it well. Only then should you try another one.
2. Begin to use each cue in conversations with people you know fairly well and with whom you are comfortable. After you are at ease doing this, consider using them with new people who enter your life.
3. Pay attention to how people respond to you when you SOFTEN. What advantages do you observe? What disadvantages? Always look for ways to correct what you are doing.

EXERCISE 8.2

**Sharing Your Interests and Ideas**

For each of the statements and topics listed, think of one or two things that you know them that you have not openly shared with an acquaintance, friend, or relative. Write them in the space provided. In your next conversation with someone, use the information to initiate a conversation and to help to keep the conversation moving along.

1. Something that you liked or disliked about a movie, television show, or book that you have experienced in the past four weeks

2. Your favorite hobby or pastime

3. An interesting person whom you have met during the past three months

4. An exciting event that occurred to you in school this year

5. An idea or thought that you have about how to make the world a better place to live in

6. An important event in your life that occurred during the past six weeks

7. An important event in your life that occurred during the last two years

8. Something that makes you afraid

EXERCISE 8.3

**Determining Your Style of Loving**

Several styles of loving were discussed in the text. This activity is designed to help you obtain a general idea of your style and its advantages and disadvantages in the relationships you have.

**Part A:** The following descriptions are based on the research literature dealing with styles of loving. Based on those provided below, rank-order the extent to which you believe each style is typical of you on a scale from 1 to 6. *Do not focus on any one phrase or sentence in the description but try to determine how the description, as a whole applies to you.* Begin by assigning a 1 to the style that is most like you and a 6 to the style that is least like you. Then rank-order the remaining styles.

_____ *Practical Lover:* Tend to rely more on logic than feelings when selecting a partner. Want to obtain the best deal in a partner and to have someone who has a background that is very similar to mine. Do take an idealistic approach to relationships and basically want someone, who will reflect well on me.

_____ *Game-Playing Lover:* Want to minimize becoming committed to and dependent upon another person. Not all that interested in getting tied down to any one person. My goal is to have a variety of partners and a good time. Enjoy the excitement and challenges of having many different partners and am sometimes guilty of playing games to gain the interest and confidence of a partner.

_____ *Erotic Lover:* Good overall physical attractiveness in a partner is very important to me. I believe in love at first sight and tend to find that sexual relations and deep personal sharing come early in a relationship. While I tend to make an intense commitment at first, it is difficult to maintain that intensity over time.

_____ *Friendship Lover:* I tend to base my relationships on sharing, mutual understanding and respect, compassion, and a concern for others. My relationships tend to develop gradually and often with someone who was previously just a good friend. Love is more of a deep friendship than an intense emotional experience.

_____ *Unselfish Lover:* Tend to place the happiness and the best interest of my partner ahead of my own. I am usually very patient, understanding, and supportive of my partner. I also feel a sense of loyalty, duty, and obligation to the person that I love.

_____ *Possessive Lover:* I tend to become dependent upon another person and require lots of attention, affection, and togetherness. Want a lot of time with my partner and tend to get jealous very easily. Would rather have my partner spend time with me than with his or her friends or family members. Overall, I find it difficult to spend time apart from my partner.

**Part B:** Rank-order each style as you think your partner would, and answer the following questions.

- Look at the two styles that best describe you. What advantages and disadvantages do they have for you in your relationship with a partner?

- In what ways are your styles similar to and different from how you see your partner?

- How are the conflicts you and a partner have related to the differences among your styles?

- How would you rank-order the profile of an "ideal" partner. Why would this person be "ideal"?

## Key Terms

*Attachment styles.*  Ways that people tend to relate to others in adult intimate relationships. Such styles reflect ways people related to their parents in childhood.

*Commitment.*  An intent to maintain a relationship in spite of the difficulties and costs that may arise.

*Companionate love.*  Less intense than romantic or passionate love and represents the steady concern, attachment, and caring we feel toward another person.

*Discrimination.*  The actions people take to treat one group differently from another based upon certain stereotypes and prejudices. Such actions often exclude one group from privileges enjoyed by another.

*Envy.*  A desire to acquire something that another person possesses.

*Intimacy.*  The sense of warmth, closeness, and sharing in a relationship.

*Jealousy.*  Emotional reaction produced by our feeling excluded from the company of someone we like or when we are afraid that our partner prefers a third party to us.

*Liking.*  Emotion characterized by a positive attitude that we have toward another person. When we like others, we trust them, enjoy their company, and admire their qualities.

*Loneliness.*  Emotional reaction to periods of isolation from other people. It might occur through a lack of friendships or separation from people close to us. When lonely, people typically report they are unhappy, their lives are somewhat bleak, and they may not have much energy for doing things.

*Love.*  A feeling characterized by our attachment to another person. Love has components of caring, respecting, trying to understand, and responding to the needs of another person.

*Passion.*  The intense sexual and erotic desire for another person.

*Prejudices.*  Strong beliefs about a person or persons that contain rigid views of what they are like and either strong positive or negative feelings. To hate teachers because they are out to get students, whites because they are untrustworthy, or women because they are undependable are examples of prejudices.

*Prejudiced attitude.*  An attitude that has rigid beliefs and strong feelings about another person.

*Romantic love.*  An intense absorption with another person in which passion and wanting to be intimate are important components of the relationship.

*Shyness.*  A tendency to avoid contact with other people. This may occur because someone is afraid of contact with others or simply does not prefer to be around others. There are different degrees of shyness. Some people might be terrified of interaction, while others are a bit timid around other people.

*Stereotypes.*  Rigid beliefs about other people. The beliefs that students are lazy, men are aggressive, or that football players are dumb are examples of stereotypes.

# CHAPTER  9

# Managing Our Relationships with Others

### Chapter Overview

Functioning effectively in relationships takes hard work and skill in managing a number of issues. How to resolve conflicts in a constructive manner is one of the concerns with which we must deal. It is also important to learn how to resist the inappropriate influence of others and to get more of our needs met by becoming more assertive in our interactions. This chapter provides information about how the latter goals can be achieved.

### Chapter Organizers

*As you read, answer the questions that follow on a separate sheet of paper, and check your responses with those provided in the summary section.*

A challenge that everyone faces is how to manage conflict constructivly. One place to begin is by analyzing the underlying components of a dispute.

1. What functions does conflict serve in your relationships?
2. Are you aware of the arenas in which a dispute is acted out?
3. Can you identify six of the common causes of conflicts?
4. Once underway, do you know what helps to support and maintain a dispute?

A variety of strategies can be employed to resolve disputes among people.

5. What are eight conflict resolution strategies that you could use ?
6. How can you determine the "best" approach to take in a situation?

Our interactions typically involve people trying to influence the thoughts, feelings, and actions of another person.

7. What tactics are employed to influence you?
8. How can you counter the influence tactics that others employ?

In face-to-face encounters with others, it is important to communicate and to take actions that help you gain control in your interactions. Using components of assertive behaviors is often helpful in achieving such goals.

9. Do you know how to deliver unexpected messages to disarm attempts to manipulate you, to make requests appropriately, and to say "no" effectively?
10. What nonverbal messages can help you to become more assertive?
11. Are you aware of your interpersonal rights?
12. What role do giving and receiving feedback play in your interactions?

## When Harry Met Sally

In spite of their successes in life, Harry and Sally were a little lonely. That is, until one sunny afternoon while jogging in the park—Harry met Sally. He wasn't sure what attracted him to her, perhaps it was the sparkle in her eyes and the pleasant way she talked. Sally also wasn't sure what attracted Harry to her. "He's good looking," she thought. "And, he is very easy to talk to."

A date for lunch was arranged, then another one for dinner, and within a few weeks Harry and Sally were known among their friends as "an item." Six months later they were engaged, and plans for a wedding were made.

Except for a couple of "minor" little habits, they liked each other. Harry showed up 15 to 20 minutes late for almost everything they did together. And Sally took too much time to decide about what clothes to wear and what to do on weekends.

Love is blind, and while irritated at each other's bad habits, neither thought it was necessary to "rock the boat." In fact, Harry and Sally were rather smug about it all. Sally once told her best friend, "Once we get married, I know I can change some of his habits." Harry had similar thoughts and firmly believed that "our love for each other will help us take care of any problems that develop."

During the first year of marriage, each tried to ignore the other's irritating habits and to keep their anger bottled up. That is, until one day Harry picked Sally up 20 minutes late after work. She was having a bad day, and his tardiness was the last straw. "How dare you. . ." she shouted almost immediately after getting into the car. For the next 45 minutes, the dam burst. A steady stream of words criticized his ability to tell time and everything else about him that irritated her. "I felt it was my duty," Harry would later tell his friends, "to also let her know that she was hardly a saint. And after I finished," he said, "she didn't like it one bit!"

Both now saw the issue as just another example of "trying to control each other's life and not allowing one another any opportunities to express their unique qualities."

Sally walked out on Harry and drove to her mother's home. She then whipped both of her parents into a frenzy, and soon every relative within Ma Bell's reach was certain "Sally was right, and Harry was wrong." Harry, in self-defense, told members of his family, and of course, most were sympathetic to Harry's version. That's the one where Harry's a saint and Sally's a sinner. A few members of each family stopped talking to each other while others decided to stay out of the fray.

Harry and Sally's attorneys were determined to get the best deal they could for their clients. "She wants my shirt," Harry cried to his attorney, while Sally could never understand why Harry thought her little demands were so unreasonable.

After the divorce, Harry and Sally periodically had bouts of "self-pity" and berated themselves for "being so stupid to have gotten married to each other in the first place." They also lived with fears that they were somehow defective because the relationship failed and wondered if they could ever remarry successfully.

———
Based upon an actual case history.

## *DEVELOPING EFFECTIVE RELATIONSHIP SKILLS*

### Dealing with Conflict

**Conflict** is the tension, frustration, and anger that occur when the actions, beliefs, motives, or goals of two or more people are incompatible. *This incompatibility might be real, and/or it can result from a misperception on the part of one or more parties.* In the case history above, Harry's behavior of showing up late was incompatible with Sally's goal of wanting to be on time. Similarly, Sally's indecisiveness was incompatible with Harry's belief that people should make quick decisions. In both cases, there was an objective reality to being late and indecisive. On the other hand, their perceptions of each other's actions and their importance were probably exaggerated.

Conflict is a very pervasive part of our everyday life. Unfortunately, too many people believe that conflict should be avoided at any cost or that it serves no useful purpose. If conflict did not serve a purpose, it most likely would have disappeared from our interactions eons ago. For better or for worse, disagreements and the negative feelings that usually follow are a natural part of spending time with another person.

Each of us faces the challenge of how to manage disputes constructively. To accomplish the latter goal, it is important to go beyond the events that are normally defined as "the conflict." A friend recently described how she and her boyfriend argued in a video store over which one of two movies to rent for the evening. The dispute she identified was something called "what videotape to rent."

"If that was the case," I asked, "then why didn't you just flip a coin."

"That wouldn't have worked," she quickly replied. "He's always getting his way in this relationship, and I was not going to give in to him again."

The conversation quickly confirmed something very important about interpersonal disputes. That is, focusing on a specific event provides only a partial understanding of the conflict. After all, would Harry and Sally agree that their conflict began when Harry showed up 20 minutes late to pick her up after work? Most disputes involve more than a single event, and often they have multiple layers. A precipitating event might represent the "straw that broke the camel's back." Perhaps it was the most recent

in a series of similar incidents. Inevitably in ongoing relationships—much more is involved. Thus, before specific strategies for managing a conflict are selected, it is important to "look before we leap" and examine underlying components of conflict. (Grasha, 1991).

## ANALYZING THE UNDERLYING COMPONENTS OF A CONFLICT

### Conflict Serves Several Functions

*Acts as an Early Warning Device* Conflicts alert us to problems in a relationship. They should not be ignored or put aside in the mistaken belief that "things will magically get better." They usually don't. Both Harry and Sally, for example, placed their concerns on a back burner and thought they could wait until after they were married.

*Serves as a Pressure Release Valve* Tensions build in relationships, and when kept within people, the anger becomes dysfunctional. Thus, some release of this tension is needed. Carol Tavris (1982), however, notes that simply releasing frustration and anger is unlikely to help. Typically, and as the case of Harry and Sally illustrates, such displays make things worse rather than better.

*Mobilizes Energy to Deal with Issues* When a dispute produces unacceptable levels of tension, people usually want to deal with it. Sometimes, the issues are brought into the open, and both parties work to find an acceptable solution. Or, as the case of Harry and Sally illustrates, there are times when ineffective courses of action are taken. This is more likely to occur when each party "blames the other for causing the problem" or when each party stubbornly tries to "win" the argument and refuses to compromise.

*Forces People to Examine and Renegotiate Existing Physical and Psychological Boundaries* New ways of relating to each other are often established. Two married friends used to argue over "whose job was more important." One day they grew weary about arguing over this issue and decided to do something about it. They now share household chores and cooperate in taking care of their son. Now when their son is sick, they alternate periods of time to stay home to watch him. As Harry and Sally's case illustrates, however, a restructuring of the relationship is not always positive. They decided to occupy different physical spaces and to communicate through their attorneys.

### Conflicts Occur Within and Across Several Arenas

*The tension a dispute produces and the time and energy spent trying to resolve a conflict occur within three arenas—the intrapersonal, interpersonal, and intergroup* (Pneuman and Bruehl, 1982; Walton, 1987). This is illustrated in Figure 9.1.

A dispute's intrapersonal arena encompasses the personal tension, and frustration within one or both parties. We are often well aware of this tension, and it is difficult to avoid thinking about what is bothering us. Susan Heitler (1990) reports that intrapersonal conflicts can be experienced in one or more of the following ways:

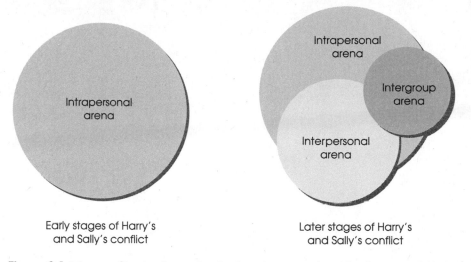

Early stages of Harry's
and Sally's conflict

Later stages of Harry's
and Sally's conflict

*Figure 9.1* *Many conflicts involve overlapping boundaries or arenas. The degree to which they overlap varies among disputes and the point in time at which the conflict is examined. Early on, Harry and Sally's conflict mostly occurred within their intrapersonal arenas. They kept things to themselves and did not involve each other or other people. After it escalated, all three arenas were involved to different degrees in the dispute. The overlap in the circles symbolizes the involvement of each arena. The relative size of each circle symbolizes how much time and energy, relatively speaking, was spent dealing with the tension and frustration the dispute produced within a given arena (based on Grasha, 1991).*

- Feeling depressed, anxious, angry, frustrated, guilty, or ashamed.
- Engaging in self-criticism.
- Focusing on the qualities we dislike in others but failing to recognize that we often possess the very same qualities we dislike in others. Such blame allows us to ignore our own deficiencies and/or contributions to a problem.
- Trying to stop thinking about the situation that bothers us.
- Trying to think about other things to take our minds off the current conflict.
- Denying that the problem is really all that bad.
- Doing nothing and hoping that the problem will go away.
- Trying to block out or dull the bad feelings by using alcohol, drugs, by eating snack foods or by overeating.

As the case of Harry and Sally illustrates, our inner tensions may be kept bottled up for a period of time, but they eventually leak into the interpersonal arena. Once they emerge, someone usually gets "blamed for the problem," arguments emerge, and people may try to make others feel guilty about causing the problem. It is not unusual to see fights or physical abuse as one party tries to dominate the other. Or one person may simply "nag" another until he or she gives in to their demands. Some people also try to get even by becoming passive-aggressive, or one or more parties decide to stop talking to one another.

As the conflict escalates, friends, neighbors, or other groups of people in the intergroup arena become involved. Coalitions of interested parties may even begin to form. They may offer advice and support to each party or otherwise become actively involved in the conflict. In the case of Harry or Sally, members of their families and subsequently their attorneys become immersed in the intergroup aspects of this conflict.

### The Severity of a Conflict Is Related to Two Things

1. *The number of arenas the conflict spans.* Conflicts that span the three arenas are much more severe than one that is largely contained to a given arena. Thus, as long as Harry and Sally kept things to themselves, the conflict was much more manageable. Once it got out into the relationship and other groups and was not handled well— things got out of hand.

2. *Within each arena the number of issues, people, and groups that are involved.* A person with four troubling thoughts on his or her mind will experience more tension than someone with one. Similarly, two people arguing about three things are likely to experience more tension than a couple trying to handle a single concern. As the number of people and groups involved escalates, so does the overall tension in a situation.

### Attempts to Resolve a Conflict Must Answer Two Questions

1. *Is the time and energy I am using to deal with the tension focused* on the proper arena? Both Harry and Sally, for example, kept their tension within their intrapersonal boundaries for a long period of time. They essentially covered up how they really felt. When their frustration erupted, very little time was spent in the interpersonal arena discussing the issues with each other. Instead, they tried to mobilize family members to "see things their way" and hired attorneys as allies to support their efforts to break up. Consequently, their attempts to manage the tension were misplaced.

2. *Does a resolution apply to each of the arenas?* Conflicts that get played out in several arenas are only resolved if the tension within each arena is resolved. Harry and Sally tried to settle their differences by getting divorced. In effect, the display of the conflict in the interpersonal area was subdued. Little attention was given to smoothing things over with their families or within themselves. The intergroup and in particular the intrapersonal arenas were ignored. They continued to suffer bouts of self-pity and berated themselves for having gotten married in the first place. They were not at peace with themselves. Each would have to work through their internal feelings before we could consider this dispute completely resolved.

## A Number of Factors Can Cause a Conflict to Occur

*Differences in Values* Values represent the important and stable beliefs that underlie our behaviors across a number of different situations in our lives. People may value beauty, independence, control, equality, or any number of other things. Because they represent ideals or desirable qualities, most of us try to model what we value in our actions.

Similar values are one of the factors that draw people together. On the other hand, when they differ, conflicts may occur. Thomas Gordon (1976) uses the term **value collision** to describe situations in which different values produce tension, frustration, or anger in a relationship. A teenager, for example, might not directly tell her mother, "I want to be independent and autonomous of you." And her mother probably would not reply with, "I don't care, I just want to control your actions and keep you dependent upon me." Instead, a conflict based on such values might be played out in arguments about curfews, the acceptability of the friends the daughter keeps, or when homework and school assignments are going to be completed.

*Expectations Are Violated*   Each party to a relationship has expectations for how the other person should behave. Conflicts often occur when certain expectations are violated. A student in one of my classes reported how she and her boyfriend got into an argument. They had agreed not to date other people, but she discovered him cheating on her.

*Unfortunately, expectations are not always explicitly shared, and what is violated are unstated assumptions about how people should act.* Consequently, conflict and anger develop, and at least one partner begins to feel used or betrayed. Among married and unmarried couples living together, concerns about spending money, work, household responsibilities, and sex lead to conflicts (Blumstein and Schwartz, 1983). These authors report that people seldom share their expectations about such things. Instead, they can be heard saying, "My partner should know what I want and how I would feel about certain things."

*Struggles for Power, Control, and Authority*   Sometimes disagreements occur over who is the more dominant or high-status person in the relationship. In effect, people struggle to maintain a "pecking order" or to establish a new one. A neighbor and his wife used to argue over who would take the garbage out for the weekly trash pickup. Alternating weeks, flipping coins, and talking about whose turn it was seldom worked. They entered therapy to work on a variety of relationship problems and soon discovered the conflict had little to do with turn-taking. Each viewed the task as demeaning. Consequently, neither wanted to be the "garbage person in the relationship." This conflict was about the "pecking order" in their marriage, with neither partner wanting to take a step down. Dealing with garbage was a task for a low-status person .

*Disagreements over Goals, Methods to Achieve Them, and How to Allocate Resources*
*There are three ways this typically happens.*

1. *Everyone does not always agree on what goals to pursue.* One partner wants to plan a wedding as soon as possible, while the other just wants to continue living together. Business partners may disagree on what new products and services to develop. A graduate student and her thesis advisor might differ on what specific research project to pursue.

2. *People may disagree on the methods used to achieve various goals.* Two business partners I knew argued about the best way to advertise a new product. One wanted to use direct mail advertising, while the other favored radio and newspaper ads. A colleague and one of her graduate students disagreed about the best method to use in gathering information about child abuse. The student favored a questionnaire, while her advisor thought that interviews would be better.

3. *Disagreements may occur about how to allocate resources.* Married couples, for example, fight about money more often than any other issue. The arguments typically involve *how money should be spent* rather than how much money each partner possesses (Blumstein and Schwartz, 1983).

*The Roles People Play Begin to Clash*   Did you ever think of yourself as an actor? You may not have starred in a play, but one way to view our daily interactions is to view our environment as a stage, with each of us playing different parts. The parts we play are called **roles.**

*During a day, people adopt multiple roles.* Individuals in my classes are students, brothers, sisters, mothers, fathers, and members of various occupational groups. I am a husband, teacher, researcher, father, consultant, writer, advisor, and president of a swim team. Roles allow us to structure our relationships with other people and prescribe certain guidelines for how to behave.

**Role conflicts** arise when difficult choices about how to behave in particular roles must be made. This can occur in three ways:

1. *We have more than one role relationship to a person or group.* A good friend found herself in a rather awkward situation. Her daughter was a member of the soccer team she coached and was misbehaving and not playing very hard in practice. Her dilemma was whether to discipline the child in her role as a parent or as a coach.

2. *People disagree on how a role other than their own should be played.* In one of my recent classes, a student became frustrated. He was angry at his best friend for talking about him behind his back. His father advised him to sever the relationship; his mother said he should try to work things out immediately; and his favorite teacher suggested waiting a couple of weeks for things to cool down before discussing the problem.

3. *Other people decide to play their roles in ways that are incompatible with our own.* Normally, the roles of husband-wife, brother-sister, student-teacher, and player-coach complement each other. Sometimes the roles become incompatible because people define them differently.

   - A basketball player was recently suspended from our university's basketball team. During practice, he decided to tell the coach how the offense "should be run."
   - A colleague and his wife divorced after 15 years of marriage. She told him that being a "traditional wife who stays home and takes care of the house and children is not what I want out of life anymore." He was not able to handle this new definition of her role.

   Table 9.1 illustrates how role conflicts can occur in a classroom.

*Boundary and Territory Violations* All creatures on this planet defend various boundaries and territories. Such boundaries can be psychological. People become angry at those who try to violate their intimate and personal space zones (cf. Chapter 7). Tangible and physical boundaries and territories also can be involved as the situations cited below illustrate. *What are some examples from your life?*

- One of my students and her sister got into a fight because "she keeps going into my closet and dresser drawers to find clothes of mine to wear."
- My brother-in-law and a neighbor have gone to court. The neighbor, without consulting my brother-in-law, had a tree cut down that rested on the line that divided their property. "I always thought of it as my tree," the neighbor said when asked why the tree was cut down.
- A friend gets mad at her boyfriend because "he keeps leaving his junk lying around my kitchen."
- A client became angry at a former business partner. "He took everything he learned from me, is starting a similar business, and is trying to steal my customers away."

## Several Factors Support and Maintain a Conflict

*Using Interpersonal Styles for Resolving Conflict Ineffectively* Figure 9.2 illustrates several **conflict resolution styles,** or preferences for dealing with others in a conflict. When overused or applied inappropriately, several of them tend to hinder finding mutually acceptable solutions. In effect, their use may support and maintain a dispute (Pruitt and Rubin, 1986; Thomas, 1992).

1. *Avoidance.* Such individuals typically avoid issues and hope they will go away. They usually do not try to have their needs met, nor do they cooperate in helping the other person. What usually happens, however, is that the situation gets worse because of the inattention. *Best used as a temporary measure to buy time, to think about things, and to figure out what to do next.*

2. *Accommodation.* The underlying attitude is "OK, I'll do it your way." While this tactic may get another person off your back, it also fails to address the underlying concerns. The person who accommodates may in time become frustrated and wonder, "When will I get some of my needs met?" *Best used occasionally to repay a favor, when the issue is not worth spending time and energy on or you want to get someone you don't have an ongoing relationship with off your back.*

3. *Competition.* One party tries to dictate solutions or attempts to overpower the opposition. A successful competitor does not allow others to have their needs met. Thus, a considerable amount of tension and frustration may ensue in the aftermath of such efforts. Those who lose are seldom gracious, and the competitor may find that their loyalty, trust, and willingness to cooperate wanes. *Best used infrequently only after other options have been exhausted. Even then, the "winner" must be strong enough to make a dictated solution stick and to handle the inevitable fallout.*

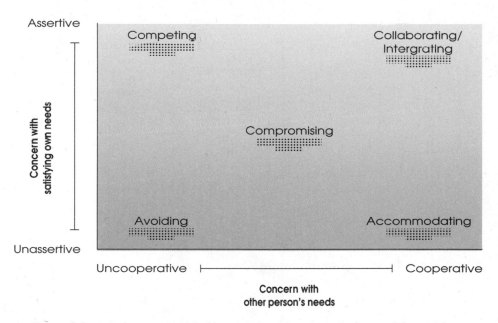

**Figure 9.2** *A dual-concern model of how people tend to approach disputes. The model assumes that individuals differ in terms of their concerns with meeting their own needs and those of other people. Various ways of trying to resolve conflicts occur depending upon how such concerns are met (Pruitt and Rubin, 1986; Thomas, 1992).*

**Table 9.1**  Role Conflicts in the College Classroom

Several ways college student and teacher roles can be interpreted are illustrated below (Fuhrmann and Grasha, 1983; Grasha, 1994). People are relatively more comfortable emphasizing some aspects of their roles more than others. *Conflict typically occurs when the demands of a situation force someone to switch from a comfortable mode.* Thus, a student who prefers a more dependent and competitive orientation will resist someone who emphasizes a facilitative or delegative style. An expert and formal-authority-oriented teacher may experience difficulties dealing with highly independent and collaborative students.

| STUDENT LEARNING STYLES | TEACHING STYLES |
|---|---|
| *Competitive:* Learns classroom material in order to perform better than others in the class. They feel they must compete for the rewards of the classroom, such as good grades or the teacher's attention. | *Expert:* Strives to maintain status as an expert by displaying detailed knowledge. Concerned with transmitting information to students and ensuring that they are well prepared. |
| *Collaborative:* Wants to learn by sharing ideas and talents. Cooperates and works well with teachers and peers. | *Formal Authority:* Concerned with providing positive and negative feedback, establishing learning goals, |

*Avoidant:* Does not participate with students and teachers in the classroom. Generally uninterested or overwhelmed by what occurs in classes.

*Participant:* Tries to meet any reasonable request of the instructor. Takes part in as much of class-related activity as possible and does little that is not part of the course outline.

*Dependent:* Shows little intellectual curiosity and learns only what is required. Relies on the teacher for guidance about how to do things.

*Independent:* Like to think for themselves, are confident in their abilities as learners, and prefer to work on their own.

expectations, and rules of conduct. Tries to maintain the correct or acceptable ways to do things.

*Personal Model:* Believes in "teaching by example." Shows students how to do things by encouraging them to "observe" and then to "emulate" the instructor's approach.

*Facilitator:* Guides and directs students by asking questions, exploring options, suggesting alternatives, and encouraging students to make informed choices.

*Delegator:* Emphasizes students working in an autonomous fashion either independently or in teams. Acts as a resource person to answer questions and to review progress.

*The Presence of "Hot Cognitions"* Ellen Siegelman (1983) labels thoughts and beliefs that help to maintain and support disputes "hot cognitions." She says they have the same effect as adding wood and gasoline to an open fire. Such beliefs stoke up the intensity of the "fire" or conflict. Examples include:

- *Thinking the worst about another person.* "Because of what she said to me, I can't trust her anymore." "Based on what he did to me, he's no better than the scum of the earth."
- *Personalizing what someone said.* "He said my school's football team sucks. Nobody gets away with talking about my school that way."
- *Blaming the other person for the dispute.* "If she hadn't screamed at me for no reason at all, I wouldn't have called her those names."
- *Thinking about retaliation rather than seeking a solution.* "There will be plenty of time to talk after I get even with him for what he did to me." "I don't give a hoot if this is settled. I just want to get back at her."

*Personal Collusion in Allowing the Conflict to Continue* All too often, people collude in keeping a dispute alive. *What they say or do and what they fail to say and do affects the course of a dispute.*

Two things contribute to this problem. *One is a tendency for someone to view him or herself as a neutral bystander in a dispute.* Here, one person typically waits around for others to "admit they were wrong" or to "do something about the mess they got us into." Disputes, however, usually develop out of successive instances of reactions and counter-reactions with both parties participating. *Second, one or both parties persist in employing ineffective thoughts and behaviors.* Someone who continues to "blame the other party for the problem" or who proceeds to use an "avoidant style" is, in effect, helping to support and maintain the dispute.

# CONFLICT RESOLUTION STRATEGIES

## Prevention—"A Stitch in Time Saves Nine"

An automobile preventive maintenance program encourages us to check and maintain the oil, fluid levels, tire pressure, and other parts so that major problems are less likely to occur. The same principle can be applied to interpersonal disputes. Jeanne Brett (1990) and her colleagues report that prevention is often an overlooked strategy. She states that it is much better to identify conditions that lead to problems and to take care of them before they erupt into a major issue. To accomplish the latter goal, she suggests that people discuss issues that may cause disputes beforehand and to try and learn from those that do occur. A list of "lessons learned" can be generated from any conflict that could help us in the future.

Several "lessons learned" for preventing conflict, from my experiences working with people, are presented in Figure 9.3. *What would you add to this list?*

*ACBD: Always Consult Before Deciding.* Avoid the temptation to take matters into your own hands in order to "save time" or because "no one will really mind anyway." Whenever possible, consult with people who are likely to be affected by a decision you want to make.

* *Fix the Problem and Not the Blame.* In working with someone, things will sometimes go wrong. Treat what happened as a problem to be solved and not as an opportunity to enter a dispute with another person

* *Instead of Becoming Defensive, Ask What's Right About What Someone Is Saying that May Be Critical of You.* It's easy to become defensive when someone does not appreciate us in some way. It is also natural and understandable to discount or ignore what they are saying. In both cases, we miss an opportunity to obtain a different perspective that may help us in the future. Use what someone says not as an opportunity to "fly off the handle," but as a chance to learn something new about yourself.

* *Count to Ten or Ten Thousand.* Whenever possible, don't react immediately to something that might cause a dispute. First distance yourself from your natural impulses and emotions. Remove yourself physically or psychologically from a situation in order to buy time to think about it. Use this time to prepare a response that has the potential to be constructive rather than destructive.

* *Take Time to Process the Things You Do with Others.* Talk to others about how tasks were accomplished, what went well and not so well, and things that need to be done differently in the future. Share expectations and make commitments for how you want to behave in the future. Such discussions often identify issues that, if left unattended, can get in the way.

*Don't Get Mad — Don't Get Even; Work to Get What You Want.* Keep your mind on what you want to accomplish. Ask yourself, "What do I really want out of this situation, and what is the most constructive thing I can do to get it?"

**Figure 9.3** *Suggestions for Preventing Disputes.*

## Take Early Action—"Nip a Conflict in the Bud"

Of course, disputes cannot always be prevented. Once they emerge, however, they are like many medical problems. The earlier they are detected and treated, the easier they are to manage. Unfortunately, conflicts are sometimes recognized, but people allow them to simmer. Like water kept in a teapot over low heat—disputes eventually begin to boil over. *This happens because over time, the issues may move from specific situations in which something was said or done to becoming a matter of principle or value.* People dig in, and their positions harden. When conflicts reach the level of "this is a matter of principle" or "this is something I really value," they become much harder to resolve. Harry and Sally might have had more success, for example, talking about specific instances of tardiness and indecisiveness early in their relationship. They waited, and the situation became a matter of principle in which each person was "trying to control the other's life and not allowing each other the opportunity to express their unique qualities."

## Using Power—"Determine Who Is the Biggest Kid on the Block"

*This is a power-based approach to resolving issues and involves a "win-lose" mentality for settling differences.* Here, the strongest party prevails and dictates his or her solution to others. Resorting to such tactics appears, on the surface, to be a fast and decisive way to settle an issue. In reality, it is neither. Typically, one party tries to gain the upper hand, and the other resists. Verbal and physical fights might break out, and the conflict persists until one side "gives in."

Even in cases in which one party is in a position to dictate a solution or to eventually "overpower" or "wear out" the opposition, losers are seldom charitable. They often take a position of, "Wait till next time," "I won't forget how you treated me," or, "I can't wait to get even." In the meantime, they resent what happened to them and may engage in passive aggressive behaviors in order to irritate the "winner." Those on the receiving end of such attacks typically view the other party as less competent in managing conflict (Canary and Spitzberg, 1990). Consequently, they do not give in easily to actions they consider inappropriate and ineffective.

A friend once used his authority to reorganize the secretarial staff in his company into a secretarial pool. The managers under him argued that the change lowered their status and made them work less effectively. The secretaries resented losing control over how they managed their work and thought the secretarial pool was too impersonal. In spite of such opposition, he told everyone, "I'm in charge here, you work for me, and you'll do what I ask." Morale and productivity quickly declined. Two of his best managers and three of the secretaries left the company. The number of errors in documents increased; customer orders were not processed as quickly; and complaints about working conditions multiplied.

The popularity of a *"win-lose"* approach to conflict is in part due to a lack of information and skill for how to resolve issues in other ways. Also, it is due to a cultural preference for competitive modes of resolving differences (Kohn, 1986). Most of us grew up playing games in which the object was to "beat the opposition." The news media are filled with reports of wars, strikes, "unfriendly corporate takeovers," and other examples of "win-lose" approaches to resolving differences. In such an atmosphere, we simply gain little experience and have little access to role models for settling disputes in other ways.

In spite of such problems, what do you do if you still think you must fight? Ian Gotlib and Catherine Colby (1988) offer some advice in Focus on Applied Research 9.1. They argue that there are ways to fight fairly.

## How to Have a Good Quarrel

Based on their experiences in helping couples to manage their differences, Ian Gotlib and Catherine Colby (1988) have identified suggestions for "fighting fairly."

### Avoid

- Evading the argument, giving the silent treatment, or walking out.
- Bringing in unrelated issues from current or past situations.
- Pretending to agree while harboring resentment.
- Attacking indirectly by criticizing someone or something the other party values.
- Using your knowledge of the other person to hit below the belt and humiliate him or her.
- Telling the other person how he or she is thinking and feeling.

### Do

- Acknowledge their viewpoint. Define the issues, and put the other person's positions in your own words.
- Keep the conversation focused on the "here and now" and not the "there and then."
- Strive to clarify where you agree and disagree and what matters most to each of you.
- Try not to feel obligated to counter the other person's anger with a direct or indirect display of your own.
- Respect the other person, and do not underestimate his or her capacity to want to find a mutually agreeable solution.
- Seek to understand the positions of the other person. Ask questions that help him or her to find words to express their concerns.

## Conciliation—"Display a Little True Grit"

Charles Osgood (1980) developed an approach to managing conflict that was conciliatory rather than retaliatory. He believed it was strong enough to discourage people from exploiting each other and to signify the determination it requires—he labeled it GRIT (*G*raduated and *R*eciprocated *I*nitiatives in *T*ension reduction). This process has been applied to a variety of interpersonal and intergroup conflicts.

To apply the GRIT process, one party takes some initiative and announces his or her intentions to reduce tensions. The words are then backed up by one or more small conciliatory acts. This modest beginning opens the door for reciprocation by the other party. If a positive gesture occurs, further positive gestures are made by the side initiating the process. If a negative gesture occurs, a negative response is then given in return. This negative reaction should not be an overreaction but one that signifies "I am serious about solving this problem, but I will not be taken advantage of." GRIT is essentially a strategy of "I've just scratched your back; now it's your turn to scratch mine." Presumably, by scratching each other's backs, people and groups begin to soften their negative attitudes and feelings towards each other. Morton Deutsch (1991) notes that it works best when both sides are "firm," "fair," and "friendly" towards each other.

This technique is based on the premise that the continuing escalation of tension and hostility only impedes the resolution of differences. It also assumes that unconditional cooperation is naive and likely to invite one party to exploit the other. Thus, the turn-taking needed to make the GRIT strategy work is designed to reduce and eventually to reverse the level of hostility and negative feelings. This can be seen in the following example.

> One of my students used the GRIT strategy to break a deadlock in his relationship with his girlfriend. They broke up after a series of arguments about dating other people. They subsequently ignored each other in class, refused to speak to each other elsewhere on campus, and said nasty things about each other to their friends. Eventually, he decided to lessen tensions and sent her a note. In it he apologized for his behaviors and agreed to stop talking about her behind her back if she did likewise. He also said he would at least like to say "hello" to her on campus and hoped she would be cordial towards him. When they passed on campus the next day, he waved at her, and she smiled and then waved back. They exchanged a few pleasant words in class, and soon they were speaking to one another. They eventually decided to remain friends but not to date each other.

Research suggests that this strategy can be successful in breaking the deadlock that often occurs when a series of "win-lose" encounters prevail between two parties. Svenn Lindskold (1988) and his associates report that announcing cooperative intent tends to boost cooperation. Conciliatory acts, when consistently applied, also breed more trust and reduce the level of hostility. However, such effects appear only when both sides decide that "it's time to stop fighting and to settle our differences." The reduction in hostility and negative feelings then makes it possible for people to talk to one another. As long as one party sees an advantage to continuing the escalation, however, the GRIT approach is less likely to work.

## Identify the Rights of Each Party—"Play by the Rules of the Game"

*"Rights based strategies" rely on such things as shared expectations, policy statements, rules, standard operating procedures, and precedents as criteria to justify particular solutions to disputes. Such things are often a matter of public record or shared as part of the formal and informal* **norms** *people use for working together (Ury, Brett, and Goldberg, 1988). For example, a judge employs rules of law and legal precedents to determine how much of a settlement each party to a divorce is entitled to have. A referee in any sport uses the official rules of the game to settle disputes between coaches or players. The criteria set forth in a job description may be applied by a department head to settle any arguments about who to hire.*

The application of a *rights-based strategy* does not have to be done in a formal manner. *In many everyday relationships, previously agreed upon expectations also can be employed as criteria to help settle disputes.* My neighbor's two daughters decided to take turns cleaning up the family room. A few weeks later, a short argument over who cleans the room was settled when one of the sisters reminded the other of the agreement. Similarly, one of my students initially resisted allowing a roommate to use her car to go shopping. She consented when reminded that she had agreed to do it the night she borrowed her roommate's favorite dress. In order for expectations to help resolve disputes, they must be explicitly shared and developed.

### Three Conditions Are Needed for This Approach to Work

1. *Each party must recognize the expectations, policies, procedures, precedents, and rules as applicable to the dispute.*
2. *Someone must insist that such criteria be used.* One or more of the parties to the dispute might initiate such a request, and/or someone in authority might "order" or "demand" that applicable criteria be employed.
3. *The criteria should be applied impartially and fairly to the issues.*

A colleague was irritated that he had to teach a 240-student section of introductory psychology. "Why do I have to teach the introductory course this year?" he asked in a faculty meeting. "I think there are other people who should teach it before I do." Our department head replied by saying, "Two years ago at the faculty retreat you attended, we voted to require everyone to teach a large section on a rotating basis. So far, everyone has complied, and your turn comes up during the fall quarter." My colleague withdrew his objection.

## Compromise—"Split the Difference"

*In order to compromise, each party works together until some acceptable "middle ground" between two positions occurs (e.g., split the difference).** This may literally mean meeting the other party halfway or at some other point between two positions that is acceptable to each party (Pruitt and Rubin, 1986). Typically, this occurs after haggling over money, resources, or ways of doing something. In order to end or avoid a stalemate, both sides offer concessions that are mutually acceptable.

A compromise provides a resolution that is not as good as someone hoped nor as bad as they could have gotten. While some of us are comfortable with it, Dean Pruitt

---

* This definition follows a convention in the conflict literature. Giving up all or part of one's demands in exchange for concessions is not a compromise. The latter strategy often involves people trying to find ways to integrate their interests and needs, as in the mutual gains model discussed later on in this chapter.

and Jeffry Rubin (1986) report that compromising is sometimes seen as "giving in" or as "losing face." These authors also suggest that people may compromise for the wrong reasons. People fail to seek more creative solutions because they get hung up on "fairness"; they are tired of working on the issue; time for a solution is running out; their aspirations are low; or they fear the dispute will worsen. On the plus side, the trade-offs involved often work to the advantage of both parties.

## Seek Mutual Gains—"All for One and One for All"

Here both parties work together to find a solution that integrates each of their interests. This is called a **mutual gains** or a **win-win** approach to resolving differences. Roger Fisher (1981, 1988) and William Ury (1988) suggest several differences between a mutual gains model and other approaches.

1. Instead of "win-lose" or "splitting the difference," the primary goal is to find solutions that *integrate* each person's interests so that both "win."
2. People work to keep statements about who is "right" or "wrong," what is "fair" or "unfair," who "deserves more or less," or other positions out of the discussion.
3. Issues are decided on their merits rather than through a haggling process that focuses on what each side says it will or will not do in response to concessions by the other party.
4. Attempts are made to base solutions on fair standards independent of the naked will of the other side.

The philosophy behind a mutual gains strategy can be illustrated by the following case of two roommates who both wanted the last lemon in their refrigerator. In the first stage of their dispute, each claimed the lemon, and the conversation quickly developed into a "win-lose" argument.

Roommate #1: "I want the lemon, I grabbed it first."

Roommate #2: "No, that's unfair, I was just going to get it before you took it."

Roommate #1: "Ok, I'll give you a little piece of it."

Roommate #2: "You're being greedy; I want at least half of it."

Roommate #1: "There you go again, calling me names."

Roommate #2: "What do you expect me to say when you refuse to share."

You can probably see that if the conversation continued this way, the situation would deteriorate further. When people take positions and play out the dispute in a "win-lose" manner, bad feelings are likely to develop, and the competitive juices flow.

The lemon problem was resolved when one of the roommates asked a very simple but powerful question: *"What do you want the lemon for, anyway?"* As it turned out, they had different needs. One person wanted the rind for a dessert while the other needed juice for a glass of iced tea. A solution that allowed them to integrate both of their needs occurred when the conversation shifted from defending their positions to exploring their needs and interests.

*Work to Integrate Your Interests with Those of the Other Party. This is somewhat different from trying to compromise.* Attempts to compromise often assume a "fixed pie." That is, each of us has to give up a piece of the pie to resolve the issue. A compromise solution in the lemon problem would have been for each roommate to agree to take one-half of the lemon. In effect, they would split the "pie." *A mutual gains approach tries to help people find solutions without having to "split the pie."* There are four ways this can occur.

1. *Look for ways both parties can have their cake and eat it, too.* In effect, this is what occurred with the lemon. Each roommate was able to have the whole lemon available for her use. Remember the nursery rhyme: Jack Sprat could eat no fat/His wife could eat no lean/And so betwixt them /They licked the platter clean. A little creativity is called for here.

2. *Expand the pie.* Time, money, space, people, and other resources often are in short supply. Instead of trying to "divide up" existing resources, creative solutions can occur by trying to increase them. Two of my neighbors argued about where to spend their two weeks of paid vacation. She wanted to spend two weeks in the mountains, while he preferred two weeks at the seashore. A solution occurred when they got their employers to give them two additional weeks of unpaid vacation time.

3. *Trade off one interest in order to get another one met.* Here one party may give up on an interest in order to have another one met. A friend agreed to allow her husband to invest part of their savings in a real estate deal if he agreed to use some of the family resources to buy the new car she wanted.

4. *Find a bridge between your interests and those of the other person.* Here something that will link two sets of interests is sought. Couples in a video store do this all the time. One wants to watch a romantic drama, while the other prefers a comedy. A romantic comedy is selected. Or, when going out to eat on a family vacation, a restaurant is selected that is reasonably priced and where each member can order something he or she likes.

The components of a mutual gains process appear in Table 9.2. In order for it to work, active listening and other communication skills discussed in Chapter 7 also must be employed.

## Develop Superordinate Goals—"Let's Do Something Together"

There are times when a common or **superordinate goal** will assist in resolving a conflict. If groups or individuals can agree on a compelling goal to pursue together, past differences may attenuate, as illustrated in Focus on Applied Research 9.2. Working toward a common goal sometimes can establish a spirit of collaboration and understanding. *This good will can then be transferred to working on other problems.* A friend of mine and his neighbor used to argue over their property lines. One day his house caught fire,

**Table 9.2**     Components of a Mutual Gains Approach

*Both parties must be willing to collaborate and view the dispute as something for which each is responsible.*

> Gary: "I admit that I have not been very pleasant about what car to buy in the past. I'm not blaming you. This is a problem that we both have to work on."

> Tammy: "I also think that we need to quit blaming each other for the impasse."

*When necessary, try to separate people from the problem.* Try to keep past or current relationship issues separated from a current problem. *A suggestion is to focus on the immediate problem and not past differences.*

> Tammy: "I know you and I have argued about major purchases in the past, but I want to focus on what car to buy in our conversation and not bring up things from the past."

> Gary: "I agree that we should let bygones be bygones."

*Or, work on building a good relationship before trying to deal with substantive issues.* Resolve relationship issues first, and/or develop guidelines for how you want to relate to each other when discussing an issue.

*Agree to take a problem-solving approach to the situation.*

> Gary: "I'd like to treat this as something both of us have to solve."

> Tammy: "I'm Ok with that."

*The interests and needs of all concerned must be clearly stated.* Self-interest often lies behind most of the conflicting demands individuals make. Such things must be recognized as legitimate, and the discussion should focus on identifying such needs.

> Tammy: "I'd like a car that is easy to drive, that gets good gas mileage, and that we can use for the children's car pools and for running errands. I don't want to pay more than $15,000 for it."

> Gary: "I also want something that looks good, that has a little power, and that is roomy and comfortable for long trips. It would not bother me if we had to pay more than $15,000 for it."

*Invent possible solutions that would integrate each person's interests.* The goal is now to be inventive, to propose options, and not to commit to any one option at this time.

> Tammy: "I think a mid-sized car like a Buick Century, a Toyota Corolla, or a station wagon would work."

> Gary: "I think a full-sized car like a Pontiac Bonneville or a mid-sized van also could give us what we want."

*Make decisions by assessing possible solutions against objective criteria.* Insist that some fair standard (e.g., market value, expert opinion, past practices and customs, rules, laws) determine the outcome. *This standard should be independent of the naked will of either side.*

> Gary: "Could we use the ratings of new cars in *Consumer Reports* to help us pick the best option?"

> Tammy: "That's alright with me."

The *Consumer Reports* magazine evaluations of new vehicles were helpful. A mid-sized van was well rated, and it allowed the two of them to have their interests met.

## The Power of a Common Goal

In a classic study of conflict, Muzafer Sherif (1966) and his colleagues formed two separate groups of 11- and 12-year-old boys from those attending a summer camp. Each group worked independently preparing meals, camping out, and fixing up a swimming hole. They also were given different names—the "Rattlers" and the "Eagles." The staff then put the groups into conflict with each other through baseball games, tugs-of-war, treasure hunts, and other games. The competitive atmosphere of the games carried over into other areas of their lives. Other intergroup and interpersonal disputes began to emerge. The boys called each other names; fistfights broke out; cabins were ransacked; and an unfriendly atmosphere prevailed.

Order occurred in this chaos when Sherif introduced a superordinate goal. He created problems where the two groups had to cooperate to achieve something each wanted. Thus the boys worked together to fix the camp's water supply, to move a truck that "broke down" on a camping trip, and to contribute money to rent a movie each wanted to see. The tensions between the groups diminished, and individuals who previously were hostile towards each other developed closer ties.

and his neighbor assisted him in putting it out. They forgot their past differences during that episode. Each felt so good about helping to avert a tragedy that they were then able to discuss the property line issue more effectively.

Superordinate goals also have been used to settle differences among couples and business executives and to promote racial harmony in the classroom. In the latter case, children work together in small groups to help each other learn information and to solve problems (Myers, 1994). Superordinate goals tend to work best when by pursuing them people are able to define a new, inclusive group that dissolves their former subgroups. Thoughts about "us" and "them" must give way to "us" (Gaertner et al., 1990). These authors also report that goals do not work as well when a large power imbalance among groups or individuals exists or when the negative feelings and hostilities are deep-seated.

Also, pursuing common goals is no panacea for all of the problems in a relationship. While people may temporarily set their differences aside, afterwards they still must deal with those that remain. This is tragically seen when a married couple decides to have a child or to buy a house to help "pull the relationship together" or to "save the marriage." While raising a child and finding and fixing up a new home are collaborative activities, they temporarily mask underlying difficulties.

## Use a Third Party—"Get a Little Help from Your Friends"

It is sometimes difficult to resolve a dispute on your own. The other party may not be very cooperative; the issues arouse too much tension; and you and the other party may have difficulty getting beyond your anger. One consequence is that ineffective ways of relating to others occurs, and the conflict cannot be resolved.

*In the latter case, the use of a neutral third party can be effective.* This might be a mutual friend who has skills in helping people to negotiate differences, a counselor or therapist, or a professional mediator. They can help set ground rules for discussions and monitor them so that everyone gets heard and the needs of both parties are discussed. *Bringing in a third party to help with a conflict is not a sign of weakness—rather, it is a sign of strength.* And many disputes may not get resolved without such help. Of course, this person must be perceived by both sides as "fair" and as "not having a vested interest in the outcome."

## Determining the Best Resolution Strategy

According to William Ury and his colleagues, any method of resolving conflicts is likely to have certain costs and benefits. This is particularly true when considering the choice of power-based, rights-based, and mutual gains approaches. Clearly, one would want to employ a strategy that yielded the most benefits in a given situation. Four questions to ask are:

1. *What are the transaction costs of a given resolution strategy?* Disputes always cost something. They take time and money; emotional energy is expended; resources are consumed; and opportunities for engaging in other productive activities are lost. Before deciding to incur such costs, ask yourself the following question.

2. *Can I live with the terms of a settlement that is dictated by the other side?* If not, then employ one of the strategies outlined in this section to help you obtain more of what you want.

3. *Is it likely that the approach I selected will lead each party to be satisfied with the outcome?* The degree of satisfaction depends primarily on the degree to which the outcomes will meet the interests of the parties involved and whether the resolution is considered fair.

4. *What effect will this approach have on my relationship with the other party?* The outcomes of conflicts and the procedures that generate those outcomes affect two things. They are the ability of each party to resolve future disputes and their ability to work together.

*Will the procedures used allow the dispute to stay resolved or to recur?* Recurrence can take three forms: same dispute—same parties; different dispute—same parties; same dispute—different parties.

Research suggests that a mutual gains approach yields higher quality solutions as well as resolutions that generally meet with the greatest acceptance among participants (Pruitt and Rubin, 1986; Ury et al., 1988; Thomas, 1992). Participants report feeling more in control of the process, and their relationships with others are not as adversely affected. Solutions obtained from them also tend to be longer lasting. This is particularly true if processes are put in place to monitor and evaluate how well agreements are working out. Power-based or competitive strategies are the least effective in this regard, while rights-based approaches are somewhere in between.

Mutual gains approaches, however, typically take more time and place a premium on people cooperating and using good but often unfamiliar communication and relationship skills. Alphie Kohn (1986) also notes that collaborative methods are not as well known to people who live in a cultural climate where competitive and more adversarial approaches to managing differences prevail. Thus, he finds that collaborative strategies are sometimes viewed as inferior and difficult to maintain in such a climate.

While collaborative ways of resolving disputes have certain benefits, the distinction between "collaborative" versus "competitive" means of resolving differences is not always easy to make. Roy Andes (1992) reports that many situations contain elements of both approaches. Mixed messages are often sent, and mixed tactics are typically employed. The attorney representing one side in a divorce settlement offers the other side her "last settlement offer of $10,000." At the same time she communicates her willingness to collaborate by being sincere and displaying a high personal regard for the other spouse and his attorney. The GRIT procedure mentioned earlier also promises collaboration as well as competition if the other party does not reciprocate in kind.

William Ury (1988; 1991) also shows that combinations of "power-based," "rights-based," and "mutual gains" approaches are typically employed in the same situation. Sometimes the nature of the dispute is complicated, and no single approach will work. Or, one strategy is employed in order to get participants to apply another that would be more helpful. Consider for a moment the following examples:

> A vice president of a business I know became frustrated with his attempts to get two of his middle managers to cooperate more. He ordered them under threats of being fired to meet with a consultant to work out their differences. He employed a "power-based strategy" in order to get them to work with a third party on a "mutual gains" settlement of their differences.

> When I was a graduate student, my landlord once demanded that I pay for water damage to a bathroom floor caused by my letting a sink overflow. We argued over the telephone about whose fault it was and who was responsible for the property. I gave in only when he later showed me a clause in my lease that clearly stated I was responsible for such damages. Initially we argued in a typical power-based "win-lose" or "I-have-my-position-and-you-have-yours" manner. The clause in the lease, however, legally spelled out who was responsible. Thus, a "rights-based" approach finally settled it.

In some situations, the question is not, "What is the best strategy to use?" Rather, the issue becomes one of, *"What combinations of strategies are best used here?"* The same criteria listed above, however, would still apply in making such determinations.

# DEALING WITH INTERPERSONAL INFLUENCE

Phillip Zimbardo and Michael Leippe (1991) view interpersonal influence as the attempts by one party to define or change the way others should think, feel, and behave. Efforts to influence are part of the normal give-and-take that occurs in our everyday interactions. The goal is to get others to think and behave in ways that one party finds desirable. Consequently, each of us faces two tasks in life. One is how to get others to do what we want. The second is how to avoid being unnecessarily influenced by other people. Such goals can only be achieved if we understand the influence tactics used and the ways to counter them.

## Social Pressure

"Come on Dena, you don't have to study now. Join the rest of us for a movie. You can study later." Surely you have had an experience in which members of a group tried to influence your attitudes and behaviors. Such influence affects all aspects of our lives, and it can be quite effective. For example, school-based antismoking and drug programs are much more productive and have longer lasting effects when run by peers (Murray et al., 1984). In another study, neighbors who recycled solid waste asked those who did not to start recycling (Burn, 1991). They converted twice as many people than did written messages left on people's doorsteps. Social pressure also has been shown to influence adherence to job safety practices, the foods people eat, what they wear, the friends they associate with and where they live (Zimbardo and Leippe, 1991). Such pressure is effective because those we admire and respect reinforce us for thinking and behaving as they do. Also, other people can make things unpleasant if we resist.

*Compliance, Identification, and Internalization* People do not always conform for the same reasons. Each of the latter three processes plays a role (Kelman, 1958). Herbert Kelman identifies **compliance** as conforming in order to receive certain rewards or to avoid sanctions. As a result, individuals who comply publicly follow the wishes of others but privately do not accept them. For example, people might dress a particular way only as long as the prospect of a reward or the threat of punishment is held over their heads. **Identification** occurs when someone finds the things others want him or her to do personally attractive or appealing in some way. Thus, the clothes worn have some intrinsic appeal to a person and allow someone to look "just like my friends." Here the motivation is to develop a certain self-image that would probably change if one's friends changed. When the thoughts and behaviors others encourage us to adopt become completely integrated into our psychological makeup—**internalization** has occurred. Thus, the types of clothes worn do not vary much when hanging out with different groups of friends. They become a statement of who you are that now transcends what others think.

## Authority and Social Power

Some individuals, because of their titles, positions in life, and status, exert a considerable amount of influence over us. Teachers, bosses, parents, ministers, and other authorities often ask students, subordinates, children, and church members to do a variety of things. Some griping and complaining may occur, and a request may not always be executed to perfection; but in the majority of cases, people do what they are told.

Sometimes following orders mindlessly has led to horrible consequences, embarrassing moments, and a willingness to "do what I'm told versus what is right for me." Each of the latter consequences is illustrated in Focus on People 9.2 Obeying authori-

---

**FOCUS ON PEOPLE 9.2**

## Obedience to Authority

### Harmful Consequences

In September of 1987, a protest against the shipment of military equipment to Nicaragua occurred outside of the Naval Weapons Station in Concord, California. Three of the protestors stretched their bodies across the railroad tracks leading out of the Naval Weapons Station to prevent a train from passing. *The civilian crew of the train had been given orders not to stop. In spite of being able to see the protestors 600 feed ahead, they never even slowed the train.* Two of the men managed to get out of the way, a third was not fast enough and had two legs severed below the knee. Naval medical corpsmen at the scene refused to treat him or allow him to be taken to the hospital in their ambulance. Onlookers tried to stop the flow of blood for 45 minutes until a private ambulance arrived (Kelman and Hamilton, 1989).

### Embarrassing Moments

A colleague sent a graduate student to be the "substitute teacher" in an introductory psychology class. The undergraduate students had never seen her before. The substitute began the class by saying, "I'm in charge today, and I want to get this session started by asking each of you to stand. Fine, now I want you to clap your hands three times and pat the person standing next to you on the shoulder five times. Now jump up and down for ten seconds. Ok, sit down and put your pen-

cils and notebooks on the floor." *Each of the 240 students in the class followed the commands of the teacher without questioning them.* My colleague then entered the room and began a well-listened-to presentation on obedience to authority.

### Doing What I'm Told Versus What's Right for Me

I was once hired by a company to be part of a workshop on making effective personal decisions. The company maintained and repaired electronic equipment used to monitor radiation levels in nuclear facilities Some technicians balked at entering an abandoned facility, fearing that it was dangerous to do so.

The company decided it only wanted to use technicians who had made an informed choice to maintain and repair the equipment. Experts in the area of radiation as well as those familiar with the site presented information and showed that the site was safe. I was asked to provide some principles of personal decision making that would help the employees decide whether or not they wanted to volunteer for the work.

Afterwards, I rode in an elevator with five of the technicians. One of them broke the silence by saying, *"You know, every one of us would have agreed to enter the facility if our boss had simply ordered us to do it. Having all of you experts brought in to talk to us only made us suspicious that the site was, in fact, dangerous."*

ty is a well-learned habit, and it becomes an acceptable alternative to asking "why am I doing this?" As the example of the technicians illustrates, some people may simply want to be told what to do. This was evident in the conclusions of a series of studies on obedience by psychologist Stanley Milgram. What stuck him was "the extreme willingness of adults to go to almost any lengths on the command of an authority" (Milgram, 1974, p. 245).

What makes someone in authority able to exert influence over others? Milgram identified several factors. *One is that they must be perceived as credible.* Otherwise we are likely to disregard their requests. *Second, all of us are socialized to obey authorities.* How many times have you heard someone say, "Respect your elders," "Do what you are told," or "Obey the law and those who enforce it." *Third, authorities also command our attention because of their ability to use several sources of social power.* Bertram Raven (1992) and his colleague John French identified several sources of social power, and these are described in Table 9.3.

Combinations of social power are typically applied. A boss who says, "I am in charge here. Do what I say or you will be fired" is using a combination of **legitimate** and **coercive power.** A parent who tells a child "Do me a favor and help me clean the bathrooms, then I will give you money for the movie" is employing **referent** and **reward power.** A classroom teacher who says, "Based on my experience, the Jones' book has the best analysis of this theory. If you read it, I will not give you a low grade" is using **expert** and **coercive power.** A salesperson providing details of how one product is superior to another in order to induce you to purchase it is using **information power.**

Research suggests that there are advantages and disadvantages to each of these

---

**Table 9.3**      Sources of Social Power and Influence

**Expert Power** Influence is based on personal knowledge and expertise that others do not possess to the same degree.

**Information Power** Influence is based upon having the information needed to be able to develop logical and/or persuasive arguments about why certain actions should be taken.

**Referent Power** Influence is based on the ability to support and nurture others and the degree to which they like you. It is fostered by the emotional commitment and identification of others with your beliefs and what you stand for in life.

**Legitimate Power** Influence is derived from the formal position that one holds within a group. Such power also develops when someone becomes dependent upon another person and becomes obligated to him or her. In the latter case, people have influence over those who owe them favors or who they have suffered or worked hard for.

**Reward Power** Influence is derived from the capacity to dispense rewards such as money, awards, social recognition and approval, and positive feelings in others.

**Coercive Power** Influence occurs through the ability to impose sanctions, to punish others, or to threaten to do such things.

Based on Raven (1992).

forms of social influence. People tend to appreciate and respond better to attempts at influence made on the basis of expert, information, and referent power. The extensive use of reward and coercive bases of social influence tends to not be as well liked by others (Podsakoff and Schriescheim, 1985; Stahelski et al., 1989).

## Appealing to Needs

Advertisers and salespeople use this technique all of the time. An advertisement in which an actor and actress promises relief from loneliness if people join the Social Clubs of America is only one illustration of this tactic. Many times there is an honest and direct relationship between the product and the need it fulfills. Food products are usually tasty, and they do satisfy our hunger or thirst. On the other hand, sometimes there is a minimal chance of our needs getting fulfilled. Toothpaste is much more effective in cleaning your teeth than in getting you dates on Saturday night. Detergents are much better at taking dirt out of clothes than they are at keeping marriages from breaking up.

People also appeal to our needs for friendship and affection or to be accepted or keep a certain image. Sometimes they tell us nice things about ourselves simply to influence us. "You really look nice today." "That was a very intelligent decision." Or they may try to show how much they share our views on things: "I also agree with your position on the Middle East." "You took the words right out of my mouth." Such attempts at influence are called flattery. A common saying is that "flattery will get you everywhere." While it sometimes works, it can also fail to get results. Andrew Colman (1980) reports that it works best with people who have a good self-image. They are more likely to believe the nice things said because it fits their image. On the other hand, people with a poor self-image are likely to reject such attempts at influence.

## Reciprocity

Social obligations are very powerful motivators. Most of us have learned that we should repay in kind what another person has provided us. We feel obligated to return favors, gifts, invitations to parties, kind words, and many other things others give us. After all, it is difficult to say "no" to someone who has previously done us a favor. Thus, a grocery store offers "free samples" of food, and people feel like they have to purchase something. A salesperson gives us a "free gift" and finds a more receptive customer. Someone we like hugs us, and we hug them back. In relationships, what is exchanged is the willingness to provide what the other person needs—when it is needed.

Research shows that people are much happier in relationships when they believe they are getting the same amount of help from a partner as they give. Those who either give more help than they receive or receive less than they had given were the most dissatisfied (Clark et al.,1986, 1989; Rook, 1987). Consequently, to keep the "give-and-take" balanced and the relationship on friendly terms, many of us end up doing favors for friends that deep down inside we would rather not do.

## Obtaining Agreement and Commitment

One of my students was engaged to get married. She had accepted the engagement ring; wedding plans were made; and invitations to the wedding were sent to friends and relatives. In the privacy of my office she broke down and told me she had made a mistake. "But it's too late now to change my mind," she said. "I feel stuck, and there's nothing I can do about it." Nothing I said seemed to make a difference. The marriage took place, and within a year they had separated and were eventually divorced.

Once we agree and commit to something we see as our own doing, it is not easy to change. Robert Cialdini (1993) reports that several processes are involved. For one thing, most of us were taught by parents, coaches, and others to "Finish what you started," "Don't give up—keep going." Or, "A person is only as good as his or her word." Also, we tend to justify our course of action to ourselves as a correct or wise choice. Otherwise, why would we agree to do something? Finally, once we agree to do something, we often feel obliged to behave consistently with that decision. No one willingly wants to appear "wishy-washy" to other people. Consequently, we mold our actions to make them consistent with our decisions.

Most of us do not agree or commit to something quickly or on the spur of the moment. Commitments seem to grow their own legs. That is, they take time to develop, and a major agreement typically grows out of a succession of smaller ones. After all, most people do not agree to marry someone after the first date. They do so only after their commitment to each other grows over time. Consequently, people trying to influence us typically begin in small ways to win us over.

## Strategies Used to Obtain Agreement and Commitment

*A Public Agreement or Commitment Is Obtained* Agreements voluntarily made in a public arena are often strongly supported. When papers and contracts are signed or other people are watching or know about what we said or did, the pressures to remain consistent with the decision are greater (Cialdini, 1993). No one wants to appear foolish in public, to back down "on what I said in front of others," or to go against a "written agreement." This is one reason my student mentioned earlier thought she couldn't back out of her engagement. Not only had she agreed to a number of relatively smaller things (e.g., to accept the ring, to select a wedding dress, to invite people to the ceremony), but all her friends and relatives knew about her promise to get married.

*Agreement Is Obtained on Unrelated Issues* Have you ever found yourself agreeing with an insurance, magazine, or clothing salesperson on such things as, "Isn't it a lovely day outside?" "Your children are so well behaved," or "You look happy today"? You soon find yourself tempted to say yes to, "Can I have your signature on this sales contract?" Ellen Langer and Carol Dweck (1973) report that by getting you to agree, the salesperson has established that the two of you have something in common. It is harder to resist a request of someone whom you think looks at the world in a similar way. A variation on this strategy is illustrated in Focus on Applied Research 9.3.

*Commitment to a Small Request Is Obtained* People are likely to agree to a large request if someone first gets them to concede to help with a small request. After all, if you agree to "spend just a minute to answer a few questions," "have a cup of coffee or a

FOCUS ON APPLIED RESEARCH 9.3
## "I'm Fine, Thank You"

Solicitors for charities often begin a telephone or door-to-door sales pitch with, "How are you feeling this evening?" or, "How are you doing today?" The intent is to get you to respond with a rather polite comment such as "I'm fine," "Things are going well today," or, "Real good." The salesperson could care less about how you feel. His or her intent is to manipulate you to make a donation.

The next statement shows their true intention. "I'm happy that things are going well with you today because I want to ask you to help those who are less fortunate than you are."

Daniel Howard (1990) reports that such introductory statements are designed to make you feel awkward, stingy, or perhaps a little guilty about refusing a request for a donation or to purchase some product. In his research study, residents of Dallas, Texas, were called on the telephone and asked if they would allow representatives from the Hunger Relief Committee to visit their homes to sell cookies. People were told that the proceeds from the sale of cookies would be used to supply meals for the needy.

When the request was not preceded with a "How are you feeling this evening?" only 18 percent of those called agreed to the request. When the latter question preceded the request, 38 percent agreed to have someone visit their home. And in a remarkable demonstration that people try to remain consistent, 89 percent of those who agreed to a home visit purchased cookies.

cigarette," or to let them use your phone, it becomes much more difficult to turn off their request for other things. One reason is that we do small favors for our friends. Thus, someone becomes almost like a friend when we comply with one or more small requests. And how many of us, for example, can resist the request of a "friend"?

*Agreement with an Analogy Is Obtained* In a classic study, William McGuire (1961) demonstrated that people were more likely to modify a belief and take action if they agreed with another issue that contained similar logic. A neighbor's wife asked if I would talk to her husband about getting a physical exam. He had not had one in several years, and she thought it was about time for a checkup. In particular, she was concerned about his tendency to overeat and to feel dizzy occasionally. Of course, he told me that he felt fine and did not need a medical exam. I asked him if an airline should check its plane engines if they appeared to run well. He said that they should. "Airplane engines may look and sound all right, but you need to periodically check them for parts that are beginning to wear." I then asked him if there was an analogy between his body and the airplane engines. He smiled and said, "Of course there is." He got a medical checkup. McGuire suggests that this procedure creates a certain amount of tension, which is often resolved by taking the requested action.

*Agreement Is Acquired Through Reactance* Most of us try to exert our personal freedom to choose a course of action whenever we feel a high degree of persuasion (Brehm and Brehm, 1981). A child who feels that his parents are trying to get him to eat spinach may decide not to eat it in order to maintain some personal control over his diet.

Similarly, a person is likely to vote against some issue in a meeting if she feels that other members of the group are trying to force her to do something else. One of the consequences of trying to persuade people is that they may do just the opposite. This process of behaving to maintain our personal freedom, to make decisions in the face of persuasive influences, is called **reactance.**

Reactance, however, can sometimes work against you. Pretend that you are talking to an encyclopedia salesperson. He says, "I bet you are really not that interested in education." "Have you ever thought that gaining knowledge was a waste of time?" "I bet you spend very little time reading." "Have you ever thought that reading was a chore?" More likely than not, you would disagree with such statements. In the process, you would begin to agree that "you have an interest in education; gaining knowledge is not a waste of time; you spend time reading"; and "reading is probably fun." By resisting the statements of the salesperson and saying just the opposite, you begin to agree with the sales presentation. How could you not buy the books after saying that you like to read, you do it often, and it's fun and educational?

## Managing Influence Tactics: Identify the Strategies Used, and Counter Them

One of the best ways to counter such influence is to identify the tactic, remind yourself that it is being used against you, and to then take appropriate action. For each of the strategies mentioned in the last section, consider how you might apply the suggestions in Table 9.4 to your life.

# GET MORE OF YOUR NEEDS MET IN RELATIONSHIPS: BECOME MORE ASSERTIVE

Are you able to exert personal control in your interactions with other people? Are you able to say what you mean, to get others to help you, and to refuse the unwanted requests of others? Or, do you find yourself putting the needs of others ahead of your own and doing things that "I don't really want to do?" Learning to become more assertive will help. Behaving assertively means that you take actions to influence other people, to limit the amount of control they have over you, and to use social skills that make you more competent. This is done without putting another person down, attacking him, or stepping over her to get what you want.

## Deliver Unexpected Messages When Necessary

Other people can use overt and subtle means to influence, control, and manipulate us only as long as we let them. Judith Stewert (1990) and Bobbie Reed (1992) point out that certain tactics will be used against us as long as we continue to make a predictable response. As long as we jump when someone says "Frog," they will continue to treat us a certain way. An unexpected message is anything that tells another person, "Things have changed, and I want you to think about what was said." Typically, we cannot change other people—they can only change themselves. What we can do is give them something to think about that might get them to change their behaviors toward us.

*Three Ways to Deliver Unexpected Messages*

1. *Give an honest and direct response to another person.* Many of us resent doing what

**Table 9.4**                          How to Counter Specific Influence Tactics

*Social Pressure.*  It is difficult to say "no" to a group of people. However, it is usually easier to say "no" to a single individual or to do so when others will support your decision. Thus, when pressured by a group to do something, buy time. "Look, I can't give you an answer right now. Which one of you can I get back to later with an answer?" Or, find one or two other people who think as you do, and together refuse the request. Also, develop your expertise in the area in which people want to apply pressure. Knowledgeable people are better able to resist the influence of others.

*Authority and Social Power.*  The key here is to not follow the dictates of authorities mindlessly. Stop and ask, "Would I do this if no one asked me to do it?" "Is it something I would tell others to do?" "Am I compromising what I believe in by taking these actions?"

*Appealing to Needs.*  Develop a skeptical stance in the face of such influence. Ask yourself questions about whether the desired outcome will occur, for example, "Would purchasing a tube of toothpaste really improve my social life?" "Am I as witty and intelligent as he says?" Focus on the self-interest of the other party. "How does the other person benefit if I do as he or she asks?" "What's in it for him or her?"

*Reciprocity.*  Once caught in its grip, it is difficult to escape from its influence. Thus, prevention is often a more helpful approach to take. When someone to whom you don't want to incur a future debt offers you something, politely decline. Ask yourself, "Do I really want to accept this and then have to do this person a favor in the future?"

*Obtaining Agreement and Commitment.*  Remember that most major commitments of time, energy, and resources begin with a succession of smaller ones. Instead of considering a positive reply to a "small request" as "no big deal," reframe it as a potential "major step" in getting a much larger commitment out of you. Then ask yourself the question, "What are the consequences of saying yes?"

A progressive chain of requests can be broken if a critical link is removed and not replaced. Thus, break one of the links. Several weeks after signing an agreement to purchase a house, a colleague realized that he had made a mistake. He simply refused the terms of the financing, and the sale was stopped.

Ask yourself, "Would I make this same choice again?" Instead of relying on your verbal response, trust the feelings that emerge. This gut reaction is likely to be a more accurate indication of your preference than your thoughts. The latter are more likely to justify the decision you already made (Cialdini, 1993, pp. 89–90).

Resist pressures to commit quickly, and demand time to think about a request. Or, say that you cannot agree until you consult with another person (e.g., friend, boss, spouse). Do a reality check. See if the request also makes sense to others.

they've asked, but we do it anyway. This leads to a halfhearted effort and feelings of being taken again. Instead, let others know what you think of their request. *Example:* John has a hard time telling people that he can't see them. Thus much of his day is spent with members of his organization that he does not really need to see. Sometimes he tries to put them off by saying, "Check with me later in the day or next week." But he still must see them later. Lately, he has been telling people, "I just don't have the time to talk to you about that." He then suggests other people in the organization who might be helpful. People are now careful when they ask to

see John. They must have a good reason, and it should be related to his area of responsibility.

2. *Say something that forces people to reconsider their actions.* The goal is to remove a predictable response and to have people reconsider what they are saying or doing. *Example:* A student, Ted, and his friend, Christine, often argued about leaving parties early. She would ask to leave, and he would get mad. One day he said, "I'd really like to stay. Take the keys to my car, and I'll get Jack to take me home later." He reports they got along fine after that.

3. " *Fog" the other person's statements.* Name-calling, guilt arousal, nagging, or just behaving obnoxiously are sometimes used to manipulate us. A helpful tactic when this occurs is to "fog" the message. You do this by agreeing in whole or in part with what others have said. *Example:* George tells Sam he is a lousy SOB if he does not help him paint his house. Sam replies, "Yes, I guess I am a lousy SOB sometimes. But I cannot help it." Diane's father constantly tells her how lazy she is about her school work. Diane replies to one such outburst, "Yes, I am lazy at times, and I suppose I don't care as much as I should about school. But I'm doing as much as I want to do now."

Afterwards, three things can occur. The other person's message does not have the desired effect, and they stop. Someone also may ask you why you think the way you do. Or, you can ask, "Can we now talk about how we see things?" In either case, you have regained more control over the situation.

## Make Requests Appropriately

Sharon and Gordon Bower (1991) describe a technique for making requests that they label DESC scripts. Each of the components is described in Table 9.5. Of course, mak-

**Table 9.5**    Using a DESC Script to Make Requests

*Describe the situation (D).* Describe the situation in behavioral terms. Let the other person know what behaviors you observed that led you to make a certain request. Concentrate on behaviors and not the motives of people when describing what is going on. *Examples:*

Damon is returning a radio that needs to be fixed. "I bought this radio from one of the salespeople in the store last week. It has only been used a week."

Laura asks her boss for a raise. "I've been working here for 18 months and have not had a raise in salary. According to my evaluations, I have apparently done a fine job during this time period and have taken on much more responsibility."

*Express your feelings about the situation (E).*
Let the other person know what feelings, if any, the situation has aroused. Do this calmly, and use "I" messages. That is, describe how you feel by saying "I feel" and not "you made me feel" a certain way. *Examples:*

Damon:  "I'm feeling disappointed that this new radio is not working after only a week."

Laura:  "I'm beginning to feel unappreciated for the work that I have been doing."

*Specify what you want (S).* Ask for the specific actions you want to see implemented or stopped. Generally request a small or reasonable amount of something, and make only one or two requests at a time. *Examples:*

Damon:  "I would like to have the radio fixed and for you to lend me another one while mine is in the shop."

Laura:  "Based on what other people in a similar position are making, I think that a $150-a-month raise would not be out of line."

*Describe the consequences associated with your request (C).*
When possible, let the other person know what the positive consequences of meeting your request are. Select something that is desirable and that is likely to be valued by the other individual. Try not to specify negative consequences, but if you must, select a reasonable punishment that you are willing to carry out. *Examples:*

Damon:  "If you do what I ask, I'll continue to feel good about the service I have come to expect from this store. And I'll be sure to let other people know how well I was treated."

Laura:  "The raise will help me to continue to be a productive employee, and I'll feel that management cares about me and the job I'm doing."

ing requests in this way does not guarantee that you will get everything you want. It only provides a clear structure for making a request. You must still, however, be willing to compromise or to help others meet their needs.

## Repeat Your Request More Than Once

Sometimes people do not hear you the first time; they choose to turn you off; or perhaps what you said was not clear. The broken-record technique, or repeating your request, is sometimes helpful. Simply repeat your request either in the same way or with minor modifications. The goal is to say what you want enough times so that you have someone acknowledge your request. Unless you are persistent, requests sometimes go in one ear and out the other. Example of the broken record:

Wife: I need you to help me fix the small leak in the dishwasher.

Husband: Sure, honey. Let me watch the baseball game first.

Wife: "There is a leak in the dishwasher and I need your help now. It cannot wait till later."

Husband: "OK. As soon as this inning is over."

Wife: "The dishwasher is leaking, and I need your help now to fix it."

Husband: "All right, if it can't wait, let's do it now."

## Exercise Your Right to Say No

People can only influence you unnecessarily if you continue to do what they want. That is, you effectively say yes to their requests. Manuel Smith (1985) and Rhonda McFarland (1992) note that saying no more often would give us more control over our time and energy. Most of us agree, however, because we are afraid that the other person will dislike or reject us; we want them to remain our friends; or we feel they will think we are petty. It is the fear of such things happening that keeps us saying "yes" when we should say no. If people are really your friends, they will not hate you, reject you, or think you are petty because you refuse a request. The following principles should help you say "no" effectively.

*Four Ways to Say "No" Effectively*

1. *Simply say "no" or "I don't want to do it."* Remember that you do not always have to give a reason for your response. In many situations, a plain "no" is all that is necessary. Giving a reason may only weaken the stand you have taken.

2. *Repeat your message until the other party accepts it.* The "broken record" technique mentioned earlier is helpful here as well. People usually continue to make the same demand because they hope you will change your mind. You must show them that you are firm.

3. *Give a reason only if you feel that the other party obviously needs or could benefit from such information.* When a pay raise request is turned down, automobile insurance is not renewed, admittance to school is denied, or a parent refuses a child's request to do something, an elaboration might help.

4. *Do not give a reason if you think the information is unlikely to help the other party or will simply allow him or her to present a number of counter arguments.* If you are sure that your decision is the one you want to make, then you do not have to give a reason.

   *Example using this principle:* A magazine salesman calls on Julie.

Salesman: "Could I interest you in a ten-year subscription to four magazines for the price of two?"

Julie: "No, thank you; I'm not interested in purchasing magazines."

Salesman: "Perhaps you don't understand the offer. What reasons do you have for refusing?"

Julie: "I understand the offer. Thanks for making it. However, I'm not interested in purchasing magazines."

Salesman: "Surely you can't be against reading and learning more, can you?"

Julie: "I'm not interested in purchasing magazines."

Salesman: "Perhaps another time. Good day."

## Use Nonverbal Messages to Help You Become More Assertive

As you can see, verbally there are a number of things you might do to behave assertively. You should not, however, ignore the nonverbal aspects of what you do. Your nonverbal behaviors need to support your verbal messages if you are to assert yourself effectively. Consider the following suggestions:

*Eye Contact* Inadequate eye contact is often interpreted by people as anxiety, dishonesty, boredom, or embarrassment. Do not stare down people you are talking with, but maintain a direct gaze while you deliver your message. Sometimes it helps to maintain as much eye contact as you can but to periodically direct your glance to different parts of the other person's face. From a distance of three or four feet, it is difficult to tell whether you are not maintaining contact.

*Facial Expressions*   Your facial expressions must match your message. It is not good to describe your anger to another person with a smile on your face. Similarly, you will not convey a relaxed posture if your teeth are tightly clenched. If you have a serious message, try to put on a serious face. The same is true of any other emotion you might want to express.

*Gestures and Posture*   Fidgeting hands, nervous shifting from one foot to another, or slumped shoulders will reduce or contradict the impact of an assertive message. Your gestures should suit the words you want to convey.

*Body Orientation*   Generally speaking, it is better to face others when talking to them. If at all possible, stand if they are standing, and sit if they are sitting. Otherwise, you might find your actions interpreted as aggressive. This is particularly true if they are sitting and you are standing. On the other hand, you will not come across as assertively if you deliver your message while you are sitting, and they are standing.

*Distance*   The discussion of personal space in Chapter 7 suggests that you need to pay attention to how far you stand away from others when communicating. You need to use the appropriate personal distance zone for the message you want to communicate. A service manager will not listen as well to your complaint if you try to talk from six to eight feet away.

| **Table 9.6** | A List of Interpersonal Rights |
|---|---|

*In interpersonal interactions, each of us has the right to:*

- say no to a request
- not give other people reasons for every action we take
- stop others from making excessive demands on us
- ask other people to listen to our point of view when we speak to them
- ask other people to correct errors they made that affect us
- change our minds
- ask other people to compromise rather than get only what they want
- ask other individuals to do things for us
- persist in making a request if people do not listen the first time
- be alone if we wish
- maintain our dignity in relationships
- evaluate our own behaviors and not just listen to evaluations that others offer
- make mistakes and accept responsibility for them
- avoid manipulation by other people
- pick our own friends without consulting our parents, peers, or anyone else
- let other people know how we are feeling
- ask that others treat us with respect
- request that someone do us a favor
- take actions that protect us from racial, sexual, or ethnic discrimination
- choose with whom and when we will have sexual relations
- follow our conscience in making popular as well as unpopular decisions
- resist demands that we think and act in a certain way

*Voice Elements*  When talking assertively, your tone of voice should not be overly loud or soft. The same is true of talking too fast or slow. You need to present your message with moderate volume and at a rate of 100 words per minute. Also watch out for distractions like the overuse of "OK," "Ya know," "Ummmm," and long pauses between sentences.

## Exercise Your Interpersonal Rights

To behave assertively is one of the rights we each have in our relationships with others. It helps us to avoid too much influence by other people and gives us a chance to decide how to spend our time and energy. There are other interpersonal rights that we have that if used, will assist us in resisting the undue influence of other people. They will also help to set us apart from others and for them to see us as unique individuals that must be treated fairly. Table 9.6 has a list of these rights. The list is based on the work of Robert Alberti and Michael Emmons (1988). Which rights in this table have you used in the past week? Which ones do you need to use more often in the future? What do you have to do to use them more in the future? One principle to keep in mind about using any interpersonal right is that other people have the same rights as you do. They are not things that only you have the authority to use. They are used much more effectively when you respect and recognize the other person's privilege to use them as well.

## Giving, Asking for, and Receiving Feedback

Providing feedback is one way we can share expectations with other people and influence the way they behave in the future. Feedback should be treated as an error-correction mechanism that can have positive effects on both the individual giving it and the person receiving it. If you change your behavior as a result of something I tell you, I am likely to behave differently toward you. Some care, however, must be taken here. Cynthia Fisher (1978) notes that feedback should be given in such a way that others do not perceive you as trying to exert too much control over their actions. Also, placing yourself in the position of always providing feedback can make someone overly dependent upon you. Consequently, they may not develop the skills to judge their own actions. People need feedback, but they also should be encouraged to monitor their own actions.

People do not always volunteer feedback. Sometimes you have to ask for it. Such information can help ensure that you obtain the information you need to correct and enhance your behaviors. Suggestions for giving and receiving feedback appear in Tables 9.7 and 9.8.

## Prepare Yourself to Behave Assertively

Assertive techniques are sometimes difficult to pick up and immediately use without some advanced preparation. A problem is that past habits can make it difficult to use them well the first time. There are several thing you can do.

*Practice in Advance.*   This can be done in three ways.

1. *Imagine yourself in the situation in which you want to use the technique.* Think about the other people that are present and what you will say. Concentrate on both the verbal and nonverbal messages you will use. What reactions do you think you will obtain from others?

2. *Rehearse in front of a mirror the verbal and nonverbal behaviors you will use.* Pay attention to what you are saying and how you look saying it. Practice until you get it right. You may want to use a videotape recording of what you are saying to help you monitor your verbal behaviors.

3. *Have one or more of your friends help you.* Ask them to role-play the person(s) with whom you want to behave assertively. Have them critique what you plan to say or do.

**Table 9.7**                Principles for Giving Feedback

*Provide feedback based on previously agreed upon goals, standards, or expectations.* When working with others, establish expectations for tasks that must be completed, who will do them, deadlines that must be met, and the level of proficiency that is required. Feedback should be directed towards such things.

*Example:* "I thought the work you did met the customers needs, but it was finished two days later than we had agreed."

*Give feedback only when you are sure the other person is ready to hear it.* If people are not ready to hear what you have to say, they are not likely to learn as much. Before giving feedback, check the other person's readiness for it.

*Example:* "Alice, I'd like to give you feedback on your performance. Can we discuss it now?"

*Give others the option to state what they would like feedback on.* This helps others to select areas of their performance that most interest them, and it also makes the feedback process more collaborative.

*Example:* "Kelly, we agreed to talk at the end of the week on how we were communicating with each other. Are there some things you might want me to comment about?"

*Focus on specific behaviors when providing feedback.* Feedback is easily misunderstood or distorted. Stating what you observed in behavioral terms gives the other person a concrete frame of reference. Feedback is specific enough when it allows the other person to plan what he or she will do in the future.

*Example:* "Your front wheel hit the sidewalk when you turned. Try to turn the steering wheel about a third of the way more to the left next time."

*Try not to be evaluative when giving feedback.* A rule of thumb here is to focus on a person's behavior, not someone's personality.

*Example:* Avoid statements like, "What a stupid thing to do" and "I've never seen such a poor performance by anyone." Keep your feedback descriptive and oriented towards specific behaviors.

*Use a frame of reference.* When providing feedback, it is often a good idea to indicate a frame of reference when making comparisons.

*Example:* "Compared to the time others took to complete this task, your time of four hours was very fast."

*Provide feedback as soon as possible.* Feedback is not likely to have as much effect when directed toward behavior that occurred in the distant past. It is best to give feedback as soon as possible after a behavior occurs. The "data" on the interaction are fresh, and the ideas can often be explored in detail.

*Give positive feedback frequently.* Even when negative feedback is called for, consider preceding it with something positive.

*Example:* "Harry, the way you summarized the client's problem was extremely effective. However, in the future you might want to wait 15 minutes before closing the interview."

**Table 9.8**                    Principles for Asking for Feedback

*Set the stage for requesting feedback.* Let the other person know you respect his or her opinion and how helpful the feedback can be to you. If possible, meet the other person in a quiet and pleasant atmosphere.

*Example:* "I have always admired how you do this task. Do you have a few minutes to show me how I can improve what I'm doing?"

*Request feedback on specific strengths and weaknesses.* Keep the other person honest by asking for specific examples of what you did well and not so well. Keep the discussion focused on specific behaviors.

*Example:* "You said that I take too much time with this task. Can you tell me exactly when and where this happens?"

*Ask people to use a frame of reference when giving feedback.* Ask the other person to indicate how your performance compares to that of other people.

*Example:* "How does my performance compare to how George and Jeanne do this task?"

*Request feedback based on previously agreed upon goals, standards, or expectations.* You should request feedback on how well such things were met.

*Example:* "When I first took this job, we talked about my beginning to supervise some of the sales people and that my personal sales on our new product line should increase over last year's. How do you see my performance in these areas so far?"

*Actively listen to what is said. Summarize, paraphrase, and validate the feedback in addition to asking questions.* These communication skills were discussed in Chapter 7. Let the other person know you really care by listening intently to what is being spoken.

*Example:* "You suggested that I have more performance reviews with people, and I agree that I have not been meeting with them as often as I could. Are there any special things that you would like me to cover in those meetings?"

*Specify next steps.* End the conversation by thinking of a few changes you will make in your actions. This tells the other person that you value what was said.

*Example:* "I'm going to schedule an additional performance review with everyone by the end of this month. I'll also work closer with the marketing department on obtaining the information I need to sell this new product line."

*Develop a Script.* You might consider writing a script for the situation. Pretend that you are going to play a role in a play. List in writing what you want to do verbally and nonverbally. Think about how the other person might react. How will you counter his or her responses?

*Follow a Role Model.* Most of us admire individuals who behave in certain ways. Think about people you know who behave assertively. Monitor their behaviors, and practice their actions in front of a mirror. Or sit down with them and discuss how they behave and see if they can give you any tips. The suggestions for using a model in Chapter 5 might help you with this task.

## *Summary of Chapter Organizers*

Suggested responses to the chapter organizers presented at the beginning of this chapter are presented below.

1. *What functions does conflict serve in your relationships?* Conflicts often serve a number of useful purposes. They act as an early warning device alerting you to problems in a relationship. Furthermore, disputes can serve as a pressure release valve to reduce tension in a relationship, provided the frustration leads to actions that help to resolve the problem. Conflicts also help us to *mobilize the energy to deal with issues and to renegotiate existing physical and psychological boundaries with others.*

2. *Are you aware of the arenas in which a dispute is acted out?* The tension in a conflict as well as the time and energy spent trying to resolve issues occur within three arenas—the intrapersonal, interpersonal, and intergroup. The severity of a conflict is related to two things: the number of arenas spanned by the conflict and, within each arena, the number of issues, people, and groups, respectively, that are involved. Typically, most conflicts are not completely resolved until participants' intrapersonal tension is reduced.

3. *Can you identify six of the common causes of conflicts?* Your disputes seldom have a single cause. While one factor might dominate, other reasons typically exist. Important triggers of conflict include:

   *Differences in values,* in which such beliefs typically collide in your interactions.

   *Violations of expectations* about how you and others are supposed to behave. Oftentimes expectations are not openly shared, and unstated assumptions about how each of you should act are violated.

   *Struggles for power, control, and authority occur* as you and others try to maintain or establish a new "pecking order" in the relationship.

   *Disagreements over goals, methods to achieve them, and how to allocate resources.*

   *The roles you play begin to clash.* This occurs because you play different roles in your relationships; disagreements occur over how such roles should be played; and other people decide to play their roles in ways that are incompatible with your own.

   *Boundary and territory violations occur.* Other people may intrude into the physical and psychological spaces that you occupy, producing tension and anger.

4. *Once underway, do you know what helps to support and maintain a dispute?* Three factors appear to be involved. Using ineffective conflict resolution styles, such as avoidance, accommodation, and competition, is one. In addition is the presence of "*hot cognitions,*" or beliefs that effectively raise the intensity of a conflict. Finally, there is *personal collusion in allowing a dispute to continue.* This occurs whenever you view yourself as a neutral bystander to a dispute or whenever ineffective thoughts and behaviors continue to be employed.

5. *What are eight conflict resolution strategies that you could use?*

   *Prevention* or taking steps to ensure that issues are identified and worked on before they can become problems.

   *Taking early actions* in order to "nip a conflict in the bud."

   *Using power* in order to gain a competitive advantage and "win" the dispute.

*Using the GRIT strategy* (Graduated and Reciprocated Initiatives in Tension reduction) to get others to follow any conciliatory gestures you might offer.

*Compromising,* or splitting the difference.

*Identifying the rights* each party has and using them as criteria for settling a dispute.

*Seeking mutual gains,* or working to integrate your interests and needs with those of the other party.

*Developing superordinate goals,* or compelling goals that allow you to pursue common interests and tasks with someone else.

*Using a third party* to help you to discuss your concerns with others.

6. *How can you determine the "best" approach to take in a situation?* All resolution strategies are likely to have certain costs and benefits. Thus, the best strategy is one that incurs the fewest costs, leads each party to be satisfied with the solution, allows everyone to work together and to resolve future disputes, and keeps the conflict from recurring. As a general rule, collaborative approaches are much more effective in that regard than are more competitive ways of resolving differences.

7. *What tactics are employed to influence you?* People trying to influence you may use social pressure and their authority, appeal to your needs, use reciprocity by doing you a favor and expecting one in return, and obtain progressive agreements and commitments to their demands.

8. *How can you counter the influence tactics that others employ?* The best ways to counter such influence are to identify the tactic, remind yourself that it is being used against you, and then take actions that directly counter it.

9. *Do you know how to deliver unexpected messages in order to disarm attempts to manipulate you, to make requests appropriately, and to say "no" effectively?* Delivering unexpected messages can occur by giving an honest and direct response to another person, saying something that forces him to reconsider his actions, or by "fogging" someone else's statements. Making requests using the DESC script process is helpful, and saying "no" is more effective if you take time to repeat the message, don't feel obliged to give reasons for your response, and do not worry about losing a friendship.

10. *What nonverbal messages can help you to become more assertive?* Assertive verbal messages must be congruent with nonverbal expressions. Therefore it helps to maintain eye contact, to make sure facial expressions and gestures suit the words you are using, and to face others. Depending upon what they are doing, sit or stand, use an appropriate personal distance zone, present a message that is free of distractions, and make sure your voice quality is not overly loud or fast.

11. *Are you aware of your interpersonal rights?* All of us have interpersonal rights, including the right to behave assertively, to say "no" to a request, to stop others from making excessive demands upon us, and to ask others to treat us with respect.

12. *What role does giving and receiving feedback play in your interactions?* Giving feedback is one of the ways you can share expectations with others and influence how they behave in the future. Receiving feedback allows you to correct personal behaviors that may interfere with your relationships.

## *Things to Do*

1. On a separate sheet of paper, select a past conflict you were engaged in, or a current conflict, and analyze it using the format in Exercise 9.3 in the next section. You may want to copy the relevant pages from the activity to help you do this.

2. The text lists the following interpersonal influence strategies: social pressure, authority and social power, appealing to needs, reciprocity, and obtaining agreement and commitment. Think of two to three examples from your life in which people have tried to influence you recently. What strategies were employed? Next think of at least two to three situations in which you need to influence someone. What strategies could you employ, and how would you use them?

3. To become more assertive, it is often necessary to practice some of the techniques discussed in the text. Consider doing one or more of the following things over the next several days. Use DESC scripts to make requests for other people to do things. Use the "broken-record" technique to get people to acknowledge an idea you have or a request you want to make. Say "no" to every request that is made of you for a day. After using each suggestion, evaluate how well you think you used it and whether it had positive or negative consequences for you. Look for opportunities to use the principles for giving and receiving feedback in Tables 9.7 and 9.8.

4. Rent a movie or watch a drama on television. As you watch it, keep a notepad handy, and identify which one or more of the sources of social power discussed in the text are used: expert, information, legitimate, referent, coercive, reward. Pay attention to when they were employed and how effective they appeared to be. Also, consider observing people interact in different settings, and look for the presence of each source of social power.

5. Read two to three descriptions of a conflict in a newspaper or national news magazine. What function does it serve, what is the cause of the conflict, and what resolution strategies are employed? How successful are the strategies used, and what transaction costs do they incur? If you were able to intervene in the conflict, what alternatives to the strategies currently employed would you use?

6. Several aspects of body language are important in behaving assertively. They include: eye contact, facial expressions, gestures, body posture, body orientation, distance, and voice elements. Pick one to work on in order to send the right signals to people. How is it currently getting in the way, and what can you do about it?

7. Table 9.6 contains a list of interpersonal rights. Select two to three that you find difficult to integrate into your life. For each of the rights you identified, answer the following questions: If you wanted to utilize each of those rights tomorrow, what factors currently prevent you from doing so? What aspects of other people, the situation, or your skills could be used to help you? Take this information and develop an action plan that you could use to make each right a part of your life.

## APPLIED ACTIVITIES

EXERCISE 9.1

**Assessing Role Conflict in the Classroom**

**Part I: Identifying Your Learning Style**

The items listed below are from the short form of the Grasha-Riechmann Student Learning Style Scales (1990). Use the rating scale listed below to rate each item. Use your typical reactions to classes in general as a frame of reference. A scoring key is provided on the next page.

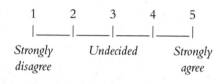

1    2    3    4    5
|____|____|____|____|
*Strongly    Undecided    Strongly*
*disagree                agree*

_____ 1. I work on class-related assignments by myself.

_____ 2. I usually have a difficult time paying attention in my classes.

_____ 3. I use the ideas of other students to help me understand course material.

_____ 4. I wish my courses were better organized.

_____ 5. I like other students to know when I have done a good job.

_____ 6. I try to participate as much as I can in all aspects of my classes.

_____ 7. I study what is important to me and not necessarily what the instructor says is important.

_____ 8. I feel like I have to attend class rather than as if I want to attend.

_____ 9. An important part my classes is learning to get along with other people.

_____ 10. I accept the structure a teacher sets for a course.

_____ 11. To get ahead in a class, sometimes you have to step on the toes of the other students.

_____ 12. I do not have trouble paying attention to what is discussed or presented.

_____ 13. I can easily determine what is important content in a course.

_____ 14. If I do not understand course material, I just forget about it.

_____ 15. I try to get to know other students on a personal basis.

_____ 16. I need clear instructions to do well.

_____ 17. Students have to be aggressive to do well in a course.

_____ 18. I get more out of going to class than staying at home.

_____ 19. I feel that my ideas about content are often as good as those in the text book.

_____ 20. I try to spend as little time as possible on a course outside of class.

_____ 21. I tend to study for tests with other students.

_____ 22. I do my assignments exactly the way my teachers say to do them.

_____ 23. I have to compete with other students to get my ideas across.

_____ 24. I am eager to learn about areas covered in a course.

**Part II: Scoring the Instrument**

Sum your ratings for the items that correspond to the learning styles listed below. *Divide your total score by 4.* Do this on a separate sheet of paper.

*Independent:* 1, 7, 13, 19     *Avoidant:* 2, 8, 14, 20
*Collaborative:* 3, 9, 15, 21     *Dependent:* 4, 10, 16, 22
*Competitive:* 5, 11, 17, 23     *Participant:* 6, 12, 18, 24

Compare your mean scores to those listed below for each age group, and then answer each of the following questions:

- Review the descriptions of each role or style in Table 9.1 to obtain a summary of the characteristics of each style.
- Check your scores against those listed below for each age group. Are you above or below the mean for your age?
- What two to three styles are most like you?

**Part III: Identifying a Possible Role Conflict in a Class**

Now think of a course you are currently taking or have taken in which you are experiencing more tension and frustration than you would like. Answer the following questions on a separate sheet of paper.

- Review the descriptions of the teaching roles or styles in Table 9.1.
- List two to three teaching styles used most often in this class.
- How are the two to three learning styles that are most like you compatible and/or incompatible with the teaching roles or styles that are employed in this course?
- What aspects of the teaching style would have to change for you to be more comfortable in this class?
- What aspects of your learning style would have to change for you to be more comfortable in this class?
- If you could be "king" or "queen" for a day and change anything you wanted, what would you do to reduce the role conflict caused by the differences in learning and teaching styles?

Norms for the Learning Style Test

| AGE | 22–28 | 29–33 | 34–40 | 41–45 | 46+ |
|---|---|---|---|---|---|
| Independent | 3.28 | 3.41 | 3.42 | 3.47 | 3.46 |
| Avoidant | 1.96 | 1.99 | 1.76 | 1.74 | 1.66 |
| Collaborative | 3.72 | 3.77 | 3.69 | 3.62 | 3.78 |
| Dependent | 3.45 | 3.37 | 3.39 | 3.42 | 3.29 |
| Competitive | 2.68 | 2.69 | 2.70 | 2.68 | 2.60 |
| Participant | 4.03 | 4.07 | 4.21 | 4.32 | 4.35 |

EXERCISE 9.2         **Using a DESC Script to Make a Request**

The DESC script technique described in the text is useful for helping to structure a request. To see how this strategy for being assertive can help you, follow the instructions listed below. Use the example in Table 9.5 to help you think through each component.

Think of someone you will ask to do something for you in the near future. Imagine that you are talking to that person, and complete the components of the DESC Script in the spaces provided.

1. *Describe the situation (D).* Specify in behavioral terms what has happened to lead you to make this request.

2. *Express your feelings about the situation (E ).* What pleasant and unpleasant feelings have been aroused by this situation? Be sure to use "I" messages when doing this.

3. *Specify what you want (S).* Ask for specific actions that you want that person to take or to stop doing.

4. *Describe the consequences associated with your request (C).* State what the positive consequences of meeting your request would be.

5. *Before using your script:* Make the script familiar to you. Practice your script in front of a mirror, with a friend or classmate, or in your imagination until you are comfortable with it. As you practice, think about how you will react to responses the person is likely to make. How will you vary what you have to say if you need to repeat the request?

EXERCISE 9.3

**How Assertive Are You?**

The items below are taken from the assertive coping subscale of the Holistic Stress Test (Grasha, 1991). Answer each one as honestly and objectively as you can. Use the following rating scale to indicate the extent to which each statement applies to your interactions with others.

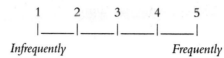

*Infrequently*           *Frequently*

_____ 1. It is easy for me to ask another person to do me a favor.

_____ 2. I hardly ever feel guilty when I refuse the requests of others.

_____ 3. When talking to someone, I am able to maintain good eye contact.

_____ 4. It is rather easy for me to accept compliments from others.

_____ 5. When I am angry at someone, I tell him or her how I feel.

_____ 6. I find it easy to give other people feedback on their performance.

_____ 7. I take a strong stand to stick up for my rights.

_____ 8. I seldom put the needs of other people ahead of my own needs.

_____ 9. When necessary, saying "no" to a friend's request is not difficult for me to do.

_____ 10. It is easy for me to tell people that I really like them.

_____ 11. In settling disputes, I believe that it is important to obtain a mutually agreeable solution.

_____ 12. I stick up for what I believe in.

_____ 13. I do not let other people take advantage of me.

_____ 14. I make requests in as clear and appropriately forceful a manner as possible.

_____ 15. I often request feedback from others to help me improve my performance.

_____ 16. When I try to assert myself, my verbal and nonverbal behaviors support each other.

**Scoring Key:**

Relatively unassertive: 16–35; Moderately assertive: 36–59; Highly assertive: 60–80

**Action Plan:**

Select one to two items from the test for which you received a relatively low score (i.e., a rating of 1 or 2). In the space below, list at least one action step you could take tomorrow to make that factor less of a problem in your life. *Use information in the text on how to behave assertively to help you develop this action plan.*

EXERCISE 9.4

**Analyzing a Personal Conflict**

Think about a conflict you are currently involved in. Select one that is important to you and that you would like to learn how to manage in an effective way. Answer the questions below. *Review the appropriate section in the text if you need additional information about the issues raised below.*

**Define the conflict:**

- Briefly specify what actions, beliefs, motives, or goals of the people involved are incompatible.

- To what extent do you believe the incompatibilities you identified are real and/or due to misperceptions.

**What Function(s) Does this Conflict Serve?**

_____ Acts as an early warning device

_____ Serves as a pressure-release valve

_____ Mobilizes energy to deal with issues

_____ Forces people to examine and renegotiate existing physical and psychological boundaries

_____ Other (please list).

Briefly state the reason(s) for your response.

**What Arenas Are Involved?**

- Draw a diagram similar to that shown in Figure 9.1 to illustrate the overlap in the involvement of the intrapersonal, interpersonal, and intergroup arenas. Use the size of each circle to symbolize the amount of time and energy spent within each arena managing the tension and frustration the dispute generated. Briefly describe the reasons for your drawing and whether or not you believe the time and energy spent on this conflict were spent in the right place.

### What Are the Causes of this Conflict?

_____ Differences in values

_____ Expectations are violated

_____ Struggle for power, control, and authority

_____ Disagreement over goals, methods to achieve them, and how to allocate resources

_____ The roles people play begin to clash

_____ Boundary and territory violations

_____ Other (please list).

- Briefly state the reason(s) you had for selecting one or more of the causes listed above.

### What Factors Appear to Support and Maintain the Conflict?

_____ Using interpersonal styles for resolving conflict ineffectively: Avoidance—Accommodation—Competition

_____ The presence of "hot cognitions"

_____ Personal collusion in allowing the conflict to continue.

- Briefly state the reason(s) you had for selecting one or more of the factors listed above.

### What Resolution Strategy(ies) Could Be Employed to Resolve It?

_____ Prevention–"A Stitch in Time Saves Nine"

_____ Take Early Action–"Nip a Conflict in the Bud"

_____ Using Power–"Determine Who Is the Biggest Kid on the Block"

_____ Conciliation–"Display a Little True GRIT"

_____ Identify the Rights of Each Party–"Play by the Rules of the Game"

_____ Compromise–"Split the Difference"

_____ Seek Mutual Gains–"All for One and One for All"

_____ Develop Superordinate Goals–"Let's Do Something Together"

_____ Use a Third Party–"Get a Little Help from Your Friends"

• What will you do to implement your strategy(ies)? Include what you will do, how you will do things, when, and where your strategy will be used.

• What are the possible transaction costs of the strategy (ies) you want to employ?

# Key Terms

*Coercive power.*   Influence occurs through the ability to impose sanctions, to punish others, as well as through threats to do such things.

*Compliance.*   Making our thoughts and actions conform to the guidelines others set for us in order to obtain a favorable reaction or to avoid unpleasant reactions.

*Compromise.*   Conflict resolution style in which each party works together to find some acceptable "middle ground" (e.g., split the difference or agree to some other mutually acceptable point between each party's position).

*Conflict.*   The tension, frustration, and anger that occur when the actions, beliefs, motives, or goals of two or more people are incompatible.

*Conflict resolution styles.*   Preferences for how we like to deal with other people when a dispute erupts, (e.g., avoid, accommodate, compete, collaborate, compromise).

*Expert power.*   Interpersonal influence is derived from one's knowledge and expertise.

*GRIT*   (Graduated and Reciprocated Initiatives in Tension reduction) A strategy for resolving differences in which one side announces that it will initiate one or more conciliatory gestures to reduce tension. This modest beginning opens the door for reciprocation by the other party.

*Identification.*   Conforming to the wishes of others in order to be just like one's friends or to create a particular image of oneself.

*Information power.*   Influence is based upon having the information needed to be able to develop logical and/or pervasive arguments about why certain actions should be taken.

*Internalization.*   Bringing one's thoughts and behaviors in line with those of others because they are personally attractive and consistent with one's beliefs.

*Interpersonal influence.*   A process of trying to define or change how someone should think, feel, or behave.

*Legitimate power.*   Influence is derived from the formal position that one holds within a group as well as from others thinking they must return favors or other social obligations.

*Mutual gains.*   A conflict resolution process in which attempts are made to integrate the needs and interests of each party.

*Norms.*   The ideas that people share that help to guide and direct their behaviors. Norms often consist of formal and informal rules, regulations, and precedents for how to behave in a situation.

*Reactance.*   Doing just the opposite of what someone wants.

*Referent power.*   Influence is based on the ability to support and nurture others and the degree to which they like you.

*Reward power.*   Influence is derived from the capacity to dispense rewards such as money, awards, social recognition and approval, and positive feelings in others.

*Roles.*   The parts that people play in daily life and that are considered appropriate for the position they occupy.

*Role conflict.*   The tension and frustration that result from playing more than one role in life or having conflicting expectations for a role.

*Superordinate goal.*   A common and very compelling goal that two or more people pursue in order to reduce tension and hostility between them.

*Values.*   The important and stable beliefs that underlie and are observed in our behaviors across a number of different situations in our lives. They represent the ideals or desirable qualities that each of us tries to obtain or to model in our lives.

*Value collision.*   When two or more people hold different values, there is a tendency for their values to clash. The result is that conflict, frustration, and anger enter a relationship.

*Win-lose conflict resolution.*   When two or more people find themselves competing for the same thing and only one party can win. Also used to describe a power based approach to trying to resolve differences.

*Win-win conflict resolution.*   When two or more people collaborate to look for ways that their needs and interests can be integrated into a resolution to a dispute. A mutual gains solution is an example of this approach.

## CHAPTER 10

# Adapting to the Demands and Challenges of Daily Living

## Chapter Overview

All of us must adapt to whatever demands and challenges life presents. To handle them, it is important to manage the stress of everyday life in an effective manner. In addition, it is often necessary to deal with the anxiety, unhappiness, and depression that occur whenever difficulties trying to cope are experienced. Finally, it is important to maintain a positive self-image in the face of life's struggles. This chapter provides suggestions to help you to achieve these goals.

## Chapter Organizers

*As you read, answer the questions that follow on a separate sheet of paper, and check your responses with those provided in the summary section.*

Everyday life has a variety of demands and challenges that test your ability to adapt.

1. What are three goals that you must achieve in order to adapt effectively?

Stress is a natural outcome of your attempts to deal with events in your life. It is something that cannot be avoided.

2. How would you define stress?
3. What are the signs of stress?

A variety of situations, events, and stimuli create stress in your life.

4. Do you know the distinction between physical and psychological stressors?
5. What steps are involved in appraising a potential stressor?
6. What characteristics of stressors make them difficult to handle?
7. Can you identify the common stressors that affect your life?

All of us try to cope with stressful events.

8. Can you identify five goals that coping responses should try to achieve?

9. What strategies for coping are related to each goal?

Anxiety and depression may develop as by-products of our attempts to manage a variety of stressors.

10. What causes anxiety and depression to occur?
11. How can you cope with these emotions?

Your self-image plays an important role in helping you to meet the demands and challenges of everyday events.

12. What are the components of your self-image?
13. How does it effect your everyday actions and the stress of daily living?
14. Are you aware of things you can do to enhance your self-image?

---

### The Struggle to Adapt: The Case of Janice

Janice was an adult student in one of my classes. She had several strikes against her from the day she was born. Her father was an alcoholic and was well known in the neighborhood for physically abusing his wife and children. She was six when her mother died and eight when her father deserted the family. Janice and her two brothers and sister were placed in numerous foster homes. Because she rarely stayed in one foster home more than a year or so, it was difficult for her to form a close relationship with adults who took care of her. "I used to cry and beg some of my foster parents I liked not to turn me over to another family."

With little support and a poor self-image, she became dissatisfied with school-work and left high school midway through her junior year. Eventually, she drifted into the wrong crowd and at 20 years of age wound up in jail for five years on a variety of robbery and receiving-stolen-property charges.

In prison, counseling sessions helped her to see that she was intelligent and had skills to make something of her life. Through contacts with the prison chaplain, she became deeply religious and spent time working with other prisoners who were having problems. She also finished her high school degree through a special program. Janice was released on probation from jail a year early and found a part-time job with the help of a family friend.

She started to take college courses in the evening and through hard work became an "A" student and eventually earned a college degree. Today, she is well into a career in social work and is married to a man she met in one of her classes. When asked to explain the turnaround in her life, she said, "I basically developed some positive attitudes and made decisions to keep me moving ahead instead of following behind in life."

---

## ADAPTING TO LIFE'S DEMANDS AND CHALLENGES

Janice overcame a rocky family life, "the wrong crowd," and prison to develop a better life for herself. Fortunately, most of us have fewer problems to overcome. But all of us have something in common with her. *We must adapt to whatever demands and challenges life presents.* How successful we become depends upon a number of things, including:

- Our skills for managing the stress various demands and challenges in our lives create
- Our capacity to manage the anxiety, unhappiness, and depression that occur when we experience difficulties trying to cope with events
- Our ability to maintain a positive self-image in the face of life's struggles.

The remainder of this chapter suggests ways to achieve the latter goals.

# MANAGING STRESS

## Stress Represents . . .

*Our Body's Reaction to Demands and Challenges* According to one point of view, **stress** is the "nonspecific response of the body to any demand made upon it" (Selye, 1976). All emergencies, illnesses, injuries, intense emotional experiences, and the challenges we face at school and work require bodily adjustments. Nonspecific physiological responses include such things as increases in blood pressure and heart and respiration rate; the release of adrenaline; increases in muscle tension; a slowing of digestive functioning to enable blood flow to be diverted to the heart, lungs, and muscles; and the mobilization of our immune system to destroy bacteria and viruses.

Our physiological responses create a state of arousal that provides the physical energy for a "fight or flight" reaction. Thus, this energy can be used to fight off an attacker or perhaps to run away from a burning building. Or, we now have the energy needed to meet a challenge such as studying for an exam, running a race, or engaging in a creative activity.

*Our Mental Reactions to Demands and Challenges* Very specific thoughts and emotions also accompany stressful events. We might become tense, frustrated, or angry at people when they irritate us or feel excited when faced with a challenge to our skills and abilities. Our thoughts might range from "I can't handle this," to "I'm really going to manage this problem very well."

*The Interaction of Mind and Body* Our mental and physical reactions to stressful events influence each other. When people are faced with heavy demands at work or school, adrenaline is released; they worry about completing tasks; they feel frustrated; and they often work at a faster pace. By taking breaks, relaxing, and instructing themselves to "calm down," they may work at a more reasonable pace on tasks. Consequently, their frustration level is likely to drop, and the level of adrenaline in their bloodstream declines. *Effective stress management helps us to learn ways to manage our mental reactions, overt responses, and the internal reactions of our bodies to the demands and challenges of everyday life.*

## Physical and Psychological Stressors Affect Our Lives

Events that produce stress are called **stressors.** Stressors may be physical stimuli (e.g., electrical shock, severe cold, loud noises, bright lights, heavy objects) or psychological (e.g., social change, poverty, arguments with friends, divorce, loss of a job). **Physical stressors** exist in the environment and naturally trigger basic physiological processes involved with illness, pain, or discomfort.

On the other hand, *our perceptions of events play an important role in determining what is stressful.* People see things differently. For some students, preparing for an exam arouses anxiety and tension. For others, it's like a walk in the park. Such events are called **psychological stressors** because they depend upon people first analyzing and then labeling them as uncomfortable (Lazarus and Folkman, 1984; Lazarus, 1991).

## Appraising Events as Stressful

This appraisal process has three components—anticipating the event, assessing our ability to cope, and evaluating the outcome of our efforts, as shown in Figure 10.1.

*1. Anticipating the Event* The event must first be categorized as either relevant or irrelevant to our lives. In other words, will something directly affect us, and is it worth spending our time and energy on it? A raging brush or forest fire hundreds of miles away may be of interest to us but unlikely to affect us. A fire in our backyard, however, is another story. Events judged as irrelevant or unimportant are usually ignored or put on a back burner just in case we need to reevaluate them in the future.

*Circumstances judged as relevant or important to us are then appraised to determine their potential to produce pleasant or unpleasant effects in our life. Potentially pleasant events* benefit us in some way or challenge us to achieve our potential or to gain something of value. *Potentially unpleasant events* lead to an immediate physical/psychological harm or loss, or they threaten to hurt us in the future.

*2. Assessing Our Ability to Cope* The issue here is whether we have the resources to cope. Or, is it likely the event will tax or exceed our capacity to manage it? Jonathan Smith (1993a) reports that Albert Bandura's ideas about self-efficacy discussed in Chapter 6 are relevant at this point in the appraisal process. **Self-efficacy** *is our judgment about our perceived capabilities to organize and execute courses of action required to handle a situation.* Such capabilities include our ability to control our thoughts, emotions, and motor skills in order to deal with a situation. Smith notes that two questions are important here: "Do I have the necessary skills and abilities?" "If I executed them, would a positive outcome occur through my efforts?" *An optimistic assessment here would contribute to our ability to manage the event as it begins to affect our lives.*

People may not be very optimistic because they lack the resources to cope, or constraints and obstacles to managing events exist. Richard Lazarus points out that we then are likely to ask, "What is the worst thing that could happen if I'm unable to cope?" And, " How likely is it that such consequences will occur?" *As you might imagine, a pessimistic outlook on our chances to cope would contribute to the frustration, anxiety, or dread inherent in the situation.*

## Appraising a Stressor

### Anticipating the Event
*Is it relevant to my life?*
*Yes - No*

*If no, no stress*
*If yes, the appraisal continues*

*Is the event potentially beneficial and / or a challenge, or is it likely to be a threat or to produce harm?*

### Assessing Your Ability to Cope
*Do I possess the necessary skills and abilities to manage this event?*
*Yes - No*

*Would I be Successful if I used my skills and abilities to cope with this event?*
*Yes - No*

*What would be the consequences if I could not cope with this event?*

### Evaluating the Outcomes of Your Efforts to Cope
*How well did I handle this situation?*
*What benefits / costs have occurred?*
*What do I need to do next?*

***Figure 10.1*** *A Summary of an Appraisal Process for Evaluating a Potential Stressor.*

*3. Evaluating the Outcomes of Our Efforts to Cope* Afterwards, we reflect and judge whether our efforts to cope were successful or unsuccessful and assess the benefits and costs that occurred. If successful, our confidence in our ability to handle a similar situation in the future is likely to increase. If unsuccessful, additional tension may occur, and we are left with a problem that still needs to be resolved. This may force us to look for other solutions or to avoid doing anything else because we feel overwhelmed by events.

*Of course, this evaluation might also help us discover that we did not exercise as much control over the situation as we could have.* In many cases, people have more control over events than they exercise. The "lessons learned" from this part of the process can help us cope more effectively in the future.

Situations that are threatening, that tax our ability to cope, and for which we fear the worst outcomes will be judged as more stressful. Also, the same event can be appraised as more stressful by one person than another. This is illustrated in Focus on People 10.1.

*Distortions and Mistakes in Appraising Events Can Occur* The result is more stress entering our lives. This can occur at any point in the process outlined above. *We might misjudge a situation as irrelevant to our lives.* A distant hurricane is perceived as "someone else's problem" until it creates tornadoes in our hometown or destroys crops raising the price of food. *Or an event is appraised as potentially having benefits, but we soon discover that a loss occurs.* Lured by fast-talking salespeople with "get rich-quick-schemes," for example, people have invested in "prime real estate in the desert," junk bonds, and

---

### FOCUS ON PEOPLE 10.1
## The End of an Era

The reactions of workers at the closing of the Norwood, Ohio, General Motors Assembly Plant illustrate the important role of cognitive appraisals in determining whether or not events are stressful. I was part of a team that worked with those affected by the layoffs to help them plan for the future.

Immediately after the layoffs were announced, a majority of those affected appraised the loss of their jobs as "the worst thing that could happen to me." They feared what the loss of income would do to their lives, and most in this group had serious doubts about being able to recover economically. Many of them also had their identies tied up in being a member of the "GM team," had given their lives to the company, and felt betrayed by General Motors. They believed the company had not treated them with the respect they deserved.

The loss of a job was appraised as producing immediate and future losses in income and self-respect. They were not confident in their ability to cope and the chances of being successful if they tried. As you might expect, members of this group had a difficult time adjusting to the loss of their jobs.

Others perceived the plant closing as an "unfortunate event" but were less worried about negative consequences. For them, the plant shut down meant "an opportunity to do other things with my life." Their identities were not totally wedded to the image of themselves as "GM employees." As one person from this group remarked, "I've worked on the line for 20 years and have always wanted to do something different. There was simply too much security here for me to make a move. Now the company has given me the incentive I always lacked and I think I can pull it off." He eventually entered a career as a travel agent.

Members of this group saw themselves as having the ability to cope and were optimistic they could do so. The consequences of losing a job were not feared as much as with the former group of employees.

other items only to discover such investments were worthless. *Our ability to cope with an event also can be underestimated.* In spite of warnings from weather forecasters, some people still try to "ride out a hurricane." Afterwards, their thoughts of "I can handle anything" turn to "never again."

*Distortions in Appraisals May Represent Defensive Pessimism* Sometimes inaccurate judgments of future events become a means of self-protection or **defensive pessimism** (Cantor and Norem, 1989). *Defensive pessimism is a self-handicapping strategy.* It occurs when people develop a "worst case scenario" before an event is experienced *even though they recognize there is little chance the event will affect them.*

A participant in a workshop held a very secure position with a company. When she heard rumors of massive layoffs, she commented to her friends, "My job is not all that secure, and I may not be able to handle getting laid off." One of my very capable students would tell his friends, "I'm going into this exam expecting the worst, even thought I know I will probably do OK." *This strategy helps people to anticipate the anxiety they might experience and to begin to cope with it.* If the worst occurs, someone can then say, "See, I told you so." Of course, if the situation turns out better than expected—they remain "pleasantly surprised."

## Stressors Interfere with Our Ability to Satisfy Needs and to Achieve Goals

A blizzard is stressful to people who dislike snow because their need to socialize with friends might be delayed and tasks at work cannot be completed. *Also, it is much more difficult to satisfy our needs and to achieve our goals when faced with stressors that are intense or of long duration and when more than one of them occurs at the same time.* A blizzard is likely to produce more havoc in people's lives than is a one-inch dusting of powdered snow. Similarly, the longer we must tolerate something we dislike (e.g., studying for final exams; remaining in a job we dislike), the more we focus on unmet needs and goals (e.g., having fun, getting ahead in life). Our levels of stress then increase. Finally, the greater the number of stressors we must "juggle" at any given time, the more difficult it is for us to manage any one of them. Tasks may get finished in a "half-baked" manner, or not at all.

*Events are more stressful when they are perceived as unpredictable and/or uncontrollable.* We then worry about whether we will be able to meet our needs or to accomplish certain goals. An approaching snowstorm is likely to create more stress if the weather report does not specify when it will arrive or how severe it is likely to be. People are left with unanswered questions: "Should I plan on school remaining open?" "Will I have time to get my grocery shopping done?" "Will I be able to get to work on time?"

*When the goal is important, the perceived impact of the stressor will be greater, and the level of stress will increase.* Obtaining a low grade on a test will be more stressful to someone who values the course than to a student who does not. Similarly, not receiving a job offer will be more stressful if the position was "very important to my career" than if it was "something to do until I find another job."

## Stressors Produce Multiple Reactions

Repeated exposure to mild physical or psychological stressors or long-lasting exposure to more severe stressors eventually decreases our ability to function effectively. *This is particularly true if our ability to cope is hampered.* Physical exhaustion and illness may occur;

our ability to work and relate to others can be hampered; we may suffer from bouts of frustration, anxiety, or depression; and critical and negative thoughts about ourselves and others increase. Let us examine in more detail some of the common reactions to stressors.

## Physiological Reactions to Stressors: The General Adaptation Syndrome

The underlying physiological responses to stressors were initially studied in pioneering work by Hans Selye (1976). He conducted research on how organisms react to stressors and proposed a general model labeled the **general adaptation syndrome**, or GAS. Selye discovered that our response to stressors involves both the nervous system and the endocrine or hormonal system. In particular, brain sites in the hypothalamus and hormones secreted by the pituitary gland help to stimulate other organs. *In spite of the variety of stressors people and other organisms experience, Selye noted that the underlying physiological responses were remarkably similar.* The components of his model as they apply to human beings are shown in Figure 10.2.

*The Alarm and Mobilization Stage* When one is confronted with the stressor, a momentary drop in blood pressure and body temperature and a temporary loss of muscle tone results. Facing an angry boss on the telephone, for example, an employee's "heart might drop" or he or she might "feel weak" and initially think, "I'm confused— what's going on here?"

The ability to resist the stressor momentarily decreases, but most of us quickly mobilize our bodies to resist the threat. An area of the brain, the hypothalamus, stimulates the pituitary gland to send a hormone or chemical messenger (Adrenocorticotropic hormone—ACTH) to the adrenal glands of the kidneys. Adrenaline is then released into the bloodstream, and our heart and respiratory systems respond by accelerating. This, in turn, supplies the muscles with more energy (oxygen), providing the strength needed to "fight or flee" as needed.

*Behaviorally, this initial stage results in a state of tension, alertness, and a readiness to respond to the stressor.* Our senses grow more responsive. Hearing becomes more acute, and taste, touch, and smell are enhanced. The pupils dilate to allow better night and peripheral vision. Mental activity also increases as our thoughts turn to ways to handle the threat. Thus, an employee might think while his or her boss screams over the telephone, "I've got to do something about this— I can't let my boss pick on me like that."

*The Resistance Stage* Instead of hanging up and going away, the employee's boss might then say, "I want to see you immediately in my office to discuss this issue further." Now the prospects of the stressor persisting increase, and ways to defend against it are needed. Consequently, from a physiological point of view, a second or resistance stage to the stressor develops. The first order of business is to obtain the additional energy in order to meet any new demands of this stressor. Our employee, for example, needs energy to keep functioning during the meeting. Someone who is physically attacked needs energy to ward off the attacker.

Powerful hormones released into the bloodstream from the adrenal glands of the kidneys come to the rescue. These hormones, glucocorticoids, elevate blood sugar (glucose) levels to fuel short bursts of energy, and the pancreas kicks in with a boost in insulin to help metabolize the blood sugar. During this stage, another adrenal gland hormone, cortisol, is released. Normally it acts to reduce inflammation that might occur from wounds or bruises if someone were physically attacked. But levels are ele-

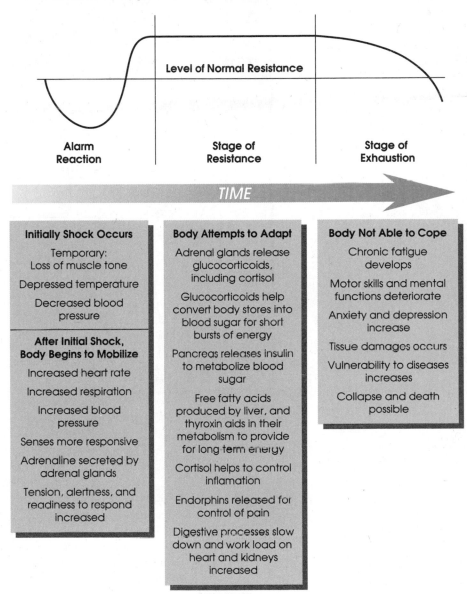

**Figure 10.2** *The General Adaptation Syndrome.*

vated anytime a threat to our physical or psychological well-being occurs (Dienstbier, 1989).

Assume for a moment that the employee's meeting with the boss did not go well. It broke up with the boss saying, "And by the way, don't think this meeting will be the end of it. We're going to have to talk about this problem for some time to come!" Now the boss will be on his or her case for some time to come. Or, perhaps an enemy has momentarily retreated but promises to return. Ways to defend against the stressor or to resist its continuing adverse effects are now needed.

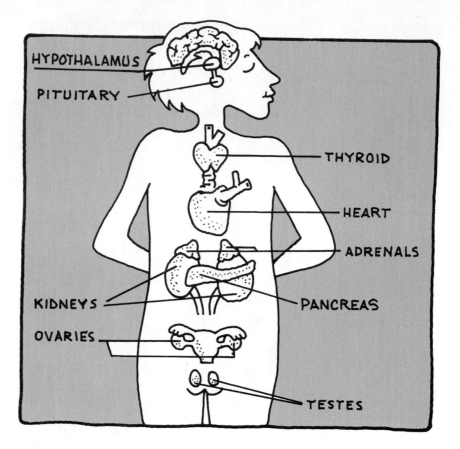

*Rather than short bursts of energy, managing an ongoing stressor demands a more stable and long-term supply of energy.* The liver responds by increasing its production of free fatty acids (cholesterol), which then become available as fuel to supplement any decreases in the supply of blood sugar. The free fatty acids, however, must be metabolized in order to provide a long-term source of energy. To do this, the thyroid gland releases the hormone thyroxine, which regulates our metabolism in order to effectively burn this additional supply of fuel.

During this resistance stage, the pituitary gland also stimulates the release of endorphins, or the body's natural painkillers. Some stressors may lead to pain and physical injury. Thus, the endorphins prevent or reduce the experience of pain and allow organisms to engage in behaviors needed to manage the stressor, for example, fleeing, fighting, or getting help.

*The Exhaustion Stage* If physical or psychological stressors continue over time, we may run out of energy or lose our ability to continue the struggle. *This can occur because the stressors are extremely powerful, and they eventually overwhelm our ability to cope. Or, the resources and skills for coping are not available or well developed.* In either case, people "spin their wheels," unable to manage various stressors, and exhaustion sets in. It is characterized by extreme fatigue, illness, high levels of anxiety and depression, impairments in motor skill and mental functions, nightmares, impaired sexual potency, and, eventually, death, if ways of managing stressors are not found.

Our employee, for example, may not have the skills to handle an overbearing boss. In time, this will take a toll on that individual's physical and emotional well-being. Tension and frustration with work may increase; that person may "dread" having to go to work; headaches, muscle tension, and physical illnesses can increase; and the adverse effects of work may spill over into other areas of his or her life. Similarly, remaining vigilant to protect oneself against an enemy and fighting periodic and largely unsuccessful skirmishes with someone eventually take a similar toll.

*Sustained Stress and Our Susceptibility to Illness* For example, research shows that a variety of stressors suppress our immune system. These include things like taking exams, separation and divorce, lack of social support, and loneliness. All can lead to a reduction in white blood cells associated with immune system functioning (Kiecolt-Glaser and Glaser, 1992). We become less able to fight off foreign organisms, to inhibit the growth of cancerous tumors, to produce antibodies, and to otherwise protect ourselves from disease. One of the internal culprits for doing this is cortisol. This hormone suppresses our immune system as part of its normal function of controlling inflammation. The problem is that it does so whether or not there is actual tissue injury to the body (Calabrese et al., 1987).

Along similar lines, various demands increase our heart rate and blood pressure. This places additional strain on our cardiovascular system, leading to a greater susceptibility to coronary problems and strokes. Finally, the release of blood sugar under stress provides for quick energy, but it also places excessive demands on the pancreas for insulin. Diabetes can be aggravated or even started if a stressor continues over time (Hanson, 1986). Finally, the increases in free fatty acids (cholesterol) lead to plaque deposits that produce hardening of the arteries and blockages in the flow of blood. Such things then become contributing factors to strokes and heart attacks.

## Behavioral, Emotional, and Cognitive Reactions to Stressors

Our responses to stressors can be examined from a physiological point of view. Or, they may be explored from the perspective of the behavioral, emotional, and cognitive responses that accompany this underlying physiology. Figure 10.3 includes a sample of the various types of reactions to stressors that are easily seen in our daily lives. *How many of them have you experienced during the past two weeks? Do some occur more often than others?*

# COMMON STRESSORS IN EVERYDAY LIFE

## Personal Qualities

*Personal Limitations* Various physical handicaps, diseases, deficiencies in social and intellectual skills, and a lack of education are personal limitations that often lead to stress. Such things interfere with achieving personal goals or prevent people from engaging in certain activities. A friend had several opportunities to become a major league baseball player. He wanted the recognition, money, and satisfaction this would provide. Unfortunately, he was in a car accident that resulted in the amputation of his right leg. He still displays a considerable amount of frustration when discussing "what could have been." Remember that our interpretation of physical and other personal limitations contributes to the amount of stress they may produce. Someone may see himself for example, as "physically handicapped" or as "physically challenged." Anyone

## Examples of Reactions to Stressors

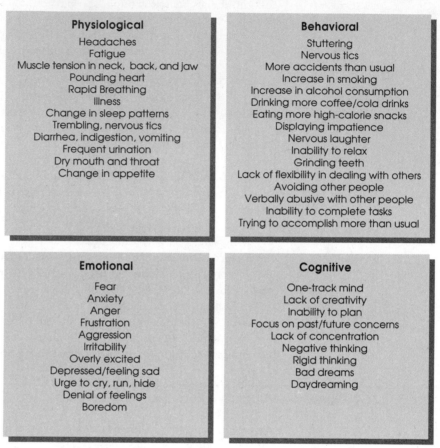

**Physiological**

Headaches
Fatigue
Muscle tension in neck, back, and jaw
Pounding heart
Rapid Breathing
Illness
Change in sleep patterns
Trembling, nervous tics
Diarrhea, indigestion, vomiting
Frequent urination
Dry mouth and throat
Change in appetite

**Behavioral**

Stuttering
Nervous tics
More accidents than usual
Increase in smoking
Increase in alcohol consumption
Drinking more coffee/cola drinks
Eating more high-calorie snacks
Displaying impatience
Nervous laughter
Inability to relax
Grinding teeth
Lack of flexibility in dealing with others
Avoiding other people
Verbally abusive with other people
Inability to complete tasks
Trying to accomplish more than usual

**Emotional**

Fear
Anxiety
Anger
Frustration
Aggression
Irritability
Overly excited
Depressed/feeling sad
Urge to cry, run, hide
Denial of feelings
Boredom

**Cognitive**

One-track mind
Lack of creativity
Inability to plan
Focus on past/future concerns
Lack of concentration
Negative thinking
Rigid thinking
Bad dreams
Daydreaming

*Figure 10.3* *Physiological, Behavioral, Emotional and Cognitive Signs of Stress.*

taking the latter perspective, however, is more likely to experience less distress and to seek ways to enhance his or her potential.

*Type A Behavior Pattern* Type A individuals are hard–driving, energetic, and impatient; they think about or try to do several things simultaneously, believe they are struggling against time, and are highly competitive. They also become hostile or angry when challenged, and they worry about other people getting ahead of them. Table 10.1 presents a list of behaviors associated with Type A individuals. Those with a **Type B behavior pattern** on the other hand are much more calm and relaxed. They are easygoing, readily satisfied, and less concerned with achievement and acquisition needs.

Individuals with a Type A personality run a much higher risk of cardiovascular problems and other stress-related illnesses. In one study, a group of 3,100 middle-aged men were followed for a period of eight and a half years. Type A men were twice as likely as Type B men to have heart attacks (Friedman and Ulmer, 1984). Other research shows that women as well as men had twice the risk of heart disease (Haynes et al., 1980). Type As also have a higher risk of other diseases that lead to debilitating illnesses and death, including strokes, diabetes, and certain types of cancers (Yakubovich, Ragland, Brand, and Syme, 1988).

*What is it about Type A individuals that makes them prone to cardiovascular problems and other illnesses?* Is it the Type A's time urgency, competitiveness, or irritability that is most

---

| **Table 10.1** | A Type A Behavior Pattern Checklist |
| --- | --- |

The items listed below are based on the research literature on the characteristics of people who possess Type A behavior patterns (Grasha, 1992). *How many apply to you?*

- I hate to sit still and do nothing.
- I tend to interrupt people when they talk.
- I finish the words and sentences of people before they can complete them.
- I tend to worry when I have a deadline.
- I don't like to waste time eating lunch.
- I check my watch or a clock to make sure I'm on schedule.
- I move from one place to another rapidly.
- I hate to watch someone do something I know I could do faster.
- I get very impatient with delays and interruptions.
- I feel like I have to compete with other people in my life.
- I lose my temper easily when people do things I dislike or they interrupt my work.
- I am impatient doing repetitive tasks like writing out checks, letters, or forms.
- I read while talking on the phone.
- I try to do as much as possible in the least amount of time.
- I take on too many responsibilities.
- I seldom take time to relax.
- I feel critical of the way other people do things.
- I find it almost impossible to slow down.
- I believe that getting ahead in life involves working long hours.
- I think that successful people must get things done faster than their peers.
- I find that I frequently do two or more activities at once.

---

important? Research suggests that Type As', irritability is the "toxic" component and the primary cause of the problem (Spielberger et al., 1985; Dembroski and Costa, 1987). It is almost as if their rage seems to lash back and strike at the heart muscle and other organ systems. Such people are often verbally aggressive as well. If you pause in the middle of a sentence, they may jump in and finish it for you.

Those who respond to life's demands with anger tend to have higher levels of physiological arousal, including muscle vasoconstriction, increased levels of norepinephrine and cholesterol, and high blood pressure. This pattern of arousal probably is not helped much by Type A's tendencies not to rest when fatigued, to carry on as usual when ill, to smoke, to drink more caffeinated beverages, and to exercise less than others (Feist and Brannon, 1988; Rice, 1987).

As shown in Figure 10.4, the roots of the Type A behavior pattern lie in the way people try to cope with insecurity. Based on experiences trying to treat the problem, Meyer Friedman and Diane Ulmer (1984) suggest that this insecurity develops in several ways. Type As may have had early childhood experiences in which they failed to form a trusting relationship with significant people in their lives. They may also have been evaluated harshly and thus acquired a fear of failure. Finally, their insecurity may be due to their high expectations and the fact they are seldom satisfied with their achievements.

*Overcommitment and Overdedication*   People with such characteristics may push themselves to the point of emotional and physical exhaustion. They burn out under the self-generated pressure to do well (Maslach, 1982). Burnout victims are often dynamic, goal-oriented, or determined perfectionists and idealists who want only the best from their marriages, jobs, children, and community. Their overcommitment and overdedication to such things eventually take their toll. They begin to question whether their efforts are worthwhile or producing effects, and they become very pessimistic about things getting better. Women tend to be more prone to burnout than

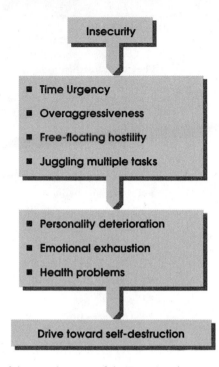

**Figure 10.4** *A Model of the Development of the Type A Behavior Pattern (based on Friedman and Ulmer, 1984).*

men, and people in the helping professions more than other occupational groups (Pines and Aronson, 1988).

Personality characteristics alone do not produce burnout. A lot depends upon the environments someone is in. For example, many work settings are ideal stages for burnout to occur. The problem is that aspects of the workplace do not adequately support the idealism, dedication, and commitment many employees and managers bring to their jobs. Characteristics of the work environment that contribute to burnout are illustrated in Table 10.2.

*Communication Style* Unfortunately, people with Type A behavior patterns and those suffering from burnout adopt styles of communication that create additional stress in their lives. Such attributes "leak out" into their interactions with others (Ganster, 1987; Burke and Greenglass, 1989). Type As, for example, tend to be more dominant and demanding and tend to elicit relatively more passive and submissive responses from others. Those suffering form burnout display much more passivity and more submissive qualities and tend to elicit more active and dominant responses from others. One of the arenas in which this struggle occurs is the college classroom, as illustrated in Focus on Applied Research 10.1.

*Major Changes in Our Lives* The death of someone close to us, marriage, divorce, disease, injury, vacations, promotions, and new jobs are stressful. Both positive and negative changes prevent us from accomplishing certain goals and may force us unexpectedly to develop new goals and objectives. In their pioneering work on life changes and stress, Thomas Holmes and Richard Rahe (1967) assigned "life change" units, or stress points, to various changes people might experience, as shown in Table

| **Table 10.2** | Burnout-Prone Workplaces |
|---|---|

The following aspects of the workplace have been identified as contributing to burnout. They tend to affect individuals who are success-oriented and who overcommit and overdedicate themselves to their jobs more than others (Pfifferling and Eckel,1982; Jackson et al., 1986). *How many apply to the place where you work?*

- Constant demands for perfection
- Workers discouraged from expressing grievances
- Expectation that employees should provide extra effort for little or no reward
- No reinforcement for suggestions about improving morale
- Staff encouraged to interact only with peers
- Repetitive work activities
- Minimal additional help provided for tasks that require extra effort
- Emotional feelings of employees downplayed
- Preachy leadership styles
- Frequent changes in policies without time to evaluate them
- Rigid role definitions for employees
- Playfulness considered unprofessional and inappropriate
- People discriminated against based on age, sex, and race
- Very little emphasis on positive feedback
- Very little concern about comfort of the work environment
- Enforcement of policies and bases of policies constantly shifting
- Attitudes of supervisors make employees feel ineffective or unappreciated
- Employee morale is low, and people feel they accomplish very little on the job

---

### FOCUS ON APPLIED RESEARCH 10.1
## Teacher Burnout, Type A Behaviors, and Student Resistance

Student resistance to teachers' efforts to gain compliance with their requests is a fundamental aspect of classroom instruction. The types of resistance strategies that college students adopt are related to whether their teachers display Type A behavior patterns or communicate a sense of feeling "burned out" (Lamude et al., 1992).

These authors suggest that college teachers with Type A behavior patterns are relentless in their pursuit of control and achievement and try to get those under them into a "fast pace." To do this, they oversupervise the efforts of students and push them to achieve high standards. Teachers who are burned out, on the other hand, and give significantly less information, less praise, are less accepting of their students' ideas, and interact less frequently with them. They also express feeling bored, are not very enthusiastic about teaching, and are chronically frustrated.

Students typically resent both types of behaviors and become frustrated. The teachers, in turn, experience more stress because they now must deal with the strategies students employ to resist them. *These authors report:*

- *When faced with a Type A teacher, students resist attempts to control them* by not participating in class, pretending to be prepared, ignoring what the teacher says, and justifying their lack of involvement by saying to themselves "this class is not as important as others I am taking."
- *When dealing with a teacher who is burned out,* students report resisting attempts to control them by threatening to go to the dean or department head, letting the teacher know he or she has problems relating to the class, telling the teacher how to run the class, and using teacher rating forms to give poor evaluations.

**Table 10.3**

## Life Change Events and Stress

Thomas Holmes and Richard Rahe assigned life change units to reflect the relative amount of stress events produced. These are shown below. Note that stress is produced by both pleasant and unpleasant events.

| FAMILY | LIFE CHANGE UNITS |
|---|---|
| Death of spouse | 100 |
| Divorce | 73 |
| Death of close family member | 63 |
| Marriage | 50 |
| Pregnancy | 40 |
| Son or daughter leaving home | 29 |
| In-law troubles | 29 |
| Spouse starting or ending work | 26 |
| **PERSONAL** | |
| Detention in jail | 63 |
| Major personal injury or illness | 53 |
| Sexual difficulties | 39 |
| Outstanding personal achievement | 28 |
| Changing to a new school | 20 |
| Change in sleeping habits | 15 |
| Change in eating habits | 13 |
| Vacation | 12 |
| Holiday season | 11 |
| **WORK** | |
| Being fired from job | 47 |
| Retirement from work | 45 |
| Major change in work responsibilities | 29 |
| Trouble with boss | 23 |
| Major change in working conditions | 20 |

Based on data reported by Holmes and Rahe (1967).

10.3. They reported that individuals with scores less than 100, for example, experienced about 1.4 illnesses during the previous six months. A score between 300 and 400 was associated with about 1.9 illnesses, and people with scores greater than 500 reported about 2.1 illnesses. Similarly, those with life change scores greater than 400 have been shown to be two to three times as likely to suffer from physical illnesses, headaches, muscle tension, bouts of anxiety and depression, and other problems than those with lower scores (De Benedittis et al., 1990; Monroe et al., 1992).

Other research suggests some modifications to the role of change and stress. While life changes disrupt the normal flow of our lives, they usually do not produce as many unpleasant stress reactions as originally thought (Sarason et al., 1985). These authors asked people to rate the degree to which life events were perceived as "positive or negative." As you might expect, negative events had a stronger impact on health than did positive ones.

| Table 10.4 | The Top Ten Hassles of Daily Living |
| --- | --- |

One hundred adult men and women kept daily records of the little irritations or hassles in their lives. The ten most frequent over a nine-month period were:

| HASSLE | PERCENT OF PEOPLE CHECKING |
| --- | --- |
| 1. Concern about weight | 52.4 |
| 2. Health of a family member | 48.1 |
| 3. Rising prices of common goods | 43.7 |
| 4. Home maintenance | 42.8 |
| 5. Too many things to do | 38.6 |
| 6. Misplacing or losing things | 38.1 |
| 7. Yard work or outside home maintenance | 38.1 |
| 8. Property, investment, or tax concerns | 37.6 |
| 9. Crime | 37.1 |
| 10. Physical appearance | 35.9 |

Based on data reported by Lazarus, 1981.

*Daily Hassles* While major changes can be stressful, so can even minor everyday "hassles." As shown in Table 10.4, the frequency, duration, and intensity of such hassles are important in determining how stressful they will become. Also, a person's mood when a hassle occurs is important. When someone is already under pressure, a petty problem that otherwise might be ignored (e.g., a misplaced pen or key, a traffic jam) can have a much greater effect. Research suggests that people with a high number of daily hassles have more respiratory infections, headaches, bad dreams, and crying spells. They also are more prone to angry outbursts, more easily excited, and more uneasy, bored, and restless than their less hassled counterparts (Folkman and Lazarus, 1988; Garrett et al., 1991).

## Unique Stressors Within the Domains of Daily Living

Events within work, school, family, and social settings also contribute to our levels of stress. Some of these were included in the examples of specific stressors associated with life changes, hassles, and personal qualities. In addition, some categories of stressors overlap each domain, including the presence of interpersonal conflicts, role conflicts, competing demands for our time, as well as having "too much to do and not enough time in which to do it." There are, however, some important stressors that are relatively unique to each domain that have not been mentioned. Examples of each are presented in Table 10.5. *Which ones affect your life within each of these domains?*

*While one might think of each domain as separate, tension and frustration in one area tends to "spill over" into another.* Perceptions of the amount of stress in school, for example, are often associated with how much tension and frustration exist in one's family and social life. Similarly, the intensity of job stress among corporate managers, employees of major businesses, students in part-time jobs, and college faculty and administrators also were affected by events in their family and social lives (Crowe and Grasha, 1993; Short and Grasha, 1994).

Among working women, Rena Repetti (1993) reports that conflicts at work and feeling overloaded on the job were important predictors of the amount of stress expe-

| | |
|---|---|
| **Table 10.5** | **Relatively Unique Stressors Associated with Work, School, Family, and Our Social Lives** |

| WORK | FAMILY |
|---|---|
| • Little input on decisions that affect my job<br>• Others try to tell me how to do my job<br>• Seldom receive regular and immediate feedback when my performance on the job is good<br>• There is little career potential and advancement in my job<br>• Promotions and pay raises have not met my expectations<br>• Concerned about my position being eliminated in the future | • Disagree with my spouse/other family members on how to spend money<br>• Do not feel loved and accepted by my spouse/other family members<br>• Quality of the time I spend with my spouse/family members is not high<br>• Sexual frustration is present in my relationship with my spouse<br>• My spouse/other family members and I are not clear about what we expect from each other |

| SCHOOL | SOCIAL LIFE |
|---|---|
| • Noisy students in class causing distractions<br>• Uncertainty about my plans after graduation<br>• Not understanding the wording of exam questions<br>• Being placed on academic probation<br>• Giving a presentation in class<br>• Studying for a test<br>• Being called on in class<br>• Receiving a D or F on a test<br>• Writing a term paper | • Not totally satisfied with the friends I have<br>• It is not easy for me to make friends<br>• My social life suffers because I have to work so much<br>• Social life is not very exciting<br>• Envy others because they have more friends that I do<br>• Social situations make me feel uncomfortable |

Items from the Holistic Stress Test (Grasha, 1989).

rienced in their family lives. Repetti observed several reasons for the overlap of tension between the two domains. One participant in her study noted, "When I've had a bad day, the first people that hit me are the people at home, so I take it out on them" (p. 117). Others reported having little physical and emotional energy after returning home from work. They talked about feeling too "tired," "washed out," or "pushed" to attend to household responsibilities. Thus, they were both less able to handle problems at home and less sensitive to the needs and feelings of family members.

## Adverse Environmental Events

Included here are events such as severe storms, famines, fires, and wars. While relatively infrequent and unpredictable, their occurrence may temporarily or permanently affect our ability to achieve certain goals. Sometimes the stress is so severe that people may experience **posttraumatic stress disorder.** This condition is characterized by nightmares, flashbacks, distress when reminded of the event, irritability, difficulty concentrating, and a general unresponsiveness (Kasl, 1990). People also report difficulties sleeping and that their use of alcohol and prescription drugs increases. Those most affected by posttraumatic stress disorder tend to ruminate passively about their problems rather than actively confronting them (Nolen-Hoeksema and Morrow, 1991).

Unpleasant but less severe environmental stimulation also is stressful. Air pollution, hot and cold weather, and noise from planes, trains, automobiles, and industrial processes contribute to feeling tense and frustrated. Such stimulation also is distracting, making it difficult to concentrate and interfering with our ability to acquire and retain information (Cohen et al., 1986).

# COPING WITH STRESS

## Five Interrelated Goals of Coping

*Prevent and Reduce Distress* In moderate amounts, stress keeps us alert and ready to respond, energizes our behaviors, and helps us to remain productive. On the other hand, when there is very little stress, boredom sets in; when there is too much, we feel overwhelmed and our responses are typically not very productive. Here, the experience of stress is labeled **distress** (Smith, 1993a). Distress, for example, often leads us to feel overly anxious and frustrated, to make mistakes, to overlook long-term solutions to problems, and to respond to rigid and inflexible ways to the demands we face.

*Create Eustress* When our responses to stressors lead to productive outcomes such as solving problems and coping constructively, our experience of stress is referred to as **eustress**. People report feeling energized, more in control of their lives, and more willing to face the challenges and demands of daily living.

Successful attempts at coping help to prevent or reduce distress and enable the experience of eustress to become a more prominent part of our everyday lives. *There is no single strategy, however, that can achieve both of these goals.* Circumstances producing stress are complicated, and appropriate combinations of various coping responses appear to work better than any strategy used in isolation.

Nealia Bruning and David Frew (1987), for example, taught coping skills to managers and employees of a large corporation to help them manage distress on their jobs. Skills included identifying problems and seeding solutions, obtaining help from others, managing time, becoming more assertive, learning relaxation skills, and increasing physical activity. Combinations of such skills were much more effective in reducing uncomfortable levels of job stress than was any strategy used alone. Similar results have been obtained in other settings including helping students to manage exams and other stressors of academic life (Smith, 1989).

*Strive to Live Within Your Comfort Zone* All of us need sufficient amounts of stress in our lives to reap the benefits it provides, but not so much that it interferes with our satisfaction and productivity. To accomplish this goal, Melvyn Kinder (1994) indicates that we must keep the level of arousal from stressors within our comfort zone. *That is, we must work to keep the intensity of arousal from stressors at subjectively moderate levels.* He finds that accomplishing the latter goal typically leads to productive levels of performance and increased satisfaction with life. Finding your comfort zone is like the task the producers of a syndicated country-western television show faced as illustrated in Focus On People 10.2.

## Putting Television Viewers into Their Comfort Zone

"Hee-Haw" was a very popular and successful country-western syndicated television show for more than 15 years. The format consisted of a series of 30-second to 5-minute segments of corny jokes, country songs, guest performers, and skits. Segments for the 26 one-hour shows were videotaped over a three-month period and then combined into a complete show.

To ensure that viewers were neither bored or overly stimulated by a show, the producers wanted to find their comfort zone. The theory was that shows perceived as "just right" would bring viewers back week after week. Thus, typical viewers were hired to rate each segment for interest, entertainment value, and humor. In effect, such viewers were telling the producers what their level of comfort was with each portion of a show.

*Segments were then combined into an hour-long show so that each program had the same average rating.* The producers wanted each program to have an overall mean rating of approximately 4.0 on interest, entertainment value, and humor. Different pieces, for example, might have rated a 1.0 (poor) on a 7-point scale on entertainment value, whereas others were given a 7.0 (excellent). To get a 4.0 average, each show combined segments that were rated relatively high and low on each criterion. *This process ensured that the overall quality of each show was well within the range of an acceptable level of viewer comfort* (Montauk and Grasha, 1993).

*Buffer and Protect Yourself from the Negative Consequences of Stress* Coping also helps us to buffer or cushion the effects of stressors and provides a certain amount of protection from them. For example, seeking help from other people helps to cushion and reduce the tension we experience. In addition, being physically fit and in good health offer some protection against the negative side effects of stress and also provide the physical energy needed to cope.

*Conserve, Replenish, and Build an Inventory of Resources Needed to Manage Stress* Steven Hobfoll (1989) views coping as a process where we spend a variety of resources. *The more resources we have to spend— the better we cope.* For example, dealing with stressors takes time, energy, and on occasion money. Without using time and expending personal energy, very few of our problems would get resolved. Similarly, some of our frustrations in life intensify when we lack material possessions. Having sufficient financial means makes it easier to handle medical bills, rent, mortgage, and car payments, and to buy food and suitable clothes to wear. A lack of money makes such things much more stressful. Other tangible resources associated with lower levels of stress include having a good education, a reasonably well paying job, suitable housing, and personal possessions such as cars, clothes, jewelry, furniture, and money in the bank.

Material resources are associated with lower levels of stress because they help us to live a healthy, productive, and more satisfying life-style. With them, people can better manage to take care of their physical needs as well as their needs for status. For example, they can buy medical care, nutritious food, as well as material possessions like stereos, cars, and clothes that signal others to their successes in life. Or when faced with a personal or legal problem, people with material resources can obtain professional advice or assistance by seeing a therapist or hiring an attorney; afford to take the time to work on issues; and purchase what they need to reduce the impact of a stressor; for example, a car to make traveling to work easier.

In Hobfoll's model, certain personal qualities also become resources for coping. They include such things as an optimistic outlook on life, beliefs that we can control events, personal resourcefulness, and having a positive self-image. The latter help us to resist stressors and to mobilize our energy to do something about a problem. Similarly, various types of knowledge, skills, and abilities promote effective coping. Included here is the information needed to succeed on exams, job interviews, or assignments at work; stress management skills; and communication and social skills. Finally it also helps to have several friends and acquaintances who can assist us when problems develop.

The wise use of resources produces important dividends in our lives. Barbara Israel (1989) and her colleagues, for example, report that people with adequate resources are less depressed, more satisfied with their jobs, and physically healthier. Similarly, students who reported possessing a larger number of the resources just described had lower levels of stress in their academic lives (Sohns, 1994).

*Because resources are so important to us, the actual loss or threat of losing them can increase the amount of distress in our lives.* Consequently, an important goal of coping is to conserve those resources we already possess, to replenish those we have used, and to increase our inventory of resources to help us meet future demands and challenges.

## ACHIEVING THE GOALS FOR COPING WITH STRESS: MANAGING DISTRESS, CREATING EUSTRESS, AND LIVING WITHIN OUR COMFORT ZONE

### Identify and Rate the Intensity of the Stress Various Events Produce

Just as segments of the "Hee-Haw" show were rated for viewer comfort, we can rate our levels of comfort with "segments of our lives." *Such ratings could acknowledge events that were outside of our comfort zone.* This would identify issues to work on in order to provide some immediate relief and to make them less of an adverse experience in the future. *The ratings also could identify situations that were within our comfort zone, suggesting the types of things we might want to experience more of in the future.* One way to accomplish the latter goal is to employ a Subjective Units of Discomfort Scale to monitor how much discomfort events produce (Montauk and Grasha, 1993). How to keep a stress journal using such a scale is described in Table 10.6 and Table 10.7.

### Engage in Constructive Thinking Processes

*Restructure How Events Are Perceived* Sometimes events are interpreted in absolute and extreme ways. Albert Ellis (1987) labels such thoughts *irrational beliefs* and shows that they also add fuel to our emotional fires. "Extreme" thoughts suggest that disaster is right around the corner and include using words to describe events like *all, every, always, awful, terrible, horrible, totally,* and *essential.* "Absolute" beliefs imply that we have no choices and include using words to describe events like *must, should, have to, need,* and *ought.* Studies show they lead to a variety of interpersonal and personal problems, including excessive worrying, depression, irritability, loneliness, excessive gambling, and conflicts with others (Hoglund and Collison, 1989; Goldberg, 1990; Walker and Phil, 1992).

Pamela Butler (1981) identified three categories of irrational beliefs—drivers, stoppers, and distorters. Examples of each are illustrated in Table 10.8. *Which ones have you used? Which ones are present in the examples shown in Table 10.8?*

| **Table 10.6** | Developing a Subjective Units of Discomfort Scale (SUDS) and Stress Journal |

*Purpose:* To determine the relative levels of stress that various events produce. It is helpful to sensitize yourself to the different emotional experiences that incidents produce, and it also produces a written record of stressful events that can be employed to analyze problems, to develop solutions, and to work towards finding levels of stress that are much more comfortable.

*Setting Up a Stress Journal:* Events are monitored for a period of time (i.e., 3-5 days) to gather a baseline on the types of stressors encountered and the relative levels of discomfort they produce. *While recording for several days is suggested, doing so for even a single day is often informative.* An alternative is to list the events of a day or two after they have occurred. While not the most desirable method because of problems forgetting details, it is acceptable if no direct recording is possible. *A description for developing a recording format follows.*

1. A small note pad that can fit in a suit or shirt pocket is needed, and *ratings of important events are recorded as soon after they occur as possible.* Important daily events are given a rating in the notebook according to the discomfort level produced. Not every event needs to be recorded. Try to concentrate on *relatively important encounters that most often occur.*
2. *A 10-point "subjective units of discomfort scale" (SUDS) is suggested* in which a 10 indicates a relatively high level of discomfort, a 5 a moderate level, and a 1 a relatively low level of discomfort.
3. *Each notation begins with:*
   a. *Time of day and a listing of the major stressor(s) encountered* (e.g., 11:15 A.M.: discussed an unexpected low grade on a test with my teacher, I was visibly upset. 1:50 P.M.: had a telephone conversation with my girlfriend about her mother getting on her case all of the time. Had a lot of other things on my mind at the time).
   b. *A rating of the relative amount of stress or discomfort associated with the event* (i.e., 1–10 rating scale) and a notation as to whether the degree of stress experienced was in the comfort zone (CZ) or outside of it (OCZ).
   c. *Label the emotional experience* and the thoughts you experienced (e.g., angry, anxious, "the worst thing that could happen to me").

Restructuring how we think about events in our lives helps to reduce distress. *Generally looking for a balanced and less extreme/absolute perspective helps.* For example, assume for a moment that a friend says, "I'm sick and tired of how you behave around me. You are a real jerk!" Instead of personalizing the remarks and thinking, "What a horrible man he was to treat me that way. He does not deserve to be my friend," appraise the situation differently. Thus, you might think, "Maybe he's having a tough day. He must be very unhappy to say such things." Or, "His getting angry at me now might help him to settle down. Then I can talk to him later about what's bothering him."

*Develop a Hardy Mental Outlook* Some people live with high levels of stress and appear not to suffer from the physical and psychological problems their peers do. Instead, they engage in better health habits, have fewer instances of illnesses, create less stress for themselves, and rate stressful events as less threatening than most other people (Funk, 1992; Pollock, 1989; Wiebe, 1991). They demonstrate hardiness in the face of stress. Research shows that they have mastered the three **C**s: **C**ommitment, **C**ontrol, and **C**hallenge (Kobassa, Maddi, and Kahn, 1982).

**Table 10.7**        Entries from a Stress Journal

Monday, February 3:

| TIME OF DAY | STRESSOR | SUDS RATING | EMOTIONS/THOUGHTS |
|---|---|---|---|
| 10:30 A.M. | Discussed customer with my boss. He was rushed for time, and I was not able to discuss the best way to handle the customer's problem. | 4 (CZ)★ | A bit frustrated: "He never takes enough time with me." |
| Noon | Presented to the out of town sales reps on the new billing policies. Speaking in public not my favorite activity, and handouts were not as good as I would prefer. | 9 (OCZ) | Anxious: "I bet everyone can see how lousy a speaker I really am." |
| 3:20 P.M. | Had a doctor's appointment, and she got on my case for not taking my medication. I told her I did not think I needed it anymore. | 6 (OCZ) | Irritated: "It seems like she enjoys picking on me." |
| 4:10 P.M. | Walked back to office and thought about my upcoming vacation. | 2 (CZ) | Relaxed: "I'd like this." |
| 4:55 P.M. | Promised wife to take her to dinner and movie. Still have about two hours' worth of work in order to get ready for tomorrow. Had to cancel our date for the evening. | 9 (OCZ) | Overwhelmed: Anxious: "I'm always doing this to my wife." |

*Analysis and Action Steps.* What coping strategies must be used to manage events outside of my comfort zone? Are there any experiences within my comfort zone I need to have more of or that suggest other constructive actions I could take?

*Example:* Need to manage my time better so that I don't have to work late and disappoint my wife. Also could stop putting myself down so much. I actually spend a lot of time with her. Need to look for ways to become a little more assertive with my boss to get what I want out of conversations. Need to get more physical activity.

★ CZ = Event Within Comfort Zone; OCZ = Event Outside of Comfort Zone

*Commitment means that hardy individuals approach life with a sense of purpose.* They enjoy what they do and do not passively go through the motions. When faced with an exam, they allow plenty of time to prepare. When faced with a new job assignment, they take the time to learn the skills needed to do well. In both cases, they approach

**Table 10.8**                    Common Types of Irrational Beliefs

**Drivers:** Keep us from a natural pace. While often rewarded in daily life, they may lead us to become fatigued, exhausted, and frustrated.

| | |
|---|---|
| *Perfectionism:* | "Be perfect in everything you do." |
| *Do it yesterday:* | "Hurry up, you don't have all the time in the world." |
| *Be Macho:* | "Be strong and put up a tough front. Never show weaknesses." |
| *Self-sacrifice:* | "Please others at any cost, or they will not like you." |
| *Push self to limit:* | "No limit to what you can do. Do as much as you can until it begins to hurt." |

**Stoppers:** Keep us from taking actions, hold us back, and otherwise make us behave as we always have. Give us a good excuse for doing nothing.

| | |
|---|---|
| *Catastrophizing:* | "This situation is utterly hopeless. Nothing will ever correct it." |
| *Negative thinking:* | "I can see nothing but gloom and doom here." |
| *Arbitrary inference:* | "My friend has not written in three weeks. She must not like me any more." |
| *Rigidity:* | "There is no reason to change how I think or feel." |
| *Living in past:* | "The old ways of doing things are always best." |
| *Waiting around:* | "I can't do anything until other people change first." |
| *Quitter:* | "I have tried everything, and nothing worked." |
| *Procrastination:* | "I have plenty of time to take care of this problem." |

**Distorters:** Lead us to develop false impressions about ourselves, other people, and events. They add confusion to our lives and keep us from obtaining a good idea of what is happening to us.

| | |
|---|---|
| *Overgeneralize:* | "I didn't do well, and thus I'll never do well." |
| *Blame others:* | "Other people are responsible for what happened." |
| *Narrow-minded:* | "I don't need more information; I have all I need." |
| *Denial:* | "This is really not a problem." |
| *Stereotype:* | "Those people are all alike. You can't trust them." |
| *Either/or thinking:* | "Either I'm a complete success, or I'm a failure." |
| *Overestimate:* | "This is the most horrible thing that has ever happened to me." |
| *Illogical thoughts:* | "My friends must support me no matter what I do." |
| *Personalization:* | "Somehow, bad things seem to happen to me no matter what I do." |

each task trying to improve themselves; they take ownership for the task and do not do something only because someone said they should.

*Hardy people also perceive themselves as controlling important aspects of their lives.* Either they know, for example, that they possess the skills to do well on exams or a new job, or they are confident they can learn such skills. *They also see problems as a challenge and not as an obstacle.* Consequently, they are willing to devote time and energy to working on them. Exams become a challenge to test their knowledge, and a new job assignment becomes a challenge for handling new responsibilities.

How can you take charge of your life and attack problems rather than retreat from them? *One way is to respond to stressors by asking questions that direct you to take charge of the situation.* You might ask, "What can I do to eliminate this stressor?" "How can I look at this problem as a potential for growth?" "In what ways does this stressor tell me something about my goals in life?" "How can I use this situation to enhance my knowledge and skills?"

*Another strategy is to get better at setting personal goals.* In particular, setting goals that provide challenges for us, to which we can commit, and over which we can exert personal control enhances our ability to adapt (Watson and Tharp, 1993). In addition, when we consciously analyze "why we want to pursue a given goal" and "our likelihood of sticking to it," our commitment and perceptions of being able to achieve it increase (Dishman et al., 1981). The section on self-renewal at the end of this chapter has several other suggestions for how to do this effectively.

*Develop a Small-Win Attitude This is the ability to take the problems we face and to divide them into smaller parts.* Thus, instead of having to "climb a mountain," we have a number of "manageable molehills" to step over. A related aspect of the "small-win attitude" is to resolve the little issues in your life. Sometimes it is the little things that hold us back from achieving our potential (Weick, 1984).

## Establish and Honor Personal Priorities for Managing Your Time

*Organize and Manage Your Time More Effectively* "If I only had more time, I could get so much more accomplished," is a common complaint. Experts in time management, however, *point out that time is not the problem.* Lucy Hedrick (1990) believes that it is unreasonable for anyone to think she can do everything she wants. She finds the important issue is to learn how to use the time we have available more effectively. This means organizing your life and establishing priorities for what you want to accomplish. People who manage their time effectively report more control over their lives, less overload and ambiguity about what they should do, less tension at work, and greater satisfaction with work and their everyday lives (Bond and Feather, 1988; Hoff-Macan et al., 1990).

There are several components of managing time. *One is to organize your activities into a schedule of what you want to accomplish.* To do this, sit down at the beginning of a day or week and list activities at work, home, and in your social life that seem important to you. *Next, allocate those activities to specific periods of time.* This often involves specific times of the day and week, but some people also are successful in just developing a "to do" list for each day and getting to things when they can. Finally, *filter your activities to determine what you really need to do.* The latter task can be accomplished by asking each of the following questions about the activities you listed (Grasha, 1987, 1992):

- *Do I have to personally "do it"?*
- *Is there a more "creative/efficient way" to do it?*
- *Can I "delegate" this to someone else?*
- *Can I "delay" taking action?*
- *Can I "dump" this activity because it's unlikely to be missed?*

Answering such questions honestly will reduce the pressure to feel like, "I have to do everything." Thus, a somewhat more leisurely, less stressful pace can be applied to those activities that remain on your schedule. Or, the additional time can be devoted to higher priority items. *An added benefit is that the questions can be applied anytime someone makes a request of you.* They can help you manage the temptation to say "yes" when you should have said "no."

The real challenge in managing time, however, is not simply developing and following a schedule. Steven Covey (1989), for example, argues that the important issue is setting and acting upon personal priorities within the time we have available. He suggests that personal priorities need to focus on:

- *Preventing problems*
- *Building relationships*
- *Acting on new opportunities for ourselves*
- *Finding time for recreation and leisure.*

Establishing rigid schedules and accounting for every minute of our day sometimes can run counter to such goals. This efficiency focus may clash with the opportunity to develop rich relationships, to meet our needs, and to enjoy spontaneous moments on a daily basis. Thus, a certain amount of flexibility needs to be a part of organizing our lives.

*Become a Little Selfish* Abraham Maslow (1970, 1971) studied the differences between individuals who were successful and growth-oriented versus those who had difficulty reaching their potential. One of the important outcomes of his work was the discovery that people in the former group (i.e., those he labeled self-actualizers) employed a somewhat "selfish" approach to life. *They took time out of their daily schedules to devote to themselves.* The time was spent "relaxing," "taking walks," "engaging in hobbies," "reading," "enhancing various skills," and in a variety of personally satisfying and growth-producing activities. The result was a much more optimistic outlook and a reduction in personal stress levels.

What is important to recognize here is that even relatively small amounts of time can be helpful. Thus, begin with 10, 20, or 30 minutes of time a day devoted to activities that are important for your personal well-being and growth. The important issue is to change your thinking from "what others want me to do is important" to "some of what I want and need also is important."

## Practice Relaxation Techniques

When daily activities become too stressful, muscle tension increases, people become anxious, and tension increases. People typically experience this as "feeling uptight" or as having tension in the muscles of the neck, lower back, or other areas of the body. Taking a break to relax helps to decrease such tension, and it slows down the physiological arousal associated with stress (Titlebaum, 1988). Various techniques for relaxing also restore energy so that you can cope better with stressful events. Those suggested by Hope Titlebaum are described in Table 10.9.

**Table 10.9**           Quick Relaxers

**Slow Rhythmic Breathing**

Sit back in a chair, or lie down if possible. Make your body as tense as you can, and remain tense for a count of ten before releasing the tension. Do this one to two additional times. This will help to release muscle tension and facilitate relaxing. Now relax your posture. Uncross your arms or legs; drop your hands to your sides; and sit or lie so that you minimize tension on your body. Exhale slowly through your nose for a count of four. Do so slowly and as naturally as you can. Inhale slowly through your nose for a count of four. Continue to do this until you get a natural and slow breathing rhythm established. Some people find it helpful to repeat a pacifier word such as calm, relax, peace, or quiet to themselves while slowly breathing. Continue this slow breathing pattern for a period of three to four minutes.

**Guided Imagery**

When relaxed and using the slow breathing exercise described above, begin to imagine a pleasant scene in your mind. Mentally place yourself into the scene, and enjoy the delights that you have imagined. You might, for example, imagine a series of scattered streams tumbling down a hillside. You follow the agitated energy of the water until it finally empties into a supremely quiet, tranquil pool or lake. The water has reached its level and now has no more need to rush and roar about. You remind yourself, while contemplating the tranquility of the deep pool, that all of us sometimes go along like the water passing through periods of seething stormy discontent. And then you see those periods of stormy discontent merging into the peacefulness of the undisturbed pool. *Some people find that once such images are practiced and associated with relaxation, simply imagining the pleasant scene helps to calm them.* Take your time going through the scenario you imagined. Pause after each event in your scenario, and reflect on what you are seeing and how it is helping to calm you.

**Disengage Yourself**

As you feel yourself becoming tense, immediately stop what you are doing and thinking about. Take a deep breath, and tell yourself to relax. Focus on some feature of the room you are in. A piece of art, a corner of the room, a chair, the floor beneath you or anything that is convenient for you to look at will suffice. Concentrate on that feature, and breath slowly. As you concentrate on the fixation point, clear your thoughts of everything. Do not make any plans, rehash a conversation, or try to solve a problem. Keep your mind as blank as possible. Do this for at least two to three minutes whenever you need a break from your concerns.

## ACHIEVING THE GOALS FOR COPING WITH STRESS: BUFFERING ITS EFFECTS AND PROTECTING OURSELVES AGAINST STRESSORS

### Seek Social Support

People who have good relationships with others suffer fewer medical and emotional problems than more isolated individuals. They also report more satisfaction with their lives. Good social support also helps us to "pull through" a variety of illnesses, medical emergencies, and other problems (Buunk and Verhoeven, 1991; Roos and Cohen, 1987). Social support appears to be an effective buffer of the stressors in our lives.

### Types of Social Support
- *Emotional support.* Others listen and talk to us about our feelings and help us explore alternative ways to handle issues. Others often display confidence in us and provide encouragement to continue working on issues.
- *Informational support.* Finally, other people can provide advice and as well as other information needed to help resolve a problem.
- *Material support.* Those we admire and trust can provide us with material support such as equipment, money, or direct assistance with a task.

***Seek Advice from Those in the Best Position to Help You***  Social support works best when it is specific to the type of problem encountered. A friend might listen to a problem and provide a feeling of "someone else cares and can appreciate how I feel." For a long-term solution, however, those in a position to give concrete advice and help are also needed. Otherwise, the problem will continue to be an irritation long after the short-term effects of "It's nice to know someone else understands" wear off. Two conditions for obtaining effective help from others are:

*1. Be clear about what you want from the person you contact.*  Specific goals can include listening to my concerns about my workload, giving advice on how to deal with my boss, providing assistance with a difficult problem, acting as an intermediary to present my concerns to another person, or any number of other things.

*2. State your goals before discussing the problem.*  For example, "I'm having a difficult time working with a my boss and wondered if you have a few minutes to listen to my concerns." Or, "I need a couple of suggestions for how to handle my frustration with the amount of work I have to do."

## Develop Physical Hardiness

Managing stress is not unlike training to participate in any sport. Those who are healthy are in good physical condition, get proper amounts of rest, and eat a healthy diet typically perform well. Such individuals have the physical endurance and strength to handle the stresses of the event. In much the same way, we need "to be in shape" to handle the demands and challenges of daily living. People who are physically fit become fatigued less easily; they remain alert to cope with the demands placed upon them; their immune systems are stronger; they possess more energy for handling events in their lives; and they are less susceptible to illnesses (Brown, 1991a; Nowack, 1991). There are several things you can do to contribute to your levels of physical hardiness.

***Integrate More Physical Activity and Exercise into Your Life***  A regular exercise program increases physical endurance, and when it includes frequent vigorous activities, it can also decrease the risk of cardiovascular problems. When physical endurance increases, people become fatigued less easily, remain alert to cope with the demands made upon them, and have more energy for handling the demands and challenges they face (Smith, 1993b).

Physical activity also takes our minds off of our problems, reduces inner tension, and improves our mood. Regular exercise makes people feel less frustrated, anxious, and depressed. It also enhances one's self-image and leads to feeling more in control of one's life (Feist and Brannon, 1988; Nowack, 1991 ). Such effects are not only present immediately after a workout, but they appear to become a regular feature in the lives of

**Calories Burned per Week by Exercise
and the Reduction in Death Risk**

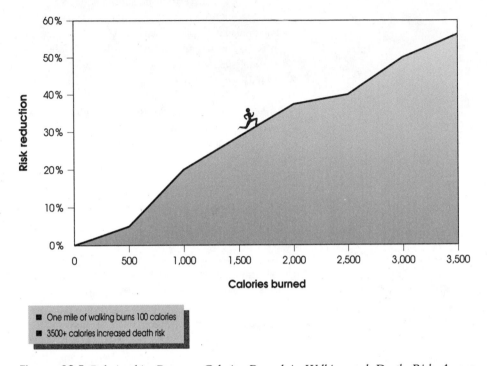

- One mile of walking burns 100 calories
- 3500+ calories increased death risk

**Figure 10.5** *Relationship Between Calories Burned in Walking and Death Risk Among 16,936 Harvard Graduates. As the number of calories used in physical activity increases up to about 3,500 calories a week, there is a progressive decrease in the risk of dying. Up to a point, exercise helps people to live longer. Another way to state this finding is that for every hour they exercised, people in this study added two hours to their expected life span. This latter fact is exactly the same increase in expected life span that would occur in the population at large if cancer were eliminated as a cause of death. When the amount of exercise is not excessive, walking and other forms of exercise produce some impressive benefits (based on Paffenbarger et al., 1986).*

those who exercise regularly (Rodin and Plante, 1989). Only one in five Americans, however, exercises enough to achieve the psychological and physical benefits of physical activity, including a reduction in their risk of dying, as shown in Figure 10.5 (Paffenbarger et al., 1986).

*Integrate a Variety of Physical Activities into Your Life-style* There are several ways to obtain the benefits of exercise (Cooper, 1989; Grasha, 1992). For short-term relief from tension and anxiety, some studies indicate that short, brisk walks of 15 to 25 minutes are very effective. For longer-term benefits, other research recommends that aerobic exercise three to four times a week is helpful. Aerobic exercise includes jogging, cross-country skiing, swimming, or any activity conducted three to four times a week that raises your heart rate to within 65 to 75 percent of its maximum for a period of 20 to 35 minutes (maximum heart rate = [220 − your age] × .65 (lower value)/.75 (upper value) [e.g., 220 − 20 years of age = 200 × .65 = 130 beats per minute].

**Table 10.10**    Common Physical Activities and Calories Consumed

The activities listed below are arranged according to the number of calories they consume. If an activity you enjoy is not listed, use those shown as a guideline to determine whether it would be a light, moderate, or heavy type of physical activity.

| LIGHT EXERCISE (4 CALORIES/MINUTE) | MODERATE EXERCISE (7 CALORIES/MINUTE) | HEAVY EXERCISE (10 CALORIES/MINUTE) |
| --- | --- | --- |
| Dancing (slow) | Badminton | Calisthenics (fast) |
| Gardening (light) | Bicycling (9.5 miles/hr.) | Climbing stairs |
| Golf | Dancing (fast) | Bicycling (12 miles/hr.) |
| Table tennis | Gardening (heavy) | Handball, racquetball |
| Volleyball | Stationary bike (moderate) | Squash |
| Walking (3 miles/hr.) | Swimming (30 yards/min.) | Jogging |
| Bowling | Tennis | Cross-country skiing |
| Downhill skiing | Walking (4.5 miles/hr.) | Skipping rope |
| Canoeing | Ice skating, roller skating | Stationary bike (fast) |
| Horseshoes | Calisthenics (moderate) | Jogging on treadmill |
| Lawn mowing (power) | | Swimming (40 yards/min.) |
| Horseback riding | | Basketball |
| Bicycling (5 miles/hr.) | | |

A third approach to physical activity proposes that whatever you do that provides a minimum of 1,500 to 2,000 calories' worth of physical activity a week will be beneficial. To help you assess how many calories you currently burn, popular activities and the energy they consume are shown in Table 10.10. The activities shown can be thought of as a smorgasbord from which you can pick those that you prefer. *Also remember that too much exercise ceases to become beneficial and instead becomes a source of stress.* In the results of Paffenbarger's study depicted in Figure 10.5, the benefit in the reduction of death risk began to decline for people who expended more than 3,500 calories per week.

While they vary in their recommendations, all of the models are clear on two points. One is that people who live sedentary life-styles need to have a thorough physical exam before initiating programs of sustained physical activity. In addition, when standards are set such as 65 to 75 percent of your maximum heart rate three to four times a week or 1,500 to 2,000 calories a week— *this does not mean the first week!* These are goals that must be reached gradually over a period of time.

Physical activity works better if you remember to do the following:

- Avoid exercise fads
- Do something you enjoy
- Engage in a variety of activities
- Use flexible schedules for exercising
- Get someone else to join you in some of your activities
- Make physical activity a part of your life-style. That is, park and walk; use stairs instead of the elevator, when possible; walk instead of driving to nearby locations.

*Eat a Healthy Diet* A good diet also helps to maintain and develop physical hardiness. Unfortunately, people tend to eat too many of the wrong foods and thus increase their chances of contracting a variety of illnesses (Feist and Brannon, 1988; Spiller, 1993 ). These authors report that foods such as eggs, cheeses, and butter are rich in serum cholesterol and thus increase the risk of a heart attack. The high salt intake at meals and in many snack foods such as pretzels and potato chips is related to high blood pressure. Diets high in fats and low in fiber have been implicated in cancer of the colon. Our immune systems are affected when our diets do not contain sufficient vitamins, minerals, and other nutrients, and thus our susceptibility to disease is lowered.

High levels of caffeine in our diets may produce restlessness, nervousness, and insomnia in some individuals. When we are under stress, such effects are enhanced, adding to the level of physiological discomfort. *How much caffeine does it take to produce*

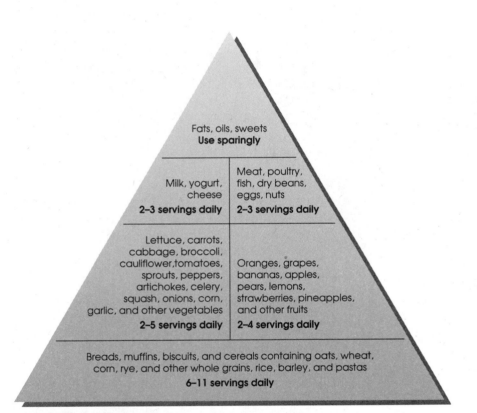

**Figure 10.6** *USDA Food Pyramid. Overall, the food pyramid emphasizes increasing the amount of whole grains, fruits, and vegetables in our diets and lowering the amount of fats and sugars. Use fats and oils sparingly. Three to five tablespoons of fat or oil a day in the foods we eat (about 21-35 grams) would be within dietary requirements for most people. Use very little saturated fats (i.e., butter fat, lard, palm oil, and coconut oil). Olive oil, peanut oil, and safflower, sunflower, corn, cottonseed, and fish oils are recommended. Single-serving sizes within each group: milk and yogurt (1 cup); cheese (1–2 ounces); meat, poultry, fish (2–3 ounces); dry beans (1–1½ cups); eggs (1–2); nuts (⅓ – ¾ cups); vegetables, cut up (½ cup); salad (1 bowl); lettuce (1 wedge); fruit, cut up (½ cup); piece of fruit (1); bread (1 slice); muffin (1); biscuit (1 ); cereal, cooked (½ – ¾ cup); dry cereal (1 cup); other grains, rice, and barley (½ – ¾ cups); pasta (½ – ¾ cup).*

*undesirable effects?* This varies among people. The only fair answer is "whatever amount brings on undesirable symptoms." For the typical adult, just 150 to 250 milligrams of caffeine are enough to produce discomfort. This is the amount in two cups of regular coffee or four to eight cans of your favorite caffeinated soft drink. A small chocolate bar, in contrast, contains about 25 milligrams of caffeine.

There is no single food or vitamin, however, that will help you to withstand the rigors of stress. *Consequently, it is important to eat a variety of foods.* In addition, *it is important to consume less fast food and processed food,* which generally contain high amounts of fats and sugars and are low in dietary fiber. Freshly prepared meals, along with fresh fruit and vegetables, are important to good nutrition and should be a regular part of our diets.

The foods to eat and the number of servings a day of each were arranged into a food pyramid by the United States Department of Agriculture (USDA) in a set of recommendations released to the general public in April 1992. The USDA pyramid was designed to suggest the components of a healthy diet, and it is illustrated in Figure 10.6. Within each food group on the pyramid, you can choose among a variety of foods to obtain the recommended number of servings.

*Maintain Good Health Habits* There are other health habits that promote physical hardiness and that protect us from developing physical illnesses and problems that would create stress in our lives. Check those listed in Table 10.11 that apply to your life.

---

**Table 10.11**            A Health Habit Checklist

---

*Which of the following health habits are a regular feature of your life-style?*

_____ Do not smoke

_____ Exercise regularly

_____ Do not engage in unprotected sexual activity

_____ Eat at fast food restaurants very infrequently

_____ Wear seat belts

_____ Regularly drive within the speed limits

_____ My weight is within the normal limits for my height and age

_____ My diet is low in fat, refined sugar, and salt and is high in fiber

_____ Have not been on a strict diet within the past 12 months

_____ Do not abuse alcohol and other hard drugs

_____ Get six to seven hours of sleep four or more times a week

_____ Find time to take breaks and to relax every day

_____ Have a medical checkup every year

_____ Frequently eat a nutritious breakfast

_____ Do not regularly drink coffee, tea, cola, or other caffeinated beverages

_____ Avoid eating high-calorie snacks and desserts on a regular basis

_____ Frequently engage in hobbies, sports, and other leisure-time activities

_____ Watch less than two hours of television a day

---

## ACHIEVING THE GOALS FOR COPING WITH STRESSORS: CONSERVE, REPLENISH, AND BUILD AN INVENTORY OF RESOURCES NEEDED TO MANAGE STRESS

In Steven Hobfoll's model introduced earlier in this section, coping forces us to spend resources. This might include the expenditure of time, energy, and money; using certain personal qualities such as a positive mental outlook to resist a stressor; and employing various types of information, skills, and abilities to resolve an issue. *Because we face a continuous parade of stressors every day, there is some risk that our supply of resources can be depleted.* There are four things you can do to avoid the latter problem.

1. *Conserve resources you already possess and replenish those that were used.* Thus some people "save money for a rainy day" or spend short amounts of time and energy on relatively unimportant problems. They also may break larger problems into smaller parts so their time and energy is more focused. Or, they may look for ways to delegate a task or delay working on an issue so that more time is available for them to tackle more important concerns. When fatigued from handling a stressor, their energies are restored by eating well and obtaining needed rest.

2. *Employ one or more resources to offset the loss of others.* A good friend's husband died in a car accident. With a major source of support in her life missing, she now sought advice from her friends. When his father lost his job, one of my students had to give his parents money he had saved to pay tuition. He resolved his frustration over meeting tuition payments by selling his car to pay his college bills.

3. *Increase your inventory of existing resources to enable you to more effectively meet future demands and challenges.* Thus, seeking a better education or job, saving money and making wise investments, forming new friendships, and acquiring additional stress management skills are factors that ultimately help people to cope better. Steven Hobfoll notes that it is better to do such things during periods of low stress so that such resources are available when we need them. (Epstein amd Katz, 1992).

4. *Evaluate your resources by answering the following questions.*

   • What resources do you currently possess? Exercise 10.1 in the Applied Activities section contains a coping resource scale that you can use to evaluate your current resources for coping.
   • Which resources do you appear to lack?
   • What actions do you need to take to build those resources?

## MANAGING ANXIETY AND DEPRESSION

**Anxiety** and **depression** often occur as by-products of our attempts to manage a variety of stressors. In particular, when we doubt our ability to handle events or experience difficulties coping, they may develop. Both emotions produce special challenges to our ability to adapt. Several signs of anxiety and depression are described in Table 10.12.

### The Causes of Anxiety

*Anxiety and the Appraisal of Stressors* This is an unpleasant feeling that occurs in response to an anticipated threat to our psychological or physical well-being. Unlike fear, which occurs in response to a real and present danger, anxiety happens in response

**Table 10.12**　　　　Signs of Anxiety and Depression

| ANXIETY | DEPRESSION |
| --- | --- |
| • Worrying about future events | • Constantly criticizing yourself |
| • Questioning competency to handle events | • Blaming yourself for the problems in your life |
| • Pacing | • Remain pessimistic about life getting better in the future |
| • Trembling knees | |
| • Extraneous hand and arm movements | • Believe that you somehow deserve the unpleasant things in your life |
| • Body swaying | • Avoiding other people |
| • Hand tremors | • Lack of interest in social life |
| • Tense facial muscles | • Lack of sexual desire |
| • Pale face | • Little interest in eating |
| • Blushing | • Normally rewarding activities are no longer fun |
| • Frequently moistening lips | |
| • Swallowing several times | • Often feel tired and fatigued and want to sleep |
| • Clearing throat several times | |
| • Breathing heavily when thinking about potential stressors | • Have little energy to do things |
| | • Tend to believe that there is little in life to live for |
| • Perspiration on forehead and palms of hands | • Focus on personal failures more than successes in life |
| • Quivering voice | |
| • Occasional stuttering | • Feel trapped by events in life |

to events that we expect to occur in the future. The appraisal process for a stressor described in Figure 10.1 can help us understand how this occurs. After evaluating a potential stressor as a threat or challenge and then assessing their ability to cope, people often must wait for it to occur. During this "wait period," worries about their ability to handle events and "second thoughts" emerge. For example, before a sports event or an artistic performance, many athletes, actresses, and musicians have "butterflies in their stomachs." They worry about how well they will do. Those who do well are able to channel their anxiety into energy that enhances their effectiveness. *If their levels of anxiety are too high, however, this emotion may interfere with their ability to think and behave appropriately.* People may "choke," "withdraw from a situation," or "forget" how to do things they knew only moments before. A basketball player misses a critical shot; an actor forgets a line; a singer is unable to remember the last verse of a song; or a student can't recall information needed to answer a question on an exam. People will typically experience less anxiety if the stressor is familiar and they have handled similar events successfully in the past.

In the appraisal process described in Figure 10.1, anxiety also can occur if we evaluated our attempts to cope as unsuccessful. Now we might worry about how our lack of success will affect us now and in future encounters with a stressor. Those who are able to put such "failures" into perspective, to put them on a back burner, and to learn from their mistakes are less bothered by anxiety.

*Anxiety and Learning* Sometimes people learn to become anxious. They encounter traumatic experiences such as a car crash, a difficult exam, or being physically attacked. Just thinking about the experience or coming into close proximity to the location where it occurred automatically triggers anxiety. Such responses are called **conditioned emotional responses**. Anxiety also can be acquired through the process of imitation learning described in Chapter 5. The daughter of one of my clients was afraid of taking trips by airplane. As a child, her mother talked about how she "feared for her husband's life" every time he took an airplane for a business trip. She also made sure her daughter read about plane crash stories in the newspapers. By example, she taught her daughter to be anxious.

## Coping with Anxiety

The strategies for coping with stress discussed earlier are also helpful for managing anxiety. Remember that situations that make us apprehensive also are likely to become sources of frustration and tension. In addition, consider how the following techniques help you to cope.

*Passive Coping*  Sometimes we try to manage the anxiety and other negative emotions associated with a stressful event without actively trying to change the situation itself. Some of those strategies include such things as learning relaxation, guided imagery, and trying not to not let a troublesome situation bother us. Christ Zois (1992) also reports that we might try to mask, shield, or cover up how we feel. This can be accomplished in a number of ways. We might wish that an anxiety-arousing situation will go away, deny that anything bad has happened, and disengage ourselves by watching television, daydreaming, sleeping, or turning to alcohol or other drugs.

*Defensive Coping*  At other times, automatic and unconscious **defense mechanisms** kick in to provide short-term relief from anxiety and other emotions a situation might evoke. Defense mechanisms are unconscious attempts at self-deception, and they are not perfect. The underlying anxiety and tension may still "leak into our conscious thoughts and behaviors in a disguised or distorted form." Common defense mechanisms and how they operate are described in Table 10.13.

*Do the Things You Fear*  Susan Jeffers (1988) reports that running away from or trying to ignore or avoid the things that make us fearful and anxious are seldom effective. All of us need to face our fears and perhaps to discover the wisdom in a quote attributed to Mark Twain, "the worst things that can happen—won't." In practice this means facing difficult challenges and trying to do the best we can. Jeffers notes that when we fall on our face, the best thing to do is to pick ourselves up and try again. Of course, we should try to learn from a mishap so we don't repeat the same mistake. Success at doing such things also reinforces new labels for describing ourselves (e.g., "I'm an anxious person" vs. "I sometimes get anxious about things, but I am usually able to take care of a situation and calm myself down."

*Sometimes gradually trying the things we fear is a useful way to face them.* A youngster who fears swimming needs to discover gradually that water is not harmful. Thus, putting one's feet into the water, wading, or even dog paddling in time can lead to learning other strokes. Doing the things we fear in small doses demonstrates that we can be successful in overcoming our problems and increases self-confidence.

*Engage in a Little Self-Coaching*  This can occur in three ways. One is to observe how someone we like and respect manages his fears. Reminding ourselves what he did and

| Table 10.13 | | Common Defense Mechanisms |
|---|---|---|
| *Repression* | | Forgetting unpleasant thoughts or emotions in order to reduce the anxiety and tension associated with them. |
| | | *Example:* Tanya is angry at her husband for not helping out more around the house. She also is anxious about telling him, because he has a bad temper. She "forgets" about her feelings. |
| *Projection* | | Attributing objectionable thoughts and feelings to other people. |
| | | *Example:* Jamal is disappointed that he lost a 1:1 basketball game to Jason. Jamal tells his wife that Jason must be angry at him. |
| *Regression* | | Using "childish" or immature behaviors to deal with a stressor. |
| | | *Example:* Manuel is frustrated with his sales staff. At a meeting he pounds his fist on the table, kicks a couple of chairs, and leaves the room screaming, "I'm sick and tired of all of you." |
| *Displacement* | | Transferring thoughts, anxieties, and tensions to a person or object that is less likely to retaliate. |
| | | *Example:* Micelle lives on a farm and worries that she will never meet anyone to marry. One day she screams at her mother, "It's all your fault that I have to live out here and have no social life." |
| *Sublimation* | | Our ability to express unacceptable thoughts and feelings in socially acceptable ways. |
| | | *Example:* Steven plays football and has a socially acceptable outlet for his aggressive tendencies. The crowd cheers, and his coach thanks him for hard-hitting style. |
| *Denial* | | Refusing to acknowledge thoughts and feelings that are unpleasant even though they are supported by convincing evidence. |
| | | *Example:* Susan's baby is diagnosed as mentally retarded. She tells her friends the condition is temporary. |
| *Rationalization* | | Using superficial explanations to justify behaviors or feelings in a situation. They often omit critical details and facts. |
| | | *Example:* David stands in a long line for movie tickets and then decides to leave. "I really didn't want to see that movie anyway," he tells a friend. |
| *Reaction Formation* | | Using socially acceptable thoughts and feelings that are just the opposite of our true but more undesirable thoughts and feelings. |
| | | *Example:* Sam is a prosecuting attorney for a large city. He built a reputation on taking owners of video and book stores to court for selling sexually explicit materials. As a child, his parents made him feel anxious and guilty about sex. Nonetheless, he often enjoys watching sexually explicit movies at home and reading novels with strong sexual themes. |

integrating appropriate parts of his behaviors into our actions is helpful. In addition, listening to the advice of people who encourage us to persist in spite of our anxieties can be helpful. Finally, "coaching" ourselves through an anxious moment is helpful. If anxious during a tough exam, it helps to repeat to yourself such things as "Relax, take it easy." "Calm down." "You can do it; you've done well on exams before." "Good job on that question—now go on to the next one and do as well on it." "Remember the rules you have to use to answer that question." Research shows that becoming your own coach can be effective in helping to enhance your ability to handle anxious moments (Meichenbaum, 1985).

Additional suggestions for self-coaching can be found in the cognitive approaches to behavior modification section of Chapter 5.

## The Causes of Depression

*Depression and the Process of Appraising Stressors*  Whereas unhappiness is a temporary sadness, depression is characterized by a more prolonged sad or apathetic mood that people perceive as never getting better. Feelings of depression may range from mild to severe, with mild depressive feelings occurring much more frequently than moderate or severe ones. Feeling depressed also is a possible outcome of the appraisal process described in Figure 10.1. As people try to meet the demands and challenges of daily living, they are not always successful. They evaluate their attempts at coping as inadequate. Some feel they are beating their heads into a brick wall, while others are at least mildly annoyed by their lack of progress.

A lack of progress runs counter to our needs to believe that we can control important events in our lives. When this experience persists, **learned helplessness** develops (Seligman, 1991). Someone comes to believe that "no matter what I do—nothing seems to work." Such beliefs are a source of unhappiness and depression.

Chris Peterson (1991) also reports that our **explanatory style**, or how we explain good and bad events in our lives, contributes to the problem. Our explanations for what happened to us can be analyzed along three dimensions:

1. The event was a stable/permanent or an unstable/temporary part of my life.
2. The event was a global/pervasive experience for me or was confined to a specific situation.
3. The event was due to personal or internal causes or was caused by external events outside of someone's control.

As the scenario below illustrates, pessimists explain bad things that happen to them as stable and pervasive experiences and as something they influenced. Optimists cope by interpreting such events as unstable, confined to a specific situation, and due to factors outside of their control. *Just the opposite occurs when people are asked to explain why good things happened to them.*

For example, optimists and pessimists would react differently after obtaining the highest grade in class on a test or being named "employee of the year." A pessimist would believe it was a "fluke" or unstable, confined to that situation alone ("This will never happen again"), and due to factors outside of her control. An optimist, on the other hand, would interpret such things as a stable and pervasive part of her life ("I'm good at what I do," "Good fortune follows me around no matter where I go") and as something she personally caused to happen.

**Scenario:**  *Stupid mistakes are made on a task at work.*

*Pessimistic:* "I'm always making mistakes like that on the job."

Stable/Permanent  |__**X**__|_____|_____|_____|  Unstable/Temporary
                                    **X**

*Optimistic:* "I've learned something. That mistake won't happen again."

*Pessimistic:* "Seems like I mess up things no matter what I try to do in life."

Global/Pervasive                                    Specific
Experience       | __X__ | ____ | ____ | ____ | Situation
                                            **X**

*Optimistic:* "I occasionally make a few mistakes on the job."

_____

*Pessimistic:* "I have no one to blame but myself for doing something foolish."

Internal Cause  | __X__ | ____ | ____ | ____ | External Cause
                                    **X**

*Optimistic:* "My boss was on my back to work faster, and I rushed things."

_____

Compared to those with a pessimistic explanatory style, Seligman and Peterson report that optimists manage stress better and that they are less anxious and depressed, in better physical health, more successful in school and their careers, and much more willing to accept challenges and explore new opportunities for themselves.

*Biological Factors* Some people are genetically predisposed to develop depression, particularly if they experience severe loss or neglect in their lives (Plomin et al., 1990). For example, relatives of people who had developed severe depression before age 20 were eight times more likely to eventually become depressed than were relatives of nondepressed individuals. Identical twins have five times the chance of developing certain depressions than do fraternal twins. In addition, certain chemicals in the brain involved in the transmission of nerve impulses, such as serotonin and norepinephrine, appear to be involved. These neurotransmitters keep our nerves firing in ways that make us feel energetic and alert. Drugs such as Elavil, Nardil, and Prozac involved in treating severe depression restore a normal balance of such neurotransmitters (Depue, 1992).

## Coping with Depression

*Disputing Pessimistic Explanations for Events* Many of the strategies for taking control of your life and reducing tension discussed in this chapter also apply to depression. Seeking small wins, learning to relax, developing social support networks, and enhancing physical hardiness are also helpful. In addition, Martin Seligman (1991) argues that *people also must learn to dispute pessimistic explanations for events.* With bad events, this means changing our internal dialogue to interpret events as unstable, confined to specific situations, and having external causes. Exercise 10.4 in the Applied Activities section is designed to help you see how to do this.

*Counseling and Drug Therapies* With extended or severe depression, counseling and psychotherapy are often necessary. People need to work through the issues that are

holding them back with a professional therapist. In some cases, antidepressant drugs are also used to reduce symptoms of severe depression. Unfortunately, drugs like Elavil and Nardil take three to four weeks to become effective and have side effects including nausea, intermittent vomiting, weight loss, diarrhea, and anxiety (Kinder, 1994). And in the case of a drug like Prozac, it works rapidly, but a serious side effect is that a small percentage of people develop intense suicidal impulses.

## THE ROLE OF OUR SELF-IMAGE IN MEETING LIFE'S DEMANDS AND CHALLENGES

All of us have ways of referring to an abstract entity labeled the **self.** We use words such as "I," "me," "myself," and can be heard to say things like: "I really like myself," "I took it upon myself to do . . . ," or "I don't feel like myself today."

Most contemporary analyses of "the self" or our **self-image** suggest that there are two parts. One aspect is our **self-concept**, or how we define ourselves. Such definitions occur in response to questions like "Who am I?" and typically include the various roles we play (e.g., employee, student, brother, sister, and husband-wife) and the personality traits we possess (e.g., impulsive, happy, obedient, cautious). The second component of our self-image is **self-esteem**, or the positive and negative feelings we have about ourselves overall (e.g., "I'm a really good person") and within specific situations (e.g., "I'm a lousy basketball player but an excellent math student"). Feedback from others as well as our estimates of how we compare to others contribute to such evaluations.

People with positive self-esteem are more successful in school and work, and they are willing to learn from their mistakes. They like other people more, do not abuse drugs, are comfortable seeking feedback from others, and are happier individuals. People with good self-esteem also have more confidence in their ability to make something productive happen in their lives. In contrast, those with a negative view of themselves do less well in school and work, are susceptible to lying and cheating, tend to be more anxious and depressed, and are much more easily manipulated by others (Baumeister, 1991; Brown, 1991b ).

## Our Self-Image Helps to Guide and Regulate Our Actions

Carl Rogers (1977) and Abraham Maslow (1971), for example, stressed the important role the image of ourselves plays in understanding how we adapt to our environment. To begin, the component of "self" labeled our self-concept is tied to the roles that we play. Such roles prescribe various guidelines for our actions, and the guidelines function as a script for how to behave. Walk into a meeting as the "group leader" or as "a member of the group," and your behaviors are different. Define yourself as a "student" or as a "teacher," and your actions in the classroom differ. *Who you think you are in a situation plays an important role in how you are going to behave.*

Of course, because our self-concept typically includes a variety of roles, the opportunities for conflict with others and feeling overwhelmed and confused about what to do in some situations can occur. Out of frustration, we might also engage in behaviors that hold us back rather than help us to grow and develop. All of this contributes to the stress in our lives (Baumeister and Scher, 1988). On the other hand, having a diverse self-concept also offers some protection against stress. When one role is lost or diminished in importance—as might happen when a job is lost, a separation occurs, or children grow up—we recognize there are other things we can do to fill the gap (Dance and Kuiper, 1987).

## Our Self-Image Helps Us to Develop and Maintain Relationships

Awareness of our self-image is important for developing relationships. Those with insights into their positive and negative characteristics are able to see other people accurately. Such individuals form attitudes about people after some reflection, and the attitudes are typically not extreme. They also are more likely to have more friendships and contacts with others. Consequently, more social support is available to help them adapt to the stressors of everyday life (Brown, 1991b).

## Enhancing Our Self-Image: Setting Goals for Self-Renewal

Self-renewal involves adopting new or changing existing roles, acquiring new or modifying existing personal characteristics (e.g., becoming assertive, more independent),

| Table 10.14 | The Top 20 Goals for Self-Renewal | |
| --- | --- | --- |

| SELF-RENEWAL GOAL | PERCENT OF PEOPLE TRYING TO MAKE THE CHANGE DURING A 12-MONTH PERIOD OF TIME |
| --- | --- |
| 1. To become a more physically fit individual | 87% |
| 2. To become a more independent person | 74% |
| 3. To become a more self-confident person | 74% |
| 4. To make and implement decisions more effectively | 66% |
| 5. To become a more sociable individual | 62% |
| 6. To become a more assertive person | 58% |
| 7. To overcome procrastination | 58% |
| 8. To become a more trusting individual | 55% |
| 9. To be able to express feelings more openly | 52% |
| 10. To become a less shy individual | 51% |
| 11. To become more comfortable with the opposite sex | 50% |
| 12. To become a more relaxed person | 50% |
| 13. To change my clothing style and appearance | 48% |
| 14. To become a less jealous person | 45% |
| 15. To become a less introverted individual | 43% |
| 16. To switch to a more satisfying vocation or major | 42% |
| 17. To become a more punctual person | 40% |
| 18. To substantially change my view of the world | 37% |
| 19. To become a less fearful and anxious person | 35% |
| 20. To become a less impulsive person | 31% |

Based on information in Klar et al., 1992.

and enhancing our self-esteem. While such things are not easy to do, a good place to start is with establishing clear goals for what you want to become.

*Six Questions to Ask*

1. *What goals for self-renewal do you want to pursue?* Yechiel Klar (1992) and his colleagues surveyed people to identify a list of the top 20 goals for self-renewal. These are shown in Table 10.14. Of the goals shown:

   • Which ones have you attempted during the past 12 months?
   • Which ones would you like to pursue?
   • What's missing from this list that you would like to pursue?

2. *Why do you want to achieve this particular goal?* The important point is whether you want to do things for yourself or to please others. If your motivation is solely to please others, you may find yourself losing interest in making changes. Most of us resist the attempts of others to control what we should think and do. Thus, personal priorities for self-renewal should reflect more of what you want to do rather than what others want for you.

## Setting Productive Personal Goals

The following ideas for setting goals are based on reviews of the literature on goal setting (Locke and Latham, 1990; Watson and Tharp, 1993). The following practices appear to be effective. As you read, think about how you can integrate them into your life.

*Set specific goals for yourself.* It is much easier to achieve goals when specific directions exist. While it is admirable to want to "do the best you can" or to "become somebody in life," such goals are too vague. "I will study four hours a day this term to get on the dean's list" or "I want to obtain a management trainee position with a corporation that manufactures and sells computers" are more direct goals.

*Set observable, measurable goals.* "I need more education" is not only a vague goal, but it is not easy to observe or measure progress or an outcome. "I need to take three courses in accounting, salesmanship, and managing people" is a much better way to establish an educational goal. Progress in each course can be assessed, and completion of the course makes it easy to determine when it is achieved. Such benchmarks are very motivational.

*Set challenging goals.* People generally perform better and are more satisfied with what they achieve if they feel challenged. This generally means not setting goals that are too easy or too difficult.

*Set attainable goals.* Personal goals should be realistic. Try not to establish extremely difficult goals to achieve, such as "I want to increase my grade point average two points next term," "I want to triple my salary in two years," or "I want to exercise two hours every day." Establishing more modest goals lowers anxiety and gives you a better chance to bask in the success of accomplishing them. As a rule of thumb, people have a better chance of achieving goals that represent a 20 to 25 percent increase over past performance than they do anything else.

*Break a complex goal into short-term, medium-term, and long-term objectives.* Finding a new job, for example, is a relatively difficult task. A long-term objective might be to get a position with the same level of responsibility and pay. A short-term objective would be to put a resumé together, call friends to let them know of one's availability, and to contact a personnel service. A medium-term objective would include mailing out a resumé, scheduling appointments with potential employers, and finding a temporary part-time job to earn money to meet basic expenses.

3. *What positive and negative effects would pursuing this goal have for your life?* Becoming clear about the positive and negative effects associated with self-renewal goals can help to increase your commitment to them. An added benefit of such an analysis is that the reasons for not pursuing certain goals also becomes apparent.

4. *Have you stated your goals in ways that will maximize your chances of achieving them?* Focus on Applied Research 10.3 has several suggestions for how to do this effectively. Remember that achieving personal goals is a great morale booster and contributes to our self-esteem.

5. *Do you possess the skills, abilities, and information needed to achieve your goals?* Sometimes personal skills and abilities are overestimated. Thus, you may need special training and experience in order to be able to accomplish your goals.

6. *In what ways can other people help you?* Perhaps they can "just be there for you to provide support" or maybe to give you feedback on the progress you are making. Or, they could act as a model for the types of changes you want to emulate.

## Summary of Chapter Organizers

Suggested responses to the chapter organizers at the beginning of this chapter are shown below.

1. *What are three goals that you must achieve in order to adapt effectively?* They include learning how to manage the stress; coping with the anxiety, unhappiness, and depression that occur if your attempts are unsuccessful; and taking steps to maintain a positive self-image in the face of life's struggles.

2. *How would you define stress?* Stress is the nonspecific response of the body to any demand placed upon it. A broader conception of stress also includes the specific behavioral, cognitive, and emotional responses to particular demands.

3. *What are the signs of stress?* Signs of stress include physiological, behavioral, emotional, and cognitive indicators. Physiological signs include such things as a rise in heart rate, blood sugar, adrenaline, headaches, and muscle tension. Several behavior signs include an inability to relax and to complete tasks. Emotionally, fear, anger, frustration, and irritability can occur, while cognitive signs include difficulty in planning and rigid thinking.

4. *Do you know the distinction between physical and psychological stressors?* Physical stressors exist outside of you and create stress because they naturally trigger basic physiological processes involved with illness, pain, or discomfort. Psychological stressors are events that first require you to cognitively appraise their capacity to become unpleasant forces in your life.

5. *What steps are involved in appraising a potential stressor? Anticipating the even*t includes determining whether it represents a potential threat or challenge. *Assessing your capacity to cope* successfully or unsuccessfully is the second part of this process. Finally the outcomes of your efforts to cope are evaluated, including assessing benefits and costs and determining what to do next.

6. *What characteristics of stressors make them difficult to handle?* Those that are perceived unpredictable and uncontrollable are troublesome, as are multiple occurrences of intense stressors and those having a long duration.

7. *Can you identify the common stressors that affect your life?* Prevalent stressors include personal qualities such as personal limitations, Type A behavior patterns, tendencies towards overcommitment and overdedication, and your communication style. Major life changes as well as everyday hassles also contribute to tension. Adverse environmental events, conflicts, competing demands for your time, and specific stressors at work, school, and within our family and social life create tension for you.

8. *Can you identify five goals that coping responses should try to achieve?* Preventing and reducing distress (i.e., stress that leads to unproductive outcomes), trying to create eustress (i.e., finding ways to respond to stress in a productive manner), living within your comfort zone, and taking actions to buffer and protect yourself from stress, and to conserve, replenish, and build and inventory of resources to manage stress.

9. *What strategies for coping are related to each goal? Managing distress, seeking eustress, and seeking our comfort zone can be obtained by*: identifying stressors; using constructive thinking processes, such as restructuring our perceptions of events; viewing events as challenges, believing you can control them, committing to your efforts, and seeking small wins; managing time more effectively; becoming a little selfish and learning relaxation strategies. *Buffering the effects of stress and protecting ourselves is*

*helped by:* seeking social support and developing physical hardiness through exercise and a good diet and health habits.

10. *What causes anxiety and depression to occur?* Anxiety may occur in the interval between evaluating a stressor and our ability to cope and then waiting for it. Depression and unhappiness can happen anytime our attempts to cope were judged inadequate. Anxiety also may arise from environmental triggers of emotional responses and through imitation learning. Depression also is produced by learned helplessness, a pessimistic explanatory style, and genetic predispositions that affect our physiological systems.

11. *How can you cope with these emotions?* The stress management strategies in this chapter can help. In addition, short-term relief from anxiety may occur through passive coping strategies such as disengaging ourselves from a situation and defense mechanisms. Doing the things you fear and engaging in self-coaching also help. With depression, trying to refute a pessimistic explanatory style is useful, as are antidepression drugs in severe cases.

12. *What are the components of your self-image?* Your self-image includes a definition of how you see yourself (i.e., your self-concept) and any positive and negative evaluations you have about yourself (i.e., your self-esteem).

13. *How does it affect your everyday actions and the stress of daily living?* Your self-image helps to guide and regulate your actions and plays a role in developing and maintaining relationships. A clear definition of self and a positive sense of self-esteem provide the confidence and self-efficacy to manage stressors.

14. *Are you aware of things you can do to enhance your self-image?* Self-renewal involves a willingness to adopt new or to modify existing roles, to acquire or modify existing personal characteristics, and to add things to your life that will lead to a more positive sense of self-esteem. Having clear and reasonable goals, understanding why you want to pursue them, taking steps to acquire needed skills and information, and consulting with others assist in such endeavors.

## Things to Do

1. The next time you feel a lot of stress, try to relax using the technique described in Table 10.9. Or consider engaging in vigorous exercise. You might want to try both suggestions at different times and assess which one tends to work best for you.

2. What is something you would like to change about yourself? To help you think about this issue, answer the six questions for self-renewal discussed in the text. Be sure to complete each part of the process.

3. List three stressful events in your life during the past two weeks. What reactions to stressors described in Figure 10.3 occurred? What needs and goals did each stressor prevent you from achieving? In what ways was each stressor perceived as unpredictable and/or uncontrollable?

4. Pick one of the events you listed in number 3 above. Describe how you attempted to cope with it. Given the information in the text on coping, what would you now do differently to handle the situation differently? List the specific strategies you would employ.

5. Watch your favorite television soap opera or dramatic series. Pay attention to characters who are anxious or depressed. What advice, based on information in the text, would you give them to manage their anxiety and bouts with depression?

6. Set up a Subjective Units Of Discomfort Scale and Stress Log as described in Tables 10.6 and 10.7 in the text. Use it for one to two days to determine action steps you need to take to better manage the levels of stress you are experiencing.

7. Pick three statements in your newspaper in which people gave detailed explanations for the good or poor actions they took. Analyze what was said for the presence of an optimistic or pessimistic explanatory style as described in the text. Show how each statement reflects the dimensions of: *Stable-Unstable; Global-Specific Situation; Internal-External Cause.* If the statement was judged to be "pessimistic," what is another possible legitimate way to reframe what happened so that the explanation was relatively more "optimistic."

8. List two to three interpretations of stressful events you have given recently. Analyze your explanation along the lines suggested in number 7 above. Be sure to indicate how you could have reframed any "pessimistic" explanations to make them more "optimistic." Why is it important to try to do this?

9. Pick three to four suggestions for increasing physical hardiness described in the text. Briefly indicate how you could begin to integrate them into your life-style tomorrow.

## APPLIED ACTIVITIES

**EXERCISE 10.1**

### Assessing Your Resources for Coping with Stressors

Steven Hobfoll (1989) suggests we acquire and protect a variety of resources that help us cope with stress. Included are psychological processes as well as tangible possessions such as a job or money in the bank. The coping resources scale from the Holistic Stress Test (Grasha, 1989; Crowe and Grasha, 1993 ) can help you assess the resources you have available to cope with stress.

**Answer "agree" or "disagree" to each of the items listed below.**

"Agree" means that the item expresses how you usually think and feel. "Disagree" means that you do not believe the item represents how you typically think and feel.

_____ 1. I tend to own expensive cars, stereos, jewelry, and other personal items.

_____ 2. I can usually find time to relax and do the things I enjoy.

_____ 3. The furniture, carpets, and other decorations in my home are adequate.

_____ 4. My wardrobe is very suitable for the different things I do in life.

_____ 5. My level of education/training is adequate for me to get ahead in life.

_____ 6. My home or apartment has enough space to meet my needs.

_____ 7. I would consider the funds I have saved to be adequate for my needs.

_____ 8. I have a close and happy relationship with at least one other person.

_____ 9. I have sufficient knowledge and skills to manage my life.

_____ 10. I am unlikely to lose my job in the near future.

_____ 11. Compared to my peers, I have accomplished a lot in life.

_____ 12. I am satisfied with the number of friends that I have.

_____ 13. I have invested money in property, stocks, bonds, and other investments.

_____ 14. When faced with a problem, I can often find people to help me out.

_____ 15. I usually can see solutions to the problems that affect me.

_____ 16. Most things that happen to me eventually work out for the best.

_____ 17. I have enough time in my life to do what I really want to do.

_____ 18. I possess enough knowledge and skill to do well at work and/or school.

_____ 19. I am optimistic about my chances of eventually getting ahead in life.

_____ 20. I am able to live relatively well on the amount of money that I earn.

_____ 21. I have the skills to effectively solve problems and make decisions.

**Scoring Key: Give yourself 1 point for each item you "agreed" with.** Research shows that as their scores increase, people report less tension and frustration with school, work, family, and events in their social life.

Generally Inadequate Resources for Coping (Scores: 1–8): Moderately Adequate Resources (Scores: 9–16); Resources For Coping Are Very Adequate (Scores: 17–21)

What are one to two resources listed above that you need to develop further in your life? What is one action step you could take tomorrow to begin this process?

EXERCISE 10.2

**The Mental ABCs of Stress Management**

### The Mental ABCs of Managing Emotions

How you think affects how your feel. Events alone do not produce stress. Our interpretation of events in any area of life is very important to the amount of stress we experience. The work of Albert Ellis discussed in the chapter suggests that absolute and extreme ways of thinking can increase our stress levels. In much the same way, obtaining a balanced perspective on issues can lower the amount of stress in our lives.

To begin to use this idea in your life, select a situation during the past one to two weeks in which you felt frustrated, tense, anxious, or any other unpleasant emotion. In selecting a situation, pick something that was particularly bothersome to you, that continues to produce negative emotions, and that you are motivated to change. *Follow the instructions listed below.*

### A. Activating Event.

Describe the event that made you feel upset. List key actors and what was said or done that upset you.

*Example:* I was at a party and overheard a friend of mine telling my boss that he thought I was a jerk. I confronted him, and we had a loud argument after the party.

### B. Beliefs.

List the self-talk (beliefs and thoughts) that went through your mind in part A above. Try to think of two to three statements.

*Example:* I have been betrayed and can never trust him again. Our relationship will never be the same after this incident. The boss will never give me the time of day or take me seriously again.

1. _____

2. _____

3. _____

### C. Emotional Consequences of Antecedent Events and Your Beliefs.

List the labels that describe the way you are feeling (e.g., anxious, tense). Also list any physical symptoms (butterflies in stomach, sweating palms) and behaviors (e.g., walked out of room) that were present in the situation.

| *Emotional Labels* | *Physical Symptoms* | *Behaviors* |
|---|---|---|
| _____ | _____ | _____ |
| _____ | _____ | _____ |
| _____ | _____ | _____ |
| _____ | _____ | _____ |

The beliefs that are particularly troublesome in creating stress are those described in the text that Albert Ellis labels irrational. The criteria for determining whether a belief is rational or irrational are listed below. For each of your self-talk statements you listed above, determine whether it is rational or irrational. If the belief meets four of the six criteria for an irrational belief, consider it irrational. Mark an **R** or an **I** next to each self-talk statement to indicate whether it is rational or irrational.

## Criteria for Rational and Irrational Beliefs

| CRITERIA | RATIONAL | IRRATIONAL |
|---|---|---|
| *Facts* | Fits the objective facts of what occurred. An instant replay on videotape would clearly show that the belief is based on the behaviors that occurred. | Based on biased and distorted interpretation of the facts. |
| *Emotions* | Leads to positive emotions. | Leads to negative emotions. |
| *Goals* | Allows you to achieve your short- and long-term goals. | Interferes with your ability to achieve your short- and long-term goals. |
| *Interactions* | Helps to maintain or enhance your ability to interact with others. | Interferes with your ability to maintain or enhance your interactions. |
| *Protection* | Allows you to protect yourself against threats to your physical, economic, and emotional well-being. | Provides limited or temporary protection against such threats. |
| *Plans* | Facilitates ability to take actions and to develop plans to work on the problem. | Interferes with ability to take actions and to develop plans to work on the problem. |

Having determined whether your beliefs were rational or irrational, turn to Table 10.8 in the text, and identify the specific type of irrational belief you are using. Put the name of the category of irrational belief next to each irrational self-talk statement you identified in part B of this activity.

## D. Dispute.

To overcome irrational beliefs, it is necessary to dispute them—that is, to prove to yourself that they are the source of your difficulty and that their influence can be diminished. In the process, the unpleasant emotions you experience should diminish.

There are two ways to do this. One is to reinterpret your self-talk so that a more balanced and rational perspective is gained on what occurred. That is, you should be able to reinterpret each irrational self-talk statement so that it would now meet four of the six criteria for a rational belief. The second is to take actions that are consistent with your new way of thinking about the situation.

*Example:* "I can never trust my friend again." *Rational Reinterpretation.* "It is unfortunate that my friend behaved as he did. However, we have been friends for a long time, and this is the first time anything like this has happened. It is possible that he was just trying to show off in front of the boss, or perhaps he was putting the boss on. One incident is no reason to put aside years of friendship. *Actions:* I will offer a peace pipe and suggest that we put the incident behind us. If my analysis is correct, it will never happen again.

For each irrational belief you identified earlier, suggest either a rational reinterpretation and/or an action step you could take to dispute it. *Integrate the rational reinterpretations and actions into your daily life.*

*Irrational Belief #1:* Rational reinterpretation and actions to dispute.

*Irrational Belief #2:* Rational reinterpretation and actions to dispute.

*Irrational Belief #3:* Rational reinterpretation and actions to dispute.

### E. Effects.

The above analysis, when integrated into your life, should help you to examine your emotions in a new light. Ellis suggests that your emotions should begin to change and your ability to cope with them should be enhanced. Try the ideas you developed, and see if this is the case in your life.

EXERCISE 10.3

**Modifying a Pessimistic Explanatory Style**

To reduce unhappiness and depression, Martin Seligman argues, pessimistic interpretations of good and bad events need to be given a more optimistic focus. The Albert Ellis model outlined in Exercise 10.2 is helpful here. When a person is depressed, a variety of irrational beliefs may prevail, including having an overly pessimistic outlook on events. Thus, the *dispute stage of the process illustrated in Exercise 10.2 also should include using a more optimistic reinterpretation of events whenever necessary.* Such interpretations also must be backed up with our actions.

**Part 1: Reinterpreting Unpleasant Events**

Write a brief three to four sentence explanation for an unpleasant event that recently happened to you. Next, analyze your explanation for the presence of the pessimism.

> *Example:* Anita tells Dontonio that she does not want to date him anymore. *Dontonio's Pessimistic Explanation:* "This is the third time this has happened to me." *(Stable/Permanent)* "I can't have a good relationship no matter what I do." *(Global/Pervasive)* "There's something wrong with me." (*Internal Cause*) *Dontonio's Optimistic Reinterpretation:* "I've also had several long-term relationships with women." *(Unstable/Temporary)* "I've never had the type of problems I had with her before." *(Specific Situation)* "She must take some responsibility for rejecting me." *(External Cause)*

*Your situation:* Write a brief description of the unpleasant event.


What aspects of pessimistic explanation for unpleasant events were present? *(Stable/Permanent, Global Experience, Internal Cause)*


Write a more optimistic explanation of the event in the space provided. *(Unstable/Temporary, Specific Situation, External Cause)*


**Part 2: Reinterpreting Pleasant Events**

Select a recent pleasant event, and analyze it for a pessimistic explanation.

*Your situation:* Write a brief description of the pleasant event.


What aspects of a pessimistic explanation for pleasant events were present? *(Unstable/Temporary, Specific Situation, External Cause)*


Write a more optimistic explanation of the event in the space provided *(Stable/Permanent, Global Experience, Internal Cause)*

EXERCISE 10.4        **Managing Your Time and Yourself More Effectively**

Use this activity to help you begin to develop new ways to manage your schedule.

**I.** Put a check mark next to the items listed below that regularly occur in your life.

_____  1. Wait until the last minute to do something

_____  2. Typically take actions only after a crisis develops

_____  3. Believe that time lost today can be made up tomorrow

_____  4. Seldom set deadlines for the work I do

_____  5. Rush to complete most tasks

_____  6. Spend a lot of time on routine and trivial tasks

_____  7. Do not complete task until it is done perfectly

_____  8. Work on the easiest tasks first, and save the hardest ones for last

_____  9. Fail to set a schedule for how I want to use my time

_____ 10. Attend meetings even when my presence is not absolutely needed

_____ 11. Do not establish priorities for the tasks I must complete

_____ 12. Cannot say "no" to requests

_____ 13. Spend time socializing instead of working

_____ 14. Read things that are unessential for completing a task

_____ 15. Do not have clear objectives for what I want to do

_____ 16. Seldom ask for help with a task

_____ 17. Fail to listen to instructions for how to do things

_____ 18. Spending time on the telephone interferes with my getting work done

Each of the items above tend to make us use time less effectively. Pick two of those you checked that you find most bothersome. *What is one action you could take tomorrow to begin to eliminate it as a problem in your life?*

1.


2.


**II.** Develop a list of things you need to do tomorrow on a separate sheet of paper. Answer the following questions about each item: *Do I have to personally do it? Is there a more creative/efficient way to do it? Can I delegate this to someone else? Can I delay taking action? Can I dump this activity because it's unlikely to be missed?*

**III.** Schedule your time for tomorrow on a separate sheet of paper, using the items on your list that remain. Also include the following two things on your schedule.

• One activity that will allow you to "be a little selfish" and to do something just for your own personal satisfaction.

• One activity that helps you to prevent a problem, build a relationship, act on a new opportunity for yourself, or to get more recreation and leisure.

**IV.** Implement your schedule. Evaluate the pros and cons at the end of the day.

## *Key Terms*

*Adaptation.*   Our ability to cope with the problems and demands of our environment.

*Anxiety.*   An emotional state of feeling fearful, apprehensive, or worried in anticipation of some danger to our psychological or physical well-being.

*Conditioned emotional response.*   An emotional response such as anxiety that is automatically triggered by stimuli associated with a situation in which some traumatic event occurred.

*Defense mechanisms.*   Automatic and unconscious attempts to adapt to stress and anxiety in our lives. They try to protect us from unpleasant thoughts and emotions through self-deception and a distortion of reality.

*Defensive pessimism.*   A self-handicapping strategy in which low expectations for success in coping are set before a stressful event is experienced.

*Depression.*   An unpleasant emotional state characterized by a prolonged sad or apathetic mood.

*Distress.*   The experience of stress when our responses to stressors create physical, emotional, and behavioral problems.

*Eustress.*   The experience of stress when our responses to stressors lead to productive outcomes, such as solving problems and coping constructively.

*Explanatory style.*   How we interpret events that happen to us in either an optimistic or pessimistic fashion.

*General adaptation syndrome.*   Model for understanding the way the body initiates and directs its resources to cope with stress.

*Learned helplessness.*   Repeatedly experiencing unpleasant events, perceiving them as impossible to control, and becoming depressed as a result.

*Physical stressor.*   Physical stressors exist outside of an individual and create unpleasant reactions because they naturally affect basic physiological processes involved with illness, pain, or discomfort (e.g., cold weather, hot objects, viruses).

*Posttraumatic stress disorder.*   Reaction to a traumatic event in which afterwards, people experience nightmares, flashbacks, distress at reminders of the event, irritability, difficulty concentrating, and a general level of unresponsiveness.

*Psychological stressor.*   Situations that acquire stressful properties because they are cognitively appraised too demanding, they tax our ability to cope, and we fear the consequences of not coping.

*Self.*   The organization of thoughts and feelings derived from life experiences that contribute to perceptions of who we currently are and what we hope to become in the future.

*Self-concept.*   Refers to the definition we have of ourselves based on the roles we play and the personality traits we possess.

*Self-efficacy.*   Belief that we can control our lives and that our actions will produce desirable effects for us.

*Self-esteem.*   The positive and negative evaluations we have about ourselves.

*Self-image.*   Another term used to refer to "the self." Our self-image would include the definitions we have of ourselves (i.e., our self-concept) and the positive and negative evaluations we have about ourselves (i.e., our sense of self-esteem).

*Stress.*    The nonspecific physiological reactions and the specific physiological, cognitive, emotional, and behavioral responses to the demands and challenges we encounter every day.

*Stressor.*    A physical or psychological event in our lives that produces distress

*Type A behavior pattern.*    Characterized by a hard-driving, energetic, impatient, competitive, and aggressive approach to daily living.

*Type B behavior pattern.*    Characterized by a more relaxed, cooperative, and less aggressive approach to daily living.

*Unconscious impulses.*    The ideas, feelings, attitudes, and conflicts of which we are not consciously aware but which continue to influence our actions.

# REFERENCES

CHAPTER 1

Abelson, R. P. (1981). Psychological status of the script concept. *American Psychologist, 36,* 715–729.

Belenky, M., Clinchy, B., Coldberser, N., and Tarug, J. (1986). *Women's ways of knowing.* New York: Basic Books.

Bienstock, E. (1989). *Creative problem solving.* Stamford, CT: Waldentapes.

Borkat, R. F. (1993). A liberating curriculum. *Newsweek,* April 12.

Damer, T. E. (1987). *Attacking faulty reasoning.* Belmont, CA: Wadsworth.

Ellis, A., and Dryden, W. (1987). *The practice of rational-emotive therapy.* New York: Springer.

Fishhoff, B. (1975). The silly certainty of hindsight. Psychology Today, 71–76.

Gilbert, D. T. (1989). Thinking lightly about others: Automatic components of the social inference process. In: J. S. Uleman and J. A. Bargh (Eds.), *Unintended thought: Limits of awareness, intention, and control.* New York: Guilford.

Gilbert, D. T., McNulty, S. E., Giuliano, T. A., and Benson, J. E. (1992). Blurry words and fuzzy deeds: The attribution of obscure behavior. *Journal of Personality and Social Psychology, 62,* 18–25.

Glaser, E. M. (1984). Education and thinking: The role of knowledge. *American Psychologist, 39,* 93–104.

Glaser, E. M. (1985). Critical thinking: Education for responsible citizenship in a democracy. *National Forum, 65,* 24–27.

Halpern, D. (1989). *Thought and knowledge: An introduction to critical thinking.* Hillsdale, NJ: Lawrence-Earlbaum.

Hawkins, S. A., and Hastie, R. (1990). Hindsight: Biased judgments of past events after the outcomes are known. *Psychological Bulletin, 107,* 311–327.

Jones, R. N. (1990). *Thinking skills: Measuring and preventing personal problems.* Pacific Grove, CA: Brooks/Cole.

Kearl, M. C., and Gordon, C. (1992). *Social psychology.* Boston: Allyn and Bacon.

Kelley, H. H., and Michela, J. L. (1980). Attribution theory and research. *Annual Review of Psychology, 31,* 457–501.

King, P. M., Kitchener, K. S., and Wood, P. K. (1985). The development of intellect and character: A longitudinal-sequential study of intellectual and moral development in young adults. *Moral Education Forum, 10,* 1–13.

Kohn, A. (1986). *No contest: The case against competition.* New York: Houghton-Mifflin Company.

Kurfiss, J. G. (1988). *Critical thinking: Theory, research, practice, and possibilities.* ASHE-ERIC Higher Education Report No. 2. Washington, D. C.: Association for the Study of Higher Education.

Langer, E. (1989a). *Mindfulness.* Reading, MA: Addison-Wesley.

Langer, E. (1989b). Minding matters. In: L. Berkowitz (Ed.), *Advances in experimental social psychology.* New York: Academic Press.

Marks, D., and Kammann, R. (1980). *The psychology of the psychic.* Buffalo, NY: Prometheus Books.

Miller, J. G. (1984). Culture and the development of everyday social explanation. *Journal of Personality and Social Psychology. 46,* 961–978.

Nelson Jones, R. (1990). *Thinking skills: Managing & preventing personal problems.* Pacific Grove, CA: Brooks/Cole.

Nickerson, R. S. (1986a). Project intelligence: An account and some reflections. In: *Facilitating cognitive development: International perspectives, programs, and practices.* M. Schwebel, and C. A. Maher (Eds.), New York: Haworth.

Nickerson, R. S. (1986b). Reasoning. In: R. F. Dillon and R. J. Steinberg (Eds.), *Cognition and instruction.* New York: Academic Press.

Norman, D. A. (1980). Post-Freudian slips. *Psychology Today,* April, 42–50.

Norman, D. A. (1988). *The psychology of everyday things.* New York: Basic Books

Myers, D. G. (1993). Social psychology. New York: McGraw-Hill.

Perkins, D. N. (1986). Knowledge as design. Hillsdale, NJ: Lawrence-Erlbaum.

Perkins, D. N. (1987). Knowledge as design: Teaching thinking through content. In: J. B. Baron and R. J. Sternberg (Eds.), *Teaching thinking skills: Theory and practice.* New York: W. H. Freeman and Company.

Perry, W. (1970). Forms of intellectual and ethical development in the college years: A scheme. New York: Holt, Rinehard & Winston.

Perry, W. (1981). Cognitive and ethical growth: The making of meaning. In A. Chickering (Ed.), *The modern American college.* San Francisco: Jossey-Bass.

Pinto, R. C., and Blair, J. A. (1993). *Reasoning: A practical guide.* Englewood Cliffs, NJ: Prentice-Hall.

Polidoro, M. (1993). Testing a psychic on Italian TV. *Skeptical Inquirer. 17,* 124–125.

Randi, J. (1982). *Flim-Flam! Psychics, unicorns and other delusions.* Buffalo, NY: Prometheus Books.

Reynolds, D. (1977). Students who haven't seen a film on sexuality and communication prefer it to a lecture on the history of psychology they haven't heard. *Teaching of Psychology, 4,* 82–83.

Rodin, J., and Langer, E. (1977). Long-term effects of a control-relevant intervention among the institutionalized aged. *Journal of Personality and Social Psychology. 35,* 897–902.

Ryan, M. P. (1984). Conceptions of prose coherence: Individual differences in epistemological standards. *Journal of Educational Psychology, 76,* 248–258.

Schneider, W., Dumais, S. T., and Shiffin, R. M. (1984). Automatic and control processing and attention. In: Parasuraman, R., Davis, R., and Beatty, J. (Eds.), *Varieties of attention.* New York: Academic Press.

Seligman, M. E. P. (1975). Helplessness: On depression, development, and death. San Francisco: W. H. Freeman.

Storms, M. D. (1973). Videotapes and the attribution process: Reversing actors' and observers' points of view. *Journal of Personality and Social Psychology. 27,* 165–175.

Wade, C., and Tavris, C. (1987). *Learning to think critically.* New York: Harper-Collins.

Wimberly, E., and Wimberly, A. (1986). *Liberation and human wholeness.* Nashville, TN: Abington Press.

Wrightsman, L. S. (1992). *Assumptions about human nature.* Newbury Park, CA.: Sage Publications.

Zechmeister, E. B., and Johnson, J. E. (1992). *Critical thinking: A functional approach.* Pacific Grove, CA: Brooks/Cole.

## CHAPTER 2

Allesandra, M. (1991). Rising hemlines historically recharge the stock market. *Newhouse News Service Special Report.* August 14.

Aronson, E., Ellsworth, P. C., Carlsmith, J. M., and Gonzales, M. H. (1990). *Methods of research in social psycholgy (2nd Edition).* New York: McGraw-Hill.

Bothwell, R. K., Brigham, J. C., and Malpass, R. S. (1989). Cross-racial identification. *Personality and Social Psychology, 15,* 19–25.

Bramel, D., and Friend, R. (1981). Hawthorne, the myth of the docile worker and class bias in psychology. *American Psychologist, 36,* 867–878.

Brown, D. (1983). The low-tar cigarette scam. Reported in United Press International News report, February 20.

Chance, J. E. (1985). *Faces, folklore, and research hypotheses.* Presidential address given at the annual meetings of the Midwestern Psychological Association, Chicago, Ill.

Cooper H., and Richardson, A. J. (1986). Unfair comparisons. *Journal of Applied Psychology, 71,* 179–184.

Crocker, J. (1981). Judgment of covariation by social perceivers. *Psychological Bulletin, 90,* 272–292.

Feder, B. (1977). How to pass without actually cheating. *Human Behavior,* June, 56–59.

Finckenauer, J. O. (1982) *Scared straight and the panacea phenomenon.* Englewood Cliffs, NJ: Prentice-Hall.

Gerena, G. (1981). Strategies in answering essay tests. *Teaching of Psychology, 8,* 53–54.

Gilovich, T., Vallone, R., and Tversky, A. (1985). The hot hand in basketball: On the misperception of random sequences. *Journal of Personality and Social Psychology, 17,* 295–314.

Gould, S. J. (1985). The median isn't the message. *Discover,* June, 40–42.

Hite, S. (1987). *Hite report: Women and love: A cultural revolution in progress.* New York: Knopf.

Levy, S. (1990). Does the Mac make you stupid? *Macworld,* November, 69–72.

Mayer, R., and Goodchild, F. (1990). *The critical thinker.* New York: Wm. C. Brown.

McDonald, P. J., and O'Neal, E. C. (1980). Classroom ecology: The effects of seating arrangement on grades and participation. *Personality and Social Psychology Bulletin, 6,* 409–412.

Platz, S. J., and Hosch, H. M. (1988). Cross-racial/ethnic eyewitness identification: A field study. *Journal of Experimental Social Psychology, 10,* 17–22.

Plous, S. (1993). *The psychology of judgment and decision making.* New York: McGraw-Hill.

Peterson, C., and Bossio, L. M. (1991). *Health and optimism*. New York: Free Press.

Richmond, P. (1993). Town without pity. *GQ Magazine*, July, 30–41.

Root-Bernstein, R. (1993). *Rethinking AIDS: The tragic cost of premature consensus*. New York: Free Press.

Schaeffer, D. L. (1984). The presidential name game. *Psychology Today*, October 12.

Skinner, N. F. (1983). Switching answers on multiple-choice questions: Shrewdness or shibboleth? *Teaching of Psychology, 10,* 220–221.

Stone, J. (1989). Lookin' for science in all the wrong places. *Discover*, October, 96–99.

Sullivan, T. (1990). Chip rivals in comedy of errors. *San Francisco Examiner*, October 5, Section B, 1-4.

Tuchfarber, A. (1990). Political and other beliefs of residents of Hamilton County, Ohio: How do they compare to a national sample? *Research Report*, February. Institute for Policy Research, University of Cincinnati.

Wolff, C. (1993). Quantitative reasoning across a curriculum. *College Teaching, 41,* 3–8.

## CHAPTER 3

Adams, J. L. (1986a). *Conceptual blockbusting: A guide to better ideas*. Reading, MA: Addison-Wesley.

Adams, J. L. (1986b). *The care and feeding of ideas: A guide to encouraging creativity*. Reading, MA: Addison-Wesley.

Amabile, T. M. (1983). *The social psychology of creativity*. New York: Springer-Verlag.

Anderson, B. F. (1980). *The complete thinker*. Englewood Cliffs, NJ.: Prentice-Hall.

Barry, J., and Charles, R. (1992). Sea of lies. *Newsweek,* July 13, 1992, 29–39.

Baxter-Magolda, M. (1987). *The affective dimension of learning: Faculty-student relationships that enhance intellectual development*. Paper presented at National Lilly Conference on College Teaching, Miami University, Oxford, OH.

Crawford, R. P. (1954). *Techniques of creative thinking*. New York: Hawthorn Books.

Dawes, R. M. (1979). The robust beauty of improper linear models in decision making. *American Psychologist, 34,* 571–582.

Dawes, R. M. (1988). *Rational choice in an uncertain world*. New York: Harcourt Brace Jovanovich.

DeBono, E. (1992a). *The five-day course in thinking*. New York: Penguin Books.

DeBono, E. (1992b). *Practical thinking*. New York: Penguin Books.

Frederiksen, N. (1984). Implications of cognitive theory for instruction in problem-solving. *Review of Educational Research, 54,* 363–407.

Garfield, P. (1974). *Creative dreaming*. New York: Simon & Schuster.

Grasha, A. F. (1990). The naturalistic approach to learning styles. *College Teaching, 38,* 106–113.

Gordon, W. J. (1970) *Synectics*. New York: HarperCollins.

Hayes, J. (1989). *The complete problem solver*. Hillsdale, NJ: Lawrence-Erlbaum.

Janis, I., and Mann, L. (1977). *Decision making*. New York: Free Press.

Johnson, S. (1993). *"Yes or No" The guide to better decisions*. New York: Harper-Collins.

Kahneman, D., Sloric, P., and Tversky, A. (1982). *Judgments made under uncertainty: Heuristics and biases*. New York: Cambridge University Press.

Keating, J. D. (1984). Triad thinking on the opportunity levels of creative problem solving. *Journal of Creative Behavior, 10,* 45–56.

Klein, G. A., and Weizenfeld, T. (1978). Improvement of skills for solving ill-defined problems. *Educational Psychologist, 13,* 31–41.

Kruglanski, A. W. (1986). Freeze-think and the Challenger. *Psychology Today*, August, 48–49.

Lopes, L. L. (1983). Observations: Some thoughts on the psychological concept of risk. *Journal of Experimental Psychology: Section on Perception and Performance, 9,* 137–144.

Mackenzie, A. (1972). *The time trap.* New York: AMACOM.

Mezof, B. (1982). Cognitive style and interpersonal behavior: A review with implications for human relations training. *Group and Organizational Studies, 7,* 13–34.

Miller, G. R. (1978). *Life choices. How to make critical decisions about your education, career, marriage, family, and lifestyle,* New York: Crowell.

Newell, A., and Simon, H. A. (1972). *Human problem solving.* Englewood Cliffs, NJ: Prentice-Hall.

Osborn, A. F. (1963). *Applied imagination.* New York: Scribner's.

Phillips, S. D., Pazienza, N. J., and Ferrin, H. H. (1984). Decision-making styles and problem-solving appraisal. *Journal of Counseling Psychology, 31,* 497–502.

Pollio, H. (1987). Practical poetry. *Teaching -Learning Issues,* No. 60, 3–18.

Prince, G. (1970). *The practice of creativity.* New York: Collier Books.

Romming, R. R., McCurdy, D., and Ballinger, R. (1984). Individual differences: A third component in problem solving instruction. *Journal of Research in Science Teaching, 21,* 71–82.

Sarason, S. B. (1978). The nature of problem solving in social action. *American Psychologist, 33,* 370–380.

Siegelman, E. Y. (1983). *Personal risk: Mastering change in love and work.* New York: HarperCollins.

Seligman, M. E. P. (1991). *Learned optimism.* New York: Knopf.

Simonton, D. K. (1988). *Scientific genius.* New York: Penguin Books.

Sontag, S. (1989). *AIDS and its metaphors.* New York: Farrart, Straus and Giroux.

Stein, M. I. (1974). *Stimulating creativity: Individual procedures.* New York: Academic Press.

Sternberg and Detterman (1986). *What is intelligence? Contemporary viewpoints on its nature and definitions.* Norwood, NJ: Ablex.

Tjosvold, D. (1984). Effects of crisis orientation on managers' approach to controversy in decision making. *Academy of Management Journal, 27,* 130–138.

Tversky, A., and Kahneman, D. (1982). Judgments of and by representativeness. In: D. Kahneman, P. Slovic, and A. Tversky (Eds.), *Judgment under uncertainty: Heuristics and biases.* Cambridge, England: Cambridge University Press.

Watzlawick, P., Weakland, J., and Fisch, R. (1974). *Change: principles of problem formation and problem resolution.* New York: Norton.

Wheeler, D., and Janis, I. L. (1980). *A practical guide for making decisions.* New York: Free Press.

Witkin, H. A., Goodenough, D. R. (1981). *Cognitive styles: Essence and origins.* New York: International Universities Press.

Zechmeister, E. B., and Johnson, J. E. (1992). *Critical thinking: A functional approach.* Pacific Grove, CA: Brooks/Cole.

CHAPTER 4

Agras, W. S. (1987). Eating disorders: *Management of obesity, bulimia, and anoxeria nervosa.* New York: Pergamon Press.

Anderson, T. H. (1980). Study strategies and adjunct aids. In: R. J. Spiro, B. C. Bruce, and W. F. Brewer (Eds.), *Theoretical issues in comprehension: Perspectives from cognitive psychology, artificial intelligence, linguistics, and education.* Hillsdale, NJ: Lawrence-Erlbaum.

Atkinson, R. C. (1975). Mnemotechnics in second language teaming. *American Psychologist, 30,* 821–828.

Atkinson, R. C., and Shiffrin, R. M. (1968). Human memory: A proposed system and its controlled processes. In: K. W. Spence and J. T. Spence (Eds.), *The psychology of learning and motivation,* Vol. 2. New York: Academic Press, pp. 89–195.

Avery, R. D., and Ivancevich, J. M. (1980). Punishment in organizations: A review, propositions, and research suggestions. *Academy of Management Review, 5,* 123–132.

Balsam, P. D., and Bondy, A. S. (1983). The negative side effects of reward. *Journal of Applied Behavioral Analysis, 16,* 283–296.

Barnett, J. E., and Seefeldt, R. W. (1989). Read something once, why read it again? Repetitive reading and recall. *Journal of Reading Behavior, 21,* 351–360.

Bilodeau, E., and Bilodeau, I. (1961). Motor skills teaming. *Annual Review of Psychology, 14,* 15–23.

Bjork, R. A. (1979). Information processing analysis of college teaching. *Educational Psychologist, 14,* 15–23.

Bonwell, C., and Eison, J. A. (1991). Active learning: Creating excitement in the classroom. ASHE-ERIC Higher Education Report No. 1. Washington, D. C.: The George Washington University School of Education and Human Development.

Bower, G. H. (1970). Analysis of a mnemonic device. *American Scientist, 58,* 496–510.

Bower, G. H. (1981). Mood and memory. *American Psychologist, 36,* 129–148.

Bower, G. H. and Clark, M. C. (1969). Narrative stories as mediators of verbal learning. *Psychonomic Science, 14,* 181–182.

Britton, B. K., and Tesser, A. (1991). Effects of time-management practices on college grades. *Journal of Educational Psychology, 83,* 405–410.

Budworth, J. (1991). *Instant recall.* Holbrook, MA: Allan Books.

Carrier, C. A., and Titus, A. (1979). The effects of notetaking: A review of studies. *Contemporary Educational Psychology, 4,* 299–314.

Chazin, S., and Neruschatz, J. S. (1990). Using a mnemonic to aid in the recall of unfamiliar information. *Perceptual and Motor Skills, 71,* 1067–1071.

Corno, L., and Mandinach, E. B. (1983). The role of cognitive engagement in classroom learning and motivation. *Educational Psychologist, 18,* 88–108.

Cowan, N. (1988). Evolving conceptions of memory storage, selective attention, and their mutual constraints within the human information processing system. *Psychological Bulletin, 104,* 163–191.

Craik, F. I. M. (1979). *Annual Review of Psychology, 30,* 63–102.

Crovitz, H. F. (1971). The capacity of memory loci in artificial memory. *Psychonomic Science, 24,* 187–188.

Demster, F. N. (1988). The spacing effect: A case study in the failure to apply the results of psychological research. *American Psychologist, 43,* 627–634.

Dessler, G. (1982). *Human Behavior. Improving performance at work.* Reston, VA: Reston Publishing.

Diamond, W. D., and Loewy, B. Z. (1991). Effects of probabilistic rewards on recycling attitudes and behavior. *Journal of Applied Social Psychology, 21,* 1590–1607.

Dickinson, D. J., and O'Connell, D. Q. (1990). Effect of quality and quantity of study on student grades. *Journal of Educational Research, 83,* 227–231.

Driskell, J. E., Willis, R. P., and Cooper, C. (1992). Effect of overlearning on retention. *Journal of Applied Psychology, 77,* 615–632.

Eaglin, J. C. (1992). *Getting students to ask questions in the classroom.* Paper presented at conference on Diversity in the Classroom, Oakland University, Oakland, MI.

Ellis, H. C., and Ashbrook, P. W. (1989). The state of "mood" and memory research: A selective review. *Journal of Social Behavior and Personality, 4,* 1–21.

Foos, P., and Clark, C. (1984). The effects of student expectations on exam scores. *Human Learning, Z* 43–48.

Garland, D. J., and Barry, J. R. (1991). Cognitive advantage in sport: The nature of perceptual structures. *American Journal of Psychology, 104,* 211–238.

Geller, E. S. (1985). Seat belt psychology. *Psychology Today,* May, 12–13.

Gfeller, K. E. (1986). Musical mnemonics for learning disabled children. *Teaching Exceptional Children, 19,* 28–30.

Gold, P. C. (1984). Cognitive mapping. *Academic Therapy, 19,* 277–284.

Goltz, S. (1992). Sequential learning analysis of decisions in organizations to escalate investments despite continuing costs of losses. *Journal of Applied Behavior Analysis, 25,* 561–574.

Hawley, W. D., Rosenholtz, S., Goodstein, H. J., and Hasselbring. T. (1984). Good schools: What research says about improving student achievement. *Peabody Journal of Education, 61,* 1–134.

Hettich, P. (1976). The journal. An autobiographical approach to learning. *Teaching of Psychology, 3,* 55–59.

Hoddes, E. (1977). Does sleep help you study? *Psychology Today,* June, 69–70.

Hyman, I. (1984). *Report on an analysis of corporal punishment cases as reported in nationwide newspapers.* National Center for the Study of Corporal Punishment and Alternatives in the Schools. Philadelphia: Temple University Press.

Hynd, C. R., Simpson, M. L., Chase, N. D. (1990). Studying narrative text: The effects of annotating vs. journal writing on test performance. *Reading Research and Instruction. 29,* 44–54.

Johnson, L. L. (1988). Effects of underlining textbook sentences on passage and sentence retention. *Reading Research and Instruction, 28,* 18–32.

Karacan, I. (1981). Dose related effects of flurazepam on human sleep-waking patterns. *Psychopharmacology, 73,* 332–339.

Kiewra, K. A., Dubois, N. F., Christian, D., and McShane, A. (1988). Providing study notes: Comparison of three types of notes for review. *Journal of Educational Psychology, 80,* 595–597.

Kirschenbaum, D. S., Malett, S. D., and Humphrey, L. (1982). Specificity of planning and maintenance of self-control: A one year follow-up of a study improvement program. *Behavior Therapy, 13,* 232–242.

Komaki, J., Heinzmann, A. T, and Lawson, L. (1980). Effect of training and feedback: Component analysis of a behavioral safety program. *Journal of Applied Psychology, 65,* 261–270.

Lindgren, H. C. (1969). *The psychology of college success: A dynamic approach.* New York: Wiley.

Lockhart, R. S., and Craik, F. I. M. (1990). Levels of processing: A retrospective commentary on a framework for memory research. *Canadian Journal of Psychology, 44,* 87–122.

Lofland, D. J. (1992). *Powerlearning.* Santa Cruz, CA: Longmeadow Press.

Loftus, E. (1980). *Memory.* Reading, MA: Addison-Wesley.

Lorayne, H. (1990). *Super memory: Super student.* Boston: Little Brown.

Luria, A. R. (1982). The mind of a mnemonist. In: Neisser, U. (Ed.), *Memory observed.* New York: Freeman.

Luthans, F., Paul, R., and Baker, D. (1981). An experimental analysis of the impact of contingent reinforcement on salespersons' performance behavior. *Journal of Applied Psychology, 66,* 314–323.

Macan, T. H., Sahani, C., Dipboye, R. L., and Phillips, A. P. (1990). College students' time management: Correlations with academic performance and stress. *Journal of Educational Psychology, 82,* 760–768.

McCagg, E. C., and Dansereau, D. F. (1991). A convergent paradigm for examining knowledge mapping as a learning strategy. *Journal of Educational Research, 84,* 317–323.

McKeachie, W. (1993). *Teaching tips.* Lexington, MA: D. C. Heath.

Melton, A. W. (1963). Implications of short-term memory for a general theory of memory. *Journal of Verbal Learning and Verbal Behavior, Z* 75–85.

Miller, D. L. and Kelley, M. L. (1991). Interventions for improving homework performance: A critical review. *School Psychology Quartery,. 3,* 174–185.

Miller, G. A. (1956). The magic number seven plus or minus two: Some limits on our capacity for processing information. *Psychological Review, 63,* 81–97.

Morrison, R. F., and Brantner, T. M. (1992). What enhances or inhibits learning a new job? A basic career issue. *Journal of Applied Psychology. 77,* 926–940.

Parke, R. D. (1977). Some effects of punishment on children's behavior: Revisited. In: E. M. Hertherington, E. M. Ross, and R. D. Parke (Eds.). *Contemporary readings in child psychology.* New York: McGraw-Hill.

Peterson, L. B., and Peterson, M. J. (1959). Short-term retention of individual items. *Journal of Experimental Psychology, 58,* 193–198.

Roberts, J. (1985). The keyword method: An alternative vocabulary strategy for developmental college readers. *Reading World,* March, 34–38.

Robinson, E. P. (1970). *How to study.* New York: HarperCollins.

Rosenheck, M. B., Levin, M. E., and Levin, J. R. (1989). Learning botany concepts mnemonically: Seeing the forest and the trees. *Journal of Educational Psychology, 81,* 196—203.

Sandstrom, R. (1990). *The ultimate memory book.* New York: Stepping Stone Books.

Schilling, R. F., and Weaver, G. E. (1983). Effect of extraneous verbal information on memory for telephone numbers. *Journal of Applied Psychology, 68,* 559–564.

Squire, L. R. (1987). *Memory and brain.* Oxford: Oxford University Press.

Snyder, M., and White, P. (1982). Mood and memories: Elation, depression, and the remembering of the events in one's life. *Journal of Personality, 50,* 149–167.

Sperling, G. (1969). The information available in brief visual presentations. *Psychological Monographs, 74* (Whole No. 498).

Stern, P. C. (1992). What psychology knows about energy conservation. *American Psychologist, 47,* 1224–1323.

Troutt-Ervin, E. D. (1990). Application of keyword mnemonics to learning terminology in the college classroom. *Journal of Experimental Education, 59,* 31–40.

Tulving, E. (1972). Episodic and semantic memory. In: E. Tulving and W. Donaldson (Eds.), *Organization of memory.* New York: Academic Press.

Underwood, B. J. (1970). A break-down of the total time law in free recall learning. *Journal of Verbal Learning and Verbal Behavior, 9,* 573–580.

Walters, C. C., and Grusec, J. E. (1977). *Punishment.* San Francisco, CA: Freeman.

Walvord, B. (1990). *Thinking and writing in college.* Urbana, IL: National Council of Teachers of English.

Worley, C. G., Bowen, J. E., and Lawler, E. E. (1992). On the relationship between objective increases in pay and employees' subjective reactions. *Journal of Organizational Behavior, 13,* 559–571.

Yalch, R. (1991). Memory in a jingle jungle: Music as a mnemonic device in comunicating advertising slogans. *Journal of Applied Psychology, 76,* 268–274.

Zechmeister, E. B., and Nyberg, S. E. (1982). *Human memory: An introduction to research and theory.* Pacific Grove, CA: Brooks/Cole.

## CHAPTER 5

Bandura, A. (1986). *Social foundations of thought and action: A social cognitive theory.* Englewood Cliffs, NJ: Prentice-Hall.

Belson, W. (1978). *Television violence and the adolescent boy.* London: Teakfield Press.

Bornstein, P. H., Hamilton, S. B., and Bornstein, M. T. (1985). Self-monitoring procedures. In: A. R. Ciminero, K. S. Calhoun, and W. E. Adams (Eds.), *Handbook of behavioral assessment (2nd Edition).* New York: Wiley.

Bushman, B. J., and Geen, R. G. (1990). Role of cognitive-emotional mediators and individual differences in the effects of media violence on aggression. *Journal of Personality and Social Psychology, 58,* 156–163.

Cervone, D., Jiwani, N., and Wood, R. (1991). Goal setting and the differential influence of self-regulatory processes on complex decision making performance. *Journal of Personality and Social Psychology, 61,* 257–266.

Cohen, S., and Lichtenstein, E. (1990). Partner behaviors that support quitting smoking. *Journal of Consulting and Clinical Psychology, 58,* 304–309.

DeVogue, J. T., Minor, T., and Karoly, P. (1981). Effects of behavioral intervention and interpersonal feedback on fear and avoidance components of severe agoraphobia: A case analysis. *Psychological Reports, 49,* 595–605.

Doyle, J. A. (1983). *The male experience.* Dubuque, IA: Brown.

Edwards, C. P. (1991). Behavioral sex differences in children of diverse cultures. The case of nurturance to infants. In: M. Piereira and L. Fairbanks (Eds.), *Juveniles: Comparative socioecology.* Oxford: Oxford University Press.

Elder, J. P., and Estey, J. D. (1992). Behavior change strategies for family planning. *Social Science Medicine, 35,* 1065–1076.

Green, R. B., Hardison, W. L., and Greene, B. F. (1984). Turning the table on advice programs parents: Using placemats to enhance family interaction at restaurants. *Journal of Applied Behavioral Analysis, 17,* 497–508.

Hall, S. M. (1980). Self-management and therapeutic maintenance: Theory and research. In: P. Karoly and J. Steffen (Eds.), *Improving the long-term effects of psychotherapy.* New York: Gardner Press, pp. 263–300.

Hearold, S. (1986). A synthesis of 1043 effects of television on social behavior. In: G. Comstock (Ed.), *Public communication and behavior,* Vol. 1. Orlando, FL: Academic Press.

Jennings, J., Geis, F. L., and Brown, J. (1980). Influence of television commercials on women's self-confidence and independent judgment. *Journal of Personality and Social Psychology, 38,* 203–210.

Johnson-O'Connor, E. J., and Kirschenbaum, D. S. (1986). Something succeeds like success: Positive self-monitoring for unskilled golfers. *Cognitive Therapy and Research, 10* 123–136.

Kirschenbaum, D. S. (1985). Proximity and specificity of planning: A position paper. *Cognitive Therapy and Research, 9,* 489–506.

Kirschenbaum, D. S., and Bale, R. M. (1980). Cognitive-behavioral skills in golf: Brain power golf. In: R. M. Suinn (Ed.), *Psychology in sports: Methods and applications.* Minneapolis, MN: Burgess.

Latham, G. P., and Saari, L. M. (1979). Application of social learning theory to training supervisors through behavioral modeling. *Journal of Applied Psychology, 64,* 239–246.

Mace, F. C., and Kratochwill, T. R. (1985). Theories of reactivity in self-monitoring. *Behavior Modification, 9,* 323–343.

Mahoney, M. J., and Auner, M. (1977). Psychology and the elite athlete: An exploratory study. *Cognitive Therapy and Research, 1,* 131–141.

Mahoney, M. J., and Lyddon, W. J. (1988). Recent developments in cognitive approaches to counseling and psychotherapy: *The Counseling Psychologist, 16, 190–234.*

Mahoney, M. J. and Thoresen, C. E. (1974). *Self-control: Power to the person.* Monterey, CA: Brooks/Cole.

Marlatt, G. A., and Gordon, J. R. (1985). *Relapse prevention: Maintenance strategies for addictive behavior change.* New York: Guilford Press.

Martin, G., and Pear, J. (1988). *Behavior modification: What it is and how to do it.* Englewood Cliffs, NJ: Prentice-Hall.

Meichenbaum, D. (1977). *Cognitive-behavior modification: An integrative approach.* New York: Plenum.

Meichenbaum, D. (1986). Cognitive-behavior modification. In: F. H. Kanfer and A. P. Goldstein (Eds.), *Helping people change.* New York: Pergamon Press.

Ollendick, T. H., and King, N. J. (1991). Origins of childhood fears: An evaluation of Rachman's theory of fear acquisition. *Behavior Research and Therapy, 29,* 117–123.

Rehm, L. P. (1988). Self-management and cognitive processes in depression. In: L. B. Alloy (Ed.), *Cognitive processes in depression.* New York: Guilford Press.

Sarason, I. G., Sarason, B. R., Pierce, G. R., Shearin, E. N., and Sayers, M. H. (1991). A social learning approach to increasing blood donations. *Journal of Applied Social Psychology, 21,* 896–918.

Seidner, M. L., and Kirschenbaum, D. S. (1980). Behavioral contracts: Effects of pretreatment information and intention statements. *Behavior Therapy, 11,* 689–698.

Shiffman, S. (1984). Coping with temptations to smoke. *Journal of Consulting and Clinical Psychology, 52,* 261–267.

Skinner, B. F. (1963). Operant behavior. *American Psychologist, 18,* 503–515.

Stevens, V. J. (1978). Increasing professional productivity while teaching full time: A case study in self-control. *Teaching of Psychology, 5,* 203–204.

Suinn, R. M. (1983). Imagery and sports. In: A. A. Sheikh (Ed.), *Imagery: Current theory, research, and application.* New York: Wiley.

Suinn, R. M. (1989). Behavioral interventions for stress management in sports. In: D. Hackfort and C. Spielberger (Eds.), *Anxiety in sports: An international perspective.* New York: Hemisphere Press.

Watson, D. L., and Tharp, R. G. (1993). *Self-directed behavior: Self-modification for personal adjustment,* Pacific Grove, CA: Brooks/Cole.

Whyte, W. F. (1972). *Skinnerian Theory in Organizations Psychology Today,* April, 27–34.

Worthington, E. L. (1979). Behavioral self-control and the contract problem. *Teaching of Psychology, 6,* 91–94.

Zecker, S. (1982). Mental practice and knowledge of results in the learning of a perceptual motor skill. *Journal of Sport Psychology, 4,* 52–63.

Zillman, D. (1989). Aggression and sex: Independent and joint operations. In: H. L. Wagner and A. S. R. Manstead (Eds.), *Handbook of psychophysiology: Emotion and social behavior.* Chichester: Wiley.

## CHAPTER 6

Adams, J. D. (1980). *Understanding and managing stress.* San Diego, CA.: University Associates.

Atkinson, J. W., and Raynor, J. O. (1978). *Personality, motivation, and achievement.* New York: Halsted Press.

Bandura, A. (1982). Self-efficacy mechanisms in human agency. *American Psychologist, 37,* 122–147.

Bandura, A. (1986). *Social foundations of thought and action:* A social cognitive theory. Englewook Cliffs, NJ: Prentice-Hall.

Bank, B. J., Biddle, B. J., and Slavings, R. L. (1992). What do undergraduates want? Expectations and undergraduate persistence. *The Sociological Quarterly, 33,* 321–335.

Bar-Tal, D. (1978). Attributional analysis of achievement-related behavior. *Review of Educational Research, 48,* 259–271.

Barry, R. G. (1975). Fear of failure in the student experience. *Personnel and Guidance Journal, 54,* 190–203.

Benassi, V. A., Sweeney, P. D., and Dufour, C. L. (1988). Is there a relation between locus of control orientation and depression? *Journal of Abnormal Psychology, 97,* 357–367.

Bolles, R. C. (1975). *Theory of motivation.* New York: HarperCollins.

Buss, D. M. (1991). Evolutionary personality theory. *Annual Review of Psychology, 42,* 459–451.

Byrne, D. (1982). Predicting human sexual behavior. In: A. G. Kraut (Ed.), *The G. Stanley Hall Lecture Series,* Vol. 2 Washington, DC: American Psychological Association.

Cartwright, R. D. (1977). *Night-life: Explorations in dreaming.* Englewood Cliffs, NJ: Prentice-Hall.

Chusmir, L. (1989). Behavior: A measure of motivation needs. *Psychology: A Journal of Human Behavior, 26,* 1–10.

Cosmides, L., and Tooby, J. (1987). From evolution to behavior: Evolutionary psychology as the missing link. In: J. Dupre (Ed.), *The latest on the best.* Cambridge, MA: MIT Press.

Dabbs, J. M., Ruback, R. B. and Besch, N. F. (1987). *Male saliva testosterone following conversations with male and female partners.* Paper presented at the annual meetings of the American Psychological Association.

Davis, S. F., Grover, C. A., Becker, A. H., and McGregor, L. N. (1992). Academic dishonesty: Prevalence, determinants, techniques, and punishments. *Teaching of Psychology, 19,* 16–20.

Deci, E. L., and Ryan, R. M. (1980). The empirical exploration of intrinsic motivational processes. In: L. Berkowitz (Ed.), *Advances in experimental social psychology.* New York: Academic Press.

Deci, E. L., and Ryan, R. M. (1985). *Intrinsic motivation and self-determination in human behavior.* New York: Plenum.

Dekker, J., and Everaerd, W. (1989). Psychological determinants of sexual arousal: A Review. *Behavior Research Therapy, 27,* 353–364.

Elizur, D. (1984). Facets of work values: A structural analysis of work outcomes. *Journal of Applied Psychology, 69,* 379–389.

Epstein, S. (1978). Avoidance-approach: The fifth basic conflict. *Journal of Consulting and Clinical Psychology, 46,* 1016–1022.

Farley, F. (1986) The world of the Type T personality. *Psychology Today,* May, 46–52.

Feather, N. (1992). Values, valences, expectations, and actions. *Journal of Social Issues, 48,* 109–124.

Feather, N., and O'Brien, G. E. (1987). Looking for employment: An expectancy-valence analysis of job-seeking behavior among young people. *British Journal of Psychology, 78,* 251–272.

Flett, G. L., Blankstein, K. R., Hewitt, P. L., and Koledin, S. (1992). Components of perfectionism and procrastination in college students. *Social Behavior and Personality. 20,* 85–94.

Ford, D. E., Wright, R. A., and Haythornwaite, J. (1985). Task performance and magnitude of goal valence. *Journal of Research in Personality, 19,* 253–260.

Franken, R. (1988). *Human motivation.* Pacific Grove, CA: Brooks/Cole.

Freud, S. (1937). *The ego and mechanisms of defense.* New York: International Universities Press.

Fried-Buchalter, S. (1992). Fear of success, fear of failure, and the imposter phenomenon. *Journal of Personality Assessment, 58,* 368–379.

Grasha, A. F., and Kirschenbaum, D. K. (1986). *Adjustment and competence: Concepts and applications.* St. Paul, MN: West Publishers.

Harvey, S. M. (1987). Female sexual behavior: Fluctuations during the menstrual cycle. *Journal of Psychosomatic Research, 31,* 101–110.

Horner, M. S. (1978). The measurement and behavioral implications of fear of success in women. In: J. W. Atkinson and J. O. Raynor (Eds.), *Personality, motivation, and achievement.* New York: Halsted Press.

Hunt, M. (1974). *Sexual behavior in the 1970's.* Chicago: Playboy Press.

Janis, I. L., and Mann, L. (1977). *Decision making.* New York: Free Press.

Jones, R. (1977). *Self-fulfilling prophecies: Social, psychological, and physiological effects of expectancies.* Hillsdale, NJ: Lawrence-Earlbaum.

Kelley, K., and Byrne, D (1991). *Human sexual behavior: An introduction.* Englewood Cliffs, NJ: Prentice-Hall.

Kulik, J. A., and Mahler, H. I. M. (1990). Stress and affiliation research: On taking the laboratory to health field settings. *Annals of Behavioral Medicine, 12,* 106–111.

Logue, A. W. (1991). *The psychology of eating and drinking.* New York: Freeman.

Maslow, A. H. (1970). *Motivation and personality.* New York: HarperCollins.

Matteson, M. T., and Ivancevich, J. M. (1987). *Controlling work stress.* San Francisco: Jossey-Bass.

Mazur, E. (1989). Predicting gender differences in same-sex friendships from affiliation motive and value. *Psychology of Women Quarterly, 1989,* 277–291.

McCabe, D. (1991). Schools for scandal. *People,* May, 103–104.

McClelland, D. C. (1975). *Power. The inner experience.* New York: Halsted Press.

McClelland, D. C. (1978). Managing motivation to expand human freedom. *American Psychologist, 33,* 201–210.

McClelland, D. C. (1985a). How motives, skills, and values determine what people do. *American Psychologist, 40,* 812–825.

McClelland, D. C. (1985b) *Human motivation.* Glenview, IL: Scott-Foresman.

Miller, P. M. (1983). *The Hilton Head metabolism diet.* New York: Warner.

Miller, P. C., Lefcourt, H. M., Holmes, J. G., Ware, E. E., and Saleh, W. E. (1986). Marital locus of control and marital problems. *Journal of Personality and Social Psychology, 51,* 161–169.

Morgan, R. R. (1978). Utilization of extrinsically manipulated grade contingencies as motivation of school learning. *Teaching of Psychology, 5,* 191–193.

Newcomb, M., and McGhee, L. (1991). Influence of sensation seeking on general deviance and specific problem behaviors from adolescence to young adulthood. *Journal of Personality and Social Psychology, 5,* 614–628.

Phares, E. J. (1973). *Locus of control: A personality determinant of behavior.* Morristown, NJ: General Learning Press.

Pinel, J. P. J. (1993). *Biopsychology.* Needham Heights, MA: Allyn and Bacon.

Reilly, R. (1993). Weight watcher. *Sports Illustrated,* September, 40–44.

Rodin, J. (1985). Insulin levels, hunger and food intake: An example of feedback loops in body weight regulation. *Health Psychology, 4,* 1–18.

Rodin, J., and Salovey, P. (1989). Health psychology. *Annual Review of Psychology, 40,* 533–579.

Rokeach, M. (1979). *Understanding human values: Individual and societal,* New York: Free Press.

Rokeach, S. J., Rokeach, M., and Grube, J. W. (1984). The great American values test. *Psychology Today,* November, 65–69.

Rotter, J. B. (1975). Some problems and misconceptions related to the construct of internal versus external control of reinforcement. *Journal of Consulting Psychology, 43,* 56–67.

Rubin, A. M. (1993). The effects of locus of control on communication motivation, anxiety, and satisfaction. *Communication Quarterly, 41,* 161–171.

Ruf, B. M., and Chusmir, L. H. (1992). Dimensions of success and motivation needs among managers. *The Journal of Psychology, 125,* 631–640.

Sass, E. J. (1989). Motivation in the college classroom: What students tell us. *Teaching of Psychology, 16,* 86–87.

Schmidt-Nielsen, K. (1994). How are control systems controlled? *American Scientist, 82,* 38–43.

Schunk, D. H. (1992). Self-efficacy and academic motivation. *Educational Psychologist, 26,* 207–231.

Schwartz, R. (1984). Body weight regulation. *University of Washington Medicine, 10,* 16–20.

Sheras, P. R., Hollier, E. A., and Brooke, J. (1983). *Dream on: A dream interpretation guide.* Englewood Cliffs, NJ: Prentice-Hall.

Suggs, R. (1962). *The hidden worlds of Polynesia.* New York: Harcourt Brace Jovanovich.

Weick, K. E. (1984). Small wins: Redefining the scale of social problems. *American Psychologist, 39,* 40–49.

Weiner, B. (1972). Attribution theory, achievement motivation, and the educational process. *Review of Educational Research, 42,* 203–215.

Wells, B. I. (1986). Predictors of female nocturnal orgasms: A multivariate analysis. *Journal of Sex Research, 22,* 421–437.

Willmuth, M. E. (1987). Sexuality after spinal cord injury: A critical review. *Clinical Psychology Review, 7,* 389–412.

Wilson, E. O. (1980). *Sociobiology: Abridged edition.* Cambridge, MA: Cambridge University Press.

Winter, D. G. (1973). *The power motive.* New York: Free Press.

Winter, D. G. (1988). The power motive in women and men. *Journal of Personality and Social Psychology, 54,* 510–519.

Wooley, S. C., Wooley, O. W., and Dyrenforth, S. R. (1979). Theoretical, practical, and applied social issues in behavioral treatments of obesity. *Journal of Applied Behavioral Analysis, 12,* 3–25.

Zuckerman, M. (1986). Sensation seeking. In: H. London and J. E. Exnex, Jr. (Eds.), *Dimensions of Personality.* New York: Wiley.

## CHAPTER 7

Althen, G. (1992). The Americans have to say everything. *Communication Quarterly, 40,* 413–421.

Anderson, P. A., & Sull, K. K. (1985). Out of touch, out of reach: Tactile predispositions as predictors of interpersonal distance. *Western Journal of Speech Communication, 49,* 52–72.

Andrews, J. D. (1989). Integrating visions of reality: Interpersonal diagnosis and the existential vision. *American Psychologist, 44,* 803–817.

Archer, D., & Akert, R. M. (1977). How well do you use body language? *Psychology Today,* October, 43–47.

Argyle, M. (1972). *The psychology of interpersonal behavior.* Middlesex, England: Pelican Books.

Bavelas, J. B., and Coates, L. (1992). How do we account for the mindfulness of face-to-face dialogue? *Communication Monographs,* 301–304.

Bonwell, C. C., and Eison, J. A. (1991). *Active learning: Creating excitement in the classroom. ASHE-ERIC* Higher Education Report No. 1. Washington, D. C.: The George Washington University, School of Education and Human Development.

Buller, D. B. (1987). Communication apprehension and reactions to proxemic violations. *Journal of Nonverbal Behavior, 11,* 13-25.

Burgoon, J. K. (1991). Relational message interpretations of touch, conversational distance, and posture. *Journal of Nonverbal Behavior, 15,* 233-259.

Burgoon, J. K., & Walther, J. B. (1992). Nonverbal expectancies and the evaluative consequences of violations. *Human Communication Research, 17,* 232-265.

Campbell, D. E., and Campbell, T. A. (1988). A new look at informal communication: The role of the physical environment. *Environment and Behavior, 20,* 211-226.

Carson, R. C. (1979). Personality and exchange in developing relationships. In: R. L. Burgess and T. L. Houston (Eds.), *Social exchange in developing relationships.* New York: Academic Press.

Christiensen, A., and Shenk, J. J. (1991). Communication conflict and psychological distance in nondistress and divorcing couples. *Journal of Consulting and Clinical Psychology, 59,* 458-463.

Covey, S. R. (1989). *The 7 habits of highly effective people.* New York: Simon and Schuster.

Devogoe, J. T. (1980). Reciprocal role training: Therapeutic transfer as viewed from a social psychology of dyads. In: P. Karoly and J. J. Steffen (Eds.), *Sources of long-term change in psychotherapy.* New York: Gardner Press.

Douglas, C. (1987). The beat goes on. *Psychology Today,* November, 37–42.

Duck, S. (1990). Relationships as unfinished business: Out of the frying pan and into the 1990s. *Journal of Social and Personal Relationships, 7,* 5–28.

Duck, S., Rutt, D. J., Hoy-Hurst, M., and Strejc, H. (1991). Some evident truths about conversations in everyday relationships: All communications are not created equal. *Human Communication Research, 18,* 228–267.

Fuhrmann, B. S., and Grasha, A. F. (1983). *A practical handbook for college teachers.* Boston: Little-Brown.

Gallaher, P. E. (1992). Individual differences in nonverbal behavior: Dimensions of style. *Journal of Personality and Social Psychology, 63,* 133–145.

Gibb, J. R. (1978). *Trust: A new view of personal and organizational development.* Los Angeles: Guild of Tutors Press.

Gifford, R. (1982). Projected interpersonal distance and orientation choices: Personality, sex, and social situation. *Social Psychology Quarterly, 45,* 145–152.

Goffman, I. (1959). *The presentation of self in everyday life.* New York: Doubleday.

Gottman, J., Notarius, C., and Markman, H. (1976). *A couple's guide to communication.* Champaign, IL: Research Press.

Graham, E. E., Barbato, C. A., and Perse, E. M. (1993). The interpersonal communication motives model. *Communication Quarterly, 41,* 172–186.

Grasha, A. F., Ichiyama, M., and Kelly, D. (1986). *Psychological size and distance in student-teacher and other interpersonal interactions.* Paper presented at Annual Meetings of American Psychological Association, Washington, D. C.

Grasha, A. F., and Ichiyama, M. (1990). *The Grasha-Ichiyama psychological size and distance scale.* Cincinnati, OH: Communication and Education Associates.

Grasha, A. F., and Homan, M. (1994). Interpersonal status and affect in the interpersonal relations of adult children of alcoholics and their alcoholic parents. *Psychological Reports, in press.*

Guilford, R. (1991). Mapping nonverbal behavior on the interpersonal circle. *Journal of Personality and Social Psychology, 61,* 279–288.

Hall, E. (1959). *The silent language.* Garden City, NY: Doubleday.

Hample, D. (1987). Communication and the unconscious. In: B. Dervin and M. J. Voigt (Eds.), *Progress in communication sciences.* Norwood, NJ: Ablex.

Hawkins, B. L., and Preston, P. (1981). *Managerial communication.* Santa Monica, CA: Goodyear Publishing.

Housel, T. J., and Davis, W. E. (1977). The reduction of upward communication distortion. *Journal of Business Communication, 14,* 49–63.

Infante, D. A., Riddle, B. L., Horvath, C. L., and Tumlin, S. A. (1992). Verbal aggressiveness: Messages and reasons. *Communication Quarterly, 40,* 116–126.

Jaska, J. A., and Stech, E. L. (1978). Communication to enhance silence: The Trappist Experience. *Journal of Communication, 28,* 75–79.

Kohn, A. (1988). Girl talk, guy talk. *Psychology Today,* February, 65–68.

Leavitt, H. J. (1951). Some effects of certain communication patterns on group performance. *Journal of Abnormal and Social Psychology, 46,* 38–50.

Lutz, W. (1989). *Doublespeak.* New York: HarperPerennial.

Mehrabian, A. (1981). *Silent messages.* Belmont, CA: Wadsworth.

Monge, P. R., Cozzens, M. D., and Contractor, N. S. (1992). Communication and motivational predictors of the dynamics of organizational innovations. *Organization Science, 3,* 250–274.

Morris, D. (1977). *Manwatching: A field guide to human behavior.* New York: Abrams.

Morrow, P. C., and McElroy, J. C. (1981). Interior office design and visitor response: A constructive replication. *Journal of Applied Psychology 66,* 646–650.

Motley, M. T. (1992). Mindfulness in solving communicators' dilemmas. *Communication Monographs, 59,* 306–313.

Mullen, B., Johnson, C., and Salas, E. (1991). Effects of communication network structure: Components of positional centrality. *Social Networks, 13,* 169–185.

Muson, H. (1982). Getting the phone's number. *Psychology Today,* October, 43–49.

Pollock, A. D., Die, A. H., and Marriott, R. G. (1990). Relationship of communication style to egalitarian marital role. *Journal of Social Psychology, 130,* 619–624.

Potash, M. (1990). *Hidden agendas.* New York: Delcorte Press.

Reik, T., (1972). *Listening with the third ear.* New York: Pyramid.

Reilly, R. (1993) Picking through the trash. *Sports Illustrated,* September 27.

Rice, B. (1981). Between the lines of threatening messages. *Psychology Today,* October, 52–62.

Rosenthal, R. (1974). Body talk and tone of voice: The language without words. *Psychology Today,* June, 34–40.

Rubin, R. B., Perse, E. M., and Barbato, C. A. (1988). Conceptualization and measurement of interpersonal communication motives. *Human Communication Research, 14,* 602–628.

Rubin, R. B., and Rubin, A. M. (1992). Antecedents of interpersonal communication motivation. *Communication Quarterly, 40,* 305–317.

Salzmann, J., and Grasha, A. F. (1991). Psychological size and distance in manager–subordinate relationships. *Journal of Social Psychology, 131,* 629–646.

Sommer, R. (1969). *Personal Space.* Englewood Cliffs, NJ: Prentice-Hall.

Snyder, M., and Ickes, W. (1985). Personality and social behavior. In: G. Lindzey and E. Aronson (Eds), *Handbook of social psychology,* Vol 2. New York: Random House.

Stamp, G. H., Vangelisti, A. L., Daly, J. A. (1992). The creation of defensiveness in social interaction, *Communication Quarterly, 40,* 177–190.

Steele, F. I. (1973). *Physical settings and organizational development.* Reading, MA: Addison Wesley.

Tesch, F., Lansky, L. M., and Lundgren, D. C. (1972). The exchange of information: One-way versus two-way communication. *Journal of Applied Behavioral Science, 8,* 169–174.

Triandis, H. (1994). *Culture and social behavior.* New York: McGraw-Hill.

## CHAPTER 8

Adams, V. (1980). Getting at the heart of jealous love. *Psychology Today,* May, 35–39.

Aronson, E., and Osherow, N. (1980). Cooperation, prosocial behavior and academic performance: Experiments in the segregated classroom. In: L. Bickman (Ed.), *Applied Social Psychology Annual,* Vol. 1. Beverly Hills, CA: Sage.

Beck, A. T., and Young, J. E. (1978). College blues. *Psychology Today,* September, 80–92.

Bell, R. A., Roloff, M. E., Van Camp, K., and Karol, S. H. (1990). Is it lonely at the top?: Career success and personal relationships. *Journal of Communication, 40,* 9–23.

Berent, J. (1993). *Beyond shyness: How to conquer social anxieties.* New York: S&F Trade.

Berscheid, E., and Fein, J. (1977). Romantic love and sexual jealousy. In: G. Clanton and L. G. Smith (Eds.), *Jealousy.* Englewood Cliffs, NJ: Prentice-Hall.

Berscheid, E., and Walster, E. (1978). *Interpersonal attraction.* Reading, MA: Addison-Wesley.

Berscheid, E. (1985). Interpersonal attraction. In: G. Lindzey and E. Aronson (Eds.), *Handbook of social psychology (3rd edition)).* New York: Random House.

Berscheid, E., Snyder, M., and Omoto, A. M. (1989). Issues in studying close relationships: Conceptualizing and measuring closeness. In: C. Hendrick (Ed.), *Review of personality and social psychology,* (Vol. 10). Newbury Park, CA: Sage.

Bierhoff-Werner, H. (1992). Twenty years of research on love: Theory, results, and prospects for the future. *The German Journal of Psychology, 15,* 95–117.

Blau, P. M. (1964). *Exchange and power in social life.* New York: Wiley.

Blumstein, P., and Schwartz, P. (1983). *American couples: Money, work, and sex.* New York: Morrow.

Brehm, S. S. (1992). *Intimate relationships.* New York: McGraw-Hill.

Brody, G. H., Neubaumn, E., and Forehand, R. (1988). Serial marriages: A heuristic analysis of an emerging family form. *Psychological Bulletin, 103,* 211–222.

Buss, D. A. (1985). Human mate selection. *American Scientist,* November, 56–68.

Clanton, G., and Smith, L. G. (1977). *Jealousy.* Englewood Cliffs, NJ: Prentice-Hall.

Devine, P. G. (1989). Stereotypes and prejudice. Their automatic and controlled components. *Journal of Personality and Social Psychology, 56,* 5–18.

Devine, P. G., and Sherman, S. J. (1992). Intuitive versus rational judgment and the role of stereotyping in the human condition: Kirk or Spock. *Psychological Inquiry, 3,* 153–193.

Dindia, K., and Allen, M. (1992). Sex differences in self-disclosure: A Meta-Analysis. *Psycholosical Bulletin, 112,* 106–124.

Feeney, J. A., and Noller, P. (1992). Attachment style and romantic love: Relationship dissolution. *Australian Journal of Psychology, 44,* 69–74.

Feingold, A. (1992). Good-looking people are not what we think. *Psychological Bulletin, 111,* 304–341.

Feld, S. L. (1991). Why your friends have more friends than you do. *American Journal of Sociology, 96,* 1464–1477.

Fishbein, H. D. (1992). The development of peer prejudice and discrimination in children. In: J. Lynch, C. Modgil, and S. Modgil (Eds.), *Cultural diversity and the schools.* Washington, D. C.: Falmer Press.

Fox, R. (1992). Evolution and stereotyping. *Psychological Inquiry, 3,* 137—152.

Grasha, A. F., and Kirschenbaum, D. S. (1986). *Adjustment and competence: Concepts and applications.* St Paul, MN: West.

Gottman, J. M., and Krokoff, L. J. (1989). Marital interaction and satisfaction: A longitudinal view. *Journal of Counsulting and Clinical Psychology, 57,* 47–52.

Gottman, J. M., and Levinson, R. (1992). Marital processes predictive of later dissolution: Behavior, psychology and health. *Journal of Personality and Social Psychology, 63,* 221–233.

Hendrick, C., and Hendrick, S. (1986). A method and theory of love. *Journal of Personality and Social Psychology, 50,* 392–402.

Hendrick, S. S., Hendrick, C., and Adler, N. L. (1988). Romantic relationships: Love, satisfaction, and staying together. *Journal of Personality and Social Psychology, 54,* 980–988.

Hendrick, C., and Hendrick, S. S. (1988). Lovers wear rose colored glasses. *Journal of Social and Personal Relationships, 5,* 161–163.

Hendrick, C. (Ed.), (1989). *Close relationships.* Newbury Park, CA: Sage.

Hill, C. T., Rubin, A., and Peplau, L. A. (1976). Breakups before marriage: The end of 103 affairs. *Journal of Social Issues, 32,* 147–168.

Holmes, J. G., and Rempel, J. K. (1989). Trust in close relationships. In: C. Hendrick (Ed.), *Close relationships,* Newbury Park, CA: Sage.

Homans, G. C. (1974). *Social behavior: Its elementary forms.* New York: Harcourt Brace Jovanovich.

Hupka, R. B., and Zaleski, Z. (1990). Romantic jealousy and romantic envy in Germany, Poland, and the United States. *Behavioral Science Research, 24,* 17–28.

Ineichen, B. (1979). The social geography of marriage. In: M. Cook and G. Wilson (Eds.), *Love and attraction.* New York: Pergamon Press.

Jackson, J., and Cochran, S. D. (1991). Loneliness and psychological distress. *The Journal of Psychology, 125,* 257–262.

Jones, M. (1991). Stereotyping hispanics and whites: Perceived differences in social roles as a determinant of ethnic stereotypes. *Journal of Social Psychology, 13,* 469–476.

Jourard, S. (1971). *Self-disclosure,* New York: Wiley.

Knapp, J. L., and Vangelist, A. L. (1992). *Interpersonal-communication and human relationships (2nd Edition).* Boston: Allyn and Bacon.

Lee, J. A. (1976). *The colors of love.* Englewood Cliffs, NJ: Prentice-Hall.

Lopez, G., and Chism, N. (1993). Classroom concerns of gay and lesbian students: The invisible minority. *College Teaching, 41,* 97–103.

Masterson, J. (1984). Divorce as a health hazard. *Psychology Today,* October, 45–52.

McClanahan, K. K. (1990). Infatuation and attraction to a dissimilar other: Why is love blind? *The Journal of Social Psychology, 130,* 433–445.

McCroskey, J. C., and Richmond, V. P. (1979). The impact of communication apprehension on individuals in organizations. *Communication Quarterly, 23,* 55–60.

Mirowsky, J., and Ross, C. E. (1989). *Social causes of psychological distress.* Hawthorne, NY: Aldine De Gruyther.

Miller, L. C. (1990). Intimacy and liking: Mutual influence and the role of unique relationships. *Journal of Personality and Social Psychology, 59,* 50–60.

Montgomery, R. L., Haemmerlie, F. M., and Edwards, M. (1991). Social, personal, and interpersonal deficits in socially anxious people. *Journal of Social Behavior and Personality, 6,* 859–872.

Murstein, B. L. (1987). A clarification and extension of the SVR theory of dyadic pairing. *Journal of Marriage and the Family, 49,* 929–933.

Nadler, A., and Dotan, I. (1992). Commitment and rival attractiveness: Their effects on male and female reactions to jealousy-arousing situations. *Sex Roles, 26,* 293–309.

Newcomb, T. (1961). *The acquaintance paradigm.* New York: Holt, Rinehart and Winston.

Peplau, A. L., and Perlman, D. (Eds.), (1982). *Loneliness: A sourcebook of current theory, research, and therapy.* New York: Wiley Interscience.

Perlman, D. (1991). Age differences in loneliness: A meta analysis. Vancouver, BC: University of British Columbia. (ERIC Document Reproduction Service No. ED 326767.)

Powell, G. N. (1992). The good manager. *Group and Organization Management, 17,* 44–56.

Rajecki, D. W., De Graaf-Kaser, R., and Rasmussen, J. L. (1992). New impressions and more discrimination: Effects of individuation on gender-label stereotypes. *Sex-Roles, 27,* 171–185.

Reisman, J. M. (1979). *Anatomy of friendship.* New York: Irvington Press.

Rempel, J. K., and Holmes, J. G. (1986). How do I trust thee? *Psychology Today,* February, 28–36.

Rubenstein, C. M. (1983). The modern art of courtly love. *Psychology Today,* July, 22–32.

Rubenstein, C. M., and Shaver, P. (1982). *In search of intimacy.* New York: Delacorte Press.

Rubin, J. (1979). Seeking a cure for loneliness. *Psychology Today,* October, 82–90.

Rubin, Z. (1973). *Liking and loving: An invitation to social psychology.* New York: Holt, Rinehart and Winston.

Saegert, S., Swop, W., and Zajonc, R. B. (1973). Exposure context and interpersonal attraction. *Journal of Personality and Social Psychology, 25,* 234–242.

Salovey, P., and Rodin, J. (1985). The heart of jealousy. *Psychology Today,* September, 24–29.

Salovey, P., and Rodin, J. (1989). Envy and jealousy in close relationships. In: C. Hendrick (Ed.), *Close relationships.* Newbury Park, CA: Sage.

Schlusher, M. P., and Anderson, C. A. (1987). When reality monitoring fails: The role of imagination in stereotype maintenance. *Journal of Personality and Social Psychology, 52,* 653–662.

Schultz, D. A. (1984). *Human sexuality.* Englewood Cliffs, NJ: Prentice-Hall.

Schwartz, R., and Schwartz, L. J. (1980). *Becoming a couple.* Englewood Cliffs, NJ: Prentice-Hall.

Shaffer, D. R., Pegalis, L. J., and Cornell, D. P. (1991). Gender and self-disclosure revisited: Personal and contextual variations in self-disclosure to same sex acquaintances. *The Journal of Social Psychology, 132,* 307–315.

Shaver, P. R., and Hazan, C. (1988). A biased overview of the study of love. *Journal of Social and Personal Relationships, 5,* 473–501.

Shaver, P. R., Hazen, C., and Bradshaw, D. (1988). Love as attachment: The integration of three behavioral systems. In: R. J. Sternberg and M. L. Barnes (Eds.), *The psychology of love.* New Haven, CT: Yale University Press.

Snodgrass, M. A. (1987). The relationships of differential loneliness, intimacy and characterological attributional style to duration of loneliness. *Journal of Social Behavior and Personality, 2,* 173–186.

Sternberg, R. (1988). Triangulating love. In: R. J. Sternberg and M. L. Barnes (Eds.), *The psychology of love.* New Haven, CT: Yale University Press.

Walster, E., and Walster, G. W. (1978). *A new look at love.* Reading, MA: Addison-Wesley.

Walster-Hatfield, E. (1988). Passionate and companionate love. In: R. J. Sternberg and M. L. Barnes (Eds.), *The psychology of love.* New Haven, CT: Yale University Press.

Wassmer, A. C. (1978). *Making contact: A guide to overcoming shyness.* New York: Dial.

Watson, D. L., and Tharp, R. G. (1993). *Self-directed behavior: Self modification for personal adjustment,* Pacific Grove, CA: Brooks/Cole.

Weiss, R. S. (1974). *Loneliness: The experience of emotional and social isolation.* Cambridge, MA: MIT Press.

Wortman, C. G., Adesman, P., Herman, E., and Greenberg, R. (1976). Self-disclosure: An attributional perspective. *Journal of Personality and Social Psychology, 33,* 184–191.

Zalkind, S. S., and Costello, T. W. (1976). Perception: Implications for administration. In: D. Kolb, I. Rubin, and J. McIntyre (Eds.), *Organizational Psychology: A book of readings. (2nd Edition).* Englewood Cliffs, NJ: Prentice-Hall.

Zimbardo, P., Pilkonis, P., and Norwood, R. (1975). The social disease called shyness. *Psychology Today,* May, 55–62.

Zimbardo, P. (1977). *Shyness.* New York: Jove

Zimbardo, P., Ebbesen, E. B., and Maslach, C. (1977). *Influencing attitudes and changing behavior.* New York: McGraw-Hill.

## CHAPTER 9

Alberti, R. E., and Emmons, M. L. (1988). *Stand up, speak out, talk back!* New York: Pocket Books.

Andes, R. (1992). Message dimensions of negotiation. *Negotiation Journal, 8,* 125–130.

Blumstein, P., and Schwartz, P. (1983). *American couples: Money, work, and sex.* New York: Morrow.

Bower, S. A., and Bower, G. H. (1991). *Asserting yourself. A practical guide to positive change.* Reading, MA: Addison-Wesley.

Brehm, S. S., and Brehm, J. W. (1981). *Psychological reactance.* New York: Academic Press.

Brett, J. M., Goldberg, S. B., and Ury, W. L. (1990). Designing systems for resolving disputes in organizations. *American Psychologist, 45,* 162–170.

Burn, S. M. (1991). Social psychology and the simulation of recycling behaviors: The block leader approach. *Journal of Applied Social Psychology, 21,* 611–629.

Canary, D. J., and Spitzberg, B. H. (1990). Attribution issues and associations between conflict strategies and competence outcomes. *Communication Monographs, 57,* 139–150.

Cialdini, R. B. (1993). *Influence: Science and practice (3rd Edition).* New York: Harper-Collins.

Clark, M. S., Mills, J., and Powell, M. (1986). Keeping track of needs in communal and exchange relationships. *Journal of Personality and Social Psychology, 51,* 403–418.

Colman, A. (1980). Flattery won't get you everywhere. *Psychology Today,* May, 34–40.

Deutsch, M. (1991). *Educating for a peaceful world.* Presidential address to the Division of Peace Psychology, Annual Meetings of the American Psychological Association.

Fisher, C. (1978). The effects of personal control, competence, and extrinsic reward systems on intrinsic motivation. *Organizational Behavior and Human Performance, 21,* 273–288.

Fisher, R., and Brown, S. (1988). *Getting together: Building relationships as we negotiate.* New York: Penguin.

Fisher, R., and Ury, W. (1981). *Getting to yes: Negotiating agreement without giving in.* New York: Penguin.

Fuhrmann, B. S., and Grasha, A. F. (1983). *A practical handbook for college teachers.* Boston: Little-Brown.

Gaertner, S. L., Mann, J., Dovidio, J. F., Murrell, A. J., and Pomare, M. (1990). How does cooperation reduce intergroup bias? *Journal of Personality and Social Psychology, 59,* 692–704.

Gordon, T. (1976). *P. E. T. in action.* New York: Wyden Books.

Gotlib, L. H., and Colby, C. A. (1988). How to have a good quarrel. In: P. Marsh (Ed.), *Eye to eye: How people interact.* Topside, MA: Salem House.

Grasha, A. F. (1990). *The Grasha-Riechmann Student Learning Style Scales.* Cincinnati, OH: Communication and Education Associates.

Grasha, A. F. (1991). *The Holistic Stress Test.* Cincinnati, OH: Communication and Education Associates.

Grasha, A. F. (1991). A systematic strategy for resolving conflict in academic departments. *The department advisor, 6,* 1–4.

Grasha, A. F. (1994). Teaching styles in the college classroom. *College Teaching* (in press).

Heitler, S. M. (1990) *From conflict to resolution.* New York: W. W. Norton.

Howard, D. J. (1990). The influence of verbal responses to common greetings on compliance behavior: The foot-in-the-mouth effect. *Journal of Applied Social Psychology, 20,* 1185–1196.

Kelman, H. C. (1958). Compliance, identification, and internalization: Three process of attitude change. *Journal of Conflict Resolution, 2,* 51–60.

Kelman, H. C., and Hamilton, V. L. (1989). *Crimes of obedience.* New Haven, CT: Yale University Press.

Kohn A. (1986). *No contest: The case against competition.* Boston: Houghton-Mifflin.

Langer, E. J., and Dweck, C. S. (1973). *Personal politics: The psychology of making it.* Englewood Cliffs, NJ: Prentice-Hall.

Lindskold, S., and Han, G. (1988). GRIT as a foundation for integrative bargaining. *Personality and Social Psychology Bulletin, 14,* 335–345.

McGuire, W. J. (1961). Resistance to counterpersuasion conferred by active and passive prior refutation of the same and alternative counter-arguments. *Journal of Abnormal and Social Psychology, 63,* 326–332.

McFarland, R. (1992). *Coping through assertiveness.* New York: Rosen Group.

Milgram, S. (1974). *Obedience to authority.* New York: HarperCollins.

Murray, D. A., Leupker, R. V., Johnson, C. A., and Mittlemark, M. B. (1984). The prevention of cigarette smoking in children: A comparison of four strategies. *Journal of Applied Social Psychology, 14,* 274–288.

Myers, D. (1994). *Exploring social psychology.* New York: McGraw-Hill.

Osgood, C. E. (1980). *GRIT: A strategy for survival in mankind's nuclear age?* Paper presented at the Pugwash Conference on New Directions in Disarmament. Racine, WI.

Pneuman, R. W., and Bruehl, M. E. (1982). *Managing conflict: A complete process-centered handbook.* Englewood Cliffs, NJ: Prentice-Hall.

Podsakoff, P. M., and Schriescheim, C. A. (1985). Field studies of French and Raven's bases of social power: Critique, reanalysis, and suggestions for future research. *Psychological Bulletin, 97,* 387–411.

Pruitt, D. G., and Rubin, J. Z. (1986). *Social conflict: Escalation, stalemate, and settlement.* New York: Random House.

Raven, B. H. (1992). A power/interaction model of interpersonal influence: French and Raven thirty years later. *Journal of Social Behavior and Personality, 7,* 217–244.

Reed, B. (1992). *Pleasing you is destroying me: How to stop being controlled by your people-pleasing addiction.* New York: Adducton.

Rook, K. S. (1987). Reciprocity of social exchange and social satisfaction among older women. *Journal of Personality and Social Psychology, 52,* 145–154.

Siegelman, E. Y. (1983). *Personal risk: Mastering change in love and work.* New York: HarperCollins.

Sherif, M. (1966). *In common predicament: Social psychology of intergroup conflict and cooperation.* Boston: Houghton Mifflin.

Smith, M. (1985). *When I say no I feel guilty.* New York: Dial.

Stahelski, A. J., Frost, D. E., and Patch, M. E. (1989). Use of socially dependent bases of power: French and Raven's theory applied to workgroup leadership. *Journal of Applied Social Psychology. 19,* 283–297.

Stewert, J. (1990). *No one's ever complained before.* London: Element Books.

Tavris, C. (1982). *Anger: The misunderstood emotion.* New York: Simon and Schuster.

Thomas, K. W. (1992). Conflict and conflict management: Reflections and update. *Journal of Organizational Behavior, 13,* 265–274.

Ury, W., Brett, J. M., and Goldberg, S. (1988). *Getting disputes resolved.* San Francisco, CA: Jossey-Bass.

Ury, W. (1991). *Getting past no: Negotiating with difficult people.* New York: Bantam.

Walton, R. E. (1987). *Managing conflict: Interpersonal dialogue and third-party roles.* Reading, MA: Addison-Wesley.

Zimbardo, P. G., and Leippe, M. R. (1991). *The psychology of attitude change and social influence.* New York: McGraw-Hill.

## CHAPTER 10

Baumeister, R. F. (1991). Self-concept and identity. In: N. J. Derlega, B. A. Winstead, and W. H. Jones (Eds.). *Personality: Contemporary theory and research.* Chicago: Nelson-Hall.

Baumeister, R. F., and Scher, S. J (1988). Self-defeating behavior patterns among normal individuals. Review and analysis of common self-destructive tendencies. *Psychological Bulletin, 104,* 3–22.

Bond, M. J., and Feather, N. T. (1988). Some correlates and purpose in the use of time. *Journal of Personality and Social Psychology, 55,* 321–329.

Brown, J. D. (1991a). Staying fit and staying well: Physical fitness as a moderator of life stress. *Journal of Personality and Social Psychology, 60,* 555–561.

Brown, J. D. (1991b). Accuracy and bias in self-knowledge. In: C. R. Snyder and D. F. Forsyth (Eds.). *Handbook of social and clinical psychology: The health perspective.* New York: Pergamon Press.

Bruning, N. S., and Frew, D. R. (1987). Effects of exercise, relaxation, and management skills training on physiological stress indicators: A field experiment. *Journal of Applied Psychology, 72,* 515–521.

Burke, R. J., and Greenglass, E. R. (1989). Psychological burnout among men and women in teaching: An examination of the Chermiss model. *Human Relations, 42,* 261–273.

Butler, P. E. (1981). *Talking to yourself.* New York: HarperCollins.

Buunk, B. P., and Verhoeven, K. (1991). Companionship and support at work: A microanalysis of the stress-reducing features of social interaction. *Basic and Applied Social Psychology, 12,* 243–258.

Calabrese, J. R., Kling, M. A., and Gold, P. W. (1987). Alterations in immunocompetence during stress, bereavement, and depression. Focus on neuroendocrine regulation. *American Journal of Psychiatry, 144,* 1123–1134.

Cantor, N., and Norem, J. K. (1989) Defensive pessimism and stress and coping. *Social Cognition, 7,* 92–112.

Cohen, S., Evans, G. W., Stokols, D., and Krantz, D. S. (1986). *Behavior, health, and environmental stress.* New York: Plenum.

Cooper, R. K. (1989). *Health and fitness excellence.* Boston: Houghton Mifflin.

Covey, S. (1989). *The 7 habits of highly effective people.* New York: Simon & Schuster.

Crow, L. S., and Grasha, A. F. (1993). *Work stress and coping styles: Comparisons across occupational groups. Proceedings of the First Annual Conference on Stress in the Workplace.* Washington, DC: American Psychological Association.

Dance, K. A., and Kuiper, N. A. (1987). Self-schemata, social roles, and a self-worth contingency model of depression. *Motivation and emotion, 11,* 251–268.

De Benedittis, G., Lornenzetti, A., and Peri, A. (1990). The role of stressful life events in the onset of chronic primary headache. *Pain, 40,* 65–75.

Dembroski, T. M, and Costa, P. T. (1987). Coronary-prone behavior: Components of the Type-A pattern and hostility. *Journal of Personality, 55,* 211–236.

Depue, R. A. (1992). *Neurobehavioral systems, personality, and psychopathology.* New York: Springer-Verlag.

Dienstbier, R. A. (1989). Arousal and physiological toughness: Implications for mental and physical health. *Psychological Review, 96,* 84–100.

Dishman, R. K., Ickes, W., and Morgan, W. P. (1981). Self-motivation and adherence to habitual physical exercise. *Journal of Applied Social Psychology, 10,* 115–132.

Ellis, A., and Dryden, W. (1987). *The practice of rational-emotive therapy.* New York: Springer.

Epstein, S., and Katz, L. (1992). Coping ability, stress, productive load, and symptoms. *Journal of Personality and Social Psychology, 62,* 813–825.

Feist, J., and Brannon, L. (1988). *Health psychology.* Belmont, CA: Wadsworth.

Folkman, V. S., and Lazarus, R. (1988). *Manual for the ways of coping questionnaire.* Palo Alto, CA: Consulting Psychologists Press.

Friedman, M., and Ulmer, D. (1984). Treating Type-A behavior and your heart. New York: Knopf.

Funk, S. C. (1992). Hardiness: A review of theory and research. *Health Psychology, 11,* 335–345.

Ganster, D. C. (1987). Type-A behavior pattern in organizations. In: J. M. Ivancevich and D. C. Ganster (Eds.). *Job stress: From theory to organization.* New York: Haworth.

Garrett, V., Brantley, P., Jones, G., and McNight, G. (1991). The relation between daily stress and Crohn's Disease. *Journal of Behavioral Medicine, 14,*187–196.

Goldberg, G. M. (1990). Irrational beliefs and three interpersonal styles. *Psychological Reports, 66,* 963–969.

Grasha, A. F. (1987). Short-term coping strategies for managing stress. In: Seldin, P (Ed.), *Coping with faculty stress.* San Francisco: Jossey-Bass.

Grasha, A. F. (1989). *Holistic stress test.* Cincinnati, OH: Communication and Education Associates.

Grasha, A. F. (1992). *Holistic stress management: A self study manual.* Cincinnati, OH: Communication and Education Associates.

Grasha, A. F., and Kirschenbaum, D. S. (1986). *Adjustment and competence: Concepts and applications.* St. Paul, MN.: West.

Hanson, P. G. (1986). *The joy of stress.* Kansas City, MO: Andrews, McMeel and Parker.

Hawking, S. (1993). *Black holes and baby universes and other essays.* New York: Bantam.

Haynes, S. G., Feinleib, M., and Kannel, W. B. (1980). The relationship of psychosocial factors to coronary heart disease in the Framingham study: III. Eight-year incidence of coronary heart disease. *American Journal of Epidemiology, 111,* 37–58.

Hedrick, L. H. (1990). *Five days to an organized life.* New York: Dell Publishing.

Hobfoll, S. E. (1989). Conservation of resources: A new attempt at conceptualizing stress. *American Psychologist, 44,* 513–534.

Hoff-Macan, T., Shahani, C., Dipboye, R. L., and Phillips, A. P. (1990). College students' time management: Correlations with academic performance and stress. *Journal of Educational Psychology, 82,* 760–768.

Hoglund, C. L., and Collison, B. B. (1989). Loneliness and irrational beliefs among college students. *Journal of College Student Development, 30,* 53–57.

Holmes, T. H., and Rahe, R. H. (1967). The social readjustment rating scale. *Journal of Psychosomatic Research, 11,* 13–218.

Israel, B. A., Schurman, S. J., Heaney, C. A., and Mero, R. P. (1989). The relation of personal resources to occupational stress, job strain, and health. *Work and Stress, 3,* 163–194.

Jackson, S. E., Schwab, R. L., and Schuler, R. S. (1986). Towards an understanding of the burnout phenomenon. *Journal of Applied Psychology, 71,* 630–640.

Jeffers, S. (1988). *Feel the fear. And do it anyway.* New York: Fawcett Columbine.

Kasl, S. V. (1990). Some considerations in the study of traumatic stress. *Journal of Applied Social Psychology, 20,* 1655–1665.

Kiecolt-Glaser, J. K., and Glaser, R. (1992). Psychoneuroimmunology: Can psychological interventions modulate immunity? *Journal of Consulting and Clinical Psychology. 60,* 569–575.

Kinder, M. (1994). *Mastering your moods.* New York: Simon and Schuster.

Klar, Y., Nadler, A., and Malloy, T. (1992). Opting to change: Students' informal self-change endeavors. In: Y. Klar, J. F. Fisher, J. M. Chinsky, and A. Nadler (Eds.) *Self change: Social psychological and clinical perspectives.* New York: Springer-Verlag.

Kobassa, S. C., Maddi, S. R., and Kahn, S. (1982). Hardiness and health: A prospective study. *Journal of Personality and Social Psychology, 42,* 168–177.

Lamude, K. G., Scudder, J., and Furno-Lamude, D. (1992). The relationship of student resistance strategies in the classroom to teacher burnout and teacher Type-A behavior. *Journal of Social Behavior and Personality, 7,* 597–610.

Lazarus, R. S. (1981). Little hassles can be hazardous to health. *Psychology Today,* July, 58–62.

Lazarus, R. S. (1991). *Emotion and adaptation.* New York: Oxford.

Lazarus, R. S., and Folkman, S. (1984). *Stress, appraisal, and coping.* New York: Springer.

Locke, E. A., and Latham, G. P. (1990). Work motivation and satisfaction: Light at the end of the tunnel, *Psychological Science, 1,* 240–246.

Macan, T. H., Sahani, C., Dipboye, R. L., and Phillips, A. P. (1990). College students time management: Correlations with academic performance and stress. *Journal of Educational Psychology, 82,* 760–768.

Maslach, C. (1982). Understanding burnout: Definitional issues in analyzing a complex phenomenon. In W. S. Paine (Ed.), *Job stress and burnout: Research, theory, and intervention perspectives.* Beverly Hills, CA: Sage.

Maslow, A. (1970). *Motivation and personality.* New York: HarperCollins.

Maslow, A. (1971). *The farther reaches of human nature.* New York: McGraw-Hill.

Meichenbaum, D. (1985). *Stress inoculation training.* New York: Pergamon Press.

Monroe, S., Thase, M., and Simmons, A. (1992). Social factors and psychobiology of depression: Relations between life stressors and rapid eye movement sleep latency. *Journal of Abnormal Psychology, 101,* 528–537.

Montauk, S., and Grasha, A. F. (1993). *Adult HIV outpatient care: A handbook for clinical teaching.* Kansas City, MO: STFM Press.

Nolen-Hoekma, S., and Morrow, J. (1991). A prospective study of depression and posttraumatic stress after a natural disaster: The 1989 Loma Prieta earthquake. *Journal of Personality and Social Psychology, 61,* 115–121.

Nowack, K. M. (1991). Psychosocial predictors of health status. *Work and Stress, 5,* 117–131.

Paffenbarger, R. S. Jr., Hyde, R. T., Wing, A. L., and Hseih, C. C. (1986). Physical activity, all cause mortality, and longevity of college alumni. *New England Journal of Medicine, 314,* 605-613.

Peterson, C., and Bossio, Lim. (1991). *Health and optimism.* New York: Free Press.

Pfifferling, J. H., and Eckel, F. M. (1982). Beyond burnout: Obstacles and prospects. In: W. S. Paine (Ed.), *Job stress and burnout: Research, theory, and intervention perspectives.* Beverly Hills, CA: Sage.

Pines, A., and Aronson, E. (1988). *Career burnout: Causes and cures.* New York: Free Press.

Plak, R. L., and Prokop, C. K. (1989). Defensive pessimism: A protective self-monitoring strategy? *Journal of Social Behavior and Personality, 4,* 285–289.

Plomin, R., and De Fries, J. C., and McClearn, G. E. (1990). *Behavioral genetics: A primer (2nd Edition).* New York: Freeman.

Pollock, S. E. (1989). The hardiness characteristic: A motivating factor in adaptation. *Advances In Nursing Science, 11,* 53–62.

Prince-Embury, S., and Rooney, F. F. (1989). Psychological symptoms of residents in the aftermath of the Three Mile Island nuclear accident and restart. *The Journal of Social Psychology, 128,* 779–790.

Prola, M. (1985). The social desirability of irrational beliefs. *Perceptual and Motor Skills, 61,* 336–338.

Repetti, R. L. (1993). Linkages between work and family roles. *Work and Stress, 4,* 105–119.

Rice, P. L. (1987). *Stress and health: Principles and practices for coping and wellness.* Monterey, CA: Brooks/Cole.

Rodin, J., and Plante, T. (1989). The psychological effects of exercise. In: R. S. Williams and A. Wellece (Eds.), *Biological effects of physical activity.* Champaign, IL: Human Kinetics.

Rogers, C. R. (1977). *Carl Rosers on personal power.* New York: Delacourt.

Roos, P. E., and Cohen, L. H. (1987). Sex roles and social support as moderators of life stress adjustment. *Journal of Personality and Social Psychology, 52,* 576–585.

Sarason, I., Sarason, B., Potter, E., and Antoni, M. (1985). Life events, social support, and illness. *Psychosomatic Medicine, 47,* 156–163.

Schutz, W. (1982). *Profound simplicity.* New York: Bantam Books.

Seligman, M. E. (1991). *Learned optimism.* New York: Knopf.

Selye, H. (1976). *The stress of life.* New York: McGraw-Hill.

Short, G. J., and Grasha, A. G. (1994). Cognitive style as a predictor of stress and coping strategies among research and development managers. *Journal of Psychological Type* (in press).

Smith, J. C. (1993a). *Understanding stress and coping.* New York: Macmillan.

Smith, J. C. (1993b). *Creative stress management.* Englewood Cliffs, NJ: Prentice-Hall.

Smith, R. E. (1989). Effects of coping skills training on generalized self-efficacy and locus of control. *Journal of Personality and Social Psychology, 56,* 228-233.

Sohns, L. J. (1994). *Students stress: The impace of life stressors, coping straegies, and personality variables.* Unpublished Masters Thesis, Univeristy of Cincinnati, Cincinnati, OH.

Spielberger, C. D., Johnson, E. H. J., Russell, S. F., Crane, R. J., Jacobs, G. A., and Worden, T. J. (1985). The experience and expression of anger. In: M. A. Chesney, S. E. Goldston, and R. H. Rosenman (Eds.). *Anger and hostility in behavioral medicine.* New York: Hemisphere McGraw-Hill.

Spiller, G. (1993). *The superpyramid eating program.* New York: Times Books.

Titlebaum, H. (1988). Relaxation. In: R. P. Zahourek (Ed.), *Relaxation and imagery: Tools for therapeutic communication and intervention.* Philadelphia: W. B. Saunders.

Walker, M. B., and Phil, D. (1992). Irrational thinking among slot machine players. *Journal of Gambling Studies, 8,* 245–261.

Watson, D. L., and Tharp, R. G. (1993) *Self-directed behavior: Self-modification for personal adjustment.* Pacific Grove, CA: Brooks/Cole.

Weick, K. E. (1984). Small wins: Redefining the scale of social problems. *American Psychologist, 39,* 40–49.

Weybrew, B. B. (1992). *The ABC's of stress.* Westport, CN: Praeger.

Wiebe, D. J. (1991). Hardiness and stress moderation: A test of proposed mechanisms. *Journal of Personality and Social Psychology, 60,* 89–99.

Yakubovich, I. S., Ragland, D. R., Brand, R. J., and Syme, S. L. (1988). Type-A behavior pattern and health status after 22 years of follow-up in the Western Collaborative Group Study. *American Journal of Epidemiology, 128,* 579–588.

Zois, C. (1992). *Think like a shrink.* New York: Warner Books.

# AUTHOR INDEX

# SUBJECT INDEX